Whole-
Language

Whole-Language

Practice and Theory

SECOND EDITION

Victor Froese, Editor
University of British Columbia

Allyn and Bacon
Boston London Toronto Sydney Tokyo Singapore

Senior Editor: Virginia Lanigan
Editorial Assistant: Nihad Farooq
Executive Marketing Manager: Kathy Hunter
Editorial-Production Administrator: Annette Joseph
Editorial-Production Service: TKM Productions
Composition Buyer: Linda Cox
Manufacturing Buyer: Megan Cochran
Cover Administrator: Suzanne Harbison

Copyright © 1996, 1991 by Allyn & Bacon
A Simon & Schuster Company
Needham Heights, MA 02194

Library of Congress Cataloging-in-Publication Data
Whole-language: practice and theory / Victor Froese, editor.
     p. . cm.
  Includes bibliographical references and index.
  ISBN 0-205-15779-3
  1. Language experience approach in education. 2. Reading
(Elementary)—Language experience approach. 3. Language arts
(Elementary) I. Froese, Victor.
  LB1573.W534 1996
  372.6—dc20   95-32108
                                  CIP

Printed in the United States of America

10 9 8 7 6 5 4 3 2 1 00 99 98 97 96

Photo Credits:
pp. 6, 45, 67, 100, 109, 207, 228, 240, 266, 280, 319, 351, 392, 413, 428, 444: Victor Froese; pp. 15, 29, 114, 379: Will Faller; pp. 165, 286, 316: Frank Siteman; p. 172: Dave Starrett; p. 260: Vancouver Public Library.

To all teachers
  who strive for liberating experiences through language,
To all students
  who celebrate empowering adventures with language, and
To all parents
  who nurture affirmative enterprises in language

Contents

Preface

Whole-Language: Practice and Theory, Second Edition, is intended as a text for prospective primary through middle-school teachers (i.e., kindergarten through grade 8) in their professional year of teacher training. It has also been found to be welcomed by experienced teachers in professional or in-service courses. Although the term *whole language* is widely used now, we begin with an operational definition so that our intentions will be clear: **Whole-language is a child-centered, literature-based approach to language teaching that immerses students in real communication situations whenever possible.** When used in this way, we hyphenate *whole-language*; when it is used in its generic sense, we do not.

This second edition of *Whole-Language: Practice and Theory* is intended to help prospective teachers to learn how to structure, plan, and execute a whole-language program. That requires considerable knowledge about how children learn and how they use language. Hence, such information is provided throughout in a practical way together with suggestions for appropriate activities. That is why *practice* is mentioned first in the book's title. However, the importance of the reasons for engaging children in meaningful learning activities is not minimized. In fact, the final chapter is unique in entry-level texts—it carefully reviews the extant research and theory on whole-language and presents it in a readable and understandable form.

There has been much change in the field of language education since the preparation of the first edition manuscript in the late 1980s. Therefore, three new chapters have been added. The field of literacy has been influenced by insights gained from critical pedagogy, feminist theory, deconstructivism, multilingualism, constructivism, and phenomonology. All have aided in the understanding and acceptance of whole language theory. The term *whole language* was not in the lexicon of most educators, but in the 1990s, it is used by the major education indices in the field: *Education Index, Current Index to Journals in Education (CIJE), The Literacy Dictionary* (Harris and Hodges, 1995), and *Australian Education Index* to cite a few key examples. *CIJE* currently lists over 300 articles related to whole language, and it is one of the five most frequently asked about topics (Smith, 1990). Between 1982 and 1987, approximately 26 dissertations were presented on some aspect of whole language; between 1988 and 1992, the number rose to 126 dissertations; and in 1993 alone, there were 50 (see the Appendix in Chapter 13). Today, whole language is a common item on professional and research-oriented conference agendas, and a growing body of research specifically on whole language is accumulating. In the last chapter of this book, we present the evidence: Whole language programs are successful, they may be more cognitively stimulating than traditional approaches, and writing skills have developed earlier than was thought possible. For example, in Loban's (1976) classic study of children's language abilities from kindergarten through grade 12, writing samples were gathered only from the fourth grade because younger children did not produce enough text to analyze.

Books such as *Whole-Language* are often criticized for their subdivisions (i.e., chapters, parts, appendices, etc.) when they claim to emphasize holistic methods. However, we believe that it is a courtesy to our readers to make it easy to locate desired information since the order in which information is required varies with the reader. Often, the reader is interested in a particular topic—how to improve writing, for example—and hence should not have to read partway through the book to discover what we have to say about the topic. The chapters in this book fall under the unified theme of whole-language and are linked by the initial chapter, which provides definitions, theoretical context, and a brief overview of all the following chapters. The second chapter, a new one in the second edition, demonstrates what whole-language looks like in practice, in a primary and middle-school classroom. Other new chapters deal with the use of technology and with children who have special needs. The remaining chapters provide insights into various aspects of whole-language from experienced educators' perspectives. Qualifications and experience of the contributors are found after this Preface.

Another reason for the present organization is that instructors of classes interested in younger children often prefer a different order of presentation than do those with classes intended for the middle years. For example, our experience is that often the former prefer to begin with an emphasis on oral language and dramatization, whereas the latter often prefer to begin with reading and writing. To some extent, the order of topics may also depend on when school experiences are scheduled in the students' program. The independence of the chapters gives the instructor considerable flexibility in using this text.

Throughout the book, we have assisted the learner in acquiring the vocabulary of instruction and learning. Each chapter begins with **Key Concepts** to be learned. **Key Vocabulary** items are indicated by boldface type for easy location and identification. We have also included a **Glossary** of terms that clarifies those words that may not have been defined adequately in context of the chapters in which they are found. At the end of each chapter, we have included **Discussion Questions** that may be used in small-group class discussions or used for individuals to test their own grasp of the chapter contents. It should, however, be noted that some of the questions ask the reader/discussant to go beyond the text, to explore or extend ideas; hence, the answers will not be found in this text. Some chapters have **appendices** to lead the reader to additional sources of practical ideas, books, and materials. Instructors should be aware that an Instructor's Manual is available for this book from the publisher. Based on many years of teaching experience by the authors, it provides very useful ideas for introducing each chapter. It provides suggestions for classroom activities, examples of learning outcomes, ways of assessing and evaluating a course based on whole-language principles, and gives additional sources of resource materials and books related to whole-language.

It is our experience that even those not initially interested in whole-language, or those who have preconceived negative understandings about it, will be able to use many of the ideas presented in this book. Further, it is not necessary to have a whole-language philosophy to benefit from the ideas in this text. Our experience does not indicate that beginning teachers start with a philosophy and then carefully structure their methodology, materials, and strategies around it. We observe, also, that teachers begin with decisions about content and activities rather than with specific objectives. This is borne out by the discussions in Borko and Niles's (1987) article on teacher planning. While classroom activities may reflect a certain type of philosophy of teaching or learning that may be deduced by inference, most often decisions about the selected activities are pragmatically rather than philosophically based. That is, teachers want to engage students in meaningful learning first. In most instances, introspection and reflective teaching come after basic teaching routines have been mastered. In short, although we encourage the development of strong philosophical views, they are not a prerequisite to whole-language-based teaching and learning. If the instructors feel that students do not have enough foundational concepts about literacy, they may wish to consider using *A Language Approach to Reading* (Froese, 1991) as a supplementary text.

This book is a testament to collaborative learning. The authors are all instructors in the Department of Language Education at the University of British Columbia, they come with school experiences in many parts of the world, and all have many years of teaching experience. All felt that a need for a rational approach to whole language was needed. We met to discuss our mutual interests, our varying views of whole language, and then we acted. We began with a dramatization of the pros and cons of whole language, which we presented to a variety of teacher groups and eventually produced in the form of a video entitled *Whole Language on Trial* (Scholastic-TAB Canada, 1988). The video presented a courtroom trial in which a teacher is charged with using a nontraditional method of instruction, thereby harming children's reading achievement, skills development, and spelling ability, and with implementing a writing program before children were supposed to be ready to write, thereby adversely affecting the development of their writing ability. The presentation consisted of the case of the prosecution, the defense, and the judge's summation. The audience became the jury and was asked to render a decision. The dramatization was often followed by break-out sessions on various aspects of whole language. The break-out session notes were expanded into chapters, and the chapters were cast into the form of a book via desktop publishing technology, and the book formed the basis of a collaboratively taught university course.

A book such as this cannot be produced without the assistance and support of many people to whom we are grateful. First, we are indebted to the teachers, administrators, and school divisions who invited us to work with them to develop and field-test our ideas about whole-language. We trust that, above all, children have benefited from these collaborations. Their projects and class work have found their way into these pages. Further, these individuals permitted the editor freedom to roam around classrooms with camera and flash to capture what was happening. Second, we are thankful for the patience of the Department of Language Education secretaries—Carol, Ginette, Anna, and Teresa—who typed, formatted, copied, and mailed pages, chapters, and draft copies of the book. Third, we must acknowledge the perseverance of the Allyn and Bacon staff, especially Virginia Lanigan, Nihad Farooq, and Annette Joseph, who guided us through the project the second time! We also would like to acknowledge the following reviewers: Janet Alcorn, University of Northern Colorado; Marti Brueggeman, Ashland University; Martha S. Kellow, East Stroudsburg University; Judith A. Meagher, University of Connecticut; Meg Philbin, State University of New York, College at Potsdam; and William E. Smith, Ohio University. Finally, we want to thank all the university students and practicing teachers who have provided us with feedback on our book and its contents. We invite further input since that is how we extend our learning. Please write to the author of your choice at the Department of Language Education, University of British Columbia, Vancouver, B.C., V6T 1Z4. Our home page address is http:\www.lane.educ.ubc,ca\.

V. F.

REFERENCES

Borko, H. & Niles, J. A. (1987). Descriptions of teacher planning: Ideas for teachers and researchers. In V. Richardson-Koehler (Ed.), *Educators' handbook: A research perspective* (pp. 167–187). White Plains, NY: Longman.

Froese, V. (1991). *A language approach to reading*. Scarborough, Ontario: Nelson Canada.

Harris, T. L. & Hodges, R. E. (Eds.) (1995). *The Literacy Dictionary: The vocabulary of reading and writing*. Newark DE: International Reading Association.

Loban, W. (1976). *Language development: Kindergarden through grade twelve*. Urbana, IL: NCTE.

Smith, C. B. (1990). Trends in reading/literacy instruction. *The Reading Teacher, 43 (9)*, 680.

Contributors

Jim Anderson
Assistant Professor, Department of Language Education, University of British Columbia
Ph.D. University of Alberta
Experience: Classroom teacher, school administrator, reading specialist, language arts consultant, assistant superintendent (curriculum)

Syd Butler
Assistant Professor, Department of Language Education, University of British Columbia
Ph.D. University of British Columbia
Experience: Classroom teacher, school librarian

Marilyn Chapman
Assistant Professor, Department of Language Education, University of British Columbia
Ph.D. University of Victoria
Experience: Classroom teacher, school administrator, school district consultant, Ministry of Education coordinator

Victor Froese
Professor & Head, Department of Language Education, University of British Columbia
Ph.D. University of Minnesota
Experience: Classroom teacher, school administrator

Lee Gunderson
Associate Professor, Department of Language Education, University of British Columbia
Ph.D. University of California, Berkeley
Experience: Nursery school, resource teacher, learning disability teacher, administrator

Ann Lukasevich
Assistant Professor, Department of Language Education, University of British Columbia
Ed.D. University of British Columbia
Experience: Classroom teacher, teacher of gifted, remedial teacher

Marion Ralston
Associate Professor, Department of Language Education, University of British Columbia
Ph.D. Walden University (California)
Experience: Classroom teacher

Jon Shapiro
Associate Professor, Department of Language Education, University of British Columbia
Ph.D. Syracuse University
Experience: Classroom teacher, preschool teacher, learning assistance teacher

Gerry Snyder
Assistant Professor, Department of Language Education, University of British Columbia
Ed.D. Oregon State University
Experience: Classroom teacher, teacher corps

Claire Staab
Associate Professor, Department of Language Education, University of British Columbia
Ph.D. Arizona State University
Experience: Classroom teacher, reading specialist, language arts consultant

Wendy Sutton
Assistant Professor, Department of Language Education, University of British Columbia
Ph.D. Michigan State University
Experience: Classroom teacher, children's literature, language arts consultant

Patrick Verriour
Associate Professor, Department of Language Education, University of British Columbia
Ph.D. University of Alberta
Experience: Classroom teacher, school administrator

Introduction to Whole-Language Teaching and Learning

VICTOR FROESE

KEY CONCEPTS

1. *Distinguishing features of a definition of whole-language and differentiating it from other common approaches to teaching language*

2. *Foundations of the linguistic, psychological, and pedagogical underpinnings of whole-language*

3. *How whole-language manifests itself in the classroom through the teacher, the student, and the materials used*

4. *The social, political, and societal motives behind particular approaches to instruction*

What Is Whole-Language and Why Is It Important?

In this book we define **whole-language** as a child-centered, literature-based approach to language teaching that immerses students in real communication situations whenever possible. The book begins with a simple definition because so much confusion about whole language is seen in the media and in the professional literature. Throughout this text we will use the term *whole-language* in its *hyphenated* form to refer to our specific operational definition (see also Gunderson, 1989). By "literature-based" we mean that textual materials of all kinds—from fiction to informational materials—are used to promote language learning. By "real communication" we mean that genuine audiences—interested listeners—are involved whenever possible in the linguistic effort. With this book we intend to assist prospective teachers in understanding the whole-language concept; to provide enough practical information and examples so that teachers are able to begin teaching in this manner; and to show that teaching and learning can be engaging, stimulating activities for everyone.

Today's journals and books are sprinkled liberally with the term *whole language* (Purcell-Gates et al., 1995; Willinsky, 1994; Piper, 1993; Ruddell, 1992; Goodman, 1992; Hydrick, 1991; Blake, 1990; Kiefer, 1990; Watson, Burke and Harste, 1989; McConaghy, 1988; Gunderson and Shapiro, 1988). What is the fascination with whole language, then? Even some of the most staunch critics have given kudos to whole language, and authorities from many fields have attested to its appeal. P. David Pearson (1989, p. 232), a prominent basal reader consultant, conceded, "There are many things I like about whole language; it has succeeded in accomplishing goals that many of us who are not part of the movement have failed to accomplish by using more conventional approaches to reform." Even one of the modern-day phonics advocates (normally considered to be the very antithesis of whole language), Marilyn Jager Adams (1990, p. 422), conceded that " 'whole language' instruction is packed with activities for developing phonological awareness, orthographic knowledge, and spelling-sound relations." Two dissenting members of Adams's advisory panel, Dorothy Strickland and Bernice Cullinan (1990, p. 433), wrote, "We believe the evidence supports a whole language and integrated language arts approach with some direct instruction, in context, on spelling-to-sound correspondence." Howard Gardner (1991, p. 211), a cognitive psychologist known especially for his theory of seven human intelligences, provided the following insights about whole language:

> Too many children have little sense of why one should read, because they reside in environments where the adults do not read. Notably, a number of programs, typically termed "whole-language" approaches, have proved

successful at setting a context for literacy activities while at the same time helping students to acquire the basics that will allow them eventually to read and write on their own. . . . A whole-language emphasis is far from being a universal practice, but it is being used in many places where it was not seen a decade ago. I believe that this small-scale pedagogical revolution has occurred because teachers themselves have discovered (or rediscovered) not only that they can write but that they actually like to write.*

Sam Crowell (1989) expressed the view that new directions emerging from a philosophy of science have much to offer in structuring education for the future. Miller (1988, p. 138) brought out another intriguing aspect of whole language—the role and support of the teacher. "The primary focus in implementing the holistic curriculum is on teacher personal growth. Of course, the curriculum is important . . ., but a holistic curriculum in the hands of a transmission-oriented teacher will become a transmission curriculum." The notion of whole language support groups, or TAWL, has become widespread. Today, aspects of holism are also appearing in psychological, philosophical, medical, theological, and engineering circles—likely as a reaction to overspecialization. In all fields, overspecialization can lead to fragmentation, as it has in education, and eventually to the realization that the effects are dehumanizing.

As is the case in the development of most concepts, whole language is related to other developments in language learning. One such development is known as language across the curriculum (LAC) which had its foundation in Britain but has evolved somewhat separately in North America. Essentially, the bases of LAC rest on three assumptions elaborated in *A Language for Life* (Bullock, 1975, p. 50): (1) all genuine learning involves discovery, (2) language has a heuristic function, and (3) to exploit the process of discovery through language in all its uses is the surest means of enabling a child to master his or her mother tongue. Even though these ideas have been discussed for almost two decades (Froese, 1994) they are still not widely applied. Heally and Barr (1991, p. 825) in defining LAC concluded, "It is ironic, however, that with a body of evidence accumulating to support a holistic view of language use as the way to promote scholastic achievement in any discipline, that language for learning activities remains unavailable to most pupils."

Most educational practices imply a theoretical or philosophical stance and whole language is not an exception. Luke (1988, p. 17) pointed out that such assumptions also prescribe functions and uses of literacy:

We see this most clearly in current debates about contending approaches to teaching reading, writing and the language arts (e.g., "whole language" versus "skills-based" approaches, "process" versus product orientations and, *alas, phonics versus word recognition methods). Often unbeknownst to participants, within such debates lies a stratum of normative assumptions not only about what is to count as literacy but about the ultimate social purpose and political potential of literacy: whether this be the ethos of, for instance, individual empowerment and personal voice, of basic morality and skill, or of rudimentary "functional" job skills and the maintenance of an industrial order.**

Piper (1993, p. 319), writing from an applied linguistic perspective concluded,

It [whole language] is discussed here because it is also the approach to language curriculum that is most consistent with our best understanding of how language acquisition occurs and the most enlightened theories of language. Since a teaching approach should be informed by both a theory of language and a theory of language learning . . . , then whole language merits special consideration in any book on language acquisition that encompasses the school years.

The whole-language approach is particularly relevant for many second-language and language-minority students. In describing some of the best ways of promoting literacy with language-minority students, Rueda advocated that students be actively engaged in constructing meaning. He stated that "in practice, this philosophy is implemented as whole-language . . . or neo-Vygotskian approaches that emphasize assisted performance" (1990, p. 95). Various sources are cited as providing evidence that the "discarding of traditional inactive approaches has led to the documentation of significant literacy improvement." McCollum (1991, p. 119) similarly concluded that learning in multicultural contexts was enhanced by social interaction and talk between participants in learning and teaching.

Clearly, then, when advocating a whole language approach to learning and teaching, we signal the fact that we prefer a different set of values than is often proposed. For example, we care as much about whether students *do* read as if they *can* read. We prefer that students understand the purposes for using language; we wish to assist them in becoming internally motivated to learn through language. We value collaborative learning and reflective teaching. We prefer evaluation to occur under real classroom learning conditions. The list could go on, but the point is that whole language reflects a view of learning and teaching that is different from other extant models of language, especially transmission models.

Refining the Meaning

Because the term *whole language* is commonly used does not mean that there is agreement on what the term means. There are several ways to approach the

*Falmer Press. Reprinted with permission.

task of clarifying the meaning. One way is to examine publications to see if there is agreement in how the term is used. Bergeron used that approach to examine 64 articles published between 1979 and 1989, then tallied under a number of attributes (for example, focus, assessment, techniques, and so on) how the term was used. Finally, based on elements found in at least 50% of the analyzed articles, she concluded that "whole language is a concept that embodies both a philosophy of language development as well as the instructional approaches embedded within, and supportive of that philosophy. This concept includes the use of real literature and writing in the context of meaningful, functional and cooperative experiences in order to develop in students motivation and interest in the process of learning" (1990, p. 319).*

While such a reductionist approach to definition is useful as a starting point, it does have certain flaws. Since not all journal authors necessarily understand whole language equally, and since some even misinterpret it rather badly (e.g., Stahl and Miller, 1989), it is necessary to treat such abstractions cautiously.

A second way to determine how the term *whole language* is used is to consult important data bases to see how items are classified. For example, the *Thesaurus of ERIC Descriptions* (1990, p. 284) began using the term in 1990 and defines it as follows: "Method of integrating language arts 'across the curriculum' that use the real literature of various age groups and subject fields to promote literacy (i.e., reading, writing, speaking, listening as well as thinking skills)."

Among the major attributes of whole language are the following:

1. Real reading and writing are initiated right from the start on the first day of school.
2. Teachers and students work collaboratively.
3. The language arts are integrated with the content areas.
4. Conferences, observation, and other forms of evaluation are used for individual and group assessment.
5. The wholeness of each literacy event is preserved.
6. Student self-assessment is promoted.
7. Literature is read daily, often out loud.
8. Reflection and learning are practiced by students and teacher.
9. A variety of teaching and learning strategies are used.
10. Nurturing, supportive, and safe learning environments are created.
11. Authentic texts are used.
12. Comprehension is a constructive process supported by interaction with other students and adults.
13. Both personal and social meaning is constructed by the individual.
14. Learning is student centered.

*Reprinted with permission of the National Reading Conference.

15. The teacher's role is to structure the learning environment, to know students, to model learning, to teach at the appropriate moment, and to be supportive.

While some of these features are also claimed by other approaches, not all are, and it is not possible to compile a complete list of characteristics at this point since whole language is still evolving in many ways. The research evidence supporting whole-language is presented in detail in Chapter 13.

Agreement and Disagreement

There is, however, consensus on some fundamental aspects of the concept. First, it is agreed that language is a naturally developing human activity, and as a result it is a social phenomenon used for communication purposes. Second, it is generally accepted that language learning and teaching must be personalized in order to respect the uniqueness and interest of the learner. Third, language learning is considered to be a part of making sense of the world; language need not be learned separately first. Language is learned holistically in context rather than in bits and pieces in isolation.

A variety of materials are useful in whole-language classrooms.

These fundamental points of consensus give way to considerable disagreement when theorists consider precisely what is entailed by whole language. Some think of it as a method or approach; others hold it to be a set of beliefs. The role of direct instruction is not clear; some advocate it, others discourage it. Some characterize it as a political activity: It shifts power away from the teacher toward the student. Still others believe that it means that all instruction should be individual rather than in small or large groups. And others have extended it to include professional development. Crowell (1989, p. 62), in fact, concluded that "whole language is an excellent example of many new paradigmatic concepts. The concept of integration, complexity, and holism are central to this approach. Process and content are intertwined, as are students and learning."

Other areas of contention have arisen from what seems to be an attempt by some to make current and traditional classroom procedures appear as though they are not very different from whole-language procedures. As a result, publishers market "whole-language" flashcards, workbooks, reading series, and other learning aids. Most of these materials are based on a learning paradigm that is antithetical to the whole-language paradigm. As well, some would argue that whole-language is another label for "whole-word" learning, which is usually compared or contrasted with phonics instruction. These arguments are basically deliberate misinterpretations of what whole language is intended to be. That is, *whole-language* refers to a child-centered, literature-based approach to language teaching that immerses students in real communication situations.

Dealing with Textbook-Based Teaching

While this book is about whole-language, we recognize that the prospective teacher is likely to encounter materials that do not fit well with whole-language teaching, such as classroom reading series, spelling series, or language series in many schools. Our intention here is simply to put these kinds of materials, and textbook-based teaching, into perspective. We will examine the differences between the assumptions behind textbook-based teaching and those behind whole-language instruction.

First, we must look at the assumptions behind the materials. Although it is commonly believed that educators have determined exactly what each student at each grade level should learn in order to become a competent language learner, one need only examine and compare different scope-and-sequence charts for any individual subject area to discover that there is only minimal agreement. If one compares across grade levels, one finds even less agreement (or, in some cases, substantial overlap). Yet many teachers, principals, and superintendents adhere to the belief that if the materials are covered, the specified skills will be learned. In fact, in most cases there is little, if any, evidence that the skills themselves exist (Froese, 1983; Johnston, 1984), and even less for the effectiveness of the sequences in which they should be taught. More recently the validity of the studies on which skills are based is being questioned (Lysynchuk, Pressley, d'Ailly, Smith, and Cake, 1989).

A second assumption is that all students must learn the proposed skills, usually in the same order and at the same time. Classroom observation reveals, of course, that groups of students do not learn in this manner. Giving any group of students a pretest on something they are supposed to learn will convince the observer that some already know the information or process, that some do not, and that some may have a partial understanding. Furthermore, not all students have a need for the skill, and those students are likely to forget it quickly even if they do learn it. For example, a report by Gunning (1988) explored the phonics processes taught and found that the skills (processes) were not used as taught. Instead, the report found that the students used a range of much more intuitive processes to develop language skills. Other studies have shown that these reading skills are infrequently modeled or demonstrated even by the teachers who claim to teach in this way (Blanton and Moorman, 1990) and that those students who were excused from skills instruction on the basis of a pretest nevertheless scored high on achievement (Taylor, Frye, and Gaetz, 1990).

Most graded series of textbooks fragment teaching and often take out of context the supposed skills to be learned. The emphasis usually is on teaching such skills as predicting outcomes, on dividing words into syllables, or on writing complete sentences. Examples are given in the textbook, practice exercises are presented, and then the student is expected to know the skill. None of these fragments has grown out of the student's experience; they are not means to an end; they do not represent problems that the student needs to solve. Interest in such activities has to be artificially induced; that is, the teacher has to try to get the students to appear interested. Shuy (1981, p. 103) has decried such practices of putting form before function in the teaching of language.

Textbook-oriented teaching does have some benefits in some people's minds. It does not require as much preparation for the teacher since the materials are already printed; it does not require much thought on the part of the teacher because the guidebook provides the directions (Goodman, Shannon, Freeman, and Murphy, 1988); and it placates the administrators because the "ground" has been covered. It is also often preferred by many teachers simply because it is the traditional method of teaching. Parents often expect such teaching since they experienced it as well.

Our position is that textbook materials may be useful at appropriate times with appropriate applications, but it is not the preferred method of instruction. When school pressures require the prospective teacher to use such materials, our suggestion would be to begin with the follow-up or enrichment activities because they can create a context for the lesson (although the Instructor's Guide usually recommends that they be used last, and then they frequently are omitted because of lack of time). Then use a pretest, or observation, to group students so that only those who need it get the textbook instruction. Others might read independently or become involved in enrichment activities. Naturally this requires additional planning and preparation, but it does have the potential of resulting in more satisfying teaching. It is rather ironic that we now are seeing textbooks on how to improve basal reader instruction (Winograd, Wixson, and Lipson, 1989) to bring it more in line with what we are suggesting in this text, rather than simply adopting whole-language, which is more in line with current theories of language development, as pointed out by Piper (1993).

Reasons Behind Whole-Language Teaching

What one teaches in language arts classes is influenced by at least three major sources of information: information from linguistics, from psychology, and from pedagogy. Linguists provide explanations and rules as to how "ideal" language users might use language; psychologists provide information about how "real" language users perform; and educators provide methods of how to accomplish language instruction in the classroom. In Figure 1.1 the areas of overlap among these three disciplines are also identified since they have become identifiable fields in themselves: psycholinguistics (the study of the mental processes underlying the acquisition and use of language), applied linguistics (linguistics applied to the teaching of languages), and educational psychology (psychology of learning and instruction). This explanation is provided only to indicate the interrelatedness of the many fields or disciplines that are brought to bear on the teaching and learning of language.

Therefore, whole-language teaching may be conceptualized as the territory where the three major disciplines coincide. Refer to Figure 1.1 for an illustration of how these three disciplines and related fields contribute to an understanding of whole-language.

The Linguistics Perspective

Thought and language are the inseparable basics of a whole-language curriculum. Children learn to use language through meaningful exchanges with other people in their environment. Thus language is learned as part of a social process,

FIGURE 1.1   *The Contribution of Various Disciplines to Whole Language*

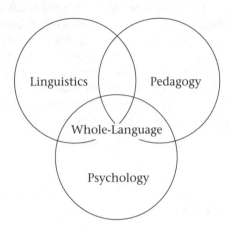

or, as Halliday (1978) has called it, a **social semiotic**. As children learn more about language and begin to talk about it and manipulate it, experts say that they are developing a **metalinguistic awareness**.

Loban (1976) has shown that a close relationship exists between listening, speaking, writing, and reading. His longitudinal study of students from kindergarten through grade 12 indicated that good oral language development is crucial to the later development of literacy. Piper (1993) also indicated that whole language is consistent with the most enlightened theories of language.

Linguists, through a study of language, have also provided educators with the basic organizational concepts of language. They have explained how the sounds of language are produced (**phonology**), how words come to represent ideas (**semantics**), how words are strung together into meaningful strings called sentences (**syntax**), and how sentences form connected discourse (**text schema**). Linguists also study **pragmatics**—that is, how language is used for communication purposes.

These linguistic concepts are certainly part of the reason why we advocate using the whole-language approach here. Because language is used for communication in real situations first, before it is formally taught, it is functional and it is used to learn about the world from very early on. Whole-language builds on the language children have already internalized, and extends it to the modalities (i.e., reading, writing) that are less developed.

The Psychological Perspective

Since *real* language users (as compared to *idealized* language users) make mistakes or miscues, do not always take into account all possible rules, and must work in "real time," they provide **psychologists** with much to study. In fact, the study of language has produced psycholinguists who specialize in the psychology of language usage. In addition, psychologists have shown how human memory is organized, what motivates one's use of language, and how language is used for different purposes (Shuell, 1986).

Educators have learned, for example, that young children have internalized information, or "rules," about language (note that these are *not* "phonics rules"), which they at first overgeneralize. A child might well say, "The mans are working on the house." This illustrates that the child has abstracted a system from hearing language used, but he or she has not yet learned the way of forming irregular nouns.

In oral reading, the child might substitute "home" for "house" because that is the term heard at home. Psycholinguists suggest that free-word association shows that patterns exist in the word combinations that come (seemingly haphazardly) to people's minds, and that there are some developmental trends

in these patterns. Semantic features that are made obvious through free association are very powerful in explaining how one learns words and the meaning that they represent in one's mind.

It is clear that language may be analyzed for structure; however, it may also be analyzed for *how it is used,* such as to control, to persuade, to inform, and so on (Tough, 1977). Whole-language takes into account the fact that language users are motivated to correct meaning rather than to correct form. Furthermore, whole-language practitioners recognize that processes such as the selection of reading materials are self-motivated (when not interfered with by peer pressure or teacher expectations).

Recently the constructivists' view of learning has been revived. This view holds that knowledge is actively built up and serves as the organization of the experiential world (von Glasersfeld, 1991, p. 31). Applied to language learning, the constructivist perspective suggests that meaning is personally "constructed" gradually through one's interaction with things, events, ideas, and so forth. Students at all ages need to be actively involved in learning, must be given opportunities to reflect on what they are doing, and must be involved in decision making. Social interaction is critical to this process. Autonomy is a major aim and the teacher's role is a facilitative one. Flavell's (1985) work in social cognition, *cognition about people and what they do*, has begun to influence literary research—research into how the writers' or readers' viewpoints are being represented is of great interest (Bonk, 1990).

The Pedagogical Perspective

Pedagogy refers to the art, science, or profession of teaching. Along with linguistic and psychological research, educational research has contributed to the development of effective language-learning strategies. Much of what is known about group processes—the selection of appropriate materials by students and by teachers, the writing process, reading as a meaning-construction procedure, curriculum organization, and observation and assessment techniques—comes from pedagogical inquiry. Additionally, many historical precedents exist for child-centered, humanistic, and progressive education (Weir, 1977).

Because collaborative learning and peer tutoring have been successful, they are used in whole-language classrooms. Because experts know that children's interests can overcome the constraints of readability, teachers should encourage students to select their own books. Because much is known about how composing, writing, and editing are accomplished, teachers should focus on the *processes* rather than the *products* alone. Finally, because it is known that invented spelling gradually begins to approximate conventional spelling, teachers should encourage children to use it.

Reading is no longer considered a *receptive* process. It is now thought of as a *constructive* or *interactive* process; the reader attempts to reconstruct or interact with the author's message, but based on his or her own experience (Spivey, 1990). Educators know that few hierarchies actually exist, so scope-and-sequence-charts have no real basis in fact. Educators have also learned that a good observer can produce a very reliable assessment even without standardized or commercial tests. And educators have learned that general strategic knowledge functions in close partnership with specialized domain knowledge (Perkins and Salomon, 1989).

The critical pedagogy of Friere, Giroux, and Apple has given rise to an area of study often known as "critical literary." This approach leads to a questioning of the social, political, and economic bases of literacy instruction (Brown, 1990). Critical feminist theory has helped to question gender issues underlying texts and schooling (Gaskell, 1992).

Since the first edition of this textbook was written (c. 1988), numerous studies specifically on whole language have found their way into the professional literature. Findings include that many classrooms exhibit some whole language type of instruction (Hollingsworth, Reutzel, and Weeks, 1990), that whole language instruction focuses on meaning rather than on small units of language (King, Crenshaw, and Watson, 1989), that students in whole language classrooms produce better reading achievement and phonics scores than those in more traditional classrooms (Eldredge, 1991), and that low-level students in whole language classrooms have a slightly better chance in catching up with their classmates (Klesius, Griffith, and Zielonka, 1991). We can truly say that educational research has influenced pedagogy.

What Whole-Language Means in Practice

Up to this point we have provided a preview of some of the attributes of whole-language, the assumptions behind whole-language, and some of the linguistic, psychological, and pedagogical reasons behind this point of view. Now we will enumerate some of the ways in which these beliefs are exemplified in classroom practice.

The Teacher's Perspective

1. Whole-language teachers believe that language is a naturally developing human activity.
2. Language is used for communication; the classroom can provide a context for "real-life" language situations.

3. Language is part of the environment and need not be separated into "subjects" to be taught (reading, composition, spelling, and so on). Large, integrated blocks of time (language arts "periods") are preferred if segmentation is required, but even wider integration with other areas such as social studies, science, or mathematics is advocated.
4. Language is learned and used holistically first; it is differentiated and refined later.
5. Classrooms should be rich learning environments and it is the teacher's responsibility to ensure that they are.
6. The whole-language teacher should be responsible for instructional and curricular decisions; these should not be dictated by the materials.
7. Teaching should be personalized, based on students' individual needs.
8. Students are taught individually, in small groups, or in large groups depending on the purpose or circumstance. Collaborative learning is encouraged.
9. Students of all ages have the ability to think critically and creatively if they are given the right opportunities and support.
10. It is the teacher's responsibility to ensure that work is assessed and evaluated, but assessment is shared with students in many ways.
11. The teacher is a model learner.
12. The learning of additional languages is generally enriching.

The Student's Perspective

1. Each student is a unique individual, different from others, and that is to be expected—it is the norm.
2. Students' interests should drive much of the daily learning. By and large, motivation is internal.
3. Students can plan their own work and make decisions about how they will accomplish it.
4. Students can assess their own work or learn to assess their own work with the teacher's guidance.
5. Students develop ownership through working with their own ideas; they develop responsibility through learning self-assessment.
6. Language is always used for some purpose, to achieve some end (hence the importance of contextualized language learning).
7. The classroom is an environment in which stimulating situations are encountered.
8. The teacher is a supportive adult in the room who assists students in learning.
9. Responses due to variations in cultural and linguistic backgrounds are acknowledged.

Both listening and speaking skills are practiced when students present information to peers.

The Materials

1. The classroom should be designed to allow the use of a variety of materials, and the furniture arrangement should be flexible.
2. All and any materials have potential as learning instruments. Graded series of textbooks are not particularly required, but they may be used when circumstances warrant them.
3. To encourage general literacy it is important to have high-quality literature of all types available—fiction, informational, and so on.
4. Much learning material is better made than bought in ready-made form.
5. It is best to acquire materials that are appropriate to the type of teaching intended. In the case of whole-language, children's own writing, tradebooks, informational books, reference books, magazines, audiovisual equipment, films, tapes, computers, games, artifacts, pictures, paper, paint, and so on are the raw materials required.
6. The "content" for most language activities, except when discussing language itself, comes from the other areas: sciences, arts, social studies, and so on.

7. Art, music, drama, and film are sources of information that have much in common with the language arts. They help people learn about the world and about themselves, as do the sciences and other humanities.
8. People in the community are among the best language resources.
9. Tests must be valid and authentic reflections of the curriculum being taught in the classroom. Summative evaluations should never be based on only *one* measure or test. For best results, teachers, students, and parents should have some input into the evaluation process. When possible, evaluation (i.e., observation, testing, conferencing) should be done under normal classroom conditions.
10. It is important to understand the underlying social, political, and persuasive purposes of commercially produced materials.

Summary

This chapter began with a definition of whole-language. It then explained what the generally agreed-upon assumptions were that underlie this type of teaching. Examples were given of why professionals from a wide range of backgrounds favor whole-language. Next, rationales for this approach were articulated from linguistic, psychological, and pedagogic perspectives. And last, a list of practical assumptions underpinning this approach in the classroom was presented.

Whole-language is based on the most enlightened theories of language and is viable today for a number of reasons. First, teachers today are very well trained and most have a degree. They can be expected to make autonomous curricular decisions. Second, materials are relatively plentiful and available. Instruction need not be centered around one common book. Third, basic skills are not enough, and literacy expectations have risen steadily. Students are expected to make important decisions for themselves. Fourth, society's expectations are that schools will produce thinking, flexible individuals who are prepared for a lifetime of learning.

Since the first edition of this book on whole-language was published, many others have appeared. Some focus on the administration and planning of whole language programs (Yatvin, 1992; Heald-Taylor, 1989), some emphasize evaluation and assessment (Goodman, Goodman, and Hood, 1989), others focus on the research behind whole language (Stephens, 1991) and still others concentrate on English as a second language (ESL) for every classroom teacher (Law and Eckes, 1990). Because of the popularity of whole language, several publications collecting either journal articles or conference proceedings have also appeared (Taylor, 1990; Kiefer, 1990; Hydrick, 1991). These are good supplementary reading for the topics indicated.

Book Overview and Use

Although we advocate a holistic approach, we did not feel it wise to compose a book with only one long chapter! So the following divisions are intended to assist you in learning, in manageable segments, the essential elements of whole-language.

To aid you in using the book, a brief overview of each chapter is provided here. The chapters in this book need not be read in the order in which they are presented, except that Chapter 1, Introduction to Whole-Language Teaching and Learning, should be read first. Teachers of kindergarten through grade 3 may wish to read the chapters in the order in which language develops; teachers of grades 4 through 8 may wish to skip to Chapter 6, Reading and Language Development, and then to Chapter 5, The Writing Connection. Others may wish to go directly to Chapter 12, Assessment: Form and Function, or to Chapter 13, Research Perspectives on Whole-Language. In short, the order of reading the chapters should be determined by need or preference. Each chapter has been planned to contribute to the whole, but each can also stand independently, providing maximum flexibility in use of this book.

You will find Key Concepts at the beginning of each chapter, Key Terms in boldface throughout each chapter, and a Glossary at the end of the text, which briefly defines each term that is not defined in context. In addition, to assist you in understanding each chapter, a set of Discussion Questions has been appended. These can be used by the instructor or by the reader to help assimilate the content, to extend it, or to apply it.

Chapter 1 presents an operational definition of whole-language and why it is important; it also presents the rationale behind it based on linguistic, psychological, and pedagogic perspectives. The first chapter enumerates some thoughts for whole-language teachers to keep in mind, student observations of the whole-language environment, and ideas for use of classroom materials.

Chapter 2 outlines what happens in two whole-language classrooms on a typical day. A representative primary classroom (kindergarten through grade 3) and an intermediate classroom (grades 4 through 8) are described in detail.

Chapter 3 stresses the role of oral language, or "talk," in the curriculum and in the classroom. Through actual classroom examples, you are introduced to the function of oral language and how it develops. Then activities for stimulating discussion and interaction are suggested.

Chapter 4 immerses the prospective teacher in children's literature of all genres, from fictional to informational. This chapter gives practical grade-level specific advice on the appropriate selection of tradebooks and how to use them in teaching appreciation for literature, and for language and concept development. Personal response is stressed.

Chapter 5 shows how written composition integrates with all of the language activities of the classroom. Part I deals with the basic principles of the writing process, and Part II discusses the implementation of this approach to writing in the classroom. Part III examines writing to learn, and Part IV provides a step-by-step demonstration of how a teacher may get started in using this approach.

Chapter 6 contains suggestions for implementing reading instruction and for furthering language development in the whole-language classroom. The close relationship of reading to the development of writing and other language abilities is explored in some detail. Included is a discussion of skills and phonics instruction within the whole-language framework.

Chapter 7 outlines active, child-centered approaches to language development through dramatic representation of ideas, stories, and texts. Even those teachers not experienced in drama can use these hands-on suggestions to motivate students to expand their expressive abilities and to actively demonstrate comprehension in various situations.

Chapter 8 provides information on how to use information technology in the whole-language classroom. Most schools have some computers available to students, others have laboratories set up for training in the technologies, and still others have sophisticated learning centers integrated into central libraries. This chapter provides some basic information for all teachers.

Chapter 9 introduces the classroom teacher to a variety of concepts needed to deal with the whole range of students with special needs, from underachievers to gifted students to English-as-a-second-language students. The information provided should assist the classroom teacher in identifying some of the special needs and to draw on other resource personnel when necessary.

Chapter 10 prepares the prospective teacher for the questions parents most often ask about whole-language instruction. The chapter explains approaches to involving parents in both in-home literacy learning and school-related learning.

Chapter 11 provides guidelines for organizing whole-language classrooms. Specific suggestions are given for organizing time, the curriculum, and classroom space; selecting materials and resources; and grouping children for whole-language learning.

Chapter 12 clarifies the reasons for assessment and evaluation in the classroom. It identifies the major issues in assessment and presents a case for the congruence of assessment procedures and curriculum content. The chapter then presents a model as well as practical procedures for evaluating the major components of language—reading, writing, speaking, and listening—in a manner consistent with the whole-language approach.

Chapter 13 interprets the research on whole-language, the relationship between reading and writing, the emergence of literacy, and the development of nontraditional reading programs. The chapter provides evidence for the basis of this volume: The whole-language approach, when applied by good teachers, can be a viable instructional alternative and can truly benefit the literacy development of children.

REFERENCES

Adams, M.J. (1989). *Beginning to read: Thinking and learning about print.* Cambridge, MA: MIT Press. (See also a summary of this book published by the Center for the Study of Reading, University of Illinois.)

Bergeron, B.S. (1990). What does the term whole language mean? Constructing a definition from the literature. *Journal of Reading Behaviour, 22, 4,* 301–329.

Blake, R.W. (Ed.). (1990). *Whole language: Explorations and applications.* Schenectady, NY: New York State English Council Monographs.

Blanton, W.E. & Moorman, G.B. (1990). The presentation of reading lessons. *Reading Research and Instruction, 29,* 35–55.

Bonk, C.J. (1990). A synthesis of social cognition and writing research. *Written Communication, 7,* 1, 136–163.

Brown, L. (1990). Literacy as politics. In S.P. Norris and L.M. Phillips (Eds.), *Foundation of literacy policy in Canada* (pp. 85–105). Calgary: Detselis.

Crowell, S. (1989). A new way of thinking: The challenge of the future. *Educational Leadership,* Sept., 60–63.

Bullock, A.B. (1975). *A language for life.* London: Her Magesty's Stationery Office.

Eldredge, L. (1991). An experiment with a modified whole language approach in first-grade classrooms. *Reading Research and Instruction, 30,* 21–38.

Flavall, J.H. (1985). *Cognitive development* (2nd ed.). Englewood Cliffs, NJ: Prentice Hall.

Froese, V. (1983). Fact and fiction about language skills. *Reading Horizons, 23,* 95–102.

Froese, V. (1994). Language across the curriculum. In N. Postlethwaite (Ed.), *International Encyclopedia of Education.* Oxford: Pergamon Press.

Gardner, H. (1991). *The unschooled mind: How children think and how schools should teach.* New York: Basic Books.

Gaskell, J. (1992). *Gender matters from school to work.* Toronto: OISE Press.

Goodman, K. (1992). I didn't found whole language. *The Reading Teacher, 46, 3,* 188–199.

Goodman, K.S., Goodman, Y.M. & Hood, W.J. (1989). *The whole language evaluation book.* Portsmouth, NH: Heinemann.

Goodman, K., Shannon, P., Freeman, Y. & Murphy, S. (1988). *Report card on the basal reader.* New York: Richard C. Owen Publisher.

Gunderson, L. (1989). *A whole language primer.* Richmond Hill, Ontario: Scholastic-TAB Publications.

Gunderson, L. & Shapiro, J. (1988). Whole language instruction: Writing in first grade. *The Reading Teacher, 41, 4,* 430–439.

Gunning, G.G. (1988). *Decoding behaviour of good and poor second grade students.* Paper presented at the 39th Annual IRA Conference, Toronto.

Halliday, M.A.K. (1978). *Language as social semiotic: The social interpretation of language and meaning.* Baltimore: University Park Press.

Heald-Taylor, G. (1989). *The administrator's guide to whole language.* Katonah, NY: Richard Owen Publishers.

Healy, M.K. & Barr, M. (1991). Language across the curriculum. In J. Flood, J.J. Jensen, D.

Lapp & J.R. Squires (Eds.), *Handbook of research on teaching English language arts* (pp. 820–826). New York: Macmillan Publishing Company.

Hollingsworth, P.M., Reutzel, D.R. & Weeks, E. (1990). Whole language practices in first grade reading instruction. *Reading Research and Instruction, 29,* 14–26.

Hydrick, J. (1991). *Whole language: Empowerment at the chalk face.* Toronto: Scholastic.

Johnston, P.H. (1984). Assessment in reading. In P.D. Pearson (Ed.), *Handbook of reading research* (pp. 147–182). New York: Longmans.

Kiefer, B. (1990). *Toward a whole language classroom: Articles from Language Arts, 1986–89.* Urbana, IL: NCTE.

King, D.F., Crenshaw, S. & Watson, D. (1989). Reading instruction: Differences in teachers' language focus. *Reading: Exploration and Discovery, 12, 1,* 38–52.

Klesius, J.P., Griffith, P.L. & Zielonka, P. (1991). A whole language and traditional instruction comparison: Overall effectiveness and development of the alphabetic principle. *Reading Research and Instruction, 30,* 47–61.

Law, B. & Eckes, M. (1990) *The more than just surviving handbook: ESL for every classroom teacher.* Winnipet, Manitoba: Peguis Publishers.

Loban, W. (1976). *Language development: Kindergarten through grade twelve.* Urbana, IL: NCTE.

Lysynchuk, L., Pressley, M., d'Ailly, H., Smith, M. & Cake, H. (1989). A methodological analysis of experimental studies of comprehension strategy instruction. *Reading Research Quarterly, 24, 4,* 458–470.

Luke, A. (1988). *Literacy, textbooks and ideology: Postwar literacy instruction and the mythology of Dick and Jane.* New York: Falmer Press.

McCollum, P. (1991). Cross-cultural perspectives on classroom discourse and literacy. In E.H. Hiebert (Ed.), *Literacy for a diverse society: Perspectives, practices, and policies* (pp. 108–121). New York: Teachers College Press.

McConaghy, T. (1988). Canada: A leader in whole-language instruction. *Phi Delta Kappan,* Dec., 336–337.

Miller, J.P. (1988). *The holistic curriculum.* Toronto: OISE Press.

Pearson, P.D. (1989). Commentary: Reading the whole language movement. *The Elementary School Journal, 90, 2,* 231–234.

Perkins, D.N. & Salomon, G. (1989). Are cognitive skills context-bound? *Educational Researcher,* Jan.-Feb., 16–25.

Piper, T. (1993). *Language for ALL our children.* Toronto: Maxwell Macmillan Canada.

Purcell-Gates, V., McIntyre, E. & Freppon, P. A. (1995). Learning written storybook language in school: A comparison of low-SES children in skills-based and whole language classrooms. *American Educational Research Journal, 32, 3,* 659–685.

Ruddell, R.B. (1992). A whole language and literature perspective: Creating a meaning-making instructional environment. *Language Arts, 69, 8,* 612–620.

Rueda, R. (1991), Characteristics of literacy programs for language-minority students. In E.H. Hiebert, (Ed.), *Literacy for a diverse society: Perspectives, practices, and policies,* (pp. 93–107). New York: Teachers College Press.

Shuell, T.J. (1986). Cognitive conceptions of learning. *Review of Educational Research, 56, 4,* 411–436.

Shuy, R.W. (1981). A holistic view of language. *Research in the Teaching of English, 15, 2,* 101–111.

Spivey, N.N. (1990). Transforming texts: Constructive processes in reading and writing. *Written Communication, 7, 2,* 256–287.

Stahl, S.A. & Miller, P.D. (1989). Whole language and language experience approaches for beginning reading: A quantitative research synthesis. *Review of Educational Research, 59, 1,* 87–116.

Stephens, D. (1991). *Research on whole language.* Katonah, NY: Richard Owen Publishers.

Strickland, D. & Cullinan, B. (1990). Afterword. In M.J. Adams *Beginning to read: Thinking and learning about print* (pp. 425–434). Cambridge, MA: MIT Press.

Taylor, B.M., Frye, B.J. & Gaetz, T.M. (1990). Reducing the number of reading skill activities in the elementary classrooms. *Journal of Reading Behaviour, 22,* 167–179.

Taylor, D. (1990). *English Education, 22, 1.* (A special issue on assessment of whole language teaching.)

Tough, J. (1977). *The development of meaning.* London: Allen & Unwin.

Thesaurus of ERIC Descriptions (12th ed.). (1990). Phoenix, AZ: ORYX Press.

von Glasersfeld, E. (1991). Constructivism in education. In A. Lewy (Ed.), *The International Encyclopedia of Curriculum.* Oxford: Pergamon Press.

Watson, D., Burke, C. & Harste, J. (1989). *Whole language: Inquiring voices.* Richmond Hill, Ontario: Scholastic-TAB Publications.

Weaver, C. (1988). *Reading process and practice: from sociopsychology to whole language.* Portsmouth, NH: Heinemann Educational Books.

Willinsky, J. (1994). Theory and meaning in whole language: Engaging Moorman, Blanton, and McLaughlin. *Reading Research Quarterly, 29,* 4, 334–339.

Winograd, P.N., Wixson, K.K. & Lipson, M.Y. (1989). *Improving basal reading instructions.* New York: Teachers College Press.

Yatvin, J. (1992). *Developing a whole language program for a whole school.* Midlothian, VA: Virginia State Reading Association.

DISCUSSION QUESTIONS

1. Compare and contrast the definition of whole-language herein with those found in other journals or books.

2. Most sources of information talk about teaching "skills." Consult a psychology text and look up what is meant by "skills." Find some examples in teaching journals and discuss whether their use of the term *skill* is similar to the psychologists'. If the word *skill* did not exist, which words would you use?

3. In your view, what are the most important aspects of whole-language con-tributed by the fields of linguistics, psychology, and pedagogy?

4. The concept of whole-language, when it is manifested in the classroom, has a different impact on teachers, on students, and on the ways in which materials are used. Consult this chapter for lists of ways in which each component of the classroom (teacher, student, text) is affected. Arrange these components in order of importance, in your view, and discuss the results in small groups.

2

Putting Theory into Practice: A Day in Two Classrooms

MARILYN CHAPMAN AND JIM ANDERSON

KEY CONCEPTS

1. *The relationships between whole-language principles and classroom practice at primary and intermediate levels*

2. *How teaching techniques compatible with whole-language principles may be used in the context of classroom life*

3. *Developing and carrying out teaching-learning activities consistent with a whole-language philosophy*

Together, we have taught for more than 30 years, from kindergarten through grade 12. In addition, we have both worked closely with many other classroom teachers in various provinces across Canada. From our personal experiences and from our colleagues, we have learned much about learning, about teaching, about children, and about the power of whole-language when appropriately and sensitively implemented. Although some of our colleagues might not even consider themselves whole-language teachers, we believe their teaching reflects what whole-language teaching may be like.

Our objective in this chapter is to provide you with a feel for what a day in two whole-language classrooms might look like. The two teachers you are about to meet in this chapter—Mr. Kim and Ms. Pratt—are fictional. However, we see them as amalgams of teachers with whom we have worked, for what we describe are vignettes that could have been lifted unadorned from their classrooms.

We begin by visiting Mr. Kim and his class of 22 6- and 7-year-olds; we then visit Ms. Pratt and her class of 28 11- and 12-year-olds. Both classes might be thought of as typical in that the children demonstrate a wide range of abilities and are at different points along a developmental continuum in the various curriculum areas. As with most public school classrooms, the students come from a variety of home backgrounds, have a range of abilities, and receive different levels of support from the home. We mention these since they are factors that teachers need to consider as they establish an appropriate atmosphere and set of expectations in their classrooms.

In Chapter 1, some general principles were articulated upon which whole-language is based. Mr. Kim and Ms. Pratt embody these principles in their practices by attempting to do the following:

- To engage all learners by having children actively involved in learning and by recognizing individual learning styles

- To make learning personal and functional by helping the learners relate what it is they are learning to their own lives

- To encourage children to take risks in their learning by providing a supportive, yet challenging, classroom environment

- To recognize the social dimensions of learning and therefore to utilize a variety of social contexts (e.g., individual, small group, whole class, child-child, child-adult)

- To use language for communication and as a tool for thinking and learning in all areas of the curriculum

- To help children develop awareness of their own thinking and learning processes

- To help children refine and expand their knowledge of the communication processes of reading, writing, speaking, listening, viewing, and representing

- To help children make connections by building on their prior knowledge, by helping them relate what is being learned in school to their own lives, and by helping them see relationships across the curriculum

- To incorporate a variety of oral and written forms of representation and genres (e.g., fiction and nonfiction literature, visual organizers, drama, and role taking)

- To provide balance between experiences such as individual/shared, interactive/reflective, and teacher-directed/self-directed

- To integrate assessment with instruction

As an overview of the "shape" of the day, we are providing the agenda for the day in each classroom (Figure 2.1a and 2.1b). We both use the agenda in our own teaching and have found it to be a valuable tool for various age groups. It provides a visual representation of the day for children, which is especially important for English-as-a-second-language (ESL) students (Early, 1989), it gives children a sense of structure (which is important in whole-language classrooms), and it also demonstrates functional use of reading and writing. For these reasons, we suggest adopting/adapting the agenda for your own classroom use.

Figure 2.1a   *Agenda: Ms. Pratt*

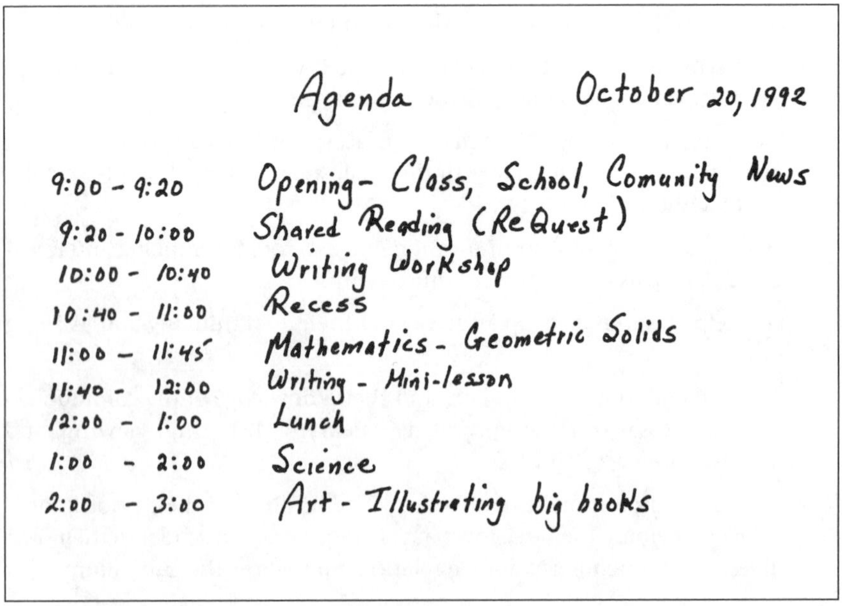

Agenda   October 20, 1992

9:00 - 9:20	Opening - Class, School, Comunity News
9:20 - 10:00	Shared Reading (ReQuest)
10:00 - 10:40	Writing Workshop
10:40 - 11:00	Recess
11:00 - 11:45	Mathematics - Geometric Solids
11:40 - 12:00	Writing - Mini-lesson
12:00 - 1:00	Lunch
1:00 - 2:00	Science
2:00 - 3:00	Art - Illustrating big books

Figure 2.1b   *Agenda: Mr. Kim*

Agenda

Group Meeting
  - Calendar
  - News
  - Shared Reading
Reading - Writing Workshop
Reading Club
Sharing
Recess
Story Time
Math
Music
Lunch
Quiet Reading
Buddy Reading
Science
Centres
Learning Logs
Sharing
  Hop on home

A Day in a Classroom with Six- and Seven-Year-Old Children

■ 9:00–9:25   Opening Activities/Sharing Time

functional language

Mr. Kim begins the day with a series of informal activities that flow from one to the other. These activities are structured to provide children with opportunities to meet and greet each other as well as to attend to administrative details such as attendance. Like many whole-language teachers, Mr. Kim realizes that the daily routines in the classroom provide functional opportunities for children to use oral and written language (Halliday, 1973; Pinnell, 1975). In the context of classroom life, such events can include authentic "workplace literacy" experiences (Mikulecky, 1983).

Sign In

functional literacy

variety of social contexts

As the children enter the classroom they put away their outdoor clothing and their snacks. Next, the children take their name tags from the "Our Class" chart by the classroom door and hang it on the "Who Is Here Today?" chart in the sharing area. Before sitting down on the carpet for opening activities, they return their books from their Take Home Reading Envelopes and select new books for tonight. (Mr. Kim realizes the importance of having children read at home and he has established a Take Home Reading Program. During his initial meeting with parents, he explained how the program works. Each day, the children take home a book to read with their parents, recording the title of the book and the date on a sheet attached to the envelope (Figure 2.2).

Attendance

language and thinking

Mr. Kim treats attendance taking as a collaborative problem-solving activity, reading and counting the name tags on the two charts with the children to help them discover how many children are present and who is away. Once the children have determined absentees, they discuss possible reasons for the absences. In this school, names of absent children are sent to the office, so Parminder, the "attendance helper," completes the form and takes it to the office while the class focuses its attention on the calendar.

Calendar

language across the curriculum

In the calendar activity, Kiko, the "calendar helper," is helped by Mr. Kim and other children to figure out the day and date and to select from preprinted cards to complete the following chart:

Yesterday was (Monday) (April) (15).

Today is (Tuesday) (April) (16).

Tomorrow will be (Wednesday) (April) (17).

Figure 2.2 *Take Home Reading Record*

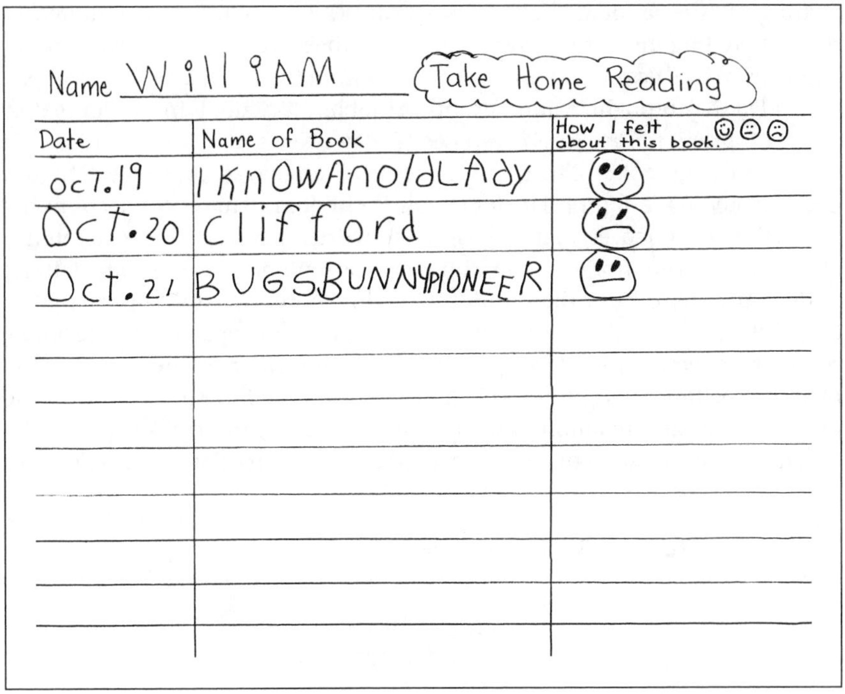
Name WilliAM Take Home Reading

Date	Name of Book	How I felt about this book.
OcT.19	I KnOwAnoldLAdy	
Oct.20	Clifford	
Oct.21	BUGSBUNNYPIONEER	

The children read the chart in unison. Mr. Kim then asks the children which of the three dates he should print on the top of the "Today's News" chart. Next, Kiko adds a stroke to a tally chart and the children figure out how many days they have been in school. Kiko prints the appropriate numeral on the "Days in School" chart, a roll of adding machine tape extending across the length of the chalkboard. Mr. Kim has incorporated many of the calendar activities suggested in *Mathematics Their Way* (Baratta-Lorton, 1976), a mathematics program based on many of the same assumptions as whole-language.

Agenda

Once the calendar is done, Mr. Kim draws the children's attention to the agenda for the day (which, of course, varies slightly from day to day to reflect the current day's events), which is printed on large chart paper (Figure 2.1b). Mr. Kim and the children read the agenda together aloud and discuss plans for the day. In the context of this shared reading activity, Mr. Kim encourages the children to make predictions about some of the words on the agenda chart and to share their thinking of how they figured the words out. Mr. Kim emphasizes good thinking, not just right answers, since he knows that good readers make predictions about text, use a variety of strategies, and focus on meaning rather than relying on a single strategy and a word accuracy focus (May, 1990).

functional literacy

awareness of thinking

News

*personal
langage*

Sharing of "special news" follows next. Mr. Kim encourages the children to share interesting things that have happened in their lives, some of their own creations, as well as favorite books and clippings from the newspaper. For example, today, D.J. has brought, Midnight, his pet rabbit, to school. In the context of the sharing activity, the class composes "Today's News" and Mr. Kim records it on a chart (Figure 2.3). Mr. Kim believes that language-experience activities (see Chapter 6) are appropriate for enabling children to make connections between their experiences, oral language, and written language. Mr. Kim "thinks aloud" as he writes (for example, "I'll start this sentence with a capital letter") to demonstrate some of the things that young writers need to think about as

*expanding
children's
knowledge of
the writing
process*

they write. He involves the children in the process by asking them to predict how some of the words might be spelled, confirming their predictions and explaining spelling conventions as appropriate. Because Mr. Kim is aware of the differences in ability among the children, he takes care to ask each child a question appropriate to his or her level of development. For example, he asks

Figure 2.3   *Today's News*

Today's News
Midnight the Bunny came to our class today. We get to keep her. D.J. thinks she is a girl rabbit. She was born on Halloween. D.J.'s mom brought Midnight to school in her car. D.J.'s Dad made a great cage. We are going to be very gentle. D.J. is going to be in charge. Laura and Evelyn are back from being sick. Gemma is moving to Owens Road.

Another teacher has students arrange word cards to demonstrate their understanding of sequence.

Ginette, a six-year-old, "How do you think *going* starts?" while to Cameron, a very capable eight-year-old, he says "Cameron, how do you think we might spell *exciting*?" Mr. Kim and the children discuss the news chart and read it aloud together. Mr. Kim also reminds the children that they may write other personal news in their journals later on. (They may do this during Reading and Writing Workshop or centers time.)

challenging children of different ability levels

■ 9:25–9:45   Shared Reading Activity (Whole Class)

The focus of language experiences in the opening activities is on connecting children's oral language with print. In the shared reading that follows, however, the focus is on helping children develop knowledge and skills related to "book language" (Holdaway, 1979). Mr. Kim wants children to become aware that written language is not just "talk written down," but is different in structure (Dyson, 1989). Today's shared reading is a new book in "big book" form, *The New Baby Calf* (Chase, 1984).

expanding children's knowledge of reading processes

Prereading

Mr. Kim begins with a schema-building activity that enables children to use their prior knowledge to make predictions about the text. Mr. Kim is aware that such activities are particularly important in today's classrooms because of

connecting with prior knowledge

the diverse backgrounds of the children. For example, children in inner-city schools may not have seen farm animals. First, Mr. Kim points out the title of the book as he reads it aloud. He encourages the children to make predictions about the book from its title and the illustration on the cover. As well as predicting the content of the book, Mr. Kim draws attention to the type of illustrations, in this case photographs of pictures created with plasticene, to encourage children to think about whether the book might be realistic/true or imaginary/fiction. Next, Mr. Kim prints the word *calf* in the center of a large piece of chart paper. The children brainstorm what they know about calves and Mr. Kim records the ideas as a **web** (Heimlich and Pittelman, 1986) (Figure 2.4). In the context of the web building, discussion ensues about whether a particular idea is true or not. (For example, the calf on the cover of the book is brown and the children debate whether all calves are brown.) Since the class questions or wonders about what colors calves can be, Mr. Kim writes "What colors are calves?" with a red pen and puts a large red question mark beside it. He then suggests that some of the children might be interested in visiting the library to find a book about cows or calves that may help them find out the answers to the questions indicated on the web or to find out other interesting things about calves that can be added to the web. (They may do this during Reading and Writing Workshop.)

Reading

supporting children

The prereading activity is followed by a shared reading of the text. Mr. Kim points to the text as he reads the book aloud. While the focus of this initial reading is *reading to* the children, Mr. Kim encourages the children to be active participants in the process, asking them to make predictions and to share their ideas about the text and to "read with" him as they are able. Some children join in and read along; other children "echo" what he has read. During this first reading of the book, Mr. Kim focuses on the meaning of the story. On subsequent days, as the class rereads the text, he will focus more on conventions of print, such as symbol/sound relationships, punctuation, spelling, and so on.

After Reading

awareness of thinking

The shared reading is followed by discussion of the story—for example, the children's predictions, and how and why they revised their thinking in the process of the reading. Because Mr. Kim is interested in helping children become aware of their own thinking processes, or **metacognition** (Paris, Wasik, and van der Westhuizen, 1988), he uses this after-reading discussion to focus on the process of reading as well as the content of the text.

The children have now been working at the carpet with Mr. Kim for 45 minutes. D.J. has spent the last few minutes over at the rabbit cage with

Figure 2.4 *Calf Web*

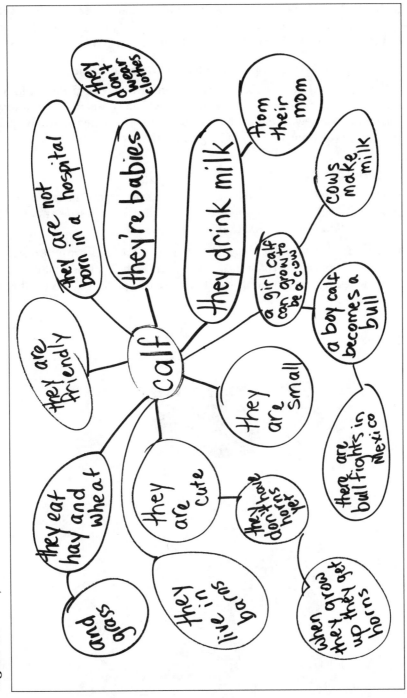

Midnight, the bunny, and some of the other children have started to fidget, so Mr. Kim brings the sharing time to a close. The children now need an opportunity for a change of pace and more self-directed activity.

■ 9:45–10:15   Individual and Small-Group Activities

variety of social contexts

Following the whole-class activities, Mr. Kim structures experiences for children to work individually or in small groups. The children are asked first to respond to the new story they have read together (an extension activity) and then to choose from a variety of language activities.

Extension Activity

During this time, the children have opportunities to respond individually to the story and Mr. Kim has an opportunity for informal assessment (anecdotal recording of informal observation, for example).

personal language

variety of representations

Children: Mr. Kim asks the children to respond to the story in two ways: by drawing and/or writing about their favorite part of the book or what they found most interesting and by writing why they chose that particular aspect of the book (Figure 2.5).

Figure 2.5   *Child's Extension Activity*

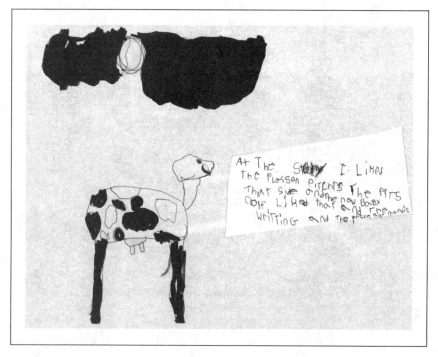

Teacher: While the children are working, Mr. Kim circulates about the room, observing the children, talking to them informally about what they are doing, and recording his observations. Today he noted that Carlos started by writing his response first and then drawing his picture. This is the first time that he has observed Carlos working in this way; previously, Carlos has started by drawing and then adding writing. Mr. Kim records his observation in anecdotal form on an "At-a-Glance Observation Sheet" (Figure 2.6), since it is a possible indicator that Carlos is becoming more at ease with written language as a medium of expression (Dyson, 1989). Mr. Kim realizes that it is important to make judgments about children's learning from multiple sources of information (Chapman, 1993). Therefore he records his observation and will take care to observe Carlos writing in a variety of contexts over the next several weeks to see if, indeed, this event signals a developmental milestone.

integrating assessment with instruction

Reading and Writing Workshop

Children: This block of time is structured to allow opportunities for the children to extend their development through independent and collaborative reading and writing. It also allows Mr. Kim to assess how they are doing. After

balanced experiences (teacher-directed and self-directed)

Figure 2.6 *Anecdotal Record—At-a-Glance Observation Sheet*

At-a-glance Observation Record

Week of: December 11 - 15		
Kiko	Reading Club - taking responsibility for returning library books. 13/12 Ashley	Ginette is reading using her knowledge of 911 to get along in the world - told everyone about the dangers of tipping chairs in news today. 11/12 Ginette
Reading Club - showed real enthusiasm for Ashley's story today. 13/12 Parminder	Cameron	Carlos
Interesting compliments to the other children in Reading Club today. 13/12 Marie-Claude	Volunteers predictions. Not always accurate but he's really listening. Very creative predictions in shared reading today. 11/12 Jamie	Michael
Manjit used the attendance sheet to check whose initials were missing from his inventory 12/12 Manjit	Following Manjit's example, Talwinder used the attendance form to check the inventory. Lots of interesting predictions in shared reading today. 12/12 Talwinder	William

the children finish the activity related to the story, they move to self-selected independent or collaborative activities, including:

*variety of
represen-
tations*

- **Reading:** Rereading the big book or accompanying small books from the morning's shared reading experience; visiting the book corner or the animal book display in the science center to select a book to read; reading classroom charts (including "Today's News" and the calf web); reading class-made books in the "Classroom Authors" center; or visiting the library to find out more about cows and calves
- **Listening:** Visiting the listening center to hear a taped story and follow the accompanying text
- **Writing:** Writing in their journals; visiting the writing center to start or continue a story of their own or to write a letter
- **Puppetry:** Visiting the puppet center to reenact the morning story or another familiar story or to to create an original puppet play
- **Science:** Working on their note-taking for their animal science projects (explained later in this section)

Reading Club

*variety of
social
contexts*

Teacher and small group: Once the children settle into their various activities, Mr. Kim begins a small-group reading conference. Mr. Kim uses a combination of group and individual conferences for reading and writing, depending on his purpose. A group reading conference (Hornsby, Sukarna, and Parry, 1986), or "Reading Club" as Mr. Kim calls it, provides him with an opportunity to hear a small group of children read and to record his observations. Mr. Kim has found that the Reading Club provides the children with meaningful practice in oral reading and an opportunity to discuss their personal reading with their peers. He has also discovered that group conferences provide many of the benefits of individual conferences yet take a lot less time. He has also found an additional benefit: The interaction among children enables them to learn from each other and share their ideas and enthusiasm. Mr. Kim had put up a sign-up chart for the week's Reading Club on Monday (Figure

*functional
literacy*

2.7) and today he is meeting with Carlos, Parminder, Ashley, Marie-Claude, and Jamie.

By now all of the children know the routine: They bring their reading logs and a book they have selected to read aloud. Some of the children will read an entire book (if it is a short one), and others who are reading longer books will read aloud a selection, such as their favorite part of a story. While the rest of the children in the class continue with their Reading and Writing Workshop activities (described previously), Mr. Kim meets the small group of children at the conference center, bringing with him his conference record sheets for the five children. The children each take a turn reading aloud for two or three min-

Figure 2.7   *Reading Club Sign-Up*

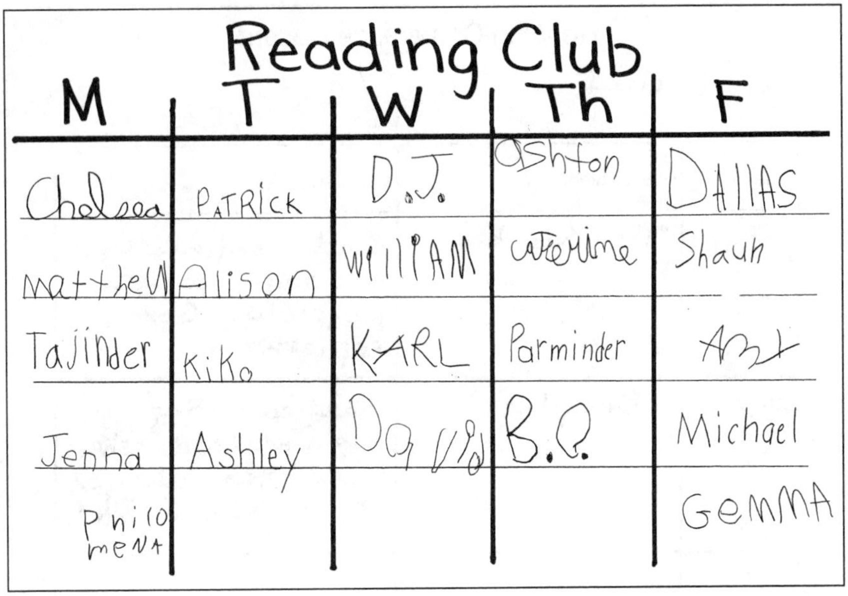

utes and then the rest of the group makes comments and asks questions about the book. Meanwhile, Mr. Kim records his observations on the conference record sheets (Figure 2.8).

Let's listen to some of the discussion:

Ashley:	[finishes reading a section from *Fox on Wheels* (Marshall, 1983)] *"Rats!" said Fox. "These aren't the wheels I had in mind!"*
Carlos:	I like the part when Carmen's cart crashed into the barrel of pickles.
Parminder:	That was funny; I like it too. And I liked when Mom said, "Hold your horses!"
Mr. Kim:	Ashley, I notice you put a lot of expression in your reading today, like when you read "Gangway!" and when you read "On your mark, get set, go!" It really sounded like you were starting a race.
Marie-Claude:	I read another story about Fox. Um, I think it was *Fox at School* (Marshall, 1983). Did you read that one?
Ashley:	No, can you help me find it?
Marie-Claude:	Okay.

Figure 2.8 *Conference Record Sheet*

Reading Conference Record

Name: Michael

Date	Title & Author	Comments
14/12/92	"The Bus Ride"	Read confidently. Knew the pattern perfectly. Good expression.
20/12/92	"Bony Legs"	Self correcting, e.g. he read "she lued" then changed it to "she liked".

Mr. Kim: Excuse me, a minute. I have to talk to Gemma and Philomena. [Mr. Kim leaves the table to talk to the two girls who are wrestling with the headphones at the listening center.]

Jamie: Can I read that book now, Ashley? Are you finished with it?

Ashley: You can have it now. You can just borrow it though, 'cause it's from the library and I have to take it back. . . .

integrating assessment with instruction

Teacher: At the end of Reading Club, the children who have participated in the group conference join the rest of the class to work independently and collaboratively on Reading and Writing Workshop activities. Meanwhile, Mr. Kim puts on his "Do Not Disturb" hat to signal to the children that he needs time for thinking. He takes about five minutes to complete his anecdotal notes on the children who participated in the group conference. Once he has done this, he circulates among the children at work and records his observations, as appropriate.

variety of social contexts

■ 10:15–10:25 Clean Up Followed by Sharing

Mr. Kim gives the children a signal to finish what they are doing, put their things away, and come to the carpet for sharing, bringing with them whatever they want to share. Rather than conducting a large group sharing session, Mr. Kim has the children form groups of two to four to share something they worked on during the morning.

■10:25–10:30 Prepare for Recess

The children get their outdoor clothing and snacks for recess. When they are ready, they go to the playground.

■ 10:30–10:45 Recess

Both children and teachers need unstructured free time. Today the children go outside to play and Mr. Kim heads to the staff room for a cup of coffee. Mr. Kim finds the rest of the morning much more productive when he is able to take time to relax away from the classroom, if only for a few minutes. He encourages the children to play outside whenever possible, since he finds they too are energized by a break, particularly in the fresh air.

■ 10:45–11:00 Story Time

After recess, the children hang up their outdoor clothes and come to the carpet for story time. Mr. Kim chooses particular stories for a variety of reasons: sometimes because the story is related to a broad theme the class is studying or to an approaching special day; at other times simply because it is a wonderful piece of literature. He often uses a story related to the mathematics lesson that follows, especially when he is working on a new concept.

Today, Mr. Kim has selected *Red Is Best* (Stinson, 1982) as a lead-in to a mathematics lesson on attribution. To begin, Mr. Kim shows the children the cover of the book, reads the title to them, and engages them in a discussion of what the book might be about. During the reading, he also encourages the children to make predictions and to comment on the story. After the reading, the class discusses the character's preference for the color red and their own color preferences.

language across the curriculum

■ 11:00–11:40 Mathematics: Introductory Lesson on Attribution

The mathematics lesson flows directly from the story reading. Mr. Kim explains to the children that color is an attribute and, through discussion, helps the children to understand that attributes might include such things as color, shape, size, and so on. In the process of discussion, the class and Mr. Kim develop a list of attributes which Mr. Kim records on a chart (Figure 2.9). To develop further the concept of attribution, he involves the children in a "people-sort" activity (Baratta-Lorton, 1976) where the children sort themselves into groups according to, in this case, the color of the shirts they are wearing. In the sorting process there is much discussion of problems such as shirts with more than one color. Next, the children participate in a people-sort based on their "lower" clothing. Mr. Kim moves a few children into a "jeans" group,

language as a tool for learning

helping children build knowledge

some others into a "shorts" group, and several others into a "skirt" group. After he has done this, he asks the other children to think individually about how he has sorted the people and to join in the group to which they think they belong. Much discussion occurs about the attribute for the people sort and about different ways in which people can be sorted—for example, by hair color, eye color, and so on.

variety of representations

Next, Mr. Kim explains to the children that they will be working in small groups to do some sorting by attributes. They are asked to find a partner and then to join another pair to make groups of four. Each foursome will select one of the many boxes and trays of manipulative objects such as buttons, attribute blocks, and so on. Each pair will sort some of the objects by an attribute of their choice and then see if their partners can determine the attribute by which the objects were sorted. They are to repeat the process choosing a different attribute each time. Once the children are clear about what to do, they choose their set of objects, find spaces in the classroom, and proceed with the activity. There is a busy hum in the room as the children become actively involved in their learning and talk about what they are doing. Mr. Kim circulates among the children at work, observing and talking with them informally. Near the end of the period, he gives the children a signal to put away their materials and come to the carpet. There is a brief discussion of the attributes children selected for their sorting. Neil tells the class that he and Justin thought of a new

Figure 2.9   *Attribute Chart*

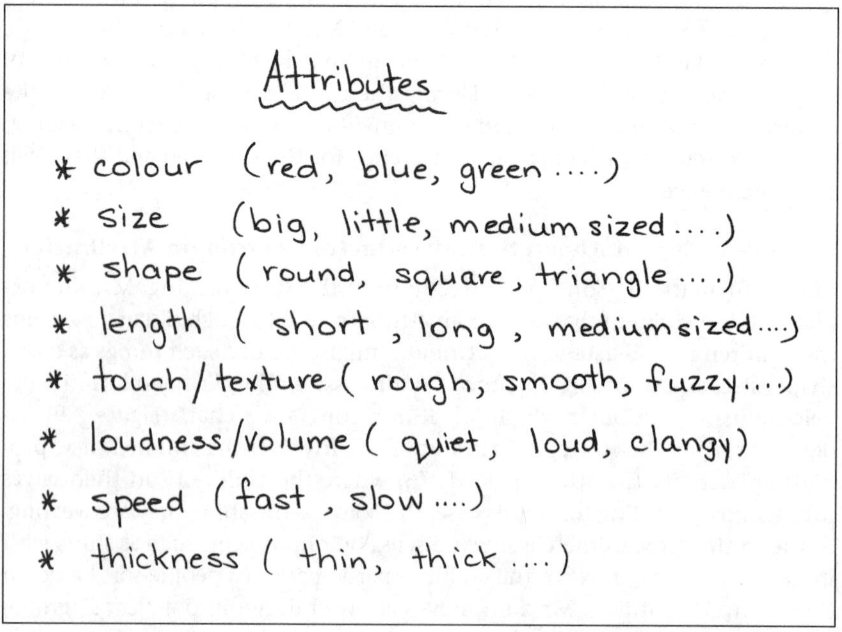

Attributes

* colour (red, blue, green ....)
* size (big, little, medium sized ....)
* shape (round, square, triangle ....)
* length (short, long, medium sized ....)
* touch / texture (rough, smooth, fuzzy ....)
* loudness / volume (quiet, loud, clangy)
* speed (fast, slow ....)
* thickness (thin, thick ....)

attribute they hadn't discussed earlier and Mr. Kim adds "height" to the attribute list. Heidi suggests that "thick and thin" could be an attribute too, so that is also added to the list. As a final activity, the children read the attribute list aloud together.

■ 11:40–12:00   Music

Mr. Kim considers music an important part of children's lives for its own sake. As well, he sees it as an opportunity to engage children in another form of literacy learning (Anderson and Ralston, 1994). Mr. Kim uses two print forms of the songs, charts and class song books. To teach a new song, Mr. Kim prefers to use a chart and afterward have the children add the page to their song books. As the year progresses, the children add more and more pages to their song books and at the end of the year they take them home. To begin, the class warms up with a couple of favorites selected by the children: "The More We Get Together" and "The Ants Go Marching." Today the children are learning a new song, "Going on a Lion Hunt." Mr. Kim has selected this song for two reasons: It relates to the animal theme they are studying and it has a repetitive pattern that enables children to learn the song easily and thus to participate fully in the musical experience.

language across the curriculum

Mr. Kim teaches the children the song using the chart. Next, Manjit and Ashley hand out the song books and the new song to be added. The children put the new pages in their books and sing the song twice more from their song books. Talwinder asks, "Can we sing 'Down by the Bay'?" Mr. Kim suggests that since it is almost lunch time, they could sing a few verses as they get ready for lunch. Also, the children often sing while getting ready to go home at the end of the day.

■ 12:00–1:00   Lunch

■ 1:00–1:15   Quiet Reading Time

As the children enter the classroom, they put their outdoor things away and find something to read. Mr. Kim has established a routine so that after children return from lunch, they take books out of their desks that they have already begun, visit the book corner to select a book, or find something from the science center such as a magazine like *Chickadee*. Because Mr. Kim is aware of the power of teacher modeling and its importance in silent reading time (McCracken and McCracken, 1978), he also reads during quiet reading time. Today, as he often does, he has brought in the newspaper from the staff room. Mr. Kim has discovered that some of the children are starting to become interested in reading the newspaper, often focusing on looking at the pictures and trying to read the captions, so he takes the newspaper apart into sections and puts them on the floor near him in the sharing area. As he does this, Marie-Claude and Soo-Yin take sections of the paper and sit on the floor nearby.

balanced experiences (interactive and individual)

■ 1:15–1:30   Shared Reading Time

variety of social contexts

After 15 minutes of independent reading, Mr. Kim tells the children that they can find one or more children with whom to share reading. Carlos and Talwinder enjoy **buddy reading** and take turns reading aloud from a single book. Kiko, Michael, Jamie, and Manjit meet in the science center to talk about and trade animal books they are reading. Marie-Claude and Kiko share their newspapers and talk about what they have found. A small group of children read and sing along with their song books, and another group congregates in the writing center to share stories they have written.

variety of represen- tations

integrating assessment with instruction

Mr. Kim uses this time as an opportunity to have individual reading or writing conferences with some of the children at the conference center. He first asks Talwinder to read to him, and then has a conference with Kiko about the draft she completed yesterday. In individual reading conferences, Mr. Kim listens to a child read orally and uses the child's **miscues** ("a reader's substi- tution, omission, insertion or repetition of a word" [May, 1990, p. 28]) to gain insight into his or her reading process (Clay, 1985; Goodman, Watson, and Burke, 1987).

In Talwinder's reading of *Rooster's Off to See the World* (Carle, 1972), Mr. Kim does not correct Talwinder's miscue when it does not alter the meaning of the text, for example:

Text:	He hadn't walked very far when he began to feel lonely.
Talwinder:	He hadn't walked very far when he began to feel lonesome.

When Talwinder's miscue does alter the meaning, however, Mr. Kim waits until Talwinder has finished the sentence, and then focuses the child's atten- tion on the meaning of the text, as the following conference excerpt shows:

Text:	. . . . the frogs saw four turtles crawling slowly down the road.
Talwinder:	. . . the frogs saw four turtles crowing slowly down the road.
Mr. Kim:	Talwinder, you read "four turtles crowing slowly down the road." Does that make sense to you? Would a turtle be crow- ing? (pauses) Have you ever seen a turtle moving?
Talwinder:	Well, it goes very slow.
Mr. Kim:	That's right, it goes very slowly, doesn't it? Can you think of a word that means going very slowly?
Talwinder:	Crawling?

helping children build knowledge of the reading process

Mr. Kim:	That would make sense here, wouldn't it? Let's check the story and see if it could be crawling. [Directs Talwinder's at- tention to the text.]
Talwinder:	Cr . . . awl . . . ing. Yes, it's crawling.

After about 10 minutes of shared reading, Mr. Kim asks the children to put away their books and come to the carpet. Informal discussion of what the children have been reading today occurs as the group that has gathered waits for the others to join them.

■ 1:30–2:10   Science

Like many primary teachers, Mr. Kim selects a science or social studies topic as a general theme through which to integrate the curriculum. He realizes that language and literacy are means through which children learn about science and social studies, so that in addition to having children engage in the processes related to science and social studies to acquire knowledge in those domains, they are also acquiring knowledge of language and literacy.

language across the curriculum

The class is currently studying the theme "animals" and writing reports about different animals. Earlier, the class had learned about whales and Mr. Kim used the whale theme as an opportunity to develop information reading and writing skills through a shared topic. Mr. Kim realizes that while children may learn much about literacy informally, they also benefit from explicit instruction at times. He believes that research skills are learned more effectively when a teacher demonstrates specific strategies and provides for guided practice (Chapman, 1994). In this instance, the children are using their knowledge from a shared experience to work on their individual animal reports. Since this is an early primary class, Mr. Kim has focused on helping the children learn how to find information in pictures and text, record the information in note form, and write drafts from their notes. Mr. Kim has shown children one form of note-taking, where the children have a paper folded into "idea boxes" and record a separate idea in each idea box (Figure 2.10).

building on prior knowledge

variety of representations

Now the children are ready to cut apart their idea boxes and sort the information into categories or main ideas. Mr. Kim has written on a large sheet of paper information about the polar bear, which he had used to review with the children a way to select and record ideas. Today Mr. Kim cuts apart his idea boxes and places them in the pocket chart. He asks the children to help him decide how to sort the ideas. The children provide advice and suggestions and Mr. Kim's ideas are sorted in a collaborative process. As this is done, there is much discussion about where ideas belong and why they go together. Next, Mr. Kim helps the children to develop the concept of *main idea* as they discuss each set of ideas. Mr. Kim pastes each set of boxes on a separate piece of chart paper and, with the children, generates headings (the main ideas) for his notes. Before the children go to work on their own ideas, Mr. Kim suggests that they may want to work in pairs and help each other with their sorting. He reviews what they are to do and requests that they cut, sort, paste, and generate headings before going on to another activity, so that they do not lose pieces of paper. After it is clear that the children know what to do, they get their note papers from their project folders and settle down to work, some children working in pairs and others working individually. Mr. Kim uses the opportunity to observe and record how the children are working, to provide assistance where needed, and so on.

expanding children's knowledge of the writing process

variety of social contexts

supporting children

Figure 2.10   *Idea Boxes*

white fur	very big	mammal	lives in the arctic
large paws and claws	dangerous	thick fur	sharp teeth
eats seals	eats arctic char	eats walrus	baby cubs
can travel on ice floes	travel long distances	live on land and ice floes	swim

■ 2:10–2:40   Centers

balanced experiences (teacher-directed and self-directed)

As the children finish their science work, they put away their materials and move into "centers time." Since the children finish their science work at different times, the start of centers time is staggered. The children have learned to take out their centers folder first and check to see what they have been working on before they decide what to work on today. Next, they go to the "choosing board" and put their name tag on the hook next to the center they have chosen. They then record in their folder the name of the center they are attending today. Mr. Kim goes to the choosing board to help anyone who needs it.

Children may select from a number of different centers, some of which are ongoing (for example, the writing center and the book corner), some of which are ongoing but with a new activity each week (for example, the art center and the listening center), some of which are brought in at various times of the year for a period of time and replaced and reintroduced as interests change (for example, the puppetry center or dress-up center) and some of which are related specifically to the theme being studied (for example, the animal science center). During centers time, Mr. Kim circulates to assist the children, to pose challenges, and so on. He also records his observations about what the children are at working on and how they are doing. (For more information about centers, see Chapter 11.)

integrating assessment with instruction

■ 2:40–2:50   Clean Up Followed by Learning Logs

At the close of centers time, Mr. Kim gives the children the signal to clean up and to get their learning logs. The learning logs provide the children with reflection time so that they can think about what they learned today. Mr. Kim has jokingly told the children that the learning logs can help them to tell their parents about what they have been learning in school so that they don't need to say "Oh, nothing" when their parents ask them what they did in school that day. This year, Mr. Kim is trying out a new idea with the learning logs: He sends them home once a week so that the children's parents can write a response to their child about his or her learning. Mr. Kim tries to incorporate many different ways of informing parents about their children's school learning, and he finds that the learning log is providing an interesting and informal opportunity for this. (Mr. Kim has discovered that Friday is not the best day for the learning logs to go home, though, since the children often forget to bring them back on Monday.) (For more information about home-school communication, see Chapter 10.)

language as a tool for thinking

language for communi-cating

After the children have finished writing in their learning logs, they find at least one friend to share the writing with before putting it away. Next, they get their Take Home Reading Envelopes with today's new books and take them to the carpet.

■ 2:50–3:00   Sharing

Today there is a notice to go home, so Mr. Kim reads it to the children, reminds them to bring back the attached form the next day, and then asks Michael to hand out notices. The children put the notice in their Take Home Reading Envelopes. The bell rings, Mr. Kim and children say their good-byes, and the children chat with each other and their teacher as they put on their coats and head for home.

functional language

Next, we illustrate what a day in a whole-language classroom with older children might look like. As with the previous description, we begin by providing an agenda to show the "shape" of the day. While there are some similarities between the two classrooms, there are also some differences that reflect the differing needs of the two age groups. Ms. Pratt is well aware of the characteristics of preadolescents and adolescents: the need to interact with peers, the ability to work more independently, and the willingness to accept increasing responsibility and leadership. Ms. Pratt deliberately creates a learning environment that capitalizes on the needs and abilities of young people of this age.

A Day in a Classroom with Eleven- and Twelve-Year-Old Children

■ 9:00–9:20   Opening—Class/School/Community News

functional language

As much as one might romantically want to conceptualize classrooms as "learning emporia" (Smith, 1983, p. 142) where nothing but scholarly work transpires, the reality in most classrooms is that a considerable amount of time is consumed by clerical and administrative procedures. There is money to be collected for the book club, attendance to be taken at the commencement of each session, and reminders about overdue library books. Many teachers like to attend to these matters during the first 5 to 10 minutes of the day. We see these as golden opportunities for students to engage in real-life "workplace literacy" events (Anderson, 1994). For example, today Ms. Pratt has assigned Vito to take attendance and he will do this for the remainder of the week and then this responsibility will be rotated to another student. After the attendance is taken, Sofia makes a series of in-class announcements, including reminders about overdue library books and plans for an upcoming field trip. To conclude this portion of the morning, Terri collects the orders for the book club. Later at lunch, she will help Ms. Pratt count the money and prepare the class order to forward to the publisher. Initially, this took very close monitoring and supervision on the part of the teacher but she believes (and our experiences suggest likewise) that most students can take on such roles with increasing sophistication and learn many important skills which are best learned by being immersed in the processes. Ms. Pratt continues to monitor these activities, explaining the rationale for procedures and ensuring that things proceed as they should.

connections with the world

While some teachers who work with children of this age group still like to do a version of the calendar, as was done with the younger children in Mr. Kim's class, Ms. Pratt prefers a less formal approach. Instead she allows 5 to 10 minutes each morning for students to share news from the class, the school, or the community, or from the state, the nation, or the world.

■ 9:20–10:00   Shared Reading (ReQuest)

active involvement

Ms. Pratt also attempts to connect what students are studying in school to the world outside school and she finds the newspaper an especially effective way to do this. Since the class is studying Mexico in social studies, today she has brought in a synopsis of a news story about the North American Free Trade Agreement and the impact it will have on Mexico. Because she will be using a comprehension strategy called ReQuest, or reciprocal questioning (Manzo, 1969), with the whole class, she will have the students read the text from the overhead. She begins by having the students read the first paragraph of the text silently (as she reads along with them, of course). After they have read the paragraph, the students then ask questions of the text.

Here, Ms. Pratt builds assessment into her instruction by closely monitoring the type of questions the students ask. If the students ask only "textually explicit" questions (Readence, Bean, and Baldwin, 1985) such as "How many . . . ?", she will model higher-level questions such as "Why did . . . ?" or "If that . . . ?" when they have read the second paragraph and it is her turn to generate the questions. Because she recognizes that students at this stage of their development tend to ask textually explicit questions and need support to move to higher-level questions, Ms. Pratt encourages a discussion of the difference between textually explicit questions and those that require students to go beyond the information given in the text. Likewise, she encourages students to ask higher-level questions when they move to the next section of the text and it is their turn. The reciprocal questioning continues until the text has been read. Today, the teacher decides to bring closure to this activity by assigning five minutes for students to begin a journal response to the text they have just read.

integrating assessment with instruction

self-directed activity

■ 10:00–10:40   Writing Workshop

After students complete their journal entries, they move into various grouping arrangements for writing workshop. Ms. Pratt has established a routine in her classroom so that during writing workshop, students go to their writing folders and pick up from where they left off the previous day. It is important to realize that different students are at different stages in the writing process (Graves, 1983). Today, for example, Monique, Juan, Katija, and Rosa are still

The teacher provides feedback to groups involved in projects.

working on the first draft of a short story they are each writing as part of a class anthology, so they go to quiet areas to work independently. Raj and John, meanwhile, have already completed a first draft, and yesterday Ms. Pratt spent time with each of them individually in a writing conference. They are now revising their pieces by incorporating suggestions that came from the conference. At another table, Leslie and Ming Hua have exchanged each other's work and are engaged in peer editing. Ms. Pratt realizes that young writers like these need guidance in editing each other's work and so she has provided them with an editing checklist. Leslie and Ming Hua have already read each other's work, concentrating on spelling, and they now are working on punctuation. Meanwhile, Lindsey and Justin are working at the computer, designing graphics that they plan to paste up to accompany the poems they are ready to publish. They have revised and edited their work and Ms. Pratt has done a final reading to correct any mechanical (e.g., spelling) or structural problems (e.g., sentence structure) that were not detected in the peer-editing stage. In the meantime, Pat has taken his research report on the use of lasers in medicine as far as he can and he is about to begin a writing conference with Ms. Pratt. (For an example of what transpires in a writing conference, see Chapter 5.)

variety of social contexts

supporting children

peer assessment

self-directed activity

■ 10:40–11:00   Recess

Like Mr. Kim, Ms. Pratt also enjoys the morning break. She finds a brisk walk invigorating and so today she and her colleague, Ms. Fernandez, go for a walk around the perimeter of the school grounds. The students in Ms. Pratt's class, like many young people of the same age, use every available opportunity to socialize, so many of them use recess as a time to catch up on the latest news of each other's social lives.

■ 11:00–11:45   Mathematics—Geometric Solids

Although school mathematics has traditionally been thought of as a precise set of hierarchically arranged procedures that students learn best through repeated drill and practice (NCTM, 1989), Ms. Pratt recognizes the importance of everyday language and communication as children learn mathematics in the classroom. One way she incorporates this is by having students work on mathematical investigations in small groups, as we will be seeing today. Also, she recognizes that students can use writing to demonstrate their current mathematical understanding and as a medium through which to learn curriculum content. She has found the journal especially beneficial as a window on children's mathematical thinking and knowledge. Earlier in the year, while completing a unit on decimal fractions, she had given the class the prompt $0.8 = 3/5$ and asked them to discuss the validity of the equation in their journals. The journal shows how a student's thinking is demonstrated through the writing (with pictorial support) in a way that would be unavailable if the student were simply required to provide an answer $8/10 > 3/5$. Thus, through journal writing, the teacher is able to "see" the child's thinking and provide the student with responses that confirm her thinking or may require her to reconsider, extend, or reconceptualize.

language across the curriculum

awareness of thinking

teacher assessment

Ms. Pratt also uses student-constructed questions (Kennedy, 1985) regularly. On occasion, she uses a small-group configuration with this procedure. Through discussion, each group composes a set of problems that require application of the current topic under study. These problems or questions are then written up and, in groups of three or four, the students solve the set of problems that has been generated by the class after which the problems and the various solutions are shared and discussed in a whole class session. Yesterday, however, she had students construct their problems and arrive at a solution independently. The example shown in Figure 2.11 was constructed by Amy.

Several benefits of student-constructed questions and problems are evident here. Through language (writing), the student has contextualized the learning by applying her mathematical knowledge to the real world. Through the writing, Amy has demonstrated her thinking and problem-solving strategies. Also significant is the metacognitive strategy of monitoring ("Oh yeah, be sure to subtract how many cards you're supposed to get by how many are missing"). It is also interesting that Amy has constructed a multistep mathematical problem here—one that is mathematically more advanced than those found in textbooks produced for students her age. Ms. Pratt's response is also quite valuable. Even though Amy has arrived at the correct solution, Ms. Pratt seeks to extend her thinking by suggesting an alternative.

awareness of thinking

Figure 2.11   *Student-Constructed Question/Problem*
Reprinted with permission by Trung Duong and Lorna Lewis.

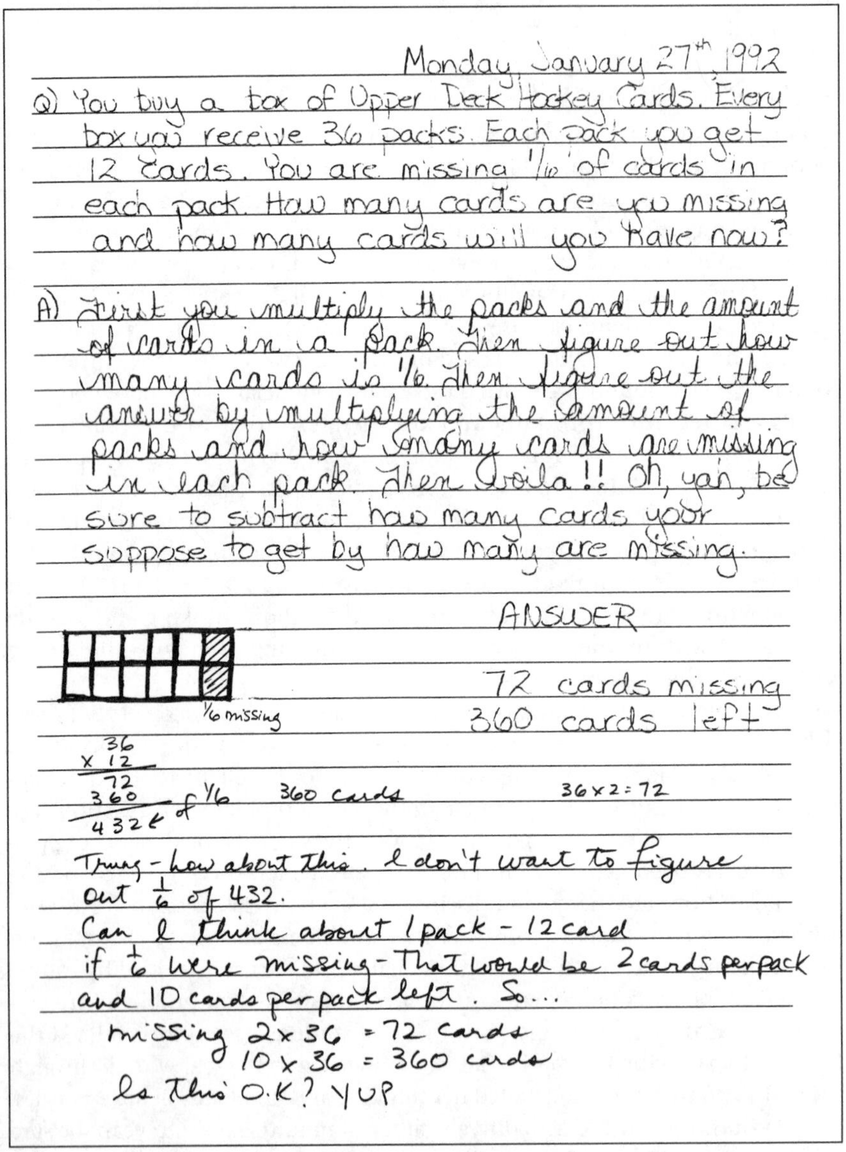

Monday, January 27th, 1992

Q) You buy a box of Upper Deck Hockey Cards. Every box you receive 36 packs. Each pack you get 12 cards. You are missing 1/6 of cards in each pack. How many cards are you missing and how many cards will you have now?

A) First you multiply the packs and the amount of cards in a pack. Then figure out how many cards is 1/6. Then figure out the answer by multiplying the amount of packs and how many cards are missing in each pack. Then Voila!! Oh, yah, be sure to subtract how many cards your suppose to get by how many are missing.

ANSWER

1/6 missing

72 cards missing
360 cards left

$$\begin{array}{r} 36 \\ \times\, 12 \\ \hline 72 \\ 360 \\ \hline 432 \end{array}$$ of 1/6   360 cards $36 \times 2 = 72$

Trung - how about this. I don't want to figure out 1/6 of 432.
Can I think about 1 pack - 12 card if 1/6 were missing - That would be 2 cards per pack and 10 cards per pack left. So...

missing $2 \times 36 = 72$ cards
$10 \times 36 = 360$ cards
Is This O.K? YUP

Today, the class is examining the properties of three-dimensional shapes in a section of a geometry unit they are completing. The objective of today's class is to have students analyze relationships within and between three-dimensional objects and to use number patterns to describe them. The class has been divided into groups of four and five and each group has been given a set of three-dimensional solids, as shown in Figure 2.12.

Let's now join Juan's group as they examine the solids and discuss their various mathematical attributes:

Juan:	I think the flat parts are the faces.
Katija:	Like the sides of a box or the top.
Billie:	Well, remember that the vertices of the triangle are the points.
Leslie:	So the vertices must be the corners.
Katija:	And these are the edges. (She glides her fingers along the perimeter of the top and sides of the rectangular solid.)

Several aspects of this conversation need to be highlighted. First, the students are using everyday language to learn mathematical concepts, as Billie and Leslie do when they use the notions of "points" and "corners" to figure out the vertices of the solid objects. Second, through talk, they are able to link previous learning about the vertices of a triangle to the present problem, the vertices of three-dimensional objects. Third, since talk permits the group to share a larger knowledge pool than that of any one individual, they are learning from each other.

language as a tool for learning

Each group has been given copies of the table shown in Figure 2.13, which Ms. Pratt has taken from the Mathematics Curriculum Guide (B. C. Ministry of Education, 1988, p. 40). Her directions to the groups are to analyze collaboratively each of the solids, to record the information on the table, and then to describe any relationships among the properties of three-dimensional solids. The various groups are at different stages in their analyses: Terri and her group have just completed the section of the table pertaining to the pentagonal row.

Terri:	Hm-m-m, it looks like the number of faces increases by 1, the vertices by 2, and the edges by 3.

Figure 2.12 *Three-Dimensional Solids*

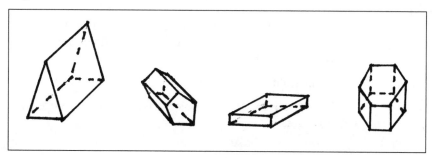

Figure 2.13   *Math Table*

Prism	Number of Faces	Number of Vertices	Number of Edges
Triangular	5	6	9
Rectangular	6	8	12
Pentagonal	7	10	15
Hexagonal	8	12	18

Raj: You're right! (as he checks columns) So, a 6-sided solid (hexagonal) will have 8 faces, 12 edges, and 18 vertices. Let's check.

They all count the sides of the hexagonal solid provided.

Teung: So, all we need to do is fill in the table for the 7-, 8-, and 9-sided ones and calculate the 10-sided one.

Ms. Pratt: Might there be a shorter way to figure it out? Look at each row for a pattern.

Terri: Wait, the top and bottom of this one is a triangle which has 3 sides, right?

Raj: So?

Terri: Well: look, 3 plus 2 equals 5—the number of faces; 3 times 2 equals 6—the number of vertices; and 3 times 3 equals 9—the number of edges.

The children check the solids to see if Terri's pattern works for the others.

Raj: That means the 10-sided object has 12 faces, 20 vertices, and 30 edges.

challenging students **Ms. Pratt:** How can you be sure?

Several functions of language are noteworthy here. In the beginning of the discussion, Terri is thinking aloud and is modeling her thinking strategies for the other students. **Scaffolding** (Wretch, 1984) is also evident here as students successively build on the previously articulated thinking of their peers. Ms. Pratt, through her first question, directs students to examine other possibilities and thus to extend their thinking. Her question at the end requires students to justify their strategies, and this invokes metacognition (Paris, Wasik, and van der Westhuizen, 1988) on the part of the students. *language for communication*

Ms. Pratt plays a crucial role here in that through listening to the group dialogue, she is able to infer how the students are thinking and therefore knows what the needs of the students are. Consequently, she is able to structure her teaching in order to meet the specific needs of her students.

■ 11:45–12:00   Writing—Mini-Lesson

Although it is sometimes asserted that whole-language teachers do not teach skills in reading and writing, Ms. Pratt realizes the fallacy of this myth (Newman and Church, 1990) and teaches skills *to students who need to be taught them.* For example, this past week, as she has been doing a final edit of students' writing, she has noted in her conference log that Terri, Justin, Raj, Katija, and John have a number of run-on sentences and sentence fragments in their writing. Since it is appropriate to expect students at this level to begin refining their use of end punctuation and, therefore, to be able to eliminate most sentence fragments and run-on sentences, Ms. Pratt has decided that these students need more explicit instruction in this area of their writing. Today she has developed a mini-lesson for the students who now need this instruction. *integrating assessment with instruction*

Adapting a procedure from Atwell (1987), Ms. Pratt uses the overhead projector so that the small group can see a writing sample (with the student's name removed to protect the anonymity of the writer) entitled "The 1/2 Bank 1/2 Hockey Story" (Figure 2.14) written by a student in her class three years ago. She finds that students generally can "hear" when end punctuation is needed, if the text is read aloud. So she reads the text aloud with appropriate intonation. She asks the students to indicate where changes in punctuation are needed and then writes these on the transparency. Care is taken to have the students discuss why a particular punctuation mark is needed and how it functions for the reader. Let's now listen to a portion of the mini-lesson, with excerpts of the text italicized: *teacher-directed activity*

Ms. Pratt:	*When I was walking down the street one day, I saw two men run into the bank wearing ski masks.* Justin, what do we need to do here?
Justin:	We need to put in a period after "masks."
Terri:	And a comma after "day."
Ms. Pratt:	Okay, let's put them in.

Figure 2.14 *The 1/2 Bank 1/2 Hockey Story*

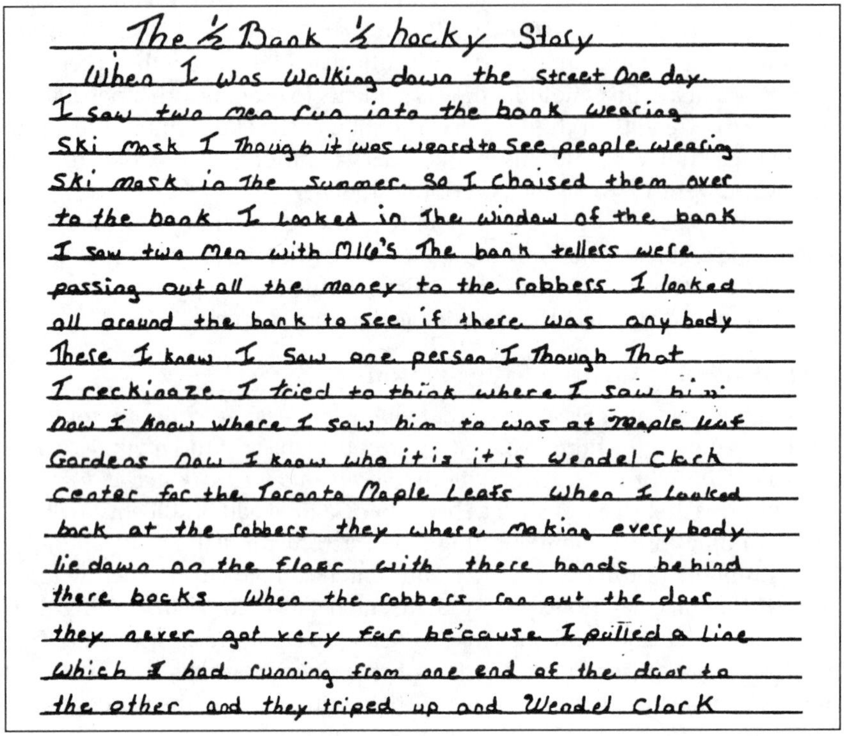
The ½ Bank ½ hocky Story
When I was walking down the street One day.
I saw two men run into the bank wearing
Ski mask I though it was weard to see people wearing
Ski mask in The summer. So I chaised them over
to the bank I Looked in The window of the bank
I saw two Men with M16's The bank tellers were
passing out all the money to the robbers. I looked
all around the bank to see if there was any body
There I knew I saw one person I though That
I reckinaze. I tried to think where I saw him
now I know where I saw him to was at Maple Leaf
Gardens now I know who it is it is Wendel Clark
center for the Toronto Maple Leafs When I looked
back at the robbers they where making every body
lie down on the floor with there hands behind
there backs When the robbers ran out the door
they never got very far be'cause I pulled a Line
Which I had running from one end of the door to
the other and they triped up and Wendel Clark

Ms. Pratt: *I thought it was weird to see people wearing ski masks in summer. So I chased them over to the bank.* What should we do here Katija?

Katija: Put a period after "bank."

Ms. Pratt: Good. Any other changes?

Terri: It reads fine now.

Ms. Pratt: Notice that the student had placed a period after "summer." Do we need the period after "summer" or should we remove the period and make this into a longer sentence?

Terri: It's fine the way it is.

Ms. Pratt: Let's try it both ways. *I thought it was weird to see people wearing a ski mask in summer. So I chased them over to the bank. . . . I thought it was weird to see people wearing ski masks in summer so I chased them over to the bank.*

Justin: I think the second way—removing the period after "summer"—reads better.

Ms. Pratt will continue the mini-lesson in this way. Notice that she does not have students focus here on other surface features such as spelling; nor does she have them engage in revising the piece. She wants them to focus on end punctuation in this lesson since this need has been demonstrated in their writing. Notice also that she does not give a lecture on a sentence being a complete thought, a fairly abstract notion that many students at this level would have trouble understanding and applying. Instead, she is modeling a strategy that students can use later on their own while at the same time encouraging students to verbalize their thinking and learn from each other. Like Atwell (1991), she will also follow up on this by having individual conferences when these students are engaged in editing their writing.

Ms. Pratt finds the mini-lesson format especially effective because she is able to address very specific needs of small groups of children. Just last week, for example, she had worked with one small group of children who were experiencing difficulty with verb tenses, while on another day the mini-lesson involved Ming Hua and Vito who were experiencing difficulty organizing their longer pieces into paragraphs. She also finds that because the lesson is connected with the students' writing, the students transfer the skills to their writing. As well, the relatively short and focused nature of the lesson encourages real engagement on the part of the students. However, the biggest benefit that she realizes in this arrangement is that because the lessons occur on a needs basis, students who already know the particular skills do not have to attend to lessons on that which they already know. And because they write every day, there are many opportunities for those who need it to practice these skills in an authentic way. For example, the students who were not involved in the mini-lesson today continued to work on the class newspaper that they are producing for Thanksgiving. Meanwhile, the students involved in the mini-lesson today may not be involved in the next one, as it will focus on a different skill that they already have learned and they may have an opportunity to work on a project such as the class newspaper.

*teacher
assessment*

■ 12:00–1:00   Lunch

■ 1:00–2:00   Science

Ms. Pratt is highly cognizant of the role that various forms of language play in learning any discipline. To that end, in science classes she provides ample opportunity for student talk in small group and large-group contexts (see Chapter 3), possibilities for students to use writing to learn science (see Chapter 5), study guides to help students learn from content area textual material (see Chapter 6), and a collection of quality literature, fiction and nonfiction (see Chapter 4), on science.

*language
across the
curriculum*

However, Ms. Pratt also realizes that reading, writing, listening, speaking, viewing, and representing—while very important in learning science—cannot replace actually "doing science." Thus, she carefully structures her science classes so that students engage in hands-on activities to allow them to "learn science by doing science as scientists do" (Edelsky, Altwerger, and Flores, 1991, p. 66).

At this point, the class is completing a unit on ecosystems and today the students will be looking at biotic communities using study plots (Yore et al., 1990, p. 341). Essentially this means that students will work in pairs to examine specific areas of an ecosystem (e.g., one square yard of the schoolyard) and observe and record the variety of plants and animals therein.

functional language

In preparation for today's exploration, Ms. Pratt had recorded the procedures to be followed on a chart (Figure 2.15), which the class read and discussed yesterday. She now returns to the chart to review the procedures to ensure that

connection with prior knowledge

students know what is expected of them. Prior to having students carry out activities such as this, Ms. Pratt encourages them to form tentative hypotheses, since she sees this as the foundation of the scientific process and an overarching objective of the science curriculum. She asks students to predict what plant and animal life they expect to find in their schoolyard. She records their answers and has the students help her organize a semantic web (Heimlich and Pittelman, 1986) (Figure 2.16). As suggestions are offered, students are encouraged to ex-

integrating language across the curriculum

plain and discuss the rationale for their predictions, again capitalizing on opportunities for talking to learn. Ms. Pratt will have students return to this web later and compare their actual findings to their predictions.

Figure 2.15 *Science Chart*

Procedure - Study Plot

Materials: Hula hoop, piece of string, clipboard and paper, pencil and trowel

1. Each pair collects materials and goes to school yard.
2. Select an area for your study plot.
3. Use string to divide hula hoop in half.
4. Place hula hoop on ground. Count and record the different kinds of plant and animal life which you find.
5. Use the trowel to dig up one scoop of soil. Again, look for and record plant/animal life.
6. Return materials to science lab at 1:55.

Figure 2.16   *Science Web*

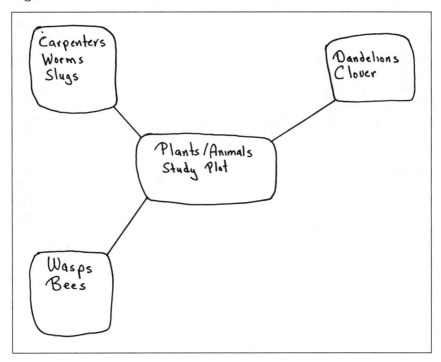

Ms. Pratt now gives each pair of students a hula hoop and a piece of string with which to divide the hoop in half, for she has found this to be an effective way for students to demarcate their study plots. As Ms. Pratt leads the students to the schoolyard, she notices that Juan and Justin are using the hula hoops to engage in horseplay. She immediately tells the students to stop the horseplay and to proceed to the schoolyard. Once she has the other students established in their groups, she takes Juan and Justin aside. Ms. Pratt discusses with the students the inappropriateness of their behavior, emphasizing safety considerations. She also discusses with them the need for students to take responsibility for their own behavior in situations, such as this field trip where greater student autonomy is desirable—indeed, necessary—if they are to get maximum benefits from the experience. The students agree that their behavior was inappropriate in this context and rejoin the groups. Each student identifies and then records each organism found in the area of the study plot in a log book format.

Following the advice of Yore (1990), Ms. Pratt has had each group bring along a plant and animal identification book and she encourages students to use this resource when they encounter organisms that they cannot identify. Similarly, she reminds the groups to look for burrows and footprints as clues to

integrating language across the curriculum

animal inhabitants. Also, to help students realize the variety of subsurface life, she has each student carefully examine a shovelful of topsoil.

Meanwhile, Ms. Pratt has a very important role to play in this activity. While some proponents of whole-language suggest that the teacher's role is that of facilitator, Ms. Pratt sees this role as far too narrow. True, establishing groups, procedures, and routines all involve a facilitating function. However, fundamental to the learning theories, such as those of Bruner (1986) and Vygotsky (1978) upon which many tenets of whole-language rest, is the structuring and mediating of learning by a more experienced and more competent significant other—a teacher in the original sense of the word. Ms. Pratt recognizes this mediating role and is able to actualize it quite effectively with her students. For example, as she looks in on each group, she notices that Juan and his group are forgetting to look underneath the flowers for animal life, so she reminds the *interactive reflective experiences* group of the necessity of doing this by showing them an insect they had missed. She capitalizes on this occasion to discuss the importance of precision and thoroughness in this type of scientific inquiry.

Later, as she works with Ming Hua's group, Ms. Pratt notices that there is a high concentration of carpenter ants in one half of the study plot in which the soil is quite moist and which contains a rotting tree root. She asks questions to help students realize that the parts of an ecosystem are interrelated. ("How is the half which Ming Hua's group is examining different from the other?" "Are the moisture and the tree stump equally necessary for the carpenter ants to live here?" "What effect will the carpenter ants have had on this soil five years from now?"). By teaching science in this manner, Ms Pratt is helping children develop scientific concepts, understand science processes, and comprehend the language of science simultaneously in an integrated fashion.

Since exploring the study plot will occupy all of today's time devoted to science, it will be necessary for Ms. Pratt and her class to do a follow-up tomorrow. She will first have each group of students compile a graph of their findings, as *variety of representations* shown in Figure 2.17. Notice here that this is a realistic and functional way of integrating bar graphing, which the students are learning in mathematics, with another discipline.

■ 2:00–3:00   Art—Illustrating Big Books

Ms. Pratt considers the role of the audience to be just as important in young people's artistic development as it is in their writing development. One especially effective way she has found to do this is to have students illustrate big books that they have written and then present them to primary classes in the school. Ms. Pratt knows that this project is also applicable for older students. For example, students in one twelfth-grade French class composed several big books in French, illustrated them, and presented them to primary classes in a neighboring school (Andrews, 1989).

Figure 2.17   *Science Graph*

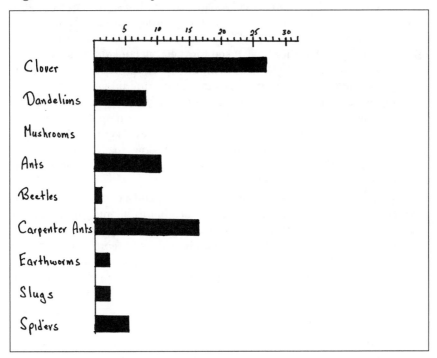

As soon as the students return from the science activity, they go to the art storage area and retrieve the group projects on which they have been working. We now look in on each group.

Terri and her group are using a collage technique similar to that used by author/illustrator Ezra Jack Keats (1962) in *A Snowy Day*. Today, they are cutting pieces of wallpaper samples as they develop a kitchen scene. There is considerable debate about which of two choices of wallpaper to use. Two of the students feel that the texture of one is too coarse, while the other three feel that the other has colors that are too deep. Ms. Pratt encourages this kind of debate, for she knows that such talk is essential as students construct meaning in this context (see Chapter 3).

Using a technique similar to that developed by Barbara Reed (the illustrator of the *The New Baby Calf*, written by Chase, [1984]), Vito and his group are cutting and shaping modeling clay as they busily put finishing touches on an illustration. They will then photograph the illustration and paste the photograph in the big book. Again, talk is an inherent part of this activity. Students discuss proportionality of one of the objects, as it appears to some members of the group that it is too large and dominates the illustration. Meanwhile, two

variety of represen- tations

variety of forms—oral

groups—Ramon's and Sofia's — are using watercolors as they create scenes emulative of Ted Harrison's bright colors and curved lines, in, for example, *A Northern Alphabet* (Harrison, 1982). Amy and her group have chosen line drawings as the medium for their book, whereas the students in Raj's group are using photographs that they have taken for their big book on bees.

integrating assessment with instruction

Of course, while the students work on their projects, Ms. Pratt is also quite busy. She circulates from group to group, monitoring progress and offering encouragement and suggestions. While she has previously demonstrated each of the techniques being used today, she also capitalizes on opportunities to reteach concepts or techniques. When working with Amy's group, for example, she noticed that several students were not using shadows to give the illustration three-dimensional perspective, so she uses this opportunity to demonstrate again how to achieve this effect.

teacher-directed activity

A project such as this requires careful planning and a great deal of work before actual production of the books begins. To help students gain a sense of audience by becoming cognizant of what appeals to young children, Ms Pratt brought in a number of good-quality children's books representing various genres. She and the class read the books and, through discussion, identified the characteristics of quality children's literature. These were recorded on chart paper, which was posted so that students could refer back to them as needed. Next, Ms. Pratt selected books that featured a number of respected illustrators of children's work and that represented a number of different media and techniques. Although many of these media were already familiar to the students (such as watercolors and line drawing), others such as Barbara Reed's use of

modeling clay were new, so Ms. Pratt taught students the use of those particular media. At that point, the students were ready to proceed with writing texts. Small groups had worked collaboratively for two weeks (using the writing process described earlier) to write the texts that they were now illustrating.

self-directed activity

Ms. Pratt uses opportunities to integrate subject matter whenever she can. She also realizes, though, that sometimes integration is not possible without trivializing the experience for students and that she can have students learn in subject-specific ways and still embody the principles of whole-language teaching in her classroom (Edelsky, Altwerger, and Flores, 1991).

Conclusion

Each day in each classroom is unique, yet there are commonalities in what each teacher is trying to achieve. Every day, teachers make hundreds of decisions about what to do in their classrooms; whole-language teachers base their decisions on the principles of whole-language learning and the structural guidelines we provided both at the beginning of this chapter and as indicated in the context of the descriptions of the two classrooms. An important aspect of the teacher's decision making is the integration of curriculum such as is seen in these two classrooms. However, it is important to realize that not everything can be integrated in a pedagogically sound manner. Likewise, not all curriculum areas can be included in a given day. For example, role drama was not evident in either of the descriptions of the classrooms in the chapter. However, we believe that role drama and other dramatic forms (discussed in Chapter 7) are essential elements in all classrooms.

Whole-language teachers plan their days yet allow for flexibility. Sometimes unexpected incidents occur that the teacher perceives as an interruption to his or her plan, yet the reality of classroom life is that these incidents must be addressed. For example, when a group of children become involved in a conflict during recess, time needs to be taken to help the children resolve their differences. At other times, events occur in the context of classroom activity that the teacher can use as opportunities for "teaching to the moment" and "going with the flow." For example, one teacher we know had planned a unit of study on rabbits. On the day that she planned to start the unit, when she came into the classroom she found the children clustered excitedly at the window. When she joined them, she saw that the focus of their attention was a newly built robin's nest with four eggs in it just outside the classroom window. Rather than proceeding with the rabbit unit, the teacher capitalized on the obvious interest of the children and decided to pursue a bird study that incorporated many of the original goals and objectives of the rabbit unit.

flexible planning

Social interaction is a basic human need and is also essential for cognitive development and language learning (Rogoff, 1990). We have incorporated this social dimension into the descriptions of both classrooms. Most school-age children have a tremendous need to socialize, as those who have taught them are acutely aware. We believe that teachers can capitalize on this by structuring the social context of the classroom so that this need can be met while students learn. We have tried to demonstrate this by having students in both Mr. Kim's and Ms. Pratt's classrooms work independently, in pairs, in small groups, and in large groups. While acknowledging and capitalizing on the social dimension of learning and teaching, however, we also recognize that the prime purpose of school is intellectual development and we have maintained the integrity of this aim throughout.

Whole-language teachers take the view that although children learn many things without direct instruction, teachers do not simply "wait and let children blossom," nor do they allow children to do whatever they want. They provide "developmental nudges" (Sulzby, 1989), negotiating a balance between accepting and acknowledging each child's current level of development on the one hand and his or her frustration level on the other (Vygotsky, 1978). They understand that one role of the teacher is to mediate children's learning.

We recognize that language in its various forms is central to learning. We have, therefore, shown examples of using language—reading, writing, listening, speaking, viewing, and representing—to learn across the curriculum. None of the language functions we suggested were superfluous or contrived; they were all genuine and integral to the learning at hand.

We have also demonstrated the centrality of teachers in whole-language classrooms. We believe that to be effective, all teachers must know how to structure opportunities for students to learn, must have a thorough knowledge of the disciplines they teach, must know how to monitor student learning, and must know when to intervene to help students learn more effectively, as well as when to give students the freedom to learn on their own.

The most important element in the two classrooms described here is that students "talk . . . read . . . imagine . . . build . . . listen"(Shanker, 1990, p. 349). They learn because they are actively engaged.

AUTHORS' NOTE:
We would like to acknowledge Debbie Bowering of St. Paul's High School in Harbour Grace, Newfoundland; Jan Johnston of Port Guichon Elementary School in Delta, B.C.; Lorna Lewis and Trung Dong of Brighouse Elementary School, Richmond, B.C.; and Colleen Politano of Wishart Elementary School, Sooke, B.C., for contributing samples of classroom work.

REFERENCES

Anderson, J. (1994). "Daddy what's a picket?": One child's emerging knowledge workplace literacy. *Early Child Development and Care, 98,* 7–20.

Anderson, J. & Ralston, S. (1994). Valuing and utilizing young children's diverse literacy experiences. *Canadian Children, 19,* 3 29–33.

Andrews, G. (Ed.). (1989). *Curriculum bulletin.* Spaniard's Bay, Newfoundland: Avalon North Integrated School Board.

Atwell, N. (1987). *In the middle: Writing, reading and learning with adolescents.* Upper Montclair, NJ: Boynton/Cook Publishers, Inc.

Atwell, N. (1991). *Side by side: Essays on teaching to learn.* Toronto, ON: Irwin Publishing.

Baratta-Lorton, M. (1976). *Mathematics their way: An activity-centered mathematics program for early childhood education.* Menlo Park, CA: Addison-Wesley.

British Columbia Ministry of Education. (1988). *Mathematics curriculum guide: 7–12.* Victoria, BC: Ministry of Education.

Bruner, J. (1986). *Actual minds, possible worlds.* Cambridge, MA: Harvard University Press.

Carle, E. (1972). *Rooster's off to see the world.* Saxonville, MA: Picture Book Studio.

Chapman, M. (1994 in press). Active teaching for active learning in the primary classroom. *Prime Areas.*

Chapman, M. (1993). Literacy assessment and evaluation: An anthropological approach. *English Quarterly, 26* (1), 30–38.

Chase, E. (1984). *The new baby calf.* Richmond Hill, ON: Scholastic.

Clay, M. M. (1985). *The early detection of reading difficulties* (3rd ed.). Auckland, NZ: Heinemann.

Dyson, A. H. (1989). *Multiple worlds of child writers: Friends learning to write.* New York: Teachers College Press.

Early, M. (1989). Using key visuals to aid E.S.L. students comprehension of content classroom texts. *Reading Canada Lecture, 7,* 202–212.

Edelsky, C., Altwerger, B. & Flores, B. (1991). *Whole language: What's the difference?* Portsmouth, NH: Heinemann.

Goodman, Y., Watson, D. & Burke, C. (1987). *Reading miscue inventory: Alternative procedures.* Portsmouth, NH: Heinemann.

Graves, D. (1983). *Writing: Teachers and children at work.* Portsmouth, NH: Heinemann.

Halliday, M. A. K. (1973). The functional basis of language. In B. Bernstein (Ed.), Class, codes and control, Volume 2. *Applied studies toward a sociology of language.* London and Boston: Routledge & Kegan Paul.

Harrison, T. (1982). *A northern alphabet.* Montreal: Tundra Books.

Heimlich, J. & Pittelman, S. (1986). *Semantic mapping: Classroom applications.* Newark, DE: International Reading Association.

Holdaway, D. (1979). *The foundations of literacy.* Sydney: Ashton Scholastic.

Hornsby, D., Sukarna, D., & Parry, J. (1986). *Read on: A conference approach to reading.* Portsmouth, NH: Heinemann.

Keats, E. J. (1962). *A snowy day.* New York: Viking.

Kennedy, B. (1985). Writing letters to learn mathematics. *Learning, 13,* 58–61.

MacKenzie, T. (Ed.). (1992). *Readers' workshops: Bridging literature and literacy.* Toronto: Irwin Publishing.

Manzo, A. (1969). The request procedure. *Journal of Reading, 13,* 123–126.

Marshall, E. (1983). *Fox at school.* New York: Dial Press.

Marshall, E. (1983). *Fox on wheels.* New York: Dial Press.

May, F. B. (1990). *Reading as communication: An interactive approach.* New York: Macmillan.

McCracken, R. A. & McCracken, M. J. (1978). Modelling is the key to sustained silent reading, *The Reading Teacher, 31 (4),* 406–408.

Mikulecky, L. (1983). Preparing students for workplace literacy demands. *Journal of Reading, 28,* 253–257.

Newman, J. & Church, S. (1990). Commentary: Myths of whole language. *The Reading Teacher, 44,* 20–26.

National Council of Teachers of Mathematics Curriculum Standards. (1989). *Curriculum and evaluation standards for school mathematics.* Reston, VA: NCTM.

Paris, S., Wasik, B. & van der Westhuizen, G. (1988). Meta-metacognition: A review of research on metacognition and reading. In J. Readance & S. Baldwin (Eds.), *Dialogues on literacy research* (pp. 143–166). Chicago: National Reading Conference.

Pinnell, G. S. (1975, December). Language in primary classrooms. *Theory into Practice, 14,* 318–332.

Rogoff, B. (1990). *Spontaneous apprenticeships: Cognitive development in social contexts.* New York: Oxford University Press.

Shanker, A. (1990). The end of the traditional model of schooling and a proposal for using incentives to restructure our public schools. *Phi Delta Kappan, 72,* 344–357.

Smith, F. (1983). *Essays into literacy.* Exeter, NH: Heinemann.

Stinson, K. (1982). *Red is best.* Toronto: Annick Press.

Sulzby, E. (1989, May). How about this new idea? In J. Schickedanz & E. Sulzby (Chairs), *Instructional roles in early literacy: Some options.* Symposium conducted at the 34th Annual Convention of the International Reading Association, New Orleans, LA.

Vygotsky, L. (1978). *Mind in society.* In M. Cole, V. John-Steiner, S. Scribner & E. Souberman (Eds.). Cambridge, MA: Harvard University Press.

Wretch, J. (1984). The zone of proximal development: Some conceptual issues. In B. Rogoff & J. Wretch (Eds.), *Children's thinking in the zone of proximal development.* San Francisco: Jossey-Bass.

Yore, L., Beugger, P. McDonald, B. & Harrison, M. (1990). *Journeys in science.* Toronto: Collier MacMillan Canada, Inc.

Talk in Whole-Language Classrooms

CLAIRE STAAB

1. *How talk is different both in terms of quantity and types of interaction patterns in whole-language classrooms*

2. *Expanding one's theory of the world, making understandings more precise, and increasing one's retention of ideas through talk*

3. *Teacher commitment to the value of talk*

4. *Oral language as a way of learning across all subject areas*

5. *Psychological atmosphere and a flexible physical atmosphere as the foundations for productive talk in the classroom*

6. *Teacher confidence in the ability to gain control of the class before control is given to students*

7. *Assessment of talk should be shared by the teacher, learner, and peers within the context of actual classroom activities*

Oral language, all forms of listening and speaking, includes the total of our oral experiences. Talk is a part of oral language defined by two important conditions:

1. It is reciprocal—one person is speaking directly to a listener who is physically present and at least potentially able to interact. Listening experiences such as listening to a film, a tape recording, or a recorded broadcast are categorized as oral language, not talk, as they are not reciprocal.
2. Talk involves the spoken word as opposed to music or some other form of communication.

Though some oral language activities are mentioned, this chapter relates primarily to talk—that is, interchange between two persons: a speaker and a listener. The following examples are typical of students' talk in an elementary classroom.

Example 1: A Grade 6 Social Studies Class

Three sixth-grade children are working together to plan a model of a well-designed town. A teacher has given previous directions but is not involved in the group's discussion:

Bobby:	Wanna put the housing developments in the north end?
Kim:	Yeah, that would make sense and then we could build parks around them.
Bobby:	Yeah, O.K.
Melinda:	Put them sort of . . . (indicates a spot on the plan).
Kim:	Wait, wait, wait, let's do the housing developments more toward the center of town. Here it's too far for people to drive.
Melinda:	Then we'll need a bus system or something.

Example 2: A Grade 3 Science Class

A small group of third-grade students are working with the teacher to determine how to complete an electrical circuit and cause a small light globe to light up:

Teacher:	Which one do you think will turn it on, Leanne?
Leanne:	Not that one.
Teacher:	What do you think, Robert?
Robert:	Hmm, I think this light bulb would work.
Teacher:	Why?
Robert:	I don't know.

Teacher:	O.K., what do you suppose would happen if I put it down on this key?
Jimmy:	It would turn on.
Teacher:	How do you know?
Jimmy:	Because Rachel told me.
Teacher:	Very interesting!

Example 3: A Kindergarten Block Center

A kindergarten child is playing alone with a toy car in the block center and talking quietly to himself.

Peter:	Turning, turning—go to the left—now to the right. Turning, turning around she goes. Now back up—backing up. Faster, faster, vroom.

In all of these examples students are using oral language to converse with themselves or communicate with others, and thus are engaging in what is commonly termed *talk*. Seldom, if ever, do students talk about talking. They use talk to make sense of their world within the context of whatever they are doing. In the classroom, they use talk to socialize and connect with other speakers, to puzzle through current projects, and to share the books they are reading, the pieces they are writing, or the representations they are making. Within these contexts and many more, talk is a way to learn in all subject areas. Talk cannot be relegated to the time we schedule as Show and Tell or the oral book report; it is at the very heart of mathematics, science, social studies, literature study, or whatever students are doing. It is a way to learn—a way to grapple with ideas and revise thoughts.

In addition to a way to learn, talk is a powerful communication tool— probably the most powerful tool humans have. Students who do not speak and listen well are seriously hampered in communicative situations. Through many and varied talking experiences, one learns such things as pronunciation and vocabulary—labels for one's experiences. One learns how sentences are formed and how changes in word order alter meaning. This formation of sentences is termed *grammar*. One learns the subtle nuances of language, as when a particular style of speech is appropriate in a given situation. One learns how to make a point and perhaps persuade others when working in small groups. One learns how to encourage others and bring them into a conversation, and one learns how to speak clearly and forcefully during public speaking situations.

Even though talk is a powerful communication tool and a means for learning content in all subject areas, the topic of talk in the classroom is still a controversial one. Some teachers praise its relevance and importance, while other teachers discourage it (Staab, 1991). In some classrooms the adage, "a quiet classroom is a productive classroom," is dying, but dying slowly. Fortunately, from the very beginning, the whole-language philosophy has validated talk in the classroom. In whole-language classrooms:

1. Talk is valued as important work.
2. There is a dual focus for talk—to learn and to empower students.
3. There is a large quantity of talk.
4. Much of the talk is student directed, as seen in several interaction patterns.

Value of Talk

Whole-language teachers facilitate talk because they are convinced of its value. They defend their "noisy" classrooms to their principal, parents, colleagues, and anyone else who will listen. These teachers realize that talk is a basic form of communication and that children need to talk in order to learn, to share ideas with others, and to have their questions answered. Children need to talk to symbolize, structure, regulate, and give meaning to experience (Booth, 1994, p. 249). Seldom are the words "Stop talking and get to work" spoken. Productive talk is a part of the students' work. The need to communicate follows people all the way through school; indeed, it follows us through life (May, 1994).

Talking takes time during the school day; it is more time consuming for students to discuss a topic than it is for teachers to simply tell them about it. My hope is to convince you that talk is important and worth the extra time, but let's be more specific. How is talk work and why should students spend work time engaged in it? Three important reasons follow (Lindfors, 1987):

1. Talk can expand a student's theory of the world.
2. Talk can make understandings more precise.
3. Talk can increase a student's retention of knowledge.

Talk Expands a Child's Theory of the World

A student's theory or cognitive structure of the world expands and changes as the student encounters others' experiences, interpretations, and ideas. These encounters often take place through language, oral or written. In school, talk is a natural medium for these encounters because no costly equipment is required and most students enter school fully prepared to participate. New questions and ideas often are created as the student engages in this interaction. The talk of another in the form of comments or questions can spark an idea or cause a student to wonder about something that he or she had not considered previously. Conversely, the availability of a conversational partner can encourage a student to express ideas that may be in the process of formulation. As the

Students participate in shelling nuts to make peanut butter—an experience they will use for a variety of language activities.

student receives feedback from this partner, ideas may be solidified, reformulated, or perhaps become the foundation for new wonderings.

In one grade 6 classroom, for example, a student named Kim shared orally a piece of her writing with the teacher and four other students. The story was about a young street boy who lived in a deserted apartment building. In Kim's story the young boy was torn between remaining with his friends while possibly pursuing a life of crime or returning to a safe but unpleasant home situation. One group member asked Kim if she had considered all the negative aspects of remaining on the street, such as being constantly cold and often hungry. Kim admitted that she had not thought of these consequences, only that the boy was now free of his mother's nagging. The talk of another student caused Kim to wonder and perhaps reformulate her ideas. This encounter happened because the teacher understood the value of talk in the classroom and provided the time and the opportunity for it to happen. In quiet classrooms where each student is instructed to work silently, this encounter would not have happened. Kim might not have had an opportunity to receive feedback and consider new possibilities.

Talk Makes Understanding More Precise

Besides expanding a student's theory of the world, talk can make understandings more precise. All of us have had the experience of knowing something but being unable to express it in words. We may have some vague notions about the idea or thought, but if we are unable to articulate our ideas, it is likely that these ideas are unclear and imprecise. As we struggle to put these ideas into words, we are actually sharpening and deepening our understandings. All teachers want students to gain a clear understanding of the concepts and ideas presented, yet many teachers fail to realize the importance of encouraging students to talk through these concepts as they search for meaning.

Following a film, for example, teachers may wish to divide students into small groups and allow time for discussion. If this process is new for students, structure needs to be provided. The teacher divides students into groups of four or five, appoints a chairperson and a secretary for each group, and decides on a time limit for the exercise. The teacher then provides three or four focus questions that can be put on the chalkboard or overhead projector. The chairperson's task is to see that the group covers the questions and sticks to the topic, and that each group member has an opportunity to participate. The secretary's task is to jot down important points with regard to each question. The questions should not be so time consuming that there is no opportunity for students to talk about other interesting ideas from the film once the focus questions have been discussed. Following the small-group discussions, the secretary from each group can then summarize important points for the class.

Talk Increases the Ability to Remember

Talk increases a student's memory. As students are able to encode their thoughts in language, their ability to remember or retrieve these thoughts improves. Many teachers have been frustrated because students don't seem to retain information over any period of time. We often hear teachers saying, "Good grief, I just taught that last month." Perhaps if students were given more time to seek meaning and formulate and reformulate ideas through talk, teachers would be pleasantly surprised at the improved retention rates. Talk is a student's work and it is important work.

Talk—A Dual Focus

As mentioned at the beginning of this chapter, as students gain the ability to use talk effectively to meet their everyday needs, this power of communication becomes available to them (Staab, 1992a). As students gain the ability to speak with adults as well as peers, to function well in a small group, or to speak in front of the class, they are appropriating the power of language. As students gain the ability to state their ideas clearly, to entertain, to negotiate, or to persuade, they are appropriating the power of language. Many of the strategies involved in effective speaking and listening can be modeled, taught, and practiced, but not in a quiet classroom. Thus talk has a dual focus—as a way to learn and as a powerful communication tool. These foci are, of course, complementary. The more students know or have thought about a topic, the more they have to say about it; and the more effective the talk, the more learning takes place. This relationship is shown by the arrow in the diagram below:

Talk

Way to Learn ◄————————► *Communication Tool*

Perhaps paradoxically, the primary focus of whole-language teachers is not on talk as a way to learn OR on talk as a communication tool. To be sure both are natural outcomes, but the primary focus in the classroom is simply on whatever the students are studying—the solar system, pioneer life, or division of fractions. As teachers try to improve learning opportunities, it is not upon the discourse (talk) that they need to concentrate but rather upon the larger context in which the talk occurs (Staab, 1992b). If students are interested in a topic or project, if an atmosphere of community and inquiry is fostered, if teachers allow and plan for students to work together, useful talk develops naturally. Within the context of this talk, teachers can then model and sometimes teach effective strategies for improved communication.

Before proceeding further, it should be mentioned that in today's classrooms all interactions must be viewed in the light of multicultural considerations. Culture can be seen as a system of values, beliefs, and standards that are learned, shared, adapted to particular circumstances, and continually changing (Au, 1993, p. 92). It is particularly important to recognize how various cultures view such classroom basics as the following: participation in class, use of time, the status/role of the teacher, listening postures, attendance, promptness, questioning, discipline, and, of course, taboos. It is my belief that much of our in-service for teachers should focus on knowledge about specific cultures as a prerequisite for considering instructional methods.

Many classrooms enroll students from as many as 5 or 10 different cultures. It is beyond the scope of this chapter to present a detailed discussion of the issues involved, but it is hoped that teachers and prospective teachers will realize that all classroom interactions must be considered in the light of various cultural beliefs and expectations. A failure to acknowledge the differences in interactional styles and to provide some means for bridging them with general classroom expectations may lead to students' confusion and ultimate failure.

Quantity of Talk

Upon entering whole-language classrooms, one usually hears students talking. Of course, quiet times exist, but during the majority of the day students are allowed and even encouraged to ask questions of each other, to talk over misunderstandings, and to solve problems jointly. Students read aloud to one another from their own writing as well as from tradebooks. Students ask the teacher for help, but they also freely seek the assistance of other students. Talk is both an integral and natural part of classroom life. Often students work in partners or small groups. These groups are sometimes formed spontaneously by the students and sometimes organized by the teacher.

Let's look at a specific example. In one grade 4 classroom, students were working in pairs to solve various problems in mathematics. One student came to the teacher with the question, "Does this equal 75?" The teacher asked the pair to discuss how they might find out. One partner stated that they might get blocks and count, but the other partner pointed out that blocks would be a very slow method with a number as large as 75. Students were attempting to work through the answers to some important questions and this process naturally involved talk. Talk is prevalent in mathematics and, in fact, over many content areas, but there are some activities in which talk seems universal.

Talk about Books

In whole-language classrooms, students read and discuss books. Discussion is used as a means to stimulate interest in the book, create involvement, and clarify misunderstandings, as well as a way to interest students in various topics or the works of particular authors.

In one first-grade classroom, for example, students became very interested in the works of the author Bill Peet. They began to read various books by Bill Peet and to meet in discussion groups to talk about what they liked about a book and how it was similar to Peet's other books. They also made a large, illustrated wall chart of their favorite books, and began to formulate questions that they wanted to ask the author about his work. The questions served as a natural stimulus for the students to write letters to Peet. Talk was a constant part of all of these activities. For a period of over one month, the children read books by Bill Peet—silently, aloud to one another, and as a presentation in front of the whole class. With no direct assignment from the teacher, they prepared choral readings (two or more students reading in unison) with a partner or short role dramas to portray a favorite plot. Reading was a social rather than a solitary event in this class, and the use of oral language was a natural consequence. Children talked to each other about their books as they read.

Besides enjoying themselves and using oral language to learn, these first-graders gained direct benefits in reading. If children are to develop higher-order literacy skills, they need to talk about their reading in ways that will help them discover the unique aspects of a particular book and to discover similarities and differences among other books and authors. Talk is beneficial in helping children to explore these ideas.

Talk about Writing

Just as students talk about what they are reading, they also talk about what they are writing. Writing can be a difficult task; many people struggle to represent meaning on paper. Often professional writers are not sure how to proceed, or if they have made their meaning clear to readers. Many writers need to try out a piece of writing on someone else or ask for help and feedback. If professional writers have these needs, surely students need a great deal of help and feedback. Why do some teachers have children write alone? In whole-language classrooms, children do not write alone. They have regular conferences with the teacher. They are also free to share their work with other students in the class and to receive comments or feedback from them. Students may talk as they write.

Because whole-language teachers believe in the importance of talk, especially as a support for literacy, they facilitate it. Talk is abundant. Students are free to share with each other and to help each other learn, both in a formal sense, such as in discussion groups created by the teacher, and in an informal sense, as when students consult with other students during work time. When one enters the classrooms, students are usually heard talking.

Student-Directed Talk across Several Interaction Patterns

In whole-language classrooms, teachers attempt to shift the locus of power and responsibility for learning so that it rests more heavily on the students. With regard to talk, this idea manifests itself in two important ways:

1. When students are talking with the teacher, students often take the lead.
2. More interaction patterns are encouraged.

By interaction patterns, I mean audiences for talk. In the classroom a limited number of interaction patterns are possible. These include student-to-teacher, student-to-student, student-to-small group, and student-to-large group. In some traditional classrooms the only interaction pattern that is observed is that of the teacher interacting with an individual student or perhaps the whole class. In either case, it is the teacher who controls both the content and format of the talk. Most, if not all, of the talk is teacher directed. As teachers begin to shift the locus of power from themselves to students, many interaction patterns seem to evolve naturally. In whole-language classrooms, many lines of communication extend from student to student, and control of the talk within the various interaction patterns often is distributed equally among students and the teacher. Teacher-directed talk is present but student-directed talk becomes important.

As teachers shift the locus of power, they still maintain many decision-making powers. Teachers ultimately take the lead in developing or guiding the curriculum, the class standards, and the day's schedule, yet whole-language teachers are always searching for ways to let the learning come from within the student. It is because of this shift in locus of power that talk in whole-language classrooms may be quite different. As students are given choices and allowed to take more responsibility for their own learning, more interaction patterns are possible and students begin to take a more active role in controlling the talk. More student-directed talk is heard. These interaction patterns will be more carefully examined here.

Student-to-Teacher Interaction

In whole-language classrooms, one might observe the student-to-teacher interaction pattern. The teacher and one student are working together to solve a problem or simply to share a personal experience. One student and the teacher are talking. Specific activities may include the following:

- Individual reading or writing conferences
- Individual instruction
- The asking or answering of questions
- The relating of personal experiences

This one-to-one interaction pattern is also common in traditional classrooms as the teacher calls individual students to the front of the room or circulates around the room during work time. The difference between student-to-teacher interaction in some traditional classrooms and student-to-teacher interaction in whole-language classrooms is subtle yet important. In whole-language classrooms, the student takes the lead in these interactions. The whole-language teacher is often concerned with finding out what the student knows or wants to know so that the teacher may provide information and guidance, as opposed to following the traditional pattern of examining the student according to specific predetermined objectives.

In a writing conference, for example, the direction of inquiry remains with the student (Hansen, 1992; Staab, 1992a). The teacher attempts to determine where the student wishes to take the story and is sensitive to how much information the student can handle.

The following example is typical of a writing conference in a whole-language classroom. Brett, a fifth-grade student, shared a piece of his writing with the teacher. His story was about a trip to Hawaii that he had taken with his family. In talking with Brett, it seemed obvious to the teacher that the focal point of Brett's trip had been a spearfishing expedition that he had taken with his father, yet his piece of writing did not in any way highlight this experience. The teacher mentioned that she found the spearfishing experience particularly exciting and that she would like to know more about it, but she left the decision of whether to highlight this portion of the story up to Brett. The teacher viewed her job as one of listener and facilitator and left the organization of the piece of writing with the student. This type of student-to-teacher interaction is quite different from the traditional conference, in which it is probable that the student would have been told how to change the story.

In a reading conference conducted in a whole-language classroom, the teacher may ask, "What did you think was the most interesting part of the story?" rather than approaching the student with five or six predetermined comprehension questions. The intent, or the desire to use language for a personal purpose, is the driving force behind all language use. If the intent belongs to the student, language flows. If the intent belongs only to the teacher, the student's language may be highly curtailed. If the student is allowed to respond only to the teacher's comprehension questions, the student may not be inclined to provide anything other than the briefest possible answer. Adults who are effective language partners in talking with students demonstrate a sensitivity to what the student is trying to say and support the student in that effort. This approach is entirely different from using a conference to correct a student's work, to force the student to display specific knowledge, or to cover items that are only on the teacher's agenda. It often takes practice to allow the student to take the lead in a conference. Teachers may wish to audiotape several conferences with students for later analysis, role-play a conference situation with a peer, or ask a peer to observe a conference with a student and provide feedback.

Student-to-Student Interaction

Besides student-to-teacher interactions, whole-language classrooms tend to have a great deal of student-to-student interactions. In many traditional classrooms, this interaction is rare, as it necessitates the delegation of responsibility to students. As teachers begin to relinquish power, they begin to concede that they are not the only audience for students' work, and also that they are not the only source of information, instruction, and help. In most whole-language classrooms, students can be seen helping other students or serving as an appreciative audience for students reading their work aloud or presenting projects. This student-to-student interaction may take the following forms:

- Buddy reading aloud—that is, two students taking turns reading to one another (primary grades) or two students discussing a piece of literature (intermediate)
- Playing a game such as Twenty Questions
- Working with a partner to solve a problem
- Consulting with other students while working

In most traditional classrooms, teachers provide instruction, followed by a time of guided group practice and then a quiet period of individual work. Students are allowed to ask questions of the teacher either by waiting at the teacher's desk or by raising their hands and waiting for the teacher to come to them. All lines of communication are between teacher and students. In most whole-language classrooms, however, students take over much of this function of helping other students. Students are allowed, in fact are encouraged, to ask spontaneous questions of other students and to share their work, such as a story in the process of being written.

Some teachers shy away from this type of interaction because they feel that students will simply waste time and not accomplish their work. Whole-language teachers generally feel that if students are given interesting tasks in which they are personally involved and in which they see meaning, talk tends to be on topic and on task. Talk is not simply what some teachers term "visiting," but it is the work of learning.

For example, in one first-grade whole-language classroom, students were engaged in a writing task, and the teacher allowed them to speak freely with one another during this time. One boy asked another boy, "How do you spell 'brachiosaurus'?" The second child answered, "Look up on the wall chart for tyrannosaurus, that's the 'saurus,' and then begin it with 'br' as in breakfast."

In whole-language classrooms, students spontaneously read aloud to other students. They do not wait for the one or two minutes a day that the teacher has time to hear them read. The teacher serves as a resource during work times, but not as the only resource. Although teachers help students, they also facilitate students helping each other, and they do not take steps to prevent this student-to-student interaction.

Another type of student-to-student interaction involves a cross-age pair. Perhaps a grade 5 student will be paired with a partner in grade 1. Usually the grade 1 and the grade 5 teachers will plan for their classes to get together for a half hour once per week over the period of a term or perhaps the whole year. Numerous activities may take place, but the most common activity is for the fifth-grade child to read to the first-grader and then for the pair to talk about the book. In addition to these weekly sessions, the two classes may go on field trips together or engage in other special activities.

Student-to-Small-Group Interaction

In many whole-language classrooms, there is an abundance of student-to-small-group interaction. Small groups are prevalent during the following activities:

- Science experiments
- Art projects
- Drama
- The study of novels

Small-group discussion, often in the form of reading groups, is also prevalent in traditional classrooms, but as with student-to-teacher interaction, one can generally see a difference in the type of discussion involved. In discussion groups in whole-language classrooms, the teacher may be a member of the group, but he or she does not dominate. This lack of domination is part of the teacher's attempt to shift the responsibility for learning to the student. In these classrooms, discussion groups are not orchestrated by the teacher, nor are they a question-and-answer session. Mehan (1979) has described typical, classroom talk as being dominated by the teacher. The teacher takes every other turn, because he or she has an initiating move to which a student responds, and then the teacher evaluates that response. This type of student-teacher interaction is illustrated in the following example:

The children have just read a story and the teacher is holding a small-group discussion.

Teacher:	Why was Tina's mother so anxious for her to go to the store?
Peter:	Because they were out of milk.
Teacher:	Good. (Then proceeds to ask another question)
OR	
Teacher:	Why was Tina's mother so anxious for her to go to the store?
Peter:	Because they were hungry.
Teacher:	Well yes, but can you tell us more, Mark? (Calls on Mark)

This type of question-answer-evaluation has been compared to the type of discussion that may go on in a whole-language classroom (Edelsky, 1987). In examining one sixth-grade whole-language class, Edelsky found that the students, rather than the teacher, sometimes control the floor in discussions, and that every remark is not necessarily addressed to the teacher. The following is an example of this type of interaction.

Four intermediate students and the teacher have formed a small group for the purpose of discussing *The Elders Are Watching* (Bouchard, 1990). All members of the group have previously read the book.

Kim:	I like the beautiful colors in the illustrations—neat.
Peter:	I think they were clean looking because the book is really about the environment—the way we're really messing it up.
Kathy:	Yeah, just look at all the paper in the streets and the mess on the beach.
Peter:	They're not talking about that—it's out of the city that is important. You know, the land—like where we are logging.
Kathy:	But the city is important too—besides we live here.
Mindy:	Have you ever been to . . . you know where all the logging goes on?
Peter:	Yeah, northern Vancouver Island, that's where it's all happening. I've been there lots of times. Just big open areas with stumps—ugly, ugly.
Teacher:	It is sad, isn't it?
Mindy:	Yeah, but it just makes me mad.

From examining this transcript, one can see that the teacher is a member of the group, but not necessarily the dominant member. Although the teacher is present, the talk is student directed. Students talk to one another and raise many issues that they feel are important and that they wish to discuss. Students are allowed to have more responsibility for the discussion.

Beginning Work in Small Groups

Successful small-group work takes patience and careful planning. An effective way to begin is with a teacher-directed whole-class experience such as the reading aloud of a piece of literature. Small groups of between three to five students can then be formed to discuss the experience or to make some type of a product, such as a picture or a model, related to the experience. The small groups then report back to the large group. This can be diagrammed as follows:

Large Group ————▶ *Small Groups* ————▶ *Large Group*

This pattern can be used over and over in a variety of activities. The teacher-directed large group provides motivation and direction, the small groups allow for participation and talk and the large group then serves as a way to report back what has happened in the small group and builds in the factors of audience and accountability. Individual learning is also possible using this pattern. After the small group has met, individual responsibilities may be assigned. Individuals must then prepare ideas and materials to bring back to the small group. The small group must produce something because it will need to be "shown." There may actually be a product such as a picture that the small group has made cooperatively, and in this case it can be shown, explained, and questions answered. Many times the "product" is simply a discussion in which case one student can be appointed to take brief notes and present a summary to the large group.

A Word about Cooperative Learning

Cooperative learning is a specialized form of small-group work in which students work together in small, heterogeneous groups for the ultimate purpose of individual learning. Because students are working together, much oral language is involved. Not only is cooperative learning a powerful tool for learning but it also presents untold opportunities to teach, model, and practice strategies needed to function successfully in small groups, thus helping students appropriate the power of language. Johnson, Johnson, and Holubec (1990) spelled out several cooperative strategies that have been divided into four categories: forming groups, managing groups, maximizing learning, and stimulating thinking.

Forming Groups	**Managing Groups**
Moving into groups	Sharing ideas
Using quiet voices	Reporting ideas
Listening to others	Watching time
Taking turns	Asking for help
Staying on task	Paraphrasing ideas
Finishing tasks	Saying how one feels
Recording ideas	Being enthusiastic
Following directions	Praising others
Using names	Helping others
Encouraging others	Expressing support

Maximizing Learning	**Stimulating Thinking**
Asking probing questions	Criticizing ideas, not people
Checking for agreement	Appreciating others' views
Directing work	Coming to consensus
Elaborating	Checking validity
Summarizing	Integrating ideas
Checking for accuracy	Asking for justification
Relieving tension	Giving reasons
Showing acceptance of others	Defending views

These strategies are not stratified into any scope and sequence but some are logically more basic than others. If groups are having trouble with the Forming strategies, it is unlikely that they will be highly successful in strategies for Stimulating Thinking. Therefore an initial step would be to help groups with Forming strategies. Sample mini-lessons and means of assessment are included under the heading A Word about Assessment.

Student-to-Large-Group Interaction

Student-to-large-group interactions are prevalent in both whole-language classrooms and some traditional classrooms. Teachers create a time in which one student may have an opportunity to relate orally to the whole class. Specific incidents of this type of interaction may include the following:

- Making announcements
- Show and tell
- News time
- Giving oral reports or presenting projects

In whole-language classrooms, teachers constantly seek opportunities to allow students this type of interaction. In one first-grade classroom, a child handled a five-minute transition time without intervention from the teacher. As the teacher began to prepare for the math lesson by placing manipulatives on children's desks, she asked one of the children to teach the class a new song that he had learned the previous day. Joshua sang the song for the class, made the class repeat the words, and then asked everyone to sing. The teacher explained that at the beginning of the year she had spent several weeks helping students to take over these kinds of responsibilities and then she had created as many opportunities as possible for students to lead the class.

In several whole-language classrooms, the practice of establishing a "teacher of the day" is used. One student each day leads the morning exercises, which normally consist of calling the roll, doing the calendar, and completing the weather chart. After two months of teacher modeling, this routine is usually highly successful even in primary classrooms. The "teacher of the day" has various other duties throughout the schoolday, such as making announcements, moderating sharing times, and helping with the distribution and collection of materials. This notion of "teacher of the day" can be extended into upper elementary levels by gradually allowing students to take over appropriate teacher duties.

Teachers attempt to make these opportunities for students to talk in front of the class as real and meaningful as possible. If students are asked to report on a news item, for example, teachers make an attempt to stimulate students' interest in a news event and to encourage them to seek information about it. In one seventh-grade classroom, students became excited about the case of the 12-year-old boy in Florida who brought a lawsuit to "divorce" his natural parents. Students scoured newspapers and magazines for information about this case and became very involved in following it. This is in sharp contrast to situations where students are assigned to bring in a news clipping once a week and report to the class. Students in this grade 7 class were not fulfilling an assignment, but were actually seeking information because they wanted to know.

Listening

Understanding the Process

As students are working with partners, in small groups, and in large groups, naturally they are listening as well as speaking. The reciprocal nature of talk has been mentioned. However, some oral language activities are useful for gathering information or creating enjoyment, yet they are not reciprocal. Some students may not have the ability to listen well during these experiences without some help from the teacher.

Wolvin and Coakley (1979) diagrammed the listening process as follows:

Stimulus ──────▶ *Stimulus is received* ──────▶ *Stimulus is attended to*

Meaning is assigned ──────▶ *Meaning is remembered*

Norton (1993) discussed this topic in terms of auditory acuity, auditory perception, auditory awareness, auditory discrimination, attention, and comprehension.

When we talk about the stimulus being received, we mean that the student actually heard the stimulus. As classroom teachers, we can do little about this condition other than to be on the alert for students who may have a hearing problem. It is our responsibility to notice when students constantly ask for oral directions to be repeated, seem to daydream during oral activities, or generally misunderstand. These conditions could suggest many things but they may be symptomatic of a hearing problem and we should refer the student immediately for medical testing.

If a hearing problem is not a factor and students still aren't paying attention, or attending to the message, one or more of the following factors may be operating:

1. The topic is of little interest to students because the student does not consider the information appropriate or useful. It may be something the students already know (too easy) or something beyond the students' present ability (too difficult). The students may see no value in listening—this

is more likely to happen when the listening experience is isolated from ongoing classroom activities.

2. There may be too much noise in the classroom, too many interruptions, or the teacher may be talking so much that the students simply "tune out."

3. There may be lack of a mental set. Students may be asking themselves, "Why am I listening to this?" or "What am I supposed to get out of this?" If you want students to listen for a particular reason, such as to discover the steps needed to construct a particular model, then you need to tell students before the listening experience.

Meaning is more likely to be assigned if the gap between what students know and what students hear is not too great. Vygotsky (1986) has termed this the **zone of proximal development**—the zone in which students must "reach" a little bit but not so much as to cause total confusion and frustration. By watching students carefully to discover what they are doing and what they can do, teachers can discover this zone.

Another way to help students assign meaning is to develop prior knowledge before a listening experience. A number of years ago I announced to my staff that I intended to take my sixth-grade class to an opera sung in Italian. Amid comments such as, "Impossible, you'll have nothing but discipline problems," and "Why, the kids won't enjoy a bit of it," I set out to develop some prior knowledge. Several weeks before the performance we began by sharing the story, role-playing a number of the critical incidents, and listening to much of the music. I was lucky in that one of my student's parents was interested in opera and had a trained singing voice. She came to class, sang several of the arias, and talked about the opera as she answered students' questions. On the day of the performance my students knew the story and had become familiar with most of the music. We all enjoyed ourselves, the students listened, and discipline problems were nonexistent. Prior knowledge helped to put the experience within the students' reach.

Once meaning is assigned, we hope students will remember the experience over a period of time. My best recipe for this is to do something with the experience—talk about it, write about it, or represent it in some way. I call all of these *demonstrations of knowing*. Not all students need to draw a picture, write a story, or fill in a worksheet. Following an experience such as the opera or the reading aloud of a novel to the class, the teacher might say, "What do you think was the most important message here—the most important thing the composer/author had to say?" Some ideas might be listed on the board. "How could you represent these ideas? Let's list some ways on the board. See if you can tell us in some way that is your own. You might draw a picture, you might get together with two or three others and do a mural, you might write a story or a play, you might do a short skit or a role drama. I will be a resource person but you decide how you will tell us what you think."

Teaching Listening

There are four primary methods for teaching listening:

1. Provide a good role model.
2. Establish a supportive and helpful environment.
3. Provide many and varied listening experiences for students.
4. Provide direct instruction, when appropriate, within the context of genuine classroom activities.

This instruction can go on during talk or during various other oral language activities.

Provide a Good Role Model

When students present oral reports to the class, are you listening and asking questions when appropriate or are you taking this opportunity to mark papers or engage in some other activity? When students speak to you on a one-to-one basis, are you concentrating on what the student is saying and maintaining eye contact or are you distracted by other things going on in the classroom? When you are part of a small group, do you truly listen to what others say or are you more concerned about what it is that you have to say? In a very real

sense you show students how to listen. The first step in teaching listening is for the teacher to be a good listener.

Establish a Conducive Environment

Further on in this chapter, we will discuss essentials for establishing a good psychological and physical environment in the classroom, but in addition to these principles we need some specific rules for listening experiences. Whole-language classrooms are not without rules; in fact, rules bring freedom. Once students have a clear idea of the expectations in the classroom, both the teacher and the students are free to get on with the business of teaching and learning. Here are some examples of rules created for different interaction patterns:

Student-to-Large Group

Maintain eye contact with the speaker.
Do not speak unless recognized by the speaker.
Raise hand and wait to be called upon.
Do not engage in other activities such as drawing while someone is speaking. When recognized by the speaker, ask questions or make comments relevant to what has been said.

Student-to-Small Group or Partner

Maintain eye contact with speaker.
Wait turn before speaking.
Be on task/topic.   Staab (1992a, p. 94)

Provide Many and Varied Listening Experiences

Again, let me stress that our focus is not on what kind of listening experiences we can provide today or this week, but rather the focus is on what students are doing/learning. Within the course of these activities we can then seek to create many opportunities for students to listen. An easy way to think of this might be in terms of varying the delivery and varying the purpose. A few examples other than listening in a large group, a small group, or to a partner are as follows:

Varying the Delivery	Varying the Purpose
Film-Television	To gain information
Guest speaker/reader	To understand directions
Audio recordings	To enjoy/be entertained
Dramatic presentations	To evaluate (information or
viewpoint)	

Let's look at an example that may put a few of these ideas together. An ungraded intermediate class is studying pioneer life. You have filled the classroom with as many resources as possible—fiction and nonfiction books depicting the period, pictures, and two films. You have also planned a field trip to a pioneer town and a pioneer day in your classroom on which you intend to invite parents, grandparents, and friends. You have decided that you will introduce the topic with one of the films followed by a small-group discussion of what life was like in pioneer times. You have also decided that after a few days of general information provided by the film, discussions, and books, you will ask the class to divide into small groups and prepare a demonstration of some aspect of pioneer life that will be displayed/presented at your class pioneer day. The groups might include pioneer houses, typical food, forms of entertainment, clothing and home life, or means of employment. Each group will study, research, and present one topic at the pioneer day. You are, of course, a resource as you circulate from group to group. The form of presentation might be a report, a dramatic production, a dance, a model, or a table of prepared food. These are the general plans formulated by the teacher. Some of the listening experiences might include:

1. Listening to novels read aloud—for information and enjoyment
2. Listening to films—for information and enjoyment
3. Listening to guest speakers on the field trip—information
4. Listening to directions—for making a model, a recipe, or learning a dance
5. Listening to a short play—for enjoyment and information

Within the course of your plans, it is wise to make time for activities that seem to spring from the students' interests. In a sense, you are planned but not *too* planned. For example, as one teacher read aloud the novel, *Mary of Mile Eighteen*, (Blades, 1976), one of her students remarked that life was better in Mary's day. Another student immediately said that wasn't so because Mary didn't have television or movies or computer games. This led to a lively discussion with many students involved. The class began to compare life today with life in pioneer times and to list some of the major differences on the board. Some of the class members seemed to be lining up with quite diverse opinions, so the teacher proposed that the class take some time to consider the question "Was life better in pioneer times?" and to have a class debate. The students took on the project enthusiastically. They talked about what a debate was and the rules for holding one. They decided who would be on each side and talked about how they needed to prepare their information ahead of time. Their purpose as speakers would be to try to persuade others to go along with their viewpoint. They talked about some methods of persuasion—giving concrete information, giving convincing arguments, and appealing to people's emotions. Twelve students took three days to prepare their arguments (the rest of the class enjoyed reading about pioneer days and writing in their journals) and on the fourth day the debate was held in front of the class. They talked briefly about how to evaluate information and arguments and decided that after the debate each class member would write out his or her opinion in the form of a short essay. This led to a profitable lesson on exactly what an essay is and much valuable information about pioneer life.

Provide Direct Instruction When Appropriate

There are several direct instructional strategies that may be used during specific listening experiences (Hoskisson and Tompkins, 1987). These include creating images, webbing, and formulating questions.

Creating Images   If a speaker's or author's message contains many visual images, details, or descriptive words, it is often helpful for listeners to create a picture in their minds. We can help students develop this ability by stopping periodically during a film or the oral reading of a novel or poem and asking students to create a mental picture of what is being described. We may share our own mental picture or invite a few student volunteers to do so as a model for the class. One upper-intermediate teacher who reads aloud to the class on a daily basis often stops and asks the class to draw or represent the image with paper and colored pencils. One word of caution—use this technique sparingly. Constantly stopping for any reason during an exciting novel can prove disruptive.

Webbing   Webbing is a technique for clustering information graphically and is often useful for activating prior knowledge or providing students with a framework for organizing knowledge. Webs can be done on the board prior to a listening experience as a way to help students organize information or after a listening experience as a memory aid. Here is an example of a simple web developed by a third-grade class as a way to organize information from a film on rocks.

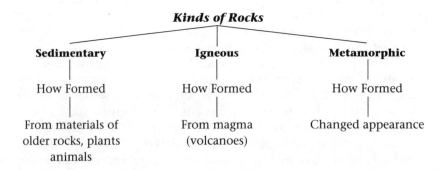

Kinds of Rocks

Sedimentary	Igneous	Metamorphic
How Formed	How Formed	How Formed
From materials of older rocks, plants animals	From magma (volcanoes)	Changed appearance

Asking Questions   Helpful questions to ask include those directed at the speaker to help clarify a message and also questions directed toward the self to determine if one is making sense of the message. The teacher can be a model for both types of questions. To encourage the first type of question, you may stop during a listening experience and ask the class if anyone has any questions. This works particularly well during films or taped presentations. To model the process, you then share your own questions.

Questions designed to monitor your own understanding can be handled in the same way. At appropriate points during a film, you can stop and ask, "What questions are you asking yourself at this point? Here is what I am asking myself." Again, all of these methods of instruction are used within the context of whatever you are doing in the classroom. The focus is on understanding pioneer life (or whatever), not on isolated exercises to teach listening.

A Word about Assessment

Chapter 12 discusses the concept of assessment in general but a word about assessment as it relates to talk in the classroom is in order. The bottom line in selecting any type of assessment for classroom use should be whether it helps students (Farr, 1992; Staab, Early, and Hunsberger, in press). Assessment of talk in the classroom should be designed to help students appropriate the power of language and to use that language for learning. Helpful assessment will pro-

vide teachers with tools for noticing what students can do with the "stuff," or content, of instruction (what students need to be able to do). This is the "what" of assessment. As you watch and listen to students talk in the classroom, what should be attracting your attention?

Perhaps the most useful and certainly the most practical way to notice what students can do and what they need to do is by teacher observation. Summaries or written copies of these observations can then be placed in students' folders or portfolios. This is the "how" of assessment. It may be helpful to videotape or make an audio recording of students talking, but I believe that this is an annual or semiannual activity—not the stuff of every day.

The What

Table 3.1 is by no means all inclusive; as you are observing students in the classroom, you may wish to include additional items for observation. The point is that you cannot simply observe students talking; you must have some reference points or things to notice. The table is divided into quadrants: talking and listening, and then the surface features and the uses of each. These will serve you well as a place to begin.

The How

As students are engaged in various large-group, small-group, or partner activities, the teacher is constantly observing students in addition to being a resource person. In recording these observations, I suggest one of two methods.

Method One

The points from Table 3.1 can be duplicated on a separate sheet of paper with room at the top for the student's name, the date, and the context of the activity. By context, I mean such things as what the interaction pattern was and what the specific activity was. The points on the chart should also be spaced sufficiently far apart so that the teacher has room for comments. The teacher then spends three to five minutes observing an individual student and recording the observations. These observations take place after the class has started to work on a project so that the teacher is free to circulate. Using this means, it is realistic to observe each student once or twice per term. One important word of caution. Oral language is appropriate to a given situation. Just because you did not observe a student summarizing, for example, does not mean that he or she cannot perform that skill. The situation may not have called for it. Your observation is only one look at a student, not the whole picture.

TABLE 3.1   *Oral Language*

Talking

Looks like/Sounds like	Use
Willing to speak in many situations to various audiences	Appropriately agrees or disagrees with others
Appropriate volume Appropriate nonverbal behavior (eye contact, etc.)	States ideas clearly Summarizes or integrates ideas
Tone of voice	Sequences ideas clearly
Appropriate quantity of talk for situation	Gives clear directions
Appropriate vocabulary	Entertains
Appropriate grammar	Socializes (initiates maintains, concludes conversations)
Absence of speech problems Displays confidence in many situations	Persuades others
	Asks for help or information

Listening

Looks like/Sounds like	Use
Willing to listen in many situations/audiences	Understands ideas
Appropriate nonverbal behavior	Follows directions
Adequate auditory acuity and discrimination	Interprets and evaluates
Synthesizes or summarizes	Enjoys various listening experiences

Method Two

Some teachers simply internalize the points on Table 3.1 and then record their observations on small "post it" tabs that can be placed in a student's folder. Teachers are busy people and we need to find a method that is profitable and realistic for us. All the forms in the world are not helpful if we never have time to fill them out. My own personal choice is to make one or two formal observations per term using the first method and then to make several informal observations on the same student using the second method. By formal observation, I mean a time when I specifically plan to watch a particular student. By informal observation, I mean any time I notice something significant and simply want to jot it down as a part of my growing information about that student.

This information can be collected on a summary sheet at the end of each grading period and can serve as a basis for reporting and for parent conferences. A sample summary sheet is as follows:

Summary—Oral Language

Student's Name: _____

Date: _____

What I have observed: _____

_____

_____

_____

_____

Conclusion drawn: _____

_____

_____

_____

Plans for action: _____

_____

_____

_____

Obviously, the preceding form includes three parts: what I saw/heard, what I think it means, and what I intend to do about it. These forms can be shared with parents, who often can be of help in drawing conclusions. Scraps of notes from observations are not helpful if the information is never pieced together for the purpose of drawing some conclusions and planning some action.

The teacher need not be the only person involved in assessment. Students as well as groups can assess themselves. These assessments, along with the teacher's assessment, can be placed in students' folders. The following forms might be used by students to evaluate themselves, particularly when working in small groups:

*Oral Language Report on Myself**

Name _____

Date _____

I was talking to _____

We were doing _____

My last improvement plan was to _____

_____

_____

_____

_____

_____

	Yes	No	Sometimes
I shared my ideas	❏	❏	❏
I listened to others	❏	❏	❏
I spoke loudly/softly enough	❏	❏	❏
I answered others' questions	❏	❏	❏
I remained on task	❏	❏	❏
I encouraged others	❏	❏	❏
I presented my ideas clearly	❏	❏	❏
I disagreed without hurting feelings	❏	❏	❏
I summarized or repeated if necessary	❏	❏	❏
I gave reasons for my opinions	❏	❏	❏

My next improvement plan will be to _____

_____

_____

_____

_____

_____

_____

(Staab, 1992, p. 63)

Students can assess themselves using this form at the end of each scheduled group discussion. The teacher should collect the forms, look them over, and then pass them back to the student for inclusion in individual folders. At the start of the next group discussion, the student should check the previous form to determine what the plan was for improvement and then be prepared to work on that strategy during the present discussion. At the end of the term, the student might put all the self-assessment forms in order of date, read them over, and then fill out the following summary form:

Summary—Oral Language Assessments

Name: _____

Date: _____

How I improved: _____

_____

_____

_____

_____

I still need to work on: _____

_____

_____

_____

_____

To work on these things I could: _____

_____

_____

_____

_____

A form such as the following might be used for assessment during those times when students give a presentation in front of the whole class:

Public Speaking—Assessment

Name: _____

Date: _____

Title of talk: _____

	Yes	No	Sometimes
The speaker (I) spoke loudly enough	❑	❑	❑
The speaker (I) had good eye contact with audience	❑	❑	❑
The speaker (I) varied the tone of voice	❑	❑	❑
The speaker (I) stood up straight	❑	❑	❑
The speaker's (my) ideas were well organized and clearly presented	❑	❑	❑

The best part was: _____

_____

_____

One suggestion is: _____

_____

_____

Students can assess themselves (thus the "I" and "my" in parentheses) or they can be assessed by a peer. In one seventh-grade classroom the teacher has three assessments for each student. Self, peer, and the teacher all assess using a form similar to the one above. Partners for the peer assessment are drawn out of a hat and the teacher works hard to emphasize that the assessment is to help the student improve, not for the purposes of criticism—only helpful comments will be accepted. Furthermore, the teacher does not begin peer assessments until a spirit of community has been established in the classroom. After all students have spoken, the teacher collects the three assessments (self, peer, and teacher). She then reviews them to make sure all comments are accurate and helpful and then uses them as a basis for a conference with the speaker.

Another form of peer assessment is for small groups to assess themselves. After a small-group discussion, the following form might be used:

Oral Language Group Report

Names: _____

Date: _____

Our task was to: _____

_____

Things we did well:

1. _____

2. _____

3. _____

4. _____

5. _____

Things on which we need help:

1. _____

2. _____

3. _____

Our worst problem was: _____

_____

_____

We might solve that problem by: _____

_____

_____

_____

Relationship between Assessment and Instruction

In order for assessment to be of help to students, the teacher must do something with the results of that assessment—something other than simply report the findings to parents, students and/or school personnel. We must look at and listen to students (assess) and then use that information as a basis for instruction.

In whole-language classrooms, instruction takes many forms, just as it does in all classrooms, but individual conferences and mini-lessons are common. Individual conferences are times when the teacher and one student or perhaps one small group get together to discuss one's strong points and specific plans for improvement. During this time, the teacher can find out what the student thinks, discuss the problem, offer suggestions, model solutions, and help the student develop a plan for improvement. This discussion often springs from a combination of a teacher's observations and the student's self-assessment.

Mini-lessons are short lessons (3–5 minutes) that the teacher provides for the whole class. From various forms of assessment the teacher realizes that students need help with a particular problem; therefore, the teacher provides input and instruction. Their content is taken from various forms of assessment. The content of a mini-lesson may be presented once or repeated several times, depending on students' need. There is no direct follow-up to a mini-lesson in the form of guided practice; the follow-up is simply more assessment to note improvement. Thus there is an endless cycle: assessment—instruction—assessment, with the overall umbrella being the curriculum (i.e., what students need to know and do—see oral language chart at the beginning of this section). Perhaps a couple of examples will help to clarify the idea of a mini-lesson.

Mini-Lesson—Example One

Teacher: Today before we get into our small groups again, we have a couple of things to talk about. In circulating around the room yesterday and in looking over your group and self-assessment forms, I noticed that many of you seem to be having a problem staying on task. Let's think about that today before we start and try to plan some strategies that would help us stay on task. First of all, what does it look like and sound like to be on task? If you were watching a group, how would you know that the group members were on task? Let's make a list on the board.

Students brainstorm some ideas as the teacher writes them down:

Looks Like	Sounds Like
Everyone has materials	Most of the talk is on topic
Everyone stays in work area	People are helping each other
Everyone is doing something to finish project	

Teacher: Good, if I saw and heard those things I would think you were on task. Now let's think about some very specific things to help us. How could we help everyone to have materials? One of the ways I know is to stop a moment before you get into your groups and to think about what you will need for today. You may not be able to think of everything but you can think about what you will need to get started. Take a moment and think about the materials you'll need—jot them down if you like. (Wait one minute.) Before you get into your groups today make sure that you have those materials. Now let's think about one other thing before we get started. How could we manage to get everyone doing something to finish the project?

Jenny: Well, yesterday some people didn't know what they were supposed to do.

Teacher: Right, I noticed that too. What about this idea? Today before you start to work, have a brief group meeting. Each member of the group can then explain what he or she hopes to accomplish today. If someone is unsure, the other members can help or remember I'm always available. Any questions? Good, let's get our materials, get into our groups, and be on task.

Mini-Lesson—Example Two

Teacher: Today before we give our oral reports on planets in our solar system, let's concentrate on improving our public speaking. We have been concentrating on keeping eye contact with all members of the audience and you have been doing that very well. What are some other things we want to remember?

Teacher lists students' suggestions on the board:

Speak loudly	Stand up straight
Include interesting visuals	Don't use a monotone

Teacher: Good list. Let's pick up on only one of those ideas—don't use a monotone; in other words, speak with expression. Listen to this. (Teacher picks up a book and reads a page using a monotone.) Did you enjoy listening to me read? Why not?

Paul: It was boring.

Teacher: Well how about this? (Teacher reads the next page with expression varying the tone of voice.) Was there a difference?

Steve: It made me want to listen.

Teacher: Yes; in other words, it held your attention. Today when we give our reports, let's remember to vary our tone of voice because that will help to hold our audience.

Getting Started

A preservice teacher, a beginning teacher, or one who is just starting a program of whole-language, may be thinking, "This is all very interesting but how do I begin? I need something for Monday morning." Since talk is viewed as an integral part of learning and a natural part of whatever is going on in a whole-language classroom, any description of a concrete activity can only serve as an illustration of an activity that a teacher might want to plan. As in the earlier example of the grade 1 teacher whose children were so interested in Bill Peet's books, this teacher knew at the beginning of the school year that she would provide an environment where children would become interested in books and in authors, but she did not plan ahead of time to use books by Bill Peet. The reading of these books and the accompanying oral and written activities grew out of the children's interests.

More important, talk in the classroom results more from the mindset of the teacher than from the planning of specific activities. If talk is viewed as a hindrance to learning rather than a way to help students learn, teachers will organize curricular activities to inhibit talk (for example, students will be asked to read and write alone). If talk is viewed as a way for students to seek meaning from their experiences, to augment their internal theories of the world, to make understandings more precise and retrievable, then students will be invited to participate with many conversational partners in many kinds of interaction patterns. It is for this reason that so much information on the value of talk was included at the beginning of the chapter. Teachers must begin with a solid belief that talk is valuable and be willing to defend that belief.

Although I have some reservations about providing specific activities because they may be misinterpreted, I have no reservations about telling you that there are some things you must do to ensure productive talk in the classroom. I have labeled these things The Musts. Following The Musts are Some Possibles—typical whole-language activities that you might like to try if they fit the needs and interests of your students.

The Musts

Establishing Control

Teachers need to establish boundaries or rules at the beginning of the school year so that all class members share common expectations. Of primary importance is a method for establishing a quiet classroom and for regaining students' attention if they have been talking in pairs or small groups. The signal for quiet should be established on the first day of school and practiced until students understand its significance and respond to it quickly. Common signals for quiet include the following:

- Blinking the classroom lights
- Playing chords on the piano
- Ringing a small bell
- Clapping the hands

Students must understand that upon hearing the signal for quiet, they must stop talking and listen. If teachers feel confident that control can be regained quickly, they feel more comfortable about giving students responsibility for learning. With some classes it may be necessary to practice this signal several times a day for a few days before the routine is working efficiently. Following each signal for quiet, teachers should include the class members in evaluating how quickly they were able to stop talking and what they might do to respond more promptly the next time.

Establishing Common Understandings

Besides the signal for quiet, several other common understandings need to be established during the first weeks of school. Some of these common understandings include the following:

- How students are to obtain, handle, and replace materials
- How students are to be responsible for keeping the classroom tidy
- How students are to treat other students and other students' property
- How students are to move into and out of discussion groups
- How student discussion groups are to be conducted

Teachers may spend several days or weeks on these understandings at the beginning of the school year, but once these common understandings are shared by all members of the class, students can engage in learning activities without wasting valuable time, and teachers can begin to shift the responsibility for learning to the students with a certain degree of comfort.

Levels of Talk

Some teachers, even those who are committed to the value of talk, may feel that the sound level in the classroom can at times become uncomfortable and distracting. Teachers may wish to work with their students to establish the following levels of talk:

- Pin drop—an absolutely quiet condition in which one can literally hear a pin drop
- Conversation—quiet voices used when two people are speaking with one another
- Discussion—projection of the voice so that one can be heard by class members sitting several feet away

As pin drop is an absolutely quiet condition, it can be used during such activities as Uninterrupted Sustained Silent Reading, viewing a film, testing, or whenever the teacher feels that the class needs silence. In any classroom there should be periods of quiet, if only to provide a rest from activity.

Conversation, or quiet talk, can be used during such activities as writing, reading, or in any situation where students are working together or helping one another. At the conversation level it is quite possible for those students who prefer to read or write in relative quiet to engage independently in these activities.

The discussion level is used when it is necessary for a student to be heard by more than one person. Such activities might include small-group discussion and large-group presentations. During these activities most class members are usually speaking or listening at any given time, so it is not important that the room remain quiet enough for some students to work independently.

The three talk levels should be explained to students on the first day of school and practiced over successive weeks. By the middle of October, students should be well acquainted with the three levels of talk and know when to use each one.

Time spent at the beginning of the school year to establish these various talk levels and understandings is not wasted. Teachers, especially beginning teachers, need confidence in their ability to provide a workable and productive structure for classroom activities. From the vantage point of this confidence, teachers can begin to encourage students to engage in various interaction patterns as discussed in this chapter, and to use talk to seek personal meaning. Without this confidence, teachers are unlikely to try many new activities or to try to encourage much student-directed talk.

Establishing an Atmosphere for Talk

The Psychological Atmosphere   Do students feel free to use talk as a way to learn and to seek personal meaning, or do they feel constrained to supply only the answers that the teacher feels are acceptable? By establishing an underlying atmosphere of acceptance and encouragement rather than one of evaluation, teachers release students to explore their own thoughts and ideas. There are, of course, times when teachers need to evaluate students to determine their basic knowledge (for example, a test on division of fractions), but there should also be times when students feel free to express their own ideas and opinions (for example, discussion of a novel). Students, like adults, are more inclined to participate and contribute in an environment where they feel secure and valued rather than in an atmosphere where they feel judged by predetermined standards.

To create this atmosphere of acceptance and encouragement, teachers can begin by allowing students to express their own opinions. Teachers can ask many questions that have no one correct answer and then respond to students' answers nonjudgmentally. Such casual remarks as, "Tell me more about your idea," "I hadn't thought of that before," and "Let's think about that," are often helpful.

In order to express original opinions or ideas, students must risk being unsure or wrong. Teachers can model this process by being honest and admitting that there are many times when they are unsure. When the teacher can establish an atmosphere of "We are here to learn together" or "How could we find out about this idea?" rather than an atmosphere of "I know all the answers and I'm trying to determine if you do," students feel freer to learn though the medium of talk.

The Physical Atmosphere   In classrooms where many interaction patterns are to be encouraged, the arrangement of the furniture becomes extremely important. Teachers will need to plan for students to engage in individual, small-group, and large-group activities easily without taking time to move desks and heavy pieces of furniture each time an activity is changed. If desks are placed in straight rows, for example, it becomes very difficult to allow space for students to work alone or in partners and to have additional room to gather in small groups or to get together as one body for a whole-class activity. A better arrangement might be to cluster desks in groups of four or six and then to provide tables for individual work along the periphery of the classroom. Space could be left for a large-group activity in front of the blackboard or in one corner of the room. Teachers need to give careful consideration to room arrangement because the very nature of the arrangement will either encourage or discourage talk. No one room arrangement will be suitable for all classes, given the furniture that the school district provides and the size of individual classrooms, but teachers can give thought to accommodating various interaction patterns regardless of whether they use individual desks or tables. Two sample diagrams of room arrangements are provided in Chapter 11, which discusses the organization of whole-language classrooms.

Grouping

Naturally, there are many times throughout the schoolday when teachers feel it is beneficial for students to work individually. This individual work normally does not elicit student talk. For talk to be stimulated, students must work in partners or in groups. Teachers need to consider when group work might be appropriate and plan for these group experiences. Most science experiments, art activities such as murals, and social studies projects such as mapping seem to lend themselves nicely to group experiences.

Children's Literature

Even though there is much variation in individual classrooms, whole-language teachers seem to share a love of good children's literature. They fill the classroom with as much of it as possible. They read aloud to students and encourage students to read to themselves every day. Integral to this love of children's literature is the talking about and the sharing of good books.

An Interesting Classroom

Once the psychological and the physical environment have been established, teachers can begin to plan activities that will encourage talk. Children seldom talk about talk. They talk about the interesting things that are happening in their environment. If the physical surroundings of the classroom are bare and sterile, there may not be much of interest to stimulate talk. It is the teacher's responsibility to provide a stimulating and exciting classroom. This can be done in a number of ways. A few of these ways leads into a discussion of Some Possibles.

Some Possibles

Collections

Bring into the classroom a personal collection. This may be anything from an extensive collection of seashells to collections that have been put together expressly for the purpose of sharing in the classroom. Collections that fall into this latter category might include various types of nails, utensils for use in the kitchen, or various types of seeds. The collection should be displayed prominently on a table in the classroom and remain there for a period of a week or so. The collector, in this case the teacher, is now the class expert with regard to this collection. The collector is responsible for explaining the collection to the class and for answering any questions that members of the class might have. The collector may even place reference books on the table so that members of the class can look up the answer to any questions that the collector is unable to answer. After the teacher has presented one or two collections and modeled the process, children in the class should be invited to bring their collections and to become the class expert.

Sometimes these collections are class collections. One spring, a particular first-grade class became interested in spiders. They brought garden spiders, house spiders, and various other forms of creeping, crawling phenomena into the classroom. The teacher set up a table at the front of the class complete with reference books, magnifying glasses, tweezers, and so on, and the class happily spent three weeks investigating and classifying spiders.

News Bulletin Board

Instead of the usual bulletin board where students place isolated items from newspapers or magazines, the teacher might try devoting an entire bulletin board to one story in which the children are interested. The 12-year-old boy in

Florida who "divorced" his parents is an example of the kind of news story that might arouse interest. This technique allows students to gather information as it is made available and to discuss each day what new developments have been presented.

Items of Interest

Whenever possible, bring into the classroom items of interest. Following a recent trip to the seashore, one teacher brought back two starfish. These items led to talk about starfish and obtaining library books to find out more information about starfish. This activity should not be done by way of an assignment but simply to arouse curiosity. Students should also be encouraged to bring in items of particular interest to them.

Pets or Plants

Pets can be a welcome addition to the classroom and provide the students with many opportunities for talk. If the class pet is a hamster, for example, students can share the responsibility for its care and feeding. Students can also chart the pet's growth or use the opportunity to find out all they can about hamsters.

Growing plants from seeds or seedlings can be a very rewarding experience and can provide the students with many opportunities for talk. Students can test and record the growth of different kinds of plants, or the same plant under different conditions such as the amount of light and water. Students may even try some transplanting experiments if space is available.

Centers

Centers are those areas in the classroom that are usually devoted to one particular subject area and that are set up with independent activities. The subject of centers is discussed more fully in Chapter 11. An art center, for example, might be set up on a back counter of the classroom and include different kinds of paper and sets of watercolor brushes. A mathematics center might consist of a pocket chart hung on the wall and filled with word problems or brain teasers for students to solve. Centers can also be organized around a theme, such as a collection of Bill Peet's books and a chart indicating which books the students liked best.

Centers that stimulate talk are those where students can work cooperatively on a project. The teacher, for example, may perform several simple science experiments as a demonstration for the class. The materials to perform these experiments can then be placed in a center and two or three students can work cooperatively to replicate the experiments. These centers where students work cooperatively may be highly structured, as in the preceding example, or left fairly unstructured, as in a kindergarten dress-up center where children create their own dramas.

A student follows a story in a book while listening to the story on headphones.

Ways to Share Good Books

Although the use and availability of children's literature is integral to every whole-language classroom, many ways to use and share that literature are possible. First, teachers who love children's literature read children's literature. Teachers who have read a particularly good book can then bring it to class and share it with the students. During this book talk, the teacher simply mentions the name of the book, the author, and a few of the highlights of the book or a short synopsis of the plot. It is important that the book then be placed in the classroom library so that interested students may read the book. After the teacher has given several of these book talks over a period of days or weeks, the teacher should then invite individual students to give book talks on books that they have read and enjoyed. This should not be an assignment such as a book report but simply a time allotted for the sharing of good books.

Second, during buddy reading, students are allowed to choose a partner and to read aloud to that partner if they wish. Students may also choose to read silently but to talk about the book or to share small bits of it with a partner.

Third, following a period of silent reading or buddy reading, certain students may wish to share parts of their book with the whole group. This should not be a long and tedious book report but simply the sharing of a particularly significant incident. It should not be an assignment but more of an opportunity to share. Four or five students may be chosen each day to share.

Fourth, in literature groups, students get together to read and discuss literature of quality (Peterson and Eeds, 1990). Teachers usually obtain five or six copies of four or five titles that they feel their students can enjoy. The teacher briefly introduces the various books and then asks students to choose which book they would like to read. First choices are given if possible. Groups are then formed on the basis of the titles chosen. In intermediate grades, the teacher may decide how many pages are to be read before the first discussion. The students read silently on their own and usually meet two or three times a week to discuss the book. During these discussions the teacher does not ask a number of questions to determine if the students understood the main points and details of the book, but rather the teacher attempts to engage the students in an actual discussion of the book, much as one would if discussing the book informally with another adult. The teacher may ask such questions as:

- What did you think of this book?
- What was your favorite part of the book?
- How did that part of the story make you feel?
- Does this book remind you of any other book you have read?

Process Writing

Process writing seems to invite student talk. As students are free to read parts of their writing to other members of the class and discuss their ideas with them, talk naturally accompanies writing. Furthermore, as students read pieces of their writing to the whole class or to small groups and receive feedback, talk is stimulated and encouraged. A full explanation of process writing is included in Chapter 4.

A Final Word

When The Musts are in place and teachers thoroughly understand the philosophy of whole-language, the list of Possibles is endless. Whatever the Possibles, or the specific activities, in whole-language classrooms one can observe students talking. Talk is a way to learn and to help students gain the power of communication. True, whole-language teachers have times for quiet and they have taken time to establish routines and rules, yet they believe in the value of talk and structure their classroom activities so that talk can happen.

Not only are students talking in whole-language classrooms but they are also talking within the context of many different talk structures. Students are talking with the teacher or other adults in the classroom (e.g., visiting parents, resource teacher, teacher's aide); they are talking in pairs; they are talking within the context of small groups; and they are talking in front of the whole class. As this talk is happening, the teacher is shifting the responsibility for learning to the student and is paying attention to the student's agenda and the student's needs. The talk is at least partially student directed. The teacher is allowing the student to seek meaning from an experience rather than testing the student for recall of the teacher's agenda. The teacher may structure the environment and provide information and help, but it is the student's search for meaning through the medium of talk that is at the center of classroom activities.

REFERENCES

Au, K. H. (1993). *Literacy instruction in multicultural settings.* Fort Worth: Harcourt Brace Jovanovich.

Blades, A. (1976). *Mary of Mile 18.* London: Bodley Head.

Booth, D. (1994). *Classroom voices: Language-based learning in the elementary school.* Toronto: Harcourt Brace.

Bouchard, D. (1990). *The elders are watching.* Tofino, B.C.: Eagle Dancer Enterprises Ltd.

Edelsky, C. (1987). Talk and context: A case of a truly intimate relationship. In C. Staab & S. Hudelson (Eds.), *The power of talk.* Unpublished manuscript.

Education Department of South Australia (1991). *Literacy assessment in practice.* Adelaide: Education Department of South Australia.

Farr, R. (1992). Putting it all together: Solving the reading assessment puzzle. *Language Arts, 46 (1),* 26–38.

Goodman, K. (1992). Why whole language is today's agenda in education. *Language Arts, 69 (5),* 354–363.

Goodman, K. (1986). *What's whole in whole language?* Toronto: Scholastic-TAB Publications.

Hansen, J. (1992). Students' evaluations bringing reading and writing together. *The Reading Teacher, 46 (2),* 100–106.

Hoskisson, K. & Tompkins, G. (1987). *Language arts content and teaching strategies.* Toronto: Merrill Publishing Co.

Johnson, D. W., Johnson, R. T. & Holubec, E. J. (1990). *Circles of learning: Cooperation in the classroom* (3rd ed.). Edina, MN: Interaction Book Co.

Lindfors, J. W. (1987). *Children's language and learning.* (2nd ed.). Englewood Cliffs, NJ: Prentice-Hall.

May, F. B. (1994). *Reading as communication* (4th ed.). New York: Macmillan.

Mehan, H. (1979). *Learning lessons.* Cambridge, MA: Harvard University Press.

Norton, D. E. (1993). *The effective teaching of language arts* (4th ed.). Toronto: Maxwell MacMillan Canada.

Peterson, R. & Eeds, M. A. (1990). *Grand conversations: Literature groups in action.* Richmond Hill, Ont.: Scholastic Canada.

Staab, C. (1991). Teachers' practices with regard to oral language. *The Alberta Journal of Educational Research, 37 (1),* 31–48.

Staab, C. (1992a). *Oral language for today's classroom.* Markham, Ontario: Pippin Press.

Staab, C. (1992b). Reflections: Interview with Gordon Wells. *Reflections on Canadian Literacy, 10 (4),* 194–197.

Staab, C., Early, M. & Hunsberger, M. (in press). Oral language. In V. Froese (Ed.), *Language across the curriculum.* Toronto: Harcourt Brace Canada.

Vygotsky, L. S. (1986). *Thought and language.* Cambridge, MA: M. I. T. Press.

Wolvin, A. & Coakley, C. (1979). *Listening instruction.* Annadale, Virginia: Speech Communication Association.

DISCUSSION QUESTIONS

1. List ways in which talk might be different in a whole-language classroom.
2. Why should talk be encouraged in a classroom? When should it be limited?
3. How might you organize the physical environment of your classroom to encourage talk?
4. Make a list of classroom activities that would require different levels of talk (i.e., pin drop, conversation, discussion).
5. Discuss ways in which various interaction patterns, as well as listening and speaking instruction, would be a natural part of a thematic unit such as pioneer life.
6. How might oral language be assessed other than what has been mentioned in the chapter?

Literature in a Whole-Language Program

MARION RALSTON AND
WENDY SUTTON

1. *Providing opportunities for students to experience a variety of literary genres and forms—all types of fiction, poetry, and nonfiction*

2. *Selecting tradebooks that have enduring qualities to share with children*

3. *Involving children in activities designed to encourage a continuing interest in literature and in reading*

4. *Recognizing that literature can be a source of personal enjoyment for children as well as a key to their understanding of their own and other cultures*

5. *Providing children with rich literary, aesthetic, and cognitive experiences with books in order to advance their language, creativity, and concept development*

6. *Being aware that wisely selected literature nourishes the imagination and introduces children to the limitless potential of language*

Introduction

This chapter addresses the following goals: (1) to provide an overview of the unique contribution of children's literature to literacy and learning in a whole-language classroom; (2) to establish that a rich program of literature for children ages 5 to 13 strengthens the communication skills and processes of the language arts curriculum; (3) to advocate a response-based approach for engaging children with literature; and (4) to suggest strategies that will assist a beginning teacher to incorporate literature effectively into all areas of the school curriculum.

Whole-language teachers are deeply committed to the belief that experiences with literature, both fiction and nonfiction, are the most effective means of helping children develop as lifelong readers and learners. Charlotte Huck and colleagues (1993) described literature as "the imaginative shaping of life and thought into the forms and structures of language." In classrooms where literature is a major focus, children experience the rich and imaginative illustrations and language of poetry, stories, and nonfiction. In addition to daily opportunities to read, talk, and write about what they read, children hear literature several times a day as they listen to a variety of literary genres their teacher hopes will engage their imaginations and stimulate them to respond in personally pleasing, creative ways—poetry selections, a chapter from an "on-going" novel, a description of recent discoveries under the sea, an interview with a well-known children's author are but a few examples.

Why Use Literature in a Whole-Language Classroom?

Educators have increased the understanding of how children become literate. The emphasis has shifted from a sequential, skills-based approach to literacy to one that provides children with the richest spectrum of literary experiences possible. This shift is in part characterized by children's spontaneous and personal responses to literature becoming the starting point for discussion. Children's responses that are freely given enable teachers to learn what is meaningful or familiar and what is important to the individuals expressing them—information that can guide instruction in important ways.

We also now recognize that "narrative," a sense of story, is the cognitive, meaning-making strategy that children use to understand their world and their place in it. We have become increasingly aware of the ways in which "real" stories and authentic texts enable children to utilize their sense of story to comprehend what they read. Arguing for a central place for story across the school curriculum, Gordon Wells (1986) wrote:

> *Stories have a role in education that goes far beyond their contribution to the acquisition of literacy. Constructing stories in the mind—or storying as it has been called—is one of the fundamental means of making meaning; as such, it is an activity that pervades all aspects of learning . . . stories and storying are relevant in all areas of the curriculum. (p. 194)*

Teachers also have become increasingly aware of the limitations placed on children if we plunge them too quickly into reading decontextualized language. For example, teachers now realize that by letting young readers first hear the texts they will attempt to read, they are providing the context of language and meaning necessary for children to become independent interpreters of written text. As Hoskisson (1979) reminded us, "Children must be immersed in stories when they learn to read, just as they were immersed in language in contextual situations when they learned to speak" (p. 491).

Whole-language teachers endeavor to choose poetry and prose that will expose children to richer language than that which normally surrounds them. Although the effects of hearing and reading literary language may not be immediately apparent, students' subsequent writing will reflect sentence patterns and picturesque phrases perhaps first discovered while listening to or reading a favorite story or poem. The "lessons" that evolve from experiences with literature extend children's awareness of the structures, vocabulary, and creative potential of language. It is upon their experiences with a variety of written discourse that students draw when endeavoring to meet their own language and expressive needs.

Literature in the Content Areas

Most teachers recognize and build upon the natural connections that exist between children's literature and the communication skills and processes of the language arts curriculum—listening, speaking, reading, writing, viewing, and representing. When they structure experiences focusing on one of these six strands, they are sensitive to the ways in which the other language and thinking abilities are also strengthened. What may not be so apparent is the contribution literature makes to other areas of the school curriculum. For example, in *Read Any Good Math Lately? Children's Books for Mathematical Learning K–6* (1992), David Whitin and Sandra Wilde detail how literature can help children value mathematics, build confidence in their own mathematical abilities, and gain a better understanding of mathematical ideas and their application to real-world situations. They identify specific books that, through their stories, can increase children's understanding of a variety of mathematical concepts such as time,

length, weight, volume, capacity, temperature, area, and money. Children's stories are also valuable for the way in which story characters and events often dramatize mathematical processes such as multiplication, subtraction, estimation, and measurement. For example, *The Dinosaur Who Lived in My Backyard* by B. D. Hennessey helps children become effective estimators by using a comparison strategy to link aspects of a dinosaur's life to objects familiar to children—its weight is compared to that of 20 pick-up trucks and its egg is as big as a basketball.

Science is another curriculum area in which learning is enhanced by children's literature. Chet Raymo (1992) has claimed that to be a good scientist "one must be able to imagine wonderful things." He presented a valuable distinction between science as information, a mass of facts, and science as "an attitude toward the world" (p.562). He maintained that it is crucial that information be conveyed to children in a way that captures their childlike curiosity. As a scientist, Raymo occasionally reviews children's science books, many of which are full of useful information, but he is concerned that such books may actually diminish the "very habits of mind that make for good science."

> *If we want to raise children who will grow up to understand science, who will be citizens who are curious, skeptical, undogmatic, imaginative, optimistic, and forward-looking, then let's . . . put into the hands of children books that feed imagination and fantasy. There is no better time to acquire scientific habits of mind, and no better instigator than quality children's books. (p. 567)*

In addition to the quality fiction and nonfiction now available are rich collections of poetry that capture children's curiosity and imagination by offering both a wealth of information and creative ways of considering phenomena of the natural world. For example, in *Beast Feast* by Douglas Florian (Harcourt Brace, 1994), the lobster, chameleon, and ant are 3 of 21 creatures described and celebrated through poetry and art. Other similar and worthwhile collections are:

All Creatures Great and Small, illuminated by Isabelle Brent. Little, Brown and Company, 1994.

Rich Lizard and Other Poems by Deborah Chandra. Farrar Strauss Giroux, 1993.

Joyful Noise: Poems for Two Voices by Paul Fleischman. Harper & Row, 1988.

Dinosaurs edited by Lee Bennett Hopkins. Harcourt Brace Jovanovich, 1987.

Animal, Vegetable, Mineral: Poems about Small Things selected by Myra Cohn Livingston, HarperCollins, 1994.

History and geography are just two of the other curriculum areas to which a variety of literary genres make a valuable contribution. Historical fiction, biography and autobiography, travel adventures, survival stories, and poetry enable children to learn about people and events of the past, gain insights into natural phenomena and countries of the world, and come to understand how information is obtained and why we understand it to be true.

Multicultural Literature

Aspects of other cultures have long been introduced to children through literature, particularly through folktales and fairy tales. A more recent development in publishing, frequently referred to as *multicultural literature,* is currently gaining recognition. This is the conscious effort on the part of authors and illustrators to create books that authentically reflect the cultures that are indigenous to various countries—those that have been established for one or more generations, and those, primarily from Asia, that have more recently begun to settle in the cities and towns of North America. Books helping children learn and care about each of these different groups are important, but in order to ensure diversity and balance, teachers need to be conscious of the particular focus and settings of the multicultural literature they select for their classrooms.

Fortunately, storytellers and illustrators will never tire of sharing their interpretations of myth, legend, folktales, and fairy tales. Illustrator Ed Young's *Lon Pon Po: A Red Riding Hood Story from China* and his *Yeh-Shen: A Cinderella Story from China,* written by Ai-Ling Louie, are two versions that impress upon children the universality and appeal of many of the familiar traditional stories. *The Orphan Boy,* a retelling by Tololwa Mollel of an East African legend about

This display case hold materials assembled by students who are studying Greece.

the planet Venus, magnificently illustrated by Paul Morin, and award-winning illustrator Gerald McDermott's *Raven: A Trickster Tale for the Pacific North West* are two recent picture books that present each respective culture in an authentic, engaging way.

Also dramatizing universal experiences and values are contemporary stories that feature members of minorities, such as *Through Moon and Stars and Night Skies* by Ann Turner, in which the gentle watercolors by James-Graham Hale chronicle a young Asian child's flight to reach his new adoptive family in America. Children will also relate to the feelings of the young African-American girl in Hoffman's *Amazing Grace* who loves dramatizing stories and desperately wants to play the part of Peter Pan in the school production. The Caldecott Medal winner *Grandfather's Journey* by Allen Say enables young readers to experience the love a Japanese immigrant to the United States has for both his new and original countries.

A third emphasis found in many multicultural books is the challenge and hardships many newcomers have to face when adapting to a new country and a new way of life. Sensitively written stories such as *Molly's Pilgrim* by Barbara Cohen, *Angel Child, Dragon Child* by Michele Maria Surat, and *A Jar of Dreams* by Yoshiko Uchida help children understand the hurt and shame that racial discrimination inflicts on others. Books about Native Americans also bear witness to many of the difficulties and indignities that they, like many newcomers, have had to endure.

Although quality books such as these encompass cultural aspects of the various groups represented, children also need books set in the countries from which these people have emigrated—books that provide insight into both the historical and contemporary life experiences of other cultures. *Shabanu: Daughter of the Wind* by Suzanne Fisher Staples, *The Clay Marble* by Minfong Ho, *Kiss the Dust* by Elizabeth Laird, and *Year of Impossible Goodbyes* by Sook Nyul Choi—set in Pakistan, Cambodia, Iraq, and North Korea, respectively—introduce upper-intermediate children to the cultural and social dimensions of each of these four countries. Children's experiences with multicultural literature will be richest if they have opportunities to read and discuss the variety of forms available.

Response-Based Teaching

Essentially, a literature-based, response-based approach to teaching is characterized by giving children genuine opportunities to respond openly and freely to a literary experience they have just had. To demonstrate the sincerity of their interest in children's personal responses, teachers need to accept and value any response a child offers. For example, not to like a story can be as sincere a response as liking it, and no expressed response is itself a form of response.

After the children have experienced the selection by listening to it or through an individual or shared reading experience, invite them to share their responses, perhaps first in small groups of two or three. Both teachers and researchers have established that, in a comfortable, risk-taking atmosphere, these initial responses will make evident the children's understanding and personal engagement with the story. Personal responses that are spontaneously and confidently given enable teachers to learn two very important things: what is familiar or meaningful and what is of interest to the individual children expressing them. In her well-known article, "What Facts Does This Poem Teach You?" (1980), Louise Rosenblatt urges teachers not to hurry young readers away from a "lived-through aesthetic experience" with a piece of literature.

> *Children's spontaneous comments should be welcomed, encouraged, and, as often as possible, made the starting point for further discussion. . . . As differing responses are heard, there can be a continuing return to the text/literature to see what in the text led to those varied interpretations or judgments. (p. 393)*

Rosenblatt (1980) has maintained that a child's personal, aesthetic, experiential growth is every bit as important as the "efferent" learning, the information that he or she takes from the reading of a text. Although she has acknowledged that both efferent and aesthetic readings are important, Rosenblatt argued that by overemphasizing factual detail and literal recall, schools have not provided sufficient opportunities for children to savor pleasurable, aesthetic experiences with literature. Our own experiences as readers tell us that reading to gain information and reading aesthetically are not mutually exclusive.

However, Rosenblatt (1980) has contended that a young reader's emotions must be engaged if a desire and love of reading is to be the result. Robert Ruddell (1992) also emphasized the "crucial importance" of aesthetic experiences with literature in developing reader interest and motivation to learn. As "meaning-making facilitators" within a whole-language, literature-based perspective, teachers must ensure that there is a balance between aesthetic and cognitive approaches to learning for both "are needed in the instructional setting but serve different purposes" (p. 616).

Suggestions for Encouraging Children to Respond Freely

The opportunity to hear the initial responses of children after a shared literary experience can be most rewarding for both the teacher and the children. While ensuring that each child feels comfortable sharing his or her initial thoughts, making a mental note of the nature of individual responses will help the teacher guide the subsequent discussion. For example, notice which children spoke of the illustrations, the language, the format of the book, aspects of the story itself, similar stories, personal experiences, and so on. As research into literary response has demonstrated, the range and forms of responses to a single text are wide and varied and shaped by the specific aspects of the experience that hold personal significance for the individual expressing them.

Following the sharing of a literary experience, it is best to let the responses come freely and randomly until the children begin to run out of things they wish to say. At that point, a productive way to keep the discussion going is to provide reminders—for example, "Kelly spoke of enjoying the way in the which the author used cut-outs so that what was on the next page could be seen. Is there anything else about the format or way in which the book has been made that someone would like to share?" or "Gillian said that this story reminded her of *Owl Moon* by Jane Yolen. Did any of you have a similar thought or were reminded of other stories?" It is preferable to invite the children to talk about the stories they were reminded of at this point rather than earlier when Gillian and others were sharing their initial responses. Thus, by enabling them to recall and build upon their own thinking, the teacher helps children extend and enrich their understanding and appreciation of literature.

The following are examples of questions or invitations that are helpful in getting the initial sharing and discussion started:

- Is there anything any of you would like to share with us that was special (about this book/story/poem) for you?
- Was there anything that surprised you/that you hadn't expected or that you thought was strange or unusual?
- Is there anything that this story made you think of as you were reading/listening to it?
- Has anyone said anything about the story that has helped you like it better or think about it differently?

Particularly among young children, responses to books are expressed in a wide variety of ways. From her ethnographic study of three elementary classes, Janet Hickman (1981) identified the following as "response events" or forms of literary response: listening behaviors such as body stance, laughter and applause, exclamations, and joining in refrains; contact with books such as browsing and keeping them at hand; impulse to share by reading together and sharing discoveries; oral responses such as storytelling and discussion; actions and drama that echoed the action, dramatic play, child- and teacher-initiated drama; making things such as pictures, constructions, games, and displays; and writing about literature, using literary models deliberately as well as unrecognizable models and sources (p. 346). Hickman's major findings were that children's willingness to express a response to a book depended on its accessibility. She also found that the occurrence, expression, and some aspects of the quality of response events were tied to the social-instructional context of the classroom and that the most powerful influence on that context was the teacher who created it.

In a recent summary of research into children's responses to literature, Miriam Martinez and Nancy Roser (1991) also identified the powerful effect that teachers modeling their responses to literature, both during and after the reading of stories, has on the subsequent responses of young children. "The teacher who conjectures, connects, appreciates, muses, challenges, and questions aloud shows the child how the mature responder interacts with text" (p. 652). These researchers stress the importance of teachers not only providing time and opportunities for children to collaborate in the constructing of individual and group meanings but also the value of their joining in meaning-making as equal partners.

Further Evidence of Literary Response

Whole-language teachers can be confident that literature is being appreciated and enjoyed when they observe children:

- *Talking* about their favorite stories and recommending them to others
- *Searching* for other books with similar plots or characters

- *Choosing* to select books to read during their free-time activities
- *Asking* to be read to more frequently throughout the school day
- *Selecting* books that have been shared aloud by the teacher

In order to encourage such responses from children, a "bridge" between children and books must be established. Children's engagement with books and learning is enhanced when all or most of the following are evident:

- *Books are visible* and displayed in an enticing manner, such as having the front cover visible.
- *New titles* are highlighted by an interesting label. For example, a new book by Beverly Cleary could have a flag reading "Ready for a good laugh? Try this one!"
- *Fiction, poetry, and nonfiction* are an integral part of all subject areas and units.
- *Provision is made* for storytelling, reading and listening to a variety of literary forms throughout the schoolday.
- *Time is provided* for visiting authors, local storytellers, and community "experts" to share their stories and knowledge with children.
- *Activities are planned* by the teacher in order to give children opportunities to respond creatively to learning experiences through composing, presenting, and representing.
- *Visits to other classrooms* are made to share favorite books or projects on topics of interest.
- *Visits are made* to the school and local community library to acquaint children with the fiction and nonfiction resources available to them.

A classroom designed to encourage a range of responses and learning from children does not happen by chance. Such an environment requires careful planning and scheduling on the part of the teacher. (Also see Chapter 11, Organizing Whole-Language Classrooms.)

Selecting Books for the Classroom

When children are offered a rich variety in both literature and related literary experiences, an excitement and expectation of what the world of books and reading holds in store is created. Such variety encompasses not only the range of literary genres introduced but the types, formats, and range of difficulty of the materials themselves. Reliable, well-written information books are also a form of children's literature for, like fiction, they offer creative, effective uses of language, have the capacity to capture children's imagination, and create a desire to learn. In her book *How Texts Teach What Readers Learn* (1988), Meek stated that "the most important single lesson that children learn from texts is the nature and variety of written discourse, the different ways that language lets a writer tell, and the many and different ways a reader reads" (p. 21).

Frank McTeague (1992) has maintained that when making decisions about the books and other instructional materials that will most effectively meet the learning needs and interests of a specific group of children, teachers also need to consider the personal backgrounds of the children they teach:

- *Ethnic, cultural, and linguistic roots*
- *Personal maturity—cognitive, affective, and ethical*
- *Previous experience which has shaped personal beliefs and attitudes about themselves and about school, books, and literature*
- *Present circumstances and expectations. (p. 9)*

Use of an Interest Inventory

An interest inventory helps the teacher discover the current interests and reading preferences of students. The results of such an inventory are valuable for selecting books for the classroom, for recommending titles to children, and for helping parents who request advice on choosing books. Also, by their omission, literary experiences are identified that would be important to introduce to children. An Interest Inventory such as the following can provide useful data for the classroom teacher, particularly if only the number of items appropriate

In order to capitalize on the strengths of students' interests, it is desirable to have a classroom library with a wide range of tradebooks.

for the children involved is administered at one time. The following questions may be used in conjunction with or in place of those in the inventory provided:

1. What is your favorite toy?
2. Do you watch a special television show? What do you like about it?
3. Do you collect anything? If you do, what is it?
4. Does someone read to you at home? Who?
5. What kinds of stories do you like to hear read aloud?
6. What is the name of your favorite book? What is it that you like about it?
7. If you were to write your own book, what would it be about?
8. What games or sports do you like?
9. What do you like to do after school and on weekends?
10. If you could have one special wish, what would it be?

With very young children, tape recording the answers they give during individual interviews will likely be the most rewarding.

GENERAL AND READING INTERESTS INVENTORY

Name: _____ Age: _____

1. What do you like to do after school?
2. What hobbies or collections do you have?
3. What are your favorite television programs?
4. What games or sports do you like best?
5. Do you belong to any clubs or other groups? Which ones?
6. What is your favorite type of movie?
7. Which subject in school do you like best? Least?
8. Do you have an up-to-date library card?
9. How often do you go to the library?
10. How many books do you own? What are some of your favorites?
11. What are some things you like to read about?
12. What do you like best about reading? What do you like least?
13. Do you subscribe to any magazines at home? Which ones?
13. Name a book you would like to read again. Why?
14. Do you read the newspaper? How often? Which section do you read first?
15. What do you like to do after you have read a book you have enjoyed?
16. Any additional thoughts on this topic?

Children's Literature Preferences

Children ages five to eight appear to be delightfully predictable in their enjoyment of concept books, such as number and alphabet books, folk and fairy tales, stories about mischievous and appealing animals such as Curious George and Paddington Bear, and humorous verse by poets such as Dennis Lee, A. A. Milne, and Shel Silverstein. As children mature, their interests extend to adventure stories such as *Hatchet* by Gary Paulsen, historical fiction such as *Number the Stars* by Lois Lowry, mysteries such as *The Other Side of Dark* by Joan Lowery Nixon, and contemporary realism such as *Maniac Magee* by Jerry Spinelli. Imaginative fiction such as fantasy, science fiction, and science fantasy is also popular with young readers, particularly boys. Other genres of children's literature that will enrich the variety available in the classroom include picture and illustrated books, myths, legends, fables, realistic fiction, poetry, biography and fictional biography, and a wide range of high-interest nonfiction.

In a whole-language classroom where the sharing of literature has already been established, integrating literature on a daily basis into other curricular areas evolves quite naturally. By planning cooperatively with fellow teachers and the teacher-librarian, fiction, poetry, and nonfiction can become an integral part of each of the subject areas. When the classroom teacher and the teacher-librarian work together as a team, the learning experiences for the children are enriched and strengthened. Knowledge of the students' interests and reading levels assists the teacher-librarian in recommending specific books to individuals. Teachers and the teacher-librarian can also work together on planning special events for seasonal topics, such as a display of mystery stories for Halloween, highlighting an author or illustrator's work, or drawing together resources to assist children in their exploration of an historical event or of scientific advances.

A shared understanding of the literary goals in a whole-language classroom also enables the teacher-librarian and the classroom teacher to create a stimulating literacy and learning environment. Such goals include the following:

- To provide pleasure for children
- To stimulate the imagination
- To present a range of views on the same topic or issue
- To promote creative expression
- To develop a sense of imagery
- To become familiar with a variety of literary styles and genres
- To extend children's sense of story
- To recognize and appreciate the potential and power of language
- To deepen awareness and understanding of ideas and topics

Engaging Children with Literature

One of the most effective ways for teachers to engage children with literature is to share their personal enthusiasm for reading and books. Read to the children every day and among your selections plan to include a favorite of theirs or yours. A well-stocked classroom library designed to meet the needs of reading aloud, shared, and independent reading will include a wide variety of fiction and nonfiction, poetry and prose. Table 4.1 suggests books for sharing with primary and intermediate children ages five to thirteen.

In addition to reading aloud, the teacher may use a variety of recordings, videocassettes, and films to introduce literary selections and informational topics. Children will enjoy hearing the taped voice of Dennis Lee as he reads his poetry from *Alligator Pie*, or shiver with delight when listening to Jack Prelutsky read from his rather ghoulish *Nightmares*. *Meet Jack Prelutsky* (1991), a videocassette, and *Something Big Has Been Here* (1991), an audiocassette, present Prelutsky reading and singing his poetry with children. A wealth of informational books, videocassettes, and CD-ROMs are also available to meet children's fascination with topics such as dinosaurs, mummies, jungle animals, ocean creatures, and mysteries of space. For example, children's interest in nature and the environment will be stimulated by watching videocassettes such as *Good Conversation! A Talk with Jean Craighead George* (1989) and *Where the Forest Meets the Sea* (1989) based upon the stunning picture book of the same title by Australian author-illustrator Jeannie Baker. Selection aids such as *School Library Journal* and *Booklist* now include reviews of audiovisual materials.

Part One focuses on children ages five through eight and Part Two focuses on children ages nine through thirteen.

Part One: Children Ages Five through Eight

Children's literature, including fiction, poetry, and nonfiction, is increasingly being acknowledged as the most valuable resource for enriching and extending children's language, imagination, and desire to learn. Young children experience and eagerly respond with all their senses to the figurative language of poetry and story. As they listen, they become aware of how authors and poets use words and sounds to create vivid images and word pictures. For many children the first imaginative use of language they ever hear comes to them from the pages of a well-written children's book. As Glenna Sloan (1984) so aptly reminded us in *The Child as Critic*:

TABLE 4.1 Broadening Children's Literary Experiences

Genres	Primary		Intermediate	
	5–6 years	7–8 years	9–10 years	11–13 years
Folk Literature	The Three Billy Goats Gruff	The Travelling Musicians	Lon Po Po	The True Story of the 3 Little Pigs by A. Wolf
Fantasy	The Magic Hockey Skates	Jumanji	The Wretched Stone	The Hobbit
Realism	Fly-Away Home	Muggie Maggie	Hatchet	Maniac Magee
Animal Stories	Make Way for Ducklings	The Stone Fox	Shiloh	Julie of the Wolves
Historical Fiction	When I Was Young in the Mountains	Sarah Plain and Tall	Number the Stars	The Sky is Falling
Poetry	Don't Eat Spiders	Have You Seen Birds?	17 Kings and 42 Elephants	A Bat is Born
Nonfiction	Baby Animals	Sunken Treasure	Exploring the Titanic	The Way Things Work

If literature is essential to the development of readers and writers who are genuinely literate, it is also essential to the education of the child's imagination. . . . Literature illustrates something essential for human beings to realize: that there are no limits for the imagination. (pp. 14–15)

Literature Supports Children's Language Development

The Sounds of Language

Children's love of rhythm and movement makes them particularly responsive to the sounds of language. As a result, writing by authors and poets who are sensitive to rhythm and sound offer opportunities for both appreciative and creative listening experiences. Repetition of words and phrases also delights young listeners and they enthusiastically respond to the invitations extended by such writing. *We're Going on a Bear Hunt* by Michael Rosen and Helen Oxenbury is an excellent example of literature that will appeal to children's love of sounds, rhythms, and repetition. Another rich language and sound adventure is provided by the strong rhythm, imaginative wordplay, and rhyme of Margaret Mahy's *17 Kings and 42 Elephants*. Rhyme, repetition, and action words are also the qualities that make *Nobody Pats a Sasquatch* by Denis Rodgers a poem children will enjoy.

> *If you meet an animal that's big and hairy,*
> *Walks like an ape and looks kind of scary,*
> *You'd better be careful,*
> *You'd better beware,*
> *He might be a sasquatch!*
> *Sasquatch!*
>
> *Sasquatch, sasquatch, sounds like a sneeze.*
> *Two flat feet and bends at the knees,*
> *Bears give hugs*
> *But 'squatches squeeze.*
> *Watch for the sasquatch,*
> *Sasquatch!*
>
> *Some like cats and some like puppies,*
> *Worms and turtles, goats and guppies.*
> *Think of an animal and you can bet*
> *Somebody wants him for a pet!*
> *Frogs are fun and mice are nice—*
> *But nobody pats a sasquatch twice,*
> *No body!* *

Reprinted by permission of Denis Rodgers.

The repetition of phrases and rhythms also characterizes the traditional literature of folk and fairy tales and invites young listeners to participate in the chants and refrains found in these age-old tales. In "Jack and the Beanstalk," the giant chants "Fee, fi-fo-fum," Henny Penny is distressed that "the sky is falling," the big, bad wolf threatens with, "I'll huff and I'll puff and I'll blow your house down!" and the gingerbread boy taunts his would-be captors with "Run! Run! As fast as you can, You can't catch me, I'm the gingerbread man!"

Predictable Story Patterns

The repetition and addition of detail in traditional cumulative tales, such as *The House That Jack Built* by Paul Galdone, enable young children to see a pattern of events evolve into a complete story. By continuously introducing a new character or event into the storyline, the author establishes an opportunity for the children to make predictions about what will happen next.

Another predictable book is *The Very Busy Spider* by Eric Carle. In this story, a series of animals ask a spider to play. Because she is very busy spinning her web, she ignores them. Each animal makes its own unique sound as it asks the spider to take part in an activity usually associated with that animal. For example, the pig grunts, "Oink, oink, want to roll in the mud?" The predictable repetition of the sentence patterns and events in stories such as these engages young listeners' participation in the story, often in the form of dramatic play.

In Barbara Reid's *Two by Two* with its humorously imaginative plasticine illustrations, the strongly patterned rhyming couplets and adding of pairs of animals draw children into the fun.

> *And in came the animals six by six,*
> *Pandas and penguins, all in a mix.*
>
>   · · ·
>
> *"All aboard!" cried Noah,*
> *"Shut the door!"*
> *And down came the rain*
> *as never before.*
> *The sky had sprung*
> *so many leaks*
> *That whales swam over*
> *mountain peaks.*[*]

Other delightful books that will actively engage young children are Wilhelmina Harper's *The Gunniwolf*, Pamela Allen's *Who Sank the Boat?*, Leo Lionni's *A Color of His Own*, and *The Judge* by Harve Zemach.

Language Patterns

In Remy Charlip's *Fortunately, Unfortunately*, there is a patterning of opposites, positive and negative. After the first few lines are shared, young children see the pattern developing and delight in the humor of the character's situations. A young boy receives an invitation to a surprise party in Florida, but unfortunately he is in New York —and the pattern begins.

Here is an example of how a child might use Charlip's style in his or her own writing:

> *Fortunately, a friend gave me a quarter.*
> *Unfortunately, it was not enough for a chocolate bar.*
> *Fortunately, my mom had put a dollar in my lunchbox.*
> *Unfortunately, it was covered with peanut butter and jelly.*

Young children may compose their own "fortunately, unfortunately" text as a group composition or as an individual effort once the book has been shared. Remy Charlip's title also works well as a "Roll Theater" type of story, where the children's illustrations are drawn on a continuous roll of paper so that the story is revealed as the cylinder unwinds.

Predictable and pattern books have been cited by many researchers as excellent sources for providing children with opportunities to acquire interesting language patterns (Holdaway, 1979; Newman, 1985; Gunderson and Shapiro, 1987). However, it is important to ensure that the patterns and repetition used encourage thinking and imagination rather than mindless substitution. For example, when imitating the pattern of Bill Martin's *Brown Bear, Brown Bear*, if children merely change the names preceding "What do you see?" their thinking and language abilities are not being challenged.

Vocabulary Enrichment

In addition to the enrichment gained from hearing stories with varying sentence patterns, children also have vocabulary introduced or reinforced, particularly when several books on the same topic are shared. For example, Harry McNaught's concept book simply entitled *Baby Animals* is an identification piece on young animal babies. Masayuki Yabuuchi's *Whose Baby?* extends the concept of animal identification by asking whose baby it is. The answer is given in striking illustrations of the baby and its respective parents. Finally, a more mature presentation of animal life is presented in the D'Aulaires' book *Animals Everywhere*. The authors describe animal life from the tropics to the Far North. The use of colorful illustrations to identify animals' natural habitats complements the simple but informative text.

Children Emulate Texts That Delight Them

Children's own stories and poems often reflect the literary texts that delight and intrigue them. Through their rich, imaginative uses of language, such texts serve as models of what is creatively possible. For example, *The Jolly Postman and Other People's Letters* by Janet and Allan Ahlberg has been joyfully emulated by children ages six to twelve. Calling their story "The Happy Mailman," one class of six- and seven-year-olds enclosed their letters in envelopes and on the interceding pages wrote:

> *Once upon a street*
> *So they say*
> *A Happy Mailman came one day*
> *From down the street*
> *And around the corner*
> *With a letter for the Seven Dwarfs. . . .*
> *Soon the Mailman*
> *We hear tell*
> *Stopped at a door we know well*
> *With a note for . . . guess who?*

An eleven-year-old girl introduced into her version of Ahlberg's narrative poem a "genie postman" who delivered one of his letters to the farmer's wife:

> MOTHER GOOSE LAW INC.
> 123 Fairytale Lane
> United States
> Call Toll Free 1-800-JUSTICE

> Mrs. Farmer
> 210 Barnyard St.
> Miceless County
> Canada

> Dear Madam,
>   My clients have accused you of betailing them for unlawful causes. They informed me that you cut off their tails because of their personal handicap. If you do not choose to reply to this letter, you will receive a summons to appear in court.

> Yours truly, J. Horner

> *Mrs. Farmer answered the door,*
> *She was full of cheer*
> *But when she read her horrid letter*
> *Her eyes filled up with fear.*

Delighted by the words and visual images of *Have You Seen Birds?* by Joanne Oppenheim, illustrated with plasticine by Barbara Reid, a class of eight- and nine-year-olds composed verses and illustrated each of them with a plasticine picture for a book titled *Have You Seen Pirates?* Here is a verse written by one of the groups:

Have you seen Pete the Pirate?
Tall as the crowsnest,
Skinny as the mast.
Screeching, squealing,
Squawking, talking.
Have you seen Pete the Pirate?

Additional Recommendations

Although the following qualities usually occur concurrently, the books suggested under each of the headings exemplify that particular focus in a special way.

A. Imaginative Thinking

Asch, F. (1982). *Happy Birthday Moon!* Englewood Cliffs, NJ: Prentice-Hall.

What do you give the moon as a special birthday gift? An understanding animal finds the present that in his eyes is just right. This imaginative situation stimulates creative thinking on the children's part.

Burningham, J. (1967). *Would You Rather . . . ?* New York: Crowell.

Creative thinking results from the choices the author presents to children. "Would you rather live with your dog in a kennel, gerbils in a cage, or a rabbit in a hutch?" After exploring the options offered by the author, children can make up their own sets of choices and present them to their classmates.

Hoberman, Mary A. (1978). *A House Is a House for Me.* New York: Viking.

"A glove is a house for a hand, and a pod is a house for a pea." Young children will delight in the new perspectives the author offers about houses. Children can make up a group list of all the houses they can imagine. A homemade house, such as a blanket draped over a card table, lends itself to dramatization as well.

Mahy, M. (1975). *The Boy Who Was Followed Home.* New York: Franklin Watts.

At first one and then hippos in growing numbers follow Robert home. After enjoying Robert's solution to his problem, encourage children to invent other preposterous scenarios requiring creative solutions.

B. Stimulate Discussion

Cohen, M. (1987). *Will I Have a Friend?* New York: Macmillan.

The concept of friendship and its importance at an early age is highlighted. After children share their responses to the story, a discussion about which qualities make a good friend may result.

Cooney, B. (1982). *Miss Rumphius.* New York: Viking.

A child is challenged to give something to the world to make it more beautiful. After exploring the children's responses to the story of Miss Rumphius's contribution, encourage them to think of ways in which they could enhance the beauty of the world.

Kroll, S. (1985). *Happy Mother's Day.* New York: Holiday House.

What mother needs is help around the house. She finally does get it after many suggestions are offered. To avoid it becoming too "heavy-handed," encourage the children to lead the discussion.

C. Focus on Language

Cohen, M. (1977). *When Will I Read?* Lillian Hoban, illus. New York: Greenwillow.

A sensitive teacher points out to Jim that he already can read signs in the room. But Jim is not really reading until he notices that one sign has been changed. This book should give your prereaders lots of ideas for making signs and writing stories together.

Martin, B., Jr. & Archambault, J. (1988). *Listen to the Rain.* New York: Henry Holt.

With strong verbs and onomatopoeia, this rhythmic, lyrical libretto for a rainy day focuses attention on language and sensitive listening.

Moore, L. (1988). *I'll Meet You at the Cucumbers.* New York: Atheneum.

At first fearful of city life, a country mouse finds friends and adventure and discovers he is a poet when he visits his city pen pal. Within the rich language of this short chapter book, Adam teaches his new friends about poetry by reciting his own poems and those of famous poets.

Williams, V. (1986). *Cherries and Cherry Pits.* New York: Greenwillow Books.

A child's sense of story is strongly evident as a young girl tells and draws stories about four distinctly individual people in her neighbourhood. The brilliant watercolor illustrations and text celebrate human diversity.

D. Invite Participation

Little, J., De Vries, M. & Gilman, P. (1991). *Once Upon a Golden Apple.* Markham, Ont.: Viking.

A father teases his children by telling a story in which he mixes up characters and events from traditional folk and fairy tales. Children will delight in contributing their "No, No, No," and "Yes!" each time the father finally gets the details right.

Zimmermann, H. W. (1898). *Henny Penny*. New York: Scholastic.

> *The humorous visual interpretation of this traditional cumulative tale will add to the fun of joining Henny Penny and her feathered friends as they go to tell the king that "the sky is falling."*

E. Language Play/Poetry

Heidbreder, R. (1985). *Don't Eat Spiders*. Toronto: Oxford University Press.

> *Nonsense and fantasy blend with Canadian themes in this charming book of verse. The images in the poetry vibrate with the sound and color of topics of interest to young children. Choral speaking is a natural activity with this collection.*

Lee, D. (1991). *The Ice Cream Store*. Toronto: HarperCollins.

> *Delightful humor and wordplay abound in this rollicking collection of nonsense verse. Both the words and David McPhail's fun-filled illustrations reflect the cultural diversity of today's society.*

Mahy, M. (1987). 17 Kings and 42 Elephants. London: Collins; New York: Dial Books.

> *The strong rhythms and imaginative language of this jungle journey are irresistible. "Umbrellaphants," "rockodiles," "hippopotomums," "baboonsters," and "gorillicans" are just a few of the colorful beasts watching and seen by the kings as they are "going on a journey through a wild wet night."*

Page, P. K., reteller (1991). *The Travelling Musicians*. Toronto: Kids Can Press Ltd.

> *This language-rich, poetic retelling of the Grimm Brothers' Musicians of Bremen with its humorous illustrations of the antics of the four music-loving animal friends is destined to be a teacher and class favorite.*

Facilitating Literary Response

1. Oral Activity

The teacher may encourage children to reflect on a story they have heard. For example, after listening to *Just a Dream* by Chris Van Allsburg, the students could be asked, "What did this book make you think about?" After they have shared their personal responses and looked more closely at the story, an interesting extension question would be, "If you could do one thing to help the world's environment, what would it be?" Some children may elect to script a favorite story and perform it for another class. Others may enjoy preparing for a panel discussion in which they evaluate a story character's actions. Flannel board cut-out figures of the main characters of a favorite story can be arranged on a felt board by younger children as they share their versions.

2. Dramatization

Dramatizing a favorite scene from a story or an historical or current event is a popular activity of many children. Folk and fairy tales that contain action and imagery are ideal for this type of response. For example, *Lon Po Po: A Red Riding Hood Story From China*, retold and illustrated by Ed Young, *The Twelve Dancing Princesses*, retold by Marianna Mayer, and *The Travelling Musicians,* retold by P. K. Page, are good examples of traditional literature that lends itself to dramatic interpretation.

3. Visual Expression

Many children elect to respond visually to a story. For these students, illustrating their favorite part of a story or making a diorama of a special scene demonstrates their appreciation of a particular narrative. Children can make dioramas or three-dimensional settings by placing large shoeboxes on one side and arranging objects and/or figures in front of scenic backdrops they have created based on the story. A cooperatively planned mural of the exciting events that actually happened or were depicted in a story may be constructed by interested students and displayed in a school hallway or library for the enjoyment of others in the school.

Much of what children draw in their response to literature reflects their enjoyment and perspective of a particular narrative. One six-year-old, when asked to draw the most important character in the story of *The Three Little Pigs,* drew a very elaborate brick chimney. When questioned by the teacher about his choice, he replied, "Well, wasn't it the chimney that caught the wolf!"

One class combined a science lesson with a class reading of *The Magic Hockey Skates* by Allen Morgan, by making the characters glide about the stage of their box theater using small magnets. The students discovered that by inserting a paper clip in the base to hold the figure upright, a magnet, attracted by the metal, allowed them to move the skaters about the setting in a natural manner. Additional dialogue and new events for the main characters were created by the students for this activity.

4. Written Expression

Establish a "Recommended Reading" folder in which the children place brief evaluations of favorite books. Encourage them to think of aspects they feel would entice classmates to read their suggestions. A different ending to a story may be written or the narrative may be retold from a minor character's point of view. On occasion, students will enjoy a particular character so much that they will want to create more adventures involving that character. During a seasonal celebration, one class decided to invite "Ramona" from the Beverly Cleary series to their Christmas party. They wrote about what they thought Ramona would bring for the occasion and what she would do as games were played. The students' ideas formed an interesting bulletin board for a visiting class who had never heard of the irrepressible character.

5. Representation

After sharing *When Summer Ends* by Susi Fowler, in which objects are associated with each season, one teacher encouraged her class to think of things they associated with each season. After the importance of the children's choices had been discussed, the students illustrated their own books of "seasons" to share with others.

Activities such as these offer children opportunities to express their responses to literature with confidence and imagination.

Part Two: Children Ages Nine through Thirteen

The whole-language approach with children ages 9 through 13 is also to surround them with all forms of literature. Most intermediate students have mastered the basic reading and language skills and hopefully have had many and varied opportunities to discover the pleasure and variety that reading and literature offer. One of the greatest challenges for teachers of children this age is to promote and sustain voluntary, recreational reading. Adventure and survival stories, real and fanciful animal stories, fantasy, science fiction, poetry, historical fiction and biography, time slip novels, mysteries, and informational books are just some of the genres and types of books available to and enjoyed by today's young readers.

The Appeal of Realistic Fiction

Contemporary realistic fiction is particularly popular with many 9- to 13-year-olds because it addresses their maturing interests and allows for identification with characters their age. The opportunity to "walk in the shoes of another" permits many readers of realistic fiction to try on different roles that often result in feelings of empathy and compassion for the story characters. Rather than glossing over situations such as dysfunctional families or the death of a family member or friend, authors treat such topics in a sensitive but often uncompromising manner. Sometimes a personal problem seems less difficult when a reader learns that others have faced similar difficulties and survived. Often a young reader feels less alone and perhaps encouraged if the story character triumphs in spite of the problem. Today, children are able to choose from a wide selection of contemporary fiction that reflects the changes in their world as it approaches the twenty-first century—stories that appear to present life as it really is. The places, people, conflicts, and resolutions presented are both plausible and possible.

Realistic fiction for young people existed over a century ago with books such as *Heidi* by Johanna Spyri, *Hans Brinker* by Mary Mapes Dodge, *Little Women* by Louisa May Alcott, and *Tom Sawyer* and *Huckleberry Finn* by Mark

Twain. These authors assumed that children were sensible, normal human beings who were interested in how other children handled the challenges of the real world.

Guiding Literary Response

Realistic fiction is not a panacea for solving children's problems but it is a genre many enjoy and relate to with great enthusiasm, primarily because it seems "real." For example, after a reading of Marion Dane Bauer's *On My Honor*, in which a young boy betrays his parents' trust, encourage students to share, preferably in small groups, their initial responses to the novel. A valuable and welcome follow-up of collaboration such as this is a more general sharing of some of the ideas that evolved within the groups. The inevitable range of student-generated ideas and questions that result will provide genuine reasons for the children to return to the content of the novel or story for a closer reading of the text. As "meaning-making facilitators" (Ruddell, 1992), teachers can also enrich students' experiences with literary texts by the kinds of questions they ask and the learning opportunities they structure.

In *Booktalk* (1985), Aidan Chambers described the "Tell Me" framework, which gives rise to two types of questions, neither of which focuses on content details for their own sake. One type is phenomenological in nature and leads the reader to comment on thoughts, feelings, and observations that took place during or after his or her reading of literature. Examples of this type of question are: "Tell me the parts you liked best," "Did anything in the story puzzle you?" and "Has anyone said something that has caused you to see the story differently?" The second type is structural in nature and helps the young reader focus on how the story is told, on literary form. Some examples of this type are: "Who is telling the story? Do you think it would make a difference if we knew/didn't know?" "How long did it take for the story to happen? Were the story events presented in the order that they happened?" and "If the author asked you what could be improved in the story, what would you say?" Having older children return to a novel or story guided by questions such as these can increase their enjoyment as well as help them become more perceptive and articulate readers.

After children have had opportunities to express and explore their initial responses to a literary text and have returned to the piece of literature for a closer, more analytical reading, some may choose to explore further the feelings, ideas, or issues arising from their experience with a particular text. The following are examples of questions that extend children's thinking beyond the literary text: "How would you go about learning more about the issues raised in this novel?" "If you were going to make a film of this novel, what are some of the decisions you would have to make?" "Which ideas or issues interested you most? How might you represent them visually?" Inquiries guided by questions such as these can help students clarify their own feelings and thinking about issues and topics that interest them.

Focus on Language

Byars, B. (1988). *The Burning Questions of Bingo Brown.* New York: Viking Kestrel.

> *Bingo is a contemporary, likable 12-year-old who uses journal writing in school to work through his anxiety and problems linked with growing up.*

Cleary, B. (1983). *Dear Mr. Henshaw.* New York: Morrow.

> *Plot and character are cleverly revealed through a series of letters as 11-year-old Leigh Botts falls into correspondence with a favorite author as the result of a school letter-writing assignment. The sequel Strider (1991) is written as a diary.*

Williams, V. B. & Williams, J. (1988). *Stringbean's Trip to the Shining Sea.* New York: Macmillan.

> *Using a variety of art styles, media and stamp designs, Stringbean describes his trip to his family on the backs of 24 postcards, challenging the reader to infer what is not stated. The visual approach begs to be imitated by children of all ages.*

Wiseman, D. (1981). *Jeremy Visick.* Boston: Houghton Mifflin.

> *Matthew thinks that the subject of history is rubbish until he discovers that the past can live again. Some students may enjoy researching and writing about a particular period in the past during which they would like to have lived.*

Van Allsburg, C. (1987). *The Z Was Zapped: A Play in Twenty-Six Acts.* Boston: Houghton Mifflin.

> *With clever alliteration, this sophisticated and sinister alphabet drama is a natural for older children who will enjoy the challenge of predicting what will happen to each letter and some will likely create their own alphabet dramas. This author-illustrator's The Mysteries of Harris Burdick is also rewardingly successful at eliciting rich, imaginative language from young people.*

Literature Response Activities

> *When children work with books in ways that are meaningful to them—through talk, making things, writing, or drama and music— many things happen. Children have greater satisfaction with and clarify personal meanings about what they have read. . . .[Teachers] plan those diverse activities that enhance children's delight in books, make them want to continue reading more and better books, and cause them to think more widely and more specifically about what they have read. (Huck, Hepler, and Hickman, 1993, p. 770)*

Although children may respond with enthusiasm to one or more of the suggested activities that follow, it must be recognized that there will be times when children choose not to respond in a public way. Often students find that some books are so special to them that they simply want to reflect in a quiet, personal way on the contents and on what the author's words have conveyed to them.

1. A Book for Sale.   Selling an interesting title to the class is a more imaginative approach than that of the formal book report. The "reader-salesperson" must convince the students that the recommended book is the best of its kind. A variation on this idea is to have two students compete in trying to sell two different books on the same subject or theme.

2. Commercial TV.   At a Book Fair or Book Sale gathering, students may show a 30-second or one-minute commercial they have made in order to sell a favorite book to the prospective buyers.

3. A Book Sale or Book Fair.   A book sale may encourage intermediate students to become involved in reviewing literature for younger children. In one classroom, the older children reviewed the Caldecott Award winners and the Honor books for the past five years for the primary grades.

4. Our Favorite Books.   Favorite books listed on a classroom chart offers students an opportunity to express their interests and preferences when shared with another class. As the students' tastes and interests broaden, additional titles are added to the chart.

5. A Class Book.   A class book may be designed in which each student has a page for writing a review of a favorite book. The review should include a brief statement of the book's contents and the reasons why it would be recommended reading for a classmate. Students should be encouraged to update their review pages when new literature titles are discovered.

6. An Art Idea.   Advertising posters and original book jackets can be made by the children to highlight seasonal or thematic choices. When grouped together, these illustrative materials provide an attractive and useful bulletin board.

7. Create a Journey.   Illustrated maps outlining a character's journey or the setting encompassed by a story may be constructed by the students. *The House at Pooh Corner* by A. A. Milne and *The Hobbit* by J. R. R. Tolkien are two examples of books that have maps accompanying them.

8. A Diary or Journal.   Accounts may be written by pupils to represent the experiences of the major protagonist in the book. A variation on this idea is to have the students write a journal or letter from the perspective of a minor character.

9. A "Time-Travel Newspaper."   Newspapers may be created to highlight a particular historical novel or a fantasy selection. Rosemary Sutcliff's novels about the Roman occupation of Britain could result in the publication of "The Roman Times." Similarly, "The Wonderland News" could reveal Alice's reactions to her unusual adventures underground.

10. Mobiles.   Mobiles may be constructed of the major characters from a story. Younger children may choose their favorite animal figures while older students may select the characters from an adventure series or science fiction genre.

11. Classroom Collage or School Mural.   Enable students to depict their favorite scenes or characters in an artistic way. This type of activity also leads to discussing the information of the collage or mural and considering what is important to be included.

12. Dioramas.   Dioramas provide children with the opportunity to interpret a scene in a three-dimensional image. The construction of a diorama also encourages children to think creatively about the selection of materials to be used to highlight a specific scene.

13. Flannelboards and Felt Board Characters.   Offer young children figures to manipulate as they retell a narrative. As this becomes a familiar activity, the students often make their own figures and improvise the dialogue and events of the original story and thus reveal their own imaginative ideas. (A useful reference for creating flannelboards and characters is *Storytelling with the Flannelboard* (1974) by Paul Anderson.)

14. Character Correspondence.   Book characters may exchange letters as the students write to one another as the characters might. A variation on this idea is to have a minor character offer his or her reasons to the author regarding a more prominent role in a novel.

15. Analogous Stories.   Analogous stories written in the style of old favorites offer a challenge to older students. Dr. Seuss's nonsense may lead to original verses and Rudyard Kipling's *Just So Stories* may encourage some creative explanations as to how and why certain animal characteristics came to be.

16. Author Research.   Biographies of favorite authors, illustrators, or poets "published" by students for the class provide interesting background material on popular writers for young people.

17. Interview Time.   Students may interview classmates role-playing as an author. Others may choose to interview members of the class who have read the same book to compare their responses.

18. Panel Discussions.   Intermediate students may discuss stories in terms of the conflicts faced by the main characters and suggest whether there was justification for the way in which the dilemmas were resolved. Would the students have handled the problem in a different way if they had been a part of a scene? Why or why not? How is each solution different from or the same as solutions mentioned by other members of the panel?

19. Puppetry.   Most children enjoy making and using puppets to enhance their storytelling. *Puppets* (1988) by Lyndie Wright is a valuable resource for teaching children to make an extensive array of puppets from everyday, easily obtained materials.

20. Quiz Show.   A literature game patterned after the television show "Jeopardy" offers a playful opportunity for intermediate students to become better acquainted with book characters. For younger children, the quiz may be kept to a simple answering game in which the character answers only "yes" or "no" to the students' questions.

21. Envelope Pockets.   Questions in envelope pockets on the class bulletin board present a challenge for children to add clues to the envelopes or to find out more about a particular story. An envelope labeled "Who am I?" might present clues about popular characters, such as "I am afraid of the dark" (*Franklin in the Dark* by Paulette Bourgeois). Another labeled "This book is about pioneer life" might include clues about events in Patricia MacLachlan's novel, *Sarah Plain and Tall*. Likely children will want to write their own riddles for the envelopes.

22. Headline Heroes.   Writing headlines about favorite heroes from literature may encourage students to interest others in their choices of interesting characters and books. For example, a headline such as "Friendship with wolves allows lost 13-year old girl to survive" (*Julie of the Wolves* by Jean George) may lead to other provocative headlines written by the students.

23. Dramatization.   Many stories and poems lend themselves well to a dramatization of a favorite scene or passage. Through such an activity, children sense the mood of the story and the emotions of the characters as they interact with the events depicted by the author. They also deepen their involvement with a literary selection when given the opportunity to select and create their own interpretation. (See also Chapter 7, Playing the Whole-Language Game of Drama.)

24. Readers Theater.   Another form of creative dramatics in which two or more students may take part is Readers Theater. Through an oral reading of a folk or fairy tale, a few children help their audience to experience literature. Costumes and back-drops as scenery are rarely used and the audience is called upon to visualize the setting. A narrator speaks directly to the listeners and introduces the theme of the narrative. The children taking part in this activity use their facial expressions and intonations of voice in order to convey the emotions, moods and actions of the characters. (A helpful reference for this activity is Sloyer, 1982).

In summary, it should be noted that students need to respond to literature in ways that have personal meaning for them. As a consequence, they have an opportunity to internalize the power of the author's words and to gain greater insight into the literary characters with whom they identify. This form of involvement with literature not only increases their understanding of them-selves and others but deepens their appreciation of the contribution and pleasure literature can offer throughout their lives.

Nonfiction in the Whole-Language Classroom

Nonfiction tradebooks have become a most welcome and essential resource for communicating information and generating interest in the vast range of topics encountered within the content areas of the school curriculum. Together with fiction and poetry, fine nonfiction offers informed insight into a vivid and believable world. Highly acclaimed author of children's literature Russell Freedman (1992) wrote: "An effective nonfiction book must animate its subject, infuse it with life. It must create a vivid and believable world that the reader will enter willingly and leave only with reluctance" (p. 3). This capacity to whet the intellectual appetite of young readers is one of the qualities that makes in-formational tradebooks so valuable in the various content areas of the curriculum.

Research has indicated that at a very early age children demonstrate an awareness that writing is used in different ways for different purposes. Although the elements and structures of story can assist their learning and remembering of information, Christine Pappas (1991) argued that, if given the opportunity, young children are also capable of acquiring the linguistic patterns of nonfic-tional materials. This position is supported by Thomas Newkirk (1989) whose research has focused on the nonstory writing of young children: "On what grounds do we say that an informational book on dinosaurs is less meaningful than *Where the Wild Things Are*" (p. 5)? However, because expository texts do not have the predictable structures of narrative with which children are fa-miliar, they often require more teacher mediation. Judith Langer (1990) offered a useful distinction between the reading of narrative text, where there is an ever-emerging "horizon of possibilities," and reading expository text. She main-tained that the knowledge sources relied on and the reasoning strategies used are substantially different for each.

> When engaged in informative reading, the reader's sense of the whole provides a steady reference point; instead of moving toward a horizon of possibilities, read-ers use a more constant sense of the whole as the focal point around which to organize their growing understanding of the text. From early on, readers establish their sense of the topic or the slant the author is taking and use this judgment to monitor their growing understandings. (p. 814)

Incorporating an array of nonfiction tradebooks into science, social studies, and other content areas of the curriculum, either to supplement or replace the textbook, provides many advantages. For example, unlike textbooks, which tend to be impersonal and overly comprehensive, tradebooks are often visually more appealing and communicate the author's enthusiasm for the subject and desire to engage the interest of the reader. The diversity in tradebooks also helps accommodate a wider range of reading ability than is possible with a prescribed textbook. With the wealth of tradebooks available, many books on the same topic can be gathered, allowing students to compare, judge, and synthesize information from a variety of sources. As a consequence, thinking skills not usually encouraged by the subject textbook are developed. A diversity of resources also enables students to study topics of personal interest in greater depth. In addition, by being exposed to and using a variety of informational materials, children will quickly learn the purpose and value of features such as the table of contents, index, and glossary to help them find information.

As is true of fiction, the abundance of nonfiction now available lends itself to being read aloud and enjoyed for its quality of writing, clarity of presentation, and richness of information. The informational content also lends itself to dramatization, particularly among young children who have the capacity to become almost anything the teacher reads about. Lynne Putnam (1991) wrote:

> *I have personally witnessed whole classes of pre-kindergartners, kindergartners, and first graders dramatize such things as bears hibernating in their dens, dinosaurs moving through swamps, volcanoes erupting, the earth rotating on its axis around the sun, plants giving off oxygen. . . .Invariably, the children appear to be thoroughly enjoying themselves, as if at play. They also appear to retain more of the information presented during the reading. (p. 464)*

According to Katherine Nelson (1986), it is a natural tendency of children to think in terms of events, and dramatizing events appears to serve as a kind of building block with "significance for many areas of their cognitive performance and development" (p. 247). Dramatizations are also effective in helping children understand and remember some of the more technical vocabulary of nonfiction because the physical actions associated with particular words help create a memorable context (Putnam, 1991). Teachers have also used Readers Theater as a medium for engaging older students with nonfiction. Terrell Young and Sylvia Vardell (1993) provided detailed guidelines for using Readers Theater as a medium to help students improve their oral reading skills, reading comprehension, and ability to select and script informational material.

There is strong evidence to support a literature-based curriculum that includes both fiction and nonfictional materials, for children need opportunities to experience the written language and structures of a wide range of genres and approaches to presenting knowledge. In the same way that children emulate the fictional texts that please them, they will model their own writing and presentation of information on nonfictional materials that capture their interest and imagination. An excellent comprehensive discussion of a wide range of topics related to nonfiction is *Using Nonfiction Trade Books in the Elementary Classroom* (1992), edited by Evelyn B. Freeman and Diane Goetz Person. Another valuable resource is *Beyond Fact: Nonfiction for Children and Young People* (1982), edited by Jo Carr.

A Selected Bibliography of Nonfiction

Concept books, informational picture books, identification books, the arts, photographic essays, life-cycle books, experiment and activity books, documents and journals, biographies and autobiographies, survey books, specialized books, and craft and how-to books are just some of the many forms that encompass the wealth of fine nonfiction currently available for children to enjoy. Although the following books are nonfiction, combining fiction and factual books dealing with a particular topic or concept greatly enhances the enjoyment and the learning.

For Children Ages Five through Eight

Bunting, J. (1995). *The Children's Visual Dictionary.* New York: Dorling Kindersley Publishing.

> *Themes as fascinating and diverse as mini-beasts and space introduce children to a wide range of words, many set in descriptive phrases, supported by outstanding color illustrations.*

Freeman, T. (1980). *Beginning Surfing.* Chicago: Children's Press.

> *Clear, full-color photographs and step-by-step explanations make this a valuable book for any beginner.*

Gibbons, G. (1988). *Sunken Treasure.* New York: Thomas Y. Crowell.

> *With attractive, interesting illustrations and text, this factual book introduces the wide variety of expertise and procedures that are involved in the finding and salvaging of sunken treasure.*

Harris, S.M. (1985). *This Is My Trunk.* New York: Atheneum.

> *The hard work and skill required to be a circus clown are the focus of this factual book. Costumes, makeup, and behind-the-scenes activity at a circus are all entertaining presented.*

Kalman, B. (1992). *Colonial Crafts.* New York: Crabtree Publishing Company. (Toronto: Oxford)

> *The wheelwright, blacksmith, gunsmith, and cooper are just a few of the craftspeople presented through colored photographs and accessible text.*

Lambert, M. (1989). *T.V. and Video Technology.* East Sussex, UK: Wayland.

> *A helpful glossary supports this description of some of the latest advances in television and video technology.*

McGrath, S. (1986) *Saving Our Animal Friends*. Washington, DC: National Geographic Society.

This book describes ways in which children and adults can work to save endangered species.

Parker, N. W. & Wright, J. R. (1987). *Bugs*. New York: Greenwillow.

Large, informative illustrations and amusing riddles introduce children to 16 different bugs.

Pope, J. (1988). *Kenneth Lilly's Animals*. New York: Lothrop, Lee & Shepard.

Sixty-two animals and their young are depicted in large, full-color paintings. The habits and habitat of each are discussed and a distribution map with each picture indicates where in the world the animal lives. A table of facts and figures and an index are also provided in this outstanding information book.

Reid, B. (1988). *Playing with Plasticine*. Toronto: Kids Can Press.

This well-known Canadian illustrator shows children how to create imaginative artwork with plasticine, a substance similar to Play-Doh.

Waters, K. & Slovenz-Low, M. (1990). *Lion Dancer: Ernie Wan's Chinese New Year*. New York: Scholastic.

Photographs illustrate this factual account of a six-year-old boy as he prepares to dance his first Lion Dance for the Chinese New Year.

Wyler, R. (1989). *Raindrops and Rainbows*. Englewood Cliffs, NJ: Julian Messner.

Guided by the teacher, children can discover how to catch a raindrop, create a rainbow, and make rain from a homemade cloud.

For Children Ages Nine through Thirteen

Apfel, N. H. (1988). *Nebulae: The Birth and Death of Stars*. New York: Lothrop, Lee & Shepard.

Full-color photographs of nebulae and supernovae accompany a detailed description of the life cycle of stars.

Ballard, R. D. (1988). *Exploring the Titanic*. Toronto: Scholastic/Madison Press Book.

This fascinating account of the loss and discovery of the Titanic is rich with illustrations and colored photographs.

Ballard, R. D. (1990). *The Lost Wreck of the Isis*. Mississauga, Ont.: Random House of Canada/Madison Press Book.

This account of the discovery of the Isis, an ancient Roman ship, combined with flashbacks to the fourth century A.D., provides the reader with a fascinating look at the world of ancient Rome and the wonders of modern technology.

Dewey, J. O. (1987). *At the Edge of the Pond*. Boston: Little, Brown.

Illustrated with detailed colored-pencil drawings, this book introduces children to the many creatures they might find in and near a pond.

Forsyth, A. (1988). *Journey through a Tropical Jungle.* Toronto: Greey de Pencier.

Vivid full-color photographs reveal the beauty of a Costa Rican rain forest and of the plants and animals that live there.

Giblin, J. C. (1990). *The Riddle of the Rosetta Stone: Key to Ancient Egypt.* New York: Thomas Y. Crowell.

The intriguing story of how scholars solved the mysteries of the Rosetta Stone and so made possible the study of the language and culture of ancient Egypt.

Kohl, H. (1981). *A Book of Puzzlements: Play and Invention with Language.* New York: Schocken Books.

A fascinating collection of language games, puzzles, codes and pictographic systems of writing. The author provides strategies for creating games and writing systems.

Lambert, M. (1986). *Living in the Future: Tomorrow's World.* New York: Bookright Press.

Supported by colored illustrations and photographs, questions are asked and answers provided about what our lives might be like in the future.

Lauber, P. (1990). *Seeing Earth from Space.* New York: Orchard Books.

Vivid scientific photographs and well-written captions are used to explain satellite photography or remote sensing.

Macaulay, D. (1988). *The Ways Things Work.* Boston: Houghton Mifflin.

Over 300 pages of detailed diagrams with humorous analogies present almost every imaginable instrument known to man. This fascinating book is organized in four sections—The Mechanics of Movement, Harnessing the Elements, Working with Waves, and Electricity and Automation.

O'Neill, C. (1985). *Computers, Those Amazing Machines.* Washington, DC: National Geographic Society.

Both the familiar and the more unusual uses of computers are examined and predictions are made about their potential for the future.

Peters, D. (1989). *A Gallery of Dinosaurs and Other Early Reptiles.* New York: Knopf.

Drawings to scale of a hundred dinosaurs serve as excellent references for a study of early reptiles.

Assessing Literature's Contribution to Children's Learning

Ongoing assessment of a successful literature-based program could include an analysis of considerations such as the following. Do children elect to:

1. Share books voluntarily and with enthusiasm?
2. Bring books from home to share with the class?

3. Extend an appreciation of a book through an enjoyable artistic, musical, or dramatic activity?
4. Voluntarily discuss favorite literary characters and events?
5. Ask you to read to them?
6. Read books in their free time?
7. Read, write, and speak with confidence and independence?

A review of these points will reveal the kind of attitudes both individuals and the class are developing toward literature.

Charlotte Huck and colleagues (1993) have stated that the best evaluation of the impact of a literature program for today's children will be their reading habits as adults. Only if they have learned to love reading before they complete their formal education are they likely to become lifelong readers. In *Foundations of Literacy* (1979), Don Holdaway asserted that "more than ever before there is a need to introduce children to a satisfying literature, to use such materials at the centre of instruction, and to develop methods of teaching which bring children the sustained and special joy from the written word that they can experience from no other activity" (p. 191).

Suggestions for Reading Aloud

For Children Ages Five through Eight

Ball, D. (1990). *Jeremy's Tail*. Sydney: Ashton-Scholastic.

A game at a birthday party leads Jeremy into an around-the-world adventure.

Carle, E. (1990). *The Very Quiet Cricket*. New York: Philomel.

This poetic cumulative tale of a search for a special sound ends with a delightful sound surprise.

Cleary, B. (1990). *Muggie Maggie*. New York: William Morrow & Co.

A third-grader who refuses to learn cursive writing relies on her computer until she makes an important discovery about the value of handwritten composition.

Demi. (1990). *The Empty Pot*. New York: Henry Holt & Company.

An Emperor of old China devises an unusual plan to help him find the most honest child in the land to be his successor.

French, F. (1990). *The Magic Vase*. Toronto: Oxford University Press.

A poor potter teaches a wealthy art collector a lesson about honesty and appreciating life's simple joys.

Lee, D. (1991). *The Ice-Cream Store*. Toronto: Macmillan Press.

Another delightful collection of nonsense verse about the child's everyday world from the pen of Canada's "Father Goose."

Mahony, E. (1991). *Vasilissa, The Beautiful*. New York: HarperCollins.

This creative retelling of a favorite folktale highlights the magical powers of a special childhood doll.

Munsch, R. (1991). *Show and Tell*. Willowdale, Ont.: Annick Press.

Michael Martchenko's humorous illustrations capture the chaos caused when Benjamin takes his baby sister to school for Show and Tell.

Page, P. K. (1991). *The Travelling Musicians*. Toronto: Kids Can Press.

This richly poetic retelling of the Brothers Grimm's The Musicians of Bremen *is beautifully complemented by the action-filled illustrations by Kady MacDonald Denton.*

Ringgold, F. (1991). *Tar Beach*. New York: Crown Publishers.

The power of positive thinking shines through this tale of a young girl's imaginary flight over a busy metropolis.

Wells, R. (1991). *Max's Dragon Shirt*. New York: Penguin Books.

A shopping expedition for a new pair of pants turns out to be an unexpected adventure for Max and his sister.

Yee, P. (1991). *Roses Sing on New Snow*. Toronto: Douglas & McIntyre.

Vancouver's Chinatown is the setting for this charming tale of a young girl's special culinary talents as she prepares for an important guest from her parents' homeland.

Yolen, J. (1987). *Owl Moon*. New York: Philomel Books. Illustrated by John Schoenherr.

The poetic prose combined with the shifting perspectives of the illustrations make this gentle story of a father and his daughter looking for owls on a snowy night a language and visual treat.

For Children Ages Nine through Thirteen

Bauer, M. (1991). *Face to Face*. New York: Clarion Books.

A "rites of passage" motif forms the plot of 13-year-old Michael Ostrom's whitewater rafting adventure.

Bell, W. (1990). *Forbidden City*. Toronto: Doubleday.

Alex, a high school student, accompanies his cameraman father to China where they are both caught up in the Tian An Men Square uprising.

Ellis, S. (1991). *Pick-up Sticks*. Toronto: Douglas & McIntyre.

A mother and teenage daughter share a comfortable existence until circumstances force a change in their lives and a reexamination of their personal values.

Jeffers, S. (1991). *Brother Eagle, Sister Sky: The Words of Chief Seattle*. New York: Dial Press.

The plea of Chief Seattle, a respected Northwest native leader, for man to value the environment is as timely today as it was when first heard a century ago. The author's pen and ink drawings highlight the ecological theme of this beautifully illustrated book.

Lowry, L. (1993). *The Giver*. Boston: Houghton Mifflin.

In a future society in which poverty, inequality, and unemployment have been eliminated, a young boy discovers the dark secrets of his seemingly ideal world.

Pearson, K. (1991). *The Sky Is Falling.* Toronto: Viking Press.

In this first book of a trilogy, Norah and her younger brother are sent for safety to Canada in 1940 when England feared an invasion by Hitler's army.

Price, L. (1990), reteller. *Aida.* Illustrated by Diane and Leo Dillon. San Diego: Harcourt Brace Jovanovich.

The conflict an Ethiopian princess faces in choosing between love and loyalty is explored in this handsomely illustrated version of the text of Verdi's classic opera.

Sutcliffe, R. (1990). *The Shining Company.* New York: Farrar, Straus and Giroux.

In 600 A.D. young Prosper is assigned to "The Shining Company," a legion composed of warriors and their shieldbearers who stop the advancing Saxons from seizing another kingdom.

Van Allsburg, C. (1991). *The Wretched Stone.* Boston: Houghton Mifflin.

The journal format provides an in-depth look at the emotions and the experiences of those who gaze upon the strange glowing object.

REFERENCES

Professional Books and Articles

Anderson, P. (1974). *Storytelling with the flannelboard.* Minneapolis: T.S. Denison & Company.

Carr, J. (1982). *Beyond fact: Nonfiction for children and young people.* Chicago: American Library Association.

Chambers, A. (1985). *Booktalk: Occasional writing on literature and children.* London: The Bodley Head.

Freedman, R. (1992). Fact or fiction? In E. B. Freeman & D. G. Person (Eds.), *Using nonfiction trade books in the elementary classroom: From ants to zeppelins.* Urbana, IL: National Council of Teachers of English.

Freeman, E. B. & Person, D. G. (1992). *Using nonfiction trade books in the elementary classroom: From ants to zeppelins.* Urbana, IL: National Council of Teachers of English.

Gunderson, L. & Shapiro, J. (1987). Some findings on whole-language instruction. *Reading-Canada-Lecture, 5,* 22–26.

Hickman, J. (1981). A new perspective on response to literature: Research in an elementary school setting. *Research in the Teaching of English, 15,* December, 343–354.

Holdaway, D. (1979). *Foundations of Literacy.* Sydney: Ashton.

Hoskisson, K. (1979). Learning to read naturally. *Language Arts, 56,* May, 491.

Huck, C. S., Hepler, S. & Hickman, J. (1993). *Children's literature in the elementary school* (5th ed.). San Diego, CA: Harcourt Brace Jovanovich.

Langer, J. (1990). Understanding literature. *Language Arts, 67,* December, 812–816.

Martinez, M. & Roser, N. L. (1991). Children's responses to literature. In J. Flood, J. M. Jensen, D. Lapp & J. R. Squire (Eds.), *Handbook of research on teaching the english language arts.* (pp. 643–654). IRA/NCTE. New York: Macmillan.

McTeague, F. (1992). *Shared reading: In the middle and high school years*. Markham, Ont.: Pembroke Publishers Limited.

Meek, M. (1988). *How texts teach what readers learn*. Stroud: The Thimble Press.

Nelson, K. (1986). *Event knowledge: Structure and function in development*. Hillsdale, NJ: Lawrence Erlbaum.

Newkirk, T. (1989). *More than stories: The range of children's writing*. Portsmouth, NH: Heinemann.

Pappas, C. C. (1991). Fostering full access to literacy by including information books. In *Language Arts, 68*, October, 449–462.

Putnam, L. (1991). Dramatizing nonfiction with emerging readers. In *Language Arts, 68*, October, 463–469.

Raymo, C. (1992). Dr. seuss and dr. einstein: Children's books and scientific imagination. In *The Horn Book Magazine, 68*, 560-567.

Rosenblatt, L. (1980). "What facts does this poem teach you?" *Language Arts, 57*, 386–394.

Ruddell, R. B. (1992). A whole language and literature perspective: Creating a meaning-making instructional environment. *Language Arts, 69*, December, 612–620.

Sloan, G. D. (1984). *The child as critic: Teaching literature in the elementary school*. New York: Teachers College Press.

Sloyer, S. (1982). *Readers theatre: Story dramatization in the classroom*. Urbana, IL: National Council of Teachers of ENglish.

Wells, G. (1986). *The meaning makers*. Portsmouth, NH: Heinemann.

Whitin, D. & Wilde, S. (1992). *Read any good math lately? Children's books for mathematical learning K–6*. Portsmouth, NH: Heinemann.

Wright, L. (1988). *Puppets*. London: Franklin Watts.

Young, T. A. & Vardell, S. (1993). Weaving readers theatre and nonfiction into the curriculum. *The Reading Teacher, 46*, February, 396–406.

Children's Books

Ahlberg, J. & Ahlberg, A. (1986). *The jolly postman and other people's letters*. Boston: Little, Brown.

Alcott, L. M. (1943). *Little women*. New York: Little, Brown. (Original work published 1868.)

Allen, P. (1982). *Who sank the boat?* London: Hamish Hamilton.

Bauer, M. D. (1986). *On my honor*. New York: Clarion Books.

Bourgeois, P. (1986). *Franklin in the dark*. Toronto: Kids Can.

Carle, E. (1984). *The very busy spider*. New York: Philomel.

Charlip, R. (1964). *Fortunately, unfortunately*. New York: Parents Magazine Press.

Choi, S. N. (1993). *Year of impossible goodbyes*. New York: Dell.

Cohen, B. (1983). *Molly's pilgrim*. New York: Lothrup.

Cole, J. (1976). *A chick hatches*. New York: Morrow.

D'Aulaire, I. & D'Aulaire, P. (1954). *Animals everywhere*. New York: Doubleday.

Dodge, M. (1915). *Hans Brinker*. New York: Scribner's. (Original work published 1865.)

Fowler, S. (1989). *When summer ends*. New York: Greenwillow Books.

Galdone, P. (1961). *The house that Jack built*. New York: McGraw-Hill.

George, J. (1972). *Julie of the wolves*. New York: Harper & Row.

Harper, W. (1967). *The gunniwolf*. New York: Dutton.

Hennessey, B. G. (1988). *The dinosaur who lived in my backyard*. New York: Viking.

Ho, M. (1991). *The clay marble*. New York: Farrar, Straus & Giroux.

Hoffman, M. (1991). *Amazing Grace*. New York: Dial.

Jarrell, R. (1978). *A bat is born*. Garden City, NY: Doubleday.

Kipling, R. (1991; 1902). *Just so stories*. New York: HarperCollins.

Laird, E. (1993). *Kiss the dust*. Mammoth.

Lee, D. (1974). *Alligator Pie*. Toronto: Macmillan.

Lionni, L. (1986). *A color of his own*. New York: Pantheon.

Louie, Ai-Ling. (1982). *Yeh-Shen: A Cinderella story from China*. New York: Philomel.

Lowry, L. (1989). *Number the stars*. Boston: Houghton Mifflin.

MacLachlan, P. (1985). *Sarah plain and tall*. New York: Harper.

Mahy, M. (1987). *17 kings and 42 elephants*. London: J. M. Dent.

Martin, B., Jr. (1967). *Brown bear, brown bear*. New York: Holt, Rinehart & Winston.

Mayer, M. (1989). *The twelve dancing princesses*. New York: Morrow.

McDermott, G. (1993). *Raven: A trickster tale from the Pacific North West*. San Diego: Harcourt Brace.

McNaught, H. (1981). *Baby animals*. New York: Random House.

Milne, A.A. (1928). *The house at Pooh Corner*. New York: Dutton.

Mollel, T. (1991). *The orphan boy*. New York: Clarion.

Morgan, A. (1991). *The magic hockey skates*. Don Mills, Ont.: Oxford University Press.

Nixon, J. L. (1986). *The other side of dark*. New York: Delacorte.

Oppenheim, J. (1986). *Have you seen birds?* Richmond Hill, Ont.: North Winds Press.

Page, P. K. (1991). *The travelling musicians*. Toronto: Kids Can.

Paulsen, G. (1987). *Hatchet*. New York: Bradbury Press.

Prelutsky, J. (1976). *Nightmares: Poems to trouble your sleep*. New York: Greenwillow.

Reid, B. (1992). *Two by two*. Richmond Hill, Ont.: North Winds Press.

Rosen, M. & Oxenbury, H. (1989). *We're going on a bear hunt*. London: Walker Books.

Say, A. (1993). *Grandfather's journey*. Boston: Houghton Mifflin.

Sendak, M.(1962). *Chicken soup with rice*. New York: Harper & Row.

Spinelli, J. (1990). *Maniac magee*. Boston: Little, Brown.

Spyri, J. (1958). *Heidi*. Philadelphia: Lippincott. (Original work published 1884.)

Staples, S. F. (1989). *Shabanu: Daughter of the wind*. New York: Alfred A. Knopf.

Surat, M. M. (1992). *Angel child, dragon child*. Staeck-Vaughn.

Tolkien, J. R. R. (1938). *The hobbit*. Boston: Houghton Mifflin.

Tresselt, A. (1947). *White snow, bright snow*. New York: Lothrop.

Turner, A. (1990). *Through moon and stars and night skies*. New York: Harper & Row.

Twain, M. (1952). *Tom Sawyer*. New York: Heritage Press. (Original work published 1876.)

Twain, M. (1952). *Huckleberry Finn*. New York: Heritage Press. (Original work published 1885.)

Uchida, Y. (1993). *A jar of dreams*. New York: Aladdin.

Van Allsburg, C. (1990). *Just a dream*. Boston: Houghton Mifflin.

Van Allsburg, C. (1984). *The mysteries of Harris Burdick*. Boston: Houghton Mifflin.

Yabuuchi, M. (1976). *Whose baby?* New York: Philomel.

Young, E. (1989). *Lon Po Po: A Red Riding Hood story from China*. New York: Philomel Books.

Zemach, H. (1969). *The judge*. New York: Farrar, Straus & Giroux.

Selected Bibliography of Professional References

Atwell, N. (1987). *In the middle: Writing, reading and learning with adolescents.* Portsmouth, NH: Heinemann.

Benton, M. & Fox, G. (1985). *Teaching literature nine to fourteen.* London: Oxford University Press.

Flood, J., Jensen, J. M., Lapp, D. & Squire, J. R. (1991). *Handbook of research on teaching the english language arts.* IRA/NCTE. New York: Macmillan Publishing Company.

Chambers, A. (1991). *The reading environment: How adults help children enjoy books.* Stroud: The Thimble Press.

Graves, D. H. (1989). *Experiment with fiction.* Portsmouth, NH: Heinemann.

Graves, D. H. (1989). *Investigate nonfiction.* Portsmouth, NH: Heinemann.

Griffiths, R. & Clyne, M. (1990). *Books you can count on: Linking mathematics and literature.* Albany, NY: Delmar Publishers.

Harrison, B. & Maguire, G. (1987). *Innocence & experience: Essays & conversations on children's literature.* New York: Lothrop, Lee & Shepard Books.

Hart-Hewins, L. & Wells, J. (1992). *Read it in the classroom! Organizing an interactive language arts program grades 4–9.* Markham, Ont.: Pembroke Publishers Limited.

Harwayne, S. (1992). *Lasting impressions: Weaving literature into the writing workshop.* Portsmouth, NH: Heinemann.

Hearne, B. (1990). *Choosing books for children.* New York: Delacorte.

Jobe, R. & Hart, P. (1991). *Canadian connections: Experiencing literature with children.* Markham, Ont.: Pembroke Publishers.

Kobrin, B. (1995). *Eyeopeners II: Children's books to answer children's questions about the world around them.* New York: Scholastic.

Meek, M. (1991). *On being literate.* Portsmouth, NH: Heinemann.

Newman, J. M. (Ed.). (1985). *Whole-language: Theory in use.* Portsmouth, NH: Heinemann Educational Books.

Norton, D. (1995). *Through the eyes of a child: An introduction to children's literature* (4th ed.). New York: Merrill/Prentice Hall.

Peterson, R. & Eeds, M. (1990). *Grand conversations: Literature groups in action.* Richmond Hill, Ont.: Scholastic-TAB.

Rief, L. (1992). *Seeking diversity: Language arts with adolescents.* Portsmouth, NH: Heinemann Educational Books.

Rosenblatt, L. (1938; 1983). *Literature as exploration.* NY: Appleton-Century.

Routman, R. (1991). *Invitations: Changing as teachers and learners, K–12.* Toronto, Ont.: Irwin Publishing/Portsmouth, NH: Heinemann.

Rudman, M. K. (1989). *Children's literature: Resource for the classroom.* Norwood, MA: Christopher-Gordon.

Short, K. G. & Pierce, K. M. (Eds). (1990). *Talking about books: Creating literate communities.* Portsmouth, NH: Heinemann.

Sloan, G. D. (1984). *The child as critic: Teaching literature in the elementary school.* New York: Teachers College Press.

Tompkins, G. E. & McGee, L. M. (1993). *Teaching reading with literature: Case studies to action plans.* Macmillan Publishing Co.

DISCUSSION QUESTIONS

1. Discuss the ways in which literature supports the development of language and literacy. Describe approaches you would use to facilitate and extend this development.

2. Discuss the values of reading aloud to

children and identify the criteria you would use to guide your selection of literature for this purpose.

3. Take each of the literary goals of a whole-language program and identify one or more activities and/or books you would use to support that goal.

4. Articulate your understanding of a response-based approach to teaching and discuss ways you would encourage, support, and extend children's responses to literature—fiction, poetry, and nonfiction.

5. Discuss the similarities and differences between the structures of fictional and nonfiction texts and consider the implications of these characteristics for your role as teacher.

6. Describe ways in which you would monitor and assess the success of a literature-based language arts program.

The Writing Connection

SYD BUTLER

1. *Understanding the importance of* being a writer *in the classroom and demonstrating that craft*

2. *Knowing the developmental stages in children's spelling and how to help children grow toward standard spelling*

3. *Developing skill as a sympathetic and encouraging coeditor, being able to help children express their ideas in the most suitable form for a particular audience*

4. *Understanding the problems of organizing* time *in the classroom and allowing children to develop their commitment to the writing process through choosing their own writing tasks*

5. *Understanding the importance of* publishing *in the classroom*

6. *Learning to evaluate children's writing, both* formatively *and* summatively *through using a variety of techniques to measure, record, and report the students' development as writers*

7. *Understanding the role of grammar and syntax in written composition as the means of helping students to overcome problems in expression*

8. *Understanding the differences in levels of usage in English composition in the varieties of social and geographic dialects*

Introduction

This chapter examines how written composition makes connections with all of the language activities of the classroom. Writing as the medium for composing in a whole-language program is one facet of language activity, along with other forms of oral expression—discussion, reports, presentations, drama—as well as the reading of literary and factual texts. Writing, in Andrew Wilkinson's words, "floats on a sea of talk" (1965). However, for English-as-a-second-language (ESL) students it is well to consider the advice of Law and Eckes (1990): "Students who are limited in their speaking ability [in English] can still compose text and learn to read" (p. 74).

In reading, the students create their meaning from a given text, whereas in writing, the students create their texts in order to make meaning—at first for themselves and then for other readers. The writing program begins with the students learning to express their own thoughts in their own language, to realize the power of the written word to make their thoughts visible. As Donald Graves (1983) pointed out, "Children want to write. They want to write the first day they attend school. This is no accident. Before they went to school they marked up walls, pavements, newspapers with crayons, chalk, pens or pencils . . . anything that makes a mark. The child's marks say, *I am.*"

Part I of this chapter deals with the basic principles of writing processes, defining written composition in its largest sense as authorship. It shows how students write to achieve a variety of purposes in a classroom organized by the teacher as a writers' workshop, using the conference/process approach. This paradigm in the teaching of writing implies that students write to become authors.

Part II deals with the implementation of this approach to writing in the classroom, beginning with the students' expressive writing as a foundation for the more formal demands of both informational and literary writing. The use of the writers' workshop, writing folders, and the writing conference are explained to show how teachers can create opportunities for real writing in their classrooms.

Part III focuses on writing to learn, in which writing is seen as a medium for learning across various subject areas: literature, social studies, mathematics, science, and art.

Part IV provides a step-by-step demonstration of how a teacher may get started in using the paradigm for teaching writing, with activities to help students overcome their writing apprehension, some heuristic techniques to help students generate ideas, and a demonstration of how these may be applied to a writing project called the "sense of place," as a foundation for further explorations in personal writing or lifewriting.

Part I: A Definition of Writing

The Craft of Writing

Writing, of course, is not a single, simple skill, nor is it, as it has been treated in traditional programs, simply a hierarchy of skills, beginning with handwriting or the drawing or copying of the letters of the alphabet. Traditionally, children were expected to master the 26 letters of the alphabet before being allowed to use these symbols to transcribe the sounds of speech. At this point, spelling became the dominant consideration, with the children's efforts being devoted to the mastery of correctly transcribing lists of common words and learning the rules of English spelling that could be applied to the basal vocabulary. The next stage was the transcription or copying of texts, again with an emphasis on the achievement of correctness in spelling, punctuation, and capitalization. The "mechanics," or surface features of the writing, are still regarded in some textbooks as the "basics" of writing, which must be mastered before the beginning writer can be allowed actually to use written language to convey meaning.

Instead, the view of writing in this chapter is that it is a holistic process of composition. Students learn the skills of handwriting, spelling, syntax, and mechanics in the process of developing their ability to express their meanings.

Authorship

Even for older writers, an emphasis on the craft of writing—sentence structure and paragraph and essay organization—falls far short of the heart of written composition, which is the authoring of texts. True authorship, as the highest definition of writing, lies in the writer's transcription of "some focused and edited version of inner speech" (Moffett, 1979). In other words, a writer writes down the words that express what he or she is thinking, but because thinking embraces a far greater quantity of thoughts than what can be captured by the pen (or the keyboard), what appears in the composition is a selected or edited version of the "stream of consciousness." For second-language students, it is recommended that the teacher not focus exclusively on mechanics, and put even more time into prewriting activities (Law and Eckes, 1990, p. 114). Moffett's concern in defining writing as the revision of inner speech is to ensure that the teaching of writing will emphasize "subject matter lying easily at hand within and around the writer—firsthand content such as feeling, fantasies, sensations, memories, and reflections, and secondhand content as drawn from interviews, stored information, and the writings of others." A student engaged in a research project may make tremendous gains in awareness by composing the story of that research in personal terms and communicating the results of the learning to peers (McGinley and Madigan, 1990).

Purposes for Writing

In a whole-language classroom, writing serves a variety of purposes, but the writer's own purpose for writing is always emphasized. The writer's purpose shows the difference between what James Britton calls "real writing" and the "dummy run." Real writing is writing that achieves a language function, whether it is to help the writer understand more clearly his or her own thoughts, feelings, and experiences, to request or record information, or to communicate his or her ideas to other audiences. Whatever the function of writing, the writer needs to use all of the skills of writing, from transcription to composing, simultaneously, but the emphasis on any one of them will vary according to the writer's purpose.

Noreen Shaver (1986) has told the story of a young writer, Michael, who, in first grade, became an enthusiastic journal writer, able to print a string of letters to record the words that would tell the story of the picture that he had drawn. While Michael's writing fell far short of adult standards of handwriting, spelling, punctuation, and sentence construction, he was able to record his messages and could read his stories to his teacher and his parents. However, when Michael decided to write a letter to Santa Claus, he was faced with a different set of constraints. Shaver reported that when Michael read his letter to her prior to mailing it in the classroom mailbox, Michael "dissolved into tears and crumpled his letter in frustration. Through the angry tears, he sobbed, 'Don't you see? I can't send this! Santa can't read Primary! He won't know what my letter says.' "

While Michael's limited command of transcription skills had served him well in the protected environment of home and classroom, in composing his letter to Santa he had come to realize that the demands of a different audience might not allow his letter to achieve its purpose. Although Michael's outburst showed that he had already learned a valuable lesson about writing for varied audiences, the incident also demonstrates the varying roles of the teacher of writing in a whole-language classroom. In traditional writing programs the teacher often acted mainly as the judge and jury. Having set the writing assignment, the teacher then waited until the children had finished their pieces of writing before marking, correcting, and grading their finished products. In this model of teaching, all writing was really a series of "dummy runs"—writing being produced mainly as exercises on which the writer is to be judged (and usually convicted). Michael's teacher, on the other hand, had adopted the primary role of the sympathetic and encouraging listener, interested foremost in what Michael had to say in his writing, knowing that Michael's transcription, sentence structure, and organizational skills would develop with the guidance that he needed to achieve his writing purposes. The Santa letter, then, provided the opportunity for the teacher to switch to another role—that of coeditor—using the expertise of an experienced writer to help Michael get his letter into an acceptable form.

The Conference/Process Approach

In a whole-language classroom, students write for a variety of purposes and for a variety of audiences. Teachers may use the conference/process approach to help students find their own topics and develop their ideas and language (Graves, 1983). Students become "real" writers in their commitment to making their meaning explicit; with help from their peers and teachers within the collaborative structure of the writers' workshop, they learn to draft and revise their writings to make them presentable for real audiences. Graves cited the example of a New Hampshire teacher, Mary Ellen Giacobbe, whose first-grade children began writing on their first day in school, and before the year was up had composed 1,300 five- to six-page booklets, of which 400 were published in hardcover for their classmates to read. A considerable body of research has also shown the determination and success of emerging writers as they persevere in composing their own stories. Lucy Calkins (1980), for example, has followed up on Donald Graves's research into the writing processes of seven-year-old children by studying the writing behaviors of children engaged in writing activities in their classrooms. The case histories of children from grades 1 to 4 show how these children develop: They first treat writing as a play activity, and then become engrossed in the craft of writing as they show increasing concern for the mastery of conventions in order to satisfy specific audiences.

In another study, Barbara Kamler (1980) followed the development of one piece of writing by one second-grade student over a period of three weeks, from the day Jill first decided to write a story about her pet cockatiel until her book was completed and had been shared with the whole class and then entered into the class library. While in the researcher's opinion, the finished book was just an ordinary piece of work, the experiences that contributed to its writing are worth noting. Throughout the process, Jill, the seven-year-old author, remained in control of her topic, which she had first chosen in the course of a short conference with the teacher. At first Jill talked about her cockatiel to the teacher. Then the next day she began to write her first draft in rapid bursts of activity, finally placing her writing folder in the bucket labeled "Ready for a Conference." This first effort was not very promising—57 words of somewhat perfunctory ideas. Nevertheless, during the following two weeks, while Jill was also engaged in the writing and revising of other books and poems, her cockatiel story was the subject of conferences with another student, with the teacher, and with a group. Before being published, the story went through five revisions, resulting in a number of changes and additions not merely to spelling and punctuation but also to the content, as Jill added and clarified information about her bird in response to the questions and suggestions made by her peers and teacher.

The genesis of Jill's story provides a good example of the conference/process approach to writing because it shows how the writer was allowed to experience her own writing process in her development as an author. Throughout, Jill retained ownership of the story. She chose her topic, her writing materials, and determined the time she would spend in composing. She also decided when she was ready to confer with the teacher or her peers about her piece of writing, and the number of changes she would make in her story. Finally, she controlled the publication stage of the process—how it would be illustrated and bound—before it was listed on a chart with the five other books that she already had published, and with the hundred or more titles by the rest of this second-grade class. This study also illustrates how the teacher was able to monitor Jill's progress and development as a writer by using a checklist on the child's writing folder to note which specific writing conventions Jill had used successfully. Jill was also able to use this list in checking whether her draft story was ready for a conference. During the conference, the teacher was able to confirm which writing skills had been mastered and which could still be improved, yet the teacher always accepted the piece of writing as something valuable and worthy of improvement.

For ESL students and students from different cultures, the teacher needs to be aware that the internalized patterns for organizing information may be different, particularly for narrative. This is particularly so for Native-American fiction and for non-Western ethnolinguistic groups. It also is important to equalize conversational rights between teachers and students, especially for the Hawaiian students studied by Au and Mason (1981). It is critical that tasks be as contextualized as possible for those with cultural and linguistically different backgrounds (Heath, 1983).

Paradigms in the Teaching of Writing

Research into the processes by which young children, and indeed all writers, actually compose texts to become authors has led to a new approach to the teaching of writing. Moreover, the work of the National Writing Project in promoting regional writing projects across North America has led Maxine Hairston to suggest that we are in the middle of a revolution in the teaching of writing. Hairston (1982) distinguished between the "current/traditional" and "modern" approaches to teaching writing to list the principal features of the new paradigm. (See Figure 5.1.)

These 12 features of writing programs are in accord with the philosophy that informs a whole-language approach in the elementary classroom. However, it is also important to involve students in planning, editing, and evaluation. In particular, it must be stressed that the writing strand of the language arts

FIGURE 5.1 *Principles of Modern Approaches to the Teaching of Writing*

1. It focuses on the writing process; instructors intervene in students' writing during the process.
2. It teaches strategies for invention and discovery; instructors help students to generate content and discover purpose.
3. It is rhetorically based; audience, purpose, and occasion figure prominently in the assignment of writing tasks.
4. Instructors evaluate the written product by how well it fulfills the writer's intention and meets the audience's needs.
5. It views writing as a recursive rather than a linear process; pre-writing, writing, and revision are activities that overlap and intertwine.
6. It is holistic, viewing writing as an activity that involves the intuitive and nonrational as well as the rational faculties.
7. It emphasizes that writing is a way of learning and developing as well as a communication skill.
8. It includes a variety of writing modes, expressive as well as expository.
9. It is informed by other disciplines, especially cognitive psychology and linguistics.
10. It views writing as a disciplined creative activity that can be analyzed and described; its practitioners believe that writing can be taught.
11. It is based on linguistic research and research in the composing process.
12. It stresses the principle that writing teachers should be people who write.

Source: From "The Winds of Change: Thomas Kuhn and the Revolution in the Teaching of Writing" by M. Hairston, 1982, *College Composition and Communication, 33(1),* pp. 76–88. Copyright 1982 by the National Council of Teachers of English. Reprinted by permission.

curriculum is treated as a means of discovery and communication rather than as a series of discrete skills to be mastered one after another. Writing in a whole-language classroom serves the needs of the children to express and clarify their ideas. The children *write to learn,* rather than *learn to write.*

Consequently, as was seen earlier in the example of Jill's classroom, the teacher's first response to children's writing is always at the level of meaning—looking at the function of the writing rather than the form, knowing that form follows function. The teacher's first efforts are directed toward helping the child clarify the purpose for the piece of writing. Once this is established, then the teacher will be able to work with the child to let the writing take its proper shape and achieve the conventional surface features of spelling, punctuation, and presentation. Given an emphasis on the making of meaning, it is easy then for the teacher to fit into the helping role of the coeditor when reading children's writing or working in conference with a young author. The teacher's task is thus to help the child make the best out of a piece of writing. With this attitude, no piece of writing can be seen as a failure; instead, the teacher focuses on whatever ideas have value and are worth sharing. All writings are seen as work in progress, or potential publications, and the teacher's expertise will be needed to help the student writer clarify or add to its meaning and put it into an acceptable format.

Writing for a Variety of Audiences

Children write for a variety of audiences at various levels of formality. In the beginning, the children write for themselves simply in order to see that their words can take on the concrete shape of words on paper. But when children are encouraged to develop their own ideas and responses to their experiences, then it will soon be necessary for the teacher to create opportunities for the children to share their writings, whether through oral presentation with a partner, in small groups, with the whole class, or in published forms such as books for the class library and letters to people and organizations in the world outside the classroom.

The Teacher as Writer

Another principle particularly germane to the whole-language classroom is the idea that the teacher must also be a writer. It would be unreasonable to expect that a teacher could contribute very much stimulation to the children's interest in reading unless he or she had some knowledge of, and interest in, children's literature. Obviously, the teacher of literature must be a reader in order to demonstrate the delights of reading. So, too, the teacher of writing must be a writer in order to demonstrate to children the trials and tribulations that all authors, even teachers, suffer as they struggle to find the words that will express their ideas accurately. Often children seem to think that being an expert writer means being able to compose a first draft that is perfect in organization and format. When children experience only the writing of professional authors in published formats, it is eminently possible for them to get the idea that these books were written without any mistakes or revisions. Children need to be witnesses to the writing processes of a mature writer in order to see that even an expert writer produces text that is full of mistakes and false starts. Children will feel better about their own inadequacies as writers once they realize that all writers, even professionals, suffer from self-doubt and "writer's block."

Consequently, the teacher will be a leader in writing rather than an instructor of writing in the classroom: "See how I write" rather than "Write as I tell you." When students write journals, so will the teacher. When the students write personal stories, so will the teacher. In fact, any form of writing tackled by the students will be an opportunity for the teacher to exhibit an adult's writing process that the students can compare to their own.

Using Computers in the Writing Program

Written composition is only one of many computer applications that can be used to enhance whole-language programs. These will be discussed in more detail in Chapter 8, Using Computers in Whole-Language Classrooms. At this point, it will be sufficient to show some of the advantages of using a word-processing program on a classroom computer.

David Dickinson (1986) recorded the impact of a single computer introduced into a first/second-grade classroom with the expectation that it would, as previous research has shown (Sheingold, Kane, and Endreweit, 1983; Riel, 1983) "enhance the children's enjoyment of writing and improve the quality of what they produce." The teacher in this study was already in the second year of implementing a process-oriented approach to writing, and during the writing time the children were accustomed to working at group tables or at individual desks on topics of their own choosing while the teacher circulated among them, holding writing conferences. When the computer arrived, the teacher first taught the commands for LOGO and allowed the children to take turns in pairs to use this program. At the same time, the children began to use a simple text editor to put their stories into the computer and print them out. Over the next few months, most of the children put in their stories, on an average about two each, but some as many as five stories. One skilled second-grader, and surprisingly, a first-grader with limited literacy skills, both girls, became the most prolific users.

The most encouraging development, however, was the emergence of collaborative writing as two children began to compose a story together. Other children collaborated to produce stories for the class book, and two boys composed a story based on the social studies lesson. In this way, the computer became integrated into the classroom writing program. Dickinson's tape-recordings of the children's talk provide evidence of how the children were able to focus on using talk to plan their stories and shape the meaning of their texts. There is also evidence of the children's self-monitoring of spelling and punctuation, their concern with style and ambiguity, and their giving and receiving responses to the writing produced, with many expressions of pride and enjoyment.

Dickinson's findings are supported by the results of another study (Butler and Cox, 1992), in which a first-grade teacher encouraged two six-year-old children to write stories using the Bank Street Writer program on an Apple microcomputer. Over a two-week period the two girls produced three stories, while a tape-recording of their talk showed how their discussion varied from dealing with the mechanics of the computer program to the planning of the story and the correction of their text. Only rarely were the children off task, and usually because of interruptions from other children. Transcripts of the children's talk show them dealing with apostrophes, phonics, sentence structure, plurals, verb endings, verb tense, the use of pronouns, and choice of words. At the story level, there were discussions of the character's name, whether their fictional first-grade girl would be able to add 10 plus 1 plus 2, what the characters would do in the story, and how it would end. There was also a lot of evidence of the children's reading and rereading their text aloud.

Young children can take charge of their writing processes with the help of a computer, which also helps to promote collaboration in the students' interactions when "milling around" the computer, which "affected both the content and the form of the students' writings" (Bruce, Michaels, and Watson-Gegeo, 1985). In this sixth-grade classroom, the students had been using the "Mailbag" system as part of the QUILL program, which emphasizes the opportunity for children to read each other's texts. The students had written critical reviews of the school's "Black History Show." In one case, the researchers were able to compare the differences between Margaret's handwritten draft and her final computer printout. While waiting her turn at the computer, Margaret had been able to read another student's critique of the show and had then incorporated some revised views into her original text.

This study illustrates one important aspect of a writing program based on a computer: the awareness of audience for public writing. But there was also a noticeable "media orientation" in this classroom with "the use of 'Press Release' announcements, written commercials for up-coming stories, markers of episodes, chapters, and series; urgings to 'stay tuned'; flashy titles; the use of pseudonyms, and deliberate use of nonconventional capitalization and punctuation for effect" (Bruce et al., 1985).

There is a general agreement that the use of a computer can only enhance a process approach to writing in the classroom. Merely providing the opportunity to edit and revise text has a beneficial effect, while the ability of students to print out their texts in clear type gives their writing a professional polish that pen and paper can never achieve. With younger children the problem of learning to use the keys on the keyboard may provide some difficulty. Some educators predict that with the increasing necessity to promote computer literacy, "keyboarding" as a basic skill for transcribing sounds into letters on the screen may complement or even supplant the focus on handwriting in the early grades.

In a whole-language classroom, the computer linked to a printer can become a work station as an integral part of the classroom structure, when students have the option of keyboarding and saving their stories and articles onto a disk. The benefits are immediate in that the students see their words transformed into electronic images and the printout can give their work a professional gloss. More important, having their texts printed out creates a "distance" between the writing and the composition, which allows the author to read a text as a reader as well as author. All writers know the advantages of being able to make slight changes in a text without the penalty of having to redo the whole thing again. A printed text also provides a good focus for the writing conference, when the author can act on advice and scribble marginal notes for additions and revisions to be incorporated into the text.

Yet the word-processing computer is much more than simply an electronic super-typewriter. Because the text is displayed on a screen, composing may become a public event that can be shared by two or more authors. One of the most important effects of having a computer in a whole-language classroom is the opportunity it provides for collaborative composition when two authors work on a single text. Students will be able to develop their own strategies for taking turns, or using dialogue, or dictating to each other. Text creation involves a great deal of screen reading when students will read what they have already composed as a springboard for the next idea to be expressed first orally and then through the keyboard. In fact, the main benefit of having a computer as a classroom learning station may well be the oral language that is generated in front of the screen. In any classroom from kindergarten onward there will be a great diversity in the knowledge and skills that the children bring to the classroom, particularly when it comes to computer use. The teacher will be able to draw upon this diversity to promote collaboration among the students when it becomes possible for the more computer-literate students to help the absolute novices.

The computer and printer will obviously have an important function in the publishing of children's stories and books. Children take a great delight in playing with fonts and formats, and the addition of a desktop publishing program may well give the students the opportunity to present their writing with a print quality that approaches that of the traditional typesetter.

A computer in the classroom, therefore, will enhance all aspects of the writing processes, from the initial idea generation and first drafting, through revision, editing, and proofreading, to the final presentations, whether on paper or through electronic mail, of the students' ideas. Ideas for other applications of the computer will be dealt with in Chapter 8.

Part II: Implementing the Writing Program

The Foundations of Writing

While the principles listed in Figure 5.1 hold true for any whole-language classroom, it is impossible to make a detailed sequential plan for writing as part of a whole-language program. What distinguishes the whole-language classroom is an attitude toward the children and their language which results in the "integration of listening, speaking, reading and writing around experiential learning" (Paulet, 1984). From this viewpoint, writing, as a function of the children's language, must be seen to grow along with other expressions of the children's ideas.

Although there is no one way for incorporating writing into the language program, the various facets of writing programs outlined here will provide the teacher with some ideas and devices to incorporate into the organizational structure of the curriculum. This section deals with various forms of personal writing—journals and USSW (Unstructured, Sustained, Silent Writing)—as a means of establishing the children's ownership of their writing. The recognition of developmental stages in spelling and the use of such organizational devices as the writers' workshop, writing folders, and writing conferences will provide the structure for exploring the opportunities for real writing in the classroom.

Expressive Writing

The research in the 1960s of James Britton and colleagues (1975) and others in the London University Institute of Education led to a theory of writing development based on language functions. This suggests that a foundation of "expressive" language ability is necessary for growth into the use of more formal demands of "transactional" (i.e., informational) and "poetic" (i.e., literary) modes of writing. Expressive writing is the language of everyday speech, the medium of personal exploration, and the tentative shaping of ideas that can occur in conversation. It is language used to express ideas close to the person, without the constraints of editorial conventions for specific formats. Free writing is seen as a means of generating and exploring ideas (Elbow, 1973).

For beginning writers, expressive writing can take the form of the language-experience chart used with a primary group, or it can be a private journal in which a student draws and labels records of experiences at home and in school. Some teachers will schedule a regular journal-writing time when the students can write about topics of their own choosing. At first these journal entries may be little more than the records of a diary, but with the interest of the teacher (who also models the journal-writing activity) children can learn to expand and develop their perceptions. Brenda Bradley (1985) recorded the following example. Every day the teacher in a second-grade class would have a 10-minute period for sustained writing during which the children were expected to devote themselves to their writing. Most of the children wrote about the day's events, until David, following the teacher's reading of some imaginative monster stories, began to write a Halloween story for himself. The breakthrough came when David began another story, on which the teacher commented, "This is an exciting story. I hope you finish it tomorrow." Consequently David continued his story for eight consecutive days. It was the first time that any of the children had realized that they were able to carry on a story from one day to the next, or even beyond one page. David's example, and the teacher's praise of his effort, led to a flurry of story writing among the class, as other students wanted to write "chapter stories."

However, it needs to be remembered that this is personal expression and that the student's own needs, experiences, and perceptions will dictate how and for what purpose he or she will write. Again, it is important to recognize that students from other cultures may find these decontextualized school activities puzzling. In the emphasis on getting students to present and publish stories for public consumption, some students seem to "get lost in the shuffle" (Tchudi, 1987). The teacher must struggle to help students find a true "voice" in their writing, before committing themselves to communicating to other audiences. Many students can make good use of the private letter format as the vehicle for expressing their own feelings and values in a wide range of experiences. The students' letters testify to "the value of language as a means of clarifying experience and working through feelings." But they also illustrate the value of using personal expression as an emotional release, and sometimes the writer needs no other response from the teacher but the sympathetic "I hear you." Tchudi provided this anonymous student's letter as a testament to the value of allowing students to express their innermost feelings in the security that their words will be accepted without correction or reproof:

> *I hate to do thing that I dont like but one thing. I have to do is some people off I five boy's in my naborhood there only one boy. I like in my naborhood which is me. I have very few friends. No one understand's it's just like living with your enemys and trying to kill your self. I dont have a way with words and if I did I still would'n't have anyone to talk to. but my self and I try to under stand my feeling and change but it's to hard. I had to let my feeling out this is way I rote about my self.*

> *the end*
> *Plese right*
> *back as soon*
> *as possible.* [*]

Journals

The important feature of journal writing is that the students are allowed to compose in their own language and retain the privacy of their writing. Most children, of course, are anxious to share their ideas, provided that the teacher respects the child's ownership of the writing. This means that the teacher must not attempt to "correct" (i.e., to mark language errors) the composition, but instead should respond to the child's message. Margaret Crocker (1982) is one

[*]*Source:* From "Writer to Reader to Self: The Personal Uses of Writing: by S. Tchudi, 1987, *Language Arts, 64*(5), pages 489–496. Copyright 1987 by the National Council of Teachers of English. Reprinted by permission.

of many teachers who has found that the "dialogue journals" that she uses with her sixth-grade class help her to understand her students more completely and to deal with some of the personal problems that they experience in the classroom. These students have a weekly 15-minute journal-writing session as a whole class activity (with the teacher, of course, also participating), and are encouraged to add extra entries at any time during the week, whenever they have something to record. Once a week the teacher collects the journals to read and comment on the students' ideas. There is no "marking" or grading involved; instead, the teacher will sometimes acknowledge what the student has written, ask or answer a question, or make a suggestion for further writing. The important point in this written dialogue is the complete acceptance by the teacher of the student's message. Any attempt to "correct" the student's language would be counterproductive to the idea that written language is a medium for genuine communication through which the teacher learns a great deal about the students' concerns, and, incidentally, about their writing abilities.

Another teacher also reported that the value of journal writing in her class goes beyond that of socialization (Tremblay, 1982). In their dialogues with the teacher, the students use their journal entries to achieve a great variety of language functions:

When students write their daily entries they are using language to relate, to inform, to explain, to describe, and to convince. They receive immediate written feedback. They see the effects of their writing. They know that language is working for them.

The acceptance of journals for pedagogical reasons at a variety of grade levels and across the whole range of disciplines has been marked by the "Guidelines for Using Journals in School Settings," a position statement prepared by the NCTE (National Council of Teachers of Education) Commission on Composition (in Fulwiler, 1987), which provides a sound rationale and suggestions for the use of journals. The Commission recommends that "teachers assign journals—and logs and thinkbooks and daybooks—for a variety of specific and practical reasons," including the following:

1. To help students find personal connections to the material they are studying in class and in textbooks
2. To provide a place for students to think about, learn, and understand course material
3. To collect observations, responses, and data
4. To allow students to practice their writing before handing it in to be graded

Among the many helpful suggestions in this statement, the Commission recommends that teachers should ask students to do "short journal writes" in class, and that the teacher should also write along with the students, and share writing with the students.

For evaluation, the Commission recommends that teachers should count, but not grade, student journals. Because students must be allowed to take risks, it is important not to grade the quality of journal entries, nor for that matter any first draft writing. Qualitative judgments about students' writing, as will be shown in Chapter 10 on Assessment, should be reserved for work that has benefited from the whole process of writing and revision. On the other hand, it is possible to award marks or bonus points in some quantitative way, to recognize the conscientious effort that goes into regular and thoughtful journal entries. Students should also be encouraged to value their journals by making an end-of-unit review of what they have achieved, numbering the pages, adding titles, making a contents page, and presenting a self-evaluative summation in order to bring a sense of closure to the project.

Megan, a third-grade student, makes an interesting case history, showing how in the course of the year she became more aware of herself as a writer and a learner, moving from the "simple basic narrative structure of child talk" to an example of "free association writing, to an imaginative participation in role play as she responded to Harriet Tubman's biography, to a record of her field trip to a local newspaper" (Fulwiler, 1987).

Seven years later, Megan, now in grade 10 and still keeping a journal, comments, "Looking back, I see that my entries became progressively more personal as I became more comfortable with writing. My journals have become a record of my life, of my growing up, of problems, pains and joys."

Beginning a Journal Project   Every student should have the opportunity at some time to try keeping a personal journal. Many, like Megan, will want to sustain it. But in the classroom, a journal project should be introduced for a limited period, perhaps four or five weeks, at the end of which the students have the opportunity to evaluate their experience and achievement. It is especially important to discuss the reasons for insisting on a certain amount of production for this project so that reasons for *quality* and *quantity* remain clearly differentiated. The instructions in Figure 5.2 will help older students in getting started, and includes an evaluative scale for them to assess its value.

FIGURE 5.2   *A Sixth-Grade Journal Project*

This project is designed to:

1. Help you become independent writers.
2. Develop your fluency in writing.
3. Show you the value of writing for a variety of purposes.
4. Let you experiment with a variety of writing forms.

Step 1. The Writing Derby   In this game everyone (including the teacher) starts with a blank piece of paper and a pen. One person sets a stopwatch to time five minutes. At the signal "GO," everyone writes as quickly as possible. Simply let your thoughts flow down on paper. Don't worry about spelling or punctuation. You can start by writing: "I don't know what I'm going to write about, but. . . ." By the time you have written that, a dozen thoughts will have passed through your mind. You can write anything you like, because nobody is going to read it. The game is to see who can write the most words in five minutes. The teacher of ESL students with limited language ability will need to be cautious in using this technique and may wish to increase the amount of time allowed.

Step 2. Make Your Private Journal   You can buy a special notebook for your journal but it's more fun to make your own. You need about 20 sheets of lined or plain paper, white or colored, and cardboard for the covers. You can bind the pages by sewing, stapling, or punching holes and using a lace to tie them together. Use colored pictures or wallpaper scraps to decorate the covers.

Step 3. Writing in Your Journal   Sometimes the teacher will set a journal-writing time, or you may do it as an alternative to Uninterrupted Sustained Silent Reading (USSR). Some people call it USSW (Unstructured Sustained Silent Writing). Or you can do it anytime you have 5 or 10 minutes to spare. You decide what you want to write. It may be about something that has just happened to you or something that happened a long time ago. Or it can be about a problem you are experiencing. Or it can be about your feelings. Often you will not know what you are going to write about until you actually start writing (just like in the Writing Derby). An entry can take any shape or form-prose, poetry, or even an imaginary dialogue. You can also use your journal to write imaginary letters to people you know or would like to know. It is always your choice.

Step 4. Reading the Journal   Your journal is primarily for YOU to read. As the weeks go by, you will be interested to read what you wrote earlier to see how your feelings changed, how problems have been solved, or to see what worries or questions you had. If you have a topic that will interest the teacher, you can ask him or her to read it. If so, the teacher will not mark or correct it; instead, he or she might answer your questions or comment on your ideas.

Step 5. Managing the Journal   Your journal will be kept at school in a safe, secure place because it is regarded as absolutely private. No one else will be allowed to read it unless you say so. At times the teacher may ask you to scan through your journal to see that you are keeping up conscientiously. At the end of the project you will be able to keep the journal, show it to your parents, or destroy it, as you wish.

Step 6. Evaluating the Journal At the end of the project you will be asked to compile a contents page or an index to the list of topics you have covered during the past month, and then write a final journal entry in which you assess what you have gained from the project. Then you and your teacher will rate your journal according to the following scales:

Journal Assessment

	Excellent		*Average*		*Weak*
Quantity	*1*	*2*	*3*	*4*	*5*
	(20 entries)				*(Less than 5)*
Regularity	*1*	*2*	*3*	*4*	*5*
Interest (to you as reader)	*1*	*2*	*3*	*4*	*5*

In addition, for the interest category you will be asked to choose your most interesting journal entry and make a good copy to show to your teacher, who will also read your final evaluation entry.

Good luck and happy writing!

The Learning Log

The learning log or learning journal may be considered either as an extension or as an alternative to the personal or dialogue journal in which students write about their personal interests. The aim of the learning log is to help students write and think reflectively about their learning in all areas of the school curriculum. It provides opportunity for students to comment on their learning—what has interested them, what difficulties they have encountered, or what insights they have gained. Above all, the learning log enables students to make connections between the content materials in the classroom and their own values and beliefs. The learning log encourages students to articulate curricular concepts in their own language, effectively making the new material a part of their whole understanding.

A particular version of the learning log is the reading log, in which students comment on the books they have read and, more importantly, write their personal responses to the characters, events, themes, and values in the book they are currently reading. The reading log enables students to express their own opinions, ask questions about characters, respond to the author, and clarify their understanding, even during the process of reading. Combined with various forms of oral discussion, the reading log provides a release for the students' affective responses to a literary work, enabling them to make connections between the fictional world created by the author and the real world of the students' experience.

One teacher has found that learning logs enable her fourth-grade students to become more consciously aware of their own learning (Sanford, 1988). As one of her students wrote, "Understanding is what counts for you." Another of her students wrote about what she had learned from a social studies lesson on pioneer life in the 1800s: "Yesterday my class talked about women being housewives. It's not fair, I thought. They should have ganged up on men to show women are as good as men." Such comments show personal engagement with the concept.

The learning log also provides the teacher with an invaluable window on the student's learning. By reading and responding to these logs, teachers can see how students are able to shape their own learning, to make sense of new concepts, and to keep track of their individual accomplishments.

Another advocate of the use of the "course journal" in her writing-to-learn classroom uses the analogy of the gardener's greenhouse to show the value of a journal as a place where ideas, observations, experiences, and memories can take root to grow in a protected environment. In this classroom the journal provides the fertile soil in which students can experiment with lists, free writing, free association, role-playing, unsent letters, questions, dialogue, and other heuristic techniques for generating ideas (Juell, 1985).

Developmental Stages in Spelling

Writing is a way of making language visible and permanent. Unfortunately, when children's language takes the written form, errors of transcription may set up a block to the adult's response to the message. In conversation we can ignore mistakes of diction and syntax in order to concentrate on the meaning of the language. In writing, however, because the message is often detached from the composer, we can be distracted by the surface imperfections of the text. With the process approach to the writing there is some comfort in knowing that spelling and punctuation can be put right later, when the piece of writing is nearing completion for publication, but some teachers worry that unless their children's writing is constantly corrected for spelling errors, the children will reinforce erroneous spelling patterns.

For some teachers the idea of invented spelling may be anathema, but Joyce Edwards's (1985) recent research has identified five developmental stages through which children move at varying rates of progress: (1) using random combinations of letters; (2) using sounds in spelling out words; (3) using phonetic patterns, sometimes omitting vowels; (4) using some rules haphazardly; and (5) internalizing spelling conventions for most common words. This is when they "have managed to incorporate their intuitive knowledge of language with the orthographic features they have learned, and print finally 'falls into place' for most students" (Edwards, 1985).

The teacher must be aware that within any one classroom there will be students at several of these spelling stages, and should recognize the learning value for a child who uses invented spelling to convey a message. It is necessary to tread a fine line between encouraging the child to develop fluency in writing by using whatever spelling seems to work and helping the child, as in Michael's case, to revise spelling errors in order to publish for a more demanding audience.

The Writers' Workshop

In a whole-language program, children write for different purposes at many different times throughout the day. In this sense, writing is a spontaneous activity, just as conversation or discussion. Nevertheless, it is useful for the teacher to designate some blocks of time or to set off a specific space as a writers' workshop where the emphasis will be on writing processes. Many teachers also establish a writing center in their classrooms as a corner or table in the classroom stocked with a variety of writing materials and references to help children write independently.

The idea of the writers' workshop, whether it is a specific time or a place in the classroom, is that children can engage themselves in a variety of writing activities according to their individual writing processes. The writers' workshop can accommodate both the solitary writer struggling to express first ideas about a subject and students working in partnerships or small groups to share their drafts with each other and to look for ways of improving them. Some students may be using resources to expand ideas, while others will be doing final proofreading and illustrations prior to publication.

In the writers' workshop the teacher's role will vary. It is a time and place for individual conferences, or the monitoring of the students' journals and writing folders. The teacher will be able to help a student suffering from writer's block, or to give advice to a group preparing a combined report or collaborative story. At times the teacher will give instructional sessions to a group of students who have been identified as needing enhanced training in some specific writing skill—handwriting, punctuation, spelling, or sentence structure.

The writers' workshop must be a part of a whole-language classroom because its flexibility accommodates a variety of writing behaviors, many of which are tied into the oral language of partnerships and small groups. The flexibility also allows for differences in individual ability in writing, recognizing that there is no one writing process for everybody, but enabling students to help each other according to their needs and abilities.

The Environment for Writing

The whole-language classroom provides an environment in which writing is an integral and valued activity. Opportunities for the oral sharing of ideas and experiences (as discussed in Chapter 3, Talk in Whole-Language Classrooms) provide the foundations for the students' writing. Some cautions with respect to ESL students were offered at the beginning of this chapter. The somewhat decontextualized nature of classroom activities is also a source of potential difficulty for students from other cultures. Such classroom talk, whether structured or unstructured, will generate ideas that need to be captured and preserved in writing in a variety of writing forms and for a variety of audiences. As Donald Graves (1975) found in his seminal study of the writing processes of seven-year-old children: "Informal environments give greater choice to children. When children are given choice as to whether they write or not, as to what to write, they write more, and to greater length than when specific writing assignments are given."

In this environment the teacher functions as a guide and model for writing, not as an instructor. The teacher will create an atmosphere in which writing is regarded as a natural activity, something that everyone (including the teacher) does. There will be a constant expectation from the teacher that the students will want to present their ideas in writing, but at the same time there is an awareness that not everyone will need to express their ideas in the same format. Whatever choices the students make, the teacher is available as a coeditor, ready to help each student achieve success. In this environment, success in writing is guaranteed for every student.

Writing Folders

If writing is to be a valued activity in a whole-language classroom, then it is necessary that children should preserve their writings for self-evaluation and also for the teacher who will use the child's accumulated writings over a period of time to assess the child's progress in writing. The teacher must be able to demonstrate growth in his or her students' writing ability to parents and administrators, and there is no better evidence for this than to show the quantity of each child's drafts and revisions, the breadth of the different forms of writing attempted, and the quality of those pieces that have been "published" or presented in some way after a number of conferences and revisions.

While there are many commercial forms of writing folders available, and some schools or school districts provide their students with their individual folders, it is valuable for teachers to design their own format and help their students make and decorate their own folders. Generally, a writing folder should be able to hold the child's drafts in a number of pockets with headings to show the different types of writing. For example, one pocket may be a collection of all first drafts, while another pocket contains the draft that is currently being worked on, and a third pocket contains finished drafts and private writings.

The construction of the folders and the labeling of the pockets are themselves a valuable lesson in the nature of writing processes and the need to preserve writings. This is also a step toward helping the children gain ownership of their writing. Pride in writing achievement can be promoted by listing on the cover the books that the author has published. The development of writing ability can also be recorded with a permanent and cumulative list of the writing skills that the child has demonstrated in the writings. Similarly, lists of new ideas to write about or lists of topics that interest the student provide useful reservoirs of writing "prompts." Please also refer to the section entitled Writing Folders in Chapter 12.

Marty Woollings (1984), in his article on writing folders, suggested that there is evidence that the folders work to encourage students to write and to take pride in their writing achievement. The result of a districtwide pilot project showed that folders made and personalized by the students helped to boost their self-esteem and promoted an individualized approach to the teaching of writing.

Writing Conferences

The heart of an individualized approach to the teaching of writing is the writing conference, which may take a variety of forms. Most generally, the conference takes place between the student writer and the teacher, and is focused on the specific piece of writing in which the student is engaged. The purpose of the conference may be to help the writer generate ideas or organize the ideas that are already there, or identify the audience for the piece of writing and

The teacher assists in group writing projects.

plan how the piece will be presented or published. The conference also provides an opportunity for the teacher to monitor the student's progress in this particular writing task and to assess the student's development of writing abilities. In practice, the conference may become a formalized meeting between teacher and student, both sitting at a recognized place in the classroom writing center, or it can be a teacher's discussion with a whole group about their individual writing projects, or it can be a casual 30-second encounter when the teacher helps a student to overcome a specific problem that has occurred in the writing process.

In her article, Glenda Bissex (1982) cited transcripts of writing conferences at various grade levels to illustrate the teacher's role in helping students clarify their intentions and realize the choices that they, as writers, can make in the composition. The following questions are offered as suggestions for the teacher/conferencer:

1. What would you like me/us to listen for and react to?
2. What part do you like the best?
3. What part gave you the most trouble?
4. What did you consider putting in and then decide against?
5. What would you like to change in your next draft?
6. What did you learn from writing this piece?

The writing conference is also central to Donald Graves's (1983) approach to the teaching of writing, and he offered six principles of scaffolding (or providing supports for the student's ideas) that will help make a successful conference:

1. The conference must be predictable in that the children must be comfortable in taking risks in their writing, secure in the knowledge that the teacher's response will help them achieve success.
2. Each conference should be focused on no more than one or two features of a child's piece of writing. At first it will be sufficient to focus on the writer's purpose for writing and how far this draft achieves that purpose. Mechanical conventions should wait until a piece is nearing completion.
3. The child must be able to expect demonstrable solutions to writing problems. It is not productive to speak in generalizations about writing. Rather it is important to show, perhaps with an overhead projector, how, for example, a sentence might be changed.
4. The child should be free to initiate questions and comments, and this role reversal ensures that the conference should be child centered rather than teacher dominated.
5. The conference also benefits from use of nomenclature, as the child needs to develop and use vocabulary about the processes and the technicalities of writing.
6. Finally, Graves emphasized the principle of playfulness in conferences. Humor is essential if children are to enjoy their writing, and it helps in

encouraging them in experimentation and in taking risks, through which they grow and develop as competent and creative writers.

Throughout the conference the principle of the child's ownership of the writing must remain supreme. Some conferencers recommend that the child retain possession of the paper in order to read it to the teacher. Moreover, the teacher should avoid making marks or corrections on the child's paper. The aim is to let the student writer know what options there are for improving the piece of writing, so that in the end it is the writer who must take responsibility for making decisions about what to change and add, about who the audience will be for the piece of writing, and about what form the presentation might take.

In a writing conference the teacher's prime function is to offer the encouragement that all writers need. Anyone who has been engaged in the struggle to discover and express his or her own ideas knows that what he or she needs above all is the reassurance that the effort is worthwhile. Errors and faults are too easy to find. In some cases it may not be necessary to do any corrections at all, because it is important, too, for students and teachers to realize that not all writings will be published. Many writings will have achieved their purpose in the discovery of ideas during the rough draft. Other papers may be concerned with personal matters that the writer will want to keep private. Some attempts at public writing may be too mundane or repetitious to be worth pursuing, and the writer will need to be guided into making a fresh start. But the student should have a place to preserve private writings, and even false starts are worth preserving in the writing folder as evidence of the student's efforts.

Peer Conferences

An important function of the writing conference between the teacher and an individual student is to model the behaviors of the sympathetic coeditor in order that students themselves will be able to learn this function. As students develop their confidence as writers, they become more adept at helping each other, and this certainly relieves the teacher's burden of being the sole arbiter of writing. One method for developing the students' abilities as coeditors is to use the peer conference group described by Marion Crowhurst (1994). In her experiment in peer response, students at various grade levels showed their ability to read and criticize each other's papers. A group of five students would sit at a table, each with a piece of writing in a draft stage. Their papers would circulate around the group, and each student would write a response slip giving the values and main idea of the writing and possibly a suggestion for improvement. After the papers had been all around the group, the response slips would be delivered to the authors so that each writer received four independently written appraisals of his or her writing.

There is no doubt that peer-to-peer writing conferences provide a major breakthrough for the teacher who wishes to establish a writing classroom. Many of the difficulties of trying to respond to the quantity of writing produced by a class of enthusiastic student writers can be overcome if students are taught how to help each other as coeditors or as sympathetic listeners. It would certainly be impossible for a busy teacher to give all of the individual help necessary, and counterproductive to try to mark and correct all of the students' draft writings. Instead, by taking time to show students how they can become good conferencers, much of the burden of responding to writing can be lifted from the teacher's shoulders.

The written response slip is one way to introduce students to the idea that they can become useful responders. Another possibility is for the teacher to share on an overhead projector a genuine piece of his or her own writing in progress, and then ask the class for helpful suggestions as to how the writing can be developed. The Bissex (1982) and Graves (1983) questions listed earlier may be too advanced for younger students. An alternative approach is to discuss with the students what they, as writers, need in the way of help and feedback, and to provide sentence frames that the students can use in their responses, whether written or oral. For example:

1. Appreciation—"I like the part about. . . ." "I like the way you. . . ."
2. Definition—"This piece will make a good. . . ." "This is an interesting story about. . . ."
3. Extension—"Can you tell me more about . . ?" "Can you give us more details about how it looked (sounded, smelled, tasted, felt)?"
4. Clarification—"Can you explain how . . ?" "What happened to the . . ?"

Intervening in Children's Writing

Barry Fox (1980) has provided an interesting case study to show how the intervention of a teacher during a writing conference helped an eight-year-old child named Lucy not only to produce a better poem, but also to become more sharply aware of the experience that had led her to write the poem. Fox has given the transcript of the writing conference between Lucy and her teacher, which illustrates some important principles the teacher followed in helping Lucy clarify her experiences by moving from generalized statements to specific images and figures of speech. After Lucy attempted her rewrite, the teacher praised her efforts and gave the poem the best verbal reading he could. Then by focusing on some of the images Lucy used, his questions helped Lucy to create more specific words to recall her original experience. The teacher's questions drew from Lucy the words that would help her realize her experience more sharply, but throughout this conference there was the implicit understanding that Lucy was in control of the process, that she retained the ownership of the poem, and that it is her contributions to the conference that would eventually improve the poem.

This conference also illustrates the importance of informal, relaxed talk between writing partners. While the teacher's questions focus on Lucy's perceptions of her experience, the result is that Lucy is able to generate more words and ideas to manifest that experience in a poetic shape.

It should be noted that in her final version, Lucy did not incorporate all of the revisions that surfaced during the course of the conference. The principle here is that suggestions can be made, alternative words or images brought to mind, or advice offered about punctuation and sentence structure, but in the end it is the writer's prerogative to accept or decline the advice as he or she decides. Lucy is the author, and it is her poem, not the teacher's. Yet as Fox (1980) pointed out, "A considerable amount of a child's potential will not be realized if teachers regularly accept their students' first offers." By involving Lucy in the process of writing, this teacher was able to promote Lucy's commitment to her piece of writing through his planned intervention.

Opportunities for Real Writing in the Classroom

One of the values of this individualized approach to the teaching of writing is that students will be able to experiment with a variety of writing forms to accommodate the variety of purposes served in their writing. It is not necessary for all students to write on the same topic in the form of the three- or five-paragraph essay. Rather, a writing program based on real writing instead of artificial exercises will show that there are many forms of expository writing that exist in the real world that the students can emulate. The guide in Figure 5.3 suggests some of the ways in which student writing can take shape.

FIGURE 5.3   *Opportunities for Real Writing in the Classroom*

1. *Journals:* personal, private notebooks to record personal experiences, feelings, and ideas; continuing-dialogue journals between teacher and student; learning journals to record the student's response to lessons and activities, etc.
2. *Personal communication:* memos to teacher, principal, peers, school staff, parents, etc.
3. *Letters:* to famous people, heroes, villains, politicians, sports and movie stars, film and TV producers, manufacturing corporations, authors, etc.
4. *Stories and poems:* to be published in individual, group, or class booklets.
5. *Class newspaper:* with news stories of family, school, and community events; reports of sporting events; interviews with notable characters; an advice column; whole-page ads; photos and captions; letters to the editor; horoscopes; opinion editorials and columns, etc.
6. *Literary magazine:* with reviews of books read, news of stories being written in the classroom; character sketches of notable authors in the classroom or school; ads for forthcoming stories and poems, etc.
7. *Casebook:* a collection of pieces by various authors on a central theme, such as the class novel, the field trip, or the current science or social studies project.

Part III: Writing to Learn Across Curriculum

In a whole-language classroom, the students learn to write because they use writing to serve their own purposes. Because they are in a school setting, one of the most important purposes is to help them learn and understand the content in all areas of the school curriculum. As Stephen and Susan Tchudi (1983) pointed out, "When students write imaginatively about scientific principles— say, using their knowledge from a unit on fuels to write a futuristic story about transportation—they will learn their subject more effectively than when they merely master the basic concepts in the textbook." Writing, of course, will also help students to achieve self-confidence through the development of their ability to express their own ideas and feelings about their personal lives. A balanced and comprehensive writing program, therefore, will help the students become aware of the many ways in which language works, and develop their abilities to use language, both oral and written, to fulfill a variety of functions.

Writing in Specific Subject Areas

Writing in Literature

With a process or workshop approach to writing in a whole-language classroom, children will be encouraged and able to make a variety of responses to their reading in all content areas. Where students are reading stories and novels of their own individual choice, it will be possible to use the sharing of their imaginative experiences in both oral and written presentations. The purpose here will be to create a sense of the breadth of reading that takes place in the classroom. Rather than work at composing the traditional, formulaic "book reports," or making dreary chapter-by-chapter plot summaries, the children will be able to experiment with a variety of oral and written ways of expressing their responses to a book.

The following suggestions will enable the children to explore a variety of written forms as a means of expressing their responses to their reading, whether it be a book or novel read as a group or by an individual student.

1. Making a poster to advertise a book provides one way to combine visual art and words to capture the main theme or most exciting episode of a novel.
2. The class may also make a cumulative card file of recommended reading by having the students write a short blurb in order to give other readers a taste of what they might enjoy.
3. The writing of letters provides a good vehicle for response to reading. A student may write an appreciative letter to the author (to be mailed in care of the publisher), or a memo to the librarian explaining why the book should or should not be on the shelves. For books authorized by the district, the students' letters may be directed to the superintendent, the school board trustees, or teachers' curriculum committees.
4. For a more extended project, a group of students may plan a campaign to have the book made into a film or TV series, writing a series of letters to TV producers about the book, with suggestions about episodes, casting, and screen titles, for example.
5. At a more imaginative level, a group of students who have been engaged by a particular novel may plan a Readers Theater production to present to the class or to record on audio or videotape. Or the students can take control of the characters in the book to plan and write a further episode to be published as their own sequel. The characters of a novel may also inspire some students to write poems or limericks about them.
6. Where a more complex novel explores a variety of interesting themes, a group of students can compile a casebook, delineating how each of the themes is treated in the book.

With poetry, the sharing of poems through oral reading can lead to the students' experimenting with a variety of poetic forms themselves. Anthologies can be compiled, combining both the students' favorite poems from noted authors and their own efforts.

Writing in Social Studies

Imaginative responses to the geographic and historical content of social studies topics will prove far better media for learning than the traditional copying of facts from resource books and encyclopedias. Here are some interesting ways of approaching social studies:

1. Dramatizations, oral presentations, discussions, and debates will all involve the development of writing skills when students use notes and scripts in their planning for class performances.
2. Students can also use the skills developing in their personal journals to put themselves imaginatively in the place of such historical figures as explorers or early settlers.
3. More complex skills of argumentation will be needed if students develop scenarios to replicate the debates or inquiries into such social problems as land claims, or environmental problems involving disparate groups.

Imaginative writing enables students to make the chronological or geographical leap that will take them to the heart of the period or area that they are studying. A variety of writing forms are available to the students: letters, requests, memos, case studies, newspaper reports, and scripts. All of these will draw upon the students' knowledge of the factual basis of the situations being studied or researched. Moreover, when students can imaginatively participate

These students are involved in a group research project.

in the lives of other peoples in different countries or different eras, there is the possibility of students understanding the human values of other cultures.

Writing in Mathematics

The learning log has already been discussed earlier as a means of enabling students to write about their own perceptions and feelings in learning new concepts, in order to personalize their knowledge, to make sense of new concepts for themselves. Linda Wason-Ellam (1987) conducted a research study in which first-grade students were asked to respond in their learning journals once a week to the question: "What did you discover this week at math centers?" This was an activity-centered classroom in which the students were allowed to experiment with hands-on approaches to dealing with number theory. The writings of these six-year-old children show that the students "created" their own language through interaction with mathematical experiences. Michael, for example, wrote: "I lrnd in sentrs today you can match the same blocks together. At the other sntrs I noticed that you can minus up dinosaurs." Tyler showed that he grasped an important concept in his comment: "Do you no how I learned to add? I used junk to learn to add. I took one group of things of junk and then another group of things and I put them together and I counted them and the numbers made a higher number than it was before. I like doing it that way."

The loosely structured expressive writing of the learning log enabled the students to speculate and reflect on their own learning, rather than simply get right answers. About the task of estimating the number of seeds in a pumpkin, Heather wrote: "I dsgvd [discovered] that the one that had the most wasn't right. It was hard to guess because you couldn't see inside the pumpkin." Jarvis wrote about how he learned to count: "we lrnd how to cownt 123456789 10 and thos hi [that's how], we want [went] to 10 and we are lrning how to do this with cubs [cubes] and with a place value board and sam times it git gin fusing [confusing] and som times I get cin fust becas sam times i cant put all the cups in to tens and we nemd [numbered] theym funny nams. and we did this becase we are soto lrn [supposed to learn] how to cawnt numbrs togetr."

Wason-Ellam (1987) suggested that this writing-to-learn technique was successful because "the students used math journals to reflect on their learning, to discover gaps in their knowledge, and to explore relationships between what they were learning and their prior experiences."

Writing in Science

Observation, recording, and reporting provide the foundation for scientific investigation. Judith Newman (1983) reported the case study of an eight-year-old student, J. P., who used his own language to record his observations of the behavior of mealworm larvae. J. P.'s drawings and captions became the basis for a published book in which J. P. showed his ability both as a scientist and as a

writer. In a series of experiments, J. P. was able to use his language to record, analyze, and predict what the larvae would do under certain conditions.
Throughout his experiments, J. P. was able to talk about his observations and
make notes and pictures about what he saw. In compiling his book, J. P. added
more information and reorganized some of the information that he had collected. Throughout this project, J. P. was going through the processes that real
authors experience because he was making language serve a practical purpose.

Newman pointed out the value of whole language in this science project,
and the learning about language that J. P. experienced as he focused on the
scientific concepts. Each of J. P.'s investigations involved him in reading and talking about his subject, making notes about what he saw, and compiling his
notes and drawings through a process of revision to publish his book. Newman
suggests that this exposure to scientific thinking and the expression of learning
about science in both oral and written language is a necessary part of learning about language in the real world.

In another experiment that was focused specifically on the development of
students' writing, George Hillocks (1975) had students working in groups to
observe, discuss, note, and write about a variety of experiences. He found that
the students made significant gains in the use of detail in their writing, an
improvement that carried over to other compositions. The types of activity
that he found useful are described in a "Theory into Practice" booklet called
Observing and Writing (NCTE, 1975). For example, in an activity called "The
Shell Game" he had the students study the peculiarities of a set of numbered
clam shells. Each group of students composed a detailed description of one of
the shells. Then the descriptions and the shells were jumbled up, and the students had to try to identify each shell according to the written descriptions.
The discussion in the debriefing session helped the students clarify how their
written descriptions worked, and they were able to internalize some important lessons about the importance of details in writing.

Writing and Art

Art and craft activities in the classroom provide a number of opportunities for
students to make their writing serve real purposes for understanding and communicating. Learning journal entries can be used by the students to help them
articulate the ideas and interpretations that inform their visual representations.
The artist's notebook or folio enables the artist to combine visual sketching
and writing. Various forms of written free response can help other artists in
the classroom understand how their works are received by an audience. At a
more formal level, introductory notes enable the artist to create a context of ideas
by which the works are to be viewed. A collection of such artists' notes could
be published as a guide to a classroom or hallway art exhibition, complete with
biographical notes on each of the artists. The notion of the artist's portfolio
has now been extended to the language arts (see Portfolios in Chapter 12).

Drawing, of course, is a composing activity in itself, and children's drawings are themselves a medium for expressing thoughts, memories, and perceptions about the world of experience. Drawing enables people to express, record, and communicate their ideas in visual forms. But drawing and sketching can also be seen as prewriting activities that allow students time to collect ideas and images to incorporate into their writing. Some students, once they have embarked on an idea for a story or article, will find it very beneficial if they make a quick sketch or line drawing as an illustration of their ideas. As a rehearsal time for ideas, it allows students to generate ideas and perceptions about their topic and to collect the words that allow them to interpret the story in writing.

Part IV: Getting Started: Writing in Whole Language

Changing Students' Attitudes

The best foundation for teachers who wish to introduce a program of real writing into the classroom is an awareness of their own writing processes combined with a willingness to share their writing with the students, even if it means exhibiting some of the inadequacies and hesitations, the false starts and failures that all writers suffer. But the basis of the process approach is a sense of trust between students and the teacher, paralleling the relationship between budding authors and their editor and publisher.

To begin, there must be some understanding of how writing functions, of how it can serve a variety of purposes of the writer, and how a piece of writing can be allowed to evolve through a series of collaborations between authors and editors, whether teacher or peers, which will guarantee the author's eventual success. Consequently, it is worthwhile to discuss with the students the reasons why people write, and what authors can achieve through their writing, in order to set some realistic goals. The overall aim is not to produce a class of 30 students who can each compose and write a 500-word essay complete with a logical paragraph structure, perfect syntax, and absolute control of surface conventions, all within the one-hour time limit of a public examination.

Rather, the goal is to let the students know that it is their ideas and perceptions that are important, that real authors write about topics and ideas that are important to them, and they do their best to publish their work for a variety of audiences. The students need to know that they can get help from the teacher and their peers at all points in the evolution of a piece of writing: while they are first generating ideas, while they are arranging and selecting ideas, while they are choosing forms and formats for their writing, and while they are readying their writing for final publication.

Beginning a Writing Project

The following plan, based on the principles outlined earlier, provides a methodology that has worked with many students at a variety of grade levels. The approach described here should not be followed slavishly. In fact, it is always better for teachers to inject their own ideas in order to get the ball rolling in the writing classroom.

Overcoming Writing Apprehension

This approach begins with two writing games to relieve the tension and anxiety, also termed writing apprehension, that students often suffer when faced with classroom writing activities. In classrooms with students from a variety of ethnolinguistic groups that have not mastered English completely, the teacher needs to exercise appropriate caution when using timed tasks such as these, or may wish to extend the time limits somewhat.

The Word Cache   The teacher can explain this game as an experiment by which the students will find out something about their writing processes. When everyone, including the teacher, is ready with a blank paper and pencil, then the teacher asks the students to look around the room to see how many different objects there are. The aim of this game is to list as many objects as possible during a two-minute time limit. Spelling does not count in this game. The students are told that if they spot some object, then they can name it or describe it; and if they are able to name it, then they are able to write it down on the paper.

With the teacher as timekeeper, everyone writes for two minutes. Afterwards, discussion should elicit how many words the students were able to collect. They should compare their lists with their neighbor's to see that everyone made a unique list. They should scan their lists to see if anyone captured an object that no one else noticed. Discussion might consider the question as to whether the writing activity actually helped the students to make more accurate and perceptive observations, and whether, through their writing, the students noticed objects in the room that were previously unnoticed.

This experiment should help the students to realize that *writing is a reflection of thinking,* that the writing helped them to see more and enabled them to record their observations. Above all, the "word cache" should help them to realize that everyone can write to achieve a purpose, which in this case was the listing of objects in the room.

The Writing Derby　　The next game or experiment takes this level of realization a stage further. The "writing derby" (Holt, 1969) or "forced writing" (Elbow, 1973) is a similar type of activity, which functions as a form of prewriting heuristic. In this experiment the students are told that they are going to try to write continuously for five minutes without letting their pens or pencils stop once. The aim is to let the thoughts flow directly onto the paper. Again, spelling and punctuation do not count. Furthermore, the students are reassured that what they write will remain absolutely private. They will not have to share it with their peers or with the teacher. When students ask, quite naturally, what they have to write about, the teacher will say: "I don't know." The students will write whatever they happen to be thinking about. They may want to start by writing, "I don't know what to write," but by the time they get to the end of the statement a myriad of thoughts will have crossed their minds, and they can continue with any one of them. They do not have to stay on the same topic for the five minutes but can switch whenever they like. When all doubts and anxieties are settled, the activity can begin. As in the "word cache," it is important that the teacher, besides being the timekeeper, is also a participating writer.

At the end of the five minutes, most students will be surprised about the number of words they have composed. Even in the early grades, students can usually manage 70 or 80 words of connected prose, while older intermediate students will be amazed that in the five minutes they will have composed a paragraph-length piece of composition. Discussion about the activity should focus on the ideas that students have expressed in this stream-of-consciousness writing. Some will have surprised themselves by mentioning ideas or topics that may be a long way from the classroom. The important realization here is that the students to become aware that their writing can be a reflection of their thinking and feeling, and that. Also, if they put aside worries about spelling and punctuation, they are better able to let their ideas flow onto paper.

A Sense of Place

The next stage is to put these two activities to work in the composition of a real piece of writing. For the "sense of place" activity, the teacher should explain that the places we live, play, and work in are a large part of a writer's experience. Now the students will be able to use the "word cache" activity to list all of the places that are important in their lives. "Places" should be interpreted as widely or loosely as possible. "Place" may mean a town or city, but it can also mean a street or park in the community or a specific room or location. It may be a place from the past or a place that is important in the present. Or it can be a place that exists only in the imagination as part of a possible future. For the listing of places it is not necessary to set a time limit, but the teacher, while engaged in the activity, should monitor the students' progress, ready to stop the writing if fatigue or boredom sets in. It is also important to monitor individual students in case any of them has difficulty in deciding on what places to list. Here, a helpful question, in effect a mini-writing conference, will help students to ensure success.

Once the students have made a tentative list of places, the next step is to ask them to select one of these places as a possible subject for further exploration. Here, modeling is a powerful teaching technique, when the teacher displays his or her own list, and explains which of the places might be chosen for further exploration. Informal talking is also a powerful motivator in the selection of ideas, and students can be paired with partners to explain to each other why each has chosen that particular place. Another prewriting technique that may be useful at this stage is to ask the students to make sketches or line-drawings of the places they have chosen. This activity creates a "thinking-space" which allows time for more ideas to be generated. The sketch also provides a focus for talk as each student can show the partner the sketch and explain the details in it. This technique was especially effective with a group of foreign students learning English as a second language (Butler, 1991).

Each of the stages in the evolution of the "sense of place" composition may occur on successive days. It is not necessary or desirable that the whole process should happen in one single session. In fact, a break between different stages will enable the teacher to monitor each student's progress and to give some helpful questions to those who might have become stuck.

Assuming that everyone, including the teacher, has made a tentative selection of an important place in his or her life, the next step is to show how some prewriting activity will help the students to collect a bank of words that they can use to describe their places. This is another use of the "word cache" applied to a real writing task. The teacher explains that in this experiment some of the students will create descriptions of their places that will make readers want to be there. And if the writing is successful, then the descriptions can be published and illustrated in a class or individual booklet, which everyone will be able to read in the class library. But first it is necessary to collect some words, to build vocabulary that can be used in the description.

Step 1   The students start with blank paper on which they write the name of the place that they are going to describe. Next the teacher asks them to imagine that they can see the place in their mind's eye, and then to list all of the objects that they can see in their place, just as they did for the "word cache" of the classroom. But now the list goes deeper. After listing objects, the list can expand to include the colors they can see in the scene. As the listing activity continues, the focus can shift to the sounds that they associate with the place. From sounds, the list can extend to tastes, smells, textures. The students can also note any wildlife, birds, or pets that they might associate with the place. Finally, the teacher's questions should bring the children back to the human dimension and the real importance of the place to them in their memory. They can list the people they connect with the place and finally write some words to describe the moods or feelings that the place conjures up.

Step 2   The next session might begin with peer conferences, in which each student shares with a partner his or her ideas and word lists about the chosen places. In effect, a lot of prewriting activity helps to delay writing, to provide what Donald Graves (1983) called "rehearsal time," when ideas and memories gradually take shape in the writer's consciousness. Many famous writers have remarked on this process of incubation, which may last months or years before a story is ready to be written. In the classroom this rehearsal for writing can often take the form of "telling" writing, when two partners tell each other about what they intend to write, and ask each other clarifying questions that will provide a scaffold of reassurance for the writing task ahead.

Individual differences among the members of any class will probably become apparent during these prewriting activities. Some students may become impatient, and having gained some confidence in their ideas, they may want to start writing immediately. Others may still feel insecure about the validity of their ideas, in which case more conferences with a partner or the teacher will be necessary. However, for this initial writing activity the teacher will probably want either the whole class or at least a sizeable group of students together to tackle the first draft. Here is when the writing derby game is applied to real writing.

Step 3   With the group the teacher may first want to discuss some possibilities for an opening sentence. An idea recommended by Donald Graves is to use the technical word *lead* to help young writers to understand the mysteries of the writer's craft. At this time the students can be encouraged to write several possible leads, and then discuss them with a partner to see which will provide the best opening. The students should also review their word caches of vocabulary associated with their choice of place, and if possible, add more words to their lists. It is important at this stage that the students perceive the teacher as a fellow writer also struggling with ideas to be expressed in this composition. The teacher should share his or her own word caches and demonstrate on the blackboard or overhead projector the composing of some different lead sentences.

Step 4   Now the technique of the writing derby or forced writing can be used to take the students over the first hurdle in the composing of an initial draft. The word caches, peer conferencing, teacher demonstrations, and group discussion should have provided a springboard from which even the most reluctant writer can take the leap into composing a description of the most important place.

Once the students have moved into the writing stage, then the divergence of their writing processes will become even more apparent, and the teacher should not try to impose a lockstep series of writing events in the futile hope that all students will compose their stories according to an imposed, external timetable. The teacher's responsibility is to ensure that time is available and to help individual students who might seem to get stuck in the process. Students who forge ahead of the others should be encouraged to have frequent conferences with a partner so that the partner can provide a sympathetic ear for the composition in progress. Students can be briefed to ask clarifying questions to help the writer become aware of how ideas are received by an audience. Questioning will also help the writer to add to the bank of ideas in order that the process of revision and reshaping also entails the further generation of ideas.

Step 5   As the students' writings begin to take shape, it is necessary that the teacher, as the classroom publisher, make the students aware of the possibilities for turning their stories into a booklet form. The aim may be to compile a class book as an anthology of these first sense-of-place stories, or the teacher can demonstrate how his or her own story has been published in an individual booklet, using cardboard covers and appropriate illustrations to make it attractive. Obviously some students will have finished the drafting and reshaping of their stories before the others, and the teacher should work with these to ensure that all of the surface imperfections of their texts—spelling, punctuation, capitalization, sentence structure, word choice, and so on—are removed by careful proofreading. The booklets that these early finishers produce will provide the "carrot" of publication to encourage the slower students to persevere with their efforts.

Continuing Writing

Now that the classroom, at least for some designated periods of time throughout the school week, has been turned into a writers' workshop, the tighter structure that the teacher provided for the beginning of the process can and should be loosened. It should be expected, and welcomed, that some students will forge ahead with their writing and publications, while others may still be slaving over their first piece of writing. The teacher's responsibility is to give help as it is needed, making time available when students can sign up for a writing conference. Record keeping is shared between teacher and student, and both keep folders or portfolios of selected works. For every student, success is guaranteed, because their writing is treated as work-in-progress, and all of the resources of a cooperative classroom are available to help every writer achieve a successful published work.

Further Developments in Personal Writing

For this initial plunge into writing processes, we have seen the classroom as a writers' workshop with the emphasis on developing the students' awareness of writing processes from incubation to publication. The combination of talking and discussion, and reading and questioning, that goes on during the writing conference is a good demonstration of whole language in action. The children's use of oral language is directed toward the purpose of creating written language, which then becomes the children's texts for further reading, and especially critical reading, when the children examine and discuss each other's ideas.

The structure of the writers' workshop provides the beginning teacher with a safe and secure environment in which the students' use of language can easily be seen to be directed toward the achievement of concrete goals, when the publication of their stories provides manifest evidence of their success and achievement, and proof of their development of writing skills. The collection and saving of the students' drafts in their writing folders will provide evidence of their mastery of skills in editing and proofreading, and also provide the teacher with the opportunity to record for each student what each has mastered and where further care or information may be necessary.

From this foundation it is possible to expand the structure of the writers' workshop to allow opportunity for the discussion and sharing of the students' reading, when the stories they have produced become a part of the classroom literary collection, and the students see themselves as published authors.

Lifewriting

Personal writing can develop in many different directions. The very apprehensive student, still unsure of his or her own abilities, now having achieved the success of publication for the first time, may feel most secure by writing about another place on the original word cache of important places. The safe route for the weaker writer is to emulate the process by keeping close to the route that produced his or her first success. Others, however, can be encouraged to branch out in other directions, by making lists of other interests and experiences that they can write about. Incidents, holidays, hobbies, relationships, and letters are all forms of **lifewriting** (Bentley and Butler, 1991). Through lifewriting, students draw upon their own experiences and memories in order to write about ideas that are important to them. For these young authors commitment and involvement in the writing task is the most important part of the writing program. Once students become committed to composing and publishing their own stories, then the problems of the improvement of writing skills become absorbed in the overall task of making meaning in the composing of text (Bentley and Butler, 1991). The concerns of the proofreader for spelling, punctuation, capitalization, and other surface conventions of writing are dealt with within the context of publication, as young authors in the classroom emulate the writing processes of mature authors in the world outside.

When students write about their own interests and experiences for sharing with each other, the teacher can expect some important gains that go far beyond the improvement of writing skills. The children learn to appreciate each other as authors. The more they learn about each other's personal experiences the more they respect each other as individuals. The value of lifewriting, in fact, may be more for its effect on the social processes of the classroom than for the development of language ability. Lifewriting encourages each person in the classroom to create and express a sense of identity. Just as the students learn more about each other, so too does the teacher develop a greater awareness of the experiences and values that the students bring to the classroom. And the teacher, being also a writer/participant in the lifewriting processes, is able to share his or her experiences with the class, with the result that the students get to know their teacher better.

Program Evaluation

The proof of the pudding is in the eating; so the best evidence of the success of a whole-language program in developing writing skills comes from the writings that the children produce. Although this writing program emphasizes the many processes of written composition, in the end it is the products of the program that testify most effectively to its success. The use of students' writing folders has been suggested as an important means of monitoring individual writing achievement, providing the constant feedback and record keeping that are essential for ongoing formative evaluation (see also Chapter 12 on Assessment). Yet the outside observer of the classroom will be less impressed with the many drafts, revisions, experiments, and false starts in the students' folders than with the presented and published pieces of writing that have received meticulous proofreading and polishing to get them into a finished format. For that reason it is important to maintain class records of all of the functional writings produced by the children, including photocopies of their letters that have been mailed to outside audiences, as well as their memos, minutes, reports, and other examples of writing put to work. In addition, there should be displays of all of the students' work that has been formally published.

One must also consider all of the other writings—scripts, plans, outlines, lists—that are important as backing for the students' oral presentations. It is not necessary for this type of writing to be put into a polished format. As long as the writing serves its purpose, there is no point in demanding artificial standards of correctness that go beyond the level of the writing's purpose. Spelling, handwriting, and punctuation are less important in writing that is presented orally, provided, of course, there are no defects that make barriers to reading. But for the purpose of program evaluation it is important to collect and preserve these more transitory forms of writing in order to complete the record of the breadth and depth of the students' writing.

When writing is put to real uses, not as a series of dummy runs or exercises, the teacher can expect with some confidence that the students will develop the skills necessary for completing their writings to a greater extent than if they were in a traditional program consisting mainly of sentence exercises, error corrections, and written compositions conforming to a given formula. In fact, there is a considerable body of evidence that strongly suggests that a knowledge of grammar obtained through this type of exercise does nothing to enhance the students' writing skills. (If knowledge of grammar did make for better writers, then perhaps we would expect that grammarians and linguists would top the bestsellers lists!)

On the other hand, George Hillocks (1986), in his meta-analysis of some 2,000 experimental research studies selected from over 6,000 studies of research in the teaching of composition published in the two decades since the Braddock Report (NCTE, 1963), concluded that "on pre-to-post measures, the environmental mode [of teaching composition] is over four times more effective than the traditional presentational mode and three times more effective than the natural process mode."

According to Hillocks (1986), the "environmental mode" is characterized by:

1. clear and specific objectives . . .;
2. materials and problems selected to engage students with each other in specifiable processes important to some particular aspect of writing; and
3. activities, such as small-group, problem-centered discussions, conducive to high levels of peer interaction concerning specific tasks.

This mode of teaching emphasizes the students' interaction with each other in order to generate ideas and learn identifiable writing skills in balance with the teacher who helps to plan activities and select materials.

The value of a whole-language program is that it can accommodate both the "natural process" and the "environmental" approaches to the teaching of writing within the workshop structure. This allows students to tackle real problems in written communication, while providing the support and encouragement that will ensure their success.

What about Mechanics?

Modern theories of children's language acquisition emphasize that children learn their language by using it to achieve real purposes. So, too, studies of children's writing suggest that children learn to solve problems of spelling, punctuation, capitalization, sentence structure, and syntax as they encounter them during the process of making their meaning clear to themselves and to their audiences. Throughout this chapter it has been stressed that the basic skill of writing is to get ideas down on paper (or cardboard, or papyrus, or stone, or a computer screen, or a wall), and that problems of mechanics are really problems associated with publication, when the composition should be presented with meticulous attention to its surface correctness. In a historical perspective it is clear that English spelling did not become regularized until long after Caxton's introduction of the printing press. Shakespeare didn't even spell his own name consistently, and the first English grammar was not published until nearly a century after his death. Paragraph indentations were an invention of eighteenth-century printers who needed to break up the solidity of a page of printed prose.

Yet the realities of the educational systems mean that children's work is often judged, not by the meanings that are expressed, but how well the writing is spelled and punctuated. Traditionalists will argue that children will not learn these skills unless they are taught and drilled in a sequential system. Direct instruction, of course, is an essential part of the whole language writing program, but instead of the blockbuster approach in which everyone has to learn and practice the same set of writing skills at the same time (and often repeating the same drills year after year), whole language means that students will learn what they need for the here and now, not what they might need next year or in high school. If a first-grade student uses dialogue, then that is the time for a teacher to show that student how to put quotation marks around spoken words. Similarly, question marks and exclamation marks can be incorporated when students need such markers.

Commas present more of a problem, but the teacher should try to keep the rules simple, realizing that even in the world of higher academics there is seldom agreement amongst expert writers about hard and fast rules for commas. Questions about the restrictive and nonrestrictive use of commas between clauses can be postponed. The old advice that commas mark the pauses in the prose sentence is an oversimplification that can lead to a comma explosion. However, most children's usages will fall into one of the following categories, which can be very easily explained in a few seconds in the context of coediting the child's piece of writing:

1. Commas are used to separate items in a list, either of single words or of groups of words.
2. Commas are used to separate the ideas (clauses and phrases) in a long sentence.
3. Commas are used in pairs to set off expanded definitions or descriptions that are added to the sense of a sentence.
4. Commas are used to separate single words, such as *yes, no, well, please, however, moreover, of course,* or people's names, that are added to the sense of a sentence.
5. Commas are sometimes needed to split up an unintentional pair of words, such as, "On the table was some bread and butter was in the fridge." In this case the expected phrase "bread and butter" needs to be split with a comma in order to help the reader recognize the two statements in the sentence.

These definitions bring us to the problem that besets the traditional English teacher: what constitutes a sentence. And the traditional bugbear, of course, is the run-on sentence.

It must be emphasized again that sentence-sense develops in the writer, as in all language-users, from the expression of ideas that matter. Whole language deals with real ideas, and it is far more valuable for a beginning writer to learn how to clarify a passage for a peer reader than to do pages of exercises in splitting up someone else's artificial run-on sentences.

So, in an editing conference the problem of the run-on sentence can be dealt with first through oral reading of the text. The writer should be asked to mark the beginning and end of each sentence and to read each one separately. When a run-on sentence is detected, whether through a comma splice or a complete absence of any break, then it is a very simple matter, without any complicated grammatical explanation, to add the necessary period and capital letter to be incorporated into the next revision.

Correct spelling is also a function of editing, but students who are proud of their writing will want it to be as near perfect as possible. Detection of spelling errors, especially in homophones, is a part of the problem. The other aspect is to help the students learn the spelling rules, patterns, or ideograms that will help them to avoid future mistakes. Personal spelling dictionaries can be started at an early age and maintained throughout the years, especially as they help students to see the great number of words they have already mastered. Teachers will also be able to recognize the type of errors that occur, many of which can be cured through direct instruction of simple phonic rules.

One of the many benefits of writing with a computer or word processor is the use of the spell-check program. Beginning writers usually experience a great feeling of relief with the knowledge that the computer will look after their spelling. Of course, such confidence is not completely justified, because most programs will not recognize the differences between homophones, while during the spelling scan the writer still has to make choices from the options proffered. Nevertheless, there is valuable learning about the nature of spelling through the use of a spell-check.

In any case, the whole language teacher seeks to avoid becoming the class proofreader. The teacher may begin a writing conference with the question: "How can I help you with this piece?" It would be very disappointing if the student replied, "Please check the spelling." If the teacher is to be regarded only as the last resort in checking spelling, then students should be encouraged to make use of other resources in the classroom, especially dictionaries, a thesaurus, and other reference books, but more important, the help of other students. Expert spellers should be identified as the best people to give a text a final spell-check before publication, but ultimately it must be emphasized that the responsibility is the writer's.

The Role of Grammar in Writing

The business of traditional English teachers has long been dangling modifiers; comma splices; parallel constructions; identifying parts of speech; split infinitives; the use of the genitive case with gerunds; the names of verb tenses; subordinate, relative, and noun clauses; distinctions between *shall* and *will,* or *lie* and *lay;* agreement between subject and verb; the use of the objective case after a preposition; and so on. All writers and most teachers carry with them the fossilized remains of past English teaching that surface occasionally in idiosyncratic prejudices about writing style. Another chapter, or many books, could be written about the value of grammar and syntax. Certainly, the study of language itself—its origins, its development, the connections amongst the members of various language families, its dialects and jargons, the development of literacy movements, its usages in various facets of social life, and, of course, its grammatical and syntactic structure—is easily justified as part of one's knowledge of our human heritage and worthy of study per se. We are all richer for knowing about the historical development of the English language and literacy; word watchers delight in the recognition of how our words have developed or how other languages are represented in our word borrowings.

However, as teachers of writing, we should heed the report of the Braddock Commission (1963), which was appointed by the National Council of Teachers of English to assess the current state of knowledge about the teaching of composition by examining some 60 years of research. The authors concluded, "The teaching of formal grammar has a negligible, or, because it usually displaces some instruction and practice in actual composition, a harmful effect on the improvement of writing skills."

Further research since then has confirmed this finding, but skeptics who think that their own knowledge of grammar enables them to be good writers should read the Elley, Barham, Lamb, and Wyllie (1979) study conducted for the New Zealand government. This carefully controlled project involved 250 students in eight classes of students for three years through grades 8 to 10. Some classes were given a traditional curriculum based on a functional approach to grammar, others followed the Oregon curriculum based on the teaching of a modern transformational-generative grammar, while other classes were given a grammar-free English curriculum based on reading and writing. All of the students took a common battery of tests each year, and at the end of the study all of the students took the New Zealand School Certificate examination. Even though the nature of the tests and exams might seem to favor the grammar-based curricula, the results showed no significant differences among the classes, except in one important regard. Attitude surveys showed that the students in the grammar-based classes were much more negative about learning English. The researchers concluded that "those pupils who studied no formal grammar for three years demonstrated competence in writing and related language skills equal to that shown by the pupils who studied transformational or traditional grammar" (p. 98). This study had a major impact on curriculum because it encouraged the New Zealand Ministry of Education to promote the sorts of practices that we now recognize as Whole Language.

In summation: *Teaching grammar does not teach writing.*

Some Unanswered Questions

The following dialogue is a compendium of questions that fellow teachers and education students have asked, either orally or in writing, in response to their reading of this chapter.

Q. How can I expect my weaker students to do worthwhile writing?

A. Everyone *can* do it, provided that the teacher allows ample time, provides help from peers, and ensures that the writing is for a real communicative purpose. All students can produce some pieces of *perfect* writing, as far as the mechanics of spelling, punctuation, capitalization, grammar/usage, and so on are concerned. These pieces are the proof of the pudding, the "published books" in the classroom, the star attractions in the writing portfolios, the products that the teacher shows to the principal, the parents, and anyone else who will read them. Weaker students need more time and more help with each piece. Because they take longer, they will not achieve as many compositions as the faster students.

Q. Does whole language mean that nobody teaches phonics?

A. Of course not. Direct instruction is a part of the whole language approach, within the context of helping students to make meaning, but *not* the instruction of skills to those who can already use them. This is when the writing portfolio is essential as a means of documenting and recording students' progress, in various modes of writing, as well as in the improvement of spelling, punctuation, capitalization, grammar, and usage. The teacher and student should look at positives first, noting when things go right. But recurring problems in a student's writing will need to be remediated by direct instruction, on a one-to-one basis perhaps, or when several students exhibit the same problem through an ad hoc group. The same principle applies to phonics, taught not as a skill in itself, but as an aid to spelling and reading.

Q. Don't students need to be taught handwriting skills?

A. Yes, students do need to be taught handwriting, but the aim is not to turn out a whole classful of Palmer-style writers. Rather, we let each student find a style that serves the purposes of self-expression and communication, in which speed and legibility are the criteria for success. Some students may well find that they are best served by a modified form of primary printing. Others may want to experiment with italic handwriting or other forms of calligraphy.

Q. Can I use drawing as a heuristic?

A. Yes, especially for early primary emergent writers and for ESL students (Butler, 1991a, 1991b). Drawing is an excellent form of prewriting, a time for rehearsing ideas and collecting words. The teacher should encourage transitions in the forms of talking, labeling, and writing captions or dialogue to expand the meaning of the drawing.

Q. How can I motivate reluctant learners?

A. True motivation can come from only within, although external prods might be necessary to get the process going. But eventually self-motivation comes from a feeling of success, making every student feel valued for the expression of real ideas.

Q. How do I grade the students' essays?

A. You don't. Formative evaluation and anecdotal reporting means the avoidance of red ink. The use of the writing portfolio provides evidence of growth over time, instead of the one-shot deal of assessment as in large-scale assessments and traditional composition exams. Reference sets (benchmarks) are also being developed in many U. S. states and Canadian provinces to provide evaluative criteria.

Q. But how am I going to give grades for my students' report cards?

A. The students' writing folios are your best evidence of the students' abilities and efforts. But it is also possible to factor into the grade some marks for each student's performance in peer group presentations and conferencing, and for maintaining a journal. In other words, grades should reflect what aspects of the writing program are valued in the classroom. If the teacher gives weighted scale-points for each dimension of the writing program, then each student's scores can be combined numerically to form a grade that has both reliability and validity as a recognition of the student's achievement in writing (Butler, 1985).

Q. Will it mean more marking?

A. No, on the contrary; the marking and correcting of students' writing is replaced by the teacher's work in conferencing as a coeditor and by a periodic assessment of the folios in conjunction with the students. The teacher's aim will be to involve the students in assessing the quality and quantity of their writings. Students have to become responsible for their own proofreading. The teacher will be reading the results, not with a red pen in hand, but as an appreciative reader. Ultimately, the goal is to have the students recognize for themselves that value of their writings so that they become partners with the teacher in assessment.

Q. If I start a whole-language writing program will everything just fall into place?

A. No. Everything does not fall into place. The teacher has to make it happen by good organization, good role modeling, good discipline, and good student watching.

Q. If my students practice writing every day, does it matter what they write? Isn't the standard of their writing more important than what they write about?

A. The students should not be *practicing* writing, they should be *really* writing every day, or many times during a day, and yes, what the students write is of supreme importance. The first response to student writing is *always* to the content. But don't think it is necessary, or desirable, or even possible, for the teacher to read everything that students write. There are as many readers in the classroom as writers.

REFERENCES

Au, K. H. & Mason, J. M. (1981). Social organizational factors in learning to read: The balance of right hypothesis. *Reading Research Quarterly, 17 (1),* 115–152.

Bentley, R. & Butler, S. (1991). *Lifewriting: Self-exploration through writing and life review.* Dubuque, IA: Kendall/Hunt.

Braddock, R. et al. (1963). *Research in written composition.* Champaign, Ill.: NCTE.

Bissex, G. L. (1982). Writing conferences: Alternatives to the red pencil. *Learning, 11 (4),* 74–77.

Bradley, B. (1985). Sensitive assignments foster student writing. *Highway One: Canadian Journal of Language Education, 9 (1),* 6–12.

Britton, J. et al. (1975). *The development of writing abilities (11–18).* London: Schools Council Research Studies.

Bruce, B., Michaels, S., & Watson-Gegeo, K. (1985). How computers can change the writing process. *Language Arts, 62 (2),* 143–149.

Butler, S. J. (1985). New bottles for new wine; Evaluation in a modern writing program.

English Quarterly, 18(2), 57–68 (ERIC Document Reproduction Service EJ327827).

Butler, S. J. (1991). Lifestorying and drawing in a Czech EFL class. *TESL Canada Journal 9 (1),* 57–66 (ERIC Document Reproduction Service ED323804).

Butler, S J. (1991). Thinking-drawing-talking-writing: The whole language connection. *The Drawing Network Newsletter, 6,* 6–7.

Butler, S. J. (1992). Literacy through lifewriting. *English Quarterly, 24,* 33–41.

Butler, S. & Cox, B. (1992). Writing with a computer in grade one. *Language Arts, 69, 633–640* (ERIC Document Reproduction Service ED314763).

Calkins, L. M. (1980). Notes and comments: Children's rewriting strategies. *Research in the Teaching of English, 14,* 331–341.

Crocker, M. (1982). Dialogue journals promote interpersonal relationships. *Highway One: Canadian Journal of Language Education, 5 (3),* 34–41.

Crowhurst, M. (1994). *Language and learning across the curriculum.* Scarborough, Ontario: Allyn and Bacon Canada.

Dickinson, D. K. (1986). Cooperation, collaboration, and a computer: Integrating a computer into a first-second grade writing program. *Research in the Teaching of English, 20 (4),* 357–378.

Edwards, J. (1985). Spelling corrections alter children's voices. *Highway One: Canadian Journal of Language Education, 8 (3),* 6–14.

Elbow, P. (1973). *Writing without teachers.* New York: Oxford University Press.

Elley, W. B., Barham, I. H., Lamb, H., & Wyllie, M. (1979). *The role of grammar in a secondary school curriculum.* Wellington: New Zealand Council for Educational Research.

Fox, B. (1980). Intervention in children's writing: What is the teacher's role? *Highway One: Canadian Journal of Language Education, 3(1),* 22–25.

Fulwiler, T. (1987). Writing and learning, grade three. In T. Fulwiler (Ed.), *The Journal Book.* Portsmouth, NH: Boynton/Cook.

Graves, D. H. (1975). An examination of the writing processes of seven-year-old children. *Research in the Teaching of English, 9 (3),* 227–241.

Graves, D. H. (1983). *Writing: Teachers and children at work.* Exeter, NH: Heinemann Educational Books.

Hairston, M. (1982). The winds of change: Thomas Kuhn and the revolution in the teaching of writing. *College Composition and Communication, 33 (1),* 76–88.

Heath, S. B. (1983). *Ways with words.* New York: Cambridge University Press.

Hillocks, G. (1975). *Observing and writing.* Urbana, IL: NCTE/ERIC.

Hillocks, G. (1986). *Research on written composition: New directions for teaching.* Urbana, IL: NCTE/ERIC.

Holt, J. (1969). *The underachieving school.* New York: Pitman.

Juell, P. (1985). The course journal. In A. R. Gere (Ed.), *Roots in the sawdust: Writing to learn across the disciplines.* Urbana, IL: NCTE.

Kamler, B. (1980). Research update: One child, one teacher, one classroom. *Language Arts, 57(6),* 680–693.

Law, B. and Eckes, M. (1990). *The more-than-just-surviving handbook: ESL for every classroom teacher.* Winnipeg, Manitoba: Peguis Publishers.

McGinley, M. and Madigan, D. (1990). The research "story": A forum for integrating reading, writing, and learning. *Language Arts, 67,* 474–483.

Moffett, J. (1979). Integrity in the teaching of writing. *Phi Delta Kappan,* 276–279.

Newman, J. (1983). J. P. becomes an eight-year-old scientific writer. *Highway One: Canadian Journal of Language Education, 6 (3),* 48–58.

Newman, J. (1987). Online: The promise and threat of computers. *Language Arts, 64 (7),* 773–777.

Paulet, R. (1984). Whole language approach: Will it be used in Quebec and Manitoba? *English Quarterly, 17 (4)*, 30–36.

Rich, S. (1985). Whole language: The inner dimension. *English Quarterly, 18 (2)*, 15–22.

Riel, M. (1983). Education and ecstasy: Computer chronicles of students writing together. *The Quarterly Newsletter of the Laboratory of Comparative Human Cognition, 3*, 59–67.

Sanford, B. (1988). Writing reflectively. *Language Arts, 65 (7)*, 652–657.

Shaver, N. (1986). Making connections: Dear Santa. *Language Arts, 63(8)*, 772–773.

Sheingold, K., Kane, J. H., & Endrewit, M. E. (1983). Microcomputer use in schools. *Harvard Educational Review, 4*, 412–432.

Staab, C. F. & Smith, K. (1986). Functions in written language. *English Quarterly, 19 (1)*, 50–57.

Tchudi, S. (1987). Writer to reader to self: The personal uses of writing. *Language Arts, 64 (5)*, 489–496.

Tchudi, S. & Tchudi, S. (1983). *Teaching writing in the content area: Elementary school.* Washington, DC: National Education Association.

Tremblay, R. (1982). Journals provide vehicle for student-teacher dialogue. *Highway One: Canadian Journal of Language Education, 5 (3)*, 43–48.

Wason-Ellam, L. (1987). Writing across the curriculum. *Canadian Journal of English Language Arts, 11(3)*, 5–23.

Wilkinson, A. M. (1965). *Spoken English.* Birmingham: University of Birmingham Press.

Woollings, M. (1984). Writing folders. *English Quarterly, 17 (3)*, 20–25.

APPENDIX: SOURCES OF INFORMATION ABOUT COMPOSITION

Ammon, P. (1985). Helping children to write in ESL. In S. W. Freedman (Ed.), *The acquisition of written language: Response and revision.* Norwood, NJ: Ablex.

Daiute, C. (1985). *Writing and computers.* Reading, MA: Addison-Wesley.

Edelsky, C. (1986). *Writing in a bilingual program. Habia una vez.* Norwood, NJ: Ablex.

Kress, G. (1994). *Learning to write* (2nd ed.). New York: Routledge.

DISCUSSION QUESTIONS

1. Discuss the individual writing processes of the members of your group—how they generate and record ideas, how they write a first draft, and how they revise and edit their texts.
2. Discuss the purpose of writing. How can writing help the writer? Why write?
3. Discuss the number of ways in which pupils' talk can be structured in the classroom to provide a foundation for writing activities.
4. What is the role of the teacher in a classroom that uses Hairston's paradigm for the teaching of written composition?
5. Discuss the earliest writing experiences of the members of the group, especially any memories of early successes or fail-

ures in composing a story or essay in the classroom.

6. Discuss the importance of providing student writers (or all writers) with feedback and encouragement during the process of composition.

7. Brainstorm with the members of your group to make a list of the many forms of writing possible in our modern world (e.g., T-shirt slogans, bumper stickers, flyers, brochures, etc.). Then choose a broad topic as a center of interest (e.g., flight, railroads, the sea, mountains, China, families, buildings, reptiles, photography, time, etc.) and discuss how these writing forms could be applied to such a theme. (See Tchudi and Tchudi [1983] for further suggestions.)

6

Reading and Language Development

LEE GUNDERSON

The discussion in this chapter focuses on reading in the whole-language classroom. It differentiates between programs designed for the primary grades (K–3) and the intermediate grades (4–8). The chapter contains suggestions for implementing reading instruction through writing, reading assessment, management strategies, individualization, and instruction in language arts/reading for primary and intermediate students. It also contains a discussion of skills and phonics instruction within a whole-language framework.

Reading and Writing: Getting Started in the Primary Grades (Kindergarten to Grade 3)

Many teachers are convinced that the learning of language arts has a definite sequence: speaking, listening, reading, and writing, and students should therefore be taught to read before they are taught to write. Published reading programs are designed to teach the hundreds of subskills that educators think are important. Reading series readers contain skills intended to be taught sequentially; those learned first purportedly form the basis of those learned later (see Chapter 1, Introduction to Whole-Language Teaching and Learning, for a discussion of textbook-based instruction). The lowest-level skills are called *readiness skills*. It is thought, for instance, that being able to recognize individual letters is a readiness skill for learning to recognize words. This view posits that a student achieves "readiness" by learning a certain number of readiness skills and is then ready to begin to learn to read. Teachers who use reading series generally believe skills should be taught directly. Whole-language teachers, on the other hand, believe that language arts should be learned in a more natural, holistic fashion, and that "readiness" is an invalid concept. In whole-language classrooms, students' writing is often the first material they read; their first reading program is their own writing. Whole-language was developed to emulate the home environments of children who learned to read and write spontaneously, without being taught (Gunderson and Shapiro, 1988).

Writing Development

When Danielle Lopez was 2½ years old she began to use crayons to scribble lines and circles on any surface she could use for writing (often the walls, to her mother's chagrin) and she could read what she wrote. That is, when she was finished, Danielle could read the "writing" even though it looked like scribbles to her mother and father. She could also read it the next day, but the message was usually different. Both of her parents were elated when she "wrote." They didn't care that the product wasn't good; they loved the process. In fact, when they talked to her grandmothers on the telephone they told all about Danielle's marvelous writing. Danielle often wrote messages to her grandmothers on the backs of the letters her mother sent them. When she talked to them on the telephone they both told her what a good writer she was. Neither of them told her she was a poor speller, mostly because there were no spelled-out words. They did get excited about the process, and so did Danielle. Indeed, she was encouraged to write more because the important people in her life were so encouraging. The most incredible day in Danielle's life was when she actually wrote letters instead of scribbles because she learned that they represented writing. Her parents also read a great deal, both to themselves and to Danielle. Danielle grew up in a literate environment filled with individuals who valued and enjoyed literacy activities and they positively rewarded her attempts to read and write.

Researchers have observed other children in environments where literacy and literacy activities are highly valued. Many children produce letters and letterlike forms spontaneously. In case after case there seems to be a developmental sequence in independent writing: scribbling (with meaning); perceiving print and drawing as synonymous; representing things with individual letters; writing initial consonants to represent words beginning with particular sounds; spacing between words; representing sounds with letters; inventing spellings; and producing the mature conventions of spelling and writing (DeFord, 1980; Dyson, 1981; Ferreiro, 1986; Hipple, 1985; Sulzby, 1986). Children also learn to "read" environmental print and can recognize and understand the significance of such visual stimuli as McDonald's "golden arches." Children read together with their parents, actively following the text as it is being read, usually chiming in when they can. They read their own material even though adults cannot. In a whole-language program, the traditional developmental sequence upon which language programs are built—listening, speaking, reading, writing—is incorrect. This is especially so for many second-language learners (Law and Eckes, 1990). Grade 1 whole-language teachers from the first day of school immerse their students in speaking, listening, reading, and writing activities and believe readiness skills need not be taught directly.

Chow (1986) studied students enrolled in whole-language classes. The teachers in her school gave students "log books" and asked them to write in them on the first day of school. Individuals who could not or would not write were encouraged to do so, but not shown how. Chow found their writing revealed five stages:

1. The pre-phonetic
2. The semi-phonetic
3. The phonetic
4. The transitional
5. The conventional or mature

The Pre-Phonetic Writer

Pre-phonetic writers produce letters, letterlike shapes, and numbers. They do not understand, however, that letters correspond to sounds or words. They read their texts, but the reading varies over time. They use a small number of

FIGURE 6.1   *The Pre-Phonetic Writer*

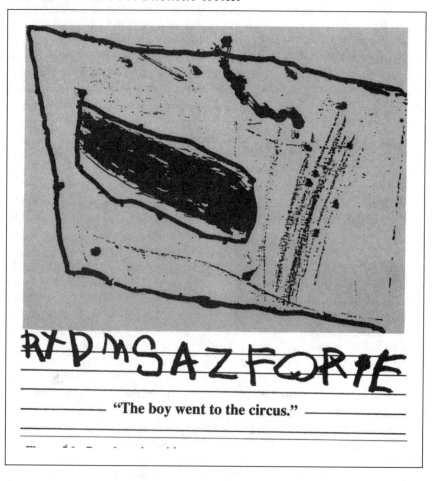

"The boy went to the circus."

capital letters and numbers to write. Figure 6.1 is an example of pre-phonetic writing. Notice that the message bears no relationship to the letters. Indeed, the student's reading of the text varies from reading to reading. These students do know that letters and numbers represent language, but they have not yet begun to understand the systematic relationships between words and symbols.

The Semi-Phonetic Writer

Semi-phonetic writers use letters to represent words or parts of words. They have begun to understand that there is a relationship between letters and sounds. Their writing is semi-phonetic because words are often represented by single letters. (See Figure 6.2.)

FIGURE 6.2   *The Semi-Phonetic Writer*

I PN RF MY SBM

W PN SQ E P

I P hm

"I am playing with my superman. We are playing soccer."

The letters they use to represent words are usually the letters corresponding to the first sounds of the words, such as *d* for daddy. This phenomenon is referred to as "making phonetic hits." Semi-phonetic writers understand there is a relationship between print and language. However, their understanding is limited to single phoneme-grapheme correspondences; that is, they perceive the initial sound of a word and are accurate in representing the word with the letter that spells the first sound. This is an important reading development since it signals that the student is beginning to understand phonics. In fact, without explicit or direct instruction the student has begun to learn some of the most consistent phonics generalizations (not necessarily the rules classroom teachers talk about)—that is, the relationship in English between initial consonant graphemes and initial consonant phonemes, that the letter *d,* for instance, represents the initial sound /d/ when a word is spelled.

The Phonetic Writer

Phonetic writers know that letters represent sounds, and know many correspondences. They have begun independently to map out phonics generalizations. Some would say they are beginning to learn phonics rules, but since they are so inconsistent it is better to refer to them as generalizations. Phonetic writers have begun to separate strings of letters into word units. (See Figure 6.3.) As can be seen, this student separates words into units, spells the words *is* and *my* correctly, and invents the spellings for *castle* and *broken*. This is another incredible development. Not only has the student not been taught phonics but she has also not been taught that words should be separated by spaces. She has learned this by observation, by watching her parents read and write, and by making inferences from the literacy materials she has seen in use.

The phonetic writer relies on knowledge of the relationship between letters and sounds to spell words and invent spellings. Such a writer knows a set of rudimentary phonics generalizations that are applied to spelling. Recent work by Dahl (1993) indicated the students in whole language classrooms are concerned with symbol/sound relations and argue with peers about them.

The Transitional Writer

Transitional writers begin to process words as visual units. Their writing contains many invented spellings; however, they also contain many conventional, nonregular spelling patterns. Figure 6.4 provides an example. This represents another milestone—the learning of irregular words—that is, those words that must be learned by sight because they do not follow any regular phonics generalization. The word *come,* for instance, is not spelled the way it is pronounced. In fact, as spelled, it should rhyme with "comb." By recognizing the word *come* from the spelling of "come" the writer has begun to learn to recognize "sight words" independently and has learned that some words are irregular in spelling or orthography. Invented spellings are very interesting because they often show that students are learning phonics relationships but overgeneralize them to irregular words.

At home the five-year-old is complimented when she invents a spelling for a word. At school such attempts are often rewarded with negative comments, sad-faced stickers, red marks, or bad grades. It's no wonder students of all ages face the typical writing assignment with trepidation.

The Mature Writer

Mature writers know many writing conventions, including "correct" spellings. They do not expend as much energy on the mechanics of writing. Their stories are longer and more complex.

FIGURE 6.3 *The Phonetic Writer*

"My castle is broken."

The examples shown in Figures 6.1 through 6.4 came from classrooms in which the teachers actively encouraged writing. However, they never imposed a writing model on students. That is, they never wrote comments on papers because they thought such a procedure would have a negative influence on students' independent writing development. However, there is another school of thought about modeling.

FIGURE 6.4 *The Transitional Writer*

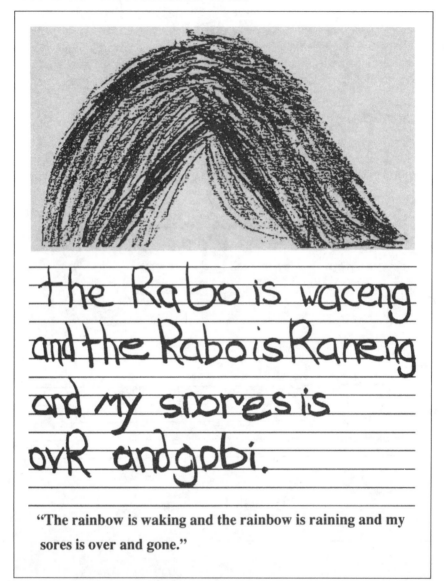

"The rainbow is waking and the rainbow is raining and my sores is over and gone."

The Teacher as Writing Model

Some whole-language teachers believe students benefit from mature writing models. The teacher may begin the school year by asking students to write. If the students indicate they cannot write, the teacher asks what they would like to write and provides the written version in the students' books. This is a kind of **language-experience activity (LEA).** Figure 6.5 shows an example of a LEA, an activity in which the teacher models mature writing for the students. This approach is contrary to the beliefs of many whole-language teachers. Parents do not write for preschool children. Rather, they encourage independent writing development, focusing on the process, not the product. Some teachers are convinced that writing development should be wholly independent, that students should be allowed the right to explore writing and to learn independently. In the school setting the teacher's model is quite powerful.

Gunderson and Shapiro (1988) found that students enrolled in programs in which teachers provided models did not exhibit the stages mentioned above. Indeed, within a month or so all of the students had become transitional writers. It would seem that the teacher's writing model accelerated students' writing development. This is not to suggest that parents should involve their children in LEA-like activities; it suggests, rather, that LEA activities are successful in

FIGURE 6.5   *Modeled Writing*

classrooms in which teachers believe in them. Parents are superb teachers and formal LEA activities would do little to improve their modeling of language.

Often, as noted earlier, students' writing does not resemble the mature model. It is important to take notes or "transcriptions" of what students write. Teachers in the first group, who did not believe in writing comments on paper, took notes at the back of students' log books or in a separate teacher log book. These notes were transcriptions of students' writing. The second group, who believed in providing students with a model, actually wrote in students' log books. They always made a positive written comment, including the essence of what students had written and, subsequently, read. (See Figure 6.6.)

FIGURE 6.6   *Teacher Emulating Writing*

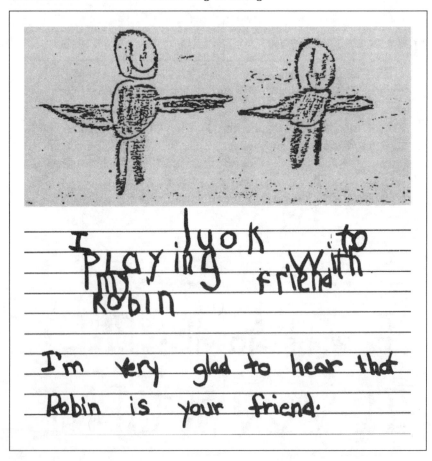

Initiating Writing in Kindergarten to Grade 3

The following is a checklist for initiating a writing program.

1. Each student is given a log book in which to write. Logs with pages divided in half, tops with no lines for illustrations, and bottoms with lines for writing are excellent.
2. All students are encouraged to write and read their writing to others every day.
3. Teachers meet with individual students to ask them to read their writing and to discuss it with them. Students are encouraged by being given positive feedback that ignores such items as invented spellings. That is, the discussion is focused on the meaning rather than the surface structure of the writing.
4. Response to students' writing is positive. Teachers who do not believe in imposing an adult model respond orally, but not in a written fashion. Those who believe in providing a model write a response containing the essence of what is written by the student.
5. Whole-language teachers keep records. Those who do not write on students' work keep careful records of what students read from their writing. Teacher transcriptions are made in the back of students' logs or in a separate teacher log book. Those who write notes on students' writing are, in effect, keeping a detailed record of growth.
6. In all cases, students' writing is dated. Indeed, the best method is to use a library dater, either borrowed from the librarian or purchased from a stationery store. (See also the section on portfolios in Chapter 12.)

In addition, students can be introduced to the microcomputer and word processor. Word processing makes it easier to rewrite, edit, and publish materials. The Bank Street Writer III is an excellent, simple word-processing program designed for grades 2 through 12. Many first-grade students as well are able to use the program. It has a spelling checker that asks writers about letter strings not found in the program's dictionary, and it focuses attention on invented spellings in a unobtrusive manner (distributed by Scholastic Inc., 1986).

Reading

The moment students begin writing, they also begin reading because they read their own materials. Whole-language teachers believe reading and writing should be enjoyable and, most importantly, meaningful, and they fill their classrooms with good books. Many critics view this procedure with some scorn, suggesting that students should be explicitly taught how to read. The essential problem is that most critics view reading as a noun and it is not, except in the sense that it is a gerund. Teaching the facts of reading like "phonics rules" is somewhat like teaching students the names of swimming strokes and expecting such knowledge to find them a place on the Olympic swimming team (see Moustafa, 1993, for example). Reading is a process and it should be taught as a process; the most efficient approach is through modeling and coaching. Elley (1991) concluded that second-language students make rapid progress when five conditions are present: incidental learning, integration, meaning focus, extensive input of meaningful print, and intrinsic motivation.

Many whole-language teachers believe language-experience activities (LEAs) help students learn to read. LEA stories are created by individuals or groups of students. The teacher tells students they are going to write a story together. Stories can be written around themes (such as holidays), classroom events, field trips, and so on, or about personal experiences. The teacher leads a discussion of the event and asks students to help create a story that the teacher writes, usually on large chart paper. LEA stories are put into books and used as part of the reading program. The traditional LEA includes teaching students to recognize words they have written. The whole-language focus, however, is on the whole story and not individual words. LEA stories, therefore, are read and discussed as wholes and, in most cases, read orally by individual students or groups of students. (LEA will be discussed later in this chapter.)

Oral Reading

Oral reading is vital to whole-language classrooms. However, the activity should be a positive experience and provide students with appropriate oral models. The teacher must not ask students to read in an unrehearsed fashion (unless it is their own writing) because it is detrimental to their reading development (see Gunderson, 1985). Parents almost never ask a three-year-old child to read aloud, unless, of course, they know the child will do it well because he or she has read it before. Their children also chime in with them as they read or reread aloud a favorite book. The bedtime story reading session is an incredible learning situation because it is positive, enjoyable, warm, nonthreatening, and supportive.

Teachers should read aloud as often as possible. As a mature reader, the teacher provides a good oral reading model. Students enjoy hearing stories read aloud. **Big books** are large-format texts, large enough for a whole class to see and to follow along or chime in. Big books can be student produced or professionally published. One of the first published big books is called *Our Big Book* and contains the story of Dick, Jane, Sally, Spot, and Puff. It was first printed in 1951 by Scott, Foresman and Company. Many adults remember this book fondly because it was the book that started them to read. As a big book it was used with whole classes or groups and it generated happy feelings of acceptance by the teacher and the other students. Indeed, this author often shows this big book to groups of adults and always gets extremely positive, often nostalgic, responses to the characters, not to the prose. In fact, the text in this big book has been criticized as being typical of reading series in that it contains bizarrely repetitious, unnatural language.

Modern big books are designed to contain stories that have more natural and interesting language. Students love to read them aloud in groups. *Impressions* (1984) is a reading program published by Holt, Rinehart and Winston; the program contains large-format big books such as *The More We Get Together,* used in shared reading sessions. Other material suitable for big book reading activities is developed by students, often stories written in themes. The stories are stapled into a big book to be shared by students. Students in one class, for instance, had written "Our Space Book." Individual students delighted in finding their particular story to be read aloud to visitors. Chapter 3, Literature in a Whole-Language Program, contains many suggestions for the use of literature, including big books. The newer form of published big books incorporates repetitive material that is written in a more natural syntactic pattern than the material in the typical basal-reader stories. Students enthusiastically chime in as the teacher reads aloud. The teacher's role in this kind of choral reading is to read with good intonation and phrasing to model good oral reading for students. If they are beginners and are not familiar with print, the teacher should track the print with a finger as it is being read. This procedure helps students track print and shows that reading should be done in phrase- and clause-length segments rather than word by word. Students can also read individual parts after they have practised.

Oral Reading Guidelines

There are two people who pay attention in the typical oral reading activity, and this does not include the teacher, as might be expected. Most of the time the teacher pays more attention to students outside the group than to the student reading, although the teacher does catch and correct bad reading. The two people who are paying attention are the reader, who has to, and the student whose turn it is to read next. The individual whose turn is coming up is counting out the number of sentences he or she thinks he or she will be asked to read. Anyone else who is paying attention, especially in the low reading group, is listening to the worst oral reading models possible, rehearsing errors. Researchers, who should know better, have discovered that teachers can get students to pay more attention by being random in the way they select students to respond. It is true, by randomly selecting students to read aloud in a reading circle, more of them are paying attention. Unfortunately, they are paying attention to the worst possible reading models. Random selection makes this deplorable situation even worse. Reading in this fashion after every story is destructive, especially for the lowest-ability readers. Some readers may indicate that, even though they are not very good at it, they enjoy reading aloud in this fashion. It's not true. Unfortunately, they have learned it's the only way they can get the teacher's attention in a nondestructive way. That is, they don't have to get into trouble to get attention.

Like choral reading, individual oral reading should always be a positive experience. Gunderson (1985) suggested three guiding principles for oral reading:

1. **Never** without preparation.
2. **Never** a great quantity.
3. **Always** in carefully structured situations.

Oral reading should always be for an audience if the goal is to improve a student's oral reading. Many traditional teachers simply have students read aloud without practice under the misguided notion that oral reading is something that should be done after every story. Their unrehearsed oral reading sessions are painful, perhaps damaging, to students. The most that can be said of them is that they take up time and do not require much planning on the teacher's part. Rather, the teacher should provide a good model to emulate so that the reader begins to focus on units larger than a word-at-a-time, fluent reading. In the simplest practice session, the teacher tells the students that they will be practicing oral reading and that they will be attempting to improve their phrasing and intonation. The following is a typical echoic reading session designed to help improve students' oral reading. Again, the goal of the lesson is not to improve comprehension, but to improve oral reading.

Teacher: Today we are going to practice and improve our oral reading skills. Please turn to page 6. Look at the first sentence. It says, "The old tiger was very unhappy with the young tiger cub." Will you please read that, Teddy?

Teddy: The old tiger was very unhappy with the young tiger cub.

Teacher: Well done, Teddy. Did you hear how well he read that sentence? Let's read it all together the same way.

The session continues in this fashion with the teacher providing the model and reinforcing the students' correct responses. As students practice oral reading in this fashion, they will improve and begin to handle larger segments of text. Often a good reader in a group can provide the model if the teacher takes care to set up the right conditions so that no invidious comparisons arise.

Students also share their reading with classmates. The atmosphere of a whole-language classroom fosters a joy of writing and reading; it produces individuals who are avid writers and readers anxious to share their work. In these cases the reading does not have to be prepared and rehearsed because students are familiar with the material since it is their own writing. Indeed, reading aloud helps students to edit their work. Listening to recordings of their own reading allows students to monitor and edit material they have written.

Language Experience

Many, but not all, whole-language teachers believe language-experience activities (LEAs) help students learn to read and write. The language-experience approach involves the teacher using students' own experiences to create stories that they dictate as students' reading material. Individual students or groups are asked to relate stories to the teacher based on their experiences in or out of the classroom. Often experiences are provided for students through field trips. Students are met individually or in small groups and are asked to tell the teacher a story, which is recorded verbatim without changes or corrections. The teacher acts as a recorder, avoiding the temptation to make corrections in students' texts. The story is then read aloud by the students. In this case, oral reading in an unrehearsed fashion is not bad because it involves their own writing. The writing functions to provide a kind of rehearsal. The teacher also reads the story aloud in order to allow students to see the words they might have in their spoken but not in their sight vocabulary.

These students are producing a new book written by members of the class. Pages have been laminated for durability.

A few days after it has been dictated, the story should be reread and discussed. The new and difficult words should be written on flashcards for sight-word practice. This means that the words are shown to the students and they read them aloud, probably practicing enough times so they accurately remember them. Practicing sight words this way is viewed by many as old fashioned. Indeed, some view it as antithetical to whole-language since the words are not practiced in context. However, since the words are personal words dictated by the student, they are meaningful. This is also the opportunity for teachers to point out particular words and spelling patterns (e.g., "Your word has the letters *ph* in it, and that's often how we spell the /f/ sound"). This is also a source of words for a personal dictionary or for spelling practice.

Individual student work can be stapled into books of collected stories. The concept of a book is quite appealing to both students and their parents. Students rehearse their stories and read them to the teacher, to their friends, to small groups of students, or to the whole class.

The teacher may wish to produce a class LEA or have small groups of students make dictations. Field trips, school assemblies, visits by the principal or the Society for the Prevention of Cruelty to Animals representative, the first snowfall of winter, the school's annual Sports Day, school holidays, world news events, and so on, all represent experiences shared by students. LEA dictations can be organized around a theme—all the monster stories, for example—to be used over and over again as they are read by students.

Vocabulary Practice and LEA

LEA stories generate many items of vocabulary that are new to students, words they should learn to recognize. They can be written on flashcards and practiced. Practice is important since the words are known to the student but may not be recognized in print. Flashing and making a game of flashing is essential.

Flashing should be thought of as a method for helping students commit to memory words that are in their working vocabulary. You cannot assume that simply showing a student a word on a flashcard means he or she has learned it. A superior approach is best summed up as: Flash, Recite, Reinforce; Flash, Recite, Reinforce, and Practice (Gunderson, 1991). This is particularly recommended for English-as-a-second language (ESL) instruction. The teacher shows the flashcard, students recite the word, and the teacher immediately reinforces the word by reciting it. It is important that the teacher reinforce correct responses orally during the practice.

Teacher:	What is this word?
Student:	Because.
Teacher:	Because, good. That word says "because."

Flashing does nothing to help students learn word meanings. Flashing is simply a method for helping students to become automatic at word recognition. Whole-language proponents suggest that vocabulary practice should focus on context. However, in this case the words are student generated so they already understand them and their task is to learn to recognize them by sight. Again, the teacher can in some cases point out particular spelling patterns.

After stories are read, including both LEA-generated stories and those published by others, the teacher often wishes to check whether students comprehended or understood them. This is the point where many teachers attempt to measure comprehension. Comprehension is much more important than being able to read aloud well, unless, of course, one is a television or radio news reader. The two are often quite separate processes. There are many students who cannot read aloud well but who comprehend the text well and there are many students who read aloud well but do not comprehend at all. The teacher should be mindful of this, especially when listening to ESL students reading. Leu and Kinzer (1991) referred to two processes: production (reading aloud) and comprehension (understanding). Most teachers believe that comprehension is the most important process.

Reading Comprehension

The goal of every twentieth-century language teacher has been to improve comprehension skills. The typical reading lesson includes the teacher asking questions before and after students read a story. Different questions require different comprehension skills. Reading educators like to refer to three or four levels of comprehension: literal, inferential, and application/evaluation comprehension. Teachers should ask questions at all levels in order to improve students' thinking skills. Indeed, it is thought that lower-level comprehension involves little more than memory.

Literal Comprehension

If students can remember details stated in text, they are comprehending at the literal level. This is the lowest level of comprehension, requiring little more than memory capacity.

Inferential Comprehension

Readers comprehend at an inferential level when they can make inferences based on material read. Answers to inferential questions are not in the surface structure of the text, but rather in the meaning or intent of the discourse.

Application/Evaluation

These terms are often separated by authors. Readers are able to read material and evaluate its worth or apply it to a new situation. The following is a sample passage and sample questions used to evaluate reading comprehension:

A Trip to School

Syd and Marion walked to school every morning, even when it was snowing heavily. One June morning the snow was blowing wildly as they neared the old wooden bridge spanning the frozen creek.

    "I don't know if we should cross in this wind," said Marion, looking down at Syd. "These winter winds are really bad this time of year." "Come on, Sis, let's try," replied Syd. The two walked onto the bridge. It vibrated in the wind. Marion panicked and stopped moving halfway across. "Don't stop now, you big chicken," screamed Syd. Marion stared at Syd, and moved. It wasn't until later while sitting at her desk that she stopped shaking.

Some Comprehension Questions

1. *How often did Syd and Marion walk to school?*
2. *Where do you think Syd and Marion live? Why?*
3. *Who was older, Syd or Marion? What makes you think so?*
4. *What would you have done if you had been Marion?*
5. *Do you think Syd's comment to Marion was appropriate? Why or why not?*

Question 1 is certainly at the literal level since the answer is stated outright in the text. Questions 2 and 3 require the reader to make an inference, a task requiring more thought. Questions 4 and 5 ask students to evaluate items in the story and apply the information to a new situation. Every reading activity should have as its goal the development of higher-level comprehension skills, unless, of course, one is reading a cookbook or an assembly manual.

The Directed Reading-Thinking Activity (DRTA)

Whole-language encourages critical thinking and independent prediction while reading. The typical textbook reading lesson does not encourage independence; the **directed reading-thinking activity (DRTA)** does. Stauffer (1971) suggested that the typical reading lesson did not encourage students to use their natural abilities to make and confirm predictions. The typical lesson, the directed reading lesson (DRL), includes the teacher directing students' comprehension of a text by teaching new vocabulary, introducing the background of a story and guiding the reading by asking them such questions as, "Read to find out, read to see if. . . ." Stauffer was convinced that the DRL put comprehension in teachers' hands. It did not allow students to take charge of their own comprehension. He developed the DRTA as an alternative to the DRL. Over the last 20 years many versions of DRTA have been developed. The version described here fits well into a whole-language lesson and has been successfully used with kindergarten through adult-level students from native English-speaking and non-native English-speaking backgrounds (Gunderson, 1984a; 1986; 1991).

The Psycholinguistic Foundations of DRTA

DRTA is based on a notion of language that features the reader as a predictor. Some years after Stauffer developed DRTA, Goodman provided a theoretical rationale based on a psycholinguistic model of language. Indeed, he proposed that reading is a "psycholinguistic guessing game" in which the reader selects "the fewest, most productive cues necessary to produce guesses which are right the first time" (Goodman, 1976, p. 498). In his view, miscues (instances in which what is read differs from what is on the page) are not always indications of poor reading. When a miscue does not alter the meaning of a sentence, it shows that the reader is comprehending what is read. Indeed, miscues show that readers are actively predicting from what they understand from print. Predictions are based on the reader's knowledge of syntax (the systematic ordering of words in English), semantics (the meaning of words), and world knowledge (knowledge gained through experience). A good illustration of the predictability of English is the sentence, "I think he is a blithering _____." I have asked hundreds of people to supply the word and have found nearly 100% agreement concerning the missing word. How? One knows from a knowledge of English syntax the word cannot be a verb or an adjective. A noun is appropriate, but not just any noun. Because the pronoun *he* comes before, an animate noun is predicted. One could not say, "I think he is a blithering door." A knowledge of semantics tells the reader that the missing word (*idiot*) is associated with a particular noun learned through experience. Nouns such as *bird, boy, rider,* or *police officer* are not appropriate.

Goodman suggested that an extremely important part of reading is "to read critically" (Goodman, 1976). He concluded, however, that "much of reading required of children in schools deters rather than promotes critical reading" (p. 496). Critical reading does not occur because students are not encouraged to predict while reading. Instead, Goodman believes, teachers teach relatively unimportant minutiae such as letter/sound correspondences. Stauffer (1971) developed the DRTA to encourage prediction.

Active prediction is the most salient feature of DRTA. This form of DRTA is extremely simple and effective. The difficult part is to find material that students have not seen before. Students are given a passage and an opaque cover. They cover the first page. They are told how much of the story to view and read at a time. For teachers in kindergarten to grade 3 classrooms, putting the story on an overhead is very effective, especially when there are students who are unable to resist the temptation to peek ahead at the story. The following will demonstrate the power of DRTA and prediction. The example is taken from a session conducted with adults. During the DRTA the teacher is allowed to ask just three questions:

1. What do you think this story is about?
2. What do you think will happen next?
3. What makes you think so?

Occasionally it is difficult to ask only these three questions. Teachers often want to ask higher-level questions. Normally, asking higher-level questions is desirable, but in DRTA, comprehension is put into the hands of students rather than teachers. Only these three questions, or variations, are allowed. All responses are accepted and only encouraging comments are made. Students are asked to uncover the title first:

The Saturday Evening Post
September-October 1973

"What do you think this story is about?" "What makes you think so?"

Typically, one receives such responses as: "It's going to be about home life because this is from a magazine that does those kinds of stories"; "It will be about life in the middle west of the United States; I think so because they did a lot of stories like that." These responses are made by adults based on their past experience. They are asked to uncover one more line of text.

Light Verse

"What do you think this story is about?" "What makes you think so?"

Many predictions are made such as, "It will contain poetry of a simple kind because of the name." More text is uncovered.

Who Can Divine the Heart of a Robot?

The predictions change at this point. The addition of an author's name also provides a great deal of information for the reader:

By Isaac Asimov

DRTA is a powerful method for developing higher-level comprehension skills at all levels. Students enjoy the activity.

DRTA—Some Questions and Answers

Q: Is DRTA a reading program?
A: DRTA is a valuable addition to a reading program, but it is not a complete reading program.

Q: How often should DRTA be used?
A: It depends, of course, on the class, but once a week is quite effective.

Q: Is DRTA effective?

A: DRTA is very effective in developing higher-level comprehension skills. The first time a teacher conducts a DRTA lesson, however, it often doesn't work too well because both teachers and students are uncertain of the procedures.

Q: Does one use DRTA with a whole class?

A: It is possible. However, DRTA works best with groups of about 10. The most effective DRTAs are conducted with interest groups. Students can be matched with stories that are of interest to them to maximize participation and motivation.

Q: How can DRTA be used with poor readers or nonreaders?

A: Passages can be read aloud to students. Teachers are constantly amazed at the predictions these students make even though they are poor readers.

Q: How does one find passages?

A: Old reading texts are good sources of stories. Old (outdated) individualized reading kits also make good DRTA passages. The May 1983 *Reading Teacher* contains a bibliography of predictable children's books (Bridge, Winograd, and Haly, 1983).

Q: What does one do about the reading problems observed during the DRTA session? Does a teacher stop to teach the skills the students are having trouble with?

A: No. This form of DRTA is dedicated to comprehension and critical reading. Nothing should interfere with making predictions and supporting them. If students have trouble with particular skills, they should be taught later, after the DRTA.

DRTA can also be used in a writing program. Students read the beginning of a story and compose an ending. After composing endings, students discuss their versions with others and compare them with the actual ending.

DRTA is not a reading program; rather, it is an exciting activity to help improve students' comprehension. DRTA is exciting because it can be extended into many different areas. Librarians use it to engage students in material they read aloud. Videotapes can be used as DRTA activities. In this case the video is stopped at different intervals and students are asked to write or respond orally to the questions noted above. DRTA can and should be used with students at all ages and of all ability levels.

Direct Approaches to Comprehension

Many teachers believe in a more direct approach to improving comprehension. The following is a sampling of ideas to increase students' comprehension based on the portion of the story presented a few pages ago. These activities are made by the teacher. As mentioned earlier, some caution must be taken, since producing comprehension activities does put students' comprehension of a story into the hands of the teacher. The following examples are based on the story "A Trip to School" referred to earlier. The first exercise focuses on higher-level comprehension.

Character Evaluation

When Syd _____*I thought he was being* _____ *because* _____.
I thought Marion was _____ *when she*
_____ *because* _____.

This exercise is open ended in that students select the character trait and support it with details they remember or infer from the story. An even more directed approach is to isolate story elements and concepts to be included in the evaluation.

Marion is Syd's older sister:

Agree   Agree   Neither Agree   Disagree   Disagree
Completely   Nor Disagree   Completely
because _____

Syd and Marion live in Canada:

Agree   Agree   Neither Agree   Disagree   Disagree
Completely   Nor Disagree   Completely
because _____

Marion was too afraid to cross the bridge:

Agree   Agree   Neither Agree   Disagree   Disagree
Completely   Nor Disagree   Completely
because _____

Students put an "X" over one of the agree statements and then support their choice with a comment. The exercise can be designed to focus on particular events or items in a story thought to be important. Of course, the teacher makes the judgment. The five categories can also be changed to represent other traits such as happy/unhappy and friendly/unfriendly.

Another measure of comprehension is a story map, one showing the sequence of events occurring in the story. The map contains statements supporting each event. Students can also be asked to judge different statements over the course of a story by making a bar graph.

Marion is afraid . . .

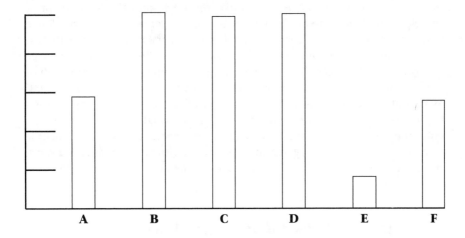

A: *As they neared the old wooden bridge.* B: *As they walked onto the bridge.*
C: *As they felt the bridge vibrate.* D: *When Syd screamed at her.* E: *After they crossed the bridge.* F: *After they arrived at school.*

A: *because* _____
B: *because* _____
C: *because* _____
D: *because* _____
E: *because* _____
F: *because* _____

Students draw in the bar graph and make supporting statements for each estimation. The activity requires the reader to make inferences and support them with statements. Readers must make inferences and critical judgments to estimate different characteristics that are not explicitly stated in text.

Activities should be designed to focus attention away from the surface structure of writing to meaning. Questions focusing on surface structure do not normally require higher-level thinking. Activities should always require students to process, think about, and judge the meaning of the material they read. There are many ideas to improve comprehension. Most are developed by teachers in response to the needs of their students. Comprehension exercises should always be designed to develop higher-level comprehension skills, unless, of course, remembering details of a particular passage is required. For example, one would certainly want a physician-to-be to be able to read an anatomy text and remember all the details of the human nervous system. Everyone has to remember details sometimes. The essential challenge is for the teacher to strike a balance in the variety of questions he asks students.

Current socio-cognitive and constructivist views of literacy suggest that students are active participants in the creation of meaning. From this view, learners interact with information and interpret it, and the learners' prior knowledge and purpose are important in making sense of the world. Since learning usually occurs in social contexts, the learners' relationship with others is an important factor in the interpretive process. Students learn language not by being told directly but by interacting with others in the completion of tasks in meaningful and functional settings (Langer, 1991; Moustafa, 1993). As a result of such current thinking, much more attention in reading comprehension is focused on bringing the background knowledge of the reader to the task, on making and confirming predictions, on schematic cues (webs, semantic maps, etc.), on mental imagery, on responding to literature in affective ways, and on learning to ask critical questions about text.

Phonics and Word Recognition

There is a mystique about phonics and phonics instruction. Some believe that there should be direct phonics instruction, that teachers should insist that classes of first-grade students learn by heart such rules as "When two vowels go walking, the first does the talking," a classic phonics generalization, because this will help them "crack the code" and learn to read. (For example, in a word like *read*—how did you pronounce it?—according to the rule, the vowel sound of the first vowel grapheme is long and therefore should be read to rhyme with *reed*.) The problem with such generalizations is quite simple. Our spelling system represents the way our English words were pronounced during the seventeenth century. The system doesn't work so well any more because symbol/sound relationships are not very regular or consistent. In fact, Clymer (1963) found that this particular phonics generalization worked about 45% of the time, and most of the time it did not work for decoding the English spelling of common first-grade words. Phonics, the system of rules advocated by many, teaches generalizations that don't qualify themselves as rules or facts because they are often inaccurate in predicting spelling.

There is another problem with the phonics method: Reading is a process and phonics instruction does not teach process. Many phonics proponents are convinced that reading teachers should get back to teaching phonics, but the truth is that in all the history of reading instruction, beginning some 3,000 years before the birth of Christ, reading teachers never have taught phonics. Ancient Greek reading teachers taught their students to read by reading aloud together, their students chiming in with them. They practiced reading syllables aloud. The ancient Roman reading teachers taught their students to read by reading aloud together, their students chimed in with them (Mathews, 1966). They made a game of reading syllables aloud. Phonics was easy because every letter represented one phoneme or sound in the language. Both Greek and Roman teachers didn't teach phonics rules, they taught students to recognize syllables (Mathews, 1966). You can learn to read Greek today in about 30 minutes. Of course, you won't understand a word, but you will be able to produce them orally, a sound at a time. The difference between oral and silent reading will be discussed later. When teachers first started to teach students to read English using the Roman alphabet, they found they had difficulties. Indeed, teaching students the alphabet didn't work well. In 1620, Charles Hoole (cited in Mathews, 1966) noted that some students who were asked to memorize the alphabet "have been thus learning a whole year together (and though they have been much chid and beaten too for want of heed) could scarce tell six of their letters at twelve months' end."

Some whole-language teachers are a bit uneasy about students learning "basic skills." They are often asked, "Is my child learning phonics?" The following section is a primer on phonics and word recognition to provide a background in terminology. This is followed by a section on skills instruction through whole-language activities. The inclusion of a phonics primer does not mean that teachers should teach phonics directly to all students. It is included to provide an overview of phonics and an introduction to phonics terminology. The teacher must judge whether phonics skills should be taught directly and to whom, a judgment based on careful observations of students' reading and writing behaviors and an understanding of the individual child's immediate and long-term needs.

A Phonics Primer

1. Phonetics: the study of speech sounds
2. Phonology: the study of the way speech sounds form patterns in language
3. Phonemes: the distinctive sounds of a particular language
4. Morphemes: minimal units of meaning
   a. Free morphemes can stand alone, e.g., *man, sick*
   b. Bound morphemes cannot stand alone, e.g., *-ist, -ly*
5. Graphemes: a visual symbol used to represent phonemes or morphemes
6. Allographs: different forms of a grapheme, e.g., *E, e*
7. Vowel graphemes: the letters *a, e, i, o, u*, sometimes *y* and *w* in English
8. Consonant graphemes: *b, c, d, f, g, h, j, k, l, m, n, p, q, r, s, t, v, w, x, z*
9. Initial consonants: consonant graphemes occurring at the beginning of words, e.g., *b*ad
10. Final consonants: consonant graphemes occurring at the end of words, e.g., ba*d*

11. Medial consonants: consonant graphemes occurring in the middle of words, e.g., bi*t*er

12. Consonant blend: two or three consonant graphemes that represent two phonemes, e.g., *br*ight and *str*ip (initial), du*mp* (final)

13. Consonant digraph: two or three consonants representing one phoneme, e.g., *sh*ip, *ch*it (initial), bun*ch*, wi*sh*, wi*tch* (final)

14. Short vowel: the vowel sounds heard in the words b*a*t, b*e*t, b*i*t, c*o*t, b*u*t

15. Long vowel: the vowel sounds heard in the words b*ai*t, b*ee*t, b*i*te, b*oa*t, c*u*te

16. Vowel digraph: two vowel graphemes producing one phoneme, e.g., b*ai*t, d*ea*d, l*ea*d

17. Diphthong: the vowel sounds heard in such words such as b*oy*, t*oy*, and av*oi*d

18. Phonogram: sometimes called word families, these are spelling patterns such as *-an, -it, -eigh, -ut*

19. Affixes: bound morphemes such as *-ly and un-*

20. Prefix: bound morphemes occurring at the beginning of words, e.g., *un*-happy, *dis*service

21. Suffix: bound morphemes occurring at the end of words, e.g., man*ly*, won-der*ful*

22. Root word: the morpheme around which more complex words are constructed, such as un*man*ly, *sign*ature, *fact*ory, and *phono*graph. Note that many root words are from Greek or Latin, as in factory and phono-graph.

23. Base word: a word to which prefixes and suffixes can be added to make new words, e.g., un*happy*

24. Phonics: the study of the relationship of graphemes and phonemes

25. Phonic generalization: sometimes called phonics or phonic rules, a generalization states a grapheme/phoneme relationship that occurs in English spelling such as "when two vowels go walking the first does the talking," meaning that in a word such as *road* the long sound of the first vowel is heard. This is phonic generalization because sometimes it doesn't work, as in the word *read* (past tense), so it can't be a rule.

26. Sight words: these are words students recognize at sight. Some teachers teach sight words because they account for a great deal of the vocabulary in reading texts. They use different words lists as sources of sight words such as *the, have, come, is,* and *was* because they are not pronounced the way they are spelled and so must be learned by memorization. The **Inner-City word list** (Gunderson,1984a), discussed next, is a good example of a corpus of words that accounts for as much as 50 to 70% of the vocabulary in initial reading texts.

Skills Instruction through Writing Activities

Students should come to understand that certain letters or letter combinations represent sounds and/or spelling patterns. Whole-language teachers generally believe students come to learn such correspondences through meaningful reading and writing activities. There is even some evidence that students learn phonics by learning and recognizing a corpus of print words first, rather than the other way around (Moustafa, 1993). Whole-language teachers know phonics and phonics terminology. They are able to observe students' writing and discover which phonic generalizations students do not know and cannot apply. It has been shown that students in whole-language programs learn to recognize and spell high-frequency words found in reading texts and word lists (Gunderson and Shapiro, 1988). Figure 6.7 is a word list produced by analyzing the writing of students in grades 2, 5, 8, and 11 in inner-city schools. The list is important because it shows that students from different backgrounds, including ESL students, produce in their writing all of the usual high-frequency vocabulary found in reading series and on other word lists. It accounts for substantial portions of vocabulary found in basal readers (Gunderson, 1984b) and can be used as a checklist to ensure that students are learning essential vocabulary. Indeed, students appear to learn to write the high-frequency words teachers believe are important for them to learn. The teacher who is afraid that students are not learning basic sight words can make a checklist of the words in this figure, and tally the words produced by their students to compare their development. In most cases, students writing their own text will correctly produce most of the important high-frequency words in English (Gunderson and Shapiro, 1988).

Some teachers have a different perspective and attempt to ensure that their students learn skills by providing activities designed to involve them directly. So, for instance, the teacher identifies a particular skill, such as knowledge of the phonics relationship of *ch* (i.e., the letters *ch* represent the voiceless alveolar fricative heard at the beginning of the word *chump*), that the students do not seem to produce accurately. It may be that six students have written words that are normally spelled with *ch* as invented spellings. The teacher wants to make certain they learn the phonic relationship:

Teacher:	Today we are going to be talking about the sounds associated with these two letters. (Shows them the word check written on a small individual chalkboard.) Does anyone know what this word is? Yes, Jenny, the word is *check*. See the letters that are underlined, they make what sound? Yes, they make the /ch/ sound. Will everyone please write another word on your chalk-

FIGURE 6.7   *Rank Order List of Inner-City Words*

the*	then*	other	talk	say*	again*
to*	get*	has	their*	wanted	an*
and*	what*	into	around*	way	call*
you*	there*	nice	ever	back	end
he*	about*	too*	everything	can't	happy
is*	all*	play*	inside	doesn't	helps
I*	good*	hope*	looked	family	knew
a*	this*	much*	most	keep*	little*
me*	see*	some*	over*	kind*	next
it*	bad*	take*	since	lot	pick*
in*	out*	father	try*	name	problem
my*	will*	something	walking	only*	same
she*	boy*	us*	come*	them	seen
was*	just*	got*	didn't	together	still
for*	saw*	could*	found*	did*	sure
of*	up*	how*	house	doing	walk*
that*	they*	even	well*	eat*	won't
your*	or*	help*	work*	goes*	year
his*	had*	no*	after*	last	big*
so*	want*	now*	each	need	class
with*	go*	life	give*	our*	close
have*	please*	might	problems	she's	coming
when*	think*	care	said*	should	door
very*	always*	he's	told	two	down*
but*	school	it's	also	use*	funny*
can*	who*	more	birthday	walked	gets
her*	from*	by*	first*	which*	gives
we*	love	fun	look*	another	left
like*	fine	home	sick	before*	let*
on*	tell*	make*	teacher	brother	living
because*	would*	sometimes	that's	food	made
not*	day*	came*	years	its*	makes
do*	at*	does*	am*	looks	night
if*	why*	were*	any*	lots	somebody
don't	man*	I'm*	anything	many*	wish
him*	as*	been*	away*	may*	write
are*	things*	money	long*	off*	wrong
know*	went*	open	looking	sister	
be*	took	put*	mom	than	
mother	going*	really	never*	thing	
one*	opened	right*	old*	yourself	

*Included on Dolch list.

Source: From "One Last Word List" by L. Gunderson, 1984, *The Alberta Journal of Educational Research, 30,* page 263. Copyright 1984. Reprinted by permisison.

	board that has the sound /ch/. Excellent, we have all written many good *ch* words. Please read your words out loud.
Students:	(Each student reads his or her word aloud. Often they are asked to explain a word.)
Teacher:	I like your word *chukul*, Darlene. When you see the word *chuckle* in a book, it looks like this. (Writes *chuckle* on a small flashcard.) Here is your word. (Hands the word card to Darlene. The teacher makes similar comments and writes each student's word on a small flashcard.) Today we are going to write stories with as many *ch* words as possible. Let's read your words again. (Each student reads his or her word.)

After each student has read his or her word aloud, the teacher directs attention to a book cover he has prepared, one containing the title "Our Great CH Book." The teacher shows the first page of the book and asks each student to paste his or her word on it. Finally, they write stories using as many words as they can containing *ch*. The pages are assembled and form another "big book." In this case, however, the book has been made by the students themselves. Students read their stories and those of others. In this manner a particular skill is introduced and reinforced through writing. This is a phonics lesson, one that is considerably more humane and effective than having students circle the *ch* in hundreds of words in a workbook or listen to a teacher lecture on digraphs.

Teachers often ask about what skills should be taught, and which are the important phonics skills and the important word recognition skills. The answer is, of course, the important skills to teach are those that the students need to learn. *The Reading Teacher's Book of Lists* by Fry, Polk, and Fountoukidis (1984) is an excellent source of phonics skills, spelling families, prefixes, suffixes, and so on. Students' work should be monitored in order to assess the skills they might have to learn. The teacher who is convinced that direct phonics instruction is important will likely focus on the most reliable phonic generalizations. Gunderson (1991) has identified a series of phonics relationships that are fairly regular and a sequence in which to teach them. He has suggested that simple CVC words such as *cat, fat, hit,* and *sit* are fairly regular and may be introduced first. His book is designed for teachers of ESL students, but the suggestions are appropriate for non-ESL students. Again, there is no good consistent evidence that the direct teaching of phonics to students results in superior reading performance. There are individuals who try to convince the public that the simple remedy for all of the ills of education is a return to phonics instruction and that there is research to support it. Neither contention is true.

Draft Books

Many teachers believe students should "practice" writing. Indeed, they believe students should learn that good writing is a result of writing, editing, and rewriting. Many whole-language teachers provide their students with "draft books" in which to master the art of writing. Chapter 5, The Writing Connection, discusses the writing process in greater detail. Primary teachers must always be cautious about having primary students rewrite because they often tire easily of the task.

Intermediate Students (Grades 4 through 8) and Whole-Language

Whole-language instruction is typically found in kindergarten to third-grade classrooms. Whole-language instruction has begun to be found in grades 4 through 8 (intermediate levels) and secondary classrooms (grades 9 through 12). In quite a number of schools there is a great tension that has developed between primary and intermediate teachers. Primary students in whole-language classes produce more complex written compositions than many fourth-grade students in non-whole-language classes because they do not dread writing but enjoy it (Gunderson, Shapiro, and Froese, 1988).

In many respects, introducing, initiating, and maintaining a whole-language program with older students is more difficult than it is with younger students because of the attitudes they have usually developed concerning writing. Typically, they associate writing with "school work"; they have learned that any writing they turn in will be scrutinized and filled with red marks and, yes, a grade. Whole-language teachers often face a great deal of negative comment from their fellow intermediate teachers. You should try to implement as many strategies as you feel comfortable doing. Writing strategies are often the easiest to implement. Again, Chapter 5 is the one to read concerning intermediate writing programs.

The following is a discussion about initiating a program with students who have already learned that school means meticulous concentration on the learning of individual skills. Intermediate students will most likely not have been enrolled in whole-language classrooms. They will have, then, the usual expectations about what is required of them in writing. It is best to explain very carefully that the whole-language approach is probably different from what they may have experienced before. The teacher should explain that he or she believes that reading and writing are the two most enjoyable and important activities in his or her life. He or she wants them to come to know the joys of reading and writing. Each student should be given a log book. It should be explained that the teacher will read the log book and react to it, but will not make any of the usual "teacher" marks and notations or "grade" it. The teacher also writes independently. On certain days, after writing what she or he thinks is an especially interesting, beautiful, or meaningful passage, the teacher reads it to the class. Students are encouraged to do the same and are made comfortable with reading their own material aloud and allowing others to read their material. In addition, students will be reading many different books, which are, for the most part, those that are of interest to them; they will not read one assigned reading text.

Individualized Reading

For years students have been grouped for reading instruction, usually into three groups. There is no real substantive rationale behind the process, but rather a belief that three groups is the most efficient way to instruct students. Many teachers, however, believe there are definite negative features attached to the approach. First, students, once placed into a group, become stigmatized if they happen to be in the low group. Second, once placed in a group, students seldom escape. That is, once they have been labeled as "low" readers, they stay that way forever. Third, regardless of the range of abilities of a group, teachers tend to "teach to the average" so that the needs of different ability levels are not, in fact, met (see Persell, 1993). One procedure that seeks to teach every student at his or her level is individualization.

For both primary and intermediate students there are three basic objectives in individualization:

1. To allow students to select their own reading material from a wide selection of appropriate material
2. To provide students with reading material that is appropriate for their abilities, skills, needs, interests, and motivations
3. To provide teachers with the opportunity to monitor, assess, and measure students' reading progress in order to plan and maintain appropriate individual instructional programs

One role of teachers in whole-language programs is to provide guidance. Their basic goal is to structure the learning environment so that it is comfortable, natural, and holistic. Teachers may guide students in choosing reading material, but they should never interfere with students' choices. Instead, teachers should inform students about interesting reading material in order to encourage students to read in new areas. Indeed, if teachers do not act as guides, students may never learn about exciting new kinds of reading. Whole-language classrooms should have collections of books, magazines, and other reading materials. Chapter 4, Literature in a Whole-Language Program, contains advice on selecting good literature. The following discussion will focus on materials that are of interest to students generally and to different subgroups of students specifically. They provide for the wide range of abilities and interests that teachers should consider when developing an individualized reading program.

Primary and Intermediate Procedures and Activities

The following discussion will focus on materials that are of interest to students generally and to different subgroups specifically at both the primary and intermediate grade levels.

Selecting and Maintaining a Classroom Reading Collection

Students' interests should be discovered as quickly as possible. The quickest method is to ask. A class is assembled and the teacher takes notes as students talk.

Teacher:	I have always been interested in stories about ghosts. I have just finished reading a book by Richard Peck that tells the story of a ghost in New Orleans. Some of the other things I am interested in are photography, skin diving, and traveling in places like Tibet. Tell me, John, what are you interested in and what have you read lately?
John:	I just read a comic book about the deceptacons. I like transformers, robots, and all kinds of science stuff about space.

As each student speaks, the teacher records comments and makes notes about students' interests and recent reading activities. Usually, about one-third of a class will not have read anything other than assigned school texts.

After students' interests are tallied, they are categorized and used to identify interest groups. The following shows a portion of an interest survey report:

	Ghosts?	Adventure?	Science Fiction?	Young Women's?
John		X	X	
Frank			X	
Ted			X	
Andrea	X			X
Louise				X
Joanne		X		

The interest survey is used to select materials and to form interest groups. For instance, Andrea and Louise can be directed to the collection of books written for their age group that are available in the "book corner" or the library. One could compose a written interest survey, but caution should be taken because students often perceive them as being just another assignment. The oral survey is more flexible than the written form since the teacher can pursue subinterests.

The school librarian and the local public librarian are invaluable resources for reading teachers. They know about high-interest low-vocabulary texts designed primarily for boys that contain highly motivating stories with limited vocabulary requirements. Fearon Pitman Publisher, in Belmont, California, publishes a series of fascinating science fiction stories that are written using easy vocabulary. The *Galaxy 5* series (1979) contains such titles as *Good-bye Earth, On the Red World, Vacation in Space, Dead Moon, Where No Sun Shines,* and *King of the Stars.* Field Educational Publications, in San Francisco, publishes *The Checkered Flag Series* (1968), containing stories about cars and racing with such titles as *Wheels, Riddler, Bearcat, Smashup,* and *Grand Prix.* The Bowmar Publishing Corporation of Glendale, California (1968 to 1971), produced high-interest very low-vocabulary texts such as *Slot Car Racing, Motorcycles, Surfing, Dune Buggy Racing, VW Bugs,* and *Drag Racing.* Often, school districts have multiple copies of these kinds of books. They can be used to form instructional groups around interests. School storerooms often have discarded but useful material such as old reading series and reading kits. Old materials, such as Individualized Reading Kits, are valuable because they contain graded material that can be used as DRTA passages or interest stories.

Integrated Reading and Writing Conferences

A whole-language program demands that the teacher keep in close contact with individual students to monitor their reading and writing progress. The conference is the most difficult part of the program. Since students read and write independently, their work is unique. Teachers respond, question, and monitor individual student progress. A teacher's conference book records who has been seen, when they were seen, and what was discussed during the meeting. The primary goal of a conference is to monitor, encourage, and guide a student's progress in reading and writing. Traditionally, conferences were held to monitor reading development. In the whole-language classroom, both reading and writing programs are individualized and must be monitored.

There are three basic systems; two of them are the regularly scheduled conference and the teacher-initiated conference based on student progress. In the first case, the teacher publishes a regular conference schedule. So, for example, Terry always meets with her teacher at 9:30 on Thursday mornings. This system is limited by its inflexibility. Often schedules are interrupted by activities such as assemblies, hot dog sales, and fire drills.

The second approach is for the teacher to monitor his or her conference log and call on students when needed. There is no regular schedule. The basic limitation of this approach is that some students may be missed if the teacher does not monitor the conference log accurately. The major complaint about the individualized approach is that teachers find there is not enough time in a week to conduct good conferences with everyone.

A third alternative is for the student to schedule a conference when help is needed with a specific task or project. At times, students will be updating their portfolios and will need to confer with the teacher on how to prepare for a student-parent conference or some other upcoming event. This alternative develops student initiative and responsibility.

Accurate and careful note taking by the teacher is the most important aspect of conferencing. The following is an example of a conference log:

Conference Log

Name _____

Date _____

Story/Chapter/Book _____

Recall _____

_____

Comprehension _____

_____

Recommendation(s) _____

_____

_____

Skills needs _____

Next reading? _____

Oral reading analysis _____

_____

Writing (Dated) _____

Subject _____

Invented spellings _____

_____

Grammar/structure _____

Suggestions _____

A three-ring binder with alphabetical tabs is a convenient conference log for recording formal conference sessions. The teacher tries to obtain as much information as possible about a student's progress and needs. The conference session may include the student reading aloud, retelling a favorite section of a book he or she is reading, reading from his or her writing log, being tested on particular skills, or being taught selected skills.

Group conferences are a possibility. Interest groups make for the best cooperative conferences. So, for instance, a teacher can have a conference with the science fiction group.

Information about students can be gained in other ways. The teacher constantly observes and monitors individuals during the day and takes notes, either mental or actual. These notes can be incorporated into the teacher's conference log or into the student-teacher cooperative log.

The Student-Teacher Cooperative Log

The student-teacher cooperative log allows students and teachers to communicate in a written fashion. It is a notebook in which students write about their daily progress. Since the students also write daily in an independent writing log about things that interest them, they in fact maintain two types of writing logs, the independent log and the student-teacher cooperative log. Many teachers reserve a 10-minute period at the end of the day for writing in cooperative logs. Teachers read the logs each day and make written responses. Students are directed to write about how they think they are progressing, what they would like to read next, what has been particularly interesting to them in their current reading, or what they think they need to learn in reading or writing. One way to monitor students' progress in reading is to direct them to answer the basic DRTA questions in their logs about stories they are reading. This is an especially good exercise for students reading novels.

Another valuable assessment tool is the teacher's clipboard. Whole-language teachers make many observations, suggestions, conclusions, assessments, and recommendations to different students during the day. An easy way to keep track of such items is to carry a clipboard with sheets of mailing labels attached. That is, the kinds of mailing labels that come on 8" x 10" sheets that can be individually pulled off. As a suggestion or observation is made, the student's name and the suggestion is written on one of the mailing labels on the top sheet of labels. At the end of the day the teacher reviews the labels and places them in appropriate places. For instance, the label that says "Bob Smith— needs new log book" goes into the teacher's planning book as a reminder. The label that says "Jane Cribbs—completed dinosaur project, needs final typing" gets placed into the student's work folder as a reminder for her to get her project to the word-processing center.

Assessment and Skills Instruction

Many teachers are uneasy about having students select and read their own books because they want to know more about students' needs, skills, and abilities. In fact, many teachers want to teach the skills that students need to learn. In this respect, conferences are important. In addition, the most important assessment involves the students' writing.

Writing—An Assessment Gold Mine

It was noted earlier that students' writing was not graded in the traditional fashion. However, students' writing should be viewed as a gold mine of vital skills information. Whole-language teachers scrutinize their students' writing, carefully noting invented spellings, grammatical errors, usage errors, and interests. In those cases in which they see consistent patterns, they use the information

These students are involved in group composing activities that will require oral presentation.

to form instructional groups. So, for instance, one teacher noted that a great many of her students were inventing different spellings for words ending with *le* as in *tumble, trouble,* and so on. She called together the group of six students who were having the difficulty and conducted a lesson similar to the *ch* lesson described earlier.

The computer can be used to generate rank-order lists of students' written vocabularies and lists of spelling difficulties for both entire classes and individual students. Using the computer to record students' writing over the period of a year also gives valuable information about skills development. This tool does require the teacher to put students' work into a computer. Local computer experts are usually willing to help find appropriate computer programs. This author, in conjunction with a computer programmer, has developed a vocabulary analysis program available on request that analyzes spelling and vocabulary development.

Many school activities involving reading have to do with students learning from text. That is, students are asked to read to learn from, say, a science book. Learning from text is important and is often referred to as *content reading*. There are thousands of content activities. Indeed, there are entire texts devoted to content reading (see, for example, *Content Area Reading* by Vacca and Vacca [1993]). The following examples help develop students' comprehension of content texts.

Prediction Activities

DRTA uses a student's ability to predict to improve comprehension. This ability can be used in another activity designed to be used with content material such as science.

Content Prediction Activity

1. Before students are given a passage, they brainstorm and list all of the things they know about the subject of the passage they are to read. This procedure works best with groups of about four to five students each. Students often work better when they have a worksheet. The following information, printed on top of a page, functions as a brainstorming worksheet. In this case, the passage to be read is about scorpions.

Scorpions

Things known and predicted   Things not predicted

2. After students have developed independent lists, they are asked to read them. As they do, the ideas are written on the chalkboard. The teacher plays "dumb" and asks students to explain their ideas, a procedure that reinforces ideas and teaches them, in a benign fashion, to other students.
3. Students are told to read a passage and to check off items they correctly predicted and note items they did not predict.
4. After students independently read the passage, they check off correct items and note new items as a group.
5. The teacher directs attention to the chalkboard and checks off items correctly predicted, asking students to clarify items for her. Any item not found in text that was predicted should be researched. Items found but not predicted are written on the chalkboard with the teacher asking for clarification of certain items.

The silent reading portion of this prediction activity is seldom silent. Students talk to each other about what they are reading, congratulating each other for making accurate predictions and noting items they did not predict, usually by saying, "I didn't know that." Students enjoy the prediction activity and learn a great deal. Indeed, the teacher can use such a session as an assessment period by monitoring students' discussions. In this manner, the teacher learns students' conceptions and misconceptions about particular subjects.

Some passages lend themselves to a different activity. The teacher identifies an issue discussed in a particular passage. For example, graphology, called the science of handwriting, has recently been discussed in newspapers. I selected an article describing the basic tenets of graphology. Before students were given the passage, they were asked to form into groups and consider the following worksheet (spread out on a standard page).

Graphology Is a Science That Can Reveal a Person's Personality

Before Reading

Agree		Disagree

After Reading

Agree		Disagree

Each group was asked to come up with as many statements as they could to support or refute the statement. The procedure is the same as the preceding one, with statements being written on the board to be discussed by the teacher. After groups have discussed, and indeed debated, the issues, the passage is handed out. After the reading, students again discuss the topic and reformulate their statements supporting or not supporting the issue. This procedure works well in such areas as social studies where students are asked to consider issues. When a group of adults read the passage on graphology, for instance, they concluded that the newspaper account was inaccurate and full of misleading statements. They had become critical readers, exactly what reading teachers should strive for.

Students can be asked to write a passage about a particular subject after they have brainstormed and discussed ideas. Each group reads its passage aloud to the class. Afterward they are given the prepared passage. Students compare their version with the actual passage. Another version includes the teacher introducing the title of the passage to be read along with a list of vocabulary words selected from the article. Students discuss the topic and the vocabulary items, then write a brief article of their own containing the words the teacher has provided. Again, the original is compared with students' versions. This procedure is an excellent activity that helps students clarify their ideas.

All of these activities could and should be adapted for different classes and different students. The brainstorming activities are wonderful for group assessments. The worksheets containing students' predictions reveal what students know about a subject. A teacher does not have to teach items that everyone already knows. Prediction activities are not quiet sessions. Students become actively interested and vocal in their reading. They talk to each other during the reading session, confirming and reconfirming ideas, exclaiming their surprise at new material and generally enjoying discovering material they did not predict.

In general, teachers should realize that there is more knowledge in the world than any one individual can or should learn. Indeed, there is a great deal of knowledge that is frankly not worth knowing. Gunderson (1995) developed a knowledge matrix to guide teachers' selection of material to be taught. The following is his knowledge matrix:

A Knowledge Matrix

	Know That	Know How
Must		
Should		
Want To		

Gunderson noted:

> *The table classifies knowledge in two basic categories; to "know that" and to "know how." The "know that" category represents basic knowledge of facts, reality. Electricity kills, London is in England, Washington is the capital of the U.S., and Water is wet are examples of the kind of knowledge found in this category. To "know how" represents such items as to know how to swim, to know how to drive a car, to know how to make bread, and to know how to read, the latter being of utmost importance to us, let's hope. As teachers we are concerned with both categories of knowledge, but in three ways: 1) knowledge that students "must" acquire; 2) knowledge that students "should" acquire (we are convinced for some good reason); and, 3) knowledge students "want" to acquire. (p. 47)*

Whole-language teachers decide what should be included in the curriculum based on many different decisions. There are several alternatives we have as teachers: "1) we can assume that our curriculum guides accurately isolate important information; 2) we can assess our curriculum guides and determine what *we* think is important to teach and for students to learn; 3) we can independently identify items we consider are important to be learned; or 4) we can evaluate the lives of our students and identify information that appears important for them to learn" (Gunderson, 1995). In addition, the teacher must teach the skills that equip students to deal with the difficult content reading skills required for them to learn from content texts.

Many teachers find the requirements of whole-language instruction, especially individualization, time consuming and extremely fatiguing (Walmsley and Adams, 1993). Publishers do produce materials and programs that can ease the teacher's burden with some aspects of their programs. A section at the end of this chapter presents an annotated bibliography of materials.

Whole-Language Programs

It may appear that whole-language teachers must design and produce their own literacy programs. Some teachers believe this is the only thoughtful way to proceed, that programs developed by other individuals are not acceptable. Some publishers, however, have begun to produce what they call "whole-language programs." Several of these programs are listed in a materials section at the end of this chapter. The reader should review them critically. One approach is to rate materials by whether they follow the principles of whole-language as outlined in the first chapter.

Student Control of Learning

Students should become empowered to take control of their own learning. The traditional classroom fosters the belief that the teacher is the ultimate expert, the one who knows all the answers. Students' primary goal is to answer teachers' questions, the correct answer being one the teacher already knows. Learning is traditionally controlled by teachers. They know what to ask; therefore, they know what students should learn. In many respects, having teachers in control trivializes learning. Indeed, it may be unnecessary to teach a student something because she already knows it. It may be a waste of time to teach a student something because it is meaningless to him. How often has the average person had to know the average rainfall in Arizona or know how many metric tons of pineapples Hawaii produces in a year? The knowledge matrix helps guide the teacher in deciding what is important for the students to learn.

Students know about their own learning and evaluation (see also Chapter 12). They can provide teachers with valuable information about their own learning to guide the teacher's planning. They should be given the time and the opportunity to take control of their own learning, to determine for themselves what they need to learn. In whole-language classrooms, students choose the books they wish to read and they choose the material they want to explore and learn about. They become empowered and take control of their own learning. The whole-language teacher's task is to help, guide, assist, and support students' efforts. It is not possible to describe everything a teacher must or must not do to encourage such student control. The process is most successful when it is slowly developed, deliberately planned, and carefully guided. Students gain control of their learning when they are able to see what learning is meaningful to them, and to view the teacher as a thoughtful resource to help guide their progress. The whole-language classroom is an environment that fosters students' independent control of learning. Students become active, interested learners who are willing to explore and take chances in learning.

Conclusion

Reading is viewed by whole-language educators as an integral part of all the language arts. Students read and write as soon as they enter the classroom. Indeed, many teachers introduce whole-language activities in kindergarten. Instructional activities focus on whole stories rather than single skills. Students read their writing to teachers, classmates, the principal, and parents. They read stories from books containing good, meaningful literature. Students share the stories they read and write. Through the act of writing, students learn word recognition and phonics skills.

Some teachers are uncomfortable with students learning reading and spelling skills independently through writing without direct instruction. They survey their students' writing to ascertain students' needs, and design programs to teach students skills in a holistic, humane manner.

Exercises to improve comprehension such as DRTA and content prediction are developed to focus on higher-level thinking processes and meaning construction. Whole-language classrooms encourage students to use their natural abilities to make and confirm predictions as they read. To improve comprehension and motivation in learning to read, whole-language teachers assess students' interests and provide a wide range of reading materials to match them. Finally, whole-language teachers maintain individualized language arts programs, designed to match the interests, motivations, needs, and skills of their students. Individualization is achieved through careful monitoring of students' progress. The whole-language teacher considers what he or she teaches to students. There is a vast amount of knowledge, some of which students must learn, need to learn, and want to learn. It is essential for teachers to understand that they must make decisions about what is to be taught and learned in the classroom.

One so-called problem with whole-language classrooms is that they encourage individual progress. In effect, they may be promoting even wider variation in student achievement since they are not restricted by common materials, especially in those cases in which they also develop students who are in control of their own learning. In a typical first-grade classroom, for instance, it is not unusual to find some students as nonreaders and some as third-grade-level readers. In the whole-language classroom, one may find some nonreaders as well as students who read at the sixth-grade level. Teachers may have a difficult time planning for the wider variation of achievement! Keeping up with students is a challenge and a joy.

REFERENCES

Bridge, C. A., Winograd, P. & Haly, D. (1983). Using predictable materials vs. preprimers to teach beginning sight words. *The Reading Teacher, 36 (9)*, 884–91.

Chow, M. (1986). Measuring the growth of writing in the kindergarten and grade one years: How are the ESL children doing? *TESL Canada Journal, 4*, 35–47.

Clymer, T. (1963) The utility of forty-five phonics generalizations. *The Reading Teacher, 6 (13)*, pp. 56–89.

Dahl, K. L. (1993). Children's spontaneous utterances during early reading and writing instruction in a whole-language classroom. *Journal of Reading Behavior, 25 (3)*, 279–294.

DeFord, D. E. (1980). Young children and their writing. *Theory Into Practice, 19*, 157–162.

Dyson, A. H. (1981). Oral language: The rooting system for learning to write. *Language Arts, 58*, 776–784.

Elley, W. B. (1991). Acquiring literacy in a second language: The effect of book-based programs. *Language Learning, 41*, 375–411.

Ferreiro, E. (1986). The interplay between information and assimilation in beginning literacy. In W. H. Teale & E. Sulzby (Eds.), *Emergent literacy: Writing and reading* (pp. 15–49). Norwood, NJ: Ablex.

Fry, E., Polk, J. & Fountoukidis, D. (1984). *The reading teacher's book of lists.* Englewood Cliffs, NJ: Prentice-Hall.

Goodman, K. S. (1976). Reading: A psycholinguistic guessing game. In H. Singer & R. Ruddell (Eds.), *Theoretical models and processes of reading.* Newark, NJ: The International Reading Association.

Gunderson, L. (1984a). Using the directed reading-thinking activity (DRTA) to improve comprehension. *Prime Areas, 26 (2)* 9–12.

Gunderson, L. (1984b). One last word list. *The Alberta Journal of Educational Research, 30*, 259–269.

Gunderson, L. (1985). Oral reading? If, when and how. *The BC Teacher, 64 (2)*, 23–26.

Gunderson, L. (1986). ESL reading teachers as facilitators of dialogue across cultures. *ATESL News*, 22–29.

Gunderson, L. (1991). *ESL literacy instruction: A guidebook to theory and practice.* Englewood Cliffs: Prentice-Hall Regents.

Gunderson, L. (1995). *Monday morning guide to comprehension.* Toronto: Pippin Publishing.

Gunderson, L. & Shapiro, J. (1988). Whole-language instruction: Writing in two grade one classrooms. *The Reading Teacher, 41*, 430–437.

Gunderson, L., Shapiro, J. & Froese, V. (1988). *The effects of models on the writing development of students in grades one and two.* Paper presented at the Annual Conference of the National Reading Conference.

Hipple, M. L. (1985). Journal writing in kindergarten. *Language Arts, 62*, 255–261.

Hunt, K. W. (1965). *Grammatical structures written at three grade levels.* Champaign, IL: NCTE.

Langer, J. (1991). Literacy and schooling: A sociocognitive perspective. In E. H. Hiebert (Ed.), *Literacy for a diverse society* (pp. 9–27). New York: Teachers College Press.

Law, B. & Eckes, M. (1990). *The more-than-just-surviving handbook: ESL for every classroom teacher.* Winnipeg, Manitoba: Peguis Publishers.

Leu, D. J. & Kinzer, C. (1991). *Effective reading instruction, K–8.* New York: Merrill.

Mathews, M. M. (1966). *Teaching to read historically considered.* Chicago: The University of Chicago Press.

Moustafa, M. (1993). Recoding in whole language reading instruction. *Language Arts, 70 (6)*, 483–487.

Persell, C. H. (1993). Social class and educational equality. In J. A. Banks & C. A. McGee Banks. *Multicultural education: Issues and perspectives.* Boston: Allyn and Bacon, pp. 71–89.

Stauffer, R. (1971). Slave, puppet or teacher? *The Reading Teacher, 25,* 24–29.

Sulzby, E. (1986). Writing and reading: Signs of oral and written organization in the young child. In W. H. Teale & E. Sulzby (Eds.), *Emergent literacy: Writing and reading* (pp. 50–89). Norwood, NJ: Ablex.

Vacca, R. T. & Vacca, J. A. (1993). *Content area reading.* (4th ed.). New York: HarperCollins.

Walmsley, S. A. and Adams, E. L. (1993). Realities of "whole language." *Language Arts, 70* (4), 272–280.

A SAMPLE OF MATERIALS LABELED AS "WHOLE LANGUAGE"

Expressways II (1984). Toronto: Gage Educational Publishing.

This program is designed for students in kindergarten to grade 6 and includes: motivators (10 large-format illustrations to encourage oral language); big books (5); 10 small-format reading books; mini-books; flip cards that are coil-bound to stimulate talk; a set of novels; student readers; and teacher's sourcebooks.

Journeys (1989). Toronto: Ginn and Company Educational Publishers, a Gulf and Western Company.

A program designed for students in kindergarten through grade 6 which contains: writing dictionaries (students are able to enter words they wish to know); writing portfolios for students' writing; listening tapes (oral readings of program stories); teacher's resource books; lap books (smaller than big books but designed for shared reading); and little books designed for "emergent reading activities."

Impressions (1984). Toronto: Holt, Rinehart and Winston of Canada, Limited.

This program contains items designed for students in kindergarten through grade 6 and contains items such as: teacher's resource book; shared reading books (big books); listening tapes; writing resource centers (a collection of activities); student books (write-in texts of student activities); word study centers (boxes of blackline masters for student activities); project books (many different projects for students); and teacher anthologies (stories designed for teachers to read aloud).

Networks (1991). Scarborough, Ontario: Nelson Canada (revision of the 1987 program).

Components designed for students in kindergarten to grade 6 include: teacher's resource books; resource center (management material); teacher's planning guides; anthologies (four per grade level); two independent readers per grade; language links (activities); action packs (blackline masters for "manipulative activities"); theme planning guide (resource units); teacher's notes.

Waves: Language Across the Curriculum (1992) Ontario: Houghton Mifflin Canada, Ltd.

A program that contains both literature and content material. Components designed for primary and elementary students include: poetry; historical fiction; social studies; favorite authors; discovery magazine; picture books, the arts; a teacher's resource booklet; radio waves (literature recorded on audio cassette tapes); and big books. Children's books are used as the starting point for making connections across subjects.

DISCUSSION QUESTIONS

1. How is a skills-based view of reading different from a whole-language-based view? How does a model of language affect classroom practice?

2. What is phonics instruction? What are some ways in which a whole-language teacher can make certain students learn phonics skills?

3. Should whole-language teachers know about phonics? If so, why? If not, why not?

4. What is individualization in a language arts/reading program? Name some of the limitations of individualization in your view.

5. Students' interests are extremely important in language arts/reading classes. How would you include students' interests in your program?

6. Whole-language teachers generally believe that reading activities should encourage and develop students' abilities to make predictions as they read. Design and describe an activity that would foster active prediction and tell how it could be used in a classroom.

7. Apply the socio-cognitive view of comprehension to a reading task. Discuss how you would help students to "construct" meaning. How would you bring student's knowledge to the task?

7

Playing the Whole-Language Game of Drama

PATRICK VERRIOUR

KEY CONCEPTS

1. *Children's natural inclination to engage in social and personal make-believe play, and their ability to construct imaginary worlds of play and story to make sense of their concerns*

2. *Structuring dramatic contexts in such a way that students' learning interests and needs are met, and opportunities are provided for them to engage in reflective thinking*

3. *The conscious use of role in teaching and learning in increasing the options available to teachers in creating new contexts for learning*

4. *Creating a supportive social climate in which children are encouraged to express their ideas freely, to respect each other's opinions, and to accept group decisions*

We got to find India, says Christopher Columbus. We got to become rich. We got to become famous. Do you think you can help us? But all Coyote can think about is playing ball. I'll let you bat first, says Coyote. No time for games, says Christopher Columbus. I'll let you make the rules, cries Coyote. But those Columbus people don't listen. They are too busy running around looking for India. Looking for stuff they can sell.

King (1992)

Introduction

Of all the different ways of learning, knowing, and understanding that are available to teachers and students in the whole language classroom there can be few so effective and yet so underused and misunderstood as drama. In this chapter, I shall examine the connections between children's spontaneous make-believe play and classroom drama, and the links between drama and other areas of the whole-language program.

Using practical examples, I shall demonstrate the central role that drama plays in the language learning process so that children not only use language in contexts that have meaning and purpose for them but also become more aware of the power of language *and* drama in their lives. In the whole-language game of drama, reading, writing, talking, signing, observing, and listening intersect in such a way that no formal distinctions are made between the student as playwright and co-creating actor or between the student as actor and co-creating audience. Therefore, the two central components of drama—the making of the art form and responding to the art form—are given equal weight and value. The use of drama in the classroom is founded on precepts central to those of whole-language teaching and learning. These include:

1. Recognizing and respecting each child's present level of language development and achievement
2. Being aware of children's individual learning styles
3. Recognizing the social and cultural context of the classroom in which students learn *through* language and *about* language both collaboratively and individually
4. Providing children with a sense of ownership *in* their learning so that they are encouraged to assume responsibility *for* their own learning
5. Offering children contexts for learning which make sense to them in terms of their own needs, interests, and social and cultural background experiences.

Most importantly, drama in the whole-language classroom challenges students intellectually, emotionally, and socially. When teachers use drama in the whole-language classroom, they are primarily concerned with finding ways in which students can identify with issues and events in their literary and language explorations at a personal level.

Therefore, the classroom becomes a forum for shared knowledge and culture, and drama a communal tool for understanding as teachers and students work together to negotiate meaning in a dramatic context they have constructed together. At the same time, I shall also emphasize that in using drama for the purpose of integrating language learning, students learn about the elements and power of the dramatic art form.

The metaphor I shall use to illustrate the implementation of drama in the language curriculum is that of a game—a game in which both teacher and students participate for the mutual satisfaction and enjoyment of the pursuit of knowledge to gain fresh understandings about themselves and the world in which they live.

The Game of Drama

From Friedrich Schiller to Jerome Bruner, writers from across the disciplines and across the centuries have drawn attention to the importance of play in intellectual and emotional development. Russian psychologist Lev Vygotsky, whose discoveries about teaching and learning are just beginning to shed fresh light on our thinking about education 60 years after his death, saw the pivotal relationship between play and intellectual and language development. "Play," he wrote, "is a leading source of (childhood) development" (Vygotsky, 1978, p. 103). In their play by themselves and with one another, children discover the symbolic properties and value of language. At school age, Vygotsky maintained that play does not die away but permeates students' attitudes to reality. "It is the essence of play that a new relation is created between the field of meaning and the visual field—that is, situations in thought and real situations" (Vygotsky, 1978, p. 105).

The ability to engage in imaginary play with others and hold the two worlds of play and "not play" firmly in mind at one and the same time is crucial to working in drama. The British educator Gavin Bolton (1992) said that the power and the fun of the dramatic playing experience for participants stems from recognizing that they are operating in two social contexts at the same time. And it is the *connections* that participants make between these two contexts or worlds that enable them to gain an understanding about important issues and concerns that face us all daily in our lives.

For example, a drama that a class of first-graders are creating with their teacher about Hans Christian Andersen's *The Ugly Duckling* provokes a lively discussion about why a parent might lavish attention on one child who is

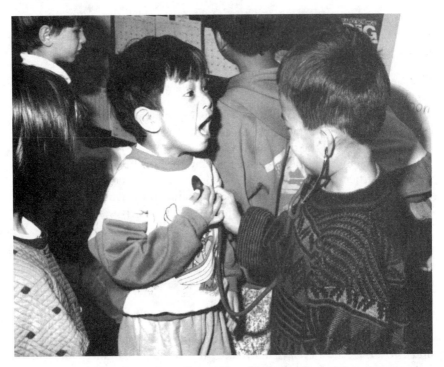

Kindergarten children learn about the world and language through spontaneous play.

different, and apparently give less attention to his or her other offspring. A sixth-grade class recreating the pioneer lives of a prairie family at the beginning of this century compares this earlier generation's concepts of what constitutes a family to present-day attitudes and beliefs. In each case, themes that are explored within the imaginary world of the drama have direct parallels with everyday life and experience.

The ways in which teachers organize and structure the game of drama provide students with opportunities to become aware of these connections and to relate them to events in their own lives. Therefore, the role that the teacher plays in classroom drama is a crucial one, and one that will be explored throughout this chapter, particularly in terms of the negotiations that occur between teacher and students.

Basic Principles and Rules

Like young children's play, participants in elementary and middle-school classroom drama are required to observe certain principles and rules to make the drama work. In approaching the work for the first time, teachers should provide opportunities for their students to learn these within the context of a drama.

Because drama is a collective experience in which the participants work collaboratively to create meaning, the basic principles of the drama game reflect this and will be understood quickly and easily by students who already appreciate the value of cooperative learning and have experience of social make-believe play. For those students who have difficulty in working together, then, the game of drama is a useful tool for fostering a spirit of cooperation in the classroom.

The following six principles for working in drama provide the underpinnings for the examples of classroom practice that are described in this chapter. As you and your class work through one or more of the dramas, you will discover the various steps that I have built in the work to ensure students fully understand these principles. For example, in the first drama the teacher enters into a *contract* with the students that clearly sets out the principles for working in the game of drama in order to seek their personal commitment (see Reading the Poem later in this chapter). The principles are:

- Participants should be predisposed to work in drama, and recognize that for the drama to succeed they should be self-motivated and self-directed.
- Participants should be willing to cooperate to make the drama work.
- There should be a desire to take different roles and think metaphorically in terms of the manipulation of signs and symbols.
- Participants should be willing to enter the "as if" world of drama, at the same time recognizing that this is not the "real" world.
- Participants should be willing to help construct and abide by the rules and conventions which govern the creation of the "as if" world.

- Opportunities should be provided for participants to reflect on their work through discussion or writing.

As each drama develops, you will also discover that there are certain rules that govern the **collective creation of a story** and the success of the drama game will largely depend on the observation of these rules. These rules are self-evolving, not prescriptive, and will likely vary according to the age level and experiential background of students. However, an awareness of these rules will enable participants in a drama to sustain the authenticity and integrity of the imaginary world that they are constructing. Therefore, the rules might include that follow, which are based on notes distributed by Jonathan Neelands at a drama workshop:

- The collective story is created by the whole class, including both teacher and students, so that any valid contribution made with regard to the unfolding of the drama should be respected by the class.
- Students should be encouraged to take different roles and adopt different perspectives in the drama.
- Assuming a role does not imply "performing" or "acting" for an audience. Sincerity and honesty in role taking should be encouraged.
- In drama, the focus of the work should be on the creation of a context that has purpose and meaning for the class. They should feel some sense of ownership of the dramatic context.
- Personal assumptions about characters or events in the story should not be voiced; the class may only hypothesize from the given facts.
- The class should not seek to resolve the story or plot too quickly (e.g., by magic). Sustaining the tension of the moment can enrich the drama.

The following workshops, discussions, teacher notes, and reflections demonstrate how the whole-language game of drama can be played based on the general principles and rules that have been outlined. In the first workshop, an intermediate class is exploring the elements of a mystery story based on a poem that the teacher has selected to use as a basis for the drama. Some of the structures in Stage Two of this drama are based on a format suggested by Jonathan Neelands.

Drama 1: Poetry and the Mystery Story

Gareth Owen's poem *Real Life* is full of all the ingredients of a mystery story complete with a hint of smugglers, an inn, and a secret underground passage. The playful, ironic tone of the poem complete with the suggestion of an opening sentence to a children's adventure story seems to imply that while often a particular place or setting might appear to have all the elements necessary for a real-life adventure, this only happens in books. In fact, the author's final line affirms this. Although I have chosen to omit the final line in presenting the poem at the beginning of the drama, it will be revealed in the final stage of the work.

Working collectively through the imaginary world of drama, the seemingly impossible can be achieved. The whole purpose of this drama is to allow the adventure to actually happen, and students to become cocreators in the development of a story that arises out of the poem. Therefore, students can bring their knowledge and understanding of story to construct a drama that will engage them intellectually and emotionally, and will enable them to explore the mystery story genre.

The poem is the story of John, who is spending his summer vacation in an old inn in the moors near a cove that had once served smugglers who could exit from the bedroom inhabited by John. He excitedly anticipates an adventure that "only happens in books" (Zola, 1990).

Reading the Poem

1. The poem is shown on the overhead projector so that the teacher can stand at the back of the class to give everyone a sense of shared ownership, as he or she reads the poem aloud.
2. After the poem has been read, the teacher tells the students that the author wrote one more line. For the time being, the poem is incomplete. Working through drama, they will discover for themselves what that final line might be. Therefore, their purpose will be to find out the connections between some of the mystery story elements in the poem to create their own story.
3. In order to secure their commitment to the work, the teacher asks the students if they are willing to create a drama about the poem. This will require them to respect other people's ideas and opinions, to take roles in the drama, and to work collectively to make the drama work for everyone. Having made this *contract* with the class, teacher and students now start constructing the dramatic context.

Stage One: Creating a Collective Image

Overview: In the first stage of the drama, teacher and students explore some of the *images* evoked by the poem.

1. To create some sense of atmosphere, the teacher asks the class to think of the sights, smells, and sounds that this poem conjures up of the old inn on the edge of the moor. These words and phrases are shared with the whole class as the teacher records them on the chalkboard.

2. To develop atmosphere and setting further, one child is asked to play the role of John sitting down later that day and writing down his first thoughts on reaching the inn. This is accomplished quite simply with "John" sitting at the front of the class at a table in a freeze position, hand poised over an open journal or diary ready to record his thoughts. The teacher takes time with the class to pose John in a writing position that is acceptable to everyone. Slowing down the drama at this point emphasizes the reflective and serious nature of the work. Questions such as, "Is everyone ready to accept that we are watching John sitting in his bedroom about to write in his diary at the end of his first day at the inn?" help set the tone for this activity. (Note: Roles in classroom drama are androgynous so that girls can play boys and boys can play girls. As an alternative to a student taking the role of John, an empty chair can be placed in the middle of the room representing John.)

3. Referring to the words and phrases that are written on the board, students now voice John's thoughts as he writes his diary. The teacher sets the scene for this activity by telling the story of the diary writing. Spoken **spontaneous narrative** is a useful way of introducing a scene, providing a link between events in a story drama, recalling incidents that might have occurred in the past, and serving as a commentary on what is happening now in the drama. At this point, the teacher says, "At the end of his first day of summer vacation at the inn, John went to his room and before he went to bed he wrote down all the thoughts that were filling his head."

The rest of the class is now invited to say his thoughts *as if* they are John. For example,

"When we first arrived I noticed the musty smell in the inn."
"The front door creaked when I opened it."
"It was very cold inside even though the sun was shining."

When one student says, "John might write he wondered if he would meet Aunt Lucy," the teacher asks him to rephrase it as John's personal thought using the personal pronoun *I*. At this early stage it is important for students to become accustomed to taking a role and operating in the "now" time of drama.

4. As the students say his thoughts, John's hand moves across the paper. (Asking the student taking the role of John to actually write down the thoughts might delay the process although the actual pace of the activity should be quite slow to allow for reflective thinking.) After a number of students have had an opportunity to contribute their ideas, the teacher asks all the students to take the role of John and write their own diary entries.

Stage Two: Taking Roles

Overview: In the next stage of the drama, the students assume the roles of police investigators with the teacher taking the role of chief investigator who presents the class with a problem to be solved. In this case the problem concerns the disappearance of John.

1. John's diary entry becomes the focus for the next stage of the drama. As the entry was not actually written down, the teacher has asked the class to re-create the diary entry from their writing. Therefore, the diary entry reads:

   What a strange place this. Just like out of a story book. There's a damp, musty smell everywhere. From my window all I can see is the flatness of the moors, and in the distance the cliffs of St. Peter's Cove. No sign of Aunt Lucy, just a note from her to my parents which my dad opened when we arrived. Uncle David read it and laughed. No one seems to know or will tell me where the secret passage is. I hope I can find a friend here.

2. For this activity, the teacher takes the role of the chief investigator of a Missing Persons Bureau meeting the other investigators, played by the students. To give the class some sense of their roles and the skills they will need to solve the mystery they will face, the teacher briefly explains that everyone will be taking a role in the drama. At this point, again the class is asked whether they are ready to go along with this. To help the students understand their roles as investigators, the teacher brainstorms with them the skills they feel a good detective needs, and records them on the chalkboard.

3. Once the class has a clear sense of the rules of the game and the roles they will be taking, the teacher in role as the chief investigator initiates this stage of the drama. If possible, the students should be seated in a circle. The teacher in role talks to them about their next case:

   Good morning, investigators. The Missing Persons Bureau is faced with a puzzling case which has just been referred to us. It seems that two nights ago between the hours of 9 P.M. and 8 A.M. the next morning, a young boy named John who was staying on holiday at an inn not many miles from here went missing. There appears to be no apparent reason for his disappearance. The only real clue that we have with regard to why and how he disappeared is his last diary entry, which he must have written that evening and which has been discovered in his room. Needless to say, his parents are extremely worried about his disappearance, and it will need all your considerable skills and talents to solve the case."

4. The teacher in role reads the diary entry and then asks the students as investigators if they have any questions. The answers of the teacher in role are

limited to information that supports what has been told in the poem or in the diary entry. Certain other details are added, for example, John's age and physical description. However questions such as, "Who was the last person to see John that evening?" are answered by saying that witnesses have not yet been interviewed. By deliberately withholding information and hinting that this is something the investigators will have to find out for themselves, the teacher introduces an element of tension and expectancy into the drama. At the end of this activity, now out of role, the teacher asks students to reflect on what they have learned thus far about John's disappearance.

5. The next drama activity opens up opportunities for students to start building on what they know. Again, the teacher talks to them in role:

What sort of questions do you think we need to ask to learn more about John's disappearance?

The teacher explains that questions that make assumptions are not permitted. For instance, questions such as, "When did Uncle David separate from Aunt Lucy?" or "What sort of contraband was smuggled through the inn?" make assumptions and should be rephrased (e.g., "Are Uncle David and Aunt Lucy related?" and "Was the inn ever used for smuggling contraband?").

The questions are brainstormed in small groups of four with one member of the group recording the questions. After each group has devised at least 6 to 10 questions, these are shared with the whole class. Each group is asked to choose what they consider to be their best question, which is then written on the board. In this way, the sharing moves quickly from group to group. If a group has a question that is very similar or the same as another group, then the other group of students eliminate it from their list. As each question is recorded, the teacher asks the whole class to consider whether or not it needs further refinement. The sharing continues until every group has had a chance to contribute at least two or three questions. The rest of the questions are read aloud, but not recorded, and saved for later.

Here are some of the students' questions written on the board:

"Who was the last person to see John?"
"Did he say anything that might indicate why he appears to have disappeared?"
"Is the secret underground passage still in existence?"
"Had John ever run away before?"
"What clothes was he wearing when he disappeared?"
"Was there anything else missing either from his room or the house?"
"What sort of search has been conducted, and has this revealed any clues?"
"Have there been any other disappearances similar to this in the neighborhood? If so, what happened?"
"How long has Aunt Lucy owned the inn and how did she acquire it?"

"Who knows about the underground passage, and is it still accessible?"
"Who is Uncle David, and why is he accompanying John and his parents on their holiday?"
"What was the inn like during the days of the smugglers?"
"What makes St. Peter's Cove inaccessible?"
"Are there any paths across the moors?"

6. Once the class has had a chance to read over the questions and reflect on them, they now start researching the story of the disappearance. In other words, the students decide who they need to talk to in order to find answers to their questions and discover *why John disappeared* and what has happened to him.

For the purposes of the drama it is important that the reasons for John's disappearance always be kept in mind as well as the story of the subsequent events. Otherwise, the drama will be more concerned with what happens next in the story rather than exploring the motives of the characters involved.

Again, suggestions solicited from the students are listed on the board. The class is warned that careful thought should be given to their list of witnesses. Often someone apparently unconnected to the story could provide more information than an actual character who is mentioned by name. For example, someone close to Aunt Lucy might be able to tell them more about her "strangeness" than Aunt Lucy herself.

Here is a list of 10 characters that the students suggest:

John's mother
John's father
Uncle David
Aunt Lucy or a friend of Aunt Lucy's
Local historian
The person who looks after the inn (possibly a housekeeper) employed by Aunt Lucy
Local fisherman
A storekeeper who supplies the inn
The local coastguard
The real estate agent who handles the renting of the inn for Aunt Lucy

7. To heighten the tension of the drama and to sharpen the focus, the teacher asks the class to select five or six characters from this list whom they think would able to provide them with more information regarding John's disappearance. Discussion about their final choices helps the class gain a clearer collective image of what they want to find out. Once this has been established, the interviewing of the witnesses proceeds.

8. In role as investigators under the direction of the teacher in role as chief investigator, the class is placed in a semi-circle around a single chair.

Using question and answer and spontaneous narrative, the teacher sets the scene:

Let's imagine that we have arrived at the inn to interview the witnesses. In what room does this take place? Let's see if we can describe the room.

After the students have given their suggestions, the teacher tells the story of their arrival using the students' ideas.

So the investigators from the Missing Persons Bureau arrived at the inn and prepared to meet the witnesses in the long, wood-paneled dining room. Through the window they could see the moors and dark clouds scurrying across the sky. As they sat in comfort, they wondered if John was somewhere out there either lost or in danger.

9. Stepping briefly out of role, the teacher now asks any student to take the role of the first witness. The student chooses any character from the final list of six on the board, and comes forward prepared to answer the investigators' questions in role as the character. Again, the rules for playing the role are similar to those that have been observed throughout the drama: the role should be played with sincerity and honesty, and although he or she will obviously contribute new information and shed fresh light on the disappearance, the person in role should not seek to solve the mystery. Wherever possible, the character should attempt to substantiate rather than refute already agreed-upon facts (e.g., John is 12 years old.) If the person in role does not wish to answer a question or does not know how to answer a question, then the reply might be, "I would prefer not to answer that."

10. Before the interviews start, the teacher advises students taking roles that as soon as they enter, they will become the character they have chosen to play. In this way, individual students are given help by the rest of the class in developing their characters. For example, the first student decides to be John's mother. The "mother" sits, legs tucked in, arms folded, and looking anxious.

    The teacher asks the class to describe how they think the mother is feeling. The teacher asks them to observe her physical posture and facial expression, and what they think she is feeling. The teacher also asks them to suggest what questions they think they will ask her. All this information helps the class to focus on the task of interviewing and at the same time helps to prepare the student taking the role of the interviewee. The teacher asks the first two or three questions to set the tone of the interview and the questioning. Here are some examples of opening questions the teacher can use:

    "I understand that you are John's mother. What is your full name?"
    "When was the last time you saw John?"
    "Did he appear to be behaving in an unusual way?"

11. Once the questioning has been turned over to the class, the teacher clarifies student in role questions or answers, and provides support for the witness whenever necessary. Occasionally the teacher stops the questioning if students flout the rules of the game (e.g., make an assumption), and discusses with them different ways of posing a question. Once the first witness has been interviewed for five minutes, another student is called forward. This student is asked to choose another character from the list, and build on what the mother has said. As the interviews proceed, a story starts emerging that will form the basis for the next stage in the drama. After all the interviews are completed, the investigators move informally among the witnesses and ask further questions. This permits a quiet student who may not have asked a question previously to ask one now.

12. To provide a summary of and a reflection on the interviews, those in the class who were investigators now write a report on what they feel they have found out about John's disappearance. Meanwhile, those who took the roles of witnesses write a diary entry recording their thoughts and feelings about the interview. In this way the information that has accumulated during the interviews is recorded for future reference in the drama.

Stage Three: Working Independently

1. Thus far, the students have been working in a whole class setting; the next stage will give them an opportunity to work independently in small groups of five to six students. Now that the class is acquiring a sense of ownership of the drama and an understanding of how the game of drama works, this activity should permit them to develop the story one step forward without actually resolving the problem of John's disappearance. The teacher asks each group to create a *still image* in which they depict an event that could provide a clue regarding John's disappearance. They are advised that their still image should not show what actually happened to John. The whole purpose of the still image will be to sustain the suspense of the drama while at the same time revealing more information about why John may have disappeared. (*Still images* are pictures frozen in time in which no one moves or speaks as the group collectively depicts the essence of an event, idea, or theme. In this case, a group of smugglers might be shown blocking up the coastal entrance to the underground passage for the last time.)

2. The use of the still image offers many opportunities for further exploration of the story, and can be a very effective and powerful teaching and learning tool. In addition to providing *protection* to the participants, as they do not have to move or speak, the rest of the class studies the still image, and

under the guidance of the teacher becomes actively involved with another group's presentation in the following ways:

- Rest of the class describes what they see in the picture. They study and describe the relationships between different characters and try to spot clues regarding John's disappearance.
- Students give a title and/or caption to the still image, describing what is happening.
- The class chooses one person in the still image to leave the picture and to say in role what is happening. A variation of this is to ask the character to imagine that he or she is looking back in time and remembering what happened. The rest of class can ask questions of this character.
- The class says what moods and feelings different characters in the still image project (e.g., anger, concern, fear).
- The students in the still image bring the picture to life and show what happens next, each character saying one line.

3. The still images can provide all sorts of useful ideas and information to help the teacher plan the future development of the drama. Here are some choices:

- Media reporters interview searchers for the latest update on the hunt for John.
- Two characters from the story (e.g., present-day smugglers) have a telephone conversation about their concerns that John has blundered into the secret passage and found their cache of smuggled goods. (This can be shown with two students sitting back to back talking to one another. If one cannot think of what to say next, the teacher can solicit ideas from the rest of the class who are watching—"How do you think they might answer that?")

An identacode picture of John could be drawn from the information gathered and circulated around the local town. Students are in role as investigators and townspeople.

An historical event related to John's disappearance could be reenacted (e.g., the disappearance of another boy at the inn a century before). To create the picture of the historical setting, both teacher and class tell stories of the inn at that time, imagining what it would be like when the smugglers used the secret passage to the cove.

- A ransom note is received by John's parents demanding a large sum of money for their son's return. In role as investigators, discuss how they determine whether or not it is a hoax.

Together with the original interviews of witnesses and still images, these activities perform the function of creating a kaleidoscope of events that surround John's disappearance. However, it is important for the class to always remember that the overall purpose of the drama is to explore the reasons for John's disappearance and discover what has happened to him. There is always a danger that they might be sidetracked into "busy work," which although interesting in itself does not maintain the focus of the drama.

Stage Four: Concluding the Drama

To conclude the drama, the teacher chooses a whole-class activity for the main reason that the students need to pool the knowledge they have gained to create an ending that makes sense to them and is truthful to what they have been trying to achieve in the drama. It *feels* authentic and lends significance to their work.

To achieve this, the teacher asks the class to create a group portrait of the people who were originally interviewed by the investigators. The picture is being taken by a newspaper photographer (teacher in role) at the conclusion of the search. All the characters in the story are waiting to hear whether John has been found. In the group picture or photograph, John is not present, so the characters are either sitting or standing around the small table or desk on which John's diary is placed. The class decides how each character should be posed simply by saying where they should be in the picture in relation to the desk. Therefore, John's parents could actually be there by the desk looking at the diary, and a more disinterested character could be some distance away looking out of the window. Their physical position and physical distance from the focal point of the picture (the diary) projects what has been found out about them during the course of the drama and how they are feeling at the end of the search. After the class has positioned the characters, students playing these roles add further alterations or adjustments either in terms of posture or distance from the desk. This gives them an opportunity to depict their own interpretation of the character they are portraying. Once the group portrait is in place, a choice is made about the ending of the drama.

The class chooses whether the search has been successful or not, and if John has been found alive or dead. Of course, he may not have been found at all, or, more intriguingly, the boy who is found is *not* John but the boy who disappeared under similar circumstances a century before. There are many possibilities and twists to the story with which the class can play, and these are some of the choices that the teacher may wish to offer students. Of course, the class will have its own suggestions too.

Strategies similar to those described in the still image are used to involve the whole class in this concluding activity, for example, by asking one character to leave the picture and reflect on the scene as if looking at it one year afterwards.

The group portrait convention is sufficiently flexible to allow the class to try different endings to the story if they are not satisfied with the one they have chosen. Students may even wish to leave the drama open ended with no resolution of the problem. However, it is important that students are given an opportunity to reflect on the drama individually, and one of the following writing activities after the group picture might help accomplish this:

1. Rereading the poem and writing the final line.
2. Writing the first sentence, paragraph, or even the whole story from the perspective of one of the characters (including John).
3. Writing the end of the story using a third person narrator.
4. Writing a report of the disappearance in role as an investigator.
5. Writing a newspaper report of the incident.

And what is the final line of the poem? Almost anticlimactic: "And he was right." There is a sense of finality and closure to this sentence. But, of course, tongue in cheek, the writer is parodying the formula mystery story. Therefore, the game of drama allows us to open up the poem to all sorts of possible interpretations and explorations.

Postdrama Discussion

Now that you have had an opportunity to read through the workshop, you will probably have a number of questions about implementing the drama in your own classroom. In addition, you may wish to know more about the connections between this drama and whole-language. To clarify both areas further I have constructed a hypothetical question and answer session to follow the workshop similar to those discussions I have had with teachers about dramas that I have either taught them or their students.

Participant:	It was easy for us to understand the poem because we know what "an inn" and "moor" are. How can my fifth-grade students create images based on the poem if they don't have any background in this kind of setting, especially those whose first language is not English?
Workshop: Leader	That's an important point, as the class should identify with the poem at a very personal level so that they can draw on their own experience to express the images that the poem evokes for them. Of course a lot will depend on the way you introduce the poem to the class. For instance, you may wish to talk to them about mystery stories they have either read or watched on television before you actually read the poem. Words such as *inn* and *moor* can be discussed in terms of their own knowledge and background experience. For example, one teacher who kindly field-tested this drama for me with her sixth-grade class found that locating the inn and moor on the nearby San Juan Islands (WA), which have a long tradition of smug-

gling, made sense of the poem for her students. At the same time, another teacher who has an English-as-a-Second-Language (ESL) class for immigrant students found her students did have some problems with the poem. After explaining the meaning of the words *inn* and *moor,* she asked them to think of their own definitions and images. One student's definition of a moor was particularly striking: "hills that never end."

P: I have a seventh-grade class with 30 students and there is very little extra space in the room in which I am teaching. How can I do drama in such a restricted area? Do you think I should do it in the gym?

WL: First, I would strongly advise against working in such a vast open space as a gym, which is associated in the students' minds with all kinds of physical sport, and will oblige you to impose controls on them to engage in the kinds of reflective thinking that are an important component of drama. As you have probably gathered from the workshop, it is a mistake to think of dramatic action simply in terms of physical action, even though I have characterized drama as a game. In the kind of improvised classroom drama game described in the workshop, the overall dramatic action refers more to the process of change effected by the sequence of different situations that occur during the course of the drama. This process of change is concerned at one level with the way in which the drama moves forward, back, or even sideways through parallel situations, to tell us more about the issues, events, and lives of the characters in the story. At another level, the process involves the students' own change of understanding that occurs as a result of their construction of and participation in the dramatic action. Therefore, a central purpose of any drama work should be to place students both inside and outside the dramatic action at one and the same time. The thoughtful, restrained quality of the work is best suited to a classroom however confined the space.

P: So what you seem to be saying is that consideration of space is an important element of planning the drama?

WL: Very much so. If you look back over the drama you will see that space plays an important role both in terms of the actual sequence of activities and the theatrical use of space in various dramatic situations. At the beginning of the first stage of the drama, the whole class brainstormed images. If there is no room for a circle in the classroom, then students will have to sit at their tables or desks. The next activity consisted of John sitting at the front of the class or perhaps in the middle of the class writing his diary. Again, the rest of the class could sit at their desks. Even when students worked in small groups creating still images, interviewing the witnesses or interviewing each other, all of these activities were conducted in quite confined spaces. At the same time, the teacher was continually drawing the students' attention to the theatrical use of space within the dramatic situation such as the way in which a witness entered the space and sat down, or the physical/ psychological distance between one character and another in a still image. Therefore, size of classroom and quantity of furniture does not necessarily have to interfere with the students' work and their understanding and appreciation of the use of space in drama.

P: In many ways the different kinds of whole-class activities and small-group activities were very similar to those we already do in our whole-language classes.

WL: That's a very important point. In a drama, the lessons move from whole-class sharing to small-group work to pairs work and so on. Each activity plays a crucial role in the development of the drama itself and the learning that takes place. For example, notice how students were asked to write their own individual diary entries after the whole-class diary writing activity. This allowed all class members to work quietly on their own for a period of time before moving on to another whole-class activity and then subsequently into small-group work. In this way each student experiences a number of different social learning situations. One thing I should stress is the importance of having the whole-class working together on a number of occasions, especially at the beginning and end of a drama, so that they work collectively. Having a long succession of small-group activities can fragment this sense of community.

P: This drama session lasted for nearly three hours. How can we possibly collapse the drama into 40- or 50-minute lessons that are constantly being interrupted by P.A. announcements and so on?

WL: One of the reasons I deliberately divided the workshop session into stages rather than lessons was to indicate that teachers have to make their own decisions about how much they think they can accomplish with their classes during the time periods they can allot to drama. Naturally I would like to see drama being used frequently over long periods of time as I believe that drama can be used to integrate learning in whole-language classrooms. However, if only short periods of time can be devoted to drama I suggest that you might adopt what Geoff Davies (1983) called the "cliff hanger" approach. In other words, the drama stops at a point when the class wants to know more or what happens next.

At the same time, time should be set aside at the end of each lesson for a few moments of reflection and/or discussion about what has taken place that day.

P: When you say drama can help integrate learning, what exactly do you mean?

WL: I think if you look at the sheer range of language activities that were covered in this drama, you will get some idea of the ways that drama can be used as a tool for integrating language learning. For instance, in addition to *listening* and *reading* the poem, students are asked to *respond* to the poem by *imagining* the inn. As John "writes" his diary, students *speak* his thoughts, and then *write in role* their own personal diary entries. All of this languaging occurs in the first stage of the drama.

In the second stage, in addition to their *negotiations in role* with the teacher and their peers, students are asked to *formulate* questions which they later *ask* the witnesses. In fact, special emphasis was given to placing students in situations where they ask questions that require them to engage in higher-level thinking skills as in the cross-examination of the witnesses. At the same time, the class is asked to *observe* and *discuss* the various signs and signals *depicted* by the students in role as witnesses. The content of the drama develops almost entirely out of the personal knowledge, background experience, feelings, and language of the students. Gillian Brown (1984) made the important point that although educators may complain that there are insufficient opportunities for students to talk to one another in the classroom, often they don't actually have anything to talk about. I believe drama provides students with the chance to engage in a whole range of language activities that have real *purpose* and *meaning* for them because they are based on the *shared knowledge* that has been accumulated within the differing *contexts* of the drama game.

P: With so many things happening in the drama and because the teacher is so actively engaged in the work, it must be very difficult to assess individual student work. How do you assess student work in drama?

WL: It would be rash for any teacher to attempt to assess all that is happening within a specific drama experience, particularly as the teacher may be taking a role working alongside the students. Therefore, I suggest that teachers focus on specific aspects of the learning. A simple way to do this is to consider the different kinds of learning that may occur in a drama activity in terms of either individual students or groups of students. If one divides the different areas of learning in drama into intellectual, emotional, social, aesthetic, and language strands, then one can concentrate on one strand at any one time.

For example, if teachers want to assess how well their classes are able to work together (social learning) in the first activity of the workshop drama, which is concerned with imaging, they might focus on their students' ability to share their ideas with one another and to accept other students' ideas. Alternatively they might be more concerned with their ability to recall past experiences, feelings, and images, and to think metaphorically (intellectual and aesthetic learning). Therefore, the kinds of assessment that are most effective in drama are those that are ongoing and formative, rather than being evaluative and summative. This kind of assessment contributes to the development of the drama learning process.

Even though it might appear that writing in role would be a useful method of evaluating student progress, one should be very clear about what one is evaluating. In most cases the writing that occurs in drama is an integral part of the drama itself and not simply a writing exercise. So any assessment of student writing must take into account the actual drama context itself. As you will recall in the workshop, the final diary entry that was used in the drama was actually a composite of the students' own writings. Whenever possible, student writing should be used in the actual drama itself.

P: In the drama, John only appeared once at the beginning of the story. Why did the teacher choose to have John disappear, and not his uncle, aunt, or one or both of his parents?

WL: There were a number of reasons for this, and they mainly concern the concepts of *distance* and *protection*. Let's consider distance first. The teacher was working with an intermediate-age class. John's age is probably very close to theirs. He could have been older or younger by one or two years. This means that the students could personally identify with John's thoughts and feelings when he first sees the inn and he writes his diary. In this way the drama is faithful to the poem, which is written from John's perspective.

If someone is to disappear, then it naturally follows that it has to be John; students already feel some sort of empathy for him. In taking the roles of adult police investigators they are invested with the power to act as adults and to cross examine the witnesses as if they are adults. The distancing from their real-life roles as children is important because this means they have to act *as if* they are someone else with the kinds of knowledge, skills, and expertise that children are not usually expected to have acquired. At the same time they probably have a great deal of knowledge about how children might react in similar circumstances. They can also construct their perceptions of how adults might react in response to John's disappearance. The concept of distance that I have outlined applies to both younger and older students working in drama, although a lot will obviously depend on the actual nature of the work, and what you hope to achieve in the drama.

Structuring the drama in this way permits students to use all that background experience and knowledge they have about missing children and parental reaction within the *protected* context of the drama. At the point the teacher in role

talks to them as fellow police investigators, the students really enter the imagined world of the drama. There is a certain tension between their real life roles and their fictional roles. In this way they are further protected in the drama because being in a fictional role offers them all sorts of opportunities to voice views and opinions that they may feel reluctant to air out of role. From the drama perspective, the continued absence of John adds suspense and different levels of tension to the drama: the tension of mystery, the tension of waiting, and the tension of an obstacle to overcome.

Drama 2: Confronting Racism

Now let's listen to two teachers planning a drama that they will team teach to an upper-intermediate class on a historical topic that still arouses controversy: the deportation of Americans of Japanese heritage from California to concentration camps during World War II. The drama work arises out of the autobiographical novel by Yoshiko Uchida, entitled *Journey Home* (Houghton Mifflin, 1989), which tells the story of a 12-year-old girl's return to Berkeley, California, after her internment with her family in an American camp in Utah.

After the teachers' planning session, each teacher's observation notes of the other teacher's drama lesson are presented.

(Teachers—T1 and T2)

Teacher 1:   The whole question is should we do the drama after we have finished reading the book with the class. Which do you think would be the most effective?

Teacher 2:   I think that to really appreciate the plight of the people in the story and the problems they were faced with after the internment was over, we should do the drama while we read the book. In that way, students will be able to explore for themselves how individual Japanese Americans felt at a very personal level based on what they have found out from the story. As the class has already read Uchida's *Journey to Topaz*, the drama could provide a link between the two books.

T1:   I like that idea. In a sense, we are creating a parallel text to the story, but I'm not very happy with the term *Japanese Americans*, even though that is used in the book. I would prefer we agree to say Americans of Japanese heritage or ancestry.

T2:   You're right. If we do emphasize that these are Americans of Japanese heritage, this underscores the fact that certain American citizens were classified as "enemy aliens" by their own government, and deprived of their constitutional rights. We should discuss this with the class.

T1:   Perhaps we could look at ways in which the main characters in the story tried to integrate themselves back into society after being so brutally rejected by a number of their fellow citizens.

T2:   I was thinking of a much broader theme which will have personal meaning for our students growing up today and facing similar, if not identical, problems: the whole notion of "survival." After all, there are other people in the story in addition to the Americans of Japanese heritage, whose lives have been deeply scarred by the war, and who have to pick up the pieces again and rebuild their lives.

T1:   Such as the Olssens who lost their son, yes. It's interesting how both books have the word *journey* in their titles. Perhaps we could link your idea of "survival" with the journey theme so that the drama is concerned with the different life journeys of the characters and how they managed to find the will to survive in spite of great odds.

T2:   I also think the drama should present the students with authentic historical material to consider as they read the story. In that way, they will be able to discover for themselves that the book is based on actual events.

T1:   Perhaps then we could use photographs. Even though the ones we have were taken 50 years ago, seeing people being deported to the camps might offer them that personal identification you are talking about.

T2:   That's a good idea. How about "before" and "after" photographs? These two photographs show first the men departing from California by train for the detention camp in Utah at the beginning of the deportation, and this one showing a group of former deportees arriving home in California after the war was over.

T1:   The men in the first picture are so well dressed and orderly. It's hard to believe they have been classified as "prisoners of war" and are being sent to concentration camps.

T2:   Well, I suppose, this reflects the attitudes of the deportees who really wanted to demonstrate to the American government and people that they were loyal, law-abiding American citizens.

Discussion of photos leads to writing and drama activities.

T1:   Yes, Uchida emphasizes that in the book: the way Yuki's father handles the agitators in the camp by helping the administration, and the fact that Ken volunteers to fight in the American army in Europe.

T2:   Also, in more subtle ways too. On the rail journey back to California, Yuki and her mother take great pains not to offend anyone, even though Yuki has to endure some really harsh, racist abuse. Notice she doesn't say anything about this experience to her mother.

T1:   So learning how to cope successfully with all the injustices inflicted on them is really part of the concept of survival on life's journey, the theme we have chosen for the drama.

T2:   Except, I hope that we don't leave students with the impression that finding the will to survive just means knuckling under and allowing oneself to be dominated or oppressed by someone more powerful than you.

T1:   No, and Yoshiko Uchido certainly doesn't imply that in her novel. Remember when Yuki tries to convince Mrs. Henley that Americans of Japanese heritage do not pose a threat. I think if we structure the drama experience in such a way that allows students to discover and see for themselves that there is always a time to speak out and resist oppression but, equally, it sometimes takes more courage to keep one's own counsel and wait for that opportunity. After all, keeping quiet doesn't prevent you from entertaining your private thoughts.

T2:   And drama really is an excellent medium to explore people's inner thought and feelings.

T1:   So that means when we look at the photograph of the men on the train, we should focus on revealing their private thoughts and feelings even though they might be saying quite different things to their families they are leaving behind. We could work with this in role.

T2:   How about me handling that lesson, and you doing the other photograph showing Americans of Japanese ancestry returning to California at the moment just before Yuki's family arrives home on the train?

Observation Notes Taken during Two Drama Lessons Based on Yoshiko Uchida's "Journey Home"

(These notes are partly based on drama taught to an upper-intermediate class about deportation and internment during World War II. Some of the verbatim answers and comments are those made by students. I am grateful to the class for permitting me to publish their thoughtful and sensitive work.)

The teacher starts the first lesson by writing two words on the overhead: *deportation* and *evacuation*. She asks the students what meanings these words have for them, what associations and images they conjure up. The general consensus in the class is that *deportation* is associated with the forced expulsion of people from a place or country, like "ethnic cleansing" in Bosnia; while *evacuation* involves the removal of people from a place where their lives are in danger. The teacher says both words have been used to describe the removal of Americans of Japanese heritage or descent from the West Coast in World War II when they were classified as enemy aliens in the event of a feared invasion by Japan even though a large percentage had been born in America.

She continues with a brief introduction retelling the story of the deportation or evacuation in 1942 or 110,000 Americans of Japanese heritage from California to the Central Utah Relocation Center at Topaz, Utah (where Yuki's family were to live), and other centers spread across the United States.

At first," she says, "the deportation was called a 'voluntary evacuation' but when most Americans of Japanese heritage stayed put, the 'voluntary evacuation' became a 'compulsory evacuation.' By and large, the people affected were expected to dispose of their property quickly and personally, including farmland, businesses, homes, furniture, and automobiles. Often these possessions were sold at a fraction of their market value to unscrupulous dealers. Each person was permitted to take only what could be carried. Anything left in storage was done so at the owner's risk. As we shall see in the story, Yuki's family lose practically everything they once owned. At first, the deportees lived in assembly areas surrounded by barbed wire and armed guards. Then in the fall of 1942, the first contingent of deportees arrived at Topaz, workers were to prepare the camp for over 8,000 Americans of Japanese heritage sent there by the end of the year."

The students are very quiet as the teacher turns on the overhead projector and a photograph of one of the train departures is flashed onto the screen.

"What do see when you look at the picture?" she asks.

The children don't hesitate to answer her.

"Men looking out of the train window while it is standing at the station."

"They are peering out from underneath the shades."

"There are more men on the platform."

"Another man in the train is smiling at someone on the platform, but you can't see who he is smiling at."

"Another man is holding up a piece of paper for someone on the platform to read."

"They all seem so well dressed. They're wearing suits and ties."

"They all seem so well dressed," echoes Joan, "I wonder if that's because they want to keep up appearances, and not look as though something unusual is happening to them. Perhaps they don't know the sort of conditions that will be awaiting them in the camps. Perhaps they don't realize that they will be doing heavy manual labor. Or perhaps there's another reason."

I am impressed with the way the children respond to the photograph. They notice important details such as the shades drawn down on the windows, and the man leaning out of the train window apparently searching in the crowd for someone special or perhaps a familiar face.

Now the teacher asks them, "What do think some of those people in the train are thinking as they say their last farewells?"

"I wonder if Keiko will be allowed to see me off."

"Young Midori does not even know why I am leaving her."

"Take care, my family. Watch over each other while I am gone."

"Why are we being treated this way? Are we not responsible American citizens?"

"I wonder what the camp will be like?"

After some more children have spoken, the teacher says, "This is obviously a very sad moment with husbands and fathers being separated from their families. When you look at that scene at the station with the train about to leave, what questions do you have about what you see?"

"Are the men outside the train saying goodbye or are they actually waiting to get on the train?"

"Where are the children and women?"

"Where did they stay when the men went?"

"Why are the men all so well dressed?"

"What will happen to them in the camp?"

After the class has created a list of questions, I take over and read them the first three pages of *Journey Home* describing Yuki's nightmare about Camp Topaz.

*   *   *   LATER   *   *   *

We have been reading the book now for 10 days in class and it has provoked some very lively discussion, thoughtful writing, and interesting drama. The students have been very motivated in their research, and we were visited by two Americans of Japanese descent who had first hand knowledge of the internment camps.

Before reading about Yuki's return to California in Chapter 6 of *Journey Home* the teacher has developed a drama activity with the class designed to mirror the activity I did when we talked about men leaving on the train from California.

To start, I read aloud to the class the first three pages describing the train journey before they reached Berkeley. I then tell the class that less than half of the 9,000 Americans of Japanese descent who left California for the camp in Topaz ever returned home. Most resettled in other states.

A photograph is flashed onto the overhead projector screen showing another train scene. In the foreground, an older woman sits on a suitcase. Eyes cast down, avoiding the eye of the camera, she is clutching a shopping bag. Behind her, two younger women and a girl stand, staring bleakly over her head in different directions. Apart from the fact they are grouped close to one another there appears to be no human contact or communication between any of these four women. Behind them stretching into the far distance, others are standing and waiting.

After a few moments of silence to allow the class to look at the picture, the teacher says, "So that we can find more what's happening to the people in this photograph, I wonder if we could recreate it here in the classroom. That means some of you will have to portray the people. Which person from the photograph should we start with? There will be others but we must build the picture slowly."

First, the class almost unanimously selects the older woman. There are at least five volunteers to play the role, and when Diane selects Sandra (a good choice) she tells the others that they will have an opportunity to play other roles. Sandra is usually very quiet, and not one to draw attention to herself. Diane asks her to study the picture, and sit on a rostrum block as if she is the elderly woman.

Meanwhile the rest of the class are asked to study Sandra and make suggestions about the way she should be sitting. The class is really engrossed in this and Mark rushes up with the bag he brings his lunch in and thrusts it into Sandra's hand.

The teacher asks the class whether they think this is a good idea. Everyone agrees to this. Now more students join the scene, and the teacher takes great care in making sure the scene is arranged to everyone's satisfaction. She switches off the overhead so that the attention of the class is focused entirely on the still image that they have created.

"When you look at this group of people, what kind of emotions do you see?"

One student says, "You can tell the woman sitting down has lost something she can never get back."

"There is anger in the eyes of the woman standing behind her."

"The girl looks hopeful."

Now the class starts asking the students in the group picture questions.

"Why do you seem so sad?" (to the old woman)

"My farm is gone."

"Why do you look so angry?" (to another character)

"They have sold all the things we've worked so hard for."

"They have taken everything," another person says.

The questioning continues as the students in the picture draw on Yuki's story and other material they have researched for their answers. There are questions about what they expect to face back home in California. There are also questions about leaving their friends who have gone to other states, and what this means to them.

Finally, the teacher asks the whole class to join the portrait in the roles of other Americans of Japanese heritage on the platform facing an uncertain future, and recalling the days spent in prison camp. I step forward, walk into the group picture and speak to them.

"As I touch you on the shoulder, say whatever you are thinking at this moment as you stand on the station platform."

The students talk about their memories of the camp, their lives before the war, and their fears of what lies ahead. If a child says nothing, I do not press them for a statement but murmur something about this person being too overcome to speak and move on. The *collage* of verbal memories that they create is very moving. To make a connection with the beginning of our work together on the story, I ask them to remember the time they first stood waiting for the train taking them to Topaz. The story has come full circle.

Then the students return to their seats and write the first paragraph of a story which will describe their arrival home in California. The paragraph may be written in the voice of any character in the book or ones that they wish to create themselves. With these moments of reflective writing, we are now ready to read the final chapters of the book and pursue the twin themes of "journey" and "survival" further.

Drama 3: Interpreting a Picture Book Story through Drama, and Exploring Other Cultural Perspectives

You will probably have noticed the emphasis given to individual personal feelings in the previous drama, and the ways in which the two teachers structured the drama experience to *protect* the students into expressing these emotions. In dealing with sensitive topics such as the deportation of the Japanese, the dramatic art form itself offers all sorts of opportunities and ways for students to explore these issues in some depth. The strategies the teacher uses in the game of drama have their roots in the *theatre* and in *literature*.

In both dramas, frequent use has been made of the *still image, group portrait,* and other forms of *"stop time" conventions* that can be most effective in their simplicity. The students *in* the still image do not have to speak, and their *depiction* of a character is often shaped by the suggestions of other students. Therefore, the whole class is deeply and significantly involved both in making and responding to the work. These are the chief constituents of any art form: making art and responding to art. In the two dramas I have described you will see the making and the responding complement each other enabling students not only to create drama but also encouraging them to reflect on their work.

These primary students are spontaneously enacting "The Billy Goat Gruff." The piano bench serves as the bridge.

One other aspect of the game of drama that should not go unrecognized concerns the importance of *story telling*. As we have seen in the two dramas, students taking roles are encouraged to speak in the direct speech of the character they are portraying, for example, "Take care, my family. Look after each other while I am gone." At the same time, there is a great deal of recounting events and recalling memories, feelings, and images anecdotally in story mode. The teachers in both dramas also use story telling to serve as an introduction to the next stage of the drama, to create a mood, to set the right tone for a moment in the work, or simply to act as a bridge between one activity and the next. Spotting different opportunities for using spontaneous story telling in classroom drama can enrich and deepen the work for everyone.

In the final series of activities I shall describe in this chapter, story telling lends special significance to the drama work. Again, like the previous dramas, this one is based on literature. However, on this occasion the art work in the book plays an important role in the exploration of the story in dramatic form.

The book is Jan Andrews's *Very Last First Time*, illustrated by Ian Wallace (Atheneum, 1986). It tells the story of an Inuit girl named Eva walking underneath the frozen sea "for the very last first time." Eva has collected mussels before with her mother under the ice, but this is the first time she goes alone into this eerie, enchanted world full of shadows, strange sounds, shapes, lights, and reflections. Author and illustrator work in harmony to evoke the feeling of the Arctic, and the sheer joy and exultation of a young girl exploring the ocean bed for the "very last first time."

Of course, students in a first-grade class who are read and shown this book may also be hearing and seeing it for the very first time. Any drama they do will not only have to enrich this experience but will also have to carry personal meaning for each and every one of them. The following drama activities are therefore intended to deepen and enhance the young child's understanding and appreciation of the lives of the two characters in the story and the rich visual images depicted in the illustrations.

1. Before reading the book to the class, the teacher talks to the students about the phrase "very last first time." What do they think this means? Can they remember things that they once could not do by themselves, and now can do without any help, such as tying shoes or putting on boots? The first time they were able to do them by themselves was the "very last first time."

   Working with a partner each child shows in **mime** the other what they can remember doing for the "very last first time." When everyone is finished, the pairs share with the rest of the class what they were showing each other. A way to accomplish this is for each partner to *tell* the class the story of what the other person was doing, and what was special about this "very last first time." Selected examples of the children's mime can be shown following the stories, focusing on noteworthy aspects of their work. For example, one child may show every detail of learning a particular skill, and holds everyone's attention. The ability to concentrate hard is an important skill that should be noted and praised. If possible, the children should be asked first what they liked about or learned from a child's work before the teacher offers comments. (A writing activity to supplement this work could involve students making a collection of all those things they remember doing for the "very last first time" in their own "Very Last First Time" books.)

2. When the story has been read to the class and students have had an opportunity to study the illustrations with their profusion of colors, images, and sea creatures, the teacher says, "I wonder what it was like the first time Eva went with her mother underneath the sea. There must have been things her mother told her to do and what not to do. Do you think she was afraid of some of the strange shadow shapes when she saw them for the first time? I wonder what her mother said to her. If I am Eva and you are all her mother, what things are you going to tell me about walking underneath the sea?"

The negotiations between teacher and students contained in this role-taking activity will allow the children to draw on their own background experience of what caregivers say to children when they are telling them about a new experience. It also encourages them to selectively use information from the story and illustrations in formulating what they will say. In addition, the *role reversal* of child playing the role of adult and teacher assuming the role of child both protects and empowers the students.

As the children give instructions, the teacher asks questions to clarify a point or to seek assurances about any fears the teacher-as-child might have, for example, "Is it slippery on the ocean bottom? What sort of animals will I see? Will I be scared? What happens if I get separated from you?"

3. Working either through the use of the children's imaginations or drawing the ocean floor on a long roll of white paper with each child being responsible for a segment of the drawing, the teacher in role as a young child is shown all the undersea wonders that the class creates.
4. Finally, Eva, now grown up and a mother herself, tells her own daughter the story of the time that she went under the frozen sea with her mother, and what her mother told her. This is either told orally by the class and written down by the teacher, or written individually by the students if they are able to do this.

The Game of Drama: A Polyphony of Voices

If you look back over the three dramas I have described, you will probably notice common threads running through all of them both in terms of content and in terms of the way they are structured as "games of drama." Each story is about a child, and deals with the thoughts, feelings, and perceptions of childhood.

Sometimes the voice of the child is very clearly heard, as in the case of Yuki's story. Sometimes, as was pointed out by the teachers planning the drama, many other voices can be heard. In the poem we hear the third-person author voice of the poet echoing the voice of a mystery writer and voicing John's unspoken thoughts in a short piece of direct speech. Finally in *Very Last First Time* we hear the author's voice, Eva's mother's voice, and Eva herself talking to her mother and to herself. We also hear Eva singing.

Each piece of literature offers a **polyphony of voices** to be explored in the game of drama because of the different perspectives, points of view, and histories that each one of those voices represents. In the mystery drama, the students create or recreate the voices of a host of characters only some of whom are briefly mentioned in the poem. In the *Journey Home* drama, we go beyond Yuki's voice and those of her family to recreate different voices: the unnamed Japanese who suffered prejudice and deportation. In the drama about walking on the ocean floor, the voices are few but there is a universal quality and a sense of continuity in their utterances: mother teaching child and child (now mother) teaching child.

The way in which classroom drama is organized and structured is designed to enable the participants in the game of drama to discover those voices for and within themselves, and, equally importantly *to express* what they hear those voices say. What voice did Elizabeth in the ESL class hear when she said, "Take care, my family, look after each other while I am gone"? The polite but tender formality of the phrasing was entirely appropriate to the person uttering those words, and to the dramatic situation itself.

The Russian writer M. M. Bakhtin, whose work in the field of literature complements that of Vygotsky in language development and psychology, said that the unique speech experience of each individual is shaped and developed "in continuous and constant interaction with others' individual utterances" (1986, p. 89). Calling this experience a process of *assimilation,* Bakhtin maintained that our speech, including our creative works, is therefore filled with other people's words, and with their tone and form of expression "which we assimilate, rework, and re-accentuate" (p. 89).

Selecting literary material for exploration in the game of drama requires one to hear the many voices that are either contained in or are suggested by the text, and it is the lives that lie behind these voices that become our concern in the drama itself. Whether it is a young boy doubting the possibility of a real-life adventure taking place in a setting ripe for adventure or a woman recalling the voices of her childhood as she rediscovers the humiliation of deportation, it is their voices, however faint, that we hear again in classroom drama assimilated and recreated by the participating students. And it is this "play" with voices and with language that makes the game of drama so important to the child's whole-language development.

Chinese Boxes and Other Sleights of Hand

One final note about each game of drama that is constructed around the poem, the autobiographical story, and the picture book is that they all involve the kinds of games and conventions that authors use. For example, each suggested ending contains a paradoxical twist:

1. The boy who reappears at the inn might not be John; instead, he could be the boy from a century before.
2. The crowd standing by the train waiting to be deported to Japan are suddenly the group of internees waiting to be transported back to their homes.

3. The mother telling the story of her walk on the ocean floor is not Eva's mother, but Eva herself talking to her child.

"I'm playing games," writes the novelist Brigid Brophy, "like a painter who includes in his picture a mirror in which he shows himself standing outside the picture painting it." If you play the whole-language game of drama, I think you will discover just how powerful the game can be once you and your students start exploring its many intriguing possibilities.

REFERENCES

Bakhtin, M. M. (1986). *Speech genres and other late essays*. Austin: University of Texas Press.

Bateson, G. (1976). A theory of play and fantasy. In *Play: Its role in education and child development*, edited by J. S. Bruner, A. Jolly, and K. Sylva. Harmondsworth, Middlesex: Penguin.

Bolton, G. (1992). *New perspectives on classroom drama*. Hemel Hempstead, Hertfordshire: Simon and Schuster.

Brown, G. (1984). *Teaching talk: Strategies for production and assessment*. New York: Cambridge University Press.

Davies, G. (1983). *Practical primary drama*. London: Heinemann.

Garvey, C. (1977). *Children's play*. Cambridge, MA: Harvard University Press.

Heath, S. B. (1983). *Ways with words*. New York: Cambridge University Press.

Vygotsky, L. S. (1978). *Mind in society. The development of higher psychological processes*. Cambridge, MA: Cambridge University Press.

Zola, M. (1990). *Poetry*. Collections 2. Toronto: Copp Clark Pitman.

HELPFUL BOOKS ABOUT DRAMA

Bolton, G. (1992). *New perspectives on classroom drama*. Hemel Hempstead, Hertfordshire: Simon and Schuster.

One of the world's leading drama teachers discusses the latest advances in the field, and describes a number of his own drama lessons.

Davies, G. (1983). *Practical primary drama*. London: Heinemann.

Many practical ideas for the primary teacher who wants to work in role.

Fox, M. (1987). *Teaching drama to young children*. Portsmouth, NH: Heinemann.

O'Neill, C., et al. (1976). *Drama guidelines*. London: Heinemann.

This invaluable teaching guide has detailed lesson plans which may be used at all levels in elementary school.

Tarlington, C. & Verriour, P. (1991). *Role drama*. Toronto: Pembroke.

A practical guide to the planning and implementation of dramas based on traditional stories in which the teacher works in role with the class.

Tarlington, C. & Verriour, P. (1983). *Offstage: Teaching elementary education through drama.* Toronto: Oxford University Press.

A lesson-by-lesson teacher's plan book of games, activities, and dramas suitable for all elementary grades.

Verriour, P. (1993). *In role: Teaching and learning dramatically.* Markham, Ont.: Pippin.

This book explains how to introduce dramatic playing into the elementary school curriculum through the use of integrated thematic units.

FILMS

Dorothy Heathcote Talks to Teachers, Parts One and Two (1974). Northwestern University, Evanston, IL. (28 mins. and 29 mins.)

Dorothy Heathcote: Building Belief, Parts One and Two (1975). Northwestern University, Evanston, IL. (30 mins. and 32 mins.)

Three Looms Waiting (1971). B.B.C. Publications, London, England. (50 mins.)

PICTURE BOOK STORIES TO EXPLORE IN DRAMA

Recommended for Students at the Primary Level

All of the following children's illustrated books explore some aspect of the human condition with sensitivity and insight, and have rich subtexts that could form the basis of classroom drama.

Andrews, J. and Reezuk, K. (1990). *The auction.* Douglas and McIntyre.

Leger, D. (1991). *The attic of all sorts.* Orca.

Little, J., De Vries, M., and Gilman, P. (1991). *Once upon a golden apple.* Viking.

McFarlane, S. and Lott, S. (1992). *Jessie's island.* Orca.

Mollel, T. and Morin, P. (1990). *The orphan boy.* Oxford University Press.

Morgan, A. and Marchenko, M. (1990). *The magic hockey skates.* Oxford University Press.

Poulin, S. (1986). *Have you seen Josephine?* Tundra Books.

Thompson, S. (1990). *Cheryl Bibalhats (Cheryl's Potlatch).* Yinka Dene Language Institute.

Wallace, I. (1991). *Chin Chiang and the dragon's dance.* Douglas and McIntyre.

STORIES FOR OLDER STUDENTS

Recommended for Students at the Intermediate Level

Here is a selection of novels written by contemporary writers which explore issues that are of interest and concern to older students and could form the basis of classroom drama at the intermediate level.

Bawden, Nina (1989). *The outside child.* Lothrop.

Brooks, Bruce (1990). *Everwhere.* Harper.

Fox, Paula (1988). *The village by the sea*. Orchard.

Garrigue, Sheila (1978). *Between friends*. Bradbury.

George, Jean Craighead (1972). *Julie of the wolves*. Harper.

Holm, Anne (1965). *North to freedom*. Harcourt.

Konigsburg, E. L (1982). *Journey to an 800 number*. Atheneum.

King, Thomas (1992). *A Coyote Columbus story*. Douglas and McIntyre.

Myers, Walter Dean (1988). *Scorpions*. Harper.

Slepian, Jan (1989). *The broccoli tapes*. Putnam.

Westhall, Robert (1976). *The machine gunners*. Greenwillow.

DISCUSSION QUESTIONS

1. List and discuss what you consider to be essential qualities and skills required of a teacher wishing to use drama as a medium of learning in the classroom.

2. The author stresses that students should feel a sense of ownership in the drama that they are constructing. Discuss the ways in which the students are encouraged to acquire ownership of the mystery drama.

3. Select a picture book story that you feel would be suitable for dramatic exploration in the K–3 classroom, and identify the different voices you "hear" in the story. What human relationships and issues do you wish to examine in the game of drama? Develop short drama activities that would allow children to gain fresh insights and understandings through taking roles and other drama conventions described in this chapter.

4. Choose a story or poem that you think could be explored through drama at the grade 4–8 level, and devise a teaching plan based on one of the two intermediate dramas described in the chapter.

Using Computers in Whole-Language Classrooms

SYD BUTLER AND
LEE GUNDERSON

Introduction

Divided into seven parts, this chapter will address the following issues: emergent literacy using computers, the computer as a tool for composing, critical literacy and computers, using a data base in the classroom, managing computer use in the whole-language classroom, recent developments in the applications of technology, and communicating in and beyond the classroom.

There will not be much discussion of particular brands of computers or particular items of software in this chapter because it would be out of date even before the book is printed. It is said there are only two types of computers: the obsolete ones you buy in stores and the up-to-date ones that are still on the designer's drawing board. This chapter is not about the technology; rather, we discuss its *uses* in the classroom that are in accord with the philosophy of whole-language. What this means is that computers, if used as described, can lead to collaborative learning, to a better understanding of authorship, to exploration of concepts and ideas not previously possible, to an understanding of how text and image are related, to modifications in and improvements to the writing process, to improved ways of storing and retrieving information, to extended ways of using the library and its newer technologies, and to new ways of communicating with real audiences in the global village.

The United Nations Educational, Scientific, and Cultural Organization (UNESCO) recently concluded a 12-country study of the metacognitive impact of computer use in schools and on children. An analysis of videotapes of computer use in these countries indicated that a variety of higher-order cognitive functionings occurred: relating a problem to previous problems, formulating appropriate questions, trying alternative approaches, evaluating one's actions, analyzing problems, recognizing relationships, generating new ideas, synthesizing information, observing central issues and problems, and comparing similarities and differences (Collis, 1993, p. 249).

Technology has always been a part of the language classroom ever since a teacher first picked up a piece of chalk to write a story on the wall or blackboard. In West Africa, teachers still scratch their written words on the ground with a stick. Forty years ago, teachers were trained in the use of spirit duplicators and filmstrip projectors, while the up-to-date educators of those times were excited about the introduction into their classrooms of 16 mm film projectors and amplified record players.

The development of technology never stands still. The past two decades have seen the introduction of video technology, first with cumbersome, black-and-white, reel-to-reel recording and playback machines, and now with the highly portable camcorder and VHS videocassette players. With audio reproduction the revolution has taken us from the fragile, scratchy 78 rpm record through the long-playing record to the modern compact disc. Audiocassette players, whether in the form of a portable audiotape player, pocket audiotape player, car stereo, or even the telephone answering machine, are now nearly as common as dust.

The computer is a fact of life. Banks, airlines, department stores, restaurants, ticket agencies, and generally all large corporations function through the computers that are on every desk or counter. Few shops are without a computer to record sales, monitor stock, and print paychecks. More and more individuals use home computers for work or for business. While many parents deplore the practice, many children visit a friend's house after school to play Nintendo.

Just as two children will quite independently play together in front of the monitor screen, so in the classroom the computer is a magnet that draws students. This chapter will show how the computer can attract students to argue and discuss options in front of the screen. Even some interactive computer games—provided we can avoid the violence, sexism, and racism too often implied in much of the software—have their value in promoting cooperative thinking skills and decision making. Moreover, there are simulation games purposely designed to make students cooperate in small groups in the making of decisions according to their assessment of sophisticated data.

For many years some doomful educators have predicted that computers might take over, when all learning will be programmed through central banks of computers, and teachers will become redundant, except to ensure that the hardware works and the software is available. Such a nightmarish *1984* or *Brave New World* view of learning envisages a future in which students are locked in front of their individual keyboards and monitor screens, with no time for human interaction.

The alternative view is that even with one or two computers in their classrooms, teachers can still be in control of the curriculum, can still have time to be with students, and can help them make use of the hardware in many creative ways. Indeed, there are already classrooms where a computer is part of the everyday curriculum, just as it is part of the everyday world of travel, government, and commerce. For students living in this technological world, computer literacy will be as important as pen-and-ink literacy.

We hope to show that a computer has a valuable place in the classroom, constituting its own learning center, on par with the reading corner, the math center, the drama and puppetry areas, the arts and crafts tables, or the science and social studies centers. Sometimes, through the judicious choice of software, the microcomputer can span many areas of the curriculum.

It is the teacher in the classroom who knows the children best, not the expert computer programmers. Although it may take a teacher time to find suitable, well-designed software for specific types of content learning, the use of generic software (especially for word processing, data processing, and desktop publishing) enables both teachers and students to be creative and imaginative. The computer is a learning tool. Students can learn *from* the computer and *with* the computer. This chapter is dedicated to both undertakings.

Emergent Literacy Using Computers

There is something magical about computers; an attraction that even kindergarten students cannot resist emanates from computer screens. Is it a kind of hypnosis, a computer-induced trance that fixes gazes to screens for hours, that compels little ones to stare at the images that fly by in glorious technicolored phantasmagorias?

There is no doubt that younger people in North America think differently than older ones. They have been trained by Nintendo, MTV, GameBoys, and home-computer-generated games to be able to perceive thousands of images a minute and to have eye-hand coordination much superior to those of us who grew up in the decades of radio and early television. In the past, teachers thought kindergarten students did not have the eye-hand coordination to become typists. To some extent, this may be true. However, they do have the coordination, the intelligence, and the desire to use the computer keyboard, the mouse, and the joystick to run programs and to play games. Unfortunately, a trip to any video arcade will reveal that the ones most addicted to computers are boys. It is interesting to note in contrast that the number of women in the workforce who use computers far exceeds the number of men who use computers—but more about that later.

The computer does have a role in the whole-language classroom. Indeed, Daiute (1992) noted that students who have trouble learning in the traditional fashion in the primary grades are often "good at learning from visual and aural sources in contexts that are meaningful to them" (p. 250). Students who cannot write find the computer and computer activities attractive. In Chapter 6, Reading and Language Development, studies of emergent literacy are described and discussed. They show that students explore reading and writing and systematically make connections between print and language. The computer can assist them in valuable ways to see how visual images, especially print, can be used to make meaning. The computer also teaches students more about literacy and literacy materials.

The Computer as Quill or Crayon

Tony Saputra is an extraordinary seven-year-old who learned how to use a computer program to generate drawings (in this case DrawPerfect 1.1 published by WordPerfect Corporation, 1990). He used a mouse to control the lines of this drawing, one of his earliest done when he was just beginning first grade. He now makes incredible drawings in color. We chose the drawing depicted in Figure 8.1 because he also added some text at the bottom. It says, "This is my dog Punky." He is using the computer to invent spellings. The computer gave him some added, important literacy information. It showed him that material can be saved or recorded and that it can be "read" later. It showed him that he could print material he had "composed." His teacher collected and collated the material that Tony produced and put it in a book. Tony learned early that he could produce books. These are all different kinds of literacy knowledge that students often do not learn until late in their schooling careers.

The drawing program allows students to manipulate visual images and to add text if they wish. Some programs provide intricate images, pictures, and patterns that can be incorporated into students' drawings. Students use the computer as they would an easel, as they do crayons to produce drawings. We have seen sixth-grade students produce intricate, multicolored drawings using computers. Early on they begin to learn the uses of the computer to generate words in written language, not simply as captions to accompany their drawing.

Figure 8.1   *"This is my dog Punky..."*

These early primary uses of the computer to compose in writing appear to adults to be painful. Students type out a single letter at a time, searching out individual letters with apparent pain and difficulty. Often, teachers, feeling great sympathy, charge in and have students dictate their stories to them. This is fine, if it does not interrupt the students' explorations. If the process is not too frustrating, it should be encouraged. It is true that primary students have some difficulty writing with a keyboard. However, it is fortunate that thoughtful keyboard inventors decided that capital letters should be used to identify the keys since we usually learn the shapes of letters first in their capital form. Indeed, they are the ones with which students are most likely to begin their independent writing. You should make the judgment on an individual basis about whether to have students dictate their stories to you or try to key in their own writing. Some exploration is wonderful. However, if the process slows the students down so significantly that they can focus only on a single letter at a time rather than whole words or sentences, then perhaps the process is not beneficial in the long run. And the computer should never substitute for the log book or journal for primary students.

The teacher must determine if working with a computer word processor is beneficial on an individual basis. For some students who would find the task exhausting, the computer may not be beneficial for writing. For others—those who enjoy the interaction of keyboard, screen, writing, and printing—the activity does allow them to explore language. Most likely the best procedure is to have students work in pairs. The use of the computer in this context is one of exploration and one of learning concepts related to emergent literacy. Its role changes from one of exploration to one of servant when students begin to use the computer as a tool for composing.

The Computer as a Tool for Composing

Word-Processing Programs for the Classroom Computer

In Chapter 5, The Writing Connection, we emphasized that written composition connects all language activities. Our view that writing floats on a sea of talk means that composing processes are often founded on discussion, interviewing, conferencing, reading, and the sharing of ideas. All writers need time, and most need social interaction, for the incubation and rehearsal of ideas. Where does the computer fit into this process?

At first it makes sense to see the computer simply as a *tool* for written composition. With its keyboard, screen, and printer, it seems analogous to a sophisticated typewriter. When you press the keys identified by letters of the alphabet, eventually those same letters appear as print on a piece of paper. Of course, the computer will do this only if it has been loaded with a word-processing program that "teaches" it to perform like a typewriter. Most modern word-processing programs will do much more than a typewriter, but the composing activities described in this section will need only a simple, basic program.

Computer Writing Processes

There is no single writing process. We cannot talk about *the* writing process or *the* computer writing process. Even with the use of pen and paper, a class of students will show a variety of ways for getting ideas into writing. The computer allows different students to develop their writing processes in a variety of ways. Picture the computer as a flexible work station in a whole-language classroom that also has a carpet for individual and group reading, shelves or racks of books for book choosing, and a variety of spaces for drama, arts and crafts, science, math, and social studies activities. The whole room signals a mixture of collaborative learning and individual responsibility as a background for the more traditional students' and the teacher's desks. The computer station is a place where one student may work privately or several students may work collaboratively.

Getting Started with a Computer

How much do students need to know about computers before they can start using one? The simple answer is nothing. Children learn by doing. They learn language by using it to achieve their own purposes. They learn to write by wanting to express their ideas in a more permanent form. They learn to spell by approximating their visual and auditory knowledge of the word with the alphabetic letters that records the word on paper. The ability to get ideas down on paper is the real basis of the writing process and is a sufficient foundation for students to begin to translate this ability into electronic formats. Students learn to use a computer by using it to achieve their communicative purposes. Computer literacy is using technology to make meaning.

The alternative answer to that question is that students need to understand how computers work, to know the terminology of computer programmers, and to learn the jargon of word-processing programs. Brenda Shynal (1984) reported that her first attempt to learn word processing followed a traditional skills approach, which gave her a clear outline of the learning objectives of the course and a sequence of activities designed, lesson by lesson, to take her through all the necessary stages. Her problems began with the first lesson when she had to learn definitions for the terminology and then learn to use certain combinations of keys. "We didn't really write anything; we played with the keys and watched the cursor. After this introduction I was sure that I was in a

Classroom computers are often used by small groups. This has the potential of stimulating both oral and written language.

foreign land and a foreign language was being spoken" (p. 36). Her problems became worse with each lesson. As the computer jargon became more and more complicated, she failed to complete a set task in correcting a given text. She then had problems in compiling a table of names and addresses, realizing that this task did not connect with any part of her life. It was another artificial exercise, a dummy run. More frustration came when she was finally to learn about printing text. Somewhere along the way she had missed an important step and had to turn to the instructor to get her out of the mess. She realized that the only interactions in the class were between student and computer, or student and instructor, because all the students worked in individual carrels, preventing them from helping each other. "This class reinforced for me that there must be a sequence of skills that one had to learn to be able to operate a computer" (p. 37). Her misfortune was that she was unable to arrive at the "right" answers and so decided that it was not within her capacity to learn the computer. Ironically, even though she had given up hope of ever learning to use a computer, she still received a certificate that, as a result of taking the course, she was qualified in word processing.

Her second course began with a lesson she and her partner were given to do: Transmit a "cookbook" of simple instructions to the instructor's electronic mail address. Again there were problems, but this time she was able to work together with her partner to create and send their messages. She failed the first course, but she was able to learn word processing in the second because it allowed her to take charge of the process in expressing her own ideas.

The whole-language approach is simple: At first the teacher switches on the computer, loads the program, and the screen is ready for the first student's message. The teacher then saves and prints the text. Within a few days these responsibilities shift to the students. Some student "experts" will be on hand to help the others. Pairing will ensure that everyone takes turns in teaching and learning the use of the hardware and software.

A more contentious issue is the problem of students learning to use the keyboard. The traditional view suggests that students have to be taught the location of the fingers on the keyboard and need an extensive course to learn to touch-type, or to use typing games on the computer to improve their skills in speed and accuracy. There is a fear that if students learn to "hunt and peck" in the early grades these habits will become ingrained and they will never learn the "correct" way to type later in high school business or secretarial courses.

Such fears are unfounded. The analogy of primary students learning first to print and later shift to cursive writing applies also to computer writing. One of the values of the computer is that young children can use their recognition of capital letters to create perfectly formed letters in their own texts. At first, this process may seem painfully slow; but then their printing with pencils is also very slow, and the results often haphazard. For these children, the computer offers a system that is, even in the early stages, at least as efficient as their handwriting. The computer models for them examples of perfectly formed letters. Moreover, for students from cultures with different writing conventions, the computer also shows them the left-to-right and top-to-bottom sequencing of words and lines of English.

Jessica Kahn and Pamela Freyd (1990) reported that in their studies of students from kindergarten to grade 8 they found that children generally wrote longer pieces with word processors while "kindergartners composed meaningful messages earlier with word processing than with pencil and paper" (p. 87). They recommended that children should be allowed to learn to keyboard incidentally as part of the larger process of writing to express their meaning. Their view is also supported by Judith Newman (1986) who described a case in which fifth-grade teachers decided to teach keyboarding for two months before allowing students to use the computer. In the same school the third-grade teachers preferred to get their students writing from the very beginning, but made some typing games available for those students who wanted to try them. By the middle of the year they found that the third-grade students were keyboarding as well as the fifth-graders and were writing longer and more fluent texts.

Kahn and Freyd offered an alternative solution to the keyboarding problem by suggesting that teachers can give a group or a whole class plasticized full-size photocopies of the layout of a computer keyboard. A few five-minute practices on these dummy keyboards will speed up the children's hunt-and-peck skills and also introduce them to the idea of "home keys" and the use of all 10 fingers.

Barbara Cox, having acquired an old computer and printer for her early primary classroom, loaded a simple word-processing program and allowed two six-year-old girls to write a story. Neither had used a computer before; neither knew anything about keyboarding. But they quickly learned what "buttons" to press and were very proud of the story they composed together (Butler and Cox, 1992).

Beginning Activities

As an introduction, students at any level can be asked, as part of their day's activities, to take a turn at the computer (which is left on with the word-processing program running) and to compose a brief message around the framework: "Hi. My name is _____. I am _____." At the end of the day the text can be printed out for shared reading. Other open-ended sentence starters can be used each day, with the aim of getting the students to compose more elaborate messages:

> I like . . . .
> My favorite . . . .
> I wish . . . .
> I have . . . .
> I hate . . . .
> Red is the color of . . . .
> If I were . . . .
> I used to . . . .
> I think that . . . .

They should be told how to form capital letters with the shift key and how to use the return key at the end of each message. These simple instructions should also be printed on a display card. At first the students may want to compose their messages on paper before going to the computer, but even at these early stages it is valuable to add ideas that come as they keyboard.

Other variations may include an adaption of the "Traveling Tale," in which the teacher gives a one-sentence story starter, and each child adds a sentence or two to continue the story. Or students can add their ideas and examples to a topic or a theme that had surfaced in their reading or in any other area of the curriculum.

As messages get longer, it will not be possible or desirable to print them all. Students will need to take ownership of their writing. This is the time to teach them to print out their own files and to store their texts on their own disks.

Once students are accustomed to using the computer station, then their computer printouts will become an integral part of their writing folders, sometimes as finished texts but also as computer drafts. Decisions about which of their written drafts are worth transferring to their computer disks will have to be made.

Another project could be based on the "Experts" idea. The starting point is that everyone knows more about some topic than anyone else in the room. Therefore, everyone has the power to give information about a particular subject, to become the class expert in that subject. We start with a brainstorming listing of who has expertise about what subjects or topics, whether it is a skill like horse riding or skateboarding, or knowledge about a very special place. Some students will choose a sport or hobby, others will select some aspect of their culture or part of a family heritage. Such a project becomes accumulative, and may involve all sorts of individual talks and demonstrations or displays, as well as a written description that can be collected on the class Experts disk.

Prewriting with a Computer

There is nothing worse for a writer than to stare at a blank screen wondering how to get started on a topic. These prewriting strategies are essentially the same as recommended for writing with pen and paper. The difference is that the teacher can provide a template with blank spaces for the student's responses, which the student can transfer onto the screen to provide a framework for

filling in ideas. This template, as in Schwartz (1983, p. 199), may be nothing more than a numbering and lettering of slots for main headings and sub-headings, as in a plan for a traditional essay.

Other heuristic techniques include **jotting** when the student simply adds line by line any random thoughts about the topic, or **freewriting** or **forced writing** when the student writes continuously for a limited period of time, as in the **Writing Derby** described in Chapter 5. The teacher can also create a computer file with a set of heuristic questions that will guide the student to think systematically through a topic. Even such questions as Where? What? Who? When? and Why? may be enough to trigger ideas and get the writing started.

Invisible writing, recommended by Stephen Marcus (1991), is done by turning off the video screen or turning down the brightness control until the screen goes dark. The student types without seeing the screen. For those students who are not expert typists it means that they can concentrate on the keyboard instead of looking to see what they have typed. The principle here is that without the distraction of the printed text on the screen, the student can focus on the topic in mind, sustain a burst of thinking and keyboarding, and then turn up the screen to see what ideas have been generated.

There are also many specialized computer programs that promote prewriting activities directly onto the screen. Most of these give some type of verbal or visual prompt and ask the student to provide lists of ideas or related words. Open-ended questions are frequently used, as well as sentence frames or sentence beginnings, which the student completes on the screen. Some of these try to build on the responses provided by the student, but the results invariably lack the delight and excitement that can come from sharing ideas with another human being. The danger with such programs is that composing can become a mechanical exercise of writing to a formula, with the consequence that the writer never really takes ownership of the text. Michael Spitzer (1989) described some of the more common commercial programs, especially in the context of college students generating ideas for writing academic essays. One advantage that the computer has over the teacher as conferencer is that students are not likely to see the computer as an authority figure, but as they find out its limitations, they realize that they have to do their own thinking.

Writing and talking activities that focus on the memories, experiences, and opinions of the members of the class make a very good preparation for further explorations into lifewriting, as described in Chapter 5. The class "Who's Who" book, or individual "All about Me" booklets can be part of an accumulative year-long project. For example, one sixth-grade class decided to take the ideas that they had generated in the "Sense of Place" activity (described in Chapter 5) and use the computer to create their own class book under this title. Every member of the class became a published author. The length of their pieces varied from a half-page to two pages of printed text, but each piece was recognizably individual and personal. For example, one student began:

My Grandparents' home is so special to me because they lived in it when I was born, and it has held all the memories of my young age. It has a special way of greeting me that makes me feel at home. It always has the smell of my favorite sweets, and has some really neat exercise equipment.

Another student described a small stream in his neighborhood, and then continued:

The stream is special to me because I can think it's mine. For it's a place to think, to pray, to thank the lord, to be alone, to have fun, to be happy. A place to love; a place for me.

Another student's "My Place" took into the realm of fantasy:

My favorite place is actually not real, it is a place in my dreams. My place doesn't have a name, it just floats out in space. You see, my place is where all my dreams are. One day I might be a pilot on a spaceship trying to destroy the evil Colonel Bishop and the Exiles. Or one day I could be a person from the past who has come into the future.

Such short explorations into personal feelings and experience build a foundation of computer writing skills.

A computer writing station provides a valuable facility that enhances the writing program. Practically anything that can be written with a pen or pencil on paper can also be written on the computer screen.

Collaborative Writing

Collaborative writing is a process that allows two or more students to produce a joint-authored text. Jane Zeni (1990), reporting on her work with the St. Louis Gateway Writing Project, recommended that teachers set the tone for computer use at their first meeting with their students:

Too many teachers resort to lessons in computer literacy, hoping that the writing process will follow. We have found that the best way to start is with a real writing experience, making computer instruction as simple, natural, and unobtrusive as we can. Our first lessons tend to have several features in common:

1. *They produce short, meaningful pieces of writing.*
2. *They require revision.*
3. *They are social or collaborative.*
4. *They result in quick, informal publication. (pp. 65–66)*

Teachers set up a writing task that gets the students to focus on their ideas and the messages they are to record. One idea is to give two students a cartoon drawing showing two figures. The students give names to each figure and then each takes one of the roles to begin a written dialogue. The only instruction needed is to begin each turn with the name of the character speaking, followed by a colon, and then to press return at the end of the speech before the partner takes over. These partnership dialogues can be saved and printed out over a few days, to give everyone a chance to participate, and then in a whole group session, possibly with the cartoon figures displayed on an overhead, the students can perform their dialogues.

In an earlier case study of collaborative writing (Daiute, 1985), two seven-year-old boys wrote eight fantasy stories over three controlled experimental sessions, four by themselves and four with each other. Two of the stories were written from terminals in separate rooms. Under this condition each child had about five minutes to add to the story transmitted by his partner over the screen before adding his next contribution. They also had face-to-face sessions when the boys composed together, both with paper and pencil and a computer, when they were allowed to make their own decisions about how to proceed. The results showed that both boys wrote more when they used the computer rather than paper and pencil. Daiute concluded from this and other studies that collaborative writing activities need to be set within a communicative context. The student pairings and collaborative strategies need careful planning to take account of individual differences in the writing process. She

This student is using a computer in the library for communication purposes.

emphasized that writers also need opportunities for solo writing with a variety of writing instruments in order to develop their own writing abilities.

Computer writing is especially useful for dealing with the demands of a school system for the traditional essay. With the computer it is easier to organize information into a formal structure. Two collaborators can make decisions about what topics should be covered in each paragraph. They can decide if each paragraph has sufficient detail and number of illustrations. They can argue about the best sequence of paragraphs, and at the end they can compose an introduction that describes what the essay is to accomplish and a conclusion that sums up their opinions. Constructing an academic essay in partnership becomes a good learning process for student writers. It will give them confidence in their ability to tackle the problem when faced with such a task in later years in the isolation of a public examination, without a computer.

Revising with a Computer

The computer provides two very important advantages for writers, both beginners and experts. First, the computer allows a *distance* between the writer and the text. Handwriting is such a personal mode of expression that a writer's handwritten text is as unique as a fingerprint. Even expert writers may be very reluctant to reread their own personal letters very thoroughly, and will resist changes to what they have expressed in a free flow of ideas. Yet because the computer transforms the writer's thoughts into a printed format on the video screen, already there is some detachment between the writer and the composed words. The writer can read the words just as if they were in someone else's text.

Second, the technology of the computer makes it easy to revise writing. Whatever the writer's propensity for making mistakes in keyboarding, spelling, vocabulary, or sentence structure, the writer can forge ahead without fear, knowing that it can all be put right in the end, without any great penalties, and with no personal recrimination from the computer. With handwritten texts it is very difficult to get students to make anything more than a clean copy. The final copy is usually just that—a neat, tidy version of the previous draft, and teachers are usually happy if all of the spelling mistakes have been caught. To ask a student to revise or make corrections after a piece has been submitted and graded will be interpreted only as a punishment. In contrast, when a teacher reads a piece of computer-produced text, the teacher knows that another draft can be produced without hardship, even if it is only to add or delete a comma.

Yet, in revision, the computer, while making it easy for a writer to revise, does not fulfill the human functions of reading and responding to ideas, which every writer needs. The writing conference—whether with a teacher, a peer, or a group of peers—is still a prerequisite for revising. Without this essential feedback, computer revision will be only superficial, just like the clean handwritten copy of written texts. In fact, some research suggests that computer writing encourages superficial editing and proofreading because even without any substantial changes, the final text looks perfect—clean, neatly printed, and correctly spelled. For beginning writers to be able to produce such a text may seem the height of achievement when there are no errors to provoke the teacher's red pen.

Feedback from another reader is essential if the writer is going to make a true second effort. There is a story of D. H. Lawrence, who having read a complete draft of his novel to some friends, then threw the whole handwritten manuscript, of which there was no copy, into the blazing fire in the hearth. It is not clear in the story whether Lawrence's listeners had showed any distaste for his writing, but it is more likely that Lawrence realized from his oral reading that his text was not creating the effect that he was striving for. Nevertheless, with his first draft now completely destroyed, Lawrence was able to rewrite the novel successfully.

In the whole-language classroom it is not necessary to have a fireplace into which students throw their completed drafts. But students should be taught, and experience will show them, that a computer draft need not be treated as sacrosanct. There are several methods that will help this process:

1. The teacher is the best person to model the process of revision by sharing with the students a piece of real writing that is in the process of being developed—that is, the teacher submits his or her writing to the scrutiny of the class as peer editors. A computer projection plate (CPP) is a very useful piece of teaching technology for this purpose. The CPP is connected to the computer just like the video screen, but instead of the image appearing on a screen, it appears on a transparent plate that fits on top of an overhead projector. The text is thus visible to a group of students or to a whole class while the teacher sits at the keyboard, and any changes are immediately visible to the whole class. Teacher and students can now read the text from the overhead screen, while the teacher at the keyboard may use blocking to highlight any sentences or ideas that the students pick out. Here is revision in action as the students ask questions or point out difficulties, while the teacher incorporates their suggestions directly into the computer text. Later, a printout of the revised text can be examined in hardcopy to see what effect the changes have had and to suggest further changes.

2. The teacher gives groups of students a text file and copies of a student's draft (but from another anonymous source, and certainly not from one of the students in the class). The challenge for each group of students is to revise the text as drastically as they like, adding and deleting ideas or changing the structure of the story or article. Each group then keyboards their version into the computer and the results are displayed on the overhead screen. In this case the class is not looking for the "correct" version, but rather to see what ideas have been changed and to compare the various versions. If a computer projection plate is not available, the same result can be achieved if each group's version is printed out and the hard copies made into overhead transparencies. Or, more simply, each group can provide the class with an oral presentation of the story.

3. Teacher and students can work together to make a list of helpful generic questions for peer conferencing. After some experience with peer conferences, the students should consider which questions seemed the most effective in highlighting areas to be revised. Sample questions could be:

a. What is the main focus of this story or article?
b. Does the opening sentence help the reader to see this focus?
c. Are there any details that are not needed?
d. Are there any ideas that are not clear to the reader?
e. Are there ideas that need illustration with examples or more details?
f. Does the story end with a good clinching sentence?

4. Once the class has agreed on a list of appropriate questions, these should be printed on cards to be mounted in the computer writing station and at the sharing table for use in peer group conferencing.

Student Awareness of Writing

One of the goals of writing is to promote the writer's meta-awareness of his or her writing processes, to make conscious the processes by which a written text is generated and revised. All writers should become their own editors. The idea of having the question-prompts constantly on view is that writers, besides using them to conference other students' writing, will also learn to use them on their own writings. Simply asking students to produce multiple drafts as proof of their revising strategies is no longer valid, when a push on a button will turn out a draft that is only marginally or cosmetically different from the previous one.

One value of computer writing is that it encourages rereading of the text, an aspect of writing many children find very difficult in a handwritten copy. Rereading is essentially a rehearsal time providing a platform for the creation and expression of the next incident in a story or a new argument in an opinion piece. As students read and reread their text, they learn to discern and correct language errors. Finally, when all other modes of revision are exhausted, the text will be ready for final editing before publication.

Most teachers recommend the use of a spell-check program for the last draft, although, as we have seen, there is no reason why a writer should not take a break from the strain of creating and expressing ideas by running a spell-check on the text already composed. There is no doubt that the beginning writer gains confidence in writing from the knowledge that spelling, and possibly grammar, word usage, and punctuation will be checked for correctness. However, students will quickly learn that spell-checkers are not infallible, and will fail to distinguish between homophones, like *no* and *know*, *pear* and *pair*, *piqued* and *peaked*, *cord* and *chord*. Indeed, it may also be a surprise to learn how many words the spell-check program does not recognize, especially proper names, slang, and colloquialisms. Ruth Betza (1987) pointed out that the deficiencies of a spell-check program provide opportunity for some valuable learning about written language.

First, because the spell-check program only signals the misspellings it has caught, and sometimes provides a list of optional replacements, the decision is left with the writer whether to make a change. The student learns that the writer is still in charge and still has the responsibility for the final appearance of the text. Second, as the program works by matching the words that the student has generated against its own built-in dictionary, there is opportunity for the student to learn from any pattern of signalled mistakes whether the program catches the repeated error in a common word or whether a particular type of error such as the double consonant or the *i* before *e* keeps recurring. Third, some spell-checkers will print out a list of the words that have been corrected, providing an accumulative list of words by which the student and teacher can measure progress, not simply in mastering simple words but also in daring to use more challenging words. Fourth, as the writer grows to realize the program's limitations, there is opportunity for the student to take charge by teaching the computer what words the writer wants the computer to spell, adding unknown words to its dictionary. However, as Betza (1987) pointed out, students need to work with standard classroom dictionaries to make sure that all added words are correctly spelled.

The same attributes also apply to the grammar- and punctuation-checking programs that are now available for some computers. Because they demand a large amount of computer power and storage capacity, it may be some time before these programs can be commonly used in the older computers that are usually relegated to classrooms. Nevertheless, whatever their limitations, these programs should be used for the same reasons as the spell-check programs. Their limitations have the effect of shifting responsibility onto the writer as the final arbiter, and as the writer becomes aware of their deficiencies, the writer will realize that his or her own built-in, unconscious knowledge of how the language works make be a more reliable guide than the computer's mechanical analysis of grammar. As one linguist said: "All grammars leak." And the grammatical system that is part of the computer's system can never be a complete guide to the complexities of a living language. Nevertheless, whatever their limitations, these programs should be used whenever possible.

Publishing with a Computer

The state of the art computer publishing programs are called *desktop publishing programs*. These programs are capable of incorporating various types of graphics, which range from simple text boxes, to graphs of various types, to illustrations from a bank of "clip art" (ready-made drawings) or illustrations created on the computer itself. The latest development is the ability to include with a text photo reproductions imported from a laser disc, stills from a videotape or television program, or even pictures taken by a special camera, which captures its images digitally on a computer disk. Some photo processing shops will save 35mm photos to a disk.

What are the limits for publication of student writing in the classroom? There is no doubt that for any group of writers, the fact of guaranteed publication is a powerful driving force, providing the external motivation that will help a writer sustain the effort needed to make a piece of writing suitable for a defined audience (Butler, 1992).

In one sense, of course, any piece of computer writing that has reached its final draft and has been shared with other readers can thus be considered "published." But it should be remembered that in Chapter 5 we suggested that not all handwritten compositions need to be published, and many, in fact, need not be taken beyond the first draft. Choosing which composition to revise and edit from among many drafts in the writing portfolio is a valuable step toward the writer's commitment to the work in progress.

With computer writing the danger is that because it is so easy to get a clean printout, then every piece of writing must be taken to its final stage, even though its content may not merit such attention. There are no hard and fast rules about the ratio of first drafts to finished pieces, but teachers and students should be aware that a great deal of writing achieves its purpose as soon as the ideas are written down.

One of the values of having a computer writing station is to review a bank of handwritten first drafts, whether in a journal or in a writing folder, to choose a piece for computer drafting and revision. We have always insisted that this is the writer's responsibility, but of course it is an aspect of our writing processes that is greatly enhanced by the encouraging ear of a peer conferencer. We should expect the student writer to sift through a number of possible writing pieces, describing the content or the purpose of each, perhaps reading a few snippets aloud to hear how they sound. The presence of the peer conferencer is necessary to make the selection process a conscious and explicit activity.

When students continually produce stories and articles in clean, competent printouts, it is the teacher's responsibility to see that they receive the recognition deserved by any author. "Publishing" them on a classroom wall or hallway bulletin board does not go very far in finding a wider readership. Some pieces will be published individually by being sent to specific readers, either as letters or reports. But for all the writing that is aimed to instruct or entertain a general audience, classroom book production is the answer, with the aim of publishing individual, group, or class anthologies that will take their place as real books on classroom or library shelves. This will involve the students in book production, using cardboard and varieties of cloth or decorative paper for covers, and learning to sew the pages. A class book will have representative compositions from every student in what could become a term-long or year-long project. In its finished form it will have a title page, contents, and an editor's introduction, together with biographies of each of the authors, probably illustrated with individual photographs. The stories themselves may be illustrated by computer-generated drawings or by pictures or photographs pasted into the book, because the book will be a unique volume, a one-of-a-kind publication with a print-run of exactly one, but one that will be treasured by authors and readers alike for its uniqueness.

Critical Literacy and Computers

The whole-language teacher's role is to produce students who are critical readers and writers. We now turn from writing to reading as we focus on critical reading skills, and especially on the development of comprehension. Chapter 6, Reading and Language Development, contains many activities that can and should be adapted to the computer. This section will contain some further suggestions that encourage critical comprehension using the computer.

The computer can be a powerful teacher. It can also be a simple-minded electronic workbook that requires students to mindlessly fill in blanks and select multiple-choice items. Kinzer (1986) referred to these kinds of activities as the drill-and-practice software. You should also be aware that many computer activities have overtones of violence (discussed later).

Comprehension

The computer can produce text and visual images. Using a basic word-processing program, one can ask students to do several activities that will promote the kinds of comprehension noted in Chapter 5. We have named one activity **Chained Storying**. The procedure is to ask students to compose a cooperative story. One alternative may be for you to write the story. Each student is asked to write independently a paragraph for the story. The simplest procedure is to give a disk to a student who writes the first introductory paragraph. The disk is passed from one student to the next until the designated conclusion-writer ends the story. The teacher makes a copy of the story and then, using the word processor's cut-and-paste function, switches and mixes the paragraphs. The mixed version is given back to students on a disk and their task, one that can be done individually or as a group, is to arrange the text so it makes sense as a story. The most effective approach is to have pairs work on the cut-and-paste activity. A public reading of the final printed versions is informative, provides a time for analysis, and is often humorous.

Some teachers are convinced that cloze activities (see Chapter 12, Assessment: Form and Function) are valuable for students because the activities put them into contact with the language of text. The computer can be used to present text that has cloze deletions, which students are asked to fill in. You should take some caution in presenting cloze activities to students because they do tend to become boring (Gunderson, 1992).

The computer can show text to students in a controlled fashion. The control has to do with the size of the screen and the total amount of information that can be presented at any one time on a screen. Gunderson (1992) has used the computer to present narrative material to students a screen at a time. At the end of each screen, students are asked to predict what they think will happen next in the story, either to each other in a paired-learning exercise or in writing in a log. Early experimentation found that switching from a text window to an answer window was too taxing for students; writing in a log was easier and resulted in superior comprehension. The one-window-at-a-time prediction activity was a little frustrating for students because it made it slightly more difficult for them to go back a page or two to reconsider some information. The biggest problem was getting the text into the computer. This also has serious implications for the teacher since copyrighted material cannot be computerized without permission.

The activities discussed so far can be set up using simple computer word-processing programs. Indeed, they are simple applications of readily available technology. More complex applications involving the possibility of using the computer to develop and encourage response to literature, sharing responses, interactive response to literature, and interactive strategies for developing comprehension do exist in CD-ROM form.

The most exciting use of computers has developed over the last several years or so. In conjunction with a video disc or CD-ROM, the computer becomes incredibly powerful. The video disc is a large format disk that contains laser-readable information that is rapidly and randomly accessible. In addition, video discs have an immense storage capacity. They allow material to be shown as still images. Video discs can contain entire encyclopedias of information. The *LASER DISC Newsletter* provides a comprehensive view of available titles (Suite 428, 496 Hudson Street, New York, NY, 10014). The information available covers almost every area of interest to an elementary teacher, including such areas as science, social studies, history, and space exploration. The computer allows the information on a video disc to be used interactively. A student can view a scene and ask for information about a particular object or action he or she has viewed, and the computer will retrieve the related information. Students who used an interactive video disc to learn about character traits also developed their own vocabulary skills, and their subsequent writing revealed that they had gained a higher knowledge of plot and character through the use of these interactive literature programs (Bransford, Kinzer, Risko, Rowe, and Vye, 1989; Kinzer, 1990). The video disc and computer combination can integrate learning across the curriculum (Bransford, Vye, Kinzer, and Risko, 1990).

The computer should be thought of as a servant of the teacher, an instrument that can help students read and comprehend text. It is not a substitute for a teacher. For reading, it does have its limitations. The reader cannot as easily flip back to find a previous page, hold the computer on the lap, or read at leisure. The computer does not make the book obsolete.

Using a Data Base in the Classroom

Using a computer data base, a data source similar to an encyclopedia, is fairly simple. It is possible to build a data base to store and organize information collected by the students about any topic. Judith Newman (1986) described an example of a classroom project in a British elementary classroom that involved creating a data base to record measurements of "conkers." These hard, nutlike seeds of the horse-chestnut tree are used by British children in a game that tests the conkers' durability, so the children had a natural interest in what made a good conker. The project included collecting specimens, determining variables to measure, debating methods of measurement, recording findings in the data base, testing hypotheses, and writing about the findings.

Such an investigation, Newman suggested, has the value of utilizing the language the students used to discuss their strategies and to write their report. "The learning was inextricably a part of the children's talking and writing together about something of real interest to them" (pp. 317–18) and hence central to whole-language.

Newman (1986) also described a poetry project. Each student is invited to choose five favorite poems to share. Titles and authors make obvious classifications to be put into the data base. In order to put this information into a data base, the class has to categorize all of the issues that crop up. In groups of four, students scanned the poems and listed the themes, then compared the results, collapsing some categories where they could find common ground. They designed a "form" or file card that simply asked for each poem's author, title, source, and major theme. The data base allows them to sort the poems by categories, making it possible to print lists of poems by author, or from the same source, or based on similar themes. At this point each group chose one of the common themes and examined the poems that were grouped within that category. They also noticed differences among the poems in the poetic form and style, the imagery used, or even the date of publication.

Just as children learn about reading by reading, so these students learned about data processing by using the computer to store, correct, and organize the data they had collected.

Alistair Ross (1984) did a collaborative social studies project by asking about people's attitudes toward work. To collect data, the class had to design a questionnaire to use as they surveyed people in the local community. For younger children a survey of the class's interests, their pets, their types of bicycles, their heroes and heroines, their favorite books, movies, and TV shows, and so on, could provide the same opportunity for developing and testing hypotheses through the collection and organization of data. Newman (1989) provided a useful plan of action to help students start out by identifying an area of general interest, and then brainstorming to identify the questions they want answered and what sort of data they will collect. In order to put the plan into operation they will have to decide on how to prepare and organize questionnaires, interviews, letters of introduction, and the like, and also plan how the data will be recorded and categorized. In the stage she calls "Pulling It Together," the students explore relationships within the data sets, develop, test, and revise their hypotheses, and summarize their work.

The Reading Inventory, a record of all of the books read by the students, is a valuable data base. We have already suggested that one of the opportunities for using the computer word-processing program is the collecting of students' written responses to their reading, which can be published periodically as a class magazine of critical reviews. The data base program allows one to take this process a stage further by getting the students to make abstracts of their reports, and then using a number of key words as subject headings to categorize the various types of books, and perhaps to award quality ratings, like movie reviews, as a number of stars the book deserves. As the number of entries increases month by month, students will be able to use the capability of the data base program to find out about their favorite reading: which types of books were most popular; what themes were explored; which books had focused on a particular theme; what qualities were most apparent in the main characters; in what localities or countries did the stories take place; what time period did the story cover.

The experience of building and using their own data bases is invaluable for preparing students to use the commercial data bases that are available on computer and compact disks. Perhaps the most important lesson to be learned is that the data base is only useful to the extent that the information entered into it is accurate and reliable—in other words, they learn the GIGO factor: garbage in, garbage out.

Data bases are a valuable resource for the whole-language teacher. Issues of confidentiality must be kept in mind, however.

Managing Computer Use in the Whole-Language Classroom

The price of computers and the peripherals that accompany them has dropped dramatically over the years. However, compared to an individual textbook or ream of paper, the computer is expensive, so you will likely not have a machine for every student. Although many computers are purchased by the schools, others are acquired with funds raised by groups of supportive parents who have donated or earned funds through various garage sales, bake sales, and drives of different sorts. These efforts are gallant, but often they result in different schools purchasing and using different computers. The essential problem that results is incompatibility.

All computers are not equal. Some run on different systems than others. Software that works on one computer will not work on another. Computers accept different-sized disks, different software, and different operating systems. Some computers are not able to operate using high-density disks, even though the disks are the same size and fit into the machinery in the same way that disks with lesser capacity do. The essential problem is that if you are not knowledgeable enough to know about compatibility, you need to find someone in the school district who will advise you. Otherwise, you may find that the beautiful word-processing program you have purchased with bake-sale money is not compatible with the computer the parents' club has purchased.

The second item to keep in mind is that most teachers, and this may include you, are afraid of computers. There is some kind of interesting phobia teachers have about computers. The basic thing to keep in mind is that when you first begin to work with a computer, *there are no stupid questions*. The first thing anyone who has ever learned how to use a computer has had to figure out is how to turn the machine on. Don't be afraid to ask any question, especially this one. Be a little brazen about it and phrase your question like this: "Whoever designed this computer hid the power switch. Where is it on this model?" The second item to remember is that students have grown up using computers; they are fearless. You will have a very long learning curve. In fact, the first few times you use the computer you may likely want to quit, but don't. The hardest part is to learn all the little things you have to do to get the machinery and the programs working. Once you learn you will be amazed that you ever had trouble. In fact, once you have learned to use one computer you will likely not want to ever change and learn another computer and its programs because it might require learning new procedures and routines.

After you have become comfortable enough with your computer and its programs so that you can begin to teach your students how to use them, you will immediately run into some potential problems. You will probably experience equipment failure. This is when the machine does not work the way it is supposed to work. This can happen for various and mysterious reasons. We have both had computers that have suddenly and unexpectedly locked up and refused to function. A dip in the electrical power will sometimes lock a machine. Usually, if you turn off the machine and then turn it back on, the computer will start up. If not, talk to your local computer expert (who may be a student in your class). Like light bulbs, computers last longer if you resist turning them on and off.

Usually software (or courseware) comes on floppy disks, either 3.5" or 5.25" in size, or on compact disk. You can experience failure for various reasons, the most serious being that the disk has been damaged and cannot be read by the computer. This kind of failure is best avoided by treating the disk with tender care. It may be worth instituting a rule that only you touch program disks. You will also experience a software failure if you try to use software that is designed for a different kind of computer than the one you have.

Gender Differences in Computer Use

Once you have become able to use a computer yourself and you have introduced them to your classroom, you will immediately notice an interesting phenomena: The boys will be attracted to your computers like flies to honey while the girls will be only moderately interested.

Elementary teachers, especially primary teachers must, absolutely must, provide equal access to boys and girls. They also must make certain that the programs they acquire and use are appropriate for both males and females. We have developed the following software checklist. Both boys and girls should learn about learning from computers, and should be involved in ethical decisions about their usage. This should be your primary goal. Here are some of the practical considerations to be made when choosing software:

1. Is the material at your students' ability and interest levels?
2. Does the software contain unnecessary or gratuitous violence?
3. Is the software equally appropriate for boys and girls?
4. Is the software needed? Does it do something that standard curriculum materials such as books cannot? In what way? Is it worth while purchasing?
5. Is the software compatible to your computer? Is the diskette the correct size and density for your computer?
6. Is the material on the software interesting?
7. Does the material on the software supplement or compliment your curriculum?
8. Can you run the software?
9. Will your students be able to independently run the software?
10. Is the software worth the expense of buying it?

The Classroom Computer Center

There is no doubt that the flickering video screen can be both an attraction and a distraction. The computer center needs to be sufficiently secluded so that computer users are not distracted by others. We know that the computer screen acts as a magnet and if the computer center is located in any sort of a traffic lane, then other students will stop to read the screen and probably make suggestions and comments. Neither should the computer users be distracted by any high-energy activity going on in the near vicinity. For example, a sharing and discussion table should be located at the other end of the room. On the other hand, computer activity is not incompatible with reading, so it might be considered as part of a reading/writing center. Location of the computer center is also determined by the source of power and by other factors such as the drinking fountain or a classroom sink. Remember that electronics and water do not mix.

The computer center should be accessible as a place where students can carry on with the usual business of the classroom. Its physical location needs to be close enough to the focus of other classroom activities so that the teacher, often engaged in working with individual students at other centers or at their desks, can keep one eye on the computer center to see that everything is functioning as it should, especially to forestall the sort of calamity that happens when a printer gets jammed or the computer loses its power.

The teacher must guard against the biggest source of technophobia—the losing of text. No one who has labored over the composing of a paragraph, or a page, or a chapter, can bear the thought of having the text disappear forever down some sort of electronic black memory hole. Yet every computer writer seems to have some horror story of losing hours of writing. The experts warn against the risks of a power failure by saying: "Save your text frequently in readiness for **when** it happens, not **if** it happens." The teacher is encouraged to set the "automatic save" feature on the word processor to about two minutes so that little will be lost in the event of equipment failure.

Children may be devastated by the loss of their creative efforts. Apart from power failure, or inadvertently switching off the computer, or pulling the power plug, most users have at some time pressed the wrong keys that have given unwanted commands and resulted in the wasting of text. Students should be warned, but not frightened, about such disasters.

Identifying student computer experts in the classroom ensures that when students encounter hardware or software problems in the computer center they need not immediately rush to the teacher. The buddy system should be part of the regular pattern of use. Partners in composing activities, whether cooperative or collaborative writing, should be encouraged to sign up together, in order to gain the benefits from learning to use the hardware.

Good storage and care of computer floppy disks is essential. Program disks should be clearly labeled and available at the center, with instructions for use clearly available on display cards. Individual text storage disks need also to be treated carefully and, if necessary, placed under some sort of security system to prevent any student interfering with another student's private disk.

If there is enough computer time available, students may be encouraged to write their journal entries directly into the computer for saving on their private disks. Selected journal entries can be transferred to the teacher's disk for reading and response directly on the screen. The electronic journal may eventually supplement the normal booklet journal with a saving in paper. Students may also swap a journal entry with their computer partner, when each student writes a response to the other's entry directly on the screen.

One advantage that the classroom computer center will have over the bank of computers in a school computer lab is that in a classroom it is easier to provide more counter space for notes and diagrams. There should also be adequate space for two or three students to sit at each computer for group responses and collaborative composition. In this sort of a center the computer itself is only one part of a space that is available for language activities—talking, drawing, planning, and drafting, as well as keyboarding and revising.

The classroom computer center also provides another link between the school and those homes that have their own computers. Students who have a computer at home will be encouraged to carry on their writing at home, and, assuming compatibility between the two systems, to transfer their work to their school disks. Students will also want to bring to school software programs that they use at home; when this happens, licensing restrictions should be strictly followed. Probably these will be some form of computer game, which the teacher should check out before allowing it for classroom use. Game playing in itself need not necessarily be a disadvantage in the classroom, especially if care is taken to see that it does not displace other forms of learning or if it is kept for recreational time. Some software programs may entail images and actions that can be interpreted as sexist or racist, and these should certainly be discouraged. Some valuable social learning is possible if such issues are made a public classroom concern, a matter for discussion and debate rather than a case of the teacher's personal censorship. The question of violence in computer games is more difficult. Games such as *Where in the World Is Carmen Sandiego?* do have an educational value, and Joseph Hacket (1991) has shown that they provide good material for group problem solving.

Teachers may also want to use interactive fiction and adventure games with small groups of students. Some of these are based on such familiar novels as *Charlotte's Web, Island of the Blue Dolphins, A Wrinkle in Time, Mrs. Frisby and the Rats of NIMH, Winnie the Pooh,* and *The Wizard of Oz.* These games must not be regarded as a substitute for reading the books themselves. There are a great number of these programs and teachers should consult a source such as Patrick Dewey's *Directory* (1988) before purchasing them.

The Future Is Now

How Many Computers Do You Have?

The bulk of this chapter has been concerned with the integration into a classroom of one or more computers, without any specification about the type or power of the computers, avoiding such questions of whether they would have a hard disk and what sorts of floppy disk drives will be installed or what peripherals would be available. We have based our suggested computer applications on a very modest idea of what a small computer and printer can do by using generic software programs for word processing and data processing. We have avoided any discussion of specialized software programs as being beyond the scope of this chapter. In fact, our aim has been to show what can be achieved by using hardware and software from the very low end of the technology—a very down-market approach, dealing with technology that can be described as the "here and now," or in some cases "then." There are certainly differences in how well schools, even in the same district, are gifted with computers. One new high school was equipped with 200 computers for 1,200 students, whereas some schools still have few or no computers.

Graphical User Interface (GUI)—Windows

Owston, Murphy, and Wideman (1992) achieved some impressive results in their study of students' computer revision strategies at the eighth-grade level when engaged in expository arguments. But in their study, the students each had individual use of an advanced GUI (graphical user interface) word processor, using a mouse to manipulate icons on the computer screen of a Macintosh computer. There is a strong suggestion that students may be better able to manipulate text when they are able to watch visual representations of the revision processes on their screens. In this case there were significantly higher mean scores for papers written and revised on computers as against those composed and revised in handwriting. The difference in quality ratings showed not only in a holistic General Competence, but also in analytic scales for Focus and Organization, Support, and Mechanics.

This study confirms what has been asserted about writing processes for many years: First, recursiveness is evidenced in the great number of text changes and the greater amounts of text scanning done by the students during the drafting stage. The students also used spell-checks more frequently in the drafting sessions rather than in the revision sessions. Second, there was a wide variety in the students' approaches to computer composition. For some competent writers the computer seemed to make little difference. Others seemed to be distracted by the computer's capabilities and spent more time in playing with the format of the text than writing it. These students were well trained in the GUI-based computers that had been extensively integrated into their seventh- and eighth-grade communications arts curricula, while in the current year of the study they had already completed a dozen or more writing tasks on computers.

Interactive CD

Some schools are already forging ahead into the realm of multimedia inquiry and composition, using a GUI computer program as the link, as in the Macintosh HyperCard, IBM Linkway, or Commodore AmigaVision. Fred D'Ignazio (1991) suggested that a classroom teacher can assemble a "Classroom Inquiry Center," using a computer with this type of link software, a VHS-VCR, a tape recorder, a video camera, a large-screen TV for class presentations, headphones for private monitoring, and a media cart to enable it to be used in many classrooms. Some schools could also add a CD-ROM player, a video digitizer that will capture images off the video camera or TV, and an audio digitizer to capture sounds from the tape recorder, radio, or classroom microphone. Such a wealth of technology "enables students to expand classroom publishing to include colorful graphics, moving images, sound effects (like crashing waves and paddle wheel foghorns), music, and written and spoken words" (p. 250).

Paul Bird (1991) showed how a computer can be linked to a stereo music system with a CD player and a monitor screen. In this case the topic was a recording of Beethoven's Ninth Symphony on the CD, but instead of simply listening to a musical performance, the teacher or students used a mouse as a remote control to shift between the recording and a data base installed in the computer that provided extensive background notes to the music. With many branching options, listeners may read historical or biographical information or a guide to the music itself, or follow the musical score on the screen. Microsoft produces several interactive CD-ROMs on great composers.

Jamie Smith (1991) uses HyperCard with his eighth-grade class to function as an open-ended data base to control interactive learning devices. Smith's students collect pictures into the data file using a camera that digitalizes them. After all of the pictures are imported into the HyperCard stacks each student typed information under the headings of Interests and Likes/Dislikes, which results in a class file of pictures and information.

The same composing processes were used for a social studies project that began with "each student being given an artifact and asked to make historical decisions regarding its use." The students used a combination of talking, writing, and computer drawing to compile their reports which were then keyboarded into the data base, and combined with the individual pictures and records. "In just 10 minutes the students were able to see the work that each one had done," which is "one of the best reasons for using computers in the classroom" (Smith, 1991, p. 675).

Another teacher, John Vallis, uses a similar computer lab for his ESL transition students who have acquired enough English to fulfill social functions but need to tackle academic structures and vocabulary. Vallis ostensibly is teaching them tenth-grade science and social studies, but really they are learning the language of these disciplines. Each student's computer is linked to the teacher's, and also to the laser disc and CD players in the classroom. In one project called "Postcards from the Edge of the Pacific" each student chose a picture from a laser disc, an electronic pictorial encyclopedia about the history of a city on the West Coast. The students were able to import the picture to their own disks, size and crop the images, and then to accumulate further information from books, maps, and other sources, including personal interviews. Not only did the students learn to generate and revise their own messages but they also shared the results with the other students in the class. Eventually their electronic "Postcards" were sent to a companion class in Japan.

Martina Lewis (1991) described how disks can be used for teaching a comparison of mythology, fairy tales, and legends. Instead of watching a 16 mm film of *The Adventures of Robin Hood*, the class views it on a video disc, taking turns with the remote control to stop and start, rerun scenes, or shift to other sources of background information. According to Lewis, "Showing them on video disc with its random access capability encourages a more in-depth and meaningful interpretation and appreciation of the film" (p. 336).

Edward Copra (1990) described a program at the California School for the Deaf in which students work with a partner in front of a video screen to write captions to a story. By touching the control panel on the screen, the children can shift to either a printed text or to a picture of an expert signer telling the story in American Sign Language (ASL). This program uses the children's ASL literacy as a bridge for developing their English print literacy. The same methodology also takes the children into several subject areas, including literature, science, and social studies.

Communicating in and Beyond the Classroom

One of the tenets of whole-language is that students write for real audiences, whether for other students in the classroom or for more general audiences in the outside world. Once a classroom computer station has been established, a telecommunications link-up will allow students to become a part of the electronic global village or worldwide web.

The principle of electronic communication was demonstrated several years ago in a study by Bertram Bruce, Sarah Michaels, and Karen Watson-Gegeo (1985) of a sixth-grade classroom, which in its writing program has an orientation toward media. The students compose press releases and commercials for their stories, which are written in chapters and published in serial form. They also produce newspapers and magazines, complete with their own advertisements. Students take turns at the classroom computer to keyboard in their handwritten copy using the QUILL program.

More recent work by Bruce and colleagues (1993) explores students conversing through local area networks and thereby creating new forms of collaboration (i.e., multiauthored works), authentic audiences, writing across the curriculum, and even new social relations. This idea is extended internationally in the University of British Columbia/Ritsumeikan Joint Academic Exchange Program where students communicate via Internet with others around the world and operate in an almost "paperless" setting (i.e., assignments are submitted electronically and instructor feedback comes via the same route). For second-language learners, for the deaf, and other special needs students, such interchanges are particularly beneficial since they continuously require a variety of language uses. Bruce and colleagues (1993) found that the student exchanges reflected more speaker/listener awareness, high levels of engagement, and a more conversational style (attributed to the medium to a large extent), freedom in getting ideas down on the page (screen), evidence of multiple drafting, and improvement in writing based on holistic scoring.

After a suitable computer (i.e., one with a hard drive for information storage) has been installed in a classroom, it is not a great expense to add a modem and software for connection to a telephone line, immediately giving students access to the wide world of telecommunications. Computerized data and messages can now be exchanged with other classrooms, other schools, other states, and other countries, for the price of a short telephone call.

Many school district administrations make an electronic bulletin board available to their schools as a basis for school networking. It is possible for one class to establish electronic contact with another class for the exchange of information on an agreed topic, or simply for the exchange of pen-pal messages between individual students, providing opportunities for both individual and collaborative writing.

Patricia Mulligan and Kay Gore (1992) described some of the networking activities that are promoted in the Central Coast area of California. With "Global Grocery List," students research the local cost of a number of foods for comparison with similar data from other areas. One Californian class, exchanging information with a school in Alaska, was surprised not only at the great difference in prices but that the Alaskan children had never eaten beans and tortillas. "Kids Connections" also provides a number of different projects that emphasize personal knowledge, the expression of opinions, the identifying of heroes, interviews with local personalities, the reporting of local news, and even a comparison of teenage slang.

There are also public networks available to schools for a modest charge. The National Geographic Society runs Kids Network for the study of science and geography in the elementary school, especially to involve students in the study of the local environment, and reporting ecological data for comparison and analysis with data from other schools. Some computer manufacturers also sponsor national and international exchange of information.

A computer in the classoom connects the students to the world of information resource technology. The computer processes that the students learn as they participate in the activities suggested in this chapter are the same as those used by adults who work with computers in so many facets of modern life. The classroom computer is a tool that gives students a tremendous power to create, process, and communicate their own information. At the same time, the computer can break down the walls of the classroom by enabling students to participate in the information sharing and networking in the world outside.

Libraries and Computers

Many schools—elementary and secondary—utilize computerized card catalogues that students must learn to use. These systems can do much more than find books for students and teachers. Many allow the user to search the library holdings for materials on specific topics with various specific conditions being specified (i.e., books about a certain topic for elementary students, etc.). Other features of use to the teacher are literature promotion, library display creation, bibliography production, library skills instruction, and access to atlases and other reference tools (Clyde, 1993). Clyde identified 474 library software packages and 142 computer-based, multifunction library management systems in existence today.

REFERENCES

Betza, R. E. (1987). Online: Computerized spelling chekers: Friends or foes? *Language Arts, 64 (4)*, 438–443.

Bird, P. (1991). *Electronic text and reading comprehension.* Conference presentation at the International Convention on Language and Literacy. University of East Anglia, Norwich, England, April.

Bransford, J. D., Kinzer, C. K., Risko, V. J., Rowe, D. W., & Vye, N. J. (1989). Designing invitations to thinking: Initial thoughts. In S. McCormick & J. Zutell (Eds.), *Cognitive and social perspectives for literacy research and instruction.* Chicago: National Reading Conference, pp. 35–54.

Bransford, J. D., Vye, N., Kinzer, C. K., and Risko, V. J. (1990). Teaching initial thinking and content knowledge: An integrated approach. In B. F. Jones and L. Idol (Eds.),

Dimensions of thinking and cognitive instruction. Hillsdale, NJ: Erlbaum, pp. 381–413.

Bruce, B., Michaels, S., & Watson-Gegeo, K. (1985). How computers can change the writing process. *Language Arts, 62,* 143–149.

Bruce, B., Peyton, J. K., and Batson, T. (1993). *Network-based classrooms: Promises and realities.* New York: Cambridge University Press.

Butler, S. (1992). Writing for posterity: writing with senior citizens. In J. Hartley (Ed.), *Technology and writing: Readings in the psychology of written communication.* London: Jessica Kingsley.

Butler, S. & Cox, B. (1992). DISKovery: Writing with a computer in grade one: A study in collaboration. *Language Arts, 69,* 633–640.

Clyde, L. A. (1993). *Computer applications in libraries: A directory of systems & software.* Port

Melbourne, Australia: Australian Library and Information Association.

Collis, B. (1993). *The ITEC project information technology in education of children.* Division of Higher Education, UNESCO.

Copra, E. R. (1990). Using interactive videodiscs for bilingual education. *Perspectives, 8,* 9–11.

Daiute, C. (1992). Multimedia composing: Extending the resources of kindergarten to writers across the grades. *Language Arts, 69,* April, 250–260.

Daiute, C. (1985). Issues in using computers to socialize the writing process. *ECTJ, 33,* 41–50.

Daiute, C. (1989). Research currents: Play and learning to write. *Language Arts, 66,* 656–664

Dewey, P. R. (1988). *Interactive fiction and adventure games for microcomputers: An annotated directory 1988.* Westport, CT.: Meckler.

D'Ignazio, F. (1991). DISKovery: The Starship Enterprise: New opportunities for learning in the 1990's. *Language Arts, 68,* 248–252.

DrawPerfect 1.1 (1990). Orem, Utah: WordPerfect Corporation.

Gunderson, L. (1992). *A study of three instructional approaches with adult ESL students.* Paper presented at the National Reading Conference, San Antonio, TX.

Hackett, J. (1991). In search of Carmen San Diego. In W. Wresch (Ed.), *The English classroom in the computer age: Thirty lesson plans.* Urbana, IL: NCTE, pp. 77–80.

Kahn, J. & Freyd, P. (1990). Online: A whole language perspective on keyboarding. *Language Arts, 67,* 84–90.

Kinzer, C. K. (1986). A five-part categorization for the use of microcomputers in reading classrooms. *The Reading Teacher, 30,* 226–232.

Kinzer, C. K. (with the Cognition and Technology Group at Vanderbilt) (1990). Anchored instruction and its relationship to situated cognition. *Educational Researcher, 19,* 2–10.

Lewis, M. E. (1991). DISKovery: Videodisc: Part of the classroom picture. *Language Arts, 68,* 333–336.

Marcus, S. (1991). Invisible writing with a computer: New sources and resources. In W. Wresch (Ed.), *The English classroom in the computer age: Thirty lesson plans.* Urbana, IL: NCTE.

Mulligan, P. A. & Gore, K. (1992). DISKovery: Telecommunications: Education's missing link? *Language Arts, 69,* 379–384.

Newman, J. M. (1986) Online: Using a database in the classroom. *Language Arts, 63 (3),* 315–319.

Newman, J. M. (1989). Online: Dealing with information. *Language Arts, 66 (1),* 58–64.

Owston, R. D., Murphy, S., & Wideman, H. H. (1992). The effects of word processing on students' writing quality and revision strategies. *Research in the Teaching of English, 26,* 249–276.

Ross, A. (1984). Learning why to hypothesize: A case study of data processing in a primary school classroom. In A. V. Kelly (Ed.), *Microcomputers and the curriculum.* London: Harper and Row.

Schwartz, H. J. (1983). Teaching organization with word processing. *Computers, Reading and Language Arts, 1 (3),* 34–36.

Shynal, B. (1984). To learn or not to learn: Two demonstrations of teaching. *Highway One: Canadian Journal of Language Education, 7 (3),* 35–40.

Smith, J. (1991). DISKovery: Going wild in HyperCard. *Language Arts, 68,* 674–680.

Spitzer, M. (1989). Incorporating prewriting software into the writing program. In C. L. Selfe, D. Rodrigues, & W. R. Oates, (Eds.), *Computers in English and the language arts: The challenge of teacher education.* Urbana, IL: NCTE., pp. 205–212.

Vibert, A. (1988). Online: Collaborative writing. *Language Arts, 65,* 74–76.

Wresch, W. (Ed.) (1991). *The English classroom in the computer age: Thirty lesson plans.* Urbana, IL: NCTE.

Zeni, J. (1990). *WritingLands: Composing with old and new writing tools.* Urbana, IL: NCTE.

Meeting Special Needs in the Whole-Language Classroom

ANN LUKASEVICH

KEY CONCEPTS

1. Realizing that although all children are alike in many ways, they are also very different in a number of other ways

2. Realizing that learners who are disabled, ESL, and gifted and talented require special instructional adaptations and/or teacher assistance beyond the norm

3. Identifying appropriate language arts materials for both teacher and student use in the classroom that will meet the needs of these students

4. Identifying which whole-language strategies can be used effectively with learners who are disabled, ESL, and gifted and talented

Introduction

This chapter will focus on the special needs of three groups of children found in most classrooms. They are learners who have disabilities, learners who speak English as a second language (ESL), and learners who are gifted and talented. Since there is such a huge literature base that addresses each of these three special groups of learners, it would be impossible to address all aspects of their school experience in this one chapter. Therefore, it is suggested that other sources of information should be read to further investigate the needs of these special learners. This chapter will also address meeting the individual needs of *all* children in whole-language classrooms, and the urgency for teachers to provide the best learning experiences and environment possible to meet children's varying needs.

Although all children are alike in many ways, they are also distinct from each other in a number of important ways. They learn at different rates and in different ways; their interests, personalities, past experiences, and home backgrounds vary as well; while some may work well on their own, others require a lot of teacher assistance. These differences, along with other individual differences, must be acknowledged by teachers, if all children are to reach their full learning potential in school. Diversity rather than homogeneity in whole-class groups is a well-proven fact.

Present findings in human growth and development research confirm the uniqueness of each child. Individuals differ greatly in their levels and rates of development. While some of these differences can be seen easily, others cannot. The most noticeable differences are physical—skin and hair color, strength, height, weight, and the like. Others, such as intellectual development, are more subtle and difficult to detect even though there is tremendous variation. For example, according to Goodlad and Anderson (1987, p. 6), children entering grade 1 may differ in mental age by approximately four full years, and this variation becomes more pronounced as children progress through the elementary grades. Those already out in front continue to move at greater and greater speeds, and as a result move further and further away from their slower-moving class peers. By the time they reach the intermediate grades, the spread is even wider. The achievement range in the various subjects now begins to approximate the mental age spread, and by the end of grades 4 and 5 it is as great or greater than the specified grade level (Goodlad and Anderson, 1987). However, teachers often fail to recognize and adapt their teaching to the wide range of ability and achievement levels found in all classrooms. In addition, individual children's achievement scores may vary greatly from subject to subject, providing classroom teachers with even greater challenges. This wide range of ability and achievement among children and within individuals strongly supports the movement to more individualized approaches to teaching and learning found in most whole-language classrooms. Because these teachers focus more on individuals, they are more apt to identify individual strengths and needs as they move about their classrooms.

While most elementary school children follow expected patterns of development and fit well into the mainstream of the whole-language classroom, others might require special instructional adaptations and/or teacher assistance because of their special learning needs (Lewis and Doorlag, 1991). Three special groups that might qualify for such assistance are children who have disabilities, children who speak English as a second language (ESL), and children who are gifted and talented. At present, there is a strong possibility that representatives from these three groups will be found in most elementary classrooms. Therefore, this chapter will describe these three special groups of children and discuss how classroom teachers can best meet their needs in the regular language arts classroom.

Learners with Disabilities

Since the implementation of the Education for all Handicapped Children Act in 1975, most children with a diversity of handicaps (disabilities) have joined their regular classroom peers. This has led to inclusive education, which is described by Andrews and Lupart (1993) "as the merger of special and regular education into a unified educational system" (p. 5). In the case of full inclusion, all students with disabilities would be included at all times with children who do not have disabilities. Although estimates vary, it is felt that about 10 to 15% of the school population consists of mainstreamed children who spend all or part of their day in the regular classroom. Therefore, most classroom teachers, at one time or another, will be asked to teach children who are mentally challenged (mild, moderate or severe), children with learning disabilities, children who have emotional impairments, children with speech disorders, as well as children who are visually impaired, hearing impaired, or physically impaired. In order to ensure that these children are given appropriate special programs, an annual individual educational program (IEP) must be written for each student by a team consisting of a local education representative, the child's teacher(s), the child's parent(s), and the child, if appropriate. These IEPs usually contain the same content learned by the child's peers who do not have disabilities. What might change is how that content is presented and adjusted, how the child will respond to that content, and the materials used.

Children with Mental (Developmental) Disabilities

The term *mentally disabled* describes students who are intellectually impaired, using a three-tiered classification system for the degree of impairment (mild, moderate, and severe). A wide range of severity exists within this classification. Incidence is approximately 3% of the total population, depending on the IQ ranges used to classify the groups. According to Searfoss and Readence (1989), mildly mentally disabled students (educable mentally retarded) include all children within a 75–50 IQ range. Other special education experts have used a range of 55–80 or 50–70 to define this highest category of mentally disabled children. Just below this category are the moderately mentally disabled (trainable mentally retarded) with an IQ range of 49–20, followed by the severely mentally disabled with an IQ below 20. Because of the wide IQ range represented by this group, their potential level of academic achievement ranges from almost none or very limited to about a fifth-grade level of achievement. Therefore, it is only with the first category, the mildly mentally retarded, that whole-language arts teachers will be mainly concerned.

Children with mild retardation are familiar to most classroom teachers. Their rate of learning is slowed, and they often have difficulty retaining information. They tend to use poor grammar and syntax, and may have difficulty with verbal expression. In addition, they exhibit a higher rate of speech impairments than the general population (Winzer, 1989). Their instruction needs to be adapted to their level of development and progress rate, which usually falls well below the norm of their peers. In addition, they may have more difficulty attending to tasks, spend more time off task, and have more difficulty making generalizations (McGee and Richgels, 1990). For these children, teachers might shorten assignments or break them down into shorter parts, depending on their individual abilities and progress rates.

Because of their below-average intelligence, they are usually not ready to begin academic instruction at the same time as their peers. And once they start, they will need more and longer participation in beginning reading and writing instruction if they are to be successful. "A focus on meaningful relevant literacy experiences is crucial" (Malicky and Norman, 1988, p. 24). In addition, teachers will need to use a variety of literacy materials to provide more needed practice with the same skills and content. For example, they will need many more repetitions of new words than their peers before the words become part of their sight vocabulary. In whole-language classrooms, this can easily be accomplished through repeated rereadings of favorite tales, verses, songs, rhymes, chants, and big books, alone, with a partner, or in a supportive group situation. Other useful practices include paired reading (with another child or adult), Readers Theatre (reading from a script), and read-along tapes in the listening center. These children should also dictate stories to the teacher or a peer, or produce their own language experience stories as a bridge to more formal reading and writing. Other writing activities at their developmental level can be done at the writing center. Posted high-frequency word lists as well as personal vocabulary word lists are useful aids for spelling. Here, they can be motivated to publish simple books and stories for enjoyment. Interesting pictures and wordless books can also be used to motivate independent writing. Used effectively, wordless books can give them a sense of story structure, increase their oral and written vocabulary, and develop sentence and story sense, as the story line is told or written with or without teacher help, depending on their level of development.

As they move up through elementary school, these children should be challenged to write longer stories and read books at a higher reading level. If they are still reading at an early primary level, many of these books will be predictable in nature. As their reading improves, other types of books can be used. It is important to use books that use easy vocabulary but are written at a high-interest level. These books should look like books written for their age level. It is also very important to include content reading material that they can read. Brainstorming and semantic map techniques are excellent ways to involve readers who have disabilities more actively in content area learning (Ford and Ohlhausen, 1988). Teachers unfamiliar with books of this type should seek the assistance of the school librarian. The 1989 IRA publication, *Easy Reading: Book Series and Periodicals* by Randall, Ryder, Graves, and Graves is also a useful source for such materials.

Other instructional strategies that have been used successfully with students who are mentally disabled include changes in the format of material discussed, changes in input and output requirements of tasks (view, read, listen), tutorial programs (peers, older buddies, aides, parents), contracts, and educational technology for writing and drill and practice (Schulz, Carpenter, and Turnbull, 1991).

Children with Learning Disabilities

The term *learning disabilities* is used to describe a number of problems that are possibly attributed to neurological dysfunction and that limit a child's ability to learn. At present, there appears to be no one universally acceptable definition of this term (Anderson and Lapp, 1988); however, simply stated, these children demonstrate a severe discrepancy between actual class achievement and the ability to learn in one or more subject areas. They may also show marked discrepancies across subject areas (Gloeckler and Simpson, 1988). For example, a child may be weak in reading but strong in math, or have trouble writing down thoughts but speak effectively. This disability includes conditions such as dyslexia and aphasia. While dyslexia describes a reading disorder (Winzer, 1989), aphasia is used to describe partial or total loss of the power to articulate speech. According to Kirk, Kliebhan, and Lerner, the two primary behaviors that characterize children with learning disabilities are indiscrimination and impulsiveness (cited in Vacca, Vacca, and Gove, 1987). Vacca, Vacca, and Gove (1987, p. 463) note that "indiscrimination is rooted in the inability to note likenesses and differences and to synthesize these observations into meaning," while the source of impulsiveness "is an inability to prioritize sensory messages" (p. 464). The result is distractibility. In addition, these children are described as hyperactive, forgetful, unpredictable, and disorganized. They usually require extensive remedial work.

Since learning disabilities are complex, and not a single condition, there is no one treatment. Ideally, these children will be placed in an individualized program geared to their needs and disability. Instruction should be based on their strengths as much as possible. For example, if they have problems processing written directions, directions should also be given orally or taped for them. Anderson and Lapp (1988) recommended the use of alternative teaching and response methods such as tape recorders, computers, or typewriters with some of these children. Others suggest structuring their environment to keep distractions to a minimum. Some teachers find that it also helps if time and work are broken down into smaller, more manageable parts. These could be written on job cards or listed on a contract.

Children with Emotional Disturbances (Disabilities)

According to Winzer (1989, p. 8), this category would include "children with behavioral disorders as well as those affected by childhood psychoses." They are significantly more aggressive or withdrawn than their peers. They are often discipline problems because they tend to act out their emotions in very unacceptable ways such as screaming, swearing, running in an uncontrolled manner, and so on, or not responding at all (withdrawal). Therefore, they will need help in learning to express their emotions in acceptable ways and to control their expressive behavior. Winzer (1989) cautioned that they will need to acquire certain social skills first, if they are to benefit from classroom instruction. Such disruptive behavior may be even more difficult to control in the whole-language classroom where children are usually given more freedom to move about the classroom. Although children with more passive behavior (anxiety, withdrawal) are less obvious and less disruptive, they can be difficult to motivate and may lack the social skills needed to make and keep friends. The use of cooperative learning groups may help in this regard.

Since these children "often experience difficulty with basic school skills" (Lewis and Doorlag, 1991, p. 56), they need to be provided with an individualized program geared to their own individual needs. The wide range of materials, strategies, and activities found in whole-language classrooms provides these children with numerous listening, speaking, reading, and writing choices that can be selected to meet their needs. One approach that is very effective with these children is the writing process (McGee and Richgels, 1990). Because it focuses on ideas first rather than spelling and mechanics, it helps to build their self-esteem and allows them to express their thoughts more freely. Because of the freedom and more relaxed sharing atmosphere found in whole-language classrooms, it is also easier for them to get help from the teacher and their peers when it is needed. It also promotes the development of more social skills, an area that is usually a problem for these children.

Children with Speech Disorders (Impairments)

"Although speech disorders are not uncommon, it is difficult to estimate their prevalence because they are often associated with other difficulties" (Winzer, 1989, p. 377). Simply stated, it is a condition that interferes with communication because of speaking (sound-producing) difficulties that may result in problems in reading and other school subjects. The type and severity of the disorder is usually diagnosed by a trained speech therapist, and can have many causes (cerebral palsy, cleft palate, for example). They generally fall into three categories: "faulty articulation, dysfluent production (stuttering), or voice disorders" (Gloeckler and Simpson, 1988, p. 22). Articulation disorders involve errors of sound production involving omissions, substitution, and distortions, while voice disorders involve problems with pitch, voice intensity, quality, and flexibility. Dysfluent production is a fluency disorder that affects the flow of speech to such a degree that it becomes difficult to hear or understand what is being said. Children with these three types of problems may hesitate to become involved in oral language activities or ask for help when they need it. Making such activities as pleasant and nonthreatening as possible is crucial. The whole-language classroom can provide this type of environment.

Within this planned environment, whole-language teachers need to provide children with many opportunities to speak in a relaxed atmosphere. Centers, found in most whole-language classrooms, are excellent places to achieve this goal. Puppets, felt-board figures, and story props can be placed in the drama center to promote the retelling of favorite stories old and new. It can also serve as an excellent area for Readers Theatre, which gives these children many opportunities to practice oral reading using prepared material. Books can be placed in the listening center along with read-along tapes, providing auditory support for children with articulation problems. In addition, many opportunities to be involved in oral shared reading activities such as choral reading, shared unison reading from big books, as well as the chanting of poems, songs, rhymes, and verses should be provided. Many of these songs, verses, and chants can be memorized and practiced orally. They can even be taped and replayed by the children for later practice. These experiences help children with speech disorders increase their vocabulary, and provide them with needed practice with correct sounds and common syntactic patterns (Winzer, 1989). With older children, cheers, raps, and favorite songs can be chanted and used for writing models. A number of songs are now available in picture books allowing children to read the words of the songs once they have learned to sing them. Some of these books are listed below.

Adams, P. (1975). *There was an old lady who swallowed a fly*. New York: Grossel and Dunlap.

Broomfield, R. (1965). *The twelve days of Christmas*. New York: McGraw-Hill.

Emberly, B. (1966). *One wide river to cross*. Englewood Cliffs, NJ: Prentice-Hall.

Glazer, T. (1982). *On top of spaghetti*. Garden City, NY: Doubleday.

Keats, E.J. (1972). *Over in the meadow*. New York: Scholastic.

Peek, M. (1981). *Roll over, a counting song*. New York: Houghton Mifflin.

Raffi (1989). *Everything grows*. New York: Crown Publishers.

Raffi (1987). *Down by the bay*. New York: Lippincott.

Quackenbush, R. (1975). *Skip to my Lou*. New York: Lippincott.

Quackenbush, R. (1972). *Old MacDonald had a farm*. New York: Lippincott.

Children with Visual Impairments

This category includes the blind as well as those children with limited or low vision (partially sighted) who require special services because of their visual problems. Those with limited vision will use it with varying degrees of competency. They are deficient in the motor areas mainly because their disability restricts or impairs mobility.

Since visual impairment has no affect on intelligence, their educational requirements are essentially the same as their peers. Therefore, the majority of these children can be mainstreamed with some classroom additions and modifications. Audio aids can be used to help those with limited and no vision learn through listening. For example, children can get information from volunteer readers, talking computers, and tapes of books, magazines, and texts. Teacher presentations can also be taped for later review. For those students with partial vision, there are large-print books, magnification devices, and even circuit television aids that can be used to enlarge material. The extensive use of large-print material in whole-language classrooms should be very helpful to the beginning reader. However, children who are blind will need to rely solely on tactile and auditory experiences. They will need to learn how to read and write using braille. Since these characters are larger than regular print, the reading of braille will be slow and tedious. Therefore, they will need to be given extra time to complete reading and writing assignments.

With students who are visually impaired, it is important to base language arts instruction on their observed functional abilities. In the area of listening, it is crucial that they develop excellent listening skills, since they will have to use them more often than their seeing peers. In the area of speaking, they tend to do as well as their peers, if their intelligence is in the normal range. However, this is not the case in reading. According to Wallace, Cohen, and Polloway (1987), it is usually their most difficult academic subject. Those with some usable residual vision should be taught to read using real print rather than braille. The print provides these children with advantages over braille in speed of reading, use of pictures and diagrams, and greater accessibility to reading materials (Wallace, Cohen, and Polloway, 1987). A multisensory approach is also recommended with an instructional shift from the visual mode to the auditory, tactile, and kinesthetic modes (Winzer, 1989). In the area of writing, a brailler could be used with the blind. Those with limited vision might use a large-print computer software program with voice or large dark felt markers with wide-lined paper. Teachers will also have to use large-print job cards at the writing center for these children. It is also important to integrate the teaching of the language arts, emphasizing the relationship of listening, speaking, reading, and writing.

Children with Hearing Impairments

The hearing impaired are deaf or hard of hearing and need special services because of their hearing loss. One or both ears can be affected. Children who are deaf receive insufficient information for speech comprehension, whereas children who are hard of hearing hear well enough to understand speech with the help of a hearing aid. Until recently, these children were seldom mainstreamed into the regular classroom. Those who are mainstreamed demonstrate varied rates of progress and achievement. "Difficulty in speech and language development is one of the major problems associated with hearing loss" (Lewis and Doorlag, 1991, p. 58). The most devastating effect of this disability may be on language acquisition, speech production, and reading skills (Anderson and Lapp, 1988). In reading, "their auditory deprivation must be compensated by building a strong sight-word vocabulary" (Winzer, 1989, p.133). Gloeckler and Simpson (1988) noted that hearing impairment, especially deafness, is often accompanied by social and psychological problems.

Perhaps the most important thing to remember about these students is that they are all individuals and cannot be expected to learn in the same way just because they have the same disability. With this thought in mind, the following suggestions are offered to teachers mainstreaming the hearing impaired.

1. Provide appropriate seating when needed.
2. Adjust your teaching style by visually reinforcing new teaching as much as possible. For example, utilize the board as much as possible before dis-

cussing new material or provide them with written previews outlining what will be covered. When speaking, it is important to face the child, enunciate clearly, and speak at a moderate rate of speed.

3. During the early stages of reading instruction, use picture books that have related pictures and text (McGee and Richgels, 1990), as well as simple concept books with limited print to develop sight vocabulary.

4. Provide filmstrips, pictures, videos, and other visual materials in the viewing center to supplement oral teaching.

5. Utilize buddies, hired aides, and/or parents as helpers or note-takers when help is needed with missed information.

6. Use the language-experience approach with younger children to enhance word recognition and comprehension (Winzer, 1989).

7. Question children often to check their comprehension of what is being taught.

Children with Physical Impairments

This category of children with disabilities "is relatively small (less than 1% of the school-aged population), but extremely diverse" (Lewis and Doorlag, 1991, p. 57). It includes children who are orthopedically impaired with such chronic conditions as muscular dystrophy, spina bifida, and missing limbs, neurologically impaired with conditions such as epilepsy, and those with special health problems such as diabetes and respiratory ailments (Gloeckler and Simpson, 1988).

There are few common learning difficulties associated with this type of disability since most of these physical impairments have no effect on cognitive ability and potential (Anderson and Lapp, 1988). Most of these children will not require vastly different language arts programs than their peers. When special needs do arise, they are more apt to be in the area of physical and technical modifications. For example, instruction materials may have to be changed for children who have difficulty writing. You may have to tape the paper down or mount it to a clipboard, and provide felt pens for writing. For those children who find writing especially difficult, computers with adaptive devices such as head-pointers, alternate switch inputs, and touch-sensitive screens and keyboard can be used. In addition, bookstands, page turners, talking books, tapes of content texts can be used by those children having difficulty turning pages and handling books. Finally, the classroom organization itself may need to be changed to ensure complete accessibility to all materials and areas of the classroom, including all learning centers. If tape recorders were available in these centers, they could be used by those with writing difficulties to tape research reports or projects, practice oral language, and tell stories.

Since the learning problems of these children may range from mentally impaired to the gifted, it is very difficult to offer teaching suggestions specific

Most children with physical disabilities do not require different language arts programs different from their peers.

to children who are physically impaired. Other suggestions already discussed in this chapter should be used with these children on an individual basis when appropriate.

English-as-a-Second-Language (ESL) Learners

Recent census figures confirm that large numbers of American and Canadian children live in homes where languages other than English are usually spoken. While some come from families with a long history in North America, others are recently arrived immigrants and refugees. In the United States, these more recent arrivals have come mainly from Asia, Latin America, and the Caribbean, and have resulted in historic levels of enrolment of immigrants in the public schools (First, 1988), of whom the majority are English-as-a-second-language (ESL) learners. At present, this rapidly growing group makes up a substantial portion of the school population in large cities throughout the

United States and Canada. In some school districts the actual number of students and languages spoken are staggering. If Bowman's (1991) 1989 prediction is right, ESL students will become the majority in the U.S. public schools by the end of the next one or two decades. Because of their ever-increasing numbers, it is now very likely that most future teachers will be teaching ESL learners in their classrooms. It is also very evident that the majority of these students will require special assistance in the language arts if they are to be successful in school. In the past, they have not done as well as their English-speaking peers.

For those bilingual students who are proficient in both English and their native (first) language, no special assistance will be required. However, those students account for only a small percentage of ESL learners (Vacca, Vacca, and Gove, 1987). This diverse group of students exhibits a wide range of competency in both their first language and English. In addition, their proficiency in their first language is apt to be better than their proficiency in English. Within this ESL group, there will also be found students who speak no English and students who are limited English proficient (LEP). It is this second group that is most frequently found in classrooms (Wallace, Cohen, and Polloway, 1987). Although support systems such as ESL programs and bilingual programs exist in many school districts with large ESL populations, the majority are mainstreamed into the regular classroom (Allen, 1986; Gunderson, 1991). According to First (1989), these special ESL services are uneven in quality. They range from simple immersion in classrooms filled with English speakers to bilingual programs designed to improve skills in both English and their native language.

At present, a number of controversies exist in relation to ESL programs. Some believe instruction should be in English alone; others believe it should be in the first language as well as in English (Glenn, 1992; McGee and Richgels, 1990). Support for bilingual programs has a long history in the United States and Canada (Cummins, 1980; Glenn, 1992; Hudelson, 1987), as well as in other English-speaking countries (Bianco, 1991/92).

Bilingual programs vary in structure and emphasis, since no universal blueprint exists for bilingual education (Hakuta and Gould, 1987). Soto (1991) identified three prevalent approaches—the transitional approach, the maintenance/developmental approach, and the two-way bilingual approach. The transitional approach relies on the students' native language for instruction only until competency is achieved in English. According to Hakuta and Gould (1987), this is the approach most often used in the United States. Reviews of research show that bilingual programs are neither better nor worse than other ESL programs (Bennett, 1986). While it may be preferable to teach ESL learners in both English and their native languages, their high numbers and the range of languages found in many schools would make this goal unattainable.

In the case of English-only programs (Chamot and O'Malley, 1989), students are often provided with intensive instruction in English language skills for part of the day by an ESL specialist. The rest of the day is spent in the regular classroom. Other programs use reception classes for periods of a few months to up to two years on school entry. Here they acquire basic proficiency in English before entering the mainstream.

Others caution that ESL students should spend all or most of their day with their English-speaking peers (Ashworth, 1989; Burgess and Gore, 1990) and work within the regular school curriculum with modifications to meet individual needs. The amount of time and help required will vary greatly. Some will need only a few years to gain the command of English to compete with their English-speaking peers (Wong-Fillmore, 1986); others will take as long as five to seven years (Ashworth, 1992; Collier, 1987; Cummins, 1984; Handscombe, 1989; Sutton, 1989).

Johnson (1988) has taken a more flexible approach to ESL programs. She wrote that such programs "can operate in a variety of contexts—in bilingual classes, in multilingual classes, and across classroom boundaries" (p. 155).

Another controversial issue in relation to ESL programs is what constitutes a good quality program. According to Handscome (1989), it is one which contains (1) an orientation program, (2) a monitoring procedure, (3) a parent involvement program, (4) a language program, and (5) an academic upgrading program. His fourth component, a language program, is also an area of great controversy. Some ESL educators believe teachers should use a structured skills-based approach to literacy; others recommend a holistic, natural, whole-language approach to literacy (Allen, 1991; Heald-Taylor, 1986; Maguire, 1991; Quintero and Huerta-Macias, 1990; Rigg and Enright, 1986; Williams and Snipper, 1990). This growing support for whole-language has resulted in changes in a number of ESL classrooms. Second-language teaching practice is now emphasizing communication over drill in informal settings, and the "learner's focus is on doing something through language" (Allen, 1986, p. 61). This allows ESL learners to acquire a second language, rather than learn it, and lays the foundation for fluency in the second language (Johns, 1988). It allows them to read, write, and speak at their own level of proficiency and rate of development. This is important since there is tremendous variation in their rate of learning English (Genishi, 1989; Hakuta and Gould, 1987). "Recent research in second-language acquisition also makes it clear that whole-language teaching strategies that benefit native speakers, are appropriate for second-language learners" (Hudelson, 1987, p. 839).

Therefore, language art teachers will need to provide ESL learners with countless opportunities to listen, to speak, to write, and to read during authentic events, using content that is familiar to them. In order to do this, they will need to learn as much as they can about their ESL learners, and how these students acquire a second language. In addition, they will need to know which whole-language strategies work best with these students, so that such knowledge can be transferred into effective classroom practice. Some of these strategies will now be addressed.

Listening and Speaking

The ESL learners found in elementary classrooms will exhibit considerable variation in their level of oral language proficiency and their rate of development. Therefore, the teacher's first responsibility will be to assess their oral proficiency as well as their inclination to learn English. In whole-language classrooms, teachers can find many opportunities to assess or informally document their level of oral language development. However, they may have to rely solely on nonverbal cues such as facial expressions if the students are recent arrivals (Genishi, 1989), since these students may not yet feel secure enough to respond orally. Once their proficiency levels have been ascertained, the teacher's responsibility is to provide them with appropriate materials and activities that will encourage meaningful oral interactions with their English-speaking peers in stimulating, informal, linguistically rich environments. These types of interactions involve both listening and speaking, and should help them to continue to develop their fluency in oral language. They should then build on the educational and personal experiences they bring to school (Early, 1990). It will be easier for them to learn a second language if they are placed in situations that are meaningful to them. Not only must this input be comprehensible, but

Kindergarten students listen to stories they cannot yet read independently.

it must be slightly beyond their current level of competence (Allen, 1991). Since they will need to feel comfortable as speakers to interact, it will only happen in classrooms where talk is risk free, valued, and oriented to success. These types of interactions are more likely to occur in whole-language classrooms where desks are usually grouped to promote meaningful oral interaction and where students often work with partners or in small collaborative groups. These grouping practices allow ESL students to become active interactors with language, rather than passive receptors of language. Teachers wishing to achieve this kind of interaction will have to become language facilitators rather than language givers.

As ESL learners move toward oral fluency, certain problems may arise. Some may become frustrated when they are unable to accomplish in English what they were able to accomplish more easily in their native language. In addition, they may be unable to process much of what they hear in the classroom. As a result, they might fail to respond to questions and may show a reluctance to speak or initiate conversations if they have been in the classroom only a short time. This more or less silent period is to be expected, since it is often a necessary feature of learning a second language (Johns, 1988; Levine, 1990). During this period, teachers will have to show more than the usual amount of patience and look for nonverbal signs of understanding or confusion. The students' primary task at this time is to develop their receptive second-language abilities in preparation for later oral communication. According to Johns (1988, p. 19), this silent period "may last from a few hours to several months." However, as their knowledge of English increases along with their confidence, so will their oral fluency. During this time, supportive oral group activities such as action verses, choral speaking, verse chanting are especially helpful with children having problems with pronunciation, use of stress, and/or intonation, and can help them gain confidence in themselves as speakers. Ashworth (1992) suggested that teachers provide their ESL students first with a buddy who can speak their language and later with a monolingual English-speaking buddy to aid the student in gaining meaning. In time, more acceptable speech patterns will evolve.

The teacher's role in this process is significant. Foremost is providing ESL students with numerous opportunities to listen and react to interesting material (songs, stories, rhymes, poetry, and so on). A variety of stories should be told and read to them while they are in large and small groups. These experiences help them to increase their listening and speaking vocabularies, develop a sense of story, make predictions, and increase their understanding of how English grammar works, as they begin to read and write in English. In classrooms, where there are a number of ESL students speaking the same first language, teachers might wish to invite parents or older ESL students to read or tell stories to them in their first language. Similar stories could also be taped and placed in the listening center along with a dual-language copy of the story.

This gives these students access to stories that they would be unable to understand in English.

During the story reading, teachers can do a great deal to increase their comprehension of the story. They can stop at key points throughout the story to discuss what has already happened, what might happen next, and so on. They can further involve students by asking questions to clarify word meaning, to encourage literal and inferential comprehension, and to relate the story to their background and experience (Hough, Nurse, and Enright, 1986). In addition, understanding can be increased through the use of real objects, charts, blackboard drawings, pictures, diagrams, photographs, story drama, and role-playing before, during, and after the reading. For those students with limited oral language proficiency, this type of literacy input is vital.

The actual books (fiction and nonfiction) selected for sharing need to be chosen carefully. Wise teachers select books with clear illustrations closely linked to the text, since illustrations play a significant role in helping ESL students attach meaning to the text. Language must also be considered. "Texts should support meaning by being predictable" (Allen, 1989, p. 59). Predictable books with repetitive refrains or predictable patterns invite listeners to complete the pattern or pick up the refrain. Many folktales and fairy tales fall into this category, and therefore are excellent choices for story telling and retelling using big books or felt-board figures. Once students become familiar with plot lines, they can retell the stories to each other over and over again using puppets, story props, and felt-board figures in the drama center. The story can also be taped as that they can listen to it as often as they wish in the listening center. In addition, they can be encouraged to tell stories based on story-type wordless books that have an appealing central character such as the one in Tomie De Paola's *Pancakes for Breakfast.* Finally, alphabet books and concept books can be used to link words to their meanings, and give students something to talk about as books are explored and shared in large and small groups.

Furthermore, teachers need to provide ESL students with many opportunities to use and hear comprehensible language that takes into account their age, interests, past experiences, and what they are doing at home and at school. These planned and unplanned social interactions should involve pairs and small cooperative groups in a variety of settings. These interactions must involve more fluent speakers of English who can act as good models of spoken English and who are prepared to provide their ESL peers with comprehensive input and support (Ashworth, 1992), to help them develop a nativelike control of English. These interactions should invite discussion, collaboration, questioning, responding, sharing, and cooperation within an encouraging, low-anxiety environment. Some suggested activities include story dramatizations, literature discussions, group projects, puppet plays, cooking experiences, group constructions, unison chanting, oral reports, science activities, role-playing, as well as the everyday oral interactions that take place in all classrooms. The richer and more frequent the exposure to such experiences, the faster oral fluency will be achieved. Teachers are reminded by Wilkes (1988) not to short-change the listening component of their programs in their haste to produce fluent speakers. He noted that an extended period of listening comprehension may have to precede as well as accompany oral language production in some cases. Finally, Handscombe (1989) reminded teachers that the use of teachers, parents, or peers who can speak the student's first language can increase both the pace and depth to which English can be acquired.

Writing

If ESL learners are to become proficient writers of English, they will need to be surrounded by people reading and writing, and by a variety of meaningful, purposeful print in an environment that promotes numerous individual and group writing experiences. There must also be meaningful input from peers and teachers. These varied experiences will need to be provided well before they have total control of their new language (Allen, 1991; Hudelson, 1986). Whenever involved in such experiences, they will make use of whatever they know about writing in English at that given time. In addition, some of them will use the knowledge they have of writing in their first language and apply it to their writing. As they learn more and more about the writing process, their writing will begin to resemble the writing of their English-speaking peers.

Like their English-speaking peers, they are able to create different kinds of texts for a variety of purposes in response to a range of whole-language strategies. Journal or diary writing has been well documented as one way of effectively moving ESL students into expressive writing. It helps them to become more competent and fluent in their writing, and encourages them to record inner feelings, personal events, as well as their thoughts about topics of interest to them. The amount of time and support teachers give to this activity can affect both the quality and quantity of their writing. Since this activity is used to encourage personal writing, it should be done without concern for correct spelling, sentence structure, punctuation, and the like. The emphasis should be on the information being conveyed.

The use of dialogue or interactive journals in which students and teachers carry on private written conversations (letters) is also highly recommended for use with ESL students (Edelsky, 1989; Hudelson, 1986; Maguire, 1991). Once set up, these journals are written in alternately by the student and teacher. Research on this type of authentic writing has shown that many ESL students who rarely respond in class become willing writers using this approach (Johnson, 1988). It is an excellent way of integrating the reading and writing process. Both problems and strengths can be easily identified by teachers, and it allows them to model correct spelling, punctuation, and syntax in their responses. Over time, student entries increase in length and fluency. It is a strategy that can be used effectively at all elementary grade levels.

ESL learners must also be given many opportunities to write literary text (stories, books, and poetry) on self-selected topics. In order to achieve this goal, some teachers set aside a block of time when everyone in the class writes. Teachers also like to set up a writing/publishing center where students can write individually as well as collaboratively in small groups. Once written, the material is usually shared in some way. It can be read to peers, displayed, or placed in the class library if it is a published book. Students should also be encouraged to display writing completed at home. Some of this writing could be in the student's native language or written as a dual language text. The stories that they hear and read will have a direct effect on what they write. They often use the framework found in such books as ABC books, counting books, folktales, fairy tales, and predictable books in their writing, and this modeling of book language helps them acquire the language of books (Allen, 1989). Wordless books can also be used in this manner to help them create stories in their own words.

Not only must ESL students write in the literary mode but also in the transactional mode (informational writing) if they are to be successful in the content areas. In this type of writing, "the aim is to present information clearly and convey a message to the reader through reporting, explanation, argumentation, persuasion, speculation, drawing conclusions, and so on" (Hudelson, 1986, p. 26).

Hadaway (1992) also highly recommended arranging letter exchanges between ESL students and English-speaking students in the same school, with another school in the district, or even in another geographic region. This activity provides them with a real task that enhances reading and writing skills. It can be done at any elementary grade level, and is one more way of providing ESL students with an English model as well as a real audience. It can also be done successfully using computers.

As ESL students learn more and more about the writing process, they go through the same developmental stages of writing (pre-phonetic, semi-phonetic, phonetic, transitional, and conventional or mature) as their English-speaking peers (Ashworth, 1992). However, they go through these stages at a slower pace. In the case of spelling, they begin with the relationship between sounds and letters, just like their peers. However, the strategies they use show that they are actively involved in working through the differences and similarities between their native language and English (Nathenson-Mejia, 1989), and that they do use conventional English spelling.

One approach that is often used with individual ESL writers is the language-experience approach (LEA). Although it is more often used to produce reading material for ESL readers (Rigg, 1989), its importance in beginning writing should not be overlooked. In this approach, text is dictated by the student to the teacher who acts as a scribe. This demonstrates the one-to-one correspondence between the speaker's oral language and the written language. Parents, volunteers, or older students can also act as scribes. Discussion precedes the dictated writing. The scribe sits parallel with the student so she or he can see the words clearly as they are written and read aloud by the scribe. Artwork often precedes the writing or may be added later. The written story is a model for letter formation, spelling, punctuation, and other mechanics of English. Once completed, the story is read to the student and then reread with the student. Finally, it is read by the student alone.

Teachers who use the LEA with individuals also use it with large and small groups. In some whole-language classrooms, this procedure is described as *shared writing*. It occurs when a group of students compose a text collaboratively with the teacher after discussing the content. It can be written on the blackboard, on chart paper, in a large book, or on an overhead transparency. These shared writing sessions give members of the group a chance to see and experience a writer at work, as well as contribute to the text. It allows the teacher to model appropriate writing practices and behaviors that he or she would like the students to adopt. Furthermore, it allows ESL students to tackle things collaboratively with their English-speaking peers that they would be unable to do individually. Once completed, the group text is read by the teacher and revised by the students if necessary. The story is then changed by the students along with the teacher. Once the students are familiar with the process, longer stories, content material, big books, report writing, letter writing, literature responses, as well as other forms of writing can be done collaboratively. Older students could be also involved in writing chapter books, class newspapers, play-scripts or content reports in small groups.

Process writing is another writing approach that has been highly recommended for use with ESL students (Ashworth, 1992; Heald-Taylor, 1986; Hudelson, 1986) as a way of improving their writing. In this approach, communication to a real audience is paramount, since writers must share their writing drafts as they work to produce a final version with the help of their peers. The process of adjusting and revising their writing in order to make ideas clearer to others is an important aspect of this approach. Most ESL writers are capable of such changes and are willing to revise their writing based on peer input (Hudelson, 1986). However, Wason-Ellam (1992) cautioned teachers that using peers as editors may be a negative experience for ESL writers, if they are forced into writing for a peer audience too soon.

Partner writing can also be used effectively with ESL writers. Writing together on paper or on a word processor enables them to pool their knowledge of the writing system, allowing ESL writers to produce a text that they could not produce without the help of their English-speaking peer. This activity is especially useful with ESL students with limited English, as it provides them with a good written model.

Once writing material has been completed, it should be published in book form, read to peers, displayed, or kept in a special writing folder or scrapbook with other dated writing samples with or without comments by the teacher. This is a good way of documenting the writing development of ESL students. Published books (stories, poems, and information books) can be displayed on a "new books" shelf in the class library. Bilingual students should be encouraged to publish in both languages. Stories and reports can also be taped and placed in the listening center for others to enjoy.

As ESL children are involved in these daily writing activities, teachers will need to respond to their writing in some way. Cumming (1985) noted that presently there are nine recommended techniques available to teachers wishing to respond to the writing of their ESL students. These are evaluation, error identification, teacher correction, marginal commentary, checklisting, oral responses, direct instruction, reformation, and peer responses (p. 59). From his review of the literature, he concluded that error identification is the most widely used technique, while teacher correction and marginal commentary are the least used. He also found that oral responses and peer responses were popularly practiced by ESL teachers.

Reading

One major issue related to learning to read in a second language is whether students should be introduced to reading in their first language before being introduced to reading in English (bilingual education), or if they should be taught to read in English alone. This practice of first teaching ESL students to read in their first language occurs with great regularity in Spanish-English programs in the United States (Hudelson, 1992). Although it might be preferable to teach ESL students to read in their first language first, for most students and teachers in the mainstream, it is not a viable option. Therefore, this chapter will not deal with these ESL students.

There appears to be no one single approach that is the best for teaching ESL learners to read (Ashworth, 1992). What is needed is a variety of materials, strategies, and activities in a supportive print-rich environment where they can interact with whole, authentic texts. As they move to reading independence, ESL students pass through sequential stages that appear to parallel the stages of language acquisition (Guckes and Kandaras, 1988). The first stage is the silent stage where ESL students receive a variety of second-language input through listening, looking, and actions (Holdaway, 1979). During this period of listening comprehension, they gain needed exposure to the phonemes and rhythms of English needed for beginning reading. This stage is followed by the oral production or prereading stage (emergent reading) which lays the foundation for initial reading experiences. During this second stage, activities focus on environmental print (school and community), story reading and telling, and reading printed commands (for example, jump, clap, run, pick up the ball). These two stages are followed by the early reading stage, the semi-independent stage, and the fluent stage.

The reading approach that is most often recommended in the ESL literature is the language-experience approach (Gunderson, 1991). It allows ESL students to create their own individual, comprehensible reading materials that are relevant to their home culture and their individual interests. The text is predictable and easy to read because it uses only their own words, their own sentence structures, and, most importantly, their own experiences. This approach also helps them to increase their sight vocabulary. Often one or more key words from the story are written on small word cards which are stored in their personal word banks. When they are later tested on the words by the teacher, the words that they have learned are retained, while those that they are unable to recognize are discarded. The words retained become a useful resource for reading and writing development.

Teachers who use the LEA with individuals also use it with large and small groups to promote reading growth. Rigg (1989) cautioned teachers not to make such groups too large. She recommended groups of four to eight, since large groups will probably result in too little participation by ESL students, and possibly result in boredom as well. The written stories deal with both home and school experiences such as the new class rabbit, a field trip, a special visitor, a special day, a favorite story, or a cooking experience. Teacher-led discussion takes place before and during the writing. Once the story has been written on the blackboard, on a chart, or in a blank big book, time may again be given to revision. It is then read by the teacher alone, and then read with the students several times as the teacher points to each word as it is read. Reading strategies are taught when needed. After it has been read several times, the material is displayed in the classroom so that it can be read later by the students individually, with a partner, or in a small group with or without the teacher. If the material was written in a blank big book, it would be placed in the class library. In addition, the material may be reproduced in a smaller size, and a copy given to each student so that they can read it on their own.

Since reading language experience materials alone will not prepare ESL students for the formal content textbooks they will have to use in the future, teachers also provide them with many opportunities to take part in shared book reading. In this approach, teachers read big books (usually predictable), either commercial or teacher made, to groups of children. During the reading, teachers reinforce reading strategies and model what good readers do when they read. Then, teachers reread (chant) the text in unison with the students several times as they point to each word as it is read. This chanting of the text allows ESL students to join in as much of the reading as they can manage. It also helps them to negotiate print, assimilate the structure of the story, and reinforce the strategies demonstrated. The multiple readings of the text provides them with the opportunity to commit parts of the text to memory and join in while it is being reread with the teacher (Hudelson, 1992). It also provides them with a good oral reading model, and helps them with pronunciation and intonation, which can be a problem for ESL students (Ashworth, 1992). Because they have the support of their English-speaking peers, they can tackle reading material slightly beyond their developmental stage. Shared reading can be done on a one-to-one basis or in a small or large group with another peer, a parent, or the teacher. In London, England, it has also been proven to be a successful home reading activity. Once the shared reading time is over, the big book is displayed prominently in or near the class library along with smaller editions if available. The students can read them later by themselves or with a peer. A read-along tape of the story along with the book could also be placed in the listening center. In addition, other independent learning materials such as sequence pictures, word games, related books, and writing activities can be placed in the centers. Poems, number verses, songs, choral verse, raps, and chants can also be used for shared reading (Holdaway, 1979). They are usually printed on the blackboard, on chart paper, or on an overhead transparency so that the words can be easily seen by the students. These can also be made into big books.

ESL students will also need to be provided with opportunities to read independently on their own as well as in small groups using good literature. Clay (1976) found that, on average, the Maori and Polynesian ESL New Zealand students she researched needed about six months to acquire the early reading behaviors they needed to begin reading books.

Once they are ready, these students should be involved in small-group, teacher-guided literature study from time to time. During this guided reading time, students will read, discuss, explore aspects of story grammar, and/or practice reading strategies. In addition, they must be given a block of daily independent reading time to read books of their own choosing. This will require an inviting well-stocked classroom library—fiction and nonfiction books, alphabet books, concept books, wordless books, dual-language texts, poetry books, magazines, and newspapers.

Readability formulas will be of little value to teachers looking for ESL reading materials (Ashworth, 1992; Rigg, 1986). What will be important is whether the students have enough background about the content so that it makes sense. These materials also need to be well organized, clearly written, and contain illustrations, charts, and diagrams that support the text, allowing them to draw upon many cues for meaning (Sutton, 1989, p. 686). Beginning ESL readers must be provided with supportive texts that have strong narratives, high predictability, repetition, and humor. Books of this type will help them to increase their sight vocabulary, develop cuing systems, and increase their chances for future success. Some of the books should be culturally familiar and others written by others from other cultures. Many good folktales and fairy tales are now readily available in versions set in different cultures and written at varying levels of difficulty. Other books and novels from the students' cultural backgrounds should be made available to older ESL students. Many excellent books from other countries have been translated into English. If some of the students are bilingual, books could also be provided in their first language.

Material for older students must be selected carefully, since ESL students tend to begin having difficulties related to meaning once they reach third or fourth grade (House, 1980; Sutton, 1989). Their problems are greatly increased because of the introduction of content texts. Teachers can help them by creating frameworks for comprehension through the use of a variety of comprehension and reading strategies and activities. Sutton (1989, p. 687) suggested teachers review unfamiliar vocabulary, provide a prereading discussion of important concepts to comprehending the text, use group assignments, and use questioning to monitor comprehension.

Before working with content material, students must be provided with prereading activities to activate their prior knowledge. Early (1989) noted that several areas identified by research show considerable potential. They are advanced organizers, purpose-setting questions, structured overview, text structures, semantic mapping, and preteaching vocabulary (p. 204).

Learners Who Are Gifted and Talented

Over time, a number of very different definitions have been used to define the gifted. Early definitions relied solely on specified scores on standardized tests of intelligence. In 1978, the term *talented* expanded the concept further with the passage of the U.S. Gifted and Talented Children's Act. Included in this group are those identified as possessing demonstrated or potential abilities (singly or in combination) in the areas of general intellectual ability, specific academic aptitude, creative or productive thinking, leadership ability, or in the visual and performing arts who by reason thereof require differentiated educational programs and/or service. This should apply to a minimum of 3 to 5% of the school population (Coleman, 1985, p. 10). At present, this U.S. federal definition is accepted in many parts of the world.

Although many schools and districts provide some form of specialized programming, most gifted and talented students will be found in the regular classroom. These students will require an appropriate, personalized, challenging language arts instructional program based on individual needs and interests that is qualitatively different than that planned for their fellow students. It should differ mainly in degree rather than kind (Tuttle, 1991). This special programming will require modifying the content to be learned, instructional strategies, the process for learning, and special materials and resources. These should be housed in a creative, responsive environment that has been well stocked with a wide range of instructional materials and resources, if they are to be motivated to think critically, deeply, and independently. Without proper nurturing and challenges, many of these students will fail to reach their creative and academic potential.

Gifted and talented learners are represented in all economic, social, racial, and cultural segments of society. Unfortunately, some of them are never identified, some become underachievers, and some even drop out of school early. Teachers of language arts must take some responsibility for their identification and nurturing, since exceptional skill in one or more of the language arts areas is frequently listed as a characteristic of these students, as well as a needed goal for their future success in other curriculum areas which are often integrated with one or more areas of the language arts. In addition, they frequently exhibit advanced verbal skills, rapid and easy learning, large vocabularies, verbal expressiveness, voracious reading, and the ability to deal with complex and abstract concepts (Feldhusen, Van Tassel-Baska, and Seeley, 1989, p. 219). They usually begin to read and use language at an earlier age than other students, and most of them will "be accelerated in vocabulary usage and understanding, in choice of words, and in use of longer and more complex sentences" (Wallace, Cohen, and Polloway, 1987, p. 479). However, not all gifted students will display all of these characteristics.

Meeting the special educational needs of this diverse group of students is not an easy task. Because they develop at a much higher level than other students, they require advance instruction, intensive involvement in individual interests, and exposure to materials and resources not usually used at their age levels. This will require the service of teachers who have a great deal of professional skill, knowledge, resourcefulness, and sensitivity (Winzer, 1989). They will also need the ability to develop activities that address various aspects of creative thinking (fluency, flexibility, originality, and elaboration). Familiarity with the six categories or levels (knowledge, comprehension, application, analysis, synthesis, and evaluation) of Bloom's Taxonomy of Cognitive Domain will also be useful to teachers, and can serve as a basis for many curriculum projects (Eby and Smutny, 1990). Since they are able to master the first two levels (knowledge and comprehension) very quickly, emphasis should be at the four higher levels. The skills involved at these four levels are precisely the ones needed to challenge their intellectual and creative potential (Smutny and Blocksom, 1990). Furthermore, teachers can provide them with enrichment using Renzulli's (1977) Enrichment Triad Model, which provides three types of activities. The highest level, Type III Activities, are especially appropriate for the gifted. It should represent original work.

Listening and Speaking

Gifted students usually possess considerable ability in listening, and their abilities in this area are often early signs of superior intellect and language skills (Wallace, Cohen, and Polloway, 1987, p. 486). At its highest levels, listening involves a good deal of critical thinking. For teachers wishing to promote this skill on a more personalized basis, an excellent technique is the learning center approach. In classroom listening centers, tapes can be used that focus on interpretive and critical listening.

Since descriptions of gifted students often stress advanced vocabulary and verbal skills, oral communication must also be given high priority. It is an activity often enjoyed by students who are gifted and talented, and one that usually develops early. Although they tend to express themselves well orally, their spoken language can be maximized further through a variety of instructional approaches. This ability is particularly crucial to them, since they will probably be required to share oral information with others more and more as they move up through the educational system. Probably, it will also have an effect on their career aspirations and future employment. For these reasons, Frith and Mims (1984) contended that teachers should take the time to teach them how to make good oral presentations.

Teachers should also provide students who are gifted with opportunities to tell stories using felt-board figures or props, to dramatize stories read or written by them, to retell stories in their own words, to use puppets to dramatize story events, to be involved in role-playing situations, to conduct meetings and interviews, and to be involved in discussion in both large and small groups. They should also be given time to present research findings using charts, overhead transparencies, diagrams, models, pictures, and media (tapes, video, slides, and films) during the later elementary grades in order to share their thoughts, information, and ideas. This should be followed by a discussion led by the student.

Speech-stimulating activities such as choral speaking and drama are especially beneficial. Drama can provide them with many opportunities to explore higher-level thinking (Gangi, 1990), and can become an integral educational tool when it is integrated with the study of literature, social studies, and history (Pigott, 1990). Pigott noted that dramatizations can also be adapted as a forum for dramatic presentations, history debates, present-day events, and biographies of great people. Students are expected to research their topic and write their own scripts. These presentations develop independence, memory, responsibility, knowledge, research skills, and public speaking ability. They also allow the students to utilize their intellectual ability along with their ability in the visual and performing arts. For example, Kathy, a gifted fifth-grade student, wrote a play about litter bugs and pollution, and then quickly convinced a number of her classmates to act in her production. They made their own costumes and scenery, and convinced the principal to let them perform it at a school assembly. After their presentation, they produced posters and implemented a schoolwide campaign to clean up the school playground.

Writing

Gifted English students usually "write fluently, often composing experimentally for their own pleasure" (West, 1980, p. 11). Although they tend to have advanced vocabularies and begin writing at an early age (Davis and Rimm, 1989), they may still require instruction in basic writing skills as well as in communicating their ideas in writing (Wallace, Cohen, and Polloway, 1987). In addition, they will require higher levels of instruction in terms of both process and content (Winzer, 1989), and should be taught how to edit their own work and the work of others. They should also be introduced to the elements of style at an early age through the sharing of good literature. When they are ready to write and/or publish, they will need an appropriate place to pursue their goal. An appropriate well-stocked writing/publishing center may be one way to achieve this goal, if it is situated near the classroom library. If a computer is available, it will be a real asset in producing the final product. Although they are most often produced in print form, they can also be presented orally or on film or video as a documentary.

At the center, these students can produce poetry, original stories and books, scripts for puppet shows and plays, letters (personal or business), invented myths, newspaper articles, tall tales, fairy tales, movable books, commentary for films and videos, and original stories modeled after published story structures. In addition, they could work collaboratively in small groups to produce a novel, which they can publish using the computer (Roush, 1992). Before starting the novel, students must be taught the mechanics of writing and the editing process. In addition, they should explore a variety of other writing modes.

For example, they will need to learn how to use research methods in the pursuit of independent study. In order to do this, they will need to learn the basic skills of research—location, acquisition, organization, recording, communication, and evaluation (Polette, 1982). Basic research skills and tools (reference books, encyclopedias, dictionaries, a thesaurus, and so on) can be introduced in a functional situation to gifted students as early as grades 2 and 3, and then developed more extensively as they move through the elementary grades. Since these students are able to use strategies used by much older students, teachers need to focus on synthesizing abilities and to provide questions and experiences that encourage connections among content, prior knowledge, and other concepts (Tuttle, 1991).

Once basic independent research skills have been mastered, students should be free to pursue self-selected topics of interest. During the beginning planning stage, some teachers like to use learning contracts to provide guidance, motivation, and a framework for the project at each successive level of independence.

Since many students who are gifted are fascinated by words, time should be taken for word study. Independent activities could deal with puns, figurative language, crossword puzzles, riddles, alliteration, synonyms, homonyms, homophones, etymology (word histories), and other word play. A variety of books deal with many of these different language aspects and can be used with the gifted and talented student. For example, *Nice or Nasty: A Book of Opposites* by Butterworth and Inkpen illustrates a number of examples of opposite concepts. Other books describe idioms and other figures of speech that are accompanied by numerous illustrations. Two excellent examples of this type of word play are *A Chocolate Moose for Dinner* and *A Little Pigeon Toad,* both by Fred Gwynne. Similar books could be produced by these students alone or with other students once they had been introduced to the concept through literature.

Reading

Gifted learners often enter elementary school already reading, and continue to be good readers as they progress through elementary school. Although they tend to be avid, proficient readers, they still require proper teacher guidance and instruction. Without this assistance, they tend to read less-than-challenging reading materials and fail to develop their full reading potential.

According to Polette (1982, p. 39), the two long-range goals of gifted reading programs should be to create readers in the full meaningful sense of the word and to expand their reading, writing, speaking, and thinking vocabularies. Many experts in the field of gifted education feel these goals can best be achieved through a literature-based reading program. They are one of the best instructional tools for gifted readers because they can be used to foster intellectual development not only at school but home as well. They are also available in every subject area at all levels of difficulty, making them an excellent resource for independent study. In addition, the field of literature abounds with excellent realistic fiction that can serve as a springboard to real-life problem-solving experiences (Polette, 1984, p.1).

Therefore, most gifted reading programs utilize a wide range of literature (fiction and nonfiction) along with a number of varied instructional approaches. In these programs there should be time for group reading as well as independent reading. Teachers can use the results of interest inventories to organize these small flexible reading groups to explore areas of interest. However, all literature is not equally appropriate for use with gifted readers. Therefore, teachers must use appropriate reference material for these kinds of resources. They must also become familiar with the best of children's literature, if they are to help their students select wisely. Baskin and Harris (1980) supplied teachers with extensive lists of intellectually demanding juvenile books that will help teachers promote the intellectual growth of their gifted readers. In addition, Polette (1984) provided them with an excellent extensive guide on 83 preschool/primary books and 47 junior novels. Furthermore, Lukasevich (1983) provided teachers with an annotated bibliography on three dozen information sources on reading for teachers working with gifted students.

Once books have been completed, these students will need to be provided with opportunities to discuss, analyze, and share their personal insights to a variety of audiences. They will also need frequent interaction, discussion, questioning, and support from the teacher. Winebrenner (1992) also suggested using reading skills and vocabulary contracts with gifted readers. These kinds of student-teacher interactions reveal their grasp of vocabulary and allow teachers to extend and clarify their understanding of what has been read. If students are not provided with these types of interactions, they may fail to understand the underlying structures of the books read, or be unable to use these structures in their own writing.

Because they enjoy and work well independently, learning centers are often recommended for use with gifted students. They require access not only to an excellent classroom library but to a school library as well. In addition, an area should be set aside in the classroom where students can research topics of interest. Wise teachers hold conferences with students before beginning such projects in order to ascertain their goals and the activities they plan to pursue, and to ensure the required materials will be available. As they progress in their independent study, they should keep a daily record of what has been accomplished, and their personal reactions to the project thus far. Polette and Hamlin (1980) suggested that such work be evaluated through the use of weekly student-teacher conferences. Self-evaluation by the students must also be undertaken at this time.

The use of good literature can contribute a great deal to the instruction of gifted readers. It can help them grow intellectually and emotionally, build problem-solving skills, and develop methods of productive teaching (Baskin and Harris (1980, p. 50). However, this can only happen with the help of a knowledgeable teacher who is willing to take the time and effort to provide students with a balanced program adapted to their individual interests and needs in a well-planned, well-stocked literacy classroom. Without such help, many gifted learners will fail to reach their full potential.

REFERENCES

Allen, V. G. (1986). Developing contexts to support second language acquisition. *Language Arts, 63 (1),* 61-66.

Allen, V. G. (1989). Literature as a support to language acquisition. In P. Rigg & V. G. Allen (Eds.), *When they don't all speak English.* Urbana, IL: National Council of Teachers of English.

Allen, V. G. (1991). Teaching bilingual and ESL children. In J. Flood, J. M. Jenson, D. Lapp, & J. B. Squire (Eds.), *Handbook of research on teaching the language arts.* New York: Macmillan Publishing Company.

Anderson, P. S. & Lapp, D. (1988). *Language skills in elementary education.* New York: Macmillan Publishing Company.

Andrews, J. & Lupart, J. (Eds.). (1993). *The inclusive classroom: Educating exceptional children.* Scarborough, ON: Nelson.

Ashworth, M. (1988). *Blessed with bilingual brains— Education of immigrant children with English as a second language.* Vancouver, B.C.: Pacific Educational Press.

Ashworth, M. (1989). A good genius for teaching. In J. H. Esling (Ed.), *Multicultural education and policy: ESL in the 1990s.* Toronto: Ontario Institute for Studies in Education.

Ashworth, M. (1992). *The first step on the longer path—Becoming an ESL teacher.* Markham, Ontario: Pippin Publishing Limited.

Baskin, B. H. & Harris, K. H. (1980). *Books for the gifted child.* New York: R. R. Bowker Company.

Bennett, W. J. (1986). *The condition of bilingual education in the nation.* Washington, DC: U.S. Department of Education.

Bianco, J. L. (1991/92). Aspects of bilingualism policy—An Australian perspective. *Language Matters, 3,* 2–9.

Bowman, B. T. (1989). Educating language-minority children: Challenges and opportunities. *Phi Delta Kappan, 71 (2),* 118–120.

Bowman, B. T. (1991). Educating language-minority children: Challenges and opportunities. In B. Persky (Ed.), *Early childhood education.* Lanham, MD: University Press of America.

Burgess, A. & Gore, L. (1990). The move from withdrawal ESL teaching to mainstream activities is necessary, possible and worthwhile. In J. Levine (Ed.), *Bilingual learners and the mainstream curriculum.* London: The Falmer Press.

Butterworth, N. & Inkpen, M. (1987). *Nice or nasty: A book of opposites.* Boston: Little, Brown.

Carr, K. S. (1984). What gifted readers need from reading instruction. *The Reading Teacher, 38 (2),* 144-146.

Chamot, A. U. & O'Malley, J. M. (1989). The cognitive academic learning approach. In P. Rigg & V. G. Allen (Eds.), *When they don't all speak English.* Urbana, IL: National Council of Teachers of English.

Clay, M. M. (1976). Early childhood and cultural diversity in New Zealand. *The Reading Teacher, 29 (4),* 333–342.

Coleman, L. J. (1985). *Schooling the gifted.* Menlo Park, CA: Addison-Wesley Publishing Company.

Collier, V. P. (1987). Age and rate of acquisition of second language for academic purposes. *TESOL Quarterly, 21,* 617–641.

Cumming, A. (1985). Responding to the writing of ESL students. *Highway One, 8 (1-2),* 58–75.

Cummins, J. (1980). Bilingualism and the ESL student. *TESL Talk, 11 (1)*, 8–13.

Cummins, J. (1984) *Bilingualism and special education: Issues in assessment and pedagogy.* Clevedon, Avon: Multilingual Matters.

Davis, G. A. & Rimm, S. B. (1989). *Education of the gifted and talented.* Englewood Cliffs, NJ: Prentice-Hall.

DePaola, T. (1978). *Pancakes for breakfast.* New York: Harcourt, Brace & Jovanovich.

Early, M. (1989). Using key visuals to aid ESL students' comprehension of content classroom texts. *Reading-Canada-Lecture, 7 (4)*, 202–212.

Early, M. (1990). Enabling first and second language learners in the classroom. *Language Arts, 67 (6)*, 567–575.

Eby, J. W. & Smutny, J. F. (1990). *A thoughtful overview of gifted education.* New York: Longman.

Edelsky, C. (1989). Putting language variation to work for you. In P. Rigg & V. G. Allen (Eds.), *When they don't all speak English.* Urbana, IL: National Council of Teachers of English.

Feldhusen, J., VanTassel-Baska, J. & Seeley, K. (1989). *Excellence in educating the gifted.* Denver, CO: Love Publishing Company.

First, J. M. (1988). Immigrant students in the U.S. public schools: Challenges with solutions. *Phi Delta Kappan, 70 (3)*, 205–210.

Ford, M. P. & Ohlhausen, M. M. (1988). Tips from reading clinicians for coping with disabled readers in regular classrooms. *The Reading Teacher, 42 (1)*, 18–22.

Frith, G. H. & Mims, A. A. (1984). Teaching gifted students to make verbal presentations. *Gifted Child Quarterly, 28 (1)*, 45–47.

Gallagher, J. J. (1985). *Teaching the gifted child.* Boston: Allyn and Bacon.

Gangi, J. M. (1990). Higher thinking skills through drama. *Gifted Child Today, 13 (1)*, 16–19.

Genishi, C. (1989). Observing the second language learner: An example of teachers' learning. *Language Arts, 66 (5)*, 509–515.

Glenn, C.L. (1992). Educating the children of immigrants. *Phi Delta Kappan, 73 (5)*, 404–408.

Gloeckler, T. & Simpson, C. (1988). *Exceptional students in regular classrooms—Challenges, services, and methods.* Mountain View, CA: Mayfield Publishing Company.

Goodlad, J. L. & Anderson, J. (1987). *The nongraded elementary school.* New York: Teachers College Press.

Guckes, L. R. & Kandaras, B. (1988). Speak it, read it: Simultaneous acquisition of language and reading skills. In R. Benya & K. E. Muller (Eds.), *Children and languages: Research, practice, and rationale for the early grades.* New York: The American Forum.

Gunderson, L. (1991). *ESL literacy instruction: A guidebook to theory and practice.* Englewood Cliffs, NJ: Prentice-Hall Regents.

Gwynne, F. (1976). *A chocolate moose for dinner.* St. Louis: Treehouse.

Gwynne, F. (1988). *A little pigeon toad.* New York: Simon & Schuster.

Hadaway, N. L. (1992). Letter to literacy—Spurring second language development across the curriculum. *Childhood Education, 69 (1)*, 24-28.

Hakuta, K. & Gould, L. J. (1987). Synthesis of research on bilingual education. *Educational Leadership, 44 (6)*, 38–45.

Handscombe, J. (1989). A quality program for learners of English as a second language. In P. Rigg & V. G. Allen (Eds.), *When they don't all speak English.* Urbana, IL: National Council of Teachers of English.

Heald-Taylor, G. (1986). *Whole language strategies for ESL primary students.* Toronto, Ontario: The Ontario Institute for Studies in Education.

Holdaway, D. (1979). *The foundation of literacy.* Sidney: Ashton Scholastic.

Hough, R. A., Nurse, J. R. & Enright, D. S. (1986). Story reading with limited English speaking children in the regular classroom. *The Reading Teacher, 39 (2)*, 510–514.

House, N. J. (1980). Comprehension and the limited English speaker. In G. Stanford (Chair), *Dealing with differences.* Urbana IL: National Council of Teachers of English.

Hudelson, S. (1986). ESL children's writing: What we've learned, what we're learning. In P. Rigg & D. S. Enright (Eds.), *Children and ESL: Integrating perspectives.* Washington, DC: Teachers of English to Speakers of Other Languages.

Hudelson, S. (1987). The role of native langauge literacy in the education of language minority children. *Language Arts, 64 (8),* 827–841.

Hudelson, S. (1992). Reading in a bilingual program. *Canadian Children, 17 (2),* 13–25.

Johns, K. M. (1988). *How children learn a second language.* Bloomington, IN: Phi Delta Kappa Educational Foundation.

Johnson, D. M. (1988). ESL children as teachers: A social view of second language use. *Language Arts, 65 (2),* 154-163.

Karnowski, L. (1989). Using LEA with process writing. *The Reading Teacher, 42 (7),* 462-465.

Levine, J. (Ed.) (1990). *Bilingual learners and the mainstream curriculum.* London: The Falmer Press.

Lewis, R. B. & Doorlag, D. H. (1991). *Teaching special students in the mainstream.* New York: Macmillan Publishing Company.

Lukasevich, A. (1983). Three dozen useful information sources on reading for the gifted. *The Reading Teacher, 36 (6),* 542–548.

Maguire, M. H. (1991). Bilingualism and whole language. *Orbit, 22 (4),* 12–16.

Malicky, G. & Norman, C. (1988). Whole language: Applications to special education. *Canadian Journal of English Language Arts, 11 (3),* 19–25.

Master, D. L. (1983). Writing and the gifted child. *Gifted Child Quarterly, 27 (4),* 162–168.

McGee, L. M. & Richgels, D. J. (1990) *Literacy's Beginnings— Supporting young readers and writers.* Boston: Allyn and Bacon.

Nathenson-Mejia, S. (1989). Writing in a second language: Negotiating meaning through invented spelling. *Language Arts, 66 (5),* 516–526.

Pigott, I. (1990). Drama in the classroom. *Gifted Child Today, 13 (1),* 2–5.

Polette, N. & Hamlin, M. (1980). *Exploring books with gifted children.* Littleton, CO: Libraries Unlimited, Inc.

Polette, N. (1982). *3R's for the gifted — Reading, writing, and research.* Littleton, CO: Libraries Unlimited Inc.

Polette, N. (1984). *Books and real life — A guide for gifted students and teachers.* Jefferson, NC: McFarland & Company, Inc.

Quintero, E. & Huerta-Macias, A. (1990). All in the family: Bilingualism and biliteracy. *The Reading Teacher, 44 (4),* 306-312.

Randall, J., Ryder, B., Graves, B. & Graves, M. F. (1989). *Easy reading: Book series and periodicals for less able readers.* Newark, DE: International Reading Association.

Renzulli, J. (1977). *The enrichment triad model: A guide for developing defensible programs for the gifted.* Wethersfield, CT: Creative Learning Press.

Rigg, P. (1986) Reading in ESL: Learning from kids. In P. Rigg & D. S. Enright (Eds.), *Children and ESL: Integrating perspectives.* Washington, DC: Teachers of English to Speakers of Other Languages.

Rigg, P. (1989). Language experience approach: Reading naturally. In P. Rigg & V. G. Allen (Eds.), *When they don't all speak English.* Urbana, IL: National Council of Teachers of English.

Rigg, P. & Allen, V. G. (Eds.) (1989) *When they don't all speak English.* Urbana, IL: National Council of Teachers of English.

Rigg, P. & Enright, D. S. (Eds.). (1986). *Children and ESL: Integrating perspectives.* Washington, DC: Teachers of English.

Roush, N. M. (1992). How to write a novel: The collaborative approach to writing. *Gifted Child Today, 15 (5),* 29–31.

Schulz, J. B., Carpenter, C. D. & Turnbull, A. P. (1991). *Mainstreaming exceptional students.* Boston, MA: Allyn and Bacon.

Searfoss, L. W. & Readence, J. E. (1989). *Helping children learn to read.* Englewood Cliffs, NJ: Prentice-Hall.

Smidt, S. (1985). Reading and our multicultural society. In C. Moon (Ed.), *Practical ways to teach reading*. Suffolk: Ward Lock Educational.

Smutny, J. F. & Blocksom, R. H. (1990). *Education of the gifted—Programs and perspectives*. Bloomington, IN: Phi Delta Kappa Educational Foundation.

Soto, L. D. (1991). Understanding bilingual/bicultural young children. *Young Children, 46 (2)*, 30–36.

Stanford, G. (Chair) (1980). *Dealing with differences*. Urbana, IL: National Council of Teachers of English.

Sutton, C. (1989). Helping the non-native English speaker with Reading. *The Reading Teacher, 42 (9)*, 684–688.

Tuttle, F. B. (1991). Teaching the gifted. In J. Flood, D. Lapp & J. B. Squire (Eds.), *Handbook of research on teaching the language arts*. New York: Macmillan Publishing Company.

Vacca, J. L., Vacca, R. T. & Gove, M. K. (1987). *Reading and learning to read*. Boston: Little, Brown and Company.

Wallace, G., Cohen, S. B. & Polloway, E. A. (1987). *Language arts—Teaching exceptional students*. Austin, TX: Pro-Ed.

Wason-Ellam, L. (1992). Tales about tales: When second language speakers become authors. *Canadian Children, 17 (2)*, 1–11.

West, W. W. (1980). *Teaching the gifted and talented in the English classroom*. Washington, DC: National Educational Association.

Wilkes, H. (1988). The aural component: What the teacher needs to know. In G. H. Irons (Ed.), *Second language acquisition*. Welland, Ontario: The Canadian Modern Language Review.

Williams, J. D. & Snipper, G. C. (1990). *Literacy and bilingualism*. New York: Longman.

Winebrenner, S. (1992). *Teaching gifted kids in the regular classroom: Strategies and techniques every teacher can use to meet the academic needs of the gifted and talented*. Minneapolis, MN: Free Spirit Publishing Inc.

Winzer, M. (1989). *Closing the gap—Special learners in regular classrooms*. Toronto: Copp Clark Pitman Ltd.

Wong, Fillmore L. (1986). Research currents: Equity or excellence. *Language Arts. 63 (5)*, 474–481.

DISCUSSION QUESTIONS

1. Invite a special needs student, ESL student, or gifted student to the classroom to tell about their school experiences. Their talk could be followed by discussion.

2. Have students bring in a multicultural book to share with their fellow students. Have them indicate why they selected the book.

3. Show a film or video on mainstreaming. Have students discuss what teachers can do to help these students.

4. Bring in a number of folktales or fairy tales written from a cultural perspective (Cinderella and Little Red Riding Hood are good choices). Have students compare and contrast different versions of the same tale.

5. Have students work in groups using picture books. Have them brainstorm questions and activities for gifted learners using Bloom's Taxonomy of Cognitive Domain. They should only use the top four levels.

10

Parents, Teachers, Children: Shared Learning

GERRY SNYDER

1. *Understanding the diversity inherent in families and family literacy backgrounds*

2. *Anticipating the questions parents may have about instructional programs and planning suitable follow-up answers and actions*

3. *Knowing a variety of procedures to enhance children's home-school literacy experiences*

4. *Expressing clear purposes for using the above procedures within the context of local communities*

5. *Planning experiences and informative sessions for parents relating to the purposes for organization and learning in the classroom*

6. *Building a collection of books, articles, videos, and experiences useful for working with parents*

Introduction

Why don't you make my child spell correctly?
How can I tell at what "level" she is reading when she doesn't even have a reader?
What do children "get" from writing, especially if it's in daily journals?
How can you possibly teach "skills" without a specific time period?
Why didn't they teach like this years ago?

Questions such as these are typically asked by parents whose children are learning in classrooms where reading, writing, listening, speaking, and thinking are integrated in busy and authentic situations. These questions cannot be answered glibly, as all come from the diverse but entrenched background experiences of concerned parents. All require a belief system of theory and practice through which a teacher can and will interpret the program, using vocabulary, example, and demonstration that parents in the community can fully understand and can willingly complement at home.

A shift from skills-oriented teaching with worksheets and right answers to learner-centered production with tolerated errors and copious writing is as difficult for many parents to accept as it is for many teachers to explain. Yet teachers must be prepared to answer questions from parents, as well as recognize and inform parents who do not know the questions to ask. Some parents may appear content to leave teaching to the teacher, but learning flourishes with home-school collaboration. This chapter deals with the parents as we find them in various communities—with their contributions to home literacy learning, with their contribution to school-related learning, and with the types of questions they often ask. An appendix provides an annotated list of useful references.

The Parents We Encounter

Many popular books, articles, and newsletters address parents as if they are a homogeneous group. However, one should remember that parents are a diverse lot, whose individual backgrounds, abilities, and special interests deserve respect and acceptance. The parents who might gain the most from these popular readings about literacy, or from the printed bulletins sent home from schools, may be those who are rarely reached. Just as children must develop a sense of audience for their writings, so must teachers develop a sense of audience in planning appropriate communication with parents.

New "Mature" Parents

"Mature" parents, as we have come to know them, are established in careers and perhaps have delayed childbearing until their late twenties or beyond. Until recently they have not been encountered in any significant numbers, but it is now imperative that we address their concerns. Articulate, educated, affluent, competitive amongst themselves and for their children, these parents often stress image and achievement as important measurements of success. They are accustomed to "how to" advice in aspects of their lives stretching from exercise to gourmet cooking, so they search out guides and information. Many of their children experience rigorous academic preschools. The parents, desirous of the best, make demands; they shop for schools and for teachers, and compare and compete with others.

Activist Parents

Activist parents are advocates for numerous causes. Some may be fundamentalists working to ban books, or asking for the removal of pagan holidays in the classroom curriculum. On the other hand, some want all Christian references removed; and yet others want all religions represented. Still others may be concerned with feminist or environmental issues, and question text content from those perspectives (Sadker & Sadker, 1994). Some are concerned with the "back-to-basics" movements. Some are health-food advocates or have special dietary restrictions. All expect much from the schools, desiring conformity to their own strong beliefs. They ask difficult questions.

Multilingual, Multicultural Groups

Multiple cultures and languages coexist in school communities. Parents are sometimes unable to communicate with school personnel (or with their own children) in English. Family ties may be strong, and there are often high expectations for academic achievement. Some parents frequently consider worksheets with corrections to be representative of academic performance and effort. Understanding diverse ethnic and cultural groups is important for teachers, and finding effective ways to develop acceptance of them and their role in classroom expectations is vital.

Special-Needs Groups

Parents of special-needs children are becoming increasingly vocal, requesting special methods and materials in regular classrooms to the meet the needs of children who are autistic, learning disabled, visually impaired, gifted, or otherwise special. As well, there are the poor, the disaffected, the hungry, families who abuse children, families so busy they barely keep home life together. Sometimes parents are functionally illiterate or are hostile toward school because of their own negative experiences.

Available Parents

Available parents are the school volunteers. They send to school the odd items requested; they accompany classes on field trips. By giving help in the classroom, they come to understand the teacher's efforts, and support them with praise and action. Even though more and more mothers are employed outside the home, some mothers or fathers should be available, and they can provide the school with important links to the community. One school refers to these parents as "the grapevine," which spreads news of school happenings to other parents. A teacher, being aware of how school news travels in her community, can plan for the news to be supportive through effective work with the volunteer parents.

Growth in Diversity

It is possible to encounter a mature, culturally different, poor, single activist who is a school volunteer and has a special-needs child. It is also possible to be teaching in a more or less homogeneous community. Acceptance on the part of school personnel of individual parental differences, however, and a willingness

to accommodate parents and students according to their circumstances, promotes the continuing success of each child. With experience, teachers begin to know and to be nonjudgmental about parent expectations, about literacy backgrounds, and about parent/child literacy experiences within the family context and culture.

Beneath children's differences in ethnicity, clothing, income background, and family structure, one can discover a multiplicity of experience with oral and written language. Even within the same family it is quite possible that one child's interactions with language and print differs from the experience of the next. Such diversity of literacy experience requires recognition of language competency within all children, and emphasizes the positive aspects of each child's unique learning capabilities (Piper, 1993). When parents accept a broadened view of literacy learning, they become increasingly involved in the educative process, as models, participants, and audience. Their children, as excited and achieving learners, become powerful influences for continued parental support, no matter what the family realities.

In-Home Literacy Learning

Many classroom practices have evolved from research on how young children develop reading and writing competencies in the home. Researchers are still busily determining home/school literacy links, but from many sources (Becher, 1985; Bissex, 1980; Ferreiro and Teberosky, 1982; Taylor, 1983; Rasinski, 1989; Snow, 1991) we can summarize important aspects.

According to Taylor (1983, p. 92), "Many of the programs designed to sensitize parents to their role as teachers of reading and writing provide them with specific suggestions on the 'how to,' yet there is nothing in the literature to suggest that children who successfully learn to read and write are specifically taught by their parents." Instead, parents take cues from the children and respond in different ways to each child's attempts to read or write, taking into consideration age, interests, and abilities. Social activities such as trips, television viewing, and shopping encompass literacy as a natural part of family life. School-related worksheet activities sent home cannot substitute for those meaningful interactions in which children use reading, writing, listening, and speaking for real purposes.

Learning Language Informally

Most language learning in the home occurs informally as parents and children read books, hold conversations, use signs, sort junk mail, search for specific places on maps, write letters, go to the library, use TV schedules, write notes or lists, use the computer, or read stories at bedtime.

Modeling

Modeling is inevitable, as children learn much from watching other family members who are often not aware of these observations. Frequently, children will replicate the activity in their play (writing orders while playing office or keeping records for a club meeting). Other times, children will interrupt to become part of the activity. One six-year-old, observing a university teacher/mother marking tests, asked to take the test too. She placed her completed effort in the unmarked stack and eventually received her "grade" (a passing one, which didn't speak well for the test!).

This incident and many like it illustrate the power of modeling: the child has an intense desire to enter into the adult's literacy world. Testing is not usually a part of the home literacy environment, but other observations show that much informal teaching does occur and that parents usually positively reinforce the child's efforts. Parents will respond to the child's questions (and tolerate much repetition) until the child is ready to move on. At home, children are given time, encouragement, background information if needed, and a chance to develop concepts.

Talking about Stories

In families, talking about stories is frequently child directed, and parents often become patient listeners. Perhaps such interactions are not recognized as teaching because of the popular notion that teaching consists of giving assignments or tests and directly telling children what and how to learn. It is not until school that "on to the next story in the reader" may become a prevailing instruction mode, even though a child may have failed to grasp nuances of previous stories.

Writing at Home

From the very beginning of writing at home, children concentrate on meaning. They demonstrate a remarkable grasp of appropriate forms of writing for different purposes, as written lists are distinguishable from letters to Uncle Bob. Children, when allowed to write freely, produce increasingly complex works that reflect their developing understanding of words, sound/symbol relationships, grammar, and punctuation (Wilde, 1992). At home, children are encouraged in what they can do without experiencing the frequently negative impact of letter grades for their efforts. Meaning and use take precedence over skill mastery as children learn new and diverse meanings and usages from each writing experience. For most children, writing at home is a wonderful activity, often pre-ceding reading.

Parent Expectations and Schooling

Parents change in their own behaviors as they interact with their children, and progress with them through their literacy experiences. Parents' language and ex-pectations become more sophisticated as their children mature. For most children and parents, the interaction takes on a different format when chil-dren enter school. Taylor (1983) suggested that the impact of school on parental expectations of their children's academic performance needs to be considered for each individual family and for each individual child. For instance, posi-tion within the family (being the oldest, middle, or youngest child) can have an effect.

In many families, older siblings can direct learning if a parent's help is re-jected. Teaching similar to this in-home activity is evident in the multiage classrooms with a structure permitting supportive interactions. Parents who attempt to assume a formal teaching role often find their efforts rejected. "Talking like a teacher" can alienate some children. Baron (1990) suggested, however, that parents who are not avid readers may influence the reasons why even children who have had good quality literacy experiences in early childhood, and who are able to read well, fail to maintain a good attitude toward reading as they mature.

Different cultures have different expectations about literacy and learning. Oral traditions and story telling may assume greater importance with some groups than do reading and writing. Teacher awareness of all aspects of lin-guistic backgrounds and communication abilities within the community is essential.

Much of the research on literacy and linguistic acquisition (Baron, 1990) in the home has involved analyses of children in middle-class settings. Often it is the researcher's own children or the children of acquaintances who are studied. One notable exception is Heath (1983), who described children and parent interactions in two quiet different working-class communities. Knowing the results of this research as well as becoming a teacher-researcher within his or her own setting enables the teacher to plan appropriate experi-ences for these children whose backgrounds might be very different. By replicating in the classroom successful practices from in-home literacy expe-riences, and communicating these practices to parents, teachers structure meaningful programs.

One fundamental point is that the absence of a rich literacy home envi-ronment does not necessarily create inept language users, nor does its presence guarantee that a child will read easily or even want to read at all.

Implications for Teacher and Parent

Practices identified as encouraging literacy learning in the home are successful in classrooms in which the emphasis is less skills oriented and more integrated by use of meaning and use of oriented strategies. This has many implications. When working with parents, keep in mind the following:

1. Language is purposeful for children, who are surrounded by print. They have access to computers, they can read signs, menus, directions, newspapers, obituaries, recipes; they write lists, notes, letters, and stories. The real reading and writing that they need to do is not from a series of graded textbooks.
2. Children learn early that reading and writing are meaningful pursuits, not skills-oriented exercises without substantive purpose. Oral language, writing, reading, and listening support one another and do not occur as isolated segments or skills.
3. Language at home is a shared experience. Children ask questions, seek information, take risks, and develop abilities in a positive climate with parents, caregivers, or siblings who accept errors as part of the learning process. Real language is not reflected in the solitary pursuits of spelling and sentence structure exercises, story-writing exercises for the teacher to correct, or reading just to get all the words right. See also the section in Chapter 1 entitled What Whole-Language Means in Practice.

Involving Parents in School-Related Literacy

Forty or fifty years ago, teachers expected parents to stay out of the business of teaching reading and writing. They believed that it was the school's duty to teach literacy skills. A parent asking about helping with reading lessons at home was told, "This would not be advisable. Teaching reading is a highly specialized job and involves many skills on the teacher's part" (Artely, 1953, p. 93).

According to another booklet produced at that time for parents, "Reading may look simple, but it is really a complicated process. It requires a highly trained person to teach it successfully. That person is your child's teacher" (Casey, 1950, p. 1). Parents today probably would not accept these statements without questioning. Casey, however, did go on to offer suggestions that are still considered valid: be good listeners; develop a sense of audience; read aloud; reading is a thought-getting process; use context to figure out new words; visit the library; and provide many children's books. The reading instruction to be left to the expert appears to be mostly phonics, not real reading.

More recently, a university student discovered the world of children's literature, devouring all the books he had missed when young. His mother had accepted the belief that introducing literature and books in the home before school was harmful, so he was deliberately kept away from such delights and not permitted to read or write at home. When he told his mother about his discovery, and about how literary experiences help children learn language, she cried, feeling she had deprived him of a rich childhood legacy. He was lucky, and will bring the real joy of literature to countless children and their parents in his teaching career. Others may not be so fortunate.

Home/school collaboration implies teachers, children, and parents working together, each doing what they do best. Parents, however, should not be expected to assume the schooling role. They can supplement, encourage, provide space and time, listen, give experiences, provide books or access to books through public libraries, give real reasons for children to read, write, listen, and speak. But encourage avoidance of school-like tasks and material such as the workbooks that have proliferated to the extent that they are now even available at supermarkets. Ideally, parents would be avid readers themselves.

Ideas for Collaboration

Newspapers and popular magazines bombard parents today with directions and suggestions as to how to teach their children to read. Some parents, who may have tried to teach their children to read without much success, or who feel they do not have the time to follow all the suggestions provided by these articles, sometimes give up entirely and consequently feel that they have failed. Being knowledgeable about the community and the parents within that community can help a teacher help those parents. The teacher might send home one or two carefully written ideas on how to proceed with at-home literacy. These ideas can harmonize with classroom themes and with the child's interests and needs. As well, children can suggest ideas for creative homework that would fit into their family situation and be productive within the precious time available for parents and children to share.

Following are some ideas for home/school collaboration that resulted from discussions with teachers.

Reading Aloud

Research confirms (Becher, 1985) that parents reading to children is commonly recommended and that many benefits are derived from the practice. In a summary of research on working with parents, the publication *What Works* (Bennett, 1988) includes the following statement:

The best way for parents to help their children become better readers is to read to them—even when they are very young. Children benefit most from reading aloud when they discuss stories, learn to identify words and letters, and talk about the meaning of words.

As the parent reads with the child, the child develops concepts of reading and the parent also learns much about reading. Suggestions from the school on how this in-home reading experience can be enhanced for older children can be provided, as this activity is recommended throughout the school years. When the parent cannot read, or cannot read in English, sensitive teachers send home books with audiotapes and cassettes, suggest siblings read together, or have children read to the parent. Schools cannot provide enough time for children to read or be read to for enjoyment and practice. Many teachers mention sending packs or bags of books home, complete with appropriate ideas for reading together.

Talking about Books

Becher (1985) indicated that parents who talk with their children about the books the children are reading on their own have children who read better and who develop and expand concepts more efficiently than those children whose parents do not hold general discussions. Warm-up questions (such as "What is this book about?") and friendly predictive questions (such as "What might happen next?") are recommended. Interrogation is very negative, as is the forced writing of questions and answers. Some teachers send home bookmarks with simple question frames for parents to use. These questions can follow a story map or can be on varying levels of thinking. Model the procedures used in your classroom, and give children help in explaining how to use them.

Family Reading Sessions

Family reading sessions, much like sustained silent reading (SSR), are planned in some families. Organized around a common theme such as boating or adventure, the sessions can accommodate most individuals with books and magazines of varying difficulties. Television programs sometimes become the impetus for collective reading endeavors since they provide interesting topics to be pursued through reading. Schools can formulate simple guidelines that are appropriate for specific parents to follow, and can suggest how family reading sessions can begin and be sustained. The family reading session centered around a theme or topic accommodates those parents who do not read in English.

Family Writing Time

Family members can be encouraged to write materials related to a chosen theme and then share these at a family gathering. With camcorders becoming more and more popular, language-experience activities can result from the video recordings of family outings, community celebrations, or other experiences. Cooperative endeavors with the computer can be encouraged also. Continuing stories are one example, where each family member can contribute a line, a paragraph, or a page. The result of that effort can be read together in a sharing session. Clay (1987) gave many suggestions for developing writing ability. As well, Chapter 5, The Writing Connection, in this book has ideas that can be adapted for family writing time.

Edwards and Maloy (1992) described an effective Writing Box program. Boxes of writing materials are sent home with suggestions for activities and methods proven to make "children two through nine effective readers."

Environmental Print

Suggestions from teachers for "environmental print walks," based on old scavenger hunt rules, promote family outings related to the pervasive print world. These adventures through lanes and parks or interesting neighborhoods involve the family in reading print on doors and posts, in windows, or on buses. Science, mathematics, and social studies concepts can become part of the learning. A family "read-in" on the beach or in the park is another good way of bringing reading out of doors.

Reading Activities

When needed, teachers can send home suggestions for effective oral reading: activities with magazines or newspapers that enhance listening and speaking vocabularies or that develop abilities in using sound/symbol relationships needed by a particular child. One teacher packages a literature book, puppet, and game related to a theme, writes simple suggestions for each kit, and encourages children to take these kits home to use with their families. These suggestions, however, must be tailored to the needs of the child and the capabilities of the parent. Sources such as *The RIF Guide to Encouraging Young Readers* provide ideas developed for "home and family life" with the message, "Relax, trust your instincts and enjoy your children" (Graves, 1987, p. 3).

Written Messages

Writing messages to children encourages them to write messages also. Teachers frequently have children write notices to parents rather than duplicating them. Even young children can write reasons for being absent or informational notes at home for the busy parent to sign before sending them to school.

One family kept a little chalkboard near the door, originally intended for the shopping list. Instead, mystery messages began to appear and a running commentary ensued, often leaving family members struggling to guess who wrote what—and why! Sharing little ideas like this prompts parents to suggest others and these, collected over the years, can be conveyed to other parents who might not realize the possibilities for spontaneous literacy practice.

Home/School Reading Program

A home reading program involving all grades enhanced community cooperation for one school (Vick, 1989). A celebrity came in to talk about the importance of reading. Book sales and trades extended otherwise limited resources. Children and their parents kept records of reading, and television watching dropped. The results of a survey indicated enthusiastic support for continuing the project. The program's success, as part of the schoolwide curriculum, is clearly attributable to enthusiastic organization and support by parents, with administrators, teachers, and children as willing collaborators. Handel (1992) described a partnership program that helped children receive a "congruent message about reading from school and home."

Scrapbooks

In school, each child is given a scrapbook in which to accumulate illustrations, riddles, stories, lists, factual accounts, and so on. The scrapbook, as a record of work, can be sent home at regular intervals to be explained to the parent by the child.

Journals

Photocopying examples of children's journals kept over time (maybe through several grade levels) provides powerful evidence of evolving competence. Parents are thrilled that the teacher's predictions of pupil growth are realized. As one teacher said, "Parents treasure journals as a record of family and school activities and of the children's development."

School Work Goes Home

Children's writing can be sent home with little notes about the positive things parents can observe: "Remember, last month Sarah was struggling to spell *because*. Notice she has mastered the word. Notice, also, the unusual and exciting ending she has created for her story."

Television

Television viewing at home can become a focus for discussion with parents and children comparing programs, retelling events, describing settings, listening for unusual vocabulary, and discussing characters. The potential for learning from television, with the amount of print that now appears on the screen, should not be overlooked. The TV guides normally contained in the local paper also provide reading opportunities.

Home Hobbies and Projects

Projects at home, such as cooking or crafts, provide children with often-overlooked opportunities to extend language through listening and talking as well as through reading and following directions.

Building Fluency in Reading

Suggest that parents tell children that they want to read a story to themselves first before they read it aloud to the children so as to be sure about the words and the story. When such preparation is made, the actual reading aloud of the story becomes much more interesting. The parent can suggest that the child can try this also, in order to become a more fluent reader. As well, indicate that prior knowledge of a story's content builds a reader's confidence in his or her reading ability.

Home Visits

Invitations to teachers to visit homes of their students provide wonderful opportunities for home/school cooperation. One group of teachers in a poor area conducted home visits to help children obtain library cards. Parents, suspicious at first, soon welcomed the visits, partly because they were not connected to the usual trouble-oriented contacts.

Parent Stories

Children enjoy stories that parents or grandparents write or tell about experiences when they were young. If the parent's time is a factor, the stories, like an oral history, can be audio-recorded. One grandmother, using significant pictures, objects, diaries, and letters, produced a video of her life much to the delight of children, grandchildren, and friends. Lifewriting, described in Chapter 5, is another option.

Shared Reading

Parents frequently complain that their own time schedules are much too crowded for reading to children, but literature can be shared throughout the day. Time need not be "set aside" for it. Parents and children can talk about stories, articles, books, and poems they have read. Parents can read the same books their children are reading. These books can be read at different times and shared, for example, while doing the laundry. Given the opportunity, many children love to suggest books for their parents to read. While making dinner, a parent can listen to a child retell or read a story or a humorous or sad paragraph. Poems from school become choral reading events while traveling to the supermarket. The driver can "chime in"! Inexpensive books can become shared surprises. One father performed "magic tricks" as the family headed for outings or vacations, with new books appearing from a car blanket, or a picnic basket, or inside his coat sleeve.

The Draft Stamp

Parents (and teachers) have difficulty in tolerating mistakes. Many teachers find that using a "DRAFT" or "WORKS IN PROGRESS" stamp on papers that are destined for home helps explain to parents that the work represents an effort to think on paper and is not considered a finished product. Individual folders of children's work can illustrate progress.

School Visits

When parents come to visit a classroom, it is the displays of children's work that allow them to see how well the school program is working. Foldout records of the students' progression from scribble, through invented spelling stages (Weiner, 1994), to conventional spelling, punctuation, and sentence formation can also be reassuring to parents. Graphic demonstrations reflect growing abilities and potential. Parents' positive responses to these demonstrated achievements can be supported by quotes from research on language learning.

Classroom displays allow parents to see the school program in action.

Invitations to visit classrooms, and written and pictorial displays of easily observable features of the program, encourage parents to feel positive about how home literacy activities become supportive of the curriculum.

Written Suggestions

Idea cards in home-bound books provide imaginative extensions of classroom studies and can be personalized for the needs of parent and child. These home activities encourage sharing in a supportive atmosphere and would be consistent with classroom strategies. Of course, children or families may sweep the idea cards aside, saying, "We don't need your suggestions, we have our own!" Add these to your own collection!

Magazines

Many excellent children's magazines are available. Compile a list suitable for various age groups and if parents ask for gift ideas, make suggestions. The publication, *Magazines and Family Reading* (1988) offers appealing ideas for choosing, using, and sharing magazines. Reading is Fundamental (RIF) publishes this as well as many other valuable resources. Write to: RIF, P.O. Box 23444, Washington, DC 20026.

Listen, Listen, Listen

Listening to children and their parents is critical, as they usually know what they can or cannot do, and may give valuable insights into home situations. Attempt to have reasonable expectations and make useful suggestions, as not all ideas are workable in every home. Careful listening helps in planning appropriate possibilities and providing acceptable learning alternatives.

Questions Parents Ask

When listening to parents and planning answers for their questions, teachers need to think from the parent's perspective. Ask, "If I were this child's parent, what would I need to know?" or, "If I were this child's parent, how could I best help her?" By reflecting on the need to answer appropriately, you can take positive actions based on a child's individual needs and on his or her actual performance in the classroom, and not on generalized-level expectations.

The questions posed at the beginning of the chapter were gleaned from a series of questions asked by parents at whole-language information sessions, and they serve as model considerations useful for framing appropriate answers and actions. Here each question is addressed and answers and actions are suggested. Collect other questions from those that other parents ask.

"Why Don't You Make My Child Spell Correctly?"

Always anticipate this question. Many parents simply cannot tolerate the idea of invented spelling, and they must be reassured.

The very phrasing of the question provides insight into parents' expectations. Many parents attended schools in which they were supposedly made to read, write, and spell. When diagnosis showed a lack of progress and many mistakes, skills and drills were prescribed, often with little real purpose readily discernible to the child.

Today's teacher may not make a child spell in the manner parents remember. Instead, through modeling, the child learns that articulating ideas is important and that spelling is a developmental process. It is interesting to note that the term *invented spelling* only came into currency in the early 1970s (Wilde, 1992). The purpose of learning to spell is to be able to communicate effectively in writing for an audience, with a reason. A teacher should show the parent that spelling competence improves through various general activities as well as through individual instruction, often in the form of mini-lessons from the teacher. Children are provided models, motivation, and opportunity to see and use words. With care and careful guidance, they will eventually spell those words conventionally.

Chow (1986) indicated that ESL children progress through spelling stages similar to other children (see Chapter 9). Visual displays of representative phases of spelling development from appropriately selected examples of children's work are very effective in showing parents how children are working toward sound/letter correspondence and spelling conventions. Assembling children's work, pointing out what they know this month that they did not last month, is important. Parents can learn to interpret invented spelling and encourage children in their writing endeavors, understanding that spelling proficiency takes time.

Parents often—perhaps unintentionally—work against their children's spelling competence by making the common excuse, "I never was a good speller." Maybe pleasurable spelling activities at home (Spill and Spell or Scrabble, for example) would be good suggestions. At Back-to-School nights, along with visual displays, give a mini-lesson for the parents to help them understand the system being used.

"How Can I Tell at What 'Level' She Is Reading When She Doesn't Even Have a Reader?"

Over the years, many teachers have inadvertently taught parents to expect children to be at certain levels in their reading, perhaps little realizing the importance parents attach to this measurement of competence. Many teachers who leave the reading series to begin literature-based, theme-oriented instruction report that some parents are upset about not being able to identify their children's reading levels.

The creation of levels was an attempt by publishers to do away with specific grade designations in a series of reading books as a way of recognizing that children in any one grade vary considerably in reading ability. Each level within a series advanced a specific set of skills, vocabulary, and content, and assumed mastery of the preceding level. Children were tested and supposedly placed at the level indicated as appropriate by the outcome of the test, often a level either above or below their grade placement. Reading progress in many classrooms, however, became material driven rather than learner oriented as all the children work through all the levels in a prescribed sequence.

Reeducating parents (and teachers) about reading levels may take time, even though observation of the child's growing competence in language is a better illustration of progress than lockstepping through the arbitrary designations of a reading series. Cadenhead (1987) suggested that structured materials and reliance on testing have convinced adults that adult reading levels do exist in materials. Therefore, adults limit, rather than promote, the development of children's minds. Given the opportunity, children will often select a wider range of material than might be indicated by their tested or assigned ability. Cadenhead asked:

> *Have the emphasis on the ease of reading, the removal of frustration and the isolation of specific skills over-shadowed such ideas as challenging students, having them puzzle out meanings for themselves? (p. 440)*

Demonstrate to parents that the use of diverse materials for reading and writing does contribute to children's literacy growth. The books children choose to read may appear difficult, yet the child's prior knowledge and interest contribute to meaning and success. Child-centered practices recognize competencies as developing from within each child and not from prescribed, arbitrarily labeled materials.

Holding information sessions and giving guidance to parents will help them understand and encourage the developing competence of each child who uses many different books and materials. However, if a parent still insists on levels after the explanations and suggestions, teachers might send home several levels of unused reading series. Many children would not object, and the level concept, while not followed in the classroom, may comfort the parent.

"What Do Children 'Get' from Writing Daily Journals?"

Again, closely analyze the phrasing of the question. In this case, one needs to consider that writing is not always getting but giving as well.

Children get a sense of competence in being able to create messages while appreciating how the power of words allows their own thoughts and experiences to assume importance. Young children, through writing in journals or diaries, are given the connections between speech, thought, writing, and reading and learn that their own words and ideas have worth. Dialogue journals—a specific type of journal kept by both student and teacher—become written conversations, providing audience for the child's writing. The teacher's responses model spelling and grammar, and give appreciation of the child's efforts.

Journals thus provide visible records of students' increased sophistication with respect to ideas and the technical aspects of language. Children certainly develop the ability to evaluate and appreciate their own progress, and as they read over their diaries, they appreciate that reading and writing work together. Children can help parents notice that what was not known last week is known today.

One worry parents may have about journal writing is the revelation of personal transactions within the family. A sensitive teacher keeps confidences. Suggest to parents that they talk over with children events and ideas that could be shared in the journal.

Diary or journal writing can develop into a worthwhile, life-long habit, but should not be recommended as a required home activity, nor be forced upon all children by parents. Some children might choose to write diaries at home, but others may be attracted to different activities, and these individual differences should be respected.

"How Can You Possibly Teach 'Skills' without a Specific Time Period?"

Answers to this question are a bit more complex, as one of the misunderstandings about the integrated classroom is that no instruction is necessary. Actual demonstrations in the classroom or those on prepared videotapes show parents how skills are learned in functional ways within the curriculum as they are needed. A series of videos prepared within the school can show how flexible grouping within large time blocks works; how children are given time to use what they know to puzzle out what they do not know; how children are free to consult one another as well as the teacher; how the teacher monitors each child's progress, noting where specific children need further assistance; how themes organize the work and allow each child to participate regardless of level; and how teachers, too, can work together to improve learning opportunities. The video technology is readily available and should be put to use to bring the parent into the classroom.

Written previews of the year's work along with time schedules help parents understand a program. And, of course, samples of work and effective parent/teacher conferences can overcome parental concerns. If a teacher cannot give concrete evidence of improvement and of learning to parents' satisfaction, re-examining classroom practices may be wise.

"Why Didn't They Teach Like This Years Ago?"

Many of the practices embodied in educational practices today were used years ago. For instance, revolts against phonic skills approaches are not new: "radical thought in the 20s held that if a child were interested at all in reading, no teaching of words by any method was necessary or justified" (Gray, 1948, p. 26). Gray suggested that in many schools neither whole words nor phonics were deemed essential. Meaning was the only consideration and children were to learn new words by "guessing" from context (Gray, 1948, p. 26). The story method was in vogue. By 1940, however, "failure of haphazard, unplanned, 'catch-as-catch-can' reading procedures brought down the wrath of parents on many schools" (Gray, 1948, p. 27). Basic, developmental reading programs were reinstated with a heavy emphasis on phonics and word-analysis skills which necessitated restricted vocabularies. The failure of the earlier, meaning-centered reading instruction appears to have resulted from misinterpretation of the methodology, with teachers presumably providing no instruction.

The enthusiasm for literature-based instruction is a result of extensive research on how children learn language, as well as an adverse reaction to literacy by fragmentation of skills. However, to excitedly tell parents that children will learn to read and write naturally (as sometimes occurred in earlier times) ignores the realities of hard work, time, knowledge, and energy demanded by the learning endeavor, be it from children, parents, or teachers. When parents today ask, "Will my child learn to read and write in a whole-language classroom?" substantiation must be forthcoming. Classroom and curriculum cannot be haphazard and unplanned. Knowledgeable teachers help children learn to use the strategies necessary for meaningful reading and writing, and enlist parents in the process. The two fundamental questions asked by parents in any situation are: "How is my child doing?" and "How can I help my child?"

Parents Speak

One might well ask if parents ever comment positively, or otherwise, on the literacy programs their children experience. Yes, they do and these comments might well be shared on back-to-school nights.

"As a teacher-parent, I appreciate the newsletters."
"I attended a workshop at our school, and after a brief introduction, we were taken through the processes of imaging, webbing, story writing, and

sharing. Walls held samples of class writing K–7. Brief write-ups described the varied stages. As a parent, I was impressed with the continuity from K–7 offered to my child."

"My child's enthusiasm and pride in projects influences my coming to the school more than just a notice about a meeting."

"The portfolio you sent home was exciting to view as my child explained each part of her work."

"I was convinced of the effectiveness of your program by having the predictions of the teacher come to life in my child's journal."

"I really enjoyed the letter my child wrote before the open house, telling me what I should look for when I visited your room."

"If you can't explain it, don't do it."

"Well, your theme week with drama, play, writing, books and school-wide presentation was very interesting, but when are the children going to get back to work?"

And an administrator asks, "Is it only parents we need to inform? Extend some the ideas to the entire community."

A child proudly boasts, "My mother and my teacher are friends."

Conclusion

Many concerned parents are demanding increased authority over the education of their children. Parents have more vested interest—in the form of their children—in the education enterprise than any other group. Teachers help a particular child for a year; parents live with the results of that child's experiences for a lifetime.

Henderson (1988), in reviewing research on parental involvement with children's education both within the family and in the school, found ample support for "well-planned, comprehensive and long-lasting" parental involvement. Advantages include improved parent/child relationships and improved child achievement. An important consideration is that "children from low income and minority families benefit the most when parents are involved in the schools, and parents do NOT have to be well educated to make a difference." (Henderson, 1988, p. 153)

It might follow, then, that appropriate strategies, with reading-writing connections, environmental language, and accessible materials, could be developed with all parents as a part of daily life.

Frank Smith (1986) echoed what many have known for years: parents have not always been welcome in schools. He suggested that parents question schools and teachers. More and more parents will be asking questions, especially as schools move away from what is remembered by parents. Many teachers pay lip service to the importance of parents in the education of their children, but they must follow through with a genuine welcome.

A total school response such as the home reading program involves everyone in a communal endeavor, but sending home one-shot explanations at the beginning of the year is inadequate. Also, long lists of suggestions are intimidating. Establishing computer files of suggestions and ideas might be one way to personalize responses when needed.

By learning to filter ideas as they relate to the children's ongoing classroom work, teachers can send home concrete but interesting suggestions to each parent, tailored to the abilities of parent and child. Provision must certainly be made for children who, for one reason or another, will not receive help at home.

Parents have the right to understand what goes on in their child's classroom and to know how changes of philosophies and procedures really will improve the education of their children. The most often question asked is, "Will my child learn?" Teachers have the responsibility to increase their knowledge about parents in the community and to enhance their ability to establish those good working relationships that bring success in shared learning. A New Age of Literacy may be center-front, but teachers must do more than a dance of enthusiasm on stage for the parental audience.

REFERENCES

Anderson, R. C., et al. (1985). *Becoming a nation of readers: The report of the Commission on Reading.* Washington, DC: National Institute of Education.

Artely, A. S. (1953). *Your child learns to read.* Glenview, IL: Scott, Foresman.

Baghban, M. (1984). *Our daughter learns to read and write.* Newark, NJ: International Reading Association.

Baron, N. (1990). *Pigeon-birds and rhyming words. (The role of parents in language learning).* Englewood Cliffs, NJ: Prentice Hall Regents.

Becher, R. M. (1985). Parent involvement and reading achievement: A review of research and implications for practice. *Childhood Education,* Sept.-Oct., *62,* 41–50.

Bennett, W. J. (1986). *What works: Research about teaching and learning.* Reston, VA: National Association of Secondary School Principals.

Bissex, G. (1980). *Gnys at work: A child learns to write and read.* Cambridge, MA: Harvard University Press.

Brogan, P. and Fox, L. (1961). *Helping children read.* New York: Holt, Rinehart and Winston.

Cadenhead, K. (1987). Reading level: A metaphor that shapes practice. *Phi Delta Kappan, 68,* 6.

Casey, S. (1950). *Ways you can help your child with reading.* Evanston, IL: Row, Peterson.

Clay, M. M. (1979). *READING: The patterning of complex behavior.* Auckland: Heinemann.

Clay, M. (1987). *Writing begins at home.* Auckland: Heinemann.

Chow, M. (1986). Nurturing the growth of writing in the kindergarten and grade one years: How are the ESL children doing? *TESL Canadian Journal/Revue TESL Du Canada, 4 (1),* 35–47.

Edwards, S. A. and Maloy, R. W. (1992). *Kids have all the write stuff: inspiring your children to put pencil to paper.* New York: Penguin.

Ferreiro, E. and Teberosky, A. (1982). *Literacy before schooling.* Portsmouth, NH: Heinemann.

Graves, R. (Ed.). (1987). *The RIF guide to encouraging young readers.* New York: Doubleday.

Gray, W. S. (1948). *On their own in reading.* Chicago: Scott, Foresman.

Hall, N. (1987). *The emergence of literacy.* Portsmouth, NH: Heinemann.

Handel, R. D. (1992). The partnership for family reading: benefits for families and schools. *The Reading Teacher, 46 (2),* 116–126.

Heath, S. B. (1983). *Ways with words.* New York: Cambridge University Press.

Henderson, A. T. (1988). Parents are a school's best friends. *Phi Delta Kappan,* October, *70,* 148–153.

Office of Educational Research and Improvement. (1988). *What works.* Washington, DC.: Department of Education (ERIC Document Reproduction Service No. ED 263 299).

Piper, T. (1993). *Language for all our children.* New York: Merrill.

Plaum, S. (1986). *The development of language and literacy in young children* (3rd ed.). Columbus, OH: Merrill.

Rasinski, T. V. (1989). Dimensions of parent involvement. *Reading Teacher, 43 (2),* 180–182.

Magazines and family reading. (1988). Washington, DC: RIF.

Sadker, D. and Sadker, M. (1994). *Failing at fairness: How America's schools cheat girls.* New York: Charles Schribner.

Smith, F. (1986). *Insult to intelligence.* New York: Arbor House.

Snow, C. E. (1991). *Unfulfilled expectations: Home and school influences on literacy.* Cambridge, MA: Harvard University Press.

Taylor, D. (1983). *Family literacy.* Exeter, NH: Heinemann.

Teale, W. and Sulzby, E. (Eds.). (1986). *Emergent literacy: Writing and reading.* Norwood: Ablex.

Tovey, D. and Kerber, J. (Eds.). (1986). *Roles in literacy learning: A new perspective.* Newark, NJ: International Reading Association.

Vick, D. (1989). *The Pineridge home/school reading program.* Unpublished manuscript, University of British Columbia.

Wilde, S. (1992). *You kan red this! Spelling and puctuation for whole language classrooms, K–6.* Portsmouth, NH: Heineman.

Weiner, S. (1994). Four first graders' description of how they spell. *Elementary School Journal, 94 (3),* 315–330.

APPENDIX: WORKING WITH PARENTS

Boehnlein, M. H. and Hager, B. H. (Compilers). (1985). *Children, parents, and reading.* Newark, NJ: International Reading Association.

An exhaustive listing of books, lists, references, and activities to support parent-school communication. An invaluable resource for all schools.

Brock, H. C. (1976). *A Practical guide—Parent volunteer programs in early childhood education.* Hamden, CT: The Shoe String Press, Inc.

Step-by-step instructions on setting up a school-parent volunteer program.

Clark, M. M. (1976). *Young fluent readers.* Portsmouth, NH: Heinemann.

Intensive and detailed analysis of 32 fluent young readers who read before formal schooling.

Clay, M. (1987). *Writing begins at home.* Auckland, NZ: Heinemann.

To help promote writing at home, use suggestions from this reference. Also presents ideas on the development of writing.

Epstein, J. L. (1986). Parent reactions to parent involvement. *The Elementary School Journal, 82,* Jan., 277–294.

Reports on a study of parents' views on their involvement in children's education. Feelings toward school are reported as positive, but parents say they want to be more involved by helping with learning activities at home.

Epstein, J. L. (Guest Editor). (1991). Parent involvement. A special section. *Phi Delta Kappan, 72,* Jan., 344–388.

Nine articles by different authors in various states who give excellent ideas about "real activities that are linking schools and homes in real communities."

Goodman, K. (1986). *What's whole in whole language?* Richmond Hill, Ontario: Scholastic-TAB Publications.

A discussion of the whole-language philosophy with descriptions of whole-language classrooms, teachers, and students.

Grinnell, P. C. (1984). How can I prepare my young child for reading? *IRA Micromonograph.* Newark, NJ: International Reading Association (ED 241906).

Discusses talking and reading to the child, letting the child read and write, modeling literacy behavior, etc., and suggests resources for parents. One of a series of useful micromonographs from IRA.

Hill, M. W. (1989). *HOME: Where reading and writing begin.* Toronto, Ontario: Scholastic-TAB Publications.

Helping the parents to value the home as a literacy-learning environment. Uses of environ-mental print and other reading-writing activities in the home are discussed.

Larrick, N. (1980). *Encourage your child to read: A parent's primer.* New York: Dell.

Provides excellent suggestions for parents on choosing books, reading at home, and a variety of other activities.

Lombana, J. H. (1983). *Home-school partnerships—Guidelines and strategies for educators.* New York: Grune and Stratton.

Overview of all aspects of home-school relationships. Useful discussion topics and suggestions for learning projects in each chapter.

Madden, L. (1976). *How to cope with your child's teacher.* Phoenix, AZ: O'Sullivan Woodside.

A different view from the "other side of the fence." Good read for both parents and teachers.

Olson, M. W. (1990). *Opening the door to classroom research.* Newark: International Reading Association.

Schickedanz, J. A. and Sullivan, M. (1984). Mom, What Does U-F-F spell? *Language Arts, 61,* 7–17.

Most literacy events in the home are child-initiated. Parents do not intentionally set out to instruct children or to ensure that literacy is not carried over from the home to the school.

Taylor, D. and Strickland, D. S. (1986). *Family storybook reading.* Portsmouth, NH: Heinemann.

Good suggestions and ideas to share with parents who may need information on reading and literature-sharing techniques.

Woodland, M. (1981). *Parents and teachers: The family as educator.* Milton Keynes, Great Britain: Open University Press.

Examines important aspects of family, school, parent, and teacher relationships.

DISCUSSION QUESTIONS

1. What questions, other than those posed in this chapter, might parents ask about whole-language in relation to their own child's learning?

2. Select a question from those formed in Question 1 and write an answer that would satisfy parents. How will you justify your decisions?

3. How might your responses to parents vary according to the type of community in which you are teaching?

4. How would you use your knowledge and understanding of whole-language to plan a back-to-school night for parents?

5. Devise a plan for you, as a teacher-researcher, to gather information about parents and about literacy in your community. Explain how you will apply the results of this research.

11

Organizing Whole-Language Classrooms

ANN LUKASEVICH

1. *Realizing that successful whole-language classrooms require careful planning and structuring to support the whole-language philosophy*

2. *Learning how whole-language teachers effectively allot classroom time*

3. *Learning how to organize effectively all or part of the curriculum into integrated themes*

4. *Organizing classroom space and materials to permit the flexibility required of a whole-language curriculum*

5. *Selecting varied appropriate whole-language materials and resources for both teacher and student use*

6. *Learning to group students effectively in whole-language classrooms*

Introduction

This chapter will describe five key aspects that must be carefully considered when planning and organizing whole-language classrooms. They are (1) organizing time, (2) organizing curriculum, (3) organizing classroom space and materials, (4) selecting materials and resources, and (5) grouping children for whole-language learning. Before dealing with these five aspects, let us review briefly the concepts behind whole-language that affect the organization of such a classroom.

Whole-language is a way of bringing together a view of language, a view of learning, and a view of people. In particular, it brings together three special groups of people: children, teachers, and parents. Whole-language begins with immersion in an environment where language is kept whole and where the language processes (listening, speaking, writing, reading, viewing, dramatizing, and so on) are integrated and learned as a means to an end, and not an end unto themselves. Such language learning is child centered as well as comprehension centered, since children use it functionally and purposefully to meet their own individual needs as they read and write daily under the guidance of their teacher. The focus is on the child as learner. This means that learning occurs as naturally as possible and children are allowed to learn through risk taking and trial and error. Skills and strategies are taught, but only when needed and only when children are ready to learn them in the context of real writing and reading. Instructional decisions are no longer prescribed by a set of graded classroom materials; they are assumed by the classroom teacher and shaped by the teacher and the children using an abundance of varied materials. As Rich (1985) noted, no one program or set of materials will satisfy the whole-language teacher. Teachers utilizing a whole-language approach to literacy integrate their children's writing with a reading program of children's literature. Whole, meaningful texts are the instructional materials, not isolated words, sounds, or vocabulary-controlled "stories" (Edelsky, Draper, and Smith, 1983). These changes result in a classroom that looks and operates much differently from the more traditional textbook-based classroom. Whole-language in its best sense implies a restructuring of the traditional school and an opening up of the curriculum (Rich, 1985). Although this is a complex, difficult task, it is not impossible.

Implementing whole-language is a complex task because no one single blueprint for doing it exists. Just as there is no one traditional textbook-based classroom, there is no one formula or model for one archetypal whole-language classroom. As a result, whole-language classrooms, like traditional classrooms, tend to be organized and conducted in distinctively different ways according to the teacher's and school's acceptance and implementation of the philosophy and goals of whole-language. These methodologies will be as varied as the teacher and children themselves. However, there are certain aspects of organizing whole-language classrooms that contrast them with traditional classrooms.

Organizing Time

Time Tabling

In order to provide their children with numerous opportunities to read, write, talk, and listen in a meaningful context, whole-language teachers allot classroom time differently from traditional teachers. They divide their teaching day into larger time blocks in which related activities can take place. Descriptions of a day in two such classrooms were presented in Chapter 2. This opening up of the timetable allows the children to practice the processes of reading and writing in a variety of group arrangements, both large and small, and as individuals. It also allows whole-language teachers to translate more easily into practice their beliefs of what constitutes a whole-language classroom. In Chapter 1, Froese notes that although there are some differences of opinion on what constitutes a whole-language classroom, many whole-language advocates would agree that there are certain aspects of these child-centered classrooms that are consistent. Therefore, when teachers develop whole-language timetables, they make sure sufficient time has been scheduled for the following whole-language components.

Read-Aloud Time

A daily read-aloud time is provided when teachers read good literature (fiction and nonfiction) to their students. This provides them with countless demonstrations of how language is used in functional and meaningful ways, surrounds them with appropriate language models, familiarizes them with book language and story structure, and introduces them to new words and ideas (*Reading in Junior Classes*, 1985).

Independent Writing

Younger children are usually given time to write in their personal journals daily, with the teacher responding regularly to what they have written. As children get older, these journals are usually changed to private diaries. Other classrooms may use dialogue journals. Unlike the traditional journal, which is usually intended for the writer alone, teacher and students converse in writing about topics that are mutually interesting.

Independent Sustained Silent Reading Time

A brief time is set aside each day when everyone reads suitable materials to himself or herself. This independent reading time when children read books of their own choosing is seen as a valued component of a whole-language program. Another acronym for this type of reading is SQUIRT—Sustained Quiet Reading Time.

Language Experience

Whole-language teachers provide their children with regular opportunities to write extensively about topics of their own choosing based on common classroom experiences or on individual personal experiences. These child-centered writings, once completed, provide the authors with meaningful reading materials. Because the words have special meaning to them, they also encourage memory for the text (*Reading in Junior Classes*, 1985). At some point in this process, the children realize that what they are creating is only a beginning that must be changed if they are to gain greater control and understanding of the writing process. It is then that they start to edit, revise, and polish the rough drafts of their favorite compositions so that they can be published for others to read. This means checking for spelling, punctuation, sentence structure, and other aspects of good writing.

Shared-Book Experience (Big Books)

The shared-book experience, as described by Don Holdaway (1979), is another key component of whole-language programs (Baskwill and Whitman, 1986; Newman, 1985). It involves incorporating repetitive materials (stories, songs, poems, or chants) that have a high predictability, a strong rhythm, and a strong story line into the reading program. The main idea behind this strategy is the support it gives early readers. Because it is most often done utilizing an enlarged edition of a regular-sized book, this procedure has also become known as the big-book experience. According to Gail Heald-Taylor (1986, p. 37), big-book experiences "introduce new syntax and vocabulary to students, support oral-language development, introduce youngsters to the reading process, and stimulate personal writing." The initial sharing is done by the teacher reading the material (a big book, chart, or overhead) to the whole class or a small group in one sitting. During the reading, pictures are discussed and outcomes and events are predicted by the children. The first reading is followed by subsequent rereadings in which the children are encouraged to read all or part of the text in unison with the teacher. Attention to detail or some key aspect of reading is provided by the teacher through the use of pointing or masking. **Masking** is a device that enables the teacher or a child to isolate a particular letter, word(s), or sentence of the text. Later still, the big book or a regular-sized edition of the big book is read with or without the teacher in a small group, with a partner, or individually. Although this approach is used mainly with younger children, it can also be used in the higher elementary grades.

Guided Reading

The New Zealand teachers' reading guide, *Reading in Junior Classes* (1985, p. 69), stresses the importance of including guided reading (a form of group instruction) in whole-language programs. It is defined by its authors as "an approach which enables a teacher and a group of children to talk, read, and think their way purposefully through a text, making possible an early introduction to silent reading." It deepens the children's understanding of the text and allows them to practice strategies that will lead to independent reading. In addition, it introduces them "to the techniques of reading new or unseen material for personal satisfaction and understanding" (Holdaway, 1979, p. 142). For the teacher, it provides many opportunities to teach specific skills as difficulties arise. In New Zealand, the government has published a series of 36 small paperback books called *Ready to Read* for teacher use during the guided reading session. Goodman (1987, p. 10) noted that these books are "as close to a basal reader as they get." This graded series of small story books was developed to provide young New Zealand children with a steady progression of reading difficulty at three broad stages of early reading development (emergent, early, and fluency). All of the books included within these three levels are also graded into levels of difficulty. Although these small books can be read independently, they are most often used during a guided reading session.

The guided reading session consists of three distinct phases according to Don Holdaway (1979):

1. *Tune-in:* A brief, lively discussion is used to arouse interest and introduce the children to the new book (relating the story to the children's background, and focusing on the central theme and unfamiliar vocabulary of the story).
2. *Reading:* The children read the story silently.
3. *Follow-up:* Postreading discussion or activities arise from the reading experience.

Shared-Language Time (Communications/Language Workshop)

The teacher-directed segment of the whole-language program when teachers model literacy strategies in a whole-class or small-group situation is defined by Baskwill and Whitman (1986) as shared-language time. Although this planned teaching time follows a definite format, its actual composition will vary greatly from classroom to classroom. It is usually scheduled early in the day and is likely to last for an hour or more. Baskwill and Whitman divide their one-hour, shared-language session into four distinct segments (warm-up, old favorite, new story, and activity), each incorporating one or more specific, related routines. This planned teaching block or related language arts time should be approximately an hour and a half long and should contain the following three activities in sequence according to Holdaway (1984).

1. Reading to/Writing for or to—input
2. Reading with/Writing with (scribing)—input/output
3. Reading by/Writing by—output

"Time and equipment," Holdaway noted, "are organized to provide for and enrich these three types of activity." The teacher, according to Holdaway, will spend approximately 40 minutes of the time block in activities 1 and 2, while the children will spend about 50 minutes in activity 3 (natural developmental practice), "while the teacher interacts naturally to provide help, sustain activity, act as V.I.P. audience, observe and note, and teach individuals or small groups." The input time would involve the "whole class as a community of learners" and allow the "children to engage in participant learning at their own levels." It should be a pleasurable time for the children. This input time may be organized in a number of ways. A pattern Holdaway found very popular with teachers used five steps (p. 36). These are:

1. *Tune-in:* Poems, songs, chants, dances, and so on are enjoyed.
2. *Old Favourite:* The story is reread on demand (usually in enlarged print).
3. *Learning about Language:* This encompasses the skill part of the time block.
4. *New Story:* Usually read one each day.
5. *Independent Reading and Activity.*

Independent Reading or Personalized Reading

The independent reading of the best in children's literature (story and content books) is an integral part of a whole-language reading program. Most programs allow each child to select his or her own reading material on the basis of interest and stage of development. These self-selected books are then read at the child's own pace with support from the teacher. The plan provides for individual reading instruction by the teacher during frequent individual conferences and small-group teaching sessions. Therefore, the sequence of strategies developed is determined by the child's own individual needs. Favorite books are often shared with others or used by the child in a creative way (written into a play format, result in an art activity, etc.). Good record keeping by both the children and the teacher is a required component of this reading approach. More details for evaluation are presented in Chapter 12 as well as in individual chapters.

The challenging question that must now be asked is: How can one best create a timetable for whole-language strategies and components? The decision, Buchanan (1980, p. 130) maintained, must be a personal one, since "no one can tell a teacher what his timetable should look like for the next day, week, month, or year." Therefore, whole-language teachers must develop their own timetables, ones that provide for the best use of their time and their children's time. To do this, they will have to consider a number of factors. They will have to make decisions about time allocations and the sequencing of teaching and learning activities. In addition, they will have to decide how their schedule can best provide for whole-class, small-group, and individual learning needs, and still provide adequate time for conferences and other forms of assessment by the teacher and the children themselves. This is a complex task that requires thoughtful work on the part of the teacher.

Teachers changing to whole-language will also have to decide how quickly they will be able to implement their whole-language program. Anderson (1984) cautioned teachers to move slowly. He recommended moving in this direction in four stages. By using his four stages, teachers may move from a more structured timetable (day) to a less structured (more flexible) day slowly, rather than trying to make the change all at once. Tyler (1987) also discussed the time factor, and noted that most implementation plans greatly underestimate the time required. He found that it took six or seven years to get a reform really working as intended. Teachers implementing change must be given opportunities to learn the new procedures required of the program change. A transition of this magnitude (from a textbook-based program to a whole-language-based program) must be done in small, well-planned steps or stages, not in one giant leap.

Although no single timetable can adequately meet the needs of all whole-language teachers, one can learn a great deal about scheduling whole-language programs by examining the format used by successful whole-language teachers. Baskwill and Whitman (1986) divided their daily grade 1/2 timetable into seven large time blocks, which are broken only by recess and lunch. The day starts with a one-hour shared language block. This is followed by large blocks of time for personal reading, a science/social studies core, personal writing, independent practice (learning-center time), physical education/music, and a math core. They (Baskwill and Whitman, 1988) divided their team-taught grade 3/4 timetable into eight large time blocks. The day starts with a 45-minute shared language block followed by blocks of time for personal reading, independent activity, physical education, science, personal writing, math, and social studies. Butler and Turbill (1984) described how three Australian teachers timetable their day. Sample timetables are included as well as one teacher's description of what happens during the first seven weeks of school. In their book, *Case Studies in Whole Language,* Vacca and Rasinski (1992) described in detail the work of six American whole-language teachers in preschool through fifth-grade classroom. They include many excellent suggestions for timetabling whole-language programs using large time blocks. The teachers are in various stages of transition in their thinking about whole language. Some schools have disbanded grade designations and moved into a nongraded organization where children work at their own pace and level.

The following timetables are suggested as two possible ways of timetabling a whole-language program.

Sample Early Elementary Timetable

9:00	Class news and announcements
9:10	Journal writing
9:30	Large-group shared language time—often thematically based (includes: chanting songs and poems; read-aloud; collaborative reading and writing; learning about language)
10:30	Recess
10:45	Center time
11:15	Math
12:00	Lunch
12:45	Independent silent reading time
1:10	Art, music, or gym
1:45	Interdisciplinary theme work
2:15	Center time
3:00	Dismissal

Sample Later Elementary Timetable

9:00	Morning announcements
9:05	Writing workshop
9:30	Large-group shared language time — often thematically based
10:15	Center time
10:45	Music or gym or art
11:15	Math
12:00	Lunch
12:45	Read-aloud
1:00	Independent silent reading time
1:30	Music or gym or art
2:00	Science/Social studies core (Integrated Curriculum)
3:00	Dismissal

Making Contracts

Some whole-language teachers never use contracts, yet others find them especially useful when students are first learning to take some responsibility for managing their own time. They are essentially an agreement negotiated between the teacher and a student (or class) about the work to be completed in a given amount of time. Contracts may range from those completely developed by the teacher to those completely developed by individual students. Contracts will vary with the age of the students involved, the material to be covered, and the purpose for which the contract was designed. They can be designed to cover one day or a week, or just one subject (center) or subjects (centers).

Because of their flexibility, their actual design and use are only limited by the teacher's imagination. If carefully designed and planned, they can be very effective in whole-language classrooms.

Ideally, the students using them should have some say in setting their own goals, selecting their own materials, deciding when activities will be completed, evaluating their own success, and in some cases even deciding what they will do. Because contracts give students greater responsibility for managing their learning, it is felt that the experience of making contracts and adhering to them helps them to become better independent learners.

Although contracts appear to work much better with older students, they can also be used effectively with very young students. The students simply can be asked to check off or date the pictorial diagrams representing their choices. Older students can be assigned more complicated forms with written instructions requiring written responses. The class contract shown in Figure 11.1 would be used by younger students during a centers period over a one-week

FIGURE 11.1 *Center-Time Contract*

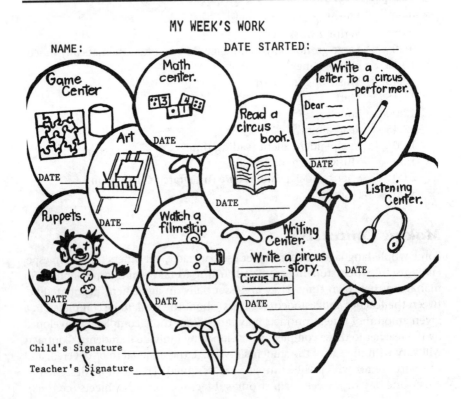

time period. When a student completes an activity, the student checks it off and colours the appropriate drawing.

Teachers wishing to set up a contracting system are advised to begin slowly. It may be more appropriate to begin with group contracts and to involve only a few areas of the curriculum or a small portion of the day. In addition, the teacher must make frequent checks to see that contracts are being properly kept and that all students are capable of meeting the specified requirements. The teacher must also take time to check completed work and record daily progress. This data, collected over time, allows the teacher to gain a better understanding of the progress and needs of the children.

Organizing Curriculum

Integrated Units/Themes/ Thematic Approach

Ken Goodman (1986, p. 31) has stated that "whole-language teachers organize the whole or a large part of the curriculum around topics or themes: What are the risks of nuclear war? Is water pollution a danger to our community?" Other topics might be bears, the gold rush, or how to take care of pets. This interdisciplinary approach to curriculum, which uses large blocks of time to explore broad areas of work, is commonly known as themes or **thematic units.** It is a strategy that intentionally integrates knowledge from many disciplines, allowing one subject matter to assist in the learning of others. The students' learning crosses subject barriers forming a cohesive whole (McFarlane, 1991). Generally, the topics are selected from social studies, science, mathematics, or literature and integrated with the language arts and the arts (music, art, physical education, and drama), as well as with each other. Although links to other subjects are brought into the unit when appropriate, it is likely that the main subject, such as science or social studies, will dominate as children use the language arts extensively to explore all aspects of the theme. Through this process they learn a great deal through language. However, if not done well it can result in a watering down of the "integrated subjects." As Routman (1991, p. 278) pointed out, "A thematic unit is an integrated unit only when the topic or theme is meaningful, relevant to the curriculum and students' lives, consistent with whole language principles, and authentic in the interrelationship of the language processes."

The selected theme provides the class with a focal point for inquiry, for language use, for problem solving, for cognitive development, and for the wealth of material found in whole-language classrooms. It builds on children's natural interests and gives them some choice in deciding which aspects of the theme will be explored. In addition, it provides a needed focus for the whole-group, shared-language sessions, as well as for the small-group and individual activities found within the classroom. It also provides a needed framework for curriculum development as listening, speaking, writing, and reading, are integrated with content in meaningful, purposeful ways. The actual amount of integration will depend to a large degree on the selected topic, the children's interest, and the availability of resources, as well as on the age and the background of the children being taught.

All selected themes are open ended, allowing the teacher and children to branch out in as many directions as possible. Their actual length will vary from a few days to over a month depending on class interest in the topic. These units may be child-initiated studies as well as teacher-initiated studies. Teachers wishing to implement a thematic approach are advised to follow the six steps discussed here regardless of the theme or content selected for study.

Brainstorming/Webbing

Once teachers select a theme, they must decide which aspects of the theme they would like to explore with their children. A useful strategy for teachers wishing to achieve this aim is to brainstorm (web) or diagram the many possible directions in which the selected topic will go. As ideas are jotted down, relationships begin to emerge and one can begin grouping ideas under specific headings on the web (or flow diagram). This webbing of possible aspects of study helps the teacher's thinking so that it is possible to go beyond the narrow confines of the theme. It is possible to keep adding to the web and increasing its complexity, ad infinitum. This brainstorming activity helps to clarify the students' and teacher's thinking and helps them to see the many varied teaching possibilities for the selected theme. It then becomes a reference bank to which the teacher can refer as the theme progresses. It should also be added to, and changed, as new thoughts and ideas occur.

The actual design or format of the web may vary greatly. Some teachers prefer to organize them around traditional subject areas (math, science, etc.); others prefer to organize them around specific topics or the individual learning centers within the classroom. In the higher elementary grades they can be developed with the children. A web for the topic "trees" is shown in Figure 11.2.

Set Valid Goals/Objectives

Once the web has been completed, the teacher must identify and list all general and specific goals for the selected theme. The strategies and concepts to be learned should also be listed at this time.

FIGURE 11.2 *Webbing: Showing Possible Theme Development*

TREES   WHERE ARE THEY FOUND?
         WHAT ARE THEY USED FOR?
         WHAT ARE THEY LIKE?

Questions such as these can lead to divergent pursuits, as illustrated below.

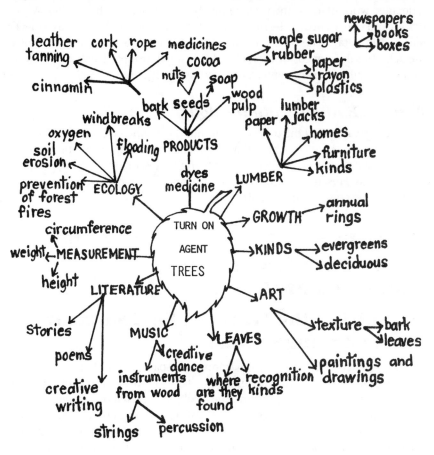

Collect Relevant Resources and Materials

When the goals have been identified and listed, it is time to gather together all relevant material for use by the teacher and the children. Possible field trips and classroom visitors should also be considered at this time. These should be listed at the beginning or the end of the unit plan.

Introduce the Topic (Launch the Theme)

Careful consideration must be given to how to best introduce the theme. This can be done by bringing in a real object, viewing a film, going on a field trip, or simply brainstorming with the children what they already know about the topic and what they would like to know about the topic.

Plan Learning Activities and Experiences

A detailed work plan for the theme must be completed by the teacher. All activities and experiences to be included in the study of the theme must now be outlined in detail. The plan must include all whole-class activities as well as the activities developed for individuals and small groups. These are often organized by subject areas, centers, or teaching strategies.

Plan an Ending (Culmination)

An effective way to end the thematic unit must be planned. This usually involves the children in some way. The children may make and display completed booklets about the theme, be involved in small-group presentations, or cooperate on a whole-class presentation to their parents or another class summarizing all aspects of the completed integrated unit.

Organizing Classroom Space and Materials

Organizing the Learning Environment (Room Arrangements)

The importance of the physical environment—space, equipment, and materials—cannot be stated strongly enough. It needs to be carefully planned, organized, and well stocked to permit the flexibility required of a whole-language curriculum. It should be an exciting, pleasing, relaxing environment where students want to read and write, and where reading and writing strategies develop naturally and purposefully. It should also be a place in which independent learning can take place, and where whole-language teachers can initiate and reinforce learning. This requires the presence of an abundance of varied, easily accessible learning materials, interesting displays, and sufficient space for whole-class work as well as for individual and small-group work. It must be rich in what Newman (1985) called "language in action." Books, charts, experience stories, pictures with captions, displays with accompanied text, samples of children's drawings and work, and the words of favourite songs can be found displayed about the classroom. This extensive use of print on the walls encourages what Massam and Kulik (1986) called "Reading the Walls" in many whole-language classrooms.

Teachers working in this type of planned learning environment use space, equipment, and materials differently from teachers working in more traditional subject-oriented classrooms. They prefer to use bookshelves, tables, and other furniture to create a number of areas or centers of learning where materials can be stored and where small groups of students can work on similar learning experiences. These experiences are organized around thematic units, which according to Goodman (1986, p. 32) "are structured to facilitate the integration of all the language processes (listening, speaking, reading, writing) with conceptual learning," thus allowing students to learn new concepts and clarify or expand old concepts through the use of language.

The actual number and physical arrangement of these centers will vary greatly from one classroom to another since no one arrangement can meet the needs of all whole-language teachers and students. While some teachers prefer to turn their whole classroom into learning centers, others prefer to set them up in the corners of their classroom and along the classroom walls. Sample room arrangements that illustrate these two types of design are shown in Figures 11.3A and 11.3B. While teachers of young children tend to prefer plan 11.3A, teachers in the higher elementary grades tend to prefer plan 11.3B.

Once the teacher has decided on the best and most suitable classroom organization, then some decisions about classroom seating need to be made. Although some teachers prefer to keep the individual desks, most whole-language teachers prefer to group some or all of the individual desks to form a table effect (four to six desks together), or to abandon them completely in favor of tables that seat four to six students. Tables or desks are usually grouped near the center of the classroom to accommodate the whole class, or they are placed in the centers that have been established in the classroom. Teachers of whole-language find that not all students are ready to work in groups at the same time. Therefore, teachers must make individual decisions on when and which students are ready for such a move.

Learning Centers

Whole-language centers provide specialized settings for students to pursue tasks on their own or in small groups as they become principal agents in their own learning. The purpose of each center will depend on the type of center established. They are most effective when they have been keyed to the particular thematic unit being studied by the student. Generally, more than one language process will be used in each center; speaking, listening, reading, and writing experiences are presented in an integrated manner to the children in meaningful whole context (Anderson, 1984).

FIGURE 11.3A   *Sample Room Arrangement: Centers Are Spaced throughout the Classroom*

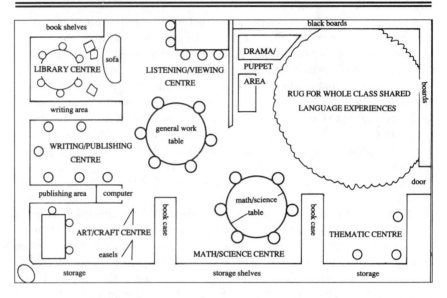

FIGURE 11.3B   *Sample Room Arrangement: Centers Are on Periphery of Classroom*

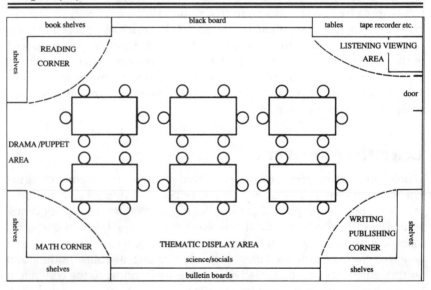

All centers should be clearly defined, well planned, and well stocked with a variety of thought-provoking materials and activities that are changed as children's needs and interests change. The actual visual effect should be attractive to arouse and sustain the interest of its users. They should be pleasing, relaxing places to work.

The exact number and variety of whole-language centers will vary from classroom to classroom; each teacher must make this decision based on needs. Initially, teachers new to whole-language may want to start with only one or two centers and then add a few more once the initial centers are well stocked and function effectively. Anderson (1984) recommended starting with one of the four basic types of centers (reading, writing, speaking, and listening) and then adding the other three until all four have been established. Once these four basic centers are being used successfully by the class, he suggested adding other content centers. Rich (1987), on the other hand, believed five centers are essential to the development and extension of a sound whole-language program. These centers—library, writing, listening, creative, and theme—can become the backbone of a whole-language program.

Library or Reading Center

An attractive, inviting library that is set off from the rest of the room by well-stocked bookshelves can do much to entice children to read many types of print. It is the focus of the whole-language program (*Reading in Junior Classes*, 1985). Ideally, it should be placed in an area of the room that has good lighting, ample space for bookshelves, and is free from interruptions. A carpeted area furnished with a comfortable sofa, old armchairs, floor cushions, or an old rocking chair can provide needed comfortable seating. The reading materials on the shelves should include a variety of tradebooks (fiction and nonfiction) on different topics and at varying levels of difficulty, as well as some big books, basal readers, magazines, pamphlets, catalogues, encyclopedias, newspapers, and dictionaries. In addition, there should be books that reflect the multicultural society. It should also include a section on poetry and original books written by the children individually or in groups. A number of these resources should be displayed on the shelves by the teacher. It is important to see that favorites are retained and nonfavorites replaced to meet changing interests and needs. Students will use this center individually and in small groups throughout the day to look at or read what they can.

Writing/Publishing Center

An attractive, inviting, well-stocked writing/publishing center can do a great deal to encourage children to write and publish in a variety of literary forms. Tasks here will focus on writing, illustrating, and publishing. Nancy Lee Cecil (1987) suggested setting up two distinct work spaces—one for the actual writing and the other for illustrating and making the books chosen for publication. A typewriter or computer with printer would be very useful at this stage in the writing process. The actual center would be equipped with a few desks placed side by side or one or two tables. It should be well stocked with paper of various sizes, colors, and shapes, as well as pens, fine markers, pencils, paint, brushes, rulers, scissors, pastels, and construction paper for covers. A large collection of writing motivators such as pictures, computer programs, job cards (or task cards, which are cards on which assignments or activities are outlined in detail), story titles, "what if" situations, and story beginnings are essential. They can act as stimuli for new stories or poems. Some of these motivators will remain in the center all year, while others will remain for only a short time. It is also wise to include examples of experience stories, published books, alphabet models, and a wide assortment of vocabulary aids and dictionaries. It should be remembered that the more attractive and stimulating the center, the more frequently the students will want to write, and the more practice they will get in the writing process.

Listening/Viewing Center

The listening/viewing center should be a quiet, comfortable place where audiovisual materials (records, tapes, read-along tapes, videos, filmstrips, etc.) and equipment (record player, tape recorder, computers, filmstrip projector) are made available to individuals and small groups. The tape recorder with six to eight headphones is a popular component, allowing groups of children to listen to tapes of whole stories, poems, parts of stories, as well as nonfictional material. While some of these tapes can be made just for pleasurable listening, others can be made to allow children to read along with the text. These read-along tapes are used on a regular basis in whole-language classrooms. Through their use, children are given increased opportunity to hear and practice reading selections on a flexible basis. While at this center, children may also view or review story filmstrips as well as filmstrips related to individual interests and class units of study.

Math Center

An imaginative, well-stocked mathematics center can do much to increase math skills and the understanding of mathematical principles and concepts. There should be such things as scales, measuring tapes, clocks, and lots of objects to manipulate—such as counters (beans, blocks, etc.), money, geoboards, attribute blocks, and calculators. There should be an emphasis on active involvement as children explore numbers, shapes, quantities, sizes, and measurement. Also included in the center would be job cards, reference books, math games, and kits.

Art Center

A variety of materials should be stored in the art center for artistic expression, projects, displays, and exhibits. There should be materials for coloring, paint-

Writing and publishing centers should be furnished comfortably to encourage students to write and illustrate their work.

ing, drawing, sculpting, and craft making. This means there must be space to store all kinds of paper, paints, brushes, crayons, cloth pieces, markers, wool, and empty boxes. At times, the center will be set up for a specific art activity, and at other times the students will be free to select an activity of their own choice. It will also be a popular center for young authors wanting to illustrate their stories, or for actors to produce costumes and props for plays they have written.

Drama/Puppet Center

The drama/puppet center should contain a variety of puppets (commercially produced and child made), a puppet theater, costumes, props, and enough space for a few actors to act out old familiar stories or plays they have written. Informal classroom drama of this type can make a major contribution to whole-language programs. Older students can also get involved in making their own costumes.

Thematic Center

The thematic center should be organized around a specific theme or topic such as dinosaurs, autumn, or Colonial America. These topics are most often selected from the science and social studies subject areas. Books, pictures, materials, and resources related to the selected theme should be stored here. In addition, the center might often contain a number of task cards or job cards that outline assignments or activities for the children to work on individually or in small groups. A center of this type should also include adequate storage areas as well as work space for the students.

Selecting Materials and Resources

A well-organized, well-stocked classroom allows students to work independently for a large part of the day, freeing the teacher to work intensively with small groups and individuals. This means that there must be a good collection of varied whole-language materials and resources in every whole-language classroom for both teacher and student use. Some of these will be discussed next.

Vocabulary/Spelling Aids

Whole-language classrooms are print rich. Displayed about the classroom will be all kinds of appropriate print-charts, experience stories, labels, signs, pictures with captions, and word lists. Students are given free access to these lists of specialized words (high-frequency words and key words related to themes), as well as their own personal word banks. Many of these specialized word lists would have been obtained through whole-class brainstorming sessions, and are conveniently displayed in the classroom on charts, bulletin boards, flash cards, or word mobiles.

Big Books

A large number of big books (purchased or teacher/student made) need to be made available in the classroom for teacher use as well as for use by small groups and individual students. Scholastic Publications, Houghton Mifflin, and Addison-Wesley are excellent sources for big books. The stories selected for big-book production are usually chosen from the student's favorite books, stories, chants, or verses. Young students enjoy reading them a great deal, while older students enjoy writing them for the younger students. There are great benefits to both groups.

Wordless Picture Books

Wordless picture books can be a valuable tool in teaching beginning readers. They provide an enjoyable vehicle for language activity as the students and teacher reconstruct the story from the sequenced pictures. These, too, can be produced as big books once the student and teacher have recorded their own personal version of the story. Later the student may "read" from the small wordless text individually or with the help of the teacher. Or the student can read the larger version with text, alone or in small groups. If the dictated text is clipped to the appropriate page of the book (rather than written in permanently), the book can be used over and over again with individual students. Older students can actually write their own version of a wordless book and then orally tell the story to others in the class. Mayer's (1974) *Frog Goes to Dinner* is an excellent choice for this type of activity. There are a large number of wordless books that can be used in this way in whole-language classrooms. Some of these are listed below. A more complete list can be found in *Using Wordless Picture Books: Authors and Activities* by Tuten-Puckett and Richey (1993).

Alexander, M. (1970). *Bobo's dream.* New York: Dial.

Anno, M. (1985). *Ann's Britain.* New York: Putnam.

Aruego, J. (1971). *Look what I can do.* New York: Scribner's.

Briggs, R. (1978). *The snowman.* London: Puffin Books.

Brown, C. (1989). *The patchwork farmer.* New York: Greenwillow.

Carle, E. (1971). *Do you want to be my friend?* New York: Crowell-Collier Press.

Day, A. (1992). *Carl's masquerade.* New York: Farrar, Straus & Giroux.

Fuchs, E. (1969). *Journey to the moon.* New York: Delacorte Press.

Goodall, J. S. (1987). *The story of a main street.* Riverside, NJ: McElderry.

Goss, J. L. & Harste, J.C. (1985). *It didn't frighten me!* Worthington, OH: Willowisp Press.

Hoban, T. (1976). *Big ones, little ones.* New York: Greenwillow.

Hutchins, P. (1971). *Changes, changes.* New York: Macmillan.

Keats, E. J. (1974). *Kitten for a day.* New York: Macmillan.

Kent, J. (1975). *The egg book.* New York: Macmillan.

Mari, L. (1969). *The magic balloon.* New York: Phillips.

Mayer, M. (1974). *Frog goes to dinner.* New York: Dial.

Mayer, M. (1967). *A boy, a dog, and a frog.* New York: Dial.

Ormerod, J. (1981). *Sunshine.* New York: Lothrop.

Simmons, E. (1970). *Family.* New York: McKay.

Spier, P. (1982). *Rain.* New York: Doubleday.

Sugita, Y. (1973). *My friend little John.* New York: McGraw-Hill.

Wezel, P. (1966). *The good bird.* New York: Harper & Row.

Wiesner, D. (1991). *Tuesday.* Burlington, MA: Houghton Mifflin.

Wiesner, D. (1988). *Free fall.* New York: Mulberry Books.

Predictable Books and Materials

Whole-language teachers like to use predictable materials such as songs, chants, nursery rhymes, verses, and stories in their classroom. Predictable books like *Three Billy Goats Gruff* or *I Know an Old Lady Who Swallowed a Fly* are especially useful to beginning readers because they help to build a sense of story for the child. They love their repetitive language and familiar content and structure. Baskwill and Whitman (1986) like to use a minimum of four predictable books on every theme covered by their grade 1/2 class. The use of predictable books can also open up story patterns to young students during creative writing time. These new stories are patterned after the original story in order to write a new original patterned story by the whole class or individual students. The character and setting may both be changed, but the story line remains the same. The following predictable books are recommended for whole classroom use.

Adams, P. (1974). *This old man.* New York: Grossett and Dunlap.

Balian, L. (1972). *Where in the world is Henry?* New York: Bradbury Press.

Becker, J. (1973). *Seven little rabbits.* New York: Scholastic.

Brown, M. (1957). *The three billy goats gruff.* New York: Harcourt Brace Jovanovich.

Brown, M. (1947). *Goodnight moon.* New York: Harper & Row.

Carle, E. (1975). *The mixed up chameleon.* New York: Crowell.

Carle, E. (1969). *The very hungry caterpillar.* Cleveland, OH: Collins World.

Galdone, P. (1969). *Henny Penny.* New York: Scholastic.

Martin, B. (1970). *Brown bear, brown bear.* New York: Holt, Rinehart & Winston.

Martin, B. (1970). *Fire! fire! said Mrs. McGuire.* New York: Holt, Rinehart & Winston.

Meyer, M. (1968). *Just for you.* New York: Golden Press.

Peppe, R. (1970). *The house that Jack built.* New York: Delacorte Press.

Preston, E.M. (1978). *Where did my mother go?* New York: Four Winds Press.

Skaar, G. (1963). *What do animals say?* New York: Scholastic.

Zolotow, C. (1958). *Do you know what I'll do?* New York: Harper & Row.

Read-Aloud Books

The whole-language teacher must have a wide knowledge of children's books. Good books must be read to the class on a daily basis. This means that the teacher must have good books of his or her own, or know where to get good books to read to the children. The librarian from the public library or the teacher's school will often willingly provide the books or lists of good books. Some sure winners are *Charlotte's Web, Alexander and the Terrible, Horrible, No Good, Very Bad Day, Where the Wild Things Are, Tales of a Fourth Grade Nothing, The Mouse on the Motorcycle,* and *Bridge to Teribithia.* Many others are listed in Chapter 4, Literature in a Whole-Language Program.

Tradebooks and Other Reading Materials

Chapter 4, Literature in a Whole-Language Program, states that in whole-language classrooms children's literature of all types (i.e., fiction and nonfiction) becomes an essential teaching tool. Tradebooks can provide students with enriching experiences and build within them a love of reading. This more positive attitude toward reading can help teachers produce children who will read as well as can read. This requires an abundance of high-quality literature (fiction and nonfiction) on a wide range of topics and covering a wide range of reading levels. These books can be collected from a number of sources. Many school libraries and public libraries will loan sets of books for several weeks. School librarians will also help teachers select books that will appeal to the grade level they are teaching. Nancy Lee Cecil (1987) included a suggested list of library books (including poetry) for grades 1 through 6 in her book *Teaching to the Heart.* Lists of recently published children's books can be obtained by consulting journals such as *The Reading Teacher* and *Language Arts.* Each fall *The Reading Teacher* publishes a list of new tradebooks that have been selected by children as the ones they liked best. Classroom libraries should also contain a good supply of magazines, newspapers, cookbooks, travel literature, pamphlets, encyclopedias, dictionaries, and reference material to add to the quantity and variety of printed material in the classroom. These materials may be organized according to topic, level of difficulty, or type.

Job Cards

Another feature often found in whole-language classrooms is the job card (activity card) on which independent learning activities are outlined. They may be used as a regular part of the program or as a supplement to it. They allow students to work independently at their own ability level and at their own pace. Although they can be made for any area of the curriculum, they are especially useful in science, social studies, and math. They invite students to explore, to think, and to engage in learning experiences—experiences that usually involve some aspect of reading and writing. The job cards should be as attractive as possible; many teachers illustrate them. In subjects such as science and mathematics they are an effective means of involving students in concrete experiences. In some whole-language classrooms, students are expected to complete a certain number of job cards a day as part of their assigned work. Some sample creative writing job cards are pictured in Figure 11.4.

FIGURE 11.4   *Creative Writing Job Cards*

BROWN BEAR'S FAVOURITE FOOD

Brown Bear's favourite food is honey! He loves it. He thinks it is delicious. He likes the way it tastes. He even likes its colour! What are your favourite foods? Write some riddles about them, and then read your riddles to a friend.

A STRANGE ADVENTURE

One hot Saturday afternoon as you are walking along the docks you hear a strange, loud, beeping noise. You decide to investigate, and find that it comes from an old deserted warehouse. You walk inside to find a large control panel with flashing GREEN lights. No one appears to be in the building. Suddenly you hear a voice coming from the panel telling you to push the flashing green button in the centre of the panel . . . .

WRITE a story telling us about your adventure.

WHAT HAPPENS NEXT?

Grouping Students for Whole-Language Learning

Whole-language teachers have a purposeful, flexible attitude toward grouping as they work with students individually, in small groups, and with the whole class to foster language development. Whole-class instruction acts as a unifying function by providing needed time for instruction in certain areas of the curriculum and the introduction and development of thematic units. Individual and small-group instruction, on the other hand, help the teacher meet individual needs, abilities, and interests. The small groups will vary in size depending on the purpose of the group and class needs. Students are often encouraged to share and discuss their work with one another and to help one another. Some of the most frequently used grouping patterns found in whole-language classrooms are interest groups, needs groups, social groups, ability groups, and working in pairs.

Their success will depend to a large extent "upon the degree to which teachers understand how to operate small groups, the commitment they have to their success, and the extent to which students regard working in groups as a significant learning strategy" (Reid, Forrestal, and Cook, 1990, p. 59).

Interest groups involve the teacher or the students grouping themselves according to an identified common interest in some topic (whales, pollution), or materials (a particular tradebook), or some child-originated interest (a puppet play).

Needs groups or instruction groups are usually formed for a short time period. The teacher selects a group of students with a similar weakness (trouble with a specific skill) and plans a program of activities for them. These are usually disbanded once the skill has been learned.

Social or friendship groups are formed when students are given an opportunity to work on an activity on the basis of friendship. Often the students are of mixed ability. Many teachers find that students accomplish more work with greater enthusiasm when they work with friends.

Ability groups may be formed occasionally. They enable students to work together at roughly the same achievement level.

Working in pairs often involves the use of student tutors. Students who have mastered a certain skill can help other children in the class who are having difficulty mastering the skill (peer tutoring). These groups are usually informal and do not last for a long period of time. The tutor can be the same age or older than the child needing help. Pairs of students can read to each other. A good reader may be matched with one that is less able. They take turns reading aloud to each other or to a group of children.

Conclusion

Ultimately, the success or failure of implementing a whole-language curriculum will rest in the hands of the classroom teacher. Although the teacher's task is complex, it is not impossible. It requires a great deal of patience, time, and effort on the part of the teacher, as well as extensive reading and continuous staff development. Teachers wishing to move in this direction will have to gain a clear understanding of the theoretical base of whole-language and know why whole-language teachers do what they are doing. They will have to carefully plan the five aspects of organizing whole-language classrooms—organizing time, organizing curriculum, organizing classroom space and materials, selecting materials and resources, and grouping children for whole-language learning. Then and only then will they be able to successfully connect theory and practice, and as a result be able to create effective whole-language classrooms.

REFERENCES

Anderson, G. S. (1984). *A whole language approach to reading*. Lanham, MD: University Press of America.

Baskwill, J. & Whitman, P. (1986). *Whole language sourcebook*. Richmond Hill, Ontario: Scholastic-TAB Publications.

Baskwill, J. & Whitman, P. (1988). *Moving on—Whole language sourcebook for grades three and four.* Richmond Hill, Ontario: Scholastic-TAB Publications.

Buchanan, E. (Ed.). (1980). *For the love of reading.* Winnipeg: The C.E.L. Group, Inc.

Butler, A. & Turbill, J. (1984). *Towards a reading-writing classroom.* Rozelle, NSW: Primary English Teaching Association.

Cecil, N. L. (1987). *Teaching to the heart.* Salem, WI: Sheffield.

Department of Education , Wellington. (1985). *Reading in junior classes.* Wellington, New Zealand: Author.

Edelsky, C., Draper, K. & Smith, K. (1983). Hookin' em in at the start of school: A "whole language" classroom. *Anthropology & Education Quarterly, 14,* 257–281.

Goodman, K. S. (1986). *What's whole in whole language?* Richmond Hill, Ontario: Scholastic-TAB Publications.

Goodman, K. S. (1987). Who can be a whole language teacher? *Teachers Networking, 1 (1),* 10–11.

Heald-Taylor, G. (1986). *Whole language strategies for ESL students.* Toronto: OISE Press.

Holdaway, D. (1979). *The foundation of literacy.* Auckland, New Zealand: Ashton Scholastic.

Holdaway, D. (1984). *Stability and change in literacy learning.* London, Ontario: University of Western Ontario.

Jewel, M. G. & Zintz, M. V. (1986). *Learning to read naturally.* Dubuque, IA: Kendall/Hunt.

Lee Cecil, N. (1987). *Teaching to the heart.* Salem, WI: Sheffield.

Massam, J. & Kulik, A. (1986). *And what else? Integrated approaches for emergent language and reading programmes.* Auckland, New Zealand: Shortland Publications.

McFarlane, C. (1991). *Theme work—A global perspective in the primary curriculum in the '90s.* Birmingham, England: Development Education Centre.

McVitty, W. (Ed.) (1986). *Getting it together—Organizing the reading-writing classroom.* Rosebery, NSW: Primary English Teaching Association.

Newman, J. M. (Ed.) (1985). *Whole language—Theory in use.* Portsmouth, NH: Heinemann Educational Books, Inc.

Reid, J., Forrestal, R. & Cook, J. (1990). *Small group learning in the classroom.* Portsmouth, NH: Heinemann Educational Books, Inc.

Rich, R. S. (1987). Learning centres—A closer look. *Whole Language Newsletter, 4 (3),* 5.

Rich, S. J. (1985). Restoring power to teachers: The impact of "whole language." *Language Arts, 62 (7),* 717–724.

Routman, R. (1991). *Invitations—Changing as teachers and learners K–12.* Portsmouth, NH: Heinemann Educational Books, Inc.

Tuten-Puckett, K. & Richey, V. H. (1993). *Using wordless picture books: Authors and activities.* Englewood, CO: Teacher Ideas Press.

Tyler, R. (1987). Education reforms. *Phi Delta Kappan, 69,* 277–280.

Vacca, R. T. & Rasinski, T. V. (1992). *Case studies in whole language.* Fort Worth, TX: Harcourt Brace Jovanovich.

RECOMMENDED READINGS

Busching, B. & Schwartz, J. (1983). *Integrating the language arts in the elementary school.* Urbana, IL: NCTE.

Cambourne, B. (1988). *The whole story.* Auckland, New Zealand: Ashton Scholastic.

Chenfeld, M. B. (1983). *Creative activities for young children.* New York: Harcourt Brace Jovanovich.

Day, B. (1988). *Early childhood education: Creative learning activities.* New York: Macmillan.

Doll, C. A. (1990). *Nonfiction books for children—Activities for thinking, learning and doing.* Englewood, CO: Teacher Ideas Press.

Forester, A. D. & Reinhard, M. (1989). *The learners' way.* Winnipeg, Manitoba: Peguis Publishers.

Loughlin, C. E. & Martin, M. D. (1987). *Supporting literacy—Developing effective learning environments.* New York: Teachers College Press.

Lukasevich, A. & Pieronek, F. (1994). *Favorites, friendships, foods, and fantasy* (Vols. One and Two). Menlo Park, CA: Addison-Wesley.

McLennan, K. (1984). *Springboard—Ideas for planning themes.* Melbourne, Australia: Thomas Nelson.

Meyen, E. L. (1981). *Developing instructional units.* Dubuque, IA: Wm. C. Brown.

Moir, H. (Ed.). (1992). *Collected perspectives—Choosing and using books for the Classroom.* Boston: Christopher-Gordon Publishers, Inc.

Piechowiak, A. B. & Cook, M. B. (1976). *Complete guide to the elementary learning centre.* New York: Parker.

Poppe, C. A. & Van Matre, N. A. (1985). *Science learning centres for the primary grades.* New York: The Center for Applied Research in Education.

Van Allen, R. & Allen, C. (1976). *Language experience activities.* Boston: Houghton Mifflin.

Wade, B. (Ed.) (1990). *Reading for real.* Milton Keynes: Open University Press.

Wendelin, K. H. & Greenlaw, M. J. (1984, 1986). *Storybook classrooms—Using children's literature in the learning centre.* Atlanta: Humanics Limited.

DISCUSSION QUESTIONS

1. Select a book or thematic topic that you feel has a rich source for developing whole-language experiences. Develop a web that builds on the strengths of the selected topic.
2. Thematic centers may be used as a focal point for whole-language themes. Design a center for a specified thematic topic, and then develop some materials to be included in the center.
3. Select a wordless book or a predictable book. Discuss how you would use this book at a specified grade level in a whole-language program.

Assessment:
Form and Function

VICTOR FROESE

1. *Understanding the* why, how, *and* who *of assessment and evaluation*

2. *Understanding the* major issues *and controversies in assessment*

3. *Understanding the classroom applications of assessment in each of the major language arts—listening, oral language, reading, and writing*

4. *Understanding some of the problems of arriving at a course grade or evaluation and writing a report card*

The language arts curriculum inevitably shrinks or expands to the boundaries of what is evaluated.

—Walter Loban (1976)

Assessment procedures are inherently political, not only because whoever controls the assessment process shapes the curriculum pedagogy and ultimately the student's life chances, but also because particular forms of assessment promote particular forms of social control within the organization, while suppressing others.

—Harold Berlak et al. (1992, p. 18)

A chapter on assessment paradoxically must begin with attention to the curriculum. It makes sense only to assess what is being taught; assessment is valid only if it pertains to what is taught. Further, as the quotation by Berlak suggests, forms of assessment represent particular views of what is important (that which is assessed) and what is unimportant (that which is not assessed). This chapter, then, must be considered in the context of the other chapters that lay out the contents of the whole-language arts program, and in the context of locally mandated curricula.

Further, it should be remembered that each of the other chapters contains specific evaluation ideas. The purpose of this chapter is to provide a larger picture of how the pieces fit together. As a result, the examples given are intended to be illustrative of the assessment concepts presented; they are not intended to be exhaustive or comprehensive in any sense.

It is important to understand that the assumptions behind whole-language extend considerably beyond that of many traditional programs (see Chapter 1). It is also important when considering assessment and evaluation to give attention to all aspects of the whole-language program, and especially to those aspects which are different. These include:

1. Documentation of students initiating language activities
2. How students collaborate during learning to extend their learning
3. Personal records of what has been accomplished by the student
4. Indications of how reference materials are used to solve problems
5. Examples of work in draft or unfinished form as well as completed work
6. Consideration of attitudes, habits, and interests
7. A balanced record of oral, written, reading, viewing, and literature activities
8. Results of student/student, student/teacher, and student/parent conferences
9. Teacher observations, reflections, summations
10. Evidence of students' synthesis of previous work samples and reflective commenting
11. Descriptions of growth over time of strategies, processes, and content
12. Evidence of students' learning of evaluation criteria
13. Examples of the development of multiple functional literacies (i.e., school, community, second and third language, etc.)
14. Evidence of being able to make critical judgments, decisions, and analysis

It is not practical or desirable to attempt to make a comprehensive list since items within the list change over time (i.e., some are important at one time but not another) and because local curricula vary and change over time. Also, the major professional organizations now support "generative" and "dynamic" standards that value "diversity" (NCTE, 1992). This is a significant change since traditional measures were norm referenced and hence valued static confor-

mity. Several complete volumes now deal exclusively with whole-language related evaluation (Baskwill and Whitman, 1988; Glazer, Searfoss, and Gentile,
1988; Goodman, Goodman and Hood, 1989; Taylor, 1990; Anthony, Johnson,
Mickelson, and Preece, 1991).

One purpose of this chapter is to outline some of the functions of assessment—*why* we assess things, *who* should do the assessing, and *how* we should
consider the results of assessment (i.e., evaluation). A second purpose is to
point out some of the major issues in assessment that relate to whole-language
instruction. Another purpose is to present a model of assessment to guide the
teacher in assuring all major aspects are addressed. The final purpose of this
chapter is to suggest methods of assessment consistent with the principles of
whole-language instruction that fit into the model presented.

Why Do We Assess Things?

The most important purpose of assessment is to provide a diagnosis for the teacher
and feedback for the student. Diagnosis is important because the teacher in a
whole-language program should teach only what is necessary. This is quite different from what is commonly found in classrooms where the same lesson is
taught to everyone regardless of whether it is needed. What is advocated here
is that through self-selection, screening procedures, diagnostic teaching, or pretest-
ing, the teacher, or a combination of teacher and student (also student and parent, and parent and teacher), plan appropriate activities. Another purpose of
assessment is to monitor progress made by an individual after a period of time
or after a particular instructional unit. These first two purposes for assessment
are said to be formative, or for teaching purposes. The following reasons are, in
contrast, considered summative since they are used for a different purpose, for
describing performance at the end of some period of time or unit.

An often unstated purpose of assessment is to allow the learner to learn
the criteria used in evaluating school achievement. In many ways this is the most
important since it allows the student to evaluate learning independently and
realistically—a strategy required for most real-life learning. Evidence from a
study involving over 30 countries indicates that students in most countries
have difficulty in accurate self-evaluation (Elley, 1992, p. 69).

Another summative purpose of assessment is to provide a grade or anecdotal
record to parents or others. This requires the teacher and student to reduce
the information gathered into a single letter grade, percentage score, or brief
comment. Schools are required to be accountable to the public through assessment and evaluation. For this purpose commercial standardized tests are
sometimes used, or, for state assessments, specially prepared instruments much
like standardized group tests are used, although currently a number of other

Watching a kindergarten student completing a puzzle gives the observant teacher much information about strategies the child is using to solve problems.

approaches are being developed (e.g., various "standards" or "indicators" projects are under development). These types of tests must be carefully evaluated to ensure that they reflect the curriculum used in the schools at the time of assessment (Froese, 1988b; Valencia et al., 1989).

We should also assess and evaluate student interests (see suggestions in other chapters), their attitudes, and their self-perceptions toward language learning since these are involved in the learning process and cannot be separated from other cognitive aspects (Raven, 1992, p. 89).

Who Should Do the Assessing?

It is too often assumed that the teacher is solely responsible for assessment, but that is an oversimplification. First, in a whole-language program, students produce so much work that the teacher cannot possibly mark it all. Second, the principles of whole-language encourage independence in learning, self-selection, and independently initiated work. This requires that the student be part of the assessment process. If a goal is to produce independent learners, then students must not only be involved in assessment, at times they must be responsible for self-assessment. Students at all grade levels are capable of self-evaluation and will improve in it if given the opportunity to discuss reasons and criteria for assessment. Sometimes cooperative assessment is the most appropriate. Most often this means that the teacher and the student together make decisions about work to be done, goals to be set, or choices to be made. This is the type of assessment often used in individual conferences. At other times it is most efficient that peers evaluate each other's work to provide feedback and to assist in the elimination of careless errors before submitting the final work.

Increasingly, parents are also directly involved in the evaluation process. In some systems students prepare and conduct student/parent conferences under the direction of the teacher. A form of "negotiated report" results when parents, teachers, and students exchange information and agree to the areas to be discussed during conference time (B.C. Primary Teachers' Association, 1992). Such involvement is most certain to lead to students and parents taking more responsibility for learning, a trend welcomed by many teachers.

Some very specialized assessment—clinical assessment—is beyond the scope of the classroom teacher, because the teacher does not have either enough time, the appropriate tests, or the required training, and hence it is considered to be beyond the scope of this text. Usually referral to a reading specialist, teacher, a psychologist, a nurse, or a speech therapist is the appropriate action when students exhibit learning difficulties that are persistent or pathological. The classroom teacher should report any observed anomalies to the available helping professions since neglect can often lead to more time-consuming remediation later, and contribute to unnecessary suffering for the student.

How Important Are Assessment Results?

Not all assessment results are equally important. One school system, for example, suggests that reports describe student development in several goal areas: emotional, social, social responsibility, physical, aesthetic, artistic, and intellectual development. Descriptions are linked to the context of the subject areas (B.C. Ministry of Education, 1991). If each area is equally important then each area would receive 1/7 of the total attention and time. It is unlikely that most teachers would give equal weight to each area, yet it is important to consider how the information from the various areas might be combined.

In another jurisdiction a report card might list spelling, reading, and so forth, but that does not mean that the spelling and reading marks are equally important. They need to be weighted in some way since spelling is only a very minor part of writing (or composition). Furthermore, in the whole-language curriculum, both process and product need to be reported on and evaluated. In short, consideration needs to be given to the relative importance of the total task of language learning, especially when the results are being used for reporting purposes. (In many states grades are not required in the elementary school, but if a grade is required, perhaps 5% might be allotted for spelling, 35% for composition, and so on.)

Another aspect to consider in assessment is to what degree a strategy, skill, process, or ability needs to be mastered. Some things need only to be recognized, others need to be used (i.e., applied), still others to be recalled, and others—perhaps aesthetic—to be appreciated.

Finally, some things are "life skills" and are basic to other learning; some are useful to have but not essential; and others are entirely optional. Obviously all of the preceding factors will determine how assessment is weighted and used.

Issues in Assessment

Holistic Assessment

Because traditional methods of teaching and assessment rely heavily on a set of skills (to know how to blend sounds, to parse sentences, to understand details, and so on), it may be inferred that students need simply learn these skills to achieve proficiency in language. Such a fragmented approach is incompatible with the whole-language approach. The reasons for this are threefold. First, there is little evidence of the usefulness of such discrete skills even though many textbooks contain long lists of them (and there is only moderate agreement what those skills are). Second, teaching and practice of the skills results mostly in better performance on the skills themselves rather than in better language performance (Hammill and McNutt, 1981). And third, holistic evaluation and assessment assumes that the affective and conative aspects of learning are always part of cognitive learning (Berlak et al., 1992). A holistic approach begins from the premise that language should be used for communication purposes first, and only when it is well internalized should it be analyzed. For example, the study of the rules of syntax is now often postponed until high school, where the structure of language is studied for its own sake. This change was required because a direct relationship between syntax and improved composition could not be verified. French is today commonly taught in an "immersion" setting because this holistic approach has been found to be more effective. The current approaches to writing and spelling are also more holistic—invented spelling is accepted from the first day of school and much writing is encouraged, however "incorrect" it may be since teachers know that it will gradually approach conventional spelling. In short, theory, curriculum goals, and assessment should be aligned (Heath, 1991; Froese, 1988a; Valencia et al., 1989); therefore, holistic assessment must accompany holistic teaching methods in order to be valid.

Student-Centered Assessment

Much current school activity is still teacher initiated, teacher directed, and teacher assessed. Many decisions are made by the teacher and little opportunity is given to students to make their own decisions—whether right or wrong. If independent learning is a goal of education, then more decision making must be shifted to students in order that they learn the criteria of self-assessment, practice them, and develop sound judgment. Student-centered approaches also require that students be allowed some choice in the selection of reading materials, writing topics, interest areas, and methods of assessment. However, not all assessment needs to be either teacher centered or student centered; cooperative assessment is another alternative. All three approaches should be used at appropriate times. Student-centered learning, however, also implies that only instruction required by the student be offered. That means that the teacher needs to be aware of each student's strengths and weaknesses, and be able to tailor instruction to individuals, small groups, or the whole class when each is appropriate.

Process-Oriented Assessment

Much assessment is product oriented; that is, marks are given for composition, spelling, giving a talk, or answering comprehension questions. However, the teacher can learn much more about the student from observing process: the process of composing (how the student makes notes of ideas and organizes them), the process of spelling (which graphemes are used to represent which sounds), the process of communication (for what purpose is language used), and the process of reading (how is context used, which experiential information is brought to the task, and so on). The more independent learning is going on in the classroom, the more opportunity the teacher has to observe individuals, to have individual conferences, and to gain insights into how students come to know things. Current research tells us much about learning processes, and teachers can learn to observe these processes. And these observations can lead to more personalized instruction.

Diagnostic Teaching and Assessment

In a whole-language program the distinction between teaching and testing is often blurred. Attempting to teach something is one of the best ways of determining what is understood and what is not understood by the student and the teacher. This is a welcome development since evidence about common teaching practices indicates that most classroom time is spent in managing students' interaction, giving assignments, or marking work rather than teaching whatever was intended. In one case (Durkin, 1978–79, p. 520) the author concluded that "practically no comprehension instruction was seen" in social studies lessons in grades 3 to 6. A more recent study (Wendler, Samuels, and Moore, 1989) found that teachers who use basal readers used only about one-third of their classroom reading time in comprehension instruction. Teachers most often give reading assignments and test comprehension; they dictate spelling lists and correct them; they assign topics and grade compositions. Much testing is done but relatively little time is spent in teaching.

The classroom teacher should spend a considerable portion of classroom time in modeling language (i.e., writing, reading, speaking, listening). In the simplest form, "thinking aloud" by the teacher is useful in explaining the language processes, especially since they can only be observed indirectly (one cannot see what a person does when he or she reads, for instance). A procedure known as *reciprocal teaching* (Palincar and Brown, 1984) involves teachers and students alternately taking these roles. Peer-tutoring is also effective since the "teacher" and the "student" have much more empathy for each other and understand each other's explanations better. Group work allows students to observe others and to learn collaboratively.

Teacher Assessment versus Standardized Measures

The most important information about whole-language programs must come from teacher observation, assessment, and evaluation since most standardized tests (California Test of Basic Skills, for example) are product measures based on the skills model. In fact, Gardner (1991, p. 132) noted, "The test is the ultimate scholastic invention, a 'decontextualized measure' to be employed in a setting that is itself decontextualized." Teachers need to know whether students do read independently, whether they have confidence in tackling new work (even at the risk of failure at times), what sort of ideas they have for writing and discussion, and whether they can realistically assess their school work. Standardized tests cannot answer such questions and they are not designed to do so. Teachers also know best the local objectives of language arts instruction and should restrict assessment to them. Finally, most assessment should be diagnostic; that is, the teacher should learn something about individuals (Froese, 1991). Information about the "group" or "class" as produced by standardized tests is only incidentally useful for the teacher since it is not specific, teaching-related information. For example, a percentile rank, stanine, or grade-equivalent score on a standardized group test does not give the teacher any information about what he or she should teach to individuals. Such information may be useful, however, to school boards in providing a measure of accountability to parents and taxpayers, provided that the tests actually reflect what is on the curriculum.

Assessment over Time

Much testing is of the "one-shot" type. That is, the teacher grades the handwriting, the composition, or the reading at one moment in time and then draws various conclusions from the results. Many authorities warn teachers against overgeneralizing from such results since learning is dynamic and often goes in spurts. As a result it is wiser to gather multiple measures of student achievement over the span of the school year and at various points of the process. The Canadian Council of Teachers of English in their policy (CCTE, 1985) suggested that "several samples of work from early draft to final product, a selection of the student's best representative work, and perhaps some of the student's experimental efforts in a variety of modes" be gathered. A joint IRA/NCTE publication (IRA/NCTE, 1989, p. 24) stated, "We know that we learn about our students over time by mentally and physically keeping track of their learning as we interact with them in the classroom." A number of techniques, such as keeping portfolios, lend themselves to gathering longitudinal data. For example, it is easy to file a sample of a student's handwriting every other month; to have students evaluate their own participation in oral-language activities; or to keep an audiotape of an individual's reading over the year. This type of cumulative record of activity is now often referred to as **portfolio assessment** (Valencia et al., 1989; Jongsma, 1989). Even an inexperienced observer can note differences in the development of most language activities and hence portfolios become particularly useful in teacher/student/parent conferences.

It is predicted that in California a majority of public school students will be Hispanic in the early part of the twenty-first century. In Vancouver, British Columbia, over one-half of the current school population consists of English-as-a-second-language (ESL) students, and because of Canada's two official languages, a significant portion of students study French as a second or third language. Furthermore, immigration into the United States and Canada, especially from Asia-Pacific regions, is having a profound effect on our populations. Cultural and linguistic diversity is no longer an exception, and the meaning of the term *language minority* may need modification.

As multilingualism is studied more carefully, the "deficit" or "subtractive" language learning models are giving way to "additive" models (Swain and Lapkin, 1991). Definitions of *literacy* are beginning to recognize the need to consider competency in languages other than English (McKay, 1993). And when broader assessment techniques are used, language-minority students show proficiency and interest in learning that was overlooked before (Miramontes and Commins, 1991). As Au (1994, p. 103) indicates, "The whole language movement along with growing evidence of the negative consequences for students and teachers associated with conventional standardized testing have made the development of alternative systems of assessment and evaluation more urgent." She consequently developed a portfolio assessment system for native Hawaiian students.

Chapman and Froese (1994) concluded after reviewing the research on literacy that "the curriculum must be inclusive of all learners, acknowledging the complexity of cultural and linguistic diversity and the need for adaptations to fit all learners."

Multiple Literacies

Increasingly it is being recognized that there is no such a thing as a generic level of literacy. One often hears that a student reads at the fourth-grade level, for example. The problem with such statements is that one does not know the context under which such reading occurred, what sort of materials were being read, or on what basis it was decided that the reading was "fourth grade." It is well known that motivation can overcome readability difficulties, and that people can be exceedingly competent in one area (computers and reading computer manuals, for example) but not in another (cookbooks, for example). A student may excel in mathematics but be incompetent in social studies. Such inconsistencies have been noticed in other subject areas as well.

From a cognitive psychology perspective it has been argued by Gardner (1991, pp. 11–12) that "students possess different kinds of minds and therefore learn, remember, perform, and understand in different ways," and "these differences challenge an educational system that assumes that everyone can learn the same materials in the same way and that a uniform, universal measure suffices to test student learning." Newer, more holistic testing and assessment theory, of course, recognizes these matters and is beginning to supply some pragmatic ways of addressing the problem (Raven, 1992). Literacy is no longer thought of as simply reading and writing. The context in which literacy is practiced must be considered, the type of text being processed must be considered, and the processes brought to bear on the task must be taken into account (for example, reasoning and computation). It is common to hear people talk about "computer literacy," "math literacy," and so on.

Diversity in Learning

As is implied by the quotation in the previous paragraph, educators must begin to find measures that are sensitive to diversity in learning rather than uniformity. In mathematics, for example, teachers generally allow different solutions to the same problem; in reading it is known that boys and girls have different interests. Traditional testing rarely takes into account such differences; it focuses on the correct answer or on a common vocabulary. Heath (1991, p. 20) clearly pointed out that "the challenge in research and teacher education is twofold: 1. to learn more about alternative and expanded genres of language and patterns of learning across cultures and situations; and 2. to enable teachers to observe, analyze, and consider the implications of alternative ways of learning and displaying knowledge in classrooms." Good observation techniques go a long way to allow the documentation of such differences.

Collaborative Learning

Traditionally, learning has been considered a solitary activity and most models of language learning do not include the function of peers or the teacher. However, Froese (1991) has shown how both other students and teachers contribute to the learning process. There are several reasons for this change of thinking. First, constructivist models of teaching indicate that teachers need to engage students in mental activities so that they can construct knowledge themselves. Often this is accomplished through discussion and responding to text. Second, if students are to go beyond "receiving knowledge to critiquing and creating it" they must interact with other students or adults (Heath, 1991, p. 21). Since peers and the teacher are always part of the school environment, it is essential that their role in learning is understood, valued, and planned.

Evaluation versus Assessment

Until now, the term *assessment* has primarily been used, but occasionally *evaluation* has also been mentioned. Although in many contexts these terms are used interchangeably, the Evaluation Policy of the Canadian Council of Teachers of English (1985) has made distinctions between these two terms:

> **Assessment** *is defined as the process or set of activities by which information is gathered so that an evaluation can be made, and* **evaluation** *is defined as the activity of making a judgement about worth or value, making a judgement whether performance or program is satisfactory, and observations or decisions based upon such judgement.*

This differentiation, although not held universally, is nevertheless useful since the teacher normally assesses a great deal more material than is evaluated. For example, the teacher may require that student journals be handed in every week, but they do not receive marks, grades, or feedback; this is a form of assessment. If the teacher writes comments back to the student, that would be evaluation since some judgment of performance was made.

Classroom Applications

A whole-language approach to assessment should center on the use of language for communication purposes in as realistic situations as are possible to arrange in the classroom. For the most part, assessment should inform instruction; in that context it is known as *formative evaluation*. When used for ranking or grading, it is known as *summative evaluation*. Both types are necessary in most school situations. At times the assessment instruments used for these purposes are different: a composition is the summative evaluation material, whereas a series of topic outlines might be the basis of a formative assessment. At other times the instrument may be the same but the manner in which the results are used is different. For example, a cloze test (a passage in which several words are deleted) could be used as a formative instrument—students could be asked to supply several synonyms for the deleted word. Or it could be used as a summative tool—the percentage of exact replications could be used as an indicator of passage difficulty. In other words, the purpose for which an instrument is used may determine the form and manner in which it is scored.

A Framework for Assessment and Evaluation

An experienced teacher reading this chapter in the first edition commented that new teachers would require a more structured and formal approach to assess students' progress. Since the author had presented a more detailed approach as part of the teacher education program, it is included here. This approach suggests three dimensions—the who, the how, and the what—to consider when planning an assessment and evaluation program. It is not a static model since each of the dimensions may be extended when required (to be explained later in this section).

Who Should Do the Assessment and Evaluation?

As has been described in earlier chapters, in a whole-language program students do far too much work for the teacher to be able to evaluate it all, so students must be brought into the process. The teacher is responsible for overall classroom evaluation, but that does not mean that the teacher should do all the evaluation. It is suggested here (see Figures 12.1 and 12.2) that a variety of activities involve the teacher, the student, peers, a combination of student and teacher, and a combination of student, teacher, and parent. Undoubtedly other combinations and extensions are possible; this is how the model is extended on this dimension.

The functions of *teachers* are perhaps best known since traditionally they do most of the assessment and evaluation. It has been previously suggested that the teacher must learn to be a good observer, but in order to have observation time students must be given opportunity to work independently at engaging tasks. The teacher should also have the training to be able to analyze students' work (compositions, oral reading, and so on) and base individual, small-group and large-group instruction on these analyses. Often checklists and rating scales are devised for such purposes, or ready-made ones are adapted (B.C. Primary Teachers' Association, 1992; *Making the Grade*, 1987). Anecdotal comments about individuals' learning processes or responses to a task may be recorded on stick-on notes and placed in the teacher's daybook for later review. Naturally, the teacher will make up quizzes and tests on units of activity, and at certain times administer formal tests for the school division or the state ministry of education.

Students play an important part in the assessment and evaluation process. Since self-assessment is encouraged, students are given the opportunity to evaluate their own work in light of criteria developed with the help of the teacher. For example, after a brief discussion of some handwriting samples, students can usually list the major components and rate their own handwriting according to these same criteria. This can be repeated several times over the span of a year together with personal goals for improvement. The student/ teacher conference can often be used to let the student set goals for a variety of tasks. Most work can be copyedited by other students or peers before being submitted to the teacher or parents, or posted on the bulletin board for public viewing. Observation sheets or checklists can be jointly developed for many activities such as oral presentations, group discussion, and so on. The byproducts of *peer evaluation* are many—students develop and learn evaluation criteria, they get personal tutoring from

FIGURE 12.1   *The Dimensions of Evaluation*

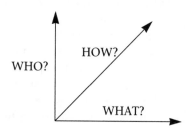

someone who sees the problem in a similar way, and they avoid the embarrassment of submitting work with mechanical mistakes. It is also becoming common to find student-led parent/teacher conferences in which the student is intimately involved in preparing for the conference and conducting it.

Increasingly, parents are becoming more involved in the assessment and evaluation process. Some schools even send home information request forms for parents to fill out. Others provide observation forms for the parent to observe the various strategies, interests, abilities, and learning needs of the student in the home setting. These are helpful in focusing parent/teacher/student interviews later on and also have inherent values independent of the conference. Parents feel more involved in the learning of their children, they learn more about the language abilities of their children, and they convey a sense of importance of education to their children. All three sets of participants can be involved in evaluating the conference.

To review, teachers, parents, peers, and students are all involved in assessment and evaluation. This forms one dimension of the program, and explains *Who* does the assessment and evaluation. It would be easy to extend this dimension by involving other people, perhaps the principal or students from another grade.

How Is Information Gathered?

Although there are many ways to classify information gathering, Cooper (1986, pp. 364–365) has suggested four main techniques used by teachers. These categories are useful for the second dimension of the assessment and evaluation approach recommended in this chapter. One category referred to as **inquiry** answers the question: What are the opinions, feelings, interests, likes, and dislikes of the student? These are the affective and conative aspects of learning mentioned earlier in this chapter. Use of interest inventories, self-evaluation checklists, and opinion ratings constitute information gathered through inquiry.

A second category, **observation,** might answer the questions: What have students accomplished? What strategies have they used to learn? and How do they get along with other students? These questions get at more cognitive products, processes, and interactions and may be somewhat more objectively observed. Anecdotal records, miscue analysis, oral presentation checklists, and group discussion evaluations are examples of this type of information gathering.

Analysis is the third category and answers the questions: What are the components of this task and which students understand each component? Which students do not understand particular components and will need to be taught them? The usual procedure is to gather samples of work, list the components involved, and under each component check off each student's accomplishments. This results in a class profile that may be used as a basis for further teaching, either individually, in groups, or with the whole class.

A fourth category of techniques may be referred to as **testing.** The questions for this category are: How does an individual respond to a task required of the group? How does the individual respond in comparison to others in the group? Most traditional tests, whether norm based or criterion based, formal or informal, are of this type. In norm based tests, scores are compared to a group average; in criterion-based tests, scores are compared to a preset standard. Most standards, such as interpreting over 50% as a pass, are completely arbitrary and often misleading since it is easy to make tests in which no one gets over 50% or everyone gets over 50%. Examples of tests are a word list that everyone is asked to pronounce or match with a meaning. In cloze tests students are asked to predict which word was omitted. In subject-specific tests students are often asked to demonstrate knowledge of strategies, facts, or sources of information.

While inquiry, observation, analysis, and testing are the major ways in which teachers classify information gathered about students, others may exist or be discovered. These would form the basis for extending this dimension of the model of assessment and evaluation described here.

What Is Being Assessed or Evaluated?

Because this is a whole-language textbook, the focus is on language assessment and evaluation. Traditionally the language arts included reading, writing, speaking, and listening, but more recently it has become common to add viewing, responding, and thinking; knowledge of children's or young people's literature is also included. Because opinions of what constitutes literacy are expanding, so will the number of elements in this category. Hence this dimension must be considered in the model.

While it is difficult to make a comprehensive list of the components of language arts, examples are given for illustrative purposes. **Reading** typically includes information about sound/symbol relationships, word meanings, word analysis, comprehension strategies, study skills, reading in the content areas, and literature. **Writing** or composition includes information about process writing (gathering information, organization, drafting, revision, proofreading, recopying, publishing), language conventions and usage, grammar, and study of various genres (narrative, description, expository, poetry, essays, reports, letters, and so on). Less attention is paid to spelling, handwriting, or word processing. Occasionally some language history is included. **Speaking** usually refers to oral language, its use, and function. Sometimes it is extended to choral speaking, story telling, dramatization, and oral reading. In secondary schools formal speech making is studied as well. **Listening** is even less familiar to most teachers. Often the same skills as listed for reading are used but with tapes, videos, or live talk. It is recognized that a variety of nonlinguistic features such as enthusiasm, gesticulation, and content affect communication through listening. Since speaking and listening work together in most social situations it is now likely that they will be discussed under "talk" in many books and journals (see also Chapter 3, Talk in Whole-Language Classrooms). Since so much of students' daily lives are taken up with watching television, seeing advertising, and other visual material, *viewing* is often dealt with in the language arts curriculum.

In short, this third dimension in the assessment and evaluation approach is composed of the language arts. The examples are provided so you may get an idea of the elements currently included.

How Is the Model Used?

The model provides the new teacher with a basis from which to form a fairly comprehensive assessment and evaluation program. If the three dimensions are understood (see Figures 12.1 and 12.2), then the teacher may devise examples of techniques in each of the major categories—the *Who*, the *How*, and

FIGURE 12.2   *A Model for Classroom Assessment and Evaluation*

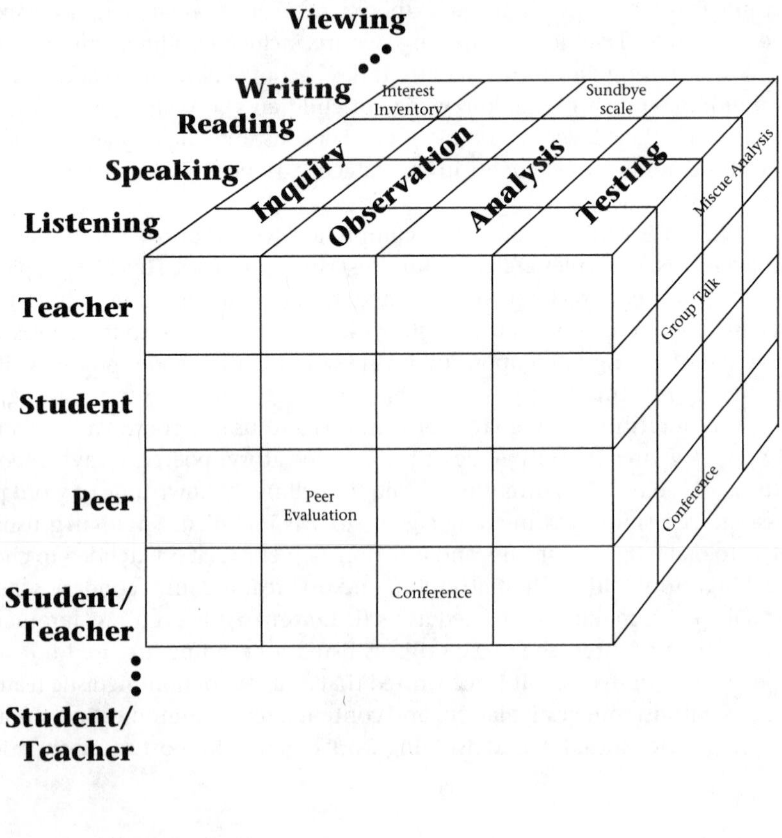

the *What*. In the following section, examples of some of the cells labeled in Figure 12.2 are provided. The teacher may intuitively construct other tasks by asking what sort of measures would fall in specific cells.

Assessment and Evaluation Techniques

The following classroom techniques are presented under four categories: listening, speaking, reading, and writing. One could easily criticize this approach as fragmenting the language arts, but it is done to assist the teacher to better understand the major purpose for using each technique. In fact, in almost every example, several language skills or processes are involved (e.g., talk and listening almost always occur together; writing and reading almost always do so as well) and no attempt has been made to isolate them. *The intent is to provide the prospective teacher with examples of the types of assessment that are possible.* First, some holistic, formative approaches will be presented; second, some methods of arriving at summative results useful for grading will be discussed; and where appropriate, observational techniques or record-keeping hints will be suggested. These assessment techniques could also be classified in terms of the size of the group—individual assessment, group assessment, whole-class assessment—or in terms of the locus of control—teacher centered, student centered, or cooperative (i.e., joint student/teacher decision). The intent here is to provide examples only; several volumes would be required for a comprehensive treatment of assessment. Following, then, are examples of holistic assessment techniques; the more they represent real communication situations (i.e., for a real purpose; to achieve some important task), the more valid they are.

Listening

Dictation and Transcription

This form of assessment has been little used recently though before photocopiers, it was very common. This is a useful global assessment technique but it should not be overused (that is, to waste classroom time because something has not been duplicated). Moffett and Wagner (1983, p. 490) referred to it as "writing without composing." They suggested taking dictations from classmates, acting as a scribe for the group (as in the DRTA procedure), taping ideas and then transcribing them, and taking down live speech (very difficult and recommended only for older students or done with use of a tape recorder). This may be a dyadic situation or a small- or large-group activity.

Retelling

Story retelling is a simple procedure that may be used on an individual basis or in a peer situation. This could be described as a speaking or listening activity; it depends on who does what. In contrast to the transcription task, it is reproducing a story without composing or decoding, and, on an individual basis, it can be used with young children.

The teacher prepares a retelling guide (a list of the major ideas in a story), the story is read to students as a group, and individuals "retell" the story either to a teacher's aide, to the teacher, or to another student. Ideally, the retelling should be to another person who has not previously heard the story (the best reason for telling a story) but that is not always possible in the classroom setting. As can be easily discerned, this task is a global one, using oral language, listening, memory, and personal experience. It allows the teacher to observe whether the student has a sense of text or story structure; that is, whether or not the main elements of a story (such as setting, initiating events, actions and reactions, and outcomes) are known.

Wilkinson Framework

This technique described by Wilkinson and his colleagues (1974, p. 66) is a useful framework for analyzing almost any listening situation. In its simplest form six questions are asked: "Who communicates what to whom, how and why, and on what occasion?" This task goes considerably beyond verbal ability—it requires students to draw on personal experience, infer the reason for the verbal exchange, speculate on the nature of the message, and guess at a setting. In short, it requires the comprehension of language in order to understand the communication act.

To initiate this procedure some pieces of real-language communication such as the following are required:

- Television or radio advertisements
- Recorded speeches (but avoid written speech read aloud)
- Recordings of class discussions or debates
- Live sportscasts
- Tapes from Grouptalk or DRTA activities (described elsewhere)

The group or class listens to these real-language situations and then individuals or groups discuss the following types of questions based on the six questions:

- **Who?**
  Who was the speaker (name, job, position, etc.)?
  What personal information do we know about the speaker?
  What do we know about the education and age of the speaker?
  What do we know about the nationality, ethnic origin, or race of the speaker?

- **What?**

  Is the speaker presenting facts, opinion, point of view?

  Is the speaker instructing, demonstrating, arguing?

  Is the speaker serious, tongue-in-cheek, etc.?

  Can the "rank" or "role" of the speaker and the audience be determined?

- **To whom?**

  Is the language suitable to occasion or audience?

  Is there an age gap (or generation gap!) between speaker and listener?

  What does the tone of voice tell us about how the speaker perceives the listener?

  If a live or television source is used, what does the body language of the speaker tell us?

- **Why?**

  What is the obvious purpose of the message?

  What is the interpreted intention?

  What is the effect of the message?

  Why is this form of address used (e.g., lecture, discussion, etc.)?

- **What occasion?**

  What is the setting in which this communication is taking place?

  What is the occasion?

  Is it an isolated event, part of a series, a celebration?

  What nonlinguistic information is accompanying the situation (e.g., handshake, gestures, long pause, etc.)?

- **How?**

  What are the speaker's facial expressions indicating?

  Does the tone of voice indicate worry, playfulness, joking?

  Is the speaker nervous or self-assured?

As can be seen, this technique can lead to a chain of communication acts—listening, speaking, writing, reading—and can simultaneously be a teaching and an assessment tool.

Speaking and Oral Language Assessment

Grouptalk

One of the most useful techniques for the teacher is Grouptalk (Whipple, 1975). It is usable at all grade levels for organizing students into workable small groups for the purpose of using language productively. Although several sessions are usually required to establish the procedure, it is well worth it since once established, it may be used for discussion purposes as well (in social studies, science, and so on).

Procedurally, the teacher divides the class into groups of about five to seven students, each group requiring a tape recorder and blank tape. Prior to the actual session, the teacher should also prepare key discussion questions written on a card large enough so that everyone in the group may see it. Groups need not have the same questions. A student leader may be appointed to hold up the question and to regulate the discussion. The actual "rules" of Grouptalk may be written on a larger class chart—starting rules, discussion rules, and ending rules (described below). It is a good idea to set a time limit of 10 to 20 minutes for the main discussion (depending on the age of the students).

The session begins by students in each group turning on the tape recorder and reading the question and clarifying any words that may not be clear or that may be ambiguous. Then they are instructed to tell others what they think the question means. The group should decide on one meaning before starting to answer the question itself. Personal experience suggests that the teacher may wish to insist that every student be required to answer during this round.

Next, the discussion proper proceeds. Some suggestions to give to students might be to stick to the topic, each contribute, listen to others, and respond to what others have said. This is the main part of the Grouptalk, providing the opportunity for each student to offer responses to the question and to be challenged by the responses of others.

To end the session, the teacher notifies the group that it is time to sum up—to try to remember the main ideas discussed. When this is done, the tape is played back and the group evaluates whether the members have followed the Grouptalk rules.

In all of this the teacher has been an observer and troubleshooter rather than a participant. Students have used oral language in a real communication situation; they have focused on controlling the discussion; and they have learned to evaluate the quality of the discussion. This is important to the teacher since eventually the groups should become self-sustaining so that the teacher may use this opportunity to observe individuals and to make notations about aspects that cause difficulties. An index card for each student should be used to keep records.

Inner-Outer Circle

The inner-outer circle procedure is a very flexible one that can be used as a follow-up exercise to something read, or with a discussion topic that is assigned directly. It helps students to understand what happens during communication and how discussion is used to achieve some purpose. A small inner circle discusses the assigned topic while the outer circle observes and evaluates the discussion using an appropriate checklist such as the following (based on Knowles, 1983, p. 236):

- Who seems really to be interested in the subject being discussed?
- What sorts of interesting words, figures of speech, and so on, are being used?

- Are the suggestions being offered good ones?
- Do individuals listen to each other's responses or is there repetition of the same information?
- Are students communicating thoughts and feelings (i.e., personal responses) rather than only what is expected?

Directed Reading-Thinking Activity

The directed reading-thinking activity (DRTA) shifts attention away from the teacher and to the students in terms of setting realistic purposes for reading. The procedure is patterned after Stauffer's (1975) reading-thinking process. Students need an essay, story, or content area piece that is several pages long. The text should be analyzed for natural segments or breaks where students will interrupt the reading and brainstorm for questions. Small groups are designated and a group recorder (one who writes down the questions) is assigned. Since the recorder role is rotated, each student will eventually have a turn.

The students in the group examine the title of the piece and make predictions about what might follow. These predictions are written down by the recorder so that after actual reading of the first segment, the predictions may be checked for accuracy. This procedure is followed for each segment of the text.

Next, the text is read individually by students (or possibly by the teacher for younger children) and a discussion follows as to which predictions were confirmed, which ones were not, and the reasons for these findings. Then, predictions for the next segment of text are suggested and recorded, the next segment is read, and a discussion follows. This is repeated until the selection is completed.

The role of the teacher is to keep the discussion moving by asking general, noncuing questions such as: "What do you think will happen? Why do you think so?" The teacher might also use a checklist (adapted) as suggested by Gillet and Temple (1982) while observing the DRTA in action. Each student could be rated under the categories of usually, occasionally, or rarely on the following issues:

Offers spontaneous predictions

Participates willingly

Makes logical predictions

Changes predictions if warranted

Explains predictions

Uses both literal and experiential information

Is tolerant to other points of view

Can locate information in the text

Uses adjunct aids (pictures, charts, headings)

Uses context to analyze vocabulary

This list could be expanded to include other items, or the teacher might look for fewer specific items in order to get some information about each student in the group

Reading Process Assessment

Oral Reading and Miscue Analysis

While it is not possible to observe much about the silent reading process (except head movement and vocalizations, both of which are not desirable), oral reading does allow the teacher to monitor the types of processing strategies used by the reader. Normally this is an individual assessment but in a group situation the teacher can use observation based on these questions to assist readers.

Moffett and Wagner (1983, p. 461) suggested questions such as the following ones:

> Which kinds of mistakes are corrected? Are they important to meaning?
>
> Which substitutions seem to constitute "reading into the text," subjective expectancies, preoccupations, or stereotypes?
>
> Is the reader involved or is the reading mechanical?
>
> Do phrasing and intonation fit the sense as well as the syntax and punctuation?
>
> Which elements of the text are ignored (word endings, punctuation, headings, phrases, phonemes, etc.)?
>
> Which combinations of sound-spellings trip up the reader (blends, vowel-consonant combinations, polysyllabic words)?

A much more comprehensive system for analyzing oral reading known as *miscue analysis* has been developed by Goodman and Burke (1972) but it is much too time consuming for the classroom teacher and requires considerable training and experience to interpret the results into classroom practice. A full-scale miscue analysis is therefore normally left to the learning assistance teacher or reading clinician, but aspects of the *Reading Miscue Inventory: Alternate Procedures* (Goodman, Watson, and Burke, 1987) are useful in raising important questions about reading for the classroom teacher.

Cloze Tests

These tests are suitable for whole-class use and are based on the psychological principle of "closure"—the tendency to complete incomplete things according to expectations. The unusual spelling *cloze* was coined as a distinctive term for tests based on the closure idea. A variety of cloze tests have been devised that assess language comprehension in general, but specific versions assess more specific things such as pronoun reference, concepts, or transitional relationships. A few types of cloze tests are described here.

Every Fifth Word Deletion   A passage of approximately 250 words (shorter for primary grades) is selected for adaptation. The first sentence is left intact but beginning with the second sentence, every fifth word is deleted and replaced by a blank of equal length (about 10 spaces) until about 50 words have been deleted. The last sentence, ideally, will be left intact as well. The student is then asked to write in the words that have been deleted. This is a difficult task and most students will get only about half of them correct. In fact, if they score between 44% and 57% correct (exact replications) one can say that the passage is at their instructional level—about right for instruction with the teacher's assistance. To make the task somewhat easier the deleted words are often scrambled at the bottom of the page, but the preceding scoring criterion should not be applied to modified cloze procedures.

Maze Cloze   This is a highly modified cloze procedure (Guthrie et al., 1974) that deletes nouns and verbs only. In the place of each deletion, three alternative responses are provided. One is the correct answer, one is a word of the same part of speech but with a different meaning, and one is a word of a different part of speech and of a different meaning.

> *Example:* One of his friends tore his
>
> a. rug
>
> b. jeans
>
> c. shiny
>
> on the fence.

This type of cloze is suitable for the primary grades but may be used at other levels as well.

Oral Cloze or Zip Cloze   A text is selected at a level appropriate for students, it is written on an overhead transparency with a permanent marker, and the target words are covered with masking tape. The teacher instructs the class members or group to read over the projected passage for general impression. Then it is reread with the class. Finally, the covered words are predicted and the tape "zipped" off for immediate feedback (Aulls, 1982).

Other forms of cloze tests delete only pronouns, others provide for synonyms to be inserted, and still others delete every tenth word (usually content-area materials). Most forms can be used for teaching or for testing. If used for testing, the exact procedures should be followed; if used for teaching, any adaptation is permissible.

Readiness for Conference—Student Self-Evaluation

Students are able to assess what they have been doing, and will improve in this process if given the opportunity. The following form may be distributed to students who are preparing for a conference (see also Hunt, 1967). They may either write the answers or prepare to discuss them with the teacher.

Instruction to Student

You should select something that you have read, and think about the following questions before meeting with your teacher in an individual conference.

A. Suitability of Book/Story
    1. Why did I choose this book or story?
    2. What made the writing hard or easy to understand?
    3. Did I have to force myself to finish it?
    4. Was it a good choice?

B. Appreciation
    1. What made this a good or poor choice?
    2. How would I compare it to other books/stories I have read?
    3. Would I read other books on the same theme or by the same author?
    4. Would I want to share this book with someone else in the class?

C. Response to Book/Story Ideas
    1. Did something happen in the book that I would like (or not like) to happen to me?
    2. Did I learn something from the book?
    3. What were the high points in the book for me?
    4. How real/fanciful was the writing?

Assessment of Writing and Composing

Although the terms *writing* and *composing* are often used carelessly and interchangeably, they are not the same thing, but they are related. Composing is the act of arranging and organizing ideas that form the basis of a composition—an essay, paragraph, poem, and so on. Composing may be done orally or in note form and may be done effectively alone or in small groups. Writing, on the other hand, denotes the actual recording of the composition and involves spelling, the development of sentences and paragraphs, editing, revising, proofreading, and handwriting or typing. Although one usually expects individually produced composition, many aspects—especially editing and proofreading—are best done with a partner or in small groups. Formative assessment of composing and writing must to some extent focus on the process; summative assessment

Group writing conferences allow the teacher to meet with more students. Such conferences are particularly appropriate ways to assess group writing projects.

often rests entirely on the product, a marked composition. The latter is not actually necessary since a final grade could well take into account a variety of items as are described in the next technique—the writing folder.

Writing Folders

Graves (1983, pp. 307–308) has very ably outlined how a writing folder assists both the teacher and the student in record keeping and assessment. The folder is not a static method of assessment and must change with changing needs. A writing folder could initially hold the following information:

> Side 1: Records of dates when each piece of writing was begun and was completed
>
> Side 2: A collection of topics of interest to the writer
>
> Side 3: A record of mastered writing and composing skills
>
> Side 4: A list of the writer's areas of expertise
>
> Side 5: Contents of writing conferences
>
> Side 6: Records of tests—dictation, pretests, etc.

Writing folders are available from many commercial sources or can be manufactured by students.

Since the purpose of record keeping and assessment is at least in part to assist the student in the process of writing, information must be meaningful to be retained. Therefore, the various sides of the folder will be changed over time to meet the student's demands. Writing folders naturally show the progress of the student and are useful to the teacher in assigning grades, if required, and for parent/teacher interviews. The ideas presented here could become part of a portfolio (described later in this chapter).

Holistic Scoring

Holistic or impressionistic scoring is a quick and reliable way of marking many papers, but it does require several individuals to mark the same paper. The most practical method is for several teachers to get together and mark each other's papers. Since very little time is required per paper, the total time required is no more than marking one set of papers independently in the normal way. Cooper and Odell (1977) suggested that holistic marking may accomplish one of several aims: papers may be matched to criterial sets of papers (good, average, poor), papers may be scored for certain features important to a particular kind of writing, or papers may be graded (using letter grades or numbers).

In one assessment program, the following five-point holistic marking scale was used:

  5 = Highly impressive—well above average in thought, sentence structure, and word choice; mostly free from error

  4 = Commendable—in command of thought, sentence structure, and word choice; relatively free from error

  3 = Questionable—probably functional in terms of thought, sentence structure, and word choice, but in need of instruction

  2 = Minimal—in need of remediation; frustration level

  1 = Insufficient material

Such grading is quick—approximately two minutes per paper—and is intended to provide general feedback to the writer. When at least three markers are used, the scoring is quite reliable.

A more detailed Descriptive Marking Scale (Manitoba Department of Education, 1979), designed for the scoring of third-grade papers, contained the following points. Such scales for older students would be modified slightly to include variety in sentence patterns, usage, and so on.

  Objectives

  A. Focus on topic
       4 = Ideas relate to topic
       3 = Fluctuation but focus is on topic

        2 = Deviates from topic
        1 = Insufficient evidence

B. Middle and ending
        4 = Includes appropriate middle and ending
        3 = Lacks one element
        2 = Lacks more than one element
        1 = Insufficient evidence

C. Organized by time (verb tense and sequence of events)
        4 = Ideas appropriately organized by time
        3 = Error in organizing by time (1 error)
        2 = Error in organizing by time (1+ errors)
        1 = Insufficient evidence

D. Descriptive words and phrases
        4 = Use of descriptive words and phrases to create impact
        3 = Word choice ordinary and functional
        2 = Insufficient use of vocabulary indicated
        1 = Insufficient evidence

E. Topic development (communicates feelings, creative)
        4 = Originality of ideas creates impact
        3 = Ideas ordinary and functional
        2 = Insufficient number of ideas
        1 = Insufficient evidence

F. Complete sentences
        4 = Writes complete sentences (no errors)
        3 = Error in writing complete sentences (1 or 2 errors)
        2 = Error in writing complete sentences (more than 2)
        1 = Insufficient evidence

G. Sentence structure
        4 = Varies sentence lengths and patterns to create impact
        3 = Varies sentence lengths and patterns but doesn't create impact
        2 = Does not use varying sentence lengths and patterns
        1 = Insufficient evidence

H. Punctuation and capitalization
        4 = Capitalizes and punctuates correctly (0–2 errors)
        3 = Errors in capitalization and punctuation (3–4 errors)
        2 = Errors in capitalization and punctuation (more than 4 errors)
        1 = Insufficient evidence

I. Spelling
        4 = Spelling attracts little or no attention
        3 = Several errors that do not detract from impact
        2 = Errors detract from readability and impression
        1 = Insufficient evidence

Handwriting: Student Self-Evaluation

The teacher may wish to put a range of handwriting examples on an overhead transparency and discuss the various aspects with students. Most of the features on the following form will come up in such a discussion. Students should complete a form at bimonthly intervals—beginning in October and following through in December, February, April, and June, for example—and file them in a folder. Previous forms should be referred to for evidence of progress and for setting new goals.

Student Self-Evaluation Form

1. Slant—Is the slant of the writing the same throughout?
_____

2. Spacing—Does the spacing between letters and words look even?
_____

3. Size—Are the small letters and tall letters even?
_____

4. Alignment—Does the writing sit on the line?
_____

5. Letter and Number Formation—Is it easy to tell one letter from another?
_____

6. Line Quality—Is the thickness of the strokes about the same throughout?
_____

Overall, how do you rate your writing sample?
Suggested scale: *5 = excellent*
                                 4 = good
                                 3 = average
                                 2 = fair
                                 1 = poor

Goal for next two months:
I will work on _____
_____
_____
_____

Sundbye Scale

A set of compositions from a small group were examined by a third-grade teacher to see which skills and strategies were being used by various students. This provided information to the teacher for subsequent lessons for particular students—a form of diagnostic teaching. (See Sundbye, 1973, for details.)

Example: Evaluation of a third-grade writing assignment

Students Uses	Derek	Robert	Leslie	Kenton	Darren
1. *Complete sentence*	yes	sometimes	sometimes	yes	no
2. *Capital letters*	yes	yes	mostly	yes	yes
3. *Periods/Question mark*	mostly	sometimes	mostly	yes	no
4. *Related ideas*	yes	yes	yes	yes	yes
5. *Time sequence*	yes	yes	yes	yes	yes
6. *Modifier for n./v.*	sometimes	yes	sometimes	yes	no
7. *Title*	yes	yes	no	yes	yes
8. *Variety in sentences*	yes	yes	yes	yes	no
9. *Coordinators*	mostly	sometimes	no	yes	yes
10. *Sounds/rhythms* *of words*	yes	yes	yes	yes	no
11. *Third person*	yes	no	yes	no	no
12. *Imaginative ideas*	mostly	yes	mostly	yes	no

Yes = consistently uses; No = not at all; Usually; Occasionally.

Using Journals

The NCTE Commission on Composition has issued "Guidelines for Using Journals in School Settings" (Fulwiler, 1986), which contains the rationale for journals and guidelines for assigning them. Among the reasons for writing journals, logs, thinkbooks, or daybooks are (1) to help students find personal connections to the material they are studying in class and textbook; (2) to provide a place for students to think about, learn, and understand course material; (3) to collect observations, responses, and data; and (4) to allow students to practice their writing before handing it in to be graded. In language arts classes, journals are kept for students "to find and explore topics; to clarify, modify, and extend those topics; to try out different writing styles; to sharpen their powers of observation; to practice fluency; and in general to become more aware of themselves as writers" (Fulwiler, 1986, p. 6). The NCTE Guidelines also suggested that students be asked to write in journals in class, that something active be done with the writing (e.g., read to share, discuss, etc.), that journals be counted in some way but that they not be graded, and that the teacher respond to selected items only.

At first glance, journals appear to present a real paradox to assessment. They should be counted but not graded; they should be required but should not impinge on individual freedom. However, if the "educated person is one who is a thinking individual, capable of making independent decisions based on analysis and reason" (B.C. Ministry of Education, March 1987, p. 2), then the journal seems to be the ideal basis for evaluating those attributes.

Portfolio Assessment and Evaluation

Portfolios may provide the best single source of assessment and evaluation information. They are a true alternative to more traditional modes of assessment because they have authentic information, they contain examples of progress over time, they have many sources of information, and they allow input by teachers and students (Tierney, Carter, and Desai, 1991; Bintz and Harste, 1991; Johns and VanLeirsburg, 1991). Further, they allow both students and teachers to make value judgments and reflect on the contents. Portfolios may contain writing samples, drafts, outlines, lists of books read, audiotapes of oral reading, personal spelling words, photographs of projects, student self-assessments, journals, collaboratively produced work, checklists of things accomplished or progress made, reflections of what has been achieved, goals aimed for, and so on. Perhaps most important, decisions about what to include are made by the students as well as by the teacher after thorough discussion.

Because so much material is accumulated, it is important to systematically review the portfolio every few months or after each reporting period, make summative reports, discard information no longer needed (or allow the student to take it home), and collect new information to add to the portfolio. Naturally, portfolios are excellent sources of information for parent/student/teacher conferences.

A survey on portfolio use by the author indicated that more teachers were keeping portfolios than students. This is probably short-sighted since the managing of portfolios is much more valuable for the student, and besides it is more time effective to have students keep their own portfolios.

Grading

At the beginning of this chapter the purposes of assessment were discussed at some length. First, you were reminded that various aspects of the language arts curriculum were not necessarily equally important (handwriting and reading, for example) and hence any attempt at grading must take the relative weighting of such things into consideration. Second, the measures used must be related to what was taught; this gives the results validity. Third, not all marks need to be provided by the teacher; self-assessment or peer evaluation in some areas of the curriculum is encouraged.

When it comes to grading—giving numeric or letter summary scores—the teacher needs to gather a minimum of three or four scores for each major area on the report card each term. Naturally, in many areas (such as writing folders) there is more information than required, but in other areas (such as listening) only observational data may be available. It is best to check on a semi-monthly basis whether enough information necessary for grading purposes has been assembled. For those using anecdotal reporting methods it is best to keep a set of index cards for each child on which weekly entries are made about the progress of individuals in the language arts. Naturally, anecdotal information needs to be supplemented with other more systematically gathered data and examples of students' work.

Currently there is a lot of interest in developing standards known as *reference sets* or *indicators*. These are descriptions of benchmarks or anchors in achievement, often with examples of students work at different developmental levels. The teacher or student compares a particular achievement in a holistic way to the benchmarks to come up with an assessment. While benchmarks developed in different places are likely to vary according to local curricula and standards, an example from the 1991 Maryland School Performance Assessment (Kapinus, Collier, and Kruglanski, 1994, p. 261), provides a useful illustration (the example is Level 1 of five levels):

Level 1 (Grade 3 Reading)

Readers at Level 1 construct, extend, and examine the meaning of third-grade-appropriate texts by:

Building a complex understanding of the text

Making judgments, connections, and extensions of the text that are substantially supported

Explicitly connecting personal experience to the text and providing substantial text support for the connections

Making extensive inferences about the author's craft and purpose with substantial text support

It is possible that parents will find such ratings, along with knowledge about the percentage of students in each class reaching the various levels, as more informative than simple letter grades or percentile ranks. Farr (1993) reported that in some classes such performance assessments made up nearly half of each student's portfolio.

A massive project funded by the U.S. Department of Education was begun in 1992 (to be completed by 1995) to develop standards for the teaching and learning of English language arts. The project involves the International Reading Association, the National Council of Teachers of English, and the Center for the Study of Reading. While it is too early to tell what the outcome will be, the intent is to describe the "kinds of curriculum experiences in which all students ought to have an opportunity to participate" (Pearson, 1993, p. 462). The project is aimed at more general accountability standards, but the result will undoubtedly filter back to the classroom level, as indicated in the quotations beginning this chapter.

Summary

This chapter began with a discussion of the purposes of assessment—why people assess things, how the results of assessment should be considered, and who should do the assessing. Then some of the current major issues in assessment were identified. It was stressed that the methods of assessment should be consistent with the principles of whole-language instruction. Next, a framework for classroom assessment and evaluation was presented. Each of the three dimensions—the Who?, the How?, and the What? of assessment—were explained. Then, examples of assessment techniques were presented for each of the major areas of the language arts—speaking, listening, reading, and writing. Some of the techniques were teacher initiated, some involved peer activities, and some were self-assessment techniques. Portfolio assessment and evaluation was presented as an alternative approach to more traditional methods. Finally, a few pointers were advanced on preparing for the grading required by some schools.

A chapter such as this can give only a few examples of the types of assessment that are possible. Consult the appendix at the end of this chapter as well as other chapters in this book for further assessment ideas.

REFERENCES

Anthony, R. J., Johnson, T. D., Mickelson, N. I. & Preece, A. (1991). *Evaluating literacy: A perspective for change.* Portsmouth, NH: Heinemann.

Au, K. H. (1994). Portfolio assessment: Experiences at the Kamehameha elementary education program. In S. H. Valencia, E. H. Hiebert, & P. P. Afflerback (Eds.), *Authentic reading assessment: Practices and possibilities.* Newark, DE: International Reading Association.

Aulls, M. (1982). *Developing readers in today's elementary school.* Toronto: Allyn & Bacon.

Balajthy, E. (1989). The printout: Holistic approaches to reading. *The Reading Teacher, 42 (4)* 324. (Suggests appropriate software.)

Baskwill, J. & Whitman, P. (1988). *Evaluation: Whole language, whole child.* Toronto: Scholastic.

B. C. Primary Teachers' Association. (1992). *Evaluation techniques and resources book II.* Van-

couver, B. C.: B. C. Primary Teachers' Association & B. C. Teachers' Federation.

B. C. Ministry of Education. (1991). *The intermediate program: Learning in British Columbia.* Victoria, B.C.: B.C. Ministry of Education.

Berlak, H., Newman, F. M., Adams, E., Archbald, D. A., Burgess, T., Raven, J. & Romberg, T. A. (1992). *Toward a new science of educational testing and assessment.* Albany, NY: SUNY Press.

Bintz, W. P. & Harste, J. (1991). Whole language evaluation: Some grounded needs, wants, and desires. In C. B. Smith, (Ed.), *Alternative assessment of performance in the language arts: Proceedings* (pp. 83–97). Bloomington, IN: ERIC.

Braun, C. (1993). *Observing and assessing young readers: Looking, listening, and learning.* Winnipeg, Manitoba: Peguis Publishers.

Canadian Council of Teachers of English. (1985). *Evaluation Policy.*

Chapman, M. and Froese, V. (1994). Literacy research, curriculum and instruction. In T. Gambell, M. C. Courtland, (Eds.), *Curriculum planning in the language arts.* (pp. 350–378).Toronto: Captus Press.

Cooper, J. M. (Ed.). (1986). *Classroom teaching skills.* Toronto: DC Heath.

Cooper, R. C. & Odell, L. (1977). *Evaluating writing.* Urbana, IL: NCTE.

Curriculum Branch, B.C. Ministry of Education (March, 1987). *Curriculum goals and principles: A position paper.*

Davies, A., Cameron, C., Politano, C., and Gregory, K. (1992). *Together is better: Collaborative assessment, evaluation, & reporting.* Winnipeg, Manitoba: Peguis Publishers.

Durkin, D. (1978–79). What classroom observations reveal about reading comprehension instruction. *Reading Research Quarterly, 14 (4),* 481–533.

Elley, W. (1992). *How in the world do students read?* The Hague: International Association for the Evaluation of Educational Achievement.

Farr, R. (1993). Writing in response to reading: A process approach to literacy assessment. In B. E. Cullinan (Ed.), *Pen in hand: Children become writers.* Newark, DE: International Reading Association.

Flood, J. & Lapp, D. (1989). Reporting reading progress: A comparison portfolio for parents. *The Reading Teacher, 42 (7),* 508–514.

Froese, V. (1991). *A language approach to reading.* Scarborough, Ontario: Nelson Canada.

Froese, V. (1988a). Language assessment: What we do and what we should do! *Canadian Journal of English Language Arts, 11 (1),* 33–44.

Froese, V. (1988b). Provincial reading/language arts assessments and evaluation. *Reading-Canada-Lecture, 6, (3),* 167–175.

Fulwiler, T. (Ed.). (1986). *The journal book.* Portsmouth, NH: Boynton/Cook Publishers.

Gardner, H. (1991). *The unschooled mind: How children think and how schools should teach.* New York: Basic Books.

Gillet, J. W. & Temple, C. (1982). *Understanding reading problems: Assessment and instruction.* Boston: Little, Brown.

Glazer, S. M., Searfoss, L. W. & Gentile, L. M. (Eds.). (1988). *Reexamining reading diagnosis: New trends and procedures.* Newark, DE: International Reading Association.

Goodman, K. S., Goodman, Y. M. & Hood, W. J. (Eds.). (1989). *The whole language evaluation book.* Portsmouth, NH: Heinemann.

Goodman, Y., Watson, D. & Burke, C. (1987). *Reading miscue inventory: Alternate procedures.* New York: Richard C. Owen Publisher.

Goodman, Y. M. & Burke, C. L. (1972). *Reading miscue inventory.* London: Collier-Macmillan.

Graves, D. H. (1983). *Writing: Teachers and children at work.* Exeter, NH: Heinemann.

Guthrie, J., Seifert, M., Burnham, N. A. & Kaplan, R. I. (1974). The maze technique to assess, monitor reading comprehension. *The Reading Teacher, 28 (2),* 161–168.

Hammill, D. D. & McNutt, G. (1981). *The correlates of reading.* Austin, TX: Pro-Ed.

Heath, S. B. (1991). The sense of being literate: Historical and cross-cultural features. In R. Barr, M. L. Kamil, B. Mosenthat, & D. Pearson (Eds.), *Handbook of reading research: Volume II* (pp. 3–25). New York: Longman.

Hunt, L. C. (1967). Evaluation through teacher-pupil conferences. In T. C. Barrett (Ed.), *The evaluation of children's reading achievement.* Newark, DE: International Reading Association, 111–125.

International Reading Association and National Council of Teachers of English. (1989). *Cases in literacy: An agenda for discussion.* Newark, DE: International Reading Association/NCTE.

Irwin, J. W. & Baker, I. (1989). *Promoting active reading comprehension strategies.* Englewood Cliffs, NJ: Prentice-Hall.

Isaak, T. & Joseph, J. (1989). Reading technology: Authoring software and teaching reading. *The Reading Teacher, 43 (3),* 254–255.

Johns, J. L. & VanLeirsburg (1991). Portfolio Assessment: A survey among professionals. In

C. B. Smith, (Ed.), *Alternative assessment of performance in the language arts: Proceedings* (pp. 242–248). Bloomington, IN: ERIC.

Jongsma, K. S. (1989). Questions and answers: Portfolio assessment. *The Reading Teacher, 43 (3),* 264–265.

Kapinus, B. A., Collier, G. V. & Kruglanski, H. (1994). The Maryland school performance assessment program: A new view of assessment. In S. H. Valencia, E. H. Hiebert, & P. P. Afflerbach (Eds.), *Authentic reading assessment: Practices and possiblities* (pp. 255–276). Newark, DE: International Reading Association.

Knowles, L. (1983). *Encouraging talk.* Toronto: Methuen.

Loban, W. (1976). *Language development: Kindergarten through grade twelve.* Urbana, IL: NCTE, Frontispiece.

Manitoba Department of Education. (1979). *Manitoba writing assessment program.* A report of the Measurement and Evaluation Branch, Department of Education, Province of Manitoba.

McKay, S. L. (1993). *Agendas for second language literacy.* New York: Cambridge University Press.

Miramontes, O. B. & Commins, N. L. (1991). Redefining literacy and literacy contexts: Discovering a community of learners. In E. H. Hiebert (Ed.), *Literacy for diverse society: Perspectives, practices, and policies* (pp. 75–89). New York: Teachers College Press.

Moffett, J. & Wagner, B. J. (1983). *Student-centered language arts and reading, K–13: A Handbook for Teachers.* Boston: Houghton Mifflin.

Muth, K. D. (1989). *Children's comprehension of text.* Newark, DE: International Reading Association.

National Council of Teachers of English. (1992). *Standards for English: Project now under way.* The Council Chronicle, September 1992: 1–2.

Palincar, A. & Brown, A. (1984). Reciprocal teaching of comprehension-fostering and comprehension-monitoring activities. *Cognition and Instruction, 1 (2),* 117–175.

Pearson, P. D. (1993). Standards for the English language arts: A policy perspective. *Journal of Reading Behavior, 25 (4),* 457–475.

Raven, J. (1992). A model of competence, motivation, and behavior, and a paradigm for assessment. In H. Berlak, et al., *Toward a new science of educational testing and assessment.* (pp. 85–116). Albany, NY: SUNY Press.

Stauffer, R. (1975). *Directing the reading-thinking process.* New York: Harper & Row.

Sundbye, N. W. (1973). Evaluation of children's composition. In King (Ed.), *A forum for focus.* (pp. 223-230). Urbana, IL: National Council of Teachers of English.

Swain, M. & Lapkin, S. (1991). Additive bilingualism and French immersion education: The roles of language proficiency and literacy. In A. G. Reynolds (Ed.), *Bilingualism, multiculturalism, and second language learning* (pp. 203–216). Hillsdale, NJ: Lawrence Erlbaum.

Taylor, D. (1990). Teaching without testing: Assessing the complexity of children's literacy learning. *English Education, 22 (1),* 4–74.

Tierney, R. J., Carter, M. A. & Desai, L. E. (1991). *Portfolio assessment in the reading-writing classroom.* Norwood, MA: Christopher-Gordon Publishers.

Valencia, S., Pearson, D., Peters, C. & Wixson, K. K. (1989). Theory and practice in state wide reading assessment: Closing the gap. *Educational Leadership, 46,* 57–63.

Wendler, D., Samuels, S. J. & Moore, V. K. (1989). Comprehension instruction of award-winning teachers, teachers with master's degrees, and other teachers. *Reading Research Quarterly, 24 (4),* 382–401.

Whipple, B. (1975). *Dynamics of discussion: Grouptalk.* Belmont, MA: Porthole Press.

Wilkinson, A., Stratta, L. & Dudley (1974). *The quality of listening.* London: Macmillan.

APPENDIX: SOURCES OF ASSESSMENT INFORMATION

Alvermann, D. E., Dillon, D. R. & O'Brien, D. G. (1987). *Using discussion to promote reading comprehension.* Newark, DE: International Reading Association.

Baskwill, J. & Whitman (1988). *Evaluation: Whole language, whole child.* Richmond Hill, Ontario: Scholastic-TAB Publications.

B.C. Primary Teachers' Association. (1992). *Evaluation techniques and resources book II.* Vancouver, B.C.: B.C. Primary Teachers' Association & B.C. Teachers' Federation.

Clay, M. M. (1990). *The early detection of reading difficulties.* Auckland, New Zealand: Heinemann Education.

De Santi, R. J., Cabergue, R. M. & Sullivan, V. G. (1986). *The De Santi cloze reading inventory.* Toronto: Allyn and Bacon.

Leslie, L. & Caldwell, J. (1990). *Qualitative reading inventory.* Glenview, IL: Scott, Foresman/Little, Brown Higher Education.

Fulwiler, T. (Ed.). (1987). *The journal book.* Portsmouth, NH: Boynton/Cook.

Gillet, J. W. & Temple, C. (1990). *Understanding reading problems: Assessment and instruction, Third Edition.* Glenview, IL: Scott, Foresman/Little Brown Higher Education.

Glazer, S. M., Searfoss, L. W. & Gentile, L. M. (Eds.) (1988). *Reexamining reading diagnosis: New trends and procedures.* Newark, DE: International Reading Association.

Goodman, K. S., Goodman, Y. M. & Hood, W. J. (Eds.). (1989). *The whole language evaluation book.* Portsmouth, NH: Heinemann.

Goodman, Y., Watson, D. & Burke, C. (1987). *Reading miscue inventory: Alternate procedures.* New York: Richard Owen Publisher.

Gourdie, T. (1981). *Handwriting made easy: A simple modern approach.* New York: Taplinger Publishing Company.

Hart, D. (1994). *Authentic assessment: A handbook for teachers.* Don Mills, Ontario: Addison-Wesley Publishing Company.

Heald-Taylor, G. (1986). *Whole language strategies for ESL primary students.* Toronto: OISE Press.

Jaggar, A. & Smith-Burke, M. T. (Eds.). (1985). *Observing the language learner.* Newark, DE: International Reading Association and NCTE.

Making the grade: Evaluating student progress. (1987). Scarborough, Ont.: Prentice Hall Canada.

Myers, M. (1980). *A procedure for writing assessment and holistic scoring.* Urbana, IL: ERIC Clearinghouse and NCTE.

Student Assessment Branch, B.C. Ministry of Education. (1988). *Enhancing and evaluating oral communication in the intermediate grades [grades 4–7]: Teacher's resource package.* Victoria: B.C. Ministry of Education.

Student Assessment Branch, B.C. Ministry of Education. (1988). *Enhancing and evaluating oral communication in the primary grades [grades 1–3]: Teacher's resource package.* Victoria: B.C. Ministry of Education.

Tierney, R. J., Carter, M. A. & Desai, L. E. (1991). *Portfolio assessment in the reading-writing classroom.* Norwood, MA: Christopher-Gordon Publishers.

DISCUSSION QUESTIONS

1. This chapter suggests that assessment and evaluation are not solely the responsibility of the teacher. How should students and peers be involved and what sorts of things could they assess and evaluate?

2. What are some of the reasons given for involving students in the assessment and evaluation process?

3. Construct an "every fifth word deletion" cloze test on some part of this textbook. Have a few friends or fellow students complete the form, and then score it as suggested. What was the range of correct answers?

4. Discuss the various divisions of language arts (spelling, composition, handwriting, etc.) discussed in your curriculum guide and how they might be combined for assessment purposes. Perhaps allotted times are given for instruction. Should the proportions be the same?

5. Compare and contrast portfolios with standardized tests. What assumptions about whole-language are likely violated when standardized tests are used?

6. What are some special considerations needed when assessing or evaluating students from a variety of cultural or linguistic groups?

Research Perspectives on Whole-Language

JON SHAPIRO

1. *Recognizing that research exists that can be used to support the implementation of whole-language programs*

2. *Understanding that whole-language programs have been found to promote positive growth in achievement and attitudes*

3. *Knowing that reading approaches that have not utilized controlled or graded materials have been found to be successful*

4. *Understanding that reading and writing are related processes and if taught in an integrated fashion they can enhance overall literacy growth*

5. *Promoting the fact that roots of literacy development are formed in the home*

6. *Knowing that young children come to school with existing knowledge about print and stories, and that they also possess emerging abilities in both reading and writing that they can utilize to construct new knowledge*

7. *Understanding that knowledge and abilities will differ somewhat from child to child and it is the responsibility of the teacher to implement programs that allow for these differences*

Introduction

It is a commonly held belief that educational research should inform class-room practices. After all, to provide accountability for his or her choices of teaching techniques and instructional materials, the teacher should be able to provide evidence that classroom practices are beneficial to the children in his or her care. Although the whole-language approach has been steadily gaining favor in North America, its growth has primarily been sparked by the personal testimony of the teachers who have been at the forefront of initiating this new direction. The actual research base underpinning whole-language has not re-ceived the attention that it should (Gunderson and Shapiro, 1988) and when research evidence is provided it has often been discounted.

The influential book, *Becoming A Nation of Readers: The Report of the Commission on Reading* (1984), paid scant attention to research from other countries which provided support for whole-language programs. The Commission preferred to view whole-language as a viable technique only for kindergarten. It implied that the successes of whole-language in New Zealand had more to do with the high literacy rates of that country than the instruction provided. When looking at North American results the Commission stated that "the results can be excellent. . . . But the average result is indifferent when compared to approaches typical in American classrooms" (p. 45). Thus, un-able to find support for the notion that traditional methods are superior when compared to whole-language, the Commission fell back to a position of dis-counting whole-language for not producing, in terms of their review of the evidence, superior results.

Another review of what was supposedly whole-language research (Stahl and Miller, 1989) was also found to be confusing and tended to discount find-ings that presented whole-language in a positive light. These authors combined an older, alternative philosophy and approach, language-experience, with whole-language programs thus confusing their attempt to compare the latter ap-proach with more traditional forms of instruction. It has also been argued (McGee and Lomax, 1990) that important studies were not included in this analysis nor were studies that examined other aspects of literacy development such as writing.

In light of the confusion that accompanies analyses of whole-language in-struction, it is not sufficient to rely on the learning and language theories that support the whole-language approach. Theoretical support alone cannot and should not be sufficient to justify large-scale commitments to new educational practice. While some might argue that whole-language philosophy and practice has only just begun to inform and promote research to determine its effec-tiveness and benefits, it cannot be said that there is insufficient research to support the whole-language approach. There is a continually growing body of whole-language research and enough existing related research to examine in order to find an accurate perspective on whole-language teaching. This chapter presents a review of this research, which, if viewed in an integrated fashion, will provide support for the belief that whole-language is an acceptable format for literacy instruction.

Whole-language programs appear to be based on four beliefs that arise from the research literature. First, the language of the child should not be dealt with in a fragmented way when he or she is learning to read. Second, the child is seen as an active participant in his or her learning. Third, reading and writing are considered to be related and mutually reinforcing activities. Fourth, instruction, and the materials of instruction, must be meaningful to the learner. Research that supports these beliefs is found in studies that have been organized around the following areas of concern:

- Whole-language classrooms
- Nontraditional reading programs
- The relationship of reading and writing
- The emergence of literacy

Each of the four sections begins with a question to alert you to the focus of the research presented in the section. The sections end with a perspective derived from the research and a list of conclusions that support that perspective. You may find it useful to start with the section question, read the perspective and conclusions, and then refer to the body of the section for the specifics of the research conducted in that area.

Whole-Language Programs

How do whole-language programs compare with more traditional means of literacy instruction and what are the effects of whole-language on the development of literacy skills?

Programs that have been characterized as whole-language have at their foundation a belief that literacy instruction should be natural and holistic. Research conducted with children before they enter school leads whole-language proponents to create classroom environments that are similar to home literacy environments (Shapiro and Doiron, 1987). While whole-language classroom research has been growing by leaps and bounds during the past few years, it is only beginning to become part of the research literature. One reason for this is that the term itself, and therefore research under the heading of "whole-language instruction," is relatively new. Since classroom practices usually drive research efforts, there has not yet been sufficient time for researchers to locate these classrooms, conduct investigations, and report on their findings. A second

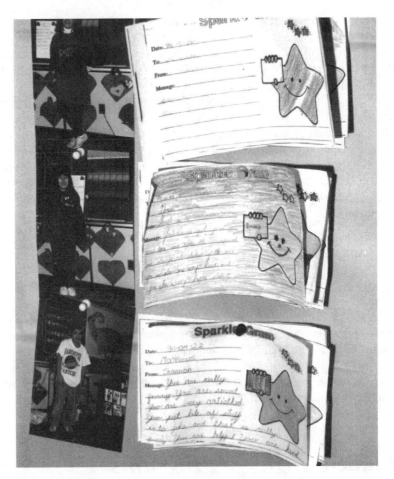

Sparkle Grams are written to individuals to indicate that their contributions to the class are appreciated by others.

reason for the difficulties in finding research on whole-language is the problem of definition. What is a whole-language program for some educators is not for others. For example, there are teachers who believe that there is no place for skills instruction in a whole-language program. Others believe it is not a question of either/or but of how and when. What appears common to various whole-language proponents is the emphasis on early and extensive writing experiences and the reading of natural language books. You may wish to refer back to Chapter 1 for a more detailed definition of whole-language. The research reviewed here was conducted in classrooms that contained these elements.

Whole-Language and Traditional Approaches

A few of the studies that fit the whole-language category are comparative in nature. That is, the researcher has compared the effects of one approach with others.

The effect of prereading kindergarten curricula on reading-related abilities of 165 children was the focus of one study (Taylor et al., 1986). Some of the kindergartens were characterized by a language- and print-rich environment in which the teachers capitalized on every opportunity to involve the children with written and oral language. Other classrooms were characterized as static, that is, displays of writing rarely changed and were not designed to be used. Regarding writing, in these latter classrooms children did not create their own books; rather, they copied print and were restricted to worksheets. Children from the language- and print-rich environments outperformed the others on tests of written language awareness, a test of basic concept knowledge, and two of three subtests of a standardized readiness test.

Similar effects for the type of program on the emerging literacy of kindergarten-age children were found by Ribowsky (1985). A whole-language kindergarten was compared to one with a code emphasis. That is, the latter classroom stressed a teacher-directed program centered on letter/name and letter/sound instruction. The amount of literacy instruction or experiences was held constant for both groups. Results favored the whole-language group on tests of language development, book-handling knowledge, and letter recognition. Dahl and Freppon (1991) found that whole-language kindergarten programs were very successful for groups of low socioeconomic children who were the least knowledgeable about written language. These children, when compared to a similar group in skills-based kindergartens, engaged in a broader range of literacy behaviors and understood that print carries meaning.

The impact of whole-language programs on the learning of the alphabetic principle is of great interest to proponents of whole-language, as well as opponents of this philosophy. The latter group often contends, without much proof, that it is only through direct instruction that awareness and command of the alphabetic principle develops. In 1988, Gunderson and Shapiro indicated that it appeared that the alphabetic principle did develop in first-grade children attending whole-language classes. However, only recently have comparative studies been reported.

Partridge, Foil, and Bitner (1991) examined the effects of a daily versus weekly story/reading and follow-up drawing/writing in kindergarten children. Using four kindergarten classes, they discovered that for both older and younger kindergartners the daily program produced significantly more awareness of the alphabetic principle as demonstrated in the daily groups' performance on a test of invented spelling.

The development of the alphabetic principle was also examined in first-grade classrooms (Klesius, Griffith, and Zielonka, 1991). Researchers compared the performance of children in three whole-language and three basal reader classes over a one-year period. Scores on spelling tests indicated that the children in whole-language classrooms, as well as those children who had received direct phonic instruction, appeared to learn the alphabetic principle.

David Doake (1980) reported on one of the earliest North American experiments with a whole-language program. This program was based on the work of Holdaway (1979), who devised the shared-book experience in New Zealand, a reading program modeled on the home reading experiences of New Zealand preschool children. This beginning reading method used "big books" containing highly predictable and natural language, with almost no vocabulary control evident. This approach is described in more detail in Chapter 6. Additional elements were a strong literature program, language-experience activities, and frequent writing by the children. While the children in the experimental program and the basal-reader program started out on an equal level, as measured by a standardized reading text, differences were seen by mid-year. By the end of grade 1 the experimental group (the whole-language group) scored nearly one-half year higher on measures of vocabulary and comprehension.

Another comparison of basal-reader and whole-language programs was carried out by DeFord (1981). In this study two basal-reader programs were included. One maintained a decoding emphasis, beginning instruction with the teaching of letters and their sounds. The other program had a more eclectic orientation, initiating instruction with the introduction of basic sight words. The whole-language classroom used the language-experience approach in conjunction with a literature program and a heavy emphasis on writing. The researcher observed these classes for a seven-month period. All children's oral reading was analyzed, and definite differences in reading strategies were apparent. Children in the decoding and eclectic basal approaches made reading miscues that demonstrated how highly dependent they were on the teachers' methods of instruction. The miscues of the whole-language group indicated that they read with more meaning; they were thinking of the message in the text. As well, they applied various strategies when dealing with unknown words, whereas the other groups were basically locked into the particular skills emphasized in their instruction. DeFord also found that the whole-language group's comprehension, as determined by their retelling of stories read, was of better quality and contained more literary devices than the other groups.

A final finding was the ability of the whole-language group to consistently write in a more storylike form. In fact, the basal groups' children often tended to write stories that resembled basal-reader story forms. DeFord concluded that children need a variety of literacy experiences, and that the provision of unnatural models (basal readers) for reading and writing might be detrimental to their growth in the language arts. She believed that her observations provided support for the notion of a reading/writing connection.

Another comparative study at the first-grade level examined the effect of the teacher's beliefs on the children. Wilucki (1984) compared a classroom with a teacher whose orientation caused an emphasis on the mechanics and skills involved in reading, and a classroom with a whole-language teacher. The former teacher did not believe that the children could read or write at entry into grade 1. The whole-language teacher believed that the children were readers and writers. The classroom environments were found to differ based on the teachers' orientation to literacy. There was quantitatively more print in the environment of the whole-language classroom. The teacher-child interaction was characterized as "child-initiated" as opposed to the "teacher-contingent" interaction of the skills-based classroom. When the children's writing was analyzed it was determined that the whole-language group wrote significantly more and that the average length of their stories was greater. These children chose the topic on which they wrote more frequently and did not need to copy adult sources as did the skills-based group.

In a study of 157 first- and second-graders, Gambrell and Palmer (1992) found that whole-language affected first-graders' metacognitive knowledge about literacy behavior, especially writing. For second-graders, whole-language produced youngsters who were more aware of strategies and reasons for reading. They also had greater knowledge about writing than did the children in conventional classrooms. Varble (1990) also found a significant impact for the writing of second-grade children. She found that the whole-language group was similar to the traditionally taught group in the mechanics of writing but the former groups' writing samples were significantly superior when they were analyzed for meaning and content.

Reutzel and Cooter (1990) studied first-graders in two different regions of the United States. Even though the traditional classrooms had a lower pupil/teacher ratio, the whole-language classes outperformed them on a standardized reading test's overall reading score, and its vocabulary and comprehension sections. While the size of the differences was considered moderate, the authors concluded they were meaningful since the type of reading assessment favored the traditional group because the tasks it presented would have been more familiar to this group.

Other researchers have compared achievement differences with children at higher grade levels. Stice and Bertrand (1988) investigated the effects of whole-language with "at risk" first-grade children coming from lower socioeconomic, non-intact families and performing poorly on standardized achievement measures. They found no significant differences between their groups in growth between administrations of the achievement test. However, the children in the whole-language classrooms made significantly greater gains in their concepts about print and books.

Whole-language type programs have also been found to be beneficial for children who speak English as a second language. Elley and Mangubhai (1983) found that children in a shared book experience program, which included writing, progressed at twice the rate of the children in the traditional program. Interestingly, at the fourth-grade level, the children taught using this approach also had superior knowledge of syntactic structures even though they were not taught directly like the traditional group.

Hagerty, Hiebert, and Owen (1989) compared children in grades 2, 4, and 6 on a number of measures after eight months of instruction. In general, the whole-language groups outperformed the children in traditional basal-reader classrooms on a measure of reading comprehension. The children receiving traditional instruction maintained their perceptions of the nature of reading and writing, while the whole-language children shifted in their views, emphasizing the meaningful nature of these areas. Surprisingly, no significant differences in writing ability, as measured by a district assessment, were found. The researchers believed this finding was due to the fact that the writing topic was imposed. They noted that at the second-grade level whole-language children produced many more books. Children in the traditional classrooms tended to write one-page compositions that were compiled into class books.

Klesius, Griffith, and Zielonka (1991) conducted a study to determine if teachers can make the transition from traditional instruction to whole-language instruction without a loss in student growth. The researchers compared the performance of first-graders in classrooms of experienced teachers, of whom three were just making the transition to a more integrated language arts curriculum. Results of countywide, mandated tests of vocabulary and comprehension indicated that the children in the classrooms of the "new" whole-language teachers, who received little in-service training, scored as well as the children in the traditional classrooms.

Another study at the first-grade level compared children's performance in a basal-reader program with a modified whole-language program (Eldridge, 1991). In three classes the whole-language program was supplemented by 15 minutes of developmental phonics instruction which included direct instruction in vowels, consonants, and blends. Children in the modified whole-language program were found to have superior scores on achievement measures. Interestingly, this group was also found to have more favorable attitudes toward reading.

A five-year study of students in grades 1 to 6 from whole-language and traditional classrooms compared performance on reading and language measures (McCallum, Moore, and Whitlow, 1992). The researchers examined the vocabulary, word attack skills, comprehension, spelling, language expression, and language mechanics of 116 children receiving whole-language instruction in an experimental program within a school and 508 youngsters in the same building's more traditional basal reader program. The results on standardized tests indicated that initially the children in the basal reader program demonstrated advantages over the whole-language group. However, with the exception of word attack skills, by third grade the advantages were reversed and the whole-language group maintained their advantages through the sixth grade.

Shapiro (1990) conducted a study which examined the relationship of instruction to the attribution of sex-role appropriateness. An attempt was made to determine if boys in whole-language kindergarten through second-grade classrooms perceived reading as an appropriate activity for themselves or more appropriate for girls and whether books were seen as a more appropriate present for girls or boys. Earlier work by May and Ollila (1981) and Shapiro (1985) had indicated that preschool-age boys saw both the activity of reading and the object, a book, as appropriate for themselves. Other research, however, indicated that as North American boys progressed through the elementary school years, they increasingly saw reading and books as inappropriate for boys (Downing et al., 1979). Results of the Shapiro (1990) study indicated that while boys in whole-language classrooms began to increasingly indicate that reading and books were more appropriate for girls as they progressed through the primary grades, at least half of the boys still saw reading and books as being appropriate for themselves also. On the other hand, boys receiving traditional basal reader instruction perceived reading and books to be more appropriate for girls.

Burns-Paterson (1991) examined first- and third-graders' concepts of reading in whole-language and traditional classrooms. These children were asked to define reading and their answers were coded into four categories. She found that the children in the whole-language classrooms gave more specific responses than those receiving basal reader instruction. The basal-reader-instructed children also tended to view reading as a school activity while the whole-language group felt that reading was an important part of their lives.

Freppon (1991) also examined first-graders' concepts of the nature and purpose of reading in two skills-based and two whole-language classrooms. While the two groups were similar in their expressed interest in learning to read and in sounding out words, they differed in their concepts of the reading process. The latter group was found to hold a broader view of reading, understood and used more stategies, and while they sounded out words less often they were more accurate than the skills-based group.

Comparisons between whole-language and traditional programs have not been limited to achievement or attitudes. Fisher and Hiebert (1988) examined the characteristics of four whole-language and four traditional classrooms at the grade 2 and grade 6 levels. They found that more time was spent on literacy tasks in the whole-language classrooms, especially in the area of writing. Furthermore, there were differences in the nature of the writing tasks. Children in the traditional classrooms spent their time completing worksheets or writing about a story just read. Writing in the whole-language classrooms tended to be in the production of individual products, generating new text, or revising drafts. Much less time was spent in the traditional classrooms on discussion of content or the process of writing. The researchers also concluded that the children in the whole-language classrooms spent more time on tasks that were higher in cognitive complexity than did the other children.

Children's ability to select books and the amount of reading done have also been examined (Mervar and Hiebert, 1988). The number of pages second-grade students read was assessed by using reading logs in the whole-language class and by the conventional teacher reporting the amount of reading since all these children read from the same books. It was found that high-achieving children in the whole-language class read significantly more than all other children. While the lower-achieving whole-language children also read more than their counterparts in the traditional class, the difference was not statistically significant.

To determine self-selection abilities two tasks were set up. In the first, the children were observed during a library visit and then interviewed about self-selection of books. The second task required the children to rank order five books in terms of their quality. Two books were described as outstanding children's literature by a panel of librarians. Two others were "supermarket" books, popular but not high in literary quality. The fifth book was a basal reader not in use in the school. The researchers found significant differences in the library task. Children from the whole-language class spent almost five times the amount of time spent by the traditional group in selecting a book. The pattern of book selection behavior that emerged for the traditional group was to go to a specific section of the library that contained familiar books and immediately pull a book from the shelf. On the other hand, with no exceptions, the children in the whole-language classroom sampled text from one or more books before making their selection. In the structured book-ranking task differences were not as clear-cut. However, the whole-language group ranked one of the high-quality books first and the basal reader last, while the traditional group ranked a "supermarket" book best and the basal reader second best.

Whole-Language Developmental Effects

Very few studies look at the long-term effects of literacy programs, and of course, this is true for newer approaches such as whole-language. However, one team of researchers has begun to disseminate results from one- and two-year studies of whole-language classrooms. This type of research sheds additional light on questions concerning the viability of this approach to literacy instruction.

Gunderson and Shapiro (1987, 1988) examined the writing of 52 first-grade students for an entire school year. From the very first day of school these children were asked to write. Just over half of the children could not write and dictated sentences or stories to the teachers instead. Ten percent wrote strings of letters that they deciphered for the teachers and that the teachers then recorded. Almost 40% wrote letter strings that did contain decipherable words. Rapid progress through writing experiences and exposure to literacy and literature were soon seen. Within a month, those who could not write began to produce texts complete with invented spellings, writing conventions such as spacing, and identifiable sentence strings. Literacy learning continued to be observed throughout the year. By year's end, most youngsters, including those who spoke English as a second language, were writing a substantial number of words. Conventional spellings and punctuation were in evidence. The level of writing sophistication that these children developed was evident at the start of grade 2. The children who had the grade 1 whole-language instruction often produced lengthy written stories. The new incoming students, on the other hand, wrote in a fashion similar to the beginning whole-language students.

These children's written vocabularies were compared to the vocabulary found in basal readers (Shapiro and Gunderson, 1988). The children produced roughly 18 times the number of words that they would have encountered in the basal system's first-grade program. High-frequency words used were similar to the basal readers and also to typical word lists. Finally, the writing vocabulary of the children revealed that the children learned to spell correctly a large number of words, and an analysis of their spelling errors indicated that they were learning phonics skills as well.

Further statistical analyses and follow-up on the writing of these students were conducted (Froese et al., 1988). Throughout the entire first-grade year, with the exception of the last school month, substantial growth was seen for the complexity of writing, the quality of writing, and the average number of words written. These same children were followed into a more conventional second-grade program. Over an entire year the only significant improvement was in the average number of words written. Writing complexity and quality was virtually static.

These same researchers then compared the performance of children receiving two different types of whole-language experiences (Gunderson et al., 1988). In one school, teachers believed that literacy skills should be allowed to develop naturally and independent of teacher intervention. These teachers believed that models for writing were implicit in children's literature, thus they never imposed a mature model of writing by commenting on the students' compositions. In another school, teachers would write for the students upon request and also place written comments on children's compositions, thus providing a mature model of writing.

The children's writing was analyzed during their grade 1 and grade 2 years. At the end of the first year, significant differences between the groups were found for quality, number of words used, and number of communication units. These results favored the children in classrooms where a mature model was provided. However, by the end of grade 2 the children without explicit models caught up. Children under both conditions demonstrated continued growth in the areas measured under both whole-language conditions. In fact, in terms of communication units, the writing of these grade 1 and 2 children compared favorably with the writing of older children in more traditional programs (Hunt, 1977).

Among the most rigorous research is that normally found in a doctoral dissertation, and that is the case for whole language as well. An examination of that source of information was undertaken by the editor via ProQuest, which allows the searching of Dissertations Abstracts International electronically. The number of theses and dissertations produced in various time periods gives some indication of the interest shown in a topic. The results indicated that during the five-year period 1982–1987, some 26 dissertations were produced; during the period 1988–1992, about 126 dissertations were reported; and in

1993 alone, 50 dissertations were completed. An examination of the 50 indicated that several were masters' theses and several dealt with postsecondary subjects, leaving 42 doctoral dissertations dealing with public school-related questions related to whole language. The appendix at the end of this chapter presents title, author, institution, type of study, and a brief comment about the study. As can be seen, whole language is being studied in universities across the country; a variety of quantitative and qualitative methods are used; and various student, teacher, and school characteristics are being studied. Clearly, support for various aspects of whole-language-language is mounting.

> *Research Perspective 1: The whole-language approach has been demonstrated to be more than capable in developing young children's all around literacy abilities, especially in the development of writing skills.*

> *This perspective is supported by research that has shown that:*

>> *Whole-language programs are successful at the kindergarten level as introductory literacy experiences.*

>> *Whole-language programs have also been successful as elementary school reading programs and may be more cognitively stimulating than traditional, basal-reader approaches.*

>> *Whole-language programs have developed children's writing skills at ages that were previously thought developmentally impossible for primary-grade students.*

Nontraditional Reading Programs

Since the majority of classrooms use basal reading programs, does that mean that there are no other acceptable ways to promote reading growth?

Reading instruction centering on a basal-reader program has been the predominant form of instruction in North America for decades. While these programs have their proponents, and most basal-reader systems are authored by highly respected reading experts, they have not been without criticism. Basal readers have long been thought to contain stilted language and to be uninteresting for young readers. Indeed, even Horace Mann in the nineteenth century was critical of the type of reading encouraged in basal readers (Gray, 1963). More recently, criticism has focused on the perceptions about reading that students develop in these programs. Research has discovered that children in basal-reader programs have a view of reading that overemphasizes decoding and accuracy in word recognition (Johns and Ellis, 1976), and that children using basal readers do not consider reading for meaning as important, nor do they find the reading interesting (Cairney, 1988).

Because of such criticisms, as well as a strong belief in child-centered education, nontraditional reading programs, those not based upon the use of a basal-reader system, have been implemented in the past. Research results for two such programs, the language-experience approach and the individualized-reading approach, will be examined.

The Language-Experience Approach

The language-experience approach has been characterized as an "open" type of instructional program (Lee and Allen, 1963). The term is meant to convey that this approach emphasizes the learner as an integral part of the program, and also emphasizes all the language arts (writing, listening, and speaking in addition to reading). The language-experience approach is based on the oral language of the child. Oral responses are recorded by the teacher at initial stages. Experiences and activities are then developed that elaborate the child's dictation. This dictation serves as the reading material and as the basis for instruction. Ashton-Warner (1963) theorized that children moved through different levels of responses that are hierarchical and developmental in nature and culminated in the ability to write and read stories. Research has confirmed the existence of these levels (Veatch et al., 1973; Blakey, 1980) and likened them to levels of metalinguistic competency, which relate to Piagetian measures of cognition (Papandropoulu and Sinclair, 1974).

The main thrust of the research on the language-experience approach has been the comparison of these programs with basal-reader programs. While the research results have been mixed, language-experience programs have usually been found to produce readers who are at least as proficient as those produced by basal-reader programs. In some studies the language-experience children have outperformed basal-reader groups on achievement, attitude, and some writing measures.

The main source for comparison of the language-experience approach versus basal-reader instructional practices was the First-Grade Studies. These studies were a large-scale investigation of the effectiveness of various beginning reading approaches during the early 1960s and were funded by the U.S. Office of Education. Of the 27 projects, 6 had a language-experience component and most of these examined over 400 first-grade students.

In the first year, there were few significant differences between language-experience groups and basal-reader groups. However, in the two studies that did not examine special populations, such as disadvantaged, Spanish-speaking children, significant differences favoring the language-experience approach were found. In a study of almost 600 children, language-experience groups scored significantly higher on various measures of reading (Vilscek et al., 1966). Superior performance was noted on word reading, paragraph meaning, vocabulary, and word study tests. Almost similar findings for word reading and paragraph meaning were reported by Stauffer (1966) in his examination of 20 first-grade classes. Stauffer's findings, which supported the language-experience approach, were replicated and extended almost a decade later. In this study, all reading performance indicators favored the language-experience groups (Stauffer, 1973).

Some of the language-experience projects were extended with five continuing into a second year and four projects following its children through grade 3. Again, findings were mixed. However, in general, the groups in the language-experience approach at the end of grades 2 and 3 were at least equal to the basal groups in reading ability, and superior on some writing measures (Harris and Morrison, 1969; Stauffer and Hammond, 1969). These findings led to the recognition of the language-experience approach as a viable teaching strategy and to the call for the inclusion of writing in the reading program (Bond and Dykstra, 1967). This call went virtually unheeded in the majority of North American classrooms.

Research on language experience has also examined issues beyond the achievement of able readers. Investigations have addressed concerns regarding the language-experience approach's affects on oral language development and vocabulary, readiness for reading, and students' attitudes toward themselves and reading.

Studies examining oral-language development have reported positive results supporting language experience. Giles (1966), investigating first-grade students' oral language, found greater gains for the language-experience groups on the diversity of vocabulary and the use of vivid and colorful expressions. In another study the focus was on the growth of oral language, determined by examining the dictated stories of the students. Significant gains were seen in the average number of words dictated, the average number of long and short sentences, the average number of pronouns and prepositions used, and the number of different words employed (Stauffer and Pikulski, 1974). These studies provide support for the linguistic growth fostered by the language-experience approach.

Vocabulary development has been the subject of several studies. Most of these investigations have shown that the vocabulary generated in the language-experience approach is comparable to the vocabulary that children would be exposed to in a basal-reader program (Henderson et al., 1972). Not only is the core vocabulary similar, but the content words have been judged to be of higher interest and are more current (Shapiro and Gunderson, 1988). Similar findings have been found for the vocabulary generated by disadvantaged students (Cohen and Kornfield, 1970). Additionally, research shows that more meaningful words are retained better by young readers (Bennett, 1971; Bridge et al., 1983). Finally, it has been discovered that the vocabulary generated in this method lends itself just as well to word analysis study as does the more controlled vocabulary found in basal readers (Dzama, 1975).

When the language-experience approach, as used at initial stages of reading, was compared to the workbook programs of basal-reader series, favorable results were also found. Kindergarten children who used experience-chart stories and other informal language experiences had higher scores on standardized reading readiness tests than workbook groups (O'Donnell and Raymond, 1972). Similar readiness-test superiority was found for beginning grade 1 students who received instruction based on experience chart stories (Brazziel and Terrell, 1962; Hall, 1965).

Remedial reading instruction has generally been based on a skills-deficit model, thus encouraging isolated skills teaching and practice. However, language experience has received some attention in this area since it is based on the utilization of the students' language, thoughts, and experiences. Favorable results from using this method in remedial programs have been reported (Kelley, 1977; Mallett, 1975; Wilson and Parkey, 1970). Often commented on in this research has been its positive effect on students' attitudes toward reading (Wasserman, 1978). In particular, boys, who are known for rejecting reading as a gender-appropriate activity (Shapiro, 1980), maintain a more positive attitude when they receive instruction by the language-experience approach (Shapiro, 1985). Better self-concept and self-esteem have also been noted for language-experience students (Mallett, 1978; Riendeau, 1973; Wilson and Parkey, 1970).

The Individualized-Reading Approach

The individualized-reading approach grew out of child-development theory (Olsen, 1952). Proponents believe that children could self-select appropriate reading material and then pace themselves at an appropriate rate to complete the material. Thus, tradebooks provide the major portion of the reading material used for instruction. Teachers determine their students' individual skill needs and provide appropriate individual and small-group instruction.

Studies that have compared individualized-reading approaches with basal-reader instruction can be traced back long before language experience. Like the language-experience approach, there have been positive comparisons reported when individualized reading, sometimes referred to as "literature based," programs have been investigated. Three summaries of research on individualized reading have been published. Vite (1963), in a review of 76 studies, found that individualized-reading programs had more favorable reading test results in 76% of these studies. It was found equal to basal-reader programs in 17% of the cases reviewed. A later summary of research examined investigations of individualized reading that took place between 1950 and 1964 (Seeber, 1969). This reviewer differentiated between well-run or tightly controlled studies and those that lacked stringent controls. Some 93% of the latter studies favored the individualized-reading approach. In the tightly controlled studies, 53%

reported more favorable gains for individualized reading while in 38% the groups were equal.

Finally, Thompson (1971) reviewed 51 studies that dated back to the 1930s. For the well-run studies, he reported that in 23 of 39 the individualized-reading groups had superior reading performance. In 15 of the studies the competing reading methods produced similar reading achievement scores. While reviews of research, like the ones described above, have consistently found results that indicated that the individualized-reading approach was at least equal to the basal-reader approach in producing reading growth, this method has not flourished. Indeed, the individualized-reading approach has received scant attention from reading researchers since the 1960s. More current research, however, has once again provided support for this method of reading instruction.

Four investigations have compared the effects of literature-based or enhanced programs and traditional basal-reader instructional schemes on reading achievement. Two studies have examined the effects of the reading program on attitudes toward reading and perceptions of reading. Cohen (1968) examined the reading performance of 130 second-grade children from lower socioeconomic status homes, taught in the conventional manner, and 155 children, of similar status, receiving literature-enhanced instruction. In the latter, the children were read to on a daily basis and had meaning-related activities, in addition to the basal-reader program. Results on standardized tests indicated that the literature-enhanced group had significantly higher scores on vocabulary and reading comprehension. Similar results were found in a later replication of the literature-enhanced program (Cullinen et al., 1974).

Eldridge and Butterfield (1984), in a controlled study of second-grade students, investigated the effects of various reading treatments and classroom groupings on reading vocabulary, comprehension, and self-image. Five experimental treatment groups, two of which were literature based, were compared to control groups receiving traditional basal-reader instruction. Results showed that the two literature-based groups made the greatest gains in reading achievement and self-image. Twenty statistically significant differences—differences that could not have occurred by chance—were found for all treatment groups when compared to the traditional basal-reader groups. Of these, 14, or 70% were achieved by the literature-based groups. A follow-up study comparing 54 grade 2 classrooms concluded that "the use of children's literature to teach children to read had a strong effect upon . . . achievement and interest . . . much greater than the traditional methods" (Bader et al., 1987, p. 65).

Shapiro and White (1991) examined the effects of a literature-based program and traditional basal-reader instruction on the attitudes and perceptions of reading for over 400 elementary school students. The literature-based program was unique in that no direct instruction was provided. Rather, the students had two daily reading periods that were comprised of individual and paired reading of tradebooks. At the primary grade level, significant differences favoring the literature-based group were found. Attitudes toward reading at home and school were greater for grades 1 through 3. Children's perceptions of their own reading ability were also better for the literature-based group. A more sophisticated attitude measure was used for the intermediate grades. Significant differences were found between programs on all attitude categories. The students in the literature-based program reported greater enjoyment of reading, looked more favorably upon school reading, reported greater uses of reading as a source of information, had less anxiety about their reading, and fewer of them suggested that they had reading difficulties.

The primary and intermediate grades were combined for the analysis of the students' perceptions of the reading process. Significant school effects were seen for questions regarding the purposes of reading, how people read, and why teachers ask questions about reading. The literature-based group, when asked "Why do we read?" gave significantly more responses that indicated reading for pleasure or knowledge. The children receiving traditional instruction gave more utilitarian and job-related responses. In regard to how they read, the traditional group was more likely to answer with a "text-driven" type response such as, "You sound out the words." The literature-based group more often included the idea of deriving meaning from print. (For example, "You

have to think about what the author meant.") Finally, the basal-reader children saw the teacher's role primarily as one of assessor and not one of assistant.

In another study, the conceptions of literacy of first-graders receiving three different forms of reading instruction were examined (Rasinski and DeFord, 1988). One teacher employed a mastery-learning, phonics-based reading program. Another utilized a more traditional basal-reading series, while the third teacher's program was based on tradebooks. The researchers found that the children in the literature-based classroom had conceptions of literacy that emphasized the meaningfulness of reading and writing activities. Children in the traditional classroom had a less holistic view but more meaningful orientation than the children in the phonics-based program who conceived of "reading and writing as something to do with words and word parts" (p. 55). Results such as these have been corroborated for children at this grade level (Boljonis and Hinchman, 1988).

Some studies have examined literature-based programs without comparing them to other approaches. Larrick (1987) studied 225 kindergarten children who were considered to have a "high risk of failure." These children came predominantly from families that were below the poverty level and non-English-speaking; in fact, 80% of the children spoke no English at kindergarten entry. The program immersed the children in literature and encouraged them to dictate and then read their own stories. Larrick found that at the end of the year, all the children could read their own dictated stories. One year later, 60% of the children were reading on or above grade level.

Tunnell (1986) used a literature-based program with older children, some of whom were reading disabled. After seven months of instruction he found the average gain in reading for the fifth-grade children was 1.1 grades on a standardized reading test. For the children who were reading-disabled the gain was 1.3 grades. Tunnell reported that there were significant changes in the negative attitudes toward books and reading that the children had at the beginning of the school year.

One other study deserves consideration. While not addressing individualized or literature-based programs per se, it does shed light on one of the issues of traditional and nontraditional approaches to reading instruction. This issue is the high quality of writing or the natural language of the tradebook and the tightly controlled, often stilted language of beginning-level basal readers. Simons and Ammon (1987) rewrote grade 1 basal-reader stories so that they would be more like the language of tradebooks. Young children's reading of the rewritten material was compared with their reading performance on the original texts. The researchers concluded that the rewritten versions were in some cases easier to read, and that they encouraged the students to read with an emphasis on meaning as opposed to pronunciation. These findings are in keeping with research concerning the comprehensibility of typical basal-reader stories versus rewritten, tradebooklike material (Beck et al., 1982, 1984; Brennan et al., 1986).

Research Perspective 2: Nontraditional reading programs have been shown to be viable means of providing reading instruction.

This perspective is supported by research that has shown that:

Many children in traditional, basal-reader programs do not have a realistic perception of reading, nor do they find reading interesting.

Language-experience programs have produced successful readers and have added benefits in the development of oral language, vocabulary, and attitudes toward reading and toward oneself.

Individualized or literature-based programs have also resulted in the promotion of reading growth, as well as in more accurate perceptions of the reading process.

The Reading/Writing Connection

In most classrooms reading and writing are taught separately, but are they related and does instruction in one have an effect on ability in the other?

For many years the various components of the language arts program were viewed as separate and distinct. Reading and writing were considered to be opposing processes. The former was thought to be a passive, receptive activity, while the latter was active and expressive. Recently, reading experts have begun to assume that reading and writing are mutually supportive because the child who is engaged in either composing or comprehending must construct meaning through print (Tierney and Pearson, 1984). It has also been suggested that many aspects of writing that cannot be taught can be learned only through wide reading (Smith, 1984). However, the researchers are not as definite about this relationship as are the theorists. In an extensive review of the reading/writing research, Belanger (1987a) supplied some moderate support for the view that reading and writing are related, and perhaps mutually reinforcing. However, he pointed out that the present measures of reading and writing abilities are not yet sophisticated enough to examine the relationship in anything but a global manner (Belanger, 1987b). Thus, caution is advised in the interpretation of this body of research.

Reading Ability and Writing Ability Are Related

In a classic, long-term longitudinal study, Loban (1963) followed hundreds of children as they progressed through school. Relationships between reading ability and writing ability were examined at various points in the children's

As part of library research, students record concepts on slips of paper, which are then arranged into semantic webs before beginning the report writing.

school careers. This was done by examining the correlations between performance on the reading and writing measures. Correlations indicate how strongly performance on one measure is related to performance on another. Correlations do not, however, indicate whether performance on one measure, or that one ability, causes proficiency on the other measure or ability. Loban did find that there were significant positive correlations, or relationships, between reading, writing, listening, and speaking. These relationships strengthened as the children progressed through the grades. Among other things, Loban found that good readers were good writers and poor readers usually wrote poorly as well. Other studies have corroborated Loban's findings that a positive relationship does exist between reading and writing. In fact, an analysis of correlational studies of the language arts conducted over a quarter of a century indicated that there was consistent support of a moderate relationship between reading and writing (Hammill and McNutt, 1980). At the elementary school level it has been reported that an individual's reading ability, as measured by standardized tests, could account for up to 43% of the difference on the student's score on a measure of writing ability, or vice versa (Shanahan, 1984).

Research has also examined the relationship between reading ability and the syntactic complexity of elementary school students' writing. A significant, positive relationship has been found at the primary-grade level (Zeman, 1969; Johnson, 1976) and at the intermediate-grade level (Evanechko et al., 1974).

These findings indicated that the higher the reading level, the more syntactically complex or mature was the writing of the students.

In a recent study with older subjects, a combined program of reading and writing rather than either taught separately was found to prompt critical thinking (Tierney et al., 1989). Thus reading and writing may be complementary processes, which have influence on thinking ability when used together.

Beginning Reading Instruction and Writing Ability

That reading and writing are interrelated also appears to be supported by studies that have examined the effects of the type of reading instruction (such as an emphasis on decoding or on word recognition) on writing ability. For the most part, reading programs that enable the child to read fluently at an early stage (primary grades), as opposed to emphasizing slow, halting reading, seem to produce better writers. These findings have held for writing vocabulary (Downing, 1967), the quality of the composition (Mazurkiewicz, 1975; Shapiro, 1973; Smith, 1968), and for writing maturity and mechanics (Duquette, 1970; Stauffer and Hammond, 1967; Willardson, 1972). These results are not correlational; rather, groups receiving different forms of reading instruction were compared on these various aspects of writing. Comparisons were usually drawn between groups receiving traditional basal-reader instruction and others such as language-experience groups, although similar results have been found for basal readers with more sophisticated sentence structure than the typical beginning basal-reader programs (Eckhoff, 1985). Since these studies have been comparative, as opposed to correlational, causality can be inferred. Thus, it can be concluded that the method of reading instruction had a direct bearing on writing ability.

Writing Instruction and Reading Ability

As more classroom attention has recently focused on the writing process, researchers have begun to examine the effects of writing instruction on reading performance. Instruction that concentrated on the analysis of writing has generally produced statistically significant gains in reading ability. On the other hand, frequent writing practice, without instruction, has not been found to affect reading performance.

The majority of this research has been at the upper elementary school level and has emphasized the structure of paragraphs and syntax (Kelley, 1984). There has been the occasional attempt to measure the influence on primary students' reading ability through specific writing instruction such as sentence organization (Weaver, 1977). Sentence-combining instruction, which also emphasizes the organization of writing, has had clear, significant effects on standardized reading-test performance (McAfee, 1980; Mackie, 1982). Other studies on sentence combining have provided partial support since not all reading measures were influenced by the sentence-combining instruction (Straw and Schreiner, 1982). Belanger (1987b) argued that grade level apparently is an important factor in determining the success of sentence-combining instruction on reading ability. Instruction at upper grade levels appears to meet with more success. As well, writing instruction may have the greatest impact on reading test scores for students of lower- or middle-level reading ability (Hughes, 1975).

> ### Research Perspective 3: Reading and writing are, to some degree, related and, to a certain extent, writing instruction can influence reading and vice versa.

This perspective is supported by research that has shown that:

> *Children who are good readers are also good writers, while poor readers are usually poor writers as well. These relationships strengthen as children progress through school (Loban, 1963; Hammill and McNutt, 1980).*

> *Reading programs promoting early fluency seem to produce better writers in terms of vocabulary, quality, and the mechanics of writing.*

> *Writing instruction at the upper elementary school level, which emphasizes sentence organization, has had positive effects on standardized reading test performance.*

The Emergence of Literacy

Does knowledge about reading and writing develop along a continuum that has its roots in the home and begins prior to school entry?

Studies in the area of the development of language in children and its relationship to schooling have had a major impact on the thinking of reading educators. These studies, as well as research on early readers—those who learned to read before school entry (Clark, 1976; Durkin, 1966)—spawned an interest in how literacy develops in young children. The term **emergent literacy,** coined by Marie Clay (1966), now represents one of the fastest growing areas of reading and writing research. The field of emergent literacy presents a new research perspective, one that focuses on the natural growth of the processes of reading and writing development.

This body of research indicates that before young children enter school, before they "formally" learn to read and write, they already know much about literacy. Young children know that the purpose of written language is to communicate, and they are developing ideas concerning the processes of reading and writing. Much of this knowledge is derived from early home and community experiences. Descriptive research studies indicate that children from homes where books are seen and used are active participants in their learning, capable of formulating, testing, and reformulating hypotheses about literacy processes (Bissex, 1980; Chomsky, 1972; Read, 1971).

Home Environment and Emergent Literacy

Early studies linked the influence of parents and the use of books in the home with success in learning to read. Durkin (1966) identified experience with books and the value placed on books by parents as key factors in the development of early readers. She found that home factors such as the amount of reading by parents were correlated with children's reading performance. The power of the parent as a reading model, which might motivate the young child to explore readinglike behavior, has also been corroborated in other studies (Clay, 1971; Keshian, 1963; Sutton, 1964). Moon and Wells (1979) found a strong relationship between parental interest in reading and attitudes toward reading with preschool children's knowledge of books and with later reading achievement.

More recent studies have also found relationships between home literacy environment and language and literacy. It appears that preschool-age children who come from homes with high-literacy environments begin to attend to the meaning of language, rather than the context in which the language occurs, sooner than do comparable children from homes with a lower-literacy environment (Reeder et al., 1988). As well, preschoolers from higher-literacy homes develop a greater sense of story, in that they appear to have an internalized knowledge of such elements of structure as setting, initiating event, and resolution (Doiron and Shapiro, 1988).

One of the most important home factors to be identified in the emergence of literacy is the role of reading to the child (Hartz, 1975; Teale, 1978). Investigations of the effects of reading aloud to children have consistently found positive correlations between this activity and the development of language skills and beginning reading proficiency (Briggs and Elkind, 1977; King and Friesen, 1972; Walker and Kuerbitz, 1979). These results indicate that when there is a high incidence of being read to as a child, scores on language and reading measures tend to be higher. The major study Literacy in Canada (1987) found that people who had been read to as children were less likely to be illiterate as adults than those who had not been read to.

Two components of the reading-aloud experience appear to be important to the child's literacy development. The effect of the language of the story itself (Heath, 1982) and the nature of the parent/child interaction during reading-aloud episodes are the key elements. In a longitudinal study spanning eight years, Wells (1985) attempted to determine the preschool literacy factors related to later school success. Using transcripts of recorded-language samples, he discovered that listening to stories was the only activity significantly related to later achievement. Wells also felt that his findings supported the notion that looking at and talking about books assists children in vocabulary development and in learning how to deal with "display questions"—those questions that are characteristic of school interactions, such as, "What do you think is going to happen next?"

Other researchers also assert that book-reading episodes assist the child in shifting from heavy dependence on contextualized language experiences to the more sophisticated abilities required in decontextualized language (Snow, 1983). The term *contextualized* suggests the child's need for the presence of the "objective event," for example, the presence of the "golden arches" in order to recognize the label "McDonalds." *Decontextualized* language, on the other hand, is the language of schooling (Olson, 1977) and the ability to use and understand decontextualized language is directly related to success in early literacy acquisition (Scollon and Scollon, 1981). Aspects of language employed by the adult while reading aloud, such as labeling objects for the child (Watson and Shapiro, 1988) and eliciting comments and questions from the child (Hess et al., 1982), have been found to be related to children's metalinguistic ability as seen in their performance on schoollike language and reading tasks. Metalinguistic ability may be thought of as children's subconscious and/or conscious knowledge of language and language tasks.

Emergent Reading

Research into the emergence of reading behavior has generally focused on two areas of children's knowledge. The area considered first, primarily because it concerns preschool-age children, is the child's concepts of print. What does the child know about the purposes and functions of print? What does the child know about how books work? The second area of research is metalinguistic awareness. What does the child know about the ways in which language works that are important for successful reading?

In a series of studies, Marie Clay (1977) observed preschool-age children's developing concepts about print. She found that print awareness in children—attention to letters and words—seemed to progress from a basic interest in print seen in the environment to a recognition that print is used to convey messages. Research has consistently demonstrated that children learn to respond to print in their environment by reading signs found in familiar contexts (Hiebert, 1978; Mason, 1980; Ylisto, 1967). Not only do children respond to environmental print but they also have been found to ask questions regarding the print found in various locations of books and about the text (Smolkin et al., 1988). Longitudinal investigations have concluded that due to the social beginnings of early literacy, young children expect reading to be meaningful (Harste et al., 1982).

Children also learn about the ways books function and how print is processed. Studies have shown that there is a developmental progression in children's understandings of how to use or handle books, the differences between print and pictures, and print directionality (Day and Day, 1979; Robeck and Wiseman, 1982; Sulzby, 1985). Further, it has been found that print concepts are related to preschoolers' understanding of speech acts such as requests and offers (Reeder et al., 1988) and children's linguistic pragmatic strategies (Reeder and Shapiro, 1993), reading ability in kindergarten and the primary grades (Day et al., 1981; Kontos and Mackley, 1985; Lomax and McGee, 1987), and writing achievement (Ollila et al., 1986). Preschool knowledge of the purposes of print has also been found to be related to later reading achievement up through grade 4 (Huba et al., 1989).

The majority of studies that have examined metalinguistic awareness have been done with young, school-age children. Thus, the principal component of metalinguistic awareness studied has been the children's knowledge that language is made up of sounds since beginning reading programs often involve the ability to deal with discrete sound/symbol relationships. The ability to segment language into increasingly smaller units appears to be developmental in nature. Younger children have more difficulty with tasks such as breaking down a sentence into its component words (Holden and MacGinitie, 1972), words into syllables (Ehri, 1975), and syllables into phonemes than do older students (Sawyer, 1983). It is also true that visual distinctions such as word boundaries (Holden and MacGinitie, 1972; Mickish, 1974) and visual/auditory tasks (Evans et al., 1979) are more easily made by older students. Segmental analysis abilities, the ability to pick out increasingly smaller units of language, have been shown to improve with age (Treiman and Baron, 1981).

The relationship between the ability to segment at the phoneme level and the ability to read has been clearly demonstrated (Ehri, 1984; Tunmer and Nesdale, 1985). Findings from research with children experiencing reading and spelling problems indicate that they often have difficulties with phonemic segmentation as well (Nix and Shapiro, 1986; Shapiro et al., 1990; Vellutino and Scanlon, 1984). This aspect of metalinguistic awareness is thought to be critical for becoming an independent reader (Juel et al., 1986) and is seen as a prerequisite for success in learning to read in reading programs containing a strong emphasis on decoding (Yopp, 1986). Finally, phonemic segmentation ability has been seen to mature in conjunction with reading instruction. In this regard, results of an Italian research study suggest that instruction that emphasizes the linguistic characteristics of the material and the unique language proficiency of the students may enhance the development of this ability (Zucchermaglio et al., 1986).

Emergent Writing

As already pointed out, reading and writing do not operate in isolation from one another. Research indicates that they often develop concurrently (Bissex, 1980; Teale and Sulzby, 1986). At one time educators felt that writing was beyond the ability of young children and should be postponed until reading ability had been acquired. However, research with young children demonstrates that writing behaviors begin prior to formal schooling (Ferreiro and Teberosky, 1982; Hall et al., 1976) and suggests that children should learn to read through the process of writing (Calkins, 1983; Chomsky, 1971; Graves, 1983).

The research literature indicates that emergent writing is developmental in nature; that is, children move through a sequence of writing stages as they acquire proficiency (Harste et al., 1982). Theories of writing acquisition have been developed through the observation and analyses of preschool-age children's writing (Clay, 1975; Ferreiro and Teberosky, 1982). These researchers believe that children construct their own knowledge of writing as they struggle to understand how print works and the conventions of print.

Clay (1975) observed the writing of five-year-olds and found that the children's writing indicated what conventions of print they had mastered. She hypothesized that children appear to follow 13 principles in their early writing. In general, according to Clay, children begin their writing development by recognizing that signs carry messages and that what they say can be written down. Children experiment with letter forms and then begin to take stock of their own learning by practicing all the words they know. Children then move from writing single words to producing groupings of words, demonstrating an awareness of space and direction.

Ferreiro and Teberosky (1982) examined the writing of three- to five-year-olds from literate and illiterate families. Unlike Clay, who did not believe that children passed through stages, these researchers discovered five distinct levels of writing acquisition. In the first level, children generate graphic character strings or scribbles of a highly similar nature. Next, children produce separate and more defined character strings that are more representative of conventional writing. The third level sees the children assigning individual letters to represent syllables of words. Level four marks the emergence of alphabetic principles as children move to a closer sound/symbol correspondence in which groups of letters are combined. Finally, at level five, children understand that each written character represents a sound value smaller than a syllable and this is seen in their alphabetic writing, which approximates conventional writing.

Other researchers have also discovered developmental levels of writing for preschoolers (DeFord, 1980; Sulzby, 1986) but not necessarily for all first-graders (Gunderson and Shapiro, 1988). This body of research, while differing as to whether children actually pass through defined levels, suggests that children acquire knowledge of writing by actively trying to reconstruct language for themselves.

Similar to the concept of metalinguistic awareness is metacognition or knowledge about one's own cognitive processes and products. This ability has been found to be of great importance in reading and writing proficiency, yet it has been assumed that young children have underdeveloped metacognitive abilities. Rowe (1988) investigated this area using ethnographic techniques. She spent three or four days per week over an eight-month period observing and interacting with three- and four-year-olds as they performed reading and writing activities. Rowe discovered that children do possess a repertoire of metacognitive abilities prior to the onset of formal instruction.

Like Rowe, other researchers have found that kindergartners can identify many writing functions: to communicate, to remember, to learn, and to express individual thoughts or feelings. Furthermore, the children also could describe negative consequences of not being able to write (Freeman and Sanders, 1989).

The use of invented spelling, common to whole-language programs, might also have a positive effect on young children's emerging literacy skills. Clarke (1988) investigated the effects of traditional spelling and invented spelling on reading, writing, and spelling ability. In a comparative study of 100 children, she found that the invented spelling group were more independent in their early writing, produced longer compositions, had greater skill in spelling as measured on a standardized test, and were better on an untimed word analysis test. Results such as these have led some educators to call for the classroom encouragement of invented spelling (Stahl et al., 1989).

Research Perspective 4: Children, as they enter school, are not "blank slates" to be filled with new information. Rather, they bring with them knowledge about print and emerging abilities in both reading and writing.

This perspective is supported by research that has shown that:

Children who have been read to as preschoolers know more about books and story structure and seem to achieve better scores on measures of language and beginning reading proficiency.

Ease of reading acquisition seems to be linked to metalinguistic awareness, that is, the child's knowledge of language.

Children appear to construct their own knowledge of writing by actively trying to reconstruct language for themselves.

Conclusion

Methods of reading instruction, especially those that do not utilize basal readers, seem to become involved in "great debates" regarding their ability to promote overall growth in reading development. Teachers and school-district officials are often loath to abandon the traditional form of reading instruction. While understandable, the hesitancy to implement new and more child-centered approaches is surprising if one considers the research on the use of basal readers, let alone their content, which has already been alluded to. It is common knowledge that in order to improve a skill, it must be practiced. So practice is crucial if a child is to become a skilled reader (Downing, 1984). Yet research indicates that many children receiving reading instruction centered on basal readers do not do much reading at all (Allington, 1983; Hiebert, 1983). In fact, an observational study (Gambrell, 1986) reported that at the first-grade level children spend an average of 3½ minutes reading during reading instruction. Students in grades 2 and 3 read for an average of 5¾ and 6¼ minutes, respectively. In less than half of the observations did students ever finish a story!

Since 1986 the body of research related to whole-language has grown at a rapid rate. If one scans the convention programs of professional reading associations since that time, this growth is readily apparent. Much of this research, both qualitative and quantitative, indicates that there are many benefits for children who are receiving their literacy instruction in whole-language classrooms. These children become effective readers. Their vocabulary increases, they employ varied strategies in word recognition, their comprehension abilities range from simple literal recall to more sophisticated judgments about authors' intent, they read for pleasure and information, and, perhaps more importantly, they have positive attitudes toward reading. In addition, these children become knowledgeable about the writing process and usually display superior writing ability.

Nontraditional reading programs have, in the past, produced reading growth and positive attitudes toward reading. A body of research on these programs provides support for educators who believe that children use complex rules of narrative production, perhaps learned from the stories they have heard, and that these structures should be built on and extended in reading instruction (Dombey, 1983). This research literature implies that children do not have to read simple stories with simplified language. Rather, "learning to read must be inextricably tied to what is read" (Fox, 1985, p. 380).

The research on emergent literacy supports the idea that children learn about reading and writing in active, not passive, ways. Children construct their own knowledge about literacy in natural contexts for their own purposes. Each child enters the elementary classroom with literacy knowledge and emerging abilities that are unique to that child. If all children are to be given the opportunity to become proficient in reading and writing, then acknowledgment of their preschool learning and the manner in which they learn must be found in the classroom (Shapiro and Doiron, 1987). Programs such as whole-language build on this knowledge and take into account the uniqueness of each individual. The research presented in this chapter should provide accurate perspectives on whole-language teaching for those teachers who desire to implement this approach or who have already done so. Research on the reading/writing relationship indicates that these are not separate and distinct aspects of language abilities. Rather, reading and writing are connected and have some impact on each other. Case studies show that when children write they are also learning to read (Graves, 1983). Walter Loban, the author of one of the most thorough studies of school children's language development, believes that research supports the notion that children must apply what they are learning "to situations in which they have something to say, a deep desire to say it, and someone to whom they genuinely want to say it" (1986, p. 614). This application is seen in a whole-language approach.

Four perspectives have been derived from the research studies reviewed in this chapter. First, the whole-language approach has already shown that it can proficiently develop young children's literacy acquisition, especially in the development of writing skills that heretofore were thought developmentally impossible for primary-grade children. Second, nontraditional reading programs (not centering on basal readers) other than whole-language have shown in the past to be a viable means of providing reading instruction in terms of fostering both growth in reading ability and the development of positive attitudes. Third, support does exist for the belief that reading and writing are related to some degree and that, to a certain extent, writing instruction can influence reading and vice versa. Fourth, as they enter school, children are not "blank slates" to be filled with new information. Rather, they bring with them knowledge about print and emerging abilities in both reading and writing and these should be taken advantage of in their early school years.

Taken as a group, these research perspectives can provide whole-language proponents with a clear view that this approach, when applied by good teachers, is a viable instructional alternative and truly benefits the literacy skills development of children. Furthermore, several implications for practice are generated by these research perspectives.

1. Oral language should be linked to written forms of language in the classroom.
2. Teachers should promote rich language experiences to increase oral language abilities and to focus on the decontextualized nature of language.

3. Instruction should build on and expand children's knowledge of reading and writing and these should be developed simultaneously.
4. Good quality children's literature should be an integral part of the classroom and the literacy program.
5. Teachers must be seen to be active users of reading/writing skills and strategies.
6. Teachers must provide a nurturing literacy environment that emulates the safe and supportive environment of the home.

REFERENCES

Allington, R. L. (1983). The reading instruction provided readers of differing ability. *The Elementary School Journal, 83,* 548–559.

Anderson, R. C., Hiebert, E. H., Scott, J. A. & Wilkinson, I. A. G. (1984). *Becoming a nation of readers: The report of the Commission on Reading.* Washington, DC: The National Institute of Education.

Ashton-Warner, S. (1963). *Teacher.* New York: Bantam Books.

Bader, L. A., Veatch, J. & Eldridge, J. L. (1987). Trade books or basal readers? *Reading Improvement, 24,* 62–67.

Beck, I., Omanson, R. & McKeown, M. (1982). An instructional redesign of reading lessons: Effects on comprehension. *Reading Research Quarterly 17,* 462–482.

Beck, I., McKeown, M., Omanson, R. & Pople, M. (1984). Improving the comprehensibility of stories: The effects of revisions that improve coherence. *Reading Research Quarterly, 19,* 263–277.

Belanger, J. (1987a). *Reading achievement and writing proficiency: A critical review of research.* Paper presented at the Canadian Council of Teachers of English, Winnipeg, Manitoba.

Belanger, J. (1987b). Theory and research into reading and writing connections: A critical review. *Reading-Canada-Lecture, 5,* 10–21.

Bennett, S. W. (1971). *The key vocabulary in organic reading: An evaluation of Ashton-Warner's assumptions of beginning reading.*

Doctoral dissertation, University of Michigan.

Bissex, G. L. (1980). *Gnys at work: A child learns to read.* Cambridge, MA: Harvard University Press.

Blakey, J. M. (1980). *An investigation of the relationship between children's key vocabulary responses and certain Piagetian concepts.* Doctoral dissertation, University of British Columbia.

Boljonis, A. & Hinchman, K. (1988). First graders' perceptions of reading and writing. In J.E. Readence and R.S. Baldwin (Eds.), *Dialogues in literacy research.* Chicago, IL: National Reading Conference.

Bond, G. L. & Dykstra, R. (1967). The cooperative program in first grade reading instruction. *Reading Research Quarterly, 2,* 5–142.

Brazziel, W. F. & Terrell, M. (1962). For first graders: A good start in school. *Elementary School Journal, 62,* 352–355.

Brennan, A., Bridge, C. & Winograd, P. (1986). The effects of structural variation on children's recall of basal reader stories. *Reading Research Quarterly, 21,* 91–104.

Bridge, C. Winograd, P. & Haley, A. (1983). Using predictable materials versus pre-primers to teach beginning sight words. *The Reading Teacher, 35,* 884–891.

Briggs, C. & Elkind, D. (1977). Characteristics of early readers. *Perceptual and Motor Skills, 44,* 1231–1237.

Burns-Paterson, A. L. (1991). *First and third graders' concepts of reading in different instructional settings.* Educational Resources Information Center, ED 339027.

Cairney, T. H. (1988). The purpose of basals: What children think. *The Reading Teacher, 41,* 420–428.

Calkins, L. (1983). *Lessons from a child: On the teaching and learning of writing.* Portsmouth, NH: Heinemann.

Chomsky, C. (1971). Write first, read later. *Childhood Education, 48,* 296–299.

Chomsky, C. (1972). Stages in language development and reading behavior. *Harvard Educational Review, 42,* 1–33.

Clark, M. M. (1976). *Young fluent readers: What can they teach us?* London: Heinemann.

Clarke, L. K. (1988). Invented versus traditional spelling in first graders' writing: Effects on learning to spell and read. *Research in the Teaching of English, 22,* 281–309.

Clay, M. (1966). *Emergent reading behavior.* Doctoral dissertation, University of Auckland, New Zealand.

Clay, M. (1971). Research on language and reading in Pakeha and Polynesian groups. In D.K. Braken and E. Malmquist (Eds.), *Improving reading ability around the world.* Newark, DE: International Reading Association.

Clay, M. (1975). *What did I write?* Exeter, NH: Heinemann.

Clay, M. (1977). *Reading: The pattern of complex behavior.* Auckland, New Zealand: Heinemann.

Cohen, D. (1968). The effect of literature on vocabulary and reading achievement. *Elementary English, 45,* 209–13, 217.

Cohen, S. A. & Kornfield, G. S. (1970). Oral vocabulary and beginning reading in disadvantaged children. *The Reading Teacher, 24,* 33–38.

Cullinen, B., Jaggar, A. & Strickland, D. (1974). Language expansion for black children in the primary grades: A research report. *Young Children, 29,* 98–112.

Dahl, K. L. & Freppon, P. A. (1991). Literacy learning in whole-language classrooms: An analysis of low socioeconomic urban children learning to read and write in kindergarten. In J. Zutell & S. McCormick (Eds.), *Learner factors/Teacher factors: Issues in literacy research and instruction.* Chicago, Ill: National Reading Conference.

Day, K. C., & Day, H. D. (1979). Development of kindergarten children's understanding of concepts about print and oral language. In M.L. Kamil and A.H. Moe (Eds.), *Reading research: Studies and applications.* Rochester, NY: National Reading Conference.

Day, K. C., Day, H. D., Spicola, R. & Griffen, M. (1981). The development of orthographic linguistic awareness in kindergarten children and the relationship of this awareness to later reading achievement. *Reading Psychology, 2,* 76–87.

DeFord, D. E. (1980). Young children and their writing. *Theory into Practice, 19,* 157–162.

DeFord, D. E. (1981). Literacy: Reading, writing, and other essentials. *Language Arts, 58,* 652–658.

Doake, D. B. (1980). Report on the shared book experience approach to learning to read. Unpublished paper, Acadia University.

Doiron, R. & Shapiro, J. (1988). Home literacy environment and children's sense of story. *Reading Psychology, 9,* 187–202.

Dombey, H. (1983). Learning the language of books. In M. Meek (Ed.), *Opening moves: Work in progress in the study of children's language development.* London: University of London Institute of Education.

Downing, J. (1967). The effects of the initial teaching alphabet on young children's written composition. *Educational Research, 9,* 137–144.

Downing, J. (1984). Task awareness in the development of reading skill. In J. Downing and R. Valtin (Eds.), *Language awareness and learning to read.* New York: Springer-Verlag.

Downing, J., Dwyer, C. A., Feitelson, D., Jansen, M., Matilhasi, H., Eggi, D. R., Sakamoto, T., Taylor, H., Thackray, D. V. & Thomson, D. (1979). A cross-national survey of cultural expectations and sex-role standards in reading. *Journal of Research in Reading, 2,* 8–23.

Duquette, R. J. (1970). *An experimental study comparing the effect of a specific program of sight vocabulary upon reading and writing achievement of selected first and second grade children.* Doctoral dissertation, Arizona State University.

Durkin, D. (1966). *Children who read early.* New York: Teachers College Press.

Dzama, M. A. (1975). Comparing use of generalizations of phonics in LEA, basal vocabulary. *The Reading Teacher, 28,* 466–472.

Eckhoff, B. (1985). *How basal reading texts effect children's writing.* Doctoral dissertation, Harvard University.

Ehri, L. C. (1975). Word consciousness in readers and prereaders. *Journal of Educational Psychology, 67,* 204–212.

Ehri, L. C. (1984). How orthography alters spoken language competencies in children learning to read and spell. In J. Downing and R. Valtin (Eds.), *Language awareness and learning to read.* New York: Springer-Verlag.

Eldridge, J. L. & Butterfield, D. (1984). *Sacred cows make good hamburger: Report on a reading research project.* ERIC Document Reproduction Service, ED 255 861.

Eldridge, L. (1991). An experiment with a modified whole-language approach in first grade classrooms. *Reading Research and Instruction, 30,* 31–38.

Elley, W. B. & Mangubhai, F. (1983). The impact of reading on second language learning. *Reading Research Quarterly, 19,* 53–67.

Evanechko, P., Ollila, L. & Armstrong, R. (1974). An investigation of the relationships between children's performance in written language and their reading ability. *Research in the Teaching of English, 8,* 315–326.

Evans, M., Taylor, N. & Blum, I. (1979). Children's written language awareness and its relation to reading acquisition. *Journal of Reading Behaviour, 11,* 7–19.

Ferreiro, E. & Teberosky, A. (1982). *Literacy before schooling.* Portsmouth, NH: Heinemann.

Fisher, C. W. & Hiebert, E. H. (1988). *Characteristics of tasks in two literacy programs.* Paper presented at the Annual Meeting of the National Reading Conference, Tucson, Arizona.

Freppon, P. (1991). Children's concepts of the nature and purpose of reading in different instructional settings. *Journal of Reading Behaviour, 23,* 139–163.

Fox, C. (1985). The book that talks. *Language Arts, 62,* 372–384.

Freeman, E. B. & Sanders, T. R. (1989). Kindergarten children's emerging concepts of writing functions in the community. *Early Childhood Research Quarterly, 4,* 331–338.

Froese, V., Gunderson, L. & Shapiro, J. (1988). *A longitudinal investigation of vocabulary development and growth in writing ability of children in whole language classrooms.* Paper presented at the Annual Reading Research Conference of the Washington Organization for Reading Development, International Reading Association, Seattle, WA.

Gambrell, L. B. & Palmer, B. M. (1992). Children's metacognitive knowledge about reading and writing in literature-based and conventional classrooms. In C.K. Kinzer & D.J. Leu (Eds.), *Literacy research, theory, and practice: Views from many perspectives.* Chicago, ILL: National Reading Conference.

Gambrell, L. B. (1986). Reading in the primary grades: How often, how long? In M.R. Sampson (Ed.), *The pursuit of literacy.* Dubuque, IA: Kendall/Hunt Publishing Company.

Giles, D. E. (1966). *The effect of two approaches to reading instruction upon the oral language development of first grade pupils.* Doctoral dissertation, North Texas State University.

Graves, D. (1983). *Writing: Children and teachers at work.* Portsmouth, NH: Heinemann.

Gray, L. (1963). *Teaching children to read.* New York: The Ronald Press Company.

Gunderson, L. & Shapiro, J. (1986). Some findings on whole language instruction. *Reading-Canada-Lecture, 5,* 22–26.

Gunderson, L. & Shapiro, J. (1988). Whole language instruction: Writing in 1st grade. *The Reading Teacher, 41,* 430–437.

Gunderson, L., Shapiro, J. & Froese, V. (1988). *The effects of implicit versus explicit modeling on the development of vocabulary, syntactic complexity, quality and topics in writing in whole language classrooms.* Paper presented at the Annual Meeting of the National Reading Conference, Tucson, Arizona.

Hagerty, P., Hiebert, E. H. & Owen, M. K. (1989). Students' comprehension, writing and perceptions in two approaches to literacy instruction. In S. McCormick & J. Zutell (Eds.), *Cognitive and Social Perspectives for Literacy Research and Instruction.* Chicago, ILL: National Reading Conference.

Hall, M. A. (1965). *The development and evaluation of a language experience approach to reading with first-grade culturally disadvantaged children.* Doctoral dissertation, University of Maryland.

Hall, M. A., Moretz, S. A. & Stratton, J. (1976). Writing before grade one—A study of early writers. *Language Arts, 53,* 582–585.

Hammill, C. & McNutt, G. (1980). Language abilities and reading: A review of the literature of their relationship. *Elementary School Journal, 80,* 269–277.

Harris, A. J. & Morrison, C. (1969). The CRAFT project: A final report. *The Reading Teacher, 22,* 335–340.

Hartz, K. R. (1975). *A comparative analysis of children who enter kindergarten reading and children of the same age who require additional readiness for reading.* Doctoral dissertation, University of Wisconsin.

Harste, J. C., Woodward, V. A. & Burke, C. (1982). Children's language and world: Initial encounters with print. In J. Langer

and M. Smith-Burke (Eds.), *Bridging the gap/reader meets author.* Newark, DE: International Reading Association.

Heath, S. B. (1982). What no bedtime story means: Narrative skills at home and at school. *Language in Society, 11,* 49–76.

Henderson, E. H., Estes, T. H. & Stonecash, S. (1972). An exploratory study of word acquisition among first-graders at midyear in a language experience approach. *Journal of Reading Behaviour, 4,* 21–31.

Hess, R. D., Holloway, S., Price, G. G. & Dickson, W. P. (1982). Family environments and the acquisition of reading skills. In L. M. Laosa and I. E. Sigel (Eds.), *Families as learning environments for children.* New York: Plenum Press.

Hiebert, E. H. (1978). Preschool children's understanding of written language. *Child Development, 49,* 1231–1234.

Hiebert, E. H. (1981). Developmental patterns and inter-relationships of preschool children's print awareness. *Reading Research Quarterly, 16,* 236–260.

Hiebert, E. H. (1983). An examination of ability grouping for reading instruction. *Reading Research Quarterly, 18,* 231–255.

Holdaway, D. (1979). *The foundations of literacy.* Sydney: Ashton Scholastic Publications.

Holden, M. H. & MacGinitie, W.H. (1972). Children's conceptions of word boundaries in speech and print. *Journal of Educational Psychology, 63,* 551–557.

Huba, M. E., Robinson, S. S. & Kontos, S. (1989). Prereaders' understanding of the purposes of print and subsequent reading achievement. *Journal of Educational Research, 82,* 210–215.

Hughes, T. O. (1975). *Sentence combining: A means of increasing reading comprehension.* ERIC Document Reproduction Service, No. ED 112 421.

Hunt, K. W. (1977). Early blooming and late blooming syntactic structures. In C. R.

Cooper and L. Odell (Eds.), *Evaluating writing*. Urbana, IL: NCTE, 91–106.

Johns, J. L. & Ellis, D. W. (1976). Reading: Children tell it like it is. *Reading World, 16,* 115–128.

Johnson, N. R. (1976). *A comparison of syntactic writing maturity with reading comprehension.* ERIC Document Reproduction Service, ED 141 794.

Juel, C., Griffith, P. L. & Gough, P. B. (1986). Acquisition of literacy: A longitudinal study of children in first and second grade. *Journal of Educational Psychology, 78,* 243–255.

Kelley, A. M. (1977). Sight vocabularies and experience stories. *Elementary English, 52,* 327–328.

Kelley, K. R. (1984). *The effect of writing instruction on reading comprehension and story writing ability.* Doctoral dissertation, University of Pittsburgh.

Keshian, J. G. (1963). The characteristics and experiences of children who learn to read successfully. *Elementary English, 40,* 615–616.

King, E. M. & Friesen, D. T. (1972). Children who read in kindergarten. *Alberta Journal of Educational Research, 18,* 147–161.

Klesius, J. P., Griffith, P. L. & Zielonka, P. (1991). A whole language and traditional instruction comparison: Overall effectiveness and development of the alphabetic principle. *Reading Research and Instruction, 30,* 47–61.

Kontos, S. & Mackley, M. (1985). *Development and inter-relationships of reading knowledge and skills during kindergarten and first grade.* Paper presented at the American Educational Research Association, Chicago, IL.

Larrick, N. (1987). Illiteracy starts too soon. *Phi Delta Kappan, 69,* 184–189.

Lee, D. M. & Allen, R. V. (1963). *Learning to read through experience,* (2nd ed.). New York: Appleton-Century-Crofts.

Literacy in Canada: A Research Report. (1987). Prepared for Southam News, Ottawa, by the Creative Research Group.

Loban, W. D. (1963). *The language of elementary school children.* NCTE Research Report No. 1. Urbana, IL: NCT.

Loban, W. D. (1986). Research currents: The somewhat stingy story of research into children's language. *Language Arts, 63,* 608–616.

Lomax, R. G. & McGee, L. M. (1987). Young children's concepts about print and reading: Toward a model of word reading acquisition. *Reading Research Quarterly, 22,* 237–256.

Mackie, B. C. (1982). *The effects of a sentence-combining program on the reading comprehension of fourth-grade students.* Doctoral dissertation, Hofstra University.

Mallett, W. G. (1975). *A comparative study of the language experience approach with junior high native Indian students.* Doctoral dissertation, Arizona State University.

Mallett, W. G. (1978). The effect of the language experience approach on attitudes of junior high native Indian remedial reading students. *Adsig Journal, 1,* 11–15.

Mason, J. (1980). When do children begin to read: An exploration of four-year-old children's letter and word reading comprehension. *Reading Research Quarterly, 15,* 203–227.

May, R. B. & Ollila, L. O. (1981). Reading sex-role attitudes in preschoolers. *Reading Research Quarterly, 16,* 583–595.

Mazurkiewicz, A. J. (1975). Comparative attitudes and achievements of the ITA and T.O. taught students in the tenth and eleventh grades. *Reading World, 15,* 242–251.

McAfee, D. C. (1980). *Effect of sentence-combining instruction on the reading and writing achievement of fifth-grade children in a suburban school.* Doctoral dissertation, Texas Women's University.

McCallum, R. D., Moore, S. & Whitlow, R. F. (1992). *Direct skills instruction in early reading: A longitudinal analysis.* Paper presented at the 42nd Annual Meeting of the National Reading Conference, San Antonio, TX.

McGee, L. M. & Lomax, R. G. (1990). On combining apples and oranges: A response to

Stahl and Miller. *Review of Educational Research, 60,* 133–140.

Mervar, K. & Hiebert, E. H. (1988). *Students' self-selection abilities and amount of reading in literature based and conventional classrooms.* Paper presented at the Annual Meeting of the National Reading Conference, Tucson, AZ.

Mickish, V. (1974). Children's perceptions of written word boundaries. *Journal of Reading Behaviour, 6,* 19–22.

Moon, C. & Wells, G. (1979). The influence of the home on learning to read. *Journal of Research in Reading, 2,* 53–62.

Morrow, L. M. (1992). The impact of a literature-based program on literacy achievement, use of literature, and attitudes of children from minority backgrounds. *Reading Research Quarterly, 27,* 250–275.

Nix, G. W. & Shapiro, J. (1986). Auditory perceptual processing in learning-assistance children. *Journal of Research in Reading, 9,* 92–102.

O'Donnell, C. M. & Raymond, D. (1972). Developing reading readiness in the kindergarten. *Elementary English, 49,* 768–771.

Ollila, L. O., Collis, B. & Yore, L. D. (1986). Predicting first-grade students' writing achievement using the Canadian Readiness Test and selected measures of cognitive development. *Journal of Educational Research, 80,* 47–52.

Olsen, W. (1952). Seeking, self-selection and pacing in the use of books by children. *The Packet, 7.* Boston: D.C. Heath.

Olson, D. R. (1977). From utterance to text: The bias of language in speech and writing. *Harvard Educational Review, 47,* 257–281.

Papandropoulu, I. & Sinclair, H. (1974). What is a word? *Human Development, 17,* 241–258.

Partridge, M. E., Foil, J. B. & Bitner, J. L. (1991). *The effects of daily opportunities to draw and write on kindergarten children's ability to represent phonemes in their spelling inventions.* Paper presented at the Annual Meeting of

the National Association for the Education of Young Children, Denver.

Rasinski, T. V. & DeFord, D. E. (1988). First graders' conceptions of literacy: A matter of schooling. *Theory Into Practice, 27,* 53–61.

Read, C. (1971). Preschool children's knowledge of English phonology. *Harvard Educational Review, 41,* 1–34.

Reeder, K., Wakefield, J. & Shapiro, J. (1988). Children's speech act comprehension and early literacy experience. *First Language, 8,* 29–48.

Reeder, K. & Shapiro, J. (1993). Relationships between early literate experience and knowledge and children's linguistic pragmatic strategies. *Journal of Pragmatics, 19,* 5–26.

Reutzel, D. R. & Cooter, B. (1990). Whole language: Comparative effects on first grade reading achievement. *Journal of Educational Research, 83,* 252–257.

Ribowsky, H. (1985). *The effects of a code emphasis approach and a whole language approach upon emergent literacy of kindergarten children.* ERIC Document Reproduction Service, ED 269 720.

Riendeau, B. A. (1973). *An exploratory investigation of the effect of two differing approaches of reading instruction on the self-social concepts of first grade children.* Doctoral dissertation, American University.

Robeck, C. P. & Wiseman, D. (1982). The development of literacy in middle-class preschool children. *Reading Psychology, 3,* 105–116.

Rowe, D. W. (1988). *Preschoolers' use of metacognitive strategies in self-selected literacy events.* Paper presented at the Annual Meeting of the National Reading Conference, Tucson, Arizona.

Sawyer, D. J. (1983). Observed patterns in the refinement of phonemic segmenting abilities among grade one boys. *Reading-Canada-Lecture, 2,* 35–44.

Scollon, R. & Scollon, S. (1981). *Narrative, literacy and face in interethnic communication.* Norwood, NJ: Ablex.

Seeber, F. (1969). The development of the individualized reading movement. In S. Duker (Ed.), *Individualized reading*. Metuchen, NJ: Scarecrow Press.

Shanahan, T. (1984). Nature of the reading-writing relation: An exploratory multivariate analysis. *Journal of Educational Psychology, 76,* 466–477.

Shapiro, B. J. (1973). The effect of reading method on compositions: I.t.a. vs. t.o. *Journal of Reading Behaviour, 5,* 82–87.

Shapiro, J. (1980). Primary children's attitudes toward reading in male and female teachers' classrooms. *Journal of Reading Behaviour, 12,* 255–258.

Shapiro, J. (1985). Preprimary children's attitudes toward reading as a sex-role appropriate activity. *Canadian Journal of Research in Early Childhood Education, 1,* 18–26.

Shapiro, J. (1990). Sex-role appropriateness of reading and reading instruction. *Reading Psychology, 11,* 241–269.

Shapiro, J. & Doiron, R. (1987). Literacy environments: Bridging the gap between home and school. *Childhood Education, 63,* 262–269.

Shapiro, J. & Gunderson, L. (1988). Language experience generated vocabulary vs. basal reader vocabulary at grade one. *Reading Research and Instruction, 27,* 40–46.

Shapiro, J., Nix, G. W. & Foster, S. F. (1990). Auditory perceptual processing in reading disabled children. *Journal of Research in Reading, 13,* 123–132.

Shapiro, J. & White, W. (1991). Attitudes and perceptions of reading in traditional and nontraditional reading programs. *Reading Research and Instruction, 30,* 52–66.

Simons, H. D. & Ammon, P. R. (1987). *The language of beginning reading texts: Final report.* Urbana, IL: National Council of Teachers of English Research Foundation.

Smith, C. B. (1968). *Relation of first grade reading and composition.* ERIC Document Reproduction Service, ED 020 080.

Smith, F. (1984). Reading like a writer. In J. M. Jensen (Ed.), *Composing and comprehending.* Urbana, IL: NCRE/ERIC.

Smolkin, L. B., Conlon, A. & Yaden, D. B. (1988). Print salient illustrations in children's picture books: The emergence of written language awareness. In J. E. Readence and R. S. Baldwin (Eds.), *Dialogues in literacy research. Thirty-seventh Yearbook of the National Reading Conference.* Chicago: The National Reading Conference, pp. 59–68.

Snow, C. (1983). Literacy and language: Relationships during the preschool years. *Harvard Educational Review, 53,* 165–189.

Stahl, S. A., Osborne, J. & Lehr, F. (1989). A summary of Adams, M. J., *Beginning to read: Thinking and learning about print.* Urbana-Champaign, IL: Center for the Study of Reading.

Stahl, S. A. & Miller, .D. (1989). Whole language and language experience approaches for beginning reading: A quantitative research synthesis. *Review of Educational Research, 59,* 87–116.

Stauffer, M. (1973). *Comparative effects of a language arts approach and basal reader approach to first grade reading achievement.* Doctoral dissertation, University of Delaware.

Stauffer, R. G. (1966). The effectiveness of language arts and basic reading approaches to first grade reading instruction. *The Reading Teacher, 20,* 18–24.

Stauffer, R. G. & Hammond, D. W. (1967). The effectiveness of language arts and basic reading approaches to first grade reading instruction—Extended into second grade. *The Reading Teacher, 20,* 740–746.

Stauffer, R. G. & Hammond, D. W. (1969). The effectiveness of language arts and basic reader approaches to first grade reading instruction—Extended into third grade. *Reading Research Quarterly, 4,* 469–499.

Stauffer, R. G., & Pikulski, J. J. (1974). A comparison and measure of oral language growth. *Elementary English, 51,* 1151–1155.

Stice, C. & Bertrand, N. (1988). *The texts and textures of literacy learning in whole language versus traditional-skills classrooms.* Paper presented at the Annual Meeting of the National Reading Conference, Tucson, AZ.

Straw, S. & Schreiner, R. (1982). The effect of sentence manipulation on subsequent measures of reading and listening comprehension. *Reading Research Quarterly, 17,* 339–352.

Sulzby, E. (1985). Children's emergent reading of favorite storybooks. *Reading Research Quarterly, 20,* 458–481.

Sulzby, E. (1986). Writing and reading: Signs of written language organization in the young child. In W. H. Teale and E. Sulzby (Eds.), *Emergent literacy: Reading and writing.* Norwood, NJ: Ablex.

Sutton, M. H. (1964). Readiness for reading at the kindergarten level. *The Reading Teacher, 17,* 234–239.

Taylor, N. E., Blum, I. H. & Logsdon, D. M. (1986). The development of written language awareness: Environmental aspects of program characteristics. *Reading Research Quarterly, 11,* 132–149.

Teale, W. H. (1978). Positive environments for learning to read: What studies of early readers tell us. *Language Arts, 55,* 922–932.

Teale, W. H. & Sulzby, E. (1986). *Emergent literacy: Reading and writing.* Norwood, NJ: Ablex.

Thompson, R. (1971). *Summarizing research pertaining to individualized reading.* ERIC Document Reproduction Service, ED 065 836.

Tierney, R. J. & Pearson, P. D. (1984). Toward a composing model of reading. In J. M. Jensen (Ed.), *Composing and comprehending.* Urbana, IL: NCRE/ERIC.

Tierney, R. J., Soter, A., O'Flahavan, J. F. & McGinley, W. (1989). The effects of reading and writing upon thinking critically. *Reading Research Quarterly, 24,* 134–169.

Treiman, R. & Baron, J. (1981). Segmental analysis ability: Development and relation to reading ability. In G. E. Mackinnon and T. G. Waller (Eds.), *Reading research—Advances*

in theory and practice. New York: Academic Press.

Tunmer, W. E. & Nesdale, A. R. (1985). Phonemic segmentation skill and beginning reading. *Journal of Educational Psychology, 77,* 417–427.

Tunnell, M. O. (1986). The natural act of reading: An effective approach. *The Advocate, 5,* 156–164.

Varble, M. E. (1990). Analysis of writing samples of students taught by teachers using whole language and traditional approaches. *Journal of Educational Research, 83,* 245–251.

Veatch, J., Sawicki, F., Elliott, E. & Blakey, J. (1973). *Key words to reading.* Columbus, OH: Merrill.

Vellutino, F. R. & Scanlon, D. M. (1984). *Phonologic coding, phonemic segmentation and code acquisition in poor and normal readers.* Paper presented at the Ninth Annual Boston University Conference on Language Development, Boston, MA.

Vilscek, E., Morgan, L. & Cleland, D. L. (1966). Coordinating and integrating language arts instruction in first grade. *The Reading Teacher, 20,* 31–37.

Vite, I. (1963). Individualized reading: Bright and promising. In J. A. Figurel (Ed.), *Reading as an intellectual activity.* Newark, DE: International Reading Association.

Walker, G. H. & Kuerbitz, I. E. (1979). Reading to preschoolers as an aid to successful beginning reading. *Reading Improvement, 16,* 154–159.

Wasserman, S. (1978). Key vocabulary: Impact on beginning reading. *Young Children, 33,* 33–38.

Watson, R. & Shapiro, J. (1988). Discourse from home to school. *Applied Psychology, 37,* 395–409.

Weaver, P. A. (1977). *Component skills in reading comprehension: An investigation of the effects of sentence organization instruction.* ERIC Document Reproduction Service, ED 136 241.

Wells, G. (1985). *The meaning makers.* London: Oxford University Press.

Willardson, M. L. (1972). *A study of the writing ability of second grade students in a communication skills through authorship program.* Doctoral dissertation, University of Idaho.

Wilson, R. M. & Parkey, N. (1970). A modified reading program in a middle school. *Journal of Reading, 13,* 447–452.

Wilucki, B. M. (1984). *The impact of teachers' orientation to literacy on children's developing concepts of written language in kindergarten.* Urbana, IL: National Council of Teachers of English Research Foundation.

Ylisto, I. (1967). *An empirical investigation of early reading responses of young children.* Doctoral dissertation, University of Michigan.

Yopp, H. (1986). *Phoneme segmentation ability: A prerequisite for phonics and sight word achievement in beginning reading?* Paper presented at the National Reading Conference, Austin, TX.

Zeman, S. S. (1969). Reading comprehension and the writing of 2nd and 3rd graders. *The Reading Teacher, 23,* 144–150.

Zucchermaglio, C., Pontecordo, C., Tonucci, F. & Blachowicz, C. L. Z. (1986). Literacy and linguistic awareness: A study of Italian first grade students. *Reading Psychology, 7,* 11–25.

DISCUSSION QUESTIONS

1. Why would reading programs that emphasize fluent reading produce better writers than programs that emphasize accuracy in word recognition?

2. Speculate on the reasons why parental interest and attitude are related to a child's later reading achievement.

3. What might be the advantages of using a nontraditional reading program?

4. Why is the view that skills instruction is a "when and how" rather than an "either/or" concern more appropriate for teachers?

APPENDIX: DOCTORAL DISSERTATIONS ON WHOLE LANGUAGE COMPLETED IN 1993

Title: The Use of and Attitudes toward Performance Assessment in a Primary Grade Program of Whole Language

Author: Powell, Larry Edward

School: Ohio University (0167) Degree: Ph. D. *Date:* 1993 *Pages:* 135

Type of Study: Comparative

Comments: Compared teachers' and students' attitudes toward performance assessment and standardized testing. Both preferred performance assessment. Experimental group did better on standardized test than regular students and showed academic improvement.

Title: Evaluation of the Meramec Valley R-III Whole Language Pilot Program
Author: Baylard-Eidson, Carrie Cunetto
School: Saint Louis University (0193) *Degree:* Ed. D. *Date:* 1993 *Pages:* 145
Type of Study: Qualitative
Comments: Analysis of pilot program concluded it had positive impact on students' learning of written language skills and reading comprehension.

Title: A Study of Transfer Efficiency in Expository Reading Tasks Using Two Methods of Rule Generation
Author: Koch, Anne Ayers
School: University of San Francisco (6019) *Degree:* Ed. D. *Date:*1993 *Pages:* 236
Type of Study: Comparative
Comments: Compared transfer of rules for comprehension of expository reading under direct instruction versus whole-language instruction. Initial performance advantage to direct instruction, but subsequent testing showed improvement under whole-language. Suggests use of combined approach.

Title: Exploring Whole-Language: Incorporating Genuine Reading and Writing opportunities in a First-Grade Classroom
Author: Mosley, Alana Jo
School: Boston University (0017)*Degree:* Ed. D. *Date:* 1993 *Pages:* 180
Type of Study: Ethnographic
Comments: 4½ month intervention; standardized achievement pre- and posttesting; study found no significant achievement improvement but student attitude improved and output increased.

Title: Teacher as Researcher: Transforming Lives through Dialogue and Dialogue Journals in an Eighth-Grade Whole Language Curriculum
Author: Truedale, Laura Saunders
School: University of South Carolina (0202) *Degree:* Ph. D. *Date:* 1993 *Pages:* 225
Type of Study: Ethnographic
Comments: Presented five case studies documenting change in students through use of journals and interaction between students.

Title: Language in Classroom Context: A Descriptive Study of Language/Literacy Learning in Kindergarten/Grade I Children Identified as SLI
Author: McErlain, Eileen Margaret
School: University of South Florida (0206) *Degree:* Ph. D. *Date:* 1993 *Pages:* 359
Type of Study: Qualitative
Comments: 2-year study showed interactive and naturalistic intervention fostered communicative competence in children with special needs in language.

Title: The Influence of the School Principal on the Reading Achievement of Urban African-American Students in Urban Elementary and Middle Schools
Author: Amory, Marion Boothe
School: Boston University (0017) *Degree:* Ed. D. *Date:* 1993 *Pages:* 204
Type of Study: Descriptive
Comments: Study found that principals of schools with successful records in reading used creative approaches, emphasized development of readers, were knowledgeable about reading and involved schools (to greater or lesser degree) in whole language or literature based programs.

Title: A Microethnography of Literature-Based Reading and Writing Instruction in a Whole Language Classroom with 'At-Risk' Adolescents
Author: Stickland, Kathleen M.
School: Indiana University of Pennsylvania (0318) *Degree:* Ph. D. *Date:* 1993 *Pages:* 377
Type of Study: Ethnographic
Comments: At-risk adolescents benefitted from literature-based approach, becoming more engaged, perceiving themselves as learners; teacher modeling considered significant.

Title: A Descriptive Study of Outstanding First-Grade Compensatory Reading Programs in South Carolina
Author: Turner, Pennie P.
School: University of South Carolina (0202) *Degree:* Ed. D. *Date:* 1993 *Pages:* 105
Type of Study: Descriptive
Comments: Analysis of successful reading programs for common characteristics: 21 basal classrooms, 19 combined, 10 that used no basals. Principals surveyed indicated teacher effectiveness most significant factor; teachers indicated belief that program, method, and material most important.

Title: Classroom Teachers' Perceptions of a Statewide Whole-Language Approach to Literacy
Author: Willett, Teresa Donohue
School: The University of Tennessee (0226) *Degree:* Ed. D. *Date:* 1993 *Pages:* 152
Type of Study: Descriptive
Comments: Survey of teachers concluded that teachers see literature-based curriculum as a positive alternative to skills-based curriculum, writing component as effective and assessment as an area of concern.

Title: Effects of Intervention on the Writing and Spelling Skills of Elementary
　　School Students with Severe Speech and Physical Impairments
Author: DeCoste, Denise Chavah
School: The George Washington University (0075) *Degree:* Ed. D. *Date:* 1993
　　Pages: 323
Type of Study: Case Study
Comments: 3 students significantly improved spelling and sentence genera-
　　tion under both skills-based and whole language instruction;
　　skills-based instruction produced slightly better spelling; students
　　preferred whole language instruction.

Title: Implementation of the English-Language Arts Framework in an Open
　　Classroom School in a Northern California School District
Author: Stokes, John Frederich
School: University of Southern California (0208) *Degree:* Ed. D. *Date:* 1992
Type of Study: Descriptive
Comments: Study found strong implementation of new framework and peda-
　　gogy. Vigorous and active involvement at all stages characterized
　　both district and school levels. Cooperative attitude of staff and
　　teacher coaching and planning in schools cited as particularly sig-
　　nificant factors.

Title: The Effects of Computer-Based Training with Multiple Theoretical
　　Perspectives on the Analysis of Cases of Reading Errors
Author: Senior-Canela, Fernando Arturo
School: University of Illinois at Urbana-Champaign (0090) *Degree:* Ph. D. *Date:*
　　1992 *Pages:* 125
Type of Study: Comparative
Comments: Results of study indicated that, regardless of treatment condition,
　　using the computer program increased the average number of the-
　　oretical perspectives subjects used per case. Additional didactic
　　instruction appeared to interfere with flexibly applying new knowl-
　　edge. Suggests more study needed.

Title: An Entry-Year Teacher's Commitment to Teaching Writing with a Whole-
　　Language Philosophy in a Traditional School System and the Socialization
　　Process She Experiences: A Case Study
Author: Buckles, Janice Deanne Davis
School: Oklahoma State University (0664) *Degree:* Ed. D. *Date:* 1992 *Pages:* 156
Type of Study: Case Study
Comments: Study documents teacher's program adjustment and professional
　　growth resulting from conflict between teacher's orientation and
　　that prevailing in the school. Concludes that socialization does af-

fect the beginning teacher but may strengthen her commitment; also concludes that process writing allows children to progress developmentally.

Title: Comparing the Self-Esteem of Early Adolescents in a Traditional Classroom with the Self-Esteem of Early Adolescents in a Whole-Language Classroom
Author: Devries, Beverly Ann
School: Oklahoma State University (0664) *Degree:* Ed. D. *Date:* 1992 *Pages:* 200
Type of Study: Comparative
Comments: In one semester no significant differences were found between most subgroups in the study. Significant differences emerged between students with high ability versus students with low ability and between boys in the traditional group and boys in the whole language group.

Title: A Descriptive Study of the Beliefs and Practices of Head Start Teachers Regarding Early Literacy Development
Author: Lind, Nancy Lessel
School: Loyola University of Chicago (0112) *Degree:* Ph. D. *Date:* 1992 *Pages:* 181
Type of Study: Descriptive/Case Study
Comments: Study found a high level of literacy activity in classrooms; most teachers described as eclectic and atheoretical; suggests that increasing children's meaningful exposure to print and more interaction between adults and individual or small groups of children around literacy behaviors would enhance literacy development.

Title: Evaluating Children's Writing: A Pen Pal Experience Between First Graders and Preservice Teachers
Author: Nieding, Deborah Ann
School: University of Missouri-Columbia (0133) *Degree:* Ph. D. *Date:* 1992 *Pages:* 267
Type of Study: Descriptive
Comments: Study analyzed students letters and reported topics and the frequency of topic use, patterns of initiating and responding to topics and progress toward standard and conventional forms of writing. Concluded that letters offered an authentic learning activity for students and provided valuable information to teachers.

Title: Usage of Whole-Language Instruction in Elementary School Classrooms: A Case Study
Author: Miller, Franklin Joe
School: University of North Texas (0158) *Degree:* Ed. D. *Date:* 1992 *Pages:* 335
Type of Study: Qualitative
Comments: Use of whole language instruction in classrooms analyzed relative to teachers commitment to and understanding of whole language.

Concluded that teachers need to become knowledgeable of whole language principles and committed personally in order to develop integrated, coherent programs. Also concluded that assessment of whole language instruction is an area of ambiguity and uncertainty for teachers in the study.

Title: Effecting Teacher Change Through Implementation of the Process Writing Component of Language Arts Curriculum
Author: Hildebrand, Charlene
School: University of Northern Colorado (0161) *Degree:* Ed. D. *Date:* 1992
   Pages: 439
Type of Study: Ethnographic
Comments: Case Study of changes in belief and practice during implementation of new holistic language arts program. Concluded that staff development critical to supporting change and to implementing new program.

Title: Spelling Growth: A Transactive Process
Author: Oglan, Gerald Richard
School: University of South Carolina (0202) *Degree:* Ph. D. *Date:* 1992 *Pages:* 383
Type of Study: Ethnographic
Comments: Case study of students' growth in spelling ability in whole language classroom. Features of a whole language classroom were identified that supported children's spelling growth over time. Spelling strategies were identified by examining writing samples over time.

Title: The Effects of Whole-Language on the Writing Ability of First-Grade Children
Author: Loshbaugh, Melodee
School: Washington State University (0251) *Degree:* Ed. D. *Date:* 1992 *Pages:* 124
Type of Study: Comparative
Comments: Study of 4 whole language and 4 traditional first-grade classrooms: after one year of instruction June writing samples were analyzed. Significant difference favored whole language students on the holistic measure; no significant difference found on other measures.

Title: School Culture and Language Arts Reform: Participant Research in an Urban Elementary School
Author: Arnett, Marjorie Joan
School: The University of Wisconsin-Milwaukee (0263) *Degree:* Ph. D. *Date:* 1992
   Pages: 195
Type of Study: Participant Research

Comments: Study analyzed process of change in one school. No dominant faculty culture existed; subgroups sharing common beliefs significantly influenced the process; 2 of 3 promoted implementation of reform.

Title: Inventing a Classroom: An Ethnographic Study of a Third Grade, Bilingual Learning Community
Author: Whitmore, Kathryn Faye
School: The University of Arizona (0009) *Degree:* Ph. D. *Date:* 1992 *Pages:* 403
Type of Study: Ethnographic
Comments: Study describes a third-grade bilingual, whole language classroom in detail and demonstrates the dynamic tension that exists between personal invention and social convention in natural learning experiences. The data suggests that classrooms that create conditions to support personal invention within natural and real-world social conventions provide intellectually challenging, socially empowering learning experiences for children.

Title: A Descriptive Study of the Implementation of an Integrated Whole Language Approach at the Fifth-Grade Level (Whole Language)
Author: Shapiro, Ardyth Rosencrantz
School: Portland State University (0180) *Degree:* Ed. D. *Date:* 1992 *Pages:* 191
Type of Study: Descriptive
Comments: Study of the implementation of curriculum change from traditional to whole language. Factors influencing the implementation were analyzed. A major conclusion was that change is an individual and developmental process. It was also concluded that significant differences between administrator and teacher interview responses were related to different knowledge and involvement levels.

Title: A Case Study of the Implementation of the English-Language Arts Framework for California Public Schools
Author: McCullough, Mary Kellett
School: University of Southern California (0208) *Degree:* Ph. D. *Date:* 1992
Type of Study: Case Study
Comments: Study analyzed level of implementation of new program and found a moderate level of implementation at the classroom level. Study suggests a number of factors that advance the implementation of change and suggests that future studies explore how classroom teachers can facilitate the change process.

Title: Situated Motivation in Literacy Instruction
Author: Turner, Julianne Christine

School: The University of Michigan (0127) *Degree:* Ph. D. *Date:* 1992
   Pages: 150
Type of Study: Comparative
Comments: Study compared the influence of traditional basal vs. whole language instruction and classroom literacy tasks on first-graders' motivated behaviors. Analysis showed that the strongest predictor of motivated behavior was the kind of literacy task. Greater learning strategy use was the only motivated behavior that distinguished whole language from basal classes.

Title: The Effects of a School's Whole Language Commitment on Reading Philosophy, Instruction, and Outcomes in Three Third-Grade Classes
Author: Lorie, Rosalina J.
School: Florida International University (1023) *Degree:* Ed. D. *Date:* 1992
   Pages: 151
Type of Study: Comparative
Comments: Study compared progress among 3 classrooms taught by 3 different teachers in a school that embraced a whole language approach. Findings indicate that a lack of significant difference was probably the result of failure to implement fully the whole language philosophy.

Title: Students' Perceptions of Literacy Activities within a Whole Language Classroom
Author: Hughes, Cheryl Kelleher
School: Indiana University (0093) *Degree:* Ph. D. *Date:* 1992 *Pages:* 171
Type of Study: Descriptive
Comments: This study analyzes literacy activities for "fit" to theoretical orientation and offers insight into evaluating theoretical consistency.

Title: Relationships between First-Grade Teachers' Theoretical Orientation to Reading, Their Reading Instructional Practice, and Students' Attitude Toward Reading
Author: Feng, Jianhua
School: Memphis State University (0124) *Degree:* Ed. D. *Date:* 1992 *Pages:* 179
Type of Study: Comparative
Comments: Study determined that most teachers held skills orientation but that all teachers who participated used a variety of teaching strategies; the most important influence on teachers' choices of strategies was classroom experience. No significant difference was found relative to students' attitude.

Title: Self-Selecting Literature: A Qualitative Study in a Sixth-Grade Classroom
Author: Sakrison, Dale L.
School: The University of North Dakota (0156) *Degree:* Ed. D. *Date:* 1992
       Pages: 311
Type of Study: Qualitative
Comments: Books, authors, genre, level of difficulty, selection techniques and
            influences on selection of books by sixth-grade students were ana-
            lyzed in this study.

Title: The Nature of Reading Instruction in a Literature-Based Reading Program
Author: Canavan, Diane Dernoncourt
School: University of North Texas (0158) *Degree:* Ph. D. *Date:* 1992 *Pages:* 202
Type of Study: Qualitative
Comments: Case study of whole language reading program. Study analyzed
            how instruction was accomplished in three domains: academic,
            social, and affective.

Title: A Comparison of the Locus-of-Control and First- and Second-Grade
       Students in Whole Language, Basal Reader, and Eclectic Instructional
       Approach Classrooms
Author: Auer, Carol Joyce
School: Northern Illinois University (0162) *Degree:* Ed. D. *Date:* 1992 *Pages:* 204
Type of Study: Comparative
Comments: Study found no significant differences among the subjects in the
            three instructional approach groups. Low achievers had signifi-
            cantly more external sense of control than average and high
            achievers; first-graders had more external sense of control than
            second-graders; there were no significant gender differences.

Title: A Study of the Commonalities and Differences of the Classroom
       Environment in Whole Language and Judicious Disciplines Classrooms
Author: Larson, Colleen May
School: Oregon State University (0172) *Degree:* Ed. D. *Date:* 1992 *Pages:* 294
Type of Study: Qualitative
Comments: Study analyzed collected data from two whole language and two ju-
            dicious discipline classrooms and found more commonalities than
            differences between the classroom environments, teacher's role
            and student's role.

Title: Incompatibility? Ethnographic Case Studies of "Learning-Disabled"
       Students in a Whole Language Classroom
Author: Rudenga, Elizabeth Ann Vanwylen

School: Purdue University (0183) *Degree:* Ph. D. *Date:* 1992 *Pages:* 264
Type of Study: Ethnographic
Comments: Study suggests that differences in testing, interpretation and setting of goals differ significantly under the skills-based remediation
program and the whole language classroom, making the two
philosophies and approaches incompatible.

Title: A Longitudinal Assessment of Elementary Students Who Participated in
a Basal Program with a Whole Language Approach to Reading Instruction
Author: Huneke, Mary Coesfeld
School: Saint Louis University (0193) *Degree:* Ph. D. *Date:* 1992 *Pages:* 81
Type of Study: Comparative
Comments: The study analyzed results of standardized testing administered
over three years and found no statistically significant interaction between year tested and level of reading ability. The three ability
groups had approximately the same change in grade equivalents
across the years tested.

Title: A Multiple Case Study of the Factors which Influence Teacher's Choice of
a Literature Based or a Traditional Basal Reading Program
Author: Palka, Laura Jane Moore
School: State University of New York at Buffalo (0656) *Degree:* Ph. D. *Date:* 1992
Pages: 255
Type of Study: Multiple Case Study
Comments: Study analyzed factors that lead teachers to choose (or not) literature-based programs and suggests that literature-based teachers
believed students need an active learning environment that provides
choice and opportunity and that such teachers perceive themselves
as designers of reading program built on framework of students'
strengths; Teachers of basal programs perceived decision making
as limited to grouping patterns, organization and lesson planning,
and worked from students' weaknesses.

Title: An Analysis of the Relationship between Political Attitudes and Theoretical
Orientation to Reading
Author: Cheek, Dallas Henderson
School: Texas A&M University (0803) *Degree:* Ph. D. *Date:* 1992 *Pages:* 103
Type of Study: Correlational
Comments: Analysis of survey results found a significant relationship between
political attitudes and theoretical orientation. The political atti-
tudes and theoretical orientation of university level teachers were
significantly different than those of both elementary teachers and

principals. There were no significant differences between the political attitudes of community school boards and the theoretical orientation to reading found within their districts.

Title: The Identification of Factors Contributing to the Development of Theoretical Orientation to Reading in Preservice Teachers
Author: Clay, Diane Mullins
School: Texas A&M University (0803) *Degree:* Ph. D. *Date:* 1992 *Pages:* 140
Type of Study:
Comments: Analysis of data revealed several factors that appear to be statistically significant in the development of a theoretical orientation that approaches the whole language end of DeFord's profile. Factors include: university instructor's orientation, writing in school, family involvement in early literacy, and reading for pleasure as an adult.

Title: Whole Language and Basal Program Reading Instruction in Two Second-Grade Classrooms: Swept Away by the Bandwagon
Author: Dubert, Lee Ann
School: The University of Wisconsin-Madison (0262) *Degree:* Ph. D. *Date:* 1992 *Pages:* 310
Type of Study: Comparative
Comments: Intent was to compare reading development and achievement of children in whole language and basal programs, but researcher concluded that integrity of the treatment conditions had been compromised and that it is virtually impossible to satisfy experimental conditions in classroom research. It is suggested that a new research paradigm is needed.

Title: The Effects of Act 178 Continuing Professional Development Law on Staff Development Plans and Activities
Author: Pennington, Lorainne Kapanak
School: University of Pittsburgh (0178) *Degree:* Ed. D. *Date:* 1992 *Pages:* 225
Type of Study: Descriptive
Comments: Analysis of survey results suggested that the Act 178 has facilitated and increased the affectiveness of local staff development programs.

Title: An Investigation of Speech-Language Pathologists' Knowledge and Perceptions of Whole Language
Author: Shaw-King, Ann E.
School: Texas Woman's University (0925) *Degree:* Ed. D. *Date:* 1992 *Pages:* 110
Type of Study: Descriptive

Comments: Although a majority agreement regarding a definition of whole language was not obtained, a majority of the participants in the survey indicated that speech-language pathologists should implement whole language and that they were implementing whole language in speech-language remediation.

Title: Testing Two Component Processing Models of Reading Acquisition
Author: Patterson, Rosemary I.
School: Simon Fraser University (Canada) (0791) *Degree:* Ph. D. *Date:* 1990
   Pages: 127
Type of Study: Comparative
Comments: Study suggests that, while phonological/orthographic coding is involved in processing to word identification, it is past the word identification level that processing related to context utilization aids passage comprehension.

Prepared by S. Froese.

Glossary

A

AFFIXES Bound morphemes, or meaning-bearing units, that cannot stand alone and hence attach to root words. Affixes are divided into prefixes, attached to the beginning of root words (e.g., unhappy), and suffixes, attached to the end of root words (e.g., happily).

ANECDOTAL RECORDS Information about individual students that describes what they know or do not know.

AUTHENTIC ASSESSMENT Assessment that takes into account context, purpose, and motivation. Also considers conative demands.

B

BIG BOOKS Large versions of books containing repetitive material (stories, songs, or chants) that have a high predictability, a strong rhythm, and a strong story line. Although big books can be read by individual children, they are most often used in a group reading situation during a shared-book experience with the teacher.

BILINGUAL Refers to the ability to use two languages proficiently.

BILINGUAL PROGRAM Refers to programs that provide instruction in the learner's native (first) language as well as in the language being learned.

BRAINSTORMING A strategy that can be used either by students alone or with the teacher to generate and record as many ideas as possible about a particular concept, idea, or topic.

C

CASE-BOOK A collection of compositions by various authors, when each provides an individual viewpoint in the treatment of a central theme or topic, perhaps a novel, a social studies project, or a field trip.

CHAINED STORYING Creating a cooperative story by having each participant add a sentence or paragraph.

CHIME IN Students read aloud with the teacher or other students. This is also sometimes referred to as "shared reading."

CLOZE PROCEDURES A method of teaching reading by omitting a number of words from a text, encouraging the reader to predict from knowledge of the context clues.

COLLABORATIVE WRITING   A written composition in which two or more authors contribute to the writing and shaping of ideas, sometimes in the form of a dialogue. Two students working in partnership will adopt this mode of authorship quite naturally when using a computer.

COMPUTER DATA BASE   A collection of facts and information, sometimes including relevant images, charts, maps, and diagrams. Some data base programs are interactive in that they allow the user to contribute information. Generic data base programs are like a computerized card-file system that allows the user to create a data base on any topic. Data processing programs allow the user to sort masses of information according to chosen categories and to show results in various formats.

COMPUTER LITERACY   The ability to use a computer, whether for entertainment, employment, business, learning, home management, correspondence, or creating. At its simplest level, computer literacy means the ability to switch the computer and screen on, and use the keyboard or mouse to run a program by following directions on the screen.

COMPUTER PROJECTION PLATE (CPP)   A peripheral attachment to the computer that can be placed on an overhead projector to enable the computer screen to be projected on a screen for public viewing.

CONATIVE (DOMAIN)   Refers to the emotional responses to tasks. It is now often assumed that the cognitive and motor domains cannot be separated from the conative.

CONFERENCE LOG   A record of a conference kept by a teacher, who makes careful notes about students' progress, needs, and abilities.

CONFERENCES   Meetings between students and teachers in order to monitor students' progress in reading and writing. There are several kinds of conferences: (1) reading conferences involving discussions about reading development of individuals; (2) group conferences involving reading discussions in small groups; (3) writing conferences in which students and teachers communicate through writing.

CONSONANTS   Refers to the letters or the sounds produced by letters that are not vowels, such as *b, c,* and *d.* (see also Grapheme and Phoneme)

CONSTRUCTIVIST   A view of learning that states that knowledge is actively built up by the learner rather than being simply received.

CONTENT READING   Reading material dealing with subjects such as science and mathematics. Students are required to read and learn from such texts. This is often referred to as "content reading" or "content area reading."

CONTRACT   An agreement (usually written) between the teacher and learner in which the learner agrees to complete stated tasks on his or her own initiative within a stated time. Ideally it is worked out mutually by the teacher and student.

CRITICAL LITERACY   A view of literacy that takes into account the underlying social, political, and economic ideologies. Critical feminist theory requires us to look at gender issues underlying text.

D

DESKTOP PUBLISHING (DTP)   Software programs that allow the computer user to shape text into magazine or newspaper formats, with columns, graphics, cutlines, etc.

DIALOGUE (INTERACTIVE) JOURNALS   In this form of journal writing, the student and teacher (or another student) read and respond to each other's writing on a continuous basis.

DISTANCING   Distance between the student and topic, student and role, or student and other participants (or the audience) can occur in both time and space. Careful consideration should be given by the teacher to the sorts of distance that might occur in a drama lesson. Distance will affect children's belief in a drama, commitment to a role, and their understanding of the themes dealt with in the drama. (For a complete description of distancing, see Verriour, P. (1985). Drama, distance, and the learning process. *Language Arts, 62 (4)*, 385–390.)

DRAMA AS A LEARNING MEDIUM   Refers to the use of drama across the curriculum as a teaching methodology for enhancing and expanding learning in any content area.

DRAMATIC PLAY   The participants are engaged in play in which there is a sense that events are happening now (in the present) and the future is not known.

DRAWING PROGRAMS   Software programs that allow the computer user to draw, shape, and "paint" in colors on the computer screen. Most of these are controlled by a mouse, although there are some that use a "light-pen" to draw directly onto the screen. Most drawing programs include a stock of "clip art," or ready-made drawings that can be incorporated into a picture or a text.

DRTA   Acronym for directed reading-thinking activity. A method to promote active prediction in reading. The term is usually credited to Russell Stauffer (*Directing the Reading-Thinking Process*. Harper & Row, 1975), who hyphenated the Reading-Thinking terms.

E

ELECTRONIC MAIL (E-MAIL)   Using a computer to send messages to another user, usually by a modem that connects the computer to a telephone line by which the sender can call the receiver's computer. The computer can also connect to a bulletin board that displays messages from a number of users, perhaps as part of a network or interconnected users.

ELECTRONIC WORKBOOK   A software program that provides the user with a number of exercises requiring simple responses from the user, usually in a multiple-choice format. The user has no control over the program. Some of these programs are enlivened by colorful graphics and sounds to reward correct answers.

EMERGENT LITERACY   The beginnings of reading and writing evolve over a period of time prior to school entrance as a result of children's experiences with meaningful print within their own social and cultural settings.

ENRICHMENT   Involves adding new material or more difficult or in-depth material to supplement a regular classroom program.

ENVIRONMENTAL PRINT   Print that is encountered outside of books and that is a persuasive part of everyday living. Street signs, package wrappers, game directions, and junk mail are examples of the print that surrounds us.

EXPRESSIVE WRITING   Writing in the language of everyday communication in which the writer is free to jump from narrative to speculation or to express opinions and feelings without restriction.

F

FORMATIVE EVALUATION   Assessment done for teaching purposes. This term is often contrasted with "summative"—assessment done for grading purposes.

FORMS OF WRITING   The infinite variety of shape that writing can take when it is composed for various purposes. Narrative can take the shape of a short story, an anecdote, a memoir, a joke, a dialogue, or even a report. Poetry has a multitude of accepted forms from the limerick and clerihew, to the more traditional ballad, ode, cinquain, diamante, tanka, haiku, sonnet, etc.

G

GRAMMAR (OR SYNTAX)   For teachers this usually means the study of the classes of words (e.g., verb, noun), their inflections, and their functions and relations in the sentence. Linguists, however, use "syntax" for that purpose and use "grammar" to refer to a description of our language system.

GRAPHEME   A letter or symbol used in writing to represent phonemes, either consonant graphemes (e.g., *b, c,* and *d*) or vowel graphemes (e.g., *a, e, i,*).

GRAPHIC USER INTERFACE (GUI)   The computer screen presents a picture or diagram, with "icons" or pictorial symbols to represent various functions of the program. The user manipulates a "mouse" to select the options, instead of typing commands on a keyboard. With a "touch-screen" system the user uses a finger to point directly to the symbols that appear on the screen.

H

HARDWARE   The actual computer and the equipment used with it. "Peripherals" or "add-ons" are other pieces of equipment connected to it, such as a printer, a modem, a TV monitor, a CD-ROM drive, a laserdisc player, a VHS recorder, or a camera.

HEURISTICS   Any method of generating ideas or problem solving, whether through "free writing" or by the use of a set of questions. Examples are listing, webbing, and cognitive mapping.

I

INDICATORS (OF ACHIEVEMENT)   "Benchmarks" in language learning against which work may be evaluated.

INDIVIDUAL EDUCATIONAL PROGRAM/PLAN (IEP)   It is a term used to describe a team-written document that outlines the special yearly educational program that has been planned for a student who has a specific disability. It may also be used with gifted and talented learners.

INDIVIDUALIZED READING   An instructional program in which each student's progress is accounted for by "personalized" programming. Instead of the traditional three instructional groups, individualized programs contain programs for each student, or for more temporary groups organized on the basis of interests, needs, or tasks.

INTENT   The purpose for which one uses language.

INTERACTION PATTERNS   The order or pattern in which child talk proceeds in the classroom (i.e., child to teacher, child to child, child to small group, and child to large group).

INTERACTIVE CD-ROM   A system that uses a standard 5-inch one-sided metal disk (just like a music CD) to provide and store information, such as a complete encyclopedia with pictures, maps, charts, etc., which can then be accessed through a keyboard.

INTEREST GROUP   An instructional group organized around students' interest, e.g., "a science fiction reading group," or based on an interest survey. (see Interest Survey)

INTEREST SURVEY   A kind of test designed to discover students' interests in reading material. See Chapter 3 for an example.

INVENTED SPELLING   Departures from conventional spelling that show the child is experimenting with knowledge of phonics and spelling patterns to record thoughts in written language, e.g., writing "cride" for cried. (see also Writing development and Phonics)

K

KEYBOARDING   The skill of being able to use the computer keyboard, often used as parts of the verb "to keyboard."

L

LANGUAGE-EXPERIENCE APPROACH (LEA)   A teaching method using stories and other writings generated by individual students or classes of students as their instructional material. The student writing is supplemented with generous supplies of trade books.

LANGUAGE PROCESS/CONCEPTUAL LEARNING   Children learn new concepts and clarify or expand old concepts through the use of language (listening, speaking, reading, and writing).

LEVELS (OR READER LEVELS)   Arbitrary and incremental designations of the complexities of print materials, particularly reading series. Any one grade may have two or more levels identified by number or by code, rather than grade level.

LIFEWRITING   Stories, anecdotes, poems, journals, etc., that record the writer's memories and perceptions of life experiences.

LITERACY   The ability to read, write, and figure in a functionally useful way.

LITERACY ATTEMPTS   Approximations or successes in reading, writing, or figuring.

LITERACY EVENTS   Activities in which reading and/or writing and/or figuring occur in the real world (i.e., actual communication situations). For example, reading a label on a shirt, writing a shopping list, and seeing print on TV are literacy events.

LITERACY EXERCISES   The practice of isolating skills (e.g., the sound of the digraph "ch") that are unrelated to an actual occurrence of reading or writing.

LOGS   Individual booklets in which students are asked to write.

LONG VOWEL   The vowel sound heard in such words as *bait* and *beet.*

M

MAINSTREAMED (INTEGRATED)   Refers to the practice of educating students who have special needs within the regular classroom for all or part of the school day to the maximum extent that it is appropriate.

MASKING   A teaching technique that enables the teacher or child to isolate and focus on a particular letter(s), word(s), or sentence of the text. This is most often done by using an open cardboard frame. When it is placed over the text, the size of the opening will determine the amount of print framed. A sliding strip can also be attached along one side of the frame. This allows the teacher to slide out the text word by word and letter by letter from beneath the mask. This technique is used mostly with big books during shared-book experiences.

MATURE WRITING   (see Writing Development)

MEDIATION   The process whereby a teacher (or another student)—through questioning, explaining, providing additional information, and so forth—helps students learn knowledge or a skill by helping them link what they already know to that which they are learning.

METALINGUISTIC AWARENESS   The process of being able to talk about, or monitor, one's language and how (or for what purpose) it is being used.

MODES OF WRITING   The familiar categories of expository, narrative, persuasive, and descriptive writing are traditionally translated into essays, stories, poems, and reports. In the real world these categories often overlap in a multitude of writing forms.

MORPHEMES   Minimal units of meaning. Bound morphemes are units of meaning that attach to free morphemes (e.g., unhappy); free morphemes may stand alone (e.g., man). Free morphemes are often root words.

O

OWNERSHIP   The principle that the writer owns or controls the writing and is the final arbiter in deciding whether to revise, extend, edit, or publish.

P

PAIRED READING   Two children of different reading abilities are paired and then take turns reading to each other. This strategy can also be utilized using a parent and a child at home or in school.

PEER CONFERENCES   A writing conference between students, possibly two students working together in partnership, or a group of students giving written feedback to the authors in their group.

PERFORMANCE   Communication to spectators or an audience that is probably not directly involved in the make-believe world of a drama.

PHONEME   Each of the distinctive sounds of a language.

PHONEMIC AWARENESS   The knowledge that spoken words contain distinguishable phonemes (sound units) and that letters symbolize the order of these phonemes in words.

PHONETIC HIT   (see Phonic Hit)

PHONETIC WRITING   (see Writing Development)

PHONETICS   The study of speech sounds.

PHONIC GENERALIZATION   A "rule" learned to help one spell or recognize words, such as, "When two vowels go walking the first does the talking." They are not called phonic rules in this text because they very often do not generalize to situations in which vocabulary is not controlled.

PHONIC HIT   Writing in which a letter or group of letters represents correctly certain phonemes, e.g., IHAF, "I have a friend."

PHONICS   Learning the relationship between graphemes (letters) and phonemes (sounds). A writer uses phonics knowledge to produce invented spellings.

PHONOGRAM   A group of letters representing a spelling pattern such as *-ate* or *-an.* Words containing such parts are often referred to as "word families."

PHONOLOGY   How the sounds of language are produced.

PORTFOLIO ASSESSMENT   A systematic collection of information over time by students or teachers, and its evaluation. Normally includes notes, drafts, students' responses to their own work, work in progress, and completed projects.

PRE-PHONETIC WRITING   (see Writing Development)

PRINTOUT   Using a printer attached to the computer to make a copy on paper of the text or graphics created by the user, or the messages sent or received by E-mail.

PROCESS WRITING   A systematic approach to teaching writing that views writing as a process, and involves children in all phases of that process, from prewriting to publishing (rehearsal-prewriting activities, drafting, reviewing-revision/editing, and publishing). See Chapter 4 for a complete definition.

PROJECTION   Projecting one's ideas, feelings, and emotions onto some other person (e.g., the student creates a statue out of another student).

PROTECTION   Students are protected into expressing or depicting feelings and emotions.

R

READERS THEATRE   In this form of drama, students read aloud from scripts as they turn a story into a play. The stories used should have a strong story line as well as a great deal of dialogue.

READING COMPREHENSION   In conventional usage it means the ability to read and understand material. Comprehension is often divided into levels: (1) literal-level comprehension involves retrieving details, a low-level skill requiring memory capacity; (2) inferential comprehension involves making inferences about material not presented in text; and (3) application/evaluation requires a reader to apply material read in text to a different context or to evaluate critically material in text. More recently, comprehension is thought of as meaning construction by the student (often in consultation with other students or adults) that combines both prior knowledge and textual information.

REAL WRITING   Writing that serves a real purpose for the writer, whether to express thoughts, feelings, or experiences, or to communicate ideas to other audiences.

REGISTER   Speech style involving choice of vocabulary, tone of voice, and nonverbal gestures. The register is selected in response to a particular context.

REQUEST   A strategy to aid comprehension of text wherein the teacher and students take turns asking questions of a text being read.

ROLE   Assuming the attitudes and feelings of an imaginary person toward a specific problem or dramatic situation.

ROOT WORD   A basic word around which more complex words are developed. Many root words are free morphemes in English. However, other root words are from Greek and Latin and are not free morphemes in English.

S

SCAFFOLDING   A principle of the writing conference by which the teacher or peer offers support and encouragement to the writer, helping the writer to sustain the effort to achieve authorship.

SCOPE AND SEQUENCE   A specific number of individual skills usually in connection with one curriculum area (e.g., reading), which are arranged in a definite order of presentation.

SEMANTIC MAPPING (WEBBING)   A procedure that can be used for a variety of purposes to visually represent relationships and develop concepts. It can be used in a variety of ways by both teachers and students.

SEMANTICS   The study of how words come to represent ideas or meaning.

SEMI-PHONETIC WRITING   (see Writing Development)

SHARED READING   Students reading material together, usually in an oral fashion.

SHORT VOWEL   The vowel sound heard in such words as *bat* and *bit*.

SOCIAL SEMIOTIC   Language is learned as part of a social process, through interaction with other people.

SOFTWARE   The "programs" or sets of instructions, bought and stored on CD-ROMs or "floppy discs," which tell the computer what to do. "Generic" software is a program, like word processing, which can serve a variety of functions. "Interactive" software allows the computer user to control the direction of the game or story. The computer reacts according to the user's responses. Many journals carry reviews of software; books and articles sometimes include software directories.

SPELL-CHECK   A software program, or a function of many word-processing programs, that scans a text, comparing each word with the words built into its memory. The program will flag any mismatches and suggest possible replacements for the user to select.

STATUS   Status enables participants in drama to determine the social standing of their role, e.g., the expert is in a high-status role if his or her expertise is being sought by someone else, who may assume a low-status role of learner.

STUDENT-CONSTRUCTED QUESTION   Questions or problems that students construct and that the other members of the class help to solve.

STUDENT-DIRECTED TALK   Student talk that is controlled by students.

SUSTAINED WRITING   Spontaneous or "free" or "forced" writing in which the writer uses the flow of language to generate ideas. (see also USSW)

SYNTAX   The study of how words are put together into meaningful strings.

T

TABLEAU   A scene is depicted or represented without speaking or movement. A tableau can start a scene and be brought to life or it may be used to stop the action in order to highlight a dramatic situation.

TEACHER-DIRECTED TALK   Student talk that is controlled by the teacher.

TEACHER-IN-ROLE   The teacher assumes a "role" with the drama to help focus and facilitate the work. In addition, "role" can be used to aid the students' reflection. The teacher should not use "role" to provide students with all the ideas.

TECHNOPHOBIA   The fear of technology, supported by a belief that machines always go wrong. A computer user may display technophobia by a wild, panic-driven pressing of keys or the frantic clicking of the mouse in the vain hope that some random combination of commands may put things right.

TEXT SCHEMA   A mental representation of how sentences form connected discourse such as stories, explanations, and so on.

TEXTUALLY EXPLICIT QUESTIONS   Questions for which the answers are explicitly stated in the text.

THEMATIC UNIT   A strategy that intentionally integrates knowledge from many disciplines in the study of a selected theme (unit) or topic. This integration allows one subject area to assist in the learning of other subject areas.

TRANSITIONAL WRITING   (see Writing Development)

U

USSW   (Unstructured, sustained, silent writing) A short period of usually 10 to 15 minutes, in which everyone, including the teacher, writes, possibly in a journal, without interruption.

V

VIDEO DISC (LASERDISC) PLAYER
A system by which films, plays, musicals, videos, or collections of pictures, are recorded digitally onto a large (12") metal platter for playback through a computer or TV monitor, providing a very high-quality picture with excellent definition, far superior to a VHS tape recording. This system has the advantage that any image or scene can be accessed instantly by numbers instead of having to run back through a long videotape. A disadvantage is that the disks are two-sided and have to be changed during the running of a long program.

VOWELS   Usually refers to the open sounds of the letters *a, e, i, o, u*, and sometimes *y*. However, there are many other vowel sounds in the English language.

W

WEB   A strategy used by teachers or students to diagram (usually through brainstorming) the many possible interconnections of selected topics of study.

WORD BANK   Once a child begins to recognize previously learned words from his or her personal writing (language experience), the teacher initiates a personal word bank of known words for that child. These words, which are often written on small individual cards, are used by the child to build up his or her sight reading and writing vocabulary.

WORD-PROCESSING PROGRAMS   Generic software programs that allow the user to type, edit, revise, format, and present texts.

WORKPLACE LITERACY   Functional reading and writing skills that are used in doing one's job.

WRITER'S BLOCK   An ailment experienced by most writers at some time or other, when the flow of ideas seems to freeze up, often during an examination period. The treatment is to change the focus of the writing activity, talk about the blockage to a helpful partner in a writing conference, or try one of the heuristic techniques.

WRITERS' WORKSHOP   A time when the classroom becomes a "press room," enabling everyone to engage in a choice of writing activity according to individual needs, whether in drafting first ideas, conferencing, editing and proofreading, or preparing for publication.

WRITING APPREHENSION   Fear of writing or, more precisely, the fear of having one's ideas scrutinized for mistakes, as in the apocryphal story of the student who complained that the essay returned by a teacher was "bleeding to death."

WRITING CENTER   A space in the classroom reserved for writing activities, stocked with a variety of resources: paper of various sizes and color; various types of pencils, crayons, and pens; reference books, including dictionaries, a thesaurus, etc.; a typewriter or microcomputer; materials for bookmaking and binding.

WRITING DEVELOPMENT   An individual's writing development appears to exhibit several stages: (1) pre-phonetic writing contains letters, numbers, and letterlike forms to represent language; however, the writer does not know any letter/sound correspondences; (2) semi-phonetic writing contains some phonics relationships as in IWMD for "I walked my dog"; (3) phonetic writing divides words into segments and is filled with invented spellings; (4) transitional writing contains any correctly spelled irregular words and many invented spellings; and (5) mature writing contains standard writing conventions with some invented spellings.

WRITING FOLDERS   A means of preserving (and thus valuing) students' writings, comparable to the artist's or photographer's folio, incorporating pockets for storing first drafts and published pieces, personal writings, work in progress, ideas for more writing, checklists of writing skills attained, etc.

WRITING TO LEARN   The writing processes used to let students express curricular concepts in their own language as a means of learning, whether in recording their observations, or for articulating questions about the topics and skills they are learning in all subject areas.

Index